MARK HUTTER

GLASSBORO STATE COLLEGE

The Changing Family:

Comparative Perspectives

SECOND EDITION

MACMILLAN PUBLISHING COMPANY
NEW YORK
Collier Macmillan Publishers
LONDON

TO LORRAINE,
DANIEL, ELIZABETH,
AND MY PARENTS

Copyright © 1988, Macmillan Publishing Company,
a division of Macmillan, Inc.

PRINTED IN THE UNITED STATES OF AMERICA

All rights reserved. No part of this book may be reproduced or
transmitted in any form or by any means, electronic or mechanical,
including photocopying, recording, or any information storage and
retrieval system, without permission in writing from the Publisher.
Earlier edition copyright © 1981, by John Wiley & Sons, Inc.

Macmillan Publishing Company
866 Third Avenue, New York, New York 10022

Collier Macmillan Canada, Inc.

Library of Congress Cataloging-in-Publication Data

Hutter, Mark, 1941–
    The changing family.

    Includes bibliographies and index.
    1. Family — Cross–cultural studies.   2. Marriage —
Cross-cultural studies.   3. Intergenerational relations —
Cross-cultural studies.   4. Family — United States.
I. Title.
HQ515.H87 1988   306.8   87–27564
    ISBN 0-02-359241-9

Printing: 1 2 3 4 5 6 7   Year: 8 9 0 1 2 3 4

Preface

This second edition continues to reflect the increased concern of the American public and of social scientists to study family change from both an historical and a cross-cultural perspective. Americans' interest in their historical and cultural roots continues unabated. In addition, the impact of worldwide revolutionary events has had a dramatic effect on all our lives, heightening our desire to gain a better understanding of other cultures.

The upsurge of significant information about the family from social history and cross-cultural scholarship has grown even more impressive since the publication of the first edition. It is no longer legitimate for sociology-of-the-family courses to focus narrowly on the contemporary American middle-class family. The approach now favored includes comparative materials from other cultures as well as from our own historical past. In addition, the diversity in American families has become the anchoring theme of sociological attention to the study of the family. Mirroring this development, instructors not only in the area of the family but also throughout the sociology curriculum are offering comparative courses that devote more time to historical and cross-cultural materials.

The first edition of this textbook was in the vanguard of this comparative emphasis. It reflected, systematized, and further enhanced these developments with new insights and a wealth of new information on the dynamics of family change and the making of the contemporary family. *The Changing Family* was and continues to be a leader among sociology-of-the-family texts that fully and systematically develop a cross-cultural perspective throughout the study of the family life cycle. It uses a wide variety of cultural and historical examples, examines selected societies, and reveals both general trends and unique variations. The reader will find the diversity of American family dynamics illuminated by these comparisons.

The topical coverage maintains this comparative view. For example, the great changes in family structure due to modernization are revealed through issues from Western and non-Western societies. The sociological perspective is similarly developed as the book explores macroscopic and microscopic concerns equally, building a balanced picture of the changing family. The text comparatively highlights changes in personal value systems, interpersonal relationships, gender-role relationships, marriage, and the structure of the family.

This new edition is characterized by increased attention to topical coverage and recent sociological analyses of the family in the United States. The historical materials found in Part I have been reorganized, presenting the theories in a more concise and more relevant fashion. Part II reflects the increased attention given to the diversity of the American family experience by including a new chapter that focuses on immigrant and ethnic family dynamics and shows the important influence of ethnicity on American family life.

The examination of contemporary American family themes has been expanded. There is added emphasis on current social issues that help the reader relate sociological theory to his or her world. This includes discussions on the feminization of poverty, teenage mothers, singlehood, the dual-career family, abortion, grandparenthood and the four-generation family, family violence, and divorce and remarriage. The timely analysis of heterosexuality, homosexuality, and the effect of AIDS on each appears in a new chapter on gender and sexuality. The implications of critical social policies on these family concerns are discussed and given added attention.

The exploration of societal and cultural similarities, using current examples, continues to illuminate comparative family dynamics. Topics covered include the Iranian revolution and the impact on women's rights and divorce; living under apartheid in South Africa; arranged marriages and the dowry system in India; work, gender roles, and policy implications in Sweden, the Soviet Union, and Israel; and industrialization and urbanization and its impact on courtship and mate-selection processes in Japan. Two chapters are still exclusively devoted to examining changing patterns of family life in non-Western societies: Chapter 6 discusses family life in sub-Saharan Africa and Chapter 18 examines the family in China. These more detailed analyses have been updated and provide three-dimensional portraits of, as well as some fascinating insights into, the impact of family change in diverse contemporary situations.

A distinctive feature of this text is the use of newspaper and newsweekly articles. New materials have been selected to illustrate concepts and theories in everyday language. There are also case studies and excerpts from popular nonfiction, which serve a useful pedagogical purpose and add to the relevance of the text. These materials reveal the impact of change on a personal level and add a human dimension to the analysis.

This second edition continues to be in the forefront of the logical evolution in the sociology-of-the-family textbook. It does not break with the past; instructors do not have to revamp their courses because the book follows tried-and-true topical patterns. Its outstanding feature is its extensive coverage of cross-cultural and historical materials from beginning to end. Instructors welcomed this emphasis in the groundbreaking first edition. Those instructors who do not emphasize the family systems of other societies will be able to elaborate on the diversity of the American family in their class lectures with the full knowledge that the comparative perspective presented in this textbook will complement and enhance their own presentation. An instructor's manual with a new feature that guides us in the usage of family history as a classroom technique is also available.

M.H.

Acknowledgments to the Second Edition

In the years that have passed since the publication of the first edition of this book, I increasingly am aware of the lifelong intellectual debt that I owe Alfred McClung Lee and Murray A. Straus. My point of view also has been influenced by Sidney Aronson, Peter L. Berger, the late Reuben Hill, the late Gregory P. Stone, and other members of the department of sociology at Brooklyn College and at the University of Minnesota. Their insights and knowledge are reflected throughout this book.

Colleagues and friends continue to enlighten me about sociology and how it should be taught. The faculty members of the sociology department at Glassboro State College are most esteemed. By name they are: Pearl W. Bartelt, Jay Chaskes, John Myers, Wilhelmina Perry, Manju Sheth, Susan Gotsch Thomson, and Flora Dorsey Young. I especially wish to thank Ted Tannenbaum for his critical reading and keen judgment that improved many a chapter. Additional significant others include Harvey A. Farberman, David Bartelt, Kathy Charmaz, R. Frank Falk, David D. Franks, Richard N. Juliani, Sandy Litvin, John Lofland, Lyn Lofland, Patrick W. Luck, Dean MacCannell, Joseph Marolla, Doreen Sternchos, Richard V. Travisano, William C. Yoels, and Margaret Zahn. The Ethnic Studies Association, the Garden State Immigration History Consortium, and The Balch Institute for Ethnic Studies are vital Delaware Valley and New Jersey institutional affiliations.

I am most grateful to the many students at Glassboro State College, the University of California, Davis, and Temple University who have fired my sociological imagination. Glassboro State College has provided numerous grants that have been invaluable in my research and writing.

This book originated with John Wiley and Sons, whose professional staff was most helpful in the publication of the first edition. A special thanks is owed to Carol Luitjens, whose enthusiasm and creative suggestions were gratifying. I re-express my gratitude to all who were involved in the editorial review process of the first edition. These included Michael Gordon, Paula M. Hudis, Elizabeth Huttman, David Kent Lee, and Hallowell Pope.

I am extremely lucky that the present staff at Macmillan has proved to be equally helpful and valuable. Sociology editor Chris Cardone has the class, sophistication, and street smarts to handle a fellow New Yorker. The production staff also is very able. Much thanks is expressed to the current reviewers, who include J. Kenneth Davidson, Sr., University of Wisconsin-Eau Claire; Gary D. Hampe, University of Wyoming; Christine A. Hope, College of Charleston; E. Doyle McCarthy, Fordham University; and Rita Phylliss Sakitt, Suffolk County Community College.

Finally, I paraphrase with love and affection my closing acknowledgment remarks of the first edition. I too often took for granted but nevertheless fully appreciate the tolerance and forbearance displayed by my wife, Lorraine, and our children, Daniel and Elizabeth, for sharing our family life with my work on *The Changing Family*. I sincerely hope that they continue to feel that the sacrifice has been justified.

Contents

PART IV

Generational Relationships   *351*

CHAPTER 13

Fertility Patterns and Parenthood   *353*

CHAPTER 14

The Family and Childhood and Adolescence   *390*

CHAPTER 15

The Family and the Elderly   *421*

CHAPTER 18
Epilogue: The Family in China   *529*

Boxes

PART I

Comparative and Theoretical Perspective

CHAPTER 1

Introduction to Comparative Family Study

"The Family" sculpture by Gustave Vigeland. This granite sculpture is located in the Vigeland Sculpture Park, Oslo, Norway.

CHAPTER OUTLINE

Change seems to be the most permanent feature in the world today. Dramatic and revolutionary changes that affect all humanity are occurring in the contemporary world in attitudes and behaviors regarding politics, economics, and social life. Fundamental ideas and values pertaining to religion, morality, and ethics are being questioned, examined, and—in some cases—re-evaluated. Massive modifications and breakdowns of societal structures and cultural values are associated with social and individual crises in which customary experience and meaning are no longer taken for granted. The conventional assumptions regarding sex-role relationships, marriage, and the family are being challenged.

Politically, we have seen the final dissolution of the colonial empires of Western European societies, some of which began over 500 years ago. In the last 50 years, new nations have arisen and begun to establish viable governmental systems; to integrate and consolidate diverse and, in some cases, antithetical cultural and social groups; and to make themselves felt as important political entities on the world scene. In addition, advanced industrially developed nations have been undergoing major political changes with resultant national identity crises and re-examinations in the light of world economic and political realignments.

Economically, the forces of industrialization and urbanization are making themselves felt in both the developed and the undeveloped nations of the world. The ramifications of these forces affect all humanity and transcend political, cultural, and national boundaries. Further, the dynamic interrelationship of energy sources is becoming so obvious that many express surprise at the myopia of those in the recent past who failed to recognize this fundamental fact of world life. The rapidity of the economic changes that are sweeping the contemporary world is almost beyond comprehension.

Social and individual changes have been as radical as those that have been occurring in the political and economic spheres. In developing societies, there is a transitory quality to all patterns of social life. The following quote from *The New York Times*—datelined Teheran, Iran, January 16, 1975—illustrates this point:

> Haji Mahmud Barzegar, a seller of songbirds, scowled at the new cars that streamed unceasingly along the avenue past his neglected shop. "The people do not buy nightingales these days," he intoned glumly. "They are too busy doing other things." (Pace, 1975)

Cross-culturally, the family is undergoing massive changes. The opening statement of William J. Goode's seminal work, *World Revolution and Family Patterns,* states:

> For the first time in world history a common set in influences—the social forces of industrialization and urbanization—is affecting every known society. Even traditional family systems in such widely separate and diverse societies as Papua, Manus, China, and Yugoslavia are reported to be changing as a result of these forces. . . . (Goode, 1963:1)

Goode emphatically declares that the worldwide changes spell doom for the old social orders and the traditional family systems. The social revolutions in Iran and China reflect the continued instability and nonpermanence of much of the changes.

These revolutionary changes have not been restricted to non-Western societies; equally radical events have occurred in the family of Western industrial societies, particularly in the United States. In recent years, the nature of marriage, family, and kinship systems in American society has been the subject of intensive scrutiny and analysis. Questions have centered on the conventional assumptions about the necessity of maintaining kinship relations and the role of the nuclear family, the inherent nature of male–female gender-role relationships, the marital relationship, and the importance and desirability of parenthood. A new, more permissive sexual morality —in part precipitated by the activities of the women's movement and some segments of the youth counterculture—is reflected in the re-examination of previously held attitudes opposed to premarital and extramarital sexual relations, out-of-wedlock pregnancies, and abortions. In fact, the very necessity, desirability, and relevancy of marriage and the family have been challenged.

Concomitantly, there has been a dramatic change in behavioral practices relating to family structure. A married couple with one or more children was the norm in American society as recently as 1960; married couples comprised three-quarters of all households, and more than half of these couples had one or more dependent children. It is estimated that, by the year 1990, a little more than half (55 percent) of American households will consist of married couples, and of these only half will contain children. Also by that time, at least one-third of the households with children will have both the wife and the husband working (Masnick and Bane, 1980). Accounting for these changes are declining marriage rates, falling birth rates, and rising divorce rates. If present trends continue, it is predicted that at least half of all marriages will end in divorce.

Occurring simultaneously with the changes in traditional family structures are the development of alternative family patterns. Current data indicate that more and more people are remaining single or postponing entry into first marriage. In addition to the increase in those choosing to live alone, there is a startling increase in the number of couples who choose to live together without marriage. According to a 1983 Census Bureau report, the number of unmarried heterosexual couples living together was slightly over half a million in 1970; thirteen years later, the figure was placed at nearly 2 million people, nearly triple the earlier figure. Cohabiting couples include college students, young working adults, middle-age people, and the elderly. The cohabiting group with the highest percentage increase contains people between the ages of 25 and 44. In addition, the number of same-sex persons living together is growing.

For those who do marry, many voluntarily choose not to have children. The number of married couples who will remain childless and not simply delay the birth of children is difficult to determine. However, a Roper survey (1980) has found that 82 percent of American women stated that children were not a necessary ingredient for a full and happy marriage. Such surveys have led to speculation that, if current trends continue, as many as 25 to 30 percent of women might remain childless.

Changes in the behavior of women have especially affected family life. Between 1970 and 1981, the number of single-parent families headed by women in the United States doubled. Much of this increase was caused by the rising divorce rate, but another major factor was the rising illegitimacy rate, despite the legalization of abortion in 1973. Also, there has been a rapid surge in married women's labor-force participation in the last 40 years. Only 14 percent of wives were gainfully employed in 1940; by 1980, a majority of them (51 percent) were employed. Further, a significant number of working wives have children, especially young children. The estimate is that about 80 percent of married women under the age of 35 hold outside-the-home jobs. Among the women who have one or more children under the age of six, 40 percent are employed.

Reactions to changes in family behavior have crystallized over the issue of legalized abortion. In 1973, the Supreme Court of the United States allowed a woman to have a legal abortion if she so desires. Although it seems evident that the legalization of abortions has had relatively little impact on the national birthrate (one demographer states that two-thirds of all legalized abortions would have been performed illegally), the law reflects the striking changes occurring in America regarding not only this issue but also many related ones concerning sexual, marital, and familial attitudes.

Another apparent change in the family has been the increase in family violence. Reports of wife, child, and elderly abuse, and—most recently—incest have led many to wonder how prevalent is such violence. Sociologists concede that domestic violence is difficult to measure because so much of it goes unreported. Researchers estimate that so many millions of people are assaulted every year by family members that the home may well be the most dangerous place in which to be.

Homosexuality is still another area that has become the debating ground for issues regarding changes in the family. The increased public character of homosexuality, as well as the panic on how to treat people suffering from AIDS and whether these people should be allowed to circulate freely in society, has coalesced divergent opinions not only on homosexuality but also on heterosexuality. In 1986, the Supreme Court ruled that states can ban sodomy between homosexuals, even if it is practiced by consenting adults in the privacy of a home. This has led many to speculate that the court's decision also has ramifications for the legality of various sexual practices for heterosexuals as well, regardless of marital status. The vehement pro and con reactions by the public, politicians, and media on this controversial decision highlight the increased importance and attention public debate has taken on sexual, marital, and family matters.

The controversy surrounding sexuality, marriage, and the family has entered the world of politics and public policy in a show of greater visibility than ever before. Laws regarding illegitimacy and regulations regarding welfare support for single-parent households containing mothers and children are being written, argued, rewritten, and reargued. Passions are ignited over the issue of abortion. Legislation regarding not only the circumstances of legally allowable abortion but also the more-fundamental level of the legality of abortion under any circumstances is constantly being tested in the courts. The same holds true for both public and private issues on the rights for homosexual activity and on the legal rights of homosexuals themselves. Politics has also intruded on the government's responsibilities to provide public support for child-care facilities, and arguments and counterarguments continuously ensue on issues of economic discrimination and women's "proper" role in the economy against their "natural" role in the family. Similarly, increased attention is being given to parallel concerns regarding men's roles vis-à-vis commitment to occupational careers and the family.

As a result of all these changes, debates, and controversies, there has been great discussion and national debate about the future of the family. A widespread view declares that the family is a dying institution and expresses much concern about the consequent implications for the "American way of life." A counter view holds that the "family" itself is not dying, but rather that one form of the family is declining and being replaced by a new type of family that will be supportive of individuals of both sexes and of all ages. This new family will usher in emancipatory and egalitarian transformations in social relations that include, but are not limited to, marital and family relations.

The aim of this book is to aid in the understanding of the causes, conditions, and consequences of these changes for the individual, the family, and the society. It seeks to answer questions on the contemporary status of the family. We believe that it is

Martha Steward/The Picture Cube

A contemporary American family: Mother and father wave goodbye to baby as the family separates for the work day.

futile to examine the family without attending to the almost continuous and radical changes occurring not only in the United States but also throughout the world. Thus, our entire analysis of the family must be grounded in change, and it particularly must be linked with the universal concomitant changes in modernization, industrialization, and urbanization.

The Whys of Comparative Analysis

Americans have been notorious for their lack of understanding and ignorance of other cultures. This is compounded by their gullible ethnocentric belief in the superiority of all things American, and not only has made them unaware of how others live and think but also has given them a distorted picture of their own way of life. In the light of today's startling changes in personal value systems and interpersonal relationships, we would argue that by using a comparative perspective we gain both a better understanding of other people and a better understanding of ourselves.

The basic aim, then, in the comparative analysis of the family is to further the understanding of the family in our own society and in other societies. The sociologist William F. Kenkel (1977:6–8) outlines four major objectives of cross-cultural comparative analysis:

1. *Appreciation of intercultural family variability and uniformity.* An examination of other societies' family systems provides knowledge about the diversity of family institutions and helps develop our own insights into the meanings a practice has for the people involved. For example, by studying polygyny (the marriage of one male to two or more females)—a practice that has had worldwide popularity as a preferred marriage form—we see its importance to the people who practice it in

their everyday life, and thus it is taken out of the realm of an ethnocentric "playboy" fantasy.

2. *Increasing objectivity.* Kenkel argues that comparative analysis develops our objectivity by placing a familiar phenomenon in an unfamiliar setting. For example, most people are able to make more-objective analytical statements about the status of other people's relationships with their parents than they are about *their* relationships with *their* parents. Likewise, a greater degree of objectivity can be gained in the comparative study of family systems than in the study of the family systems of our own society. We gain much objectivity and emotional detachment through comparative analysis, and thus the task of self-examination becomes easier.

3. *Increased sensitivity toward the American family.* The diverse and idiosyncratic features of contemporary American society come into greater focus when we compare it with other societies. For example, we can gain a better understanding of the dating and courtship patterns of Americans by comparing these patterns with the different customs and practices surrounding mate selection in other societies.

4. *Formulation and hypotheses.* Comparative analysis gives us a different perspective and increases our perception and analytical ability to examine the family. Through the process of comparative analysis, the observer begins to be able to develop hypotheses concerning the family in its relationship with other institutions in society and also in the relationship that family members have with each other. For example, the study of the family life of the Hutterites or the Amish may provide us with insights into the development of hypotheses concerning the relationship between religion and the family. Kenkel concludes that whether hypotheses developed through comparative analysis "prove to be original, or commonplace, testable or untestable, is not nearly so important as the fact that scientific curiosity about the family has been stimulated and an attempt has been made to channel it" (Kenkel, 1977:8).

John Sirjamaki succinctly summarizes the major rationale for the use of the comparative method in the sociology of the family:

> Used in family studies, the comparative method makes possible a cultural and historical analysis of family organization and institutions in societies. It permits cross-cultural generalizations about families which reveal their universal character in world societies and their particular character in individual societies in the same or different regions or periods. It provides a means to interpret historical changes in families, and to relate these to other social and cultural changes in societies. These functions of comparative analysis are of enormous importance; they make the comparative method indispensable to the scientific understanding of the family. (Sirjamaki, 1964:34)

Robert Marsh (1967) has made a similar point. He argues that many of the sociological propositions that have been treated as universal explanatory relationships and generalizations were based on data gathered in the United States and thus may have validity only in the United States and not be applicable cross-culturally. However, many persons view these propositions as being universal. This criticism seems particularly true for the sociology of the family. Systematic comparative analysis of the family is vital; many of the assertions about the family must be examined and investigated with data from cross-cultural societal settings. This is of crucial importance in testing generalizable assertions about family processes and structures.

The main reason, then, for the comparative analysis of the family is to see which assertions are universal and which are unique, and, if the latter, what accounts for their uniqueness. This is of crucial significance if we wish to answer questions about family processes and structures and their relationships to other societal institutions. Brigitte Berger (1971) has stated that the marked rapid economic, political, and social changes characteristic of the contemporary world have forced social scientists to understand these changes—not only for pragmatic and political reasons but also because comparative sociology contributes to the development of sociological theory even for those who are not primarily interested in the problems of social change. It is our firm belief that the wisdom of her remarks is of particular relevance to the sociology of the family.

Aims of This Book

This book does not claim to present an encyclopedic account of comparative family forms. Our selections and illustrations are designed to aid in the understanding of present-day family structures and processes in a world of change. Further, they are used to highlight such changes and to indicate the similarities and diversities of families and individuals in the United States and other societies.

This book is not intended to be exhaustive; it does not contain an account of every society in the world today. We have been selective in our choice of the societies we discuss, preferring to deal with a few in depth rather than to provide a comprehensive cross-cultural account. Our aim in this approach is to establish some general themes, to identify the nature of family change, and to provide the means for a better understanding of future changes.

Another aim of this selective approach is to bring to life in the mind of the reader the family systems we discuss. For many, the image of a different society is so abstract and "foreign" that they cannot relate to it. We discuss different family systems so that the reader will have a fuller and deeper understanding of them and will be able to use them comparatively in the analysis of American society. Thus, by attempting to examine other family systems in comparison to our own, we hope to shed light on the worldwide changes that are affecting all family systems.

It is not our intention to overburden the reader with a seemingly endless presentation of family and kinship classification terms. Rather, we will sketch out the variations in kinship systems to highlight how family relationships have implications not only for the individual but also for the preservation and continuation of societal patterns. We must also caution the reader to keep in mind that some of this discussion may not be of immediate apparent usefulness; however, the material introduced here will be elaborated on in the following chapters. With this cautionary note, let us proceed.

The Family in Cross-Cultural Perspective: A Brief Sketch

Throughout history, the family has been the social institution that has stood at the very center of society. For most individuals, the family is the most important group to which they belong; it provides intimate and enduring interaction, acts as a mediator between themselves and the larger society from birth until death, and transmits the traditional ways of a culture to each new generation. The family fulfills human needs as few other institutions can. It is the primary socializing agent as well as a continuous force in shaping the course of our lives. It is through the family that men and women satisfy most of their sexual, emotional, and affiliational needs. Children, inevitably raised in their families, provide a tangible link with future generations. For the society, the family provides the necessary link between it and the individual; the family motivates the individual to serve the needs of the society and its members. It is through the family that the society determines the everyday interactional patterns of the individual. In many societies, it is the family that provides the bonds of mutuality that define their members' occupations, religious lives, political roles, and economic positions (Keniston, 1965).

It is true that every society may develop its own variations on these universal themes. Yet, as the French anthropologist, Claude Lévi-Strauss (1971), has so astutely observed, one central feature emerges in all structural variations of the family: The family links individuals into an intermeshed network of social relationships. It regulates and defines social relationships through contractual marital relationships. The incest taboo may be seen as functioning to assure patterned forms of marital exchange between families instead of within families. The division of labor between husband and wife serves to enhance their dependency on one another, just as the marriage of man to woman serves the development of reciprocal ties between family groups. The continued accumulation of reciprocal obligations linking man to woman, family to family, and kinship groups to the wider social system is seen as the very basis for the social structure of a given society.

We can get a better appreciation of this perspective by examining the cross-cultural variations of the family. By paying particular attention to how the family interrelates the individual to the societal matrix through kinship structures, the importance of the orientation becomes clear. Further, if we keep in mind that there is now occurring what Goode (1963) has called a "world revolution in family patterns," we can more readily understand why it is so vitally necessary to understand the role of the family in the world today.

Family, the first and most important term in our study, is so familiar that it does not seem to warrant clarification. However, when we take a closer look at family systems in other societies as well as the diversity of forms in our society, we come to realize that the familiar can be rather complex; there is no universal family form, but many forms and variations. However, each form and structure of the family serves important functions for a given society and its members. The student, while noting these variations, should pay close attention to the purposes these forms serve rather than simply memorize and catalog them.

George Murdock suggested that "The family is a social group characterized by common residence, economic cooperation, and reproduction; it includes adults of both sexes, at least two of whom maintain a socially approved sexual relationship, and one or more children, own or adopted, of the sexually cohabiting pair" (Murdock, 1949:2–3). This definition has been questioned in that there are families that contain neither cohabiting adults nor adults who work and live together.

Exceptions to Murdock's definition have led sociologists to modify the definition and to stress the predominant characteristics of the family arrangement. These definitions usually refer to the fact that the family finds its origin in marriage, which is an institutionally sanctioned union between a man and a woman that assumes some permanence and conformity to societal norms. A primary function of the family is the reproduction of legitimate offspring, their care and socialization into the traditions and norms of the society, and the acquisition of a set of socially sanctioned statuses and roles acquired through marriage and procreation.

The definition lays down guidelines that emphasize the social arrangements relating to marriage and the family and de-emphasize the human biological aspects of the family. For humans, unlike animals, social determinants set limits, constraints, and meanings on biological determinants. Marriage and the family should not be confused with biological mating and resultant offspring.

> The mating phenomenon is shared with other animals, whereas marriage is strictly human. Mating, even on the human level, may be quite impersonal, random, and temporary. Marriage, on the other hand, is a social institution, and it assumes some permanence and conformity to societal norms. Marriage is society's way of controlling sex and fixing responsibility for adult sexual matings. In this connection it is

worth noting that all societies, both past and present, prescribe marriage for the majority of their members. Marriage, in other words, is a universal social institution, and, although extramarital sexual contacts frequently are permitted, it is the marriage arrangement that is most strongly sanctioned for most men and women during most of their life spans. (Christensen, 1964:4)

Thus, although the family is based on biological processes, these processes are channeled by a society to conform to its traditions, rules, and attitudes.

Stephens (1963), in his influential examination of the family in cross-cultural perspective, developed definitions of marriage and the family that place proper emphasis on social and cultural characteristics as opposed to biological characteristics. Stephens defines marriage as "(a) socially legitimate sexual union, begun with (b) a public announcement, undertaken with (c) some idea of permanence, and assumed with a more or less explicit (d) marriage contract, which spells out reciprocal rights and obligations between spouses, and between the spouses and their future children" (1963:7). The definition of the family builds on the one for marriage: "The family is a social arrangement based on marriage and the marriage contract, including recognition of the rights and duties of parenthood, common residence for husband, wife and children, and reciprocal economic obligations between husband and wife" (Stephens, 1963:8).

Forms of Marriage and the Family

Sexual interaction and children occur biologically, but they are socially defined. The family can also be analyzed from several vantage points, depending on its structural characteristics.

1. The family can be classified according to the form of marriage allowed by a given society:

Monogamy:	One man to one woman
Polygamy:	A plurality of spouses for one man or one woman
Polygyny:	One man to two or more women
Polyandry:	One woman to two or more men
Group Marriage:	Two or more men to two or more women

Monogamy is the only form of marriage that is universally accepted by all societies; it is the predominant form even in those societies that accept other forms of marriage. In those societies that do permit other marriage forms, economic conditions usually prevent an individual from having more than one spouse. George Murdock, in his comprehensive surveys of marital and family forms, found that monogamy was the preferred and exclusive form of marriage for only 43 (18 percent) of the 238 societies in his 1949 sample and 135 (24 percent) of the 554 societies in his 1957 world ethnographic sample.

Murdock (1949, 1957) observed that polygyny existed in 193 (81 percent) of the societies he sampled in 1949 and 415 (75 percent) of the societies in the expanded 1957 sample. For men in polygynous-allowing societies, the privilege of having multiple spouses is restricted to a small minority, usually members of the higher social strata. William N. Stephens (1963) states that polygyny serves as a status distinction, a mark of prestige, by virtue of the economic and political advantages of having several wives; that is, when women have economic and political value, there is greater

Christine Spengler/Sygma

Two Moslem women, in traditional chador, pose for the camera in front of a wedding shop.

demand for polygyny than monogamy. Polygyny is also often associated with societies in which ideologies of male power and authority — patriarchy — predominate.

Another reason that most persons in polygynous societies remain monogamous relates to the biological factor relating to sex ratios. The sex ratio is the number of men per 100 women in the society, with the denominator of the fraction usually not stated. If, for example, there are 110 men to every 100 women in a given society, the sex ratio is 110. Likewise, if there are 97 men to every 100 women, the resultant sex ratio is 97. The biological fact of life is that the sex ratio for each of the world's societies is 100; that is, 100 men to every 100 women. This equal proximation of males and females places great demographic pressure on the society for monogamous marriage. When the society allows for polygyny, and a given male has two or three wives, one or two men do not have any. The result is that, while polygyny is preferred and valued in the vast majority of societies, monogamy is more widely practiced.

Polyandry, which is relatively rare (only one percent — two and four societies respectively in Murdock's two samples), tends to be prevalent where there is a limited amount of land, conditions are hard, and wives are not economic assets. Where it occurs, the society is characterized by severe economic conditions, female infanticide, and a marked lack of jealousy among the cohusbands, who frequently are related. In the polyandrous marital system, there is a patriarchal (male dominant) organization in which one male agrees to share his wife in common with other men in exchange for the men's work services. Group marriage has not been a permanent characteristic of societal family patterns. Frequently, a polyandrous-allowing community takes on this form. It occasionally occurs during periods of societal turmoil and transition or in short-time-span experimental forms, as in the case of the Oneida community in New York from the 1840s to the 1880s and the briefer but well-publicized hippie communal groups of the late 1960s and early 1970s.

The family can be classified according to one point of reference. The family that one is born into and from which the individual receives his or her initial and most basic socialization is called the family of orientation. The family of procreation refers to the family established by the individual through marriage and childbearing. The salience of these different family forms leads us to our next categorization.

2. The family can be categorized in terms of the family formed:

Nuclear Family:	Husband, wife, and children
Conjugal Family	A form of nuclear family in which the emphasis is on the marital bond
Extended Family:	Persons related by common descent
Consanguineal Family	A form of extended family in which the emphasis is on blood relatives

In the structure of kinship, priority can be given to either marital relationships or generational relationships. The nuclear family is composed of a husband and wife and their children; the extended family is composed of combined nuclear families through the parent – child relationship. This results in family units of three or more generations — at least grandparents, parents, and children.

Although the nuclear family is a recognizable unit in most societies, there is great variation in its autonomy. When it is relatively autonomous from extended family ties and the marital bond is of primary importance, it is referred to as a *conjugal* family. In contrast, when there is an emphasis on blood ties between generations or between siblings, the extended family is referred to as a *consanguineal* family. The nuclear family has less autonomy when it is part of a functioning consanguineal family system. In such circumstances, it is inappropriate to refer to the nuclear family as a conjugal family.

Thinking of the conjugal family and the consanguineal family as two systems of extremes, or polar types, contrasting patterns can be delineated. Conjugal families, consisting of only two generations, are more transitory and fragile than consanguineal families; they are more fragile and transitory in that they are susceptible to such potentially disruptive events as death, illness, divorce, and separation. For example, the death of a parent can mean fundamental reworking of the remaining parent's role relationships with children as well as dealing with economic readjustments.

In contrast, consanguineal families are in a sense immortal; they encompass all blood relations from at least three generations. The continued existence of the consanguineal family is relatively less dependent on any one person or nuclear family. For example, the death of a parent can be compensated for by the presence and involvement of other kin stepping in to fill the various facets of the parental role. Similarly, financial and economic difficulties can best be handled through the multiple resources of the consanguineal family system. Consanguineal families are better able to acquire property and material wealth and tend to transmit it intact to future generations. Conjugal families tend to split such wealth and property at each generation.

The conjugal family, with its focus on the marital relationship, emphasizes the importance of individualism with freedom of mate choice, romantic love, separate residence, and strong husband-and-wife relationships and parent–child involvements. In the consanguineal system, the family is more likely to arrange the marriage of offsprings, the residence of the husband and wife will be with either of their extended families, and children will be socialized by extended kin as well as by the parents.

The conjugal family gives greater emphasis and larger autonomy to the individual and also relieves that person of most formal commitments, obligations, and duties to other family members. While this gives the individual greater independence from familial involvements, it may have deleterious effects on those extended kin who may be economically disadvantaged or physically or mentally handicapped. For example, in our society the conjugal family does not have a good "track record" in providing for the psychological, social, and economic needs of aged family members.

The other classifications of the family are based on the dominance and authority of family members, on the manner in which descent is reckoned, and on the residence of the nuclear family:

3. Authority:

Patriarchal — Authority held by the male (eldest male, usually the father)

Matriarchal — Authority held by the female (eldest female, usually the mother)

Egalitarian — Husband and wife share equally

4. Descent

Patrilineal — Names, property, obligations, and duties descend through father's line

Matrilineal — Names, property, obligations, and duties descend through mother's line

Bilineal — Names, property, obligations, and duties descend through both lines

5. Residence

Patrilocal — Newly married couple resides with husband's consanguineal family

| Matrilocal | Newly married couple resides with wife's consanguineal family |
| Neolocal | Newly married couple sets up own household |

Patriarchy, by far, is the most common authority arrangement. Older men have the right to make those decisions that affect the overall operation of the family and the community at large. Its prevalence is attributed to the males' size and strength and, perhaps most important, to the fact that men are not encumbered by pregnancy and the burdens of infant and child care.

Patriarchy does not mean only the subservience of women to men. It also means the submission and obedience of the young, both boys and girls, to the old. Where authority is based on age and kinship, children have little freedom and can take little initiative in determining their future. This includes the freedom of choosing marriage partners.

Bernard Farber (1964) points out that individuals' rights and obligations are specified through lineage membership. The reckoning of descent determines inheritance, authority, economic privilege, ceremonial and ritual rights of participation, choice of marital partners, and warfare and conflict alliances and opponents.

The most common form of descent, patrilineage, focuses on the man's lineage only. Men reckon their kinship obligations and duties through their father's relatives. They have minimal formal involvements with their mother's kinship groups. Women marry into their husband's family and their male children belong to their spouse's family.

Matrilineage is *not* the mirror image of patrilineal descent. Even though lineage is traced through the female line, authority and responsibility for the maintenance of the line is held by men (especially the mother's brother). The marital relationship has little significance. The biological father-ties to children are solely through affectional bonds. The maternal uncle serves as the predominant authority figure and is in fact the child's social father.

A second variation, pointed out by Farber (1964), that contrasts matrilineage from patrilineage is the role of the woman vis-à-vis the man. The man in a matrilineal society retains supervisory obligation over his own lineage; however, the woman in a patrilineal system does not have these same rights. She does not take part in any of the decisions of her own lineage after she marries. The rationale is to enhance her incorporation into her husband's lineage group. Thus, the woman in a patrilineal society does not have authoritative influence, nor does she have it in a matrilineal society.

Children in a patrilineage are the property of the father's lineage. They thus serve as the replacement population for that lineage. The wife's lineage has no rights to these children. In contrast, in matrilineal societies the wife's lineage in the person of her brother controls her children. Further, although the husband has the right of sexual access to his wife, he does not have the right to raise his children; he must raise his sister's children.

In societies characterized by consanguineal family relationships, on marriage, which is usually arranged by the respective extended-family systems, the couple usually resides in the residence of one of their families. The residential pattern is patrilocal when the couple resides within the husband's family home or matrilocal when the couple resides within the wife's family home. In either case, the married couple and their children are subservient to the larger extended-family system. The emphasis is on the consanguineal organization and its continuation, as opposed to the autonomy of the nuclear family.

Farber (1964) sees marital rules of residence along with lineage as instrumental in delineating kinship continuity. Marital residence is important in that children can be supervised and socialized by the given lineage group. In the patrilocal situation, the wife comes as a stranger to live with her husband and his family. As a result, she is at a distinct disadvantage in maintaining control over her children, who are thus raised in the social traditions and the norms and values of her husband's family. The children have minimal contact and involvement with their mother's lineage. The reverse holds true in the matrilocal situation.

There are also rules of residence governing where children and youths are to reside. In some societies, children are separated from their families as they mature. These societies are characterized by marked differentiation of age groups. During their earlier years, boys reside with their parents, but as they get older they are separated from their parents and are reared in villages populated solely with their age cohorts. Such age-differentiated societies are characterized by rigid rules, obligations, and duties that govern generational relationships, with the younger generations subsumed under the authority of the older ones.

In summary, according to Murdock (1949), the majority of the world's societies have been characterized by an emphasis on the consanguineal family form and have extended kinship structures organized in blood-related clans or tribes. These extended kinship organizations have served as the major structural units in most societies of the world. Through kinship lineages and authority and residence patterns, inheritance as well as economic and status patterns are determined. These controlled marital and sexual partnerships and relationships determine child-rearing patterns.

This prefatory examination outlines the major cross-cultural variations and normative patterns governing family systems. It suggests why the family is of vital importance to the society and to the individual. It should be apparent that changes in the family either precipitated by internal factors or influenced by external processes of social change will have serious ramifications for a given society and its people. Social scientists have increasingly observed that there is now a worldwide trend toward variants of the conjugal family. These families are characterized by egalitarian patterns of authority, bilineal descent, and neolocal residence.

The sources of these changes stem from the major social, economic, religious, political, and familial upheavals that began making themselves felt on a universal scale in the nineteenth century. Our study begins with the examination of social change and the family systems existing in Western societies a century ago. Integral to this discussion is the analysis of sociological thought that not only sought to understand these changes but also became influential in directing that change in the nineteenth as well as in the twentieth century.

Evolutionary Theory and the Origin of the Family: Setting the Stage

Sociological interest in the study of social change and the family was very strong in the mid-nineteenth century in Western Europe. There are a number of important factors to help account for this involvement. First, the fabric of Western European and American society was undergoing major changes. Societies were rapidly industrializing and urbanizing. The old social-class systems were being reworked and a new class structure was developing. Family relationships were also undergoing radical changes. The individual's rights, duties, and obligations to the family and, in turn, to the larger community were being questioned and challenged.

Second, Western colonial expansionism and imperialism were developed fully. Unknown and hitherto unsuspected cultural systems with strange and diverse ways of life were discovered and analyzed. Family systems were found to have differences almost beyond imagination.

Third, an intellectual revolution was occurring. The controversy surrounding evolutionary theory was sweeping Western Europe and America. It led to ramifications on the nature and place of the human species and affected the traditional institutions of the church, the state, and the family. Coinciding with the doctrine of evolutionism was the development of individualism and democracy.

Developing out of this social and intellectual ferment was the application of evolutionary thought to the analysis and understanding of the social origins of the human species. This discussion is concerned with the resultant theories of social change and their applicability to the study of family change.

Evolutionary Theory: The Social Darwinists

Social Darwinism was characterized by nineteenth-century evolutionary theories and was associated with, among others, the names of Herbert Spencer (*The Principles of Sociology,* 1897), J.J. Bachofen (*Das Mutterecht* [The Mother Right], 1861/1948), Henry Sumner Maine (*Ancient Law,* 1861/1960), and Lewis Henry Morgan (*Ancient Society,* 1877/1963). As Robert H. Lowie (1937) has pointed out, the idea of progressive development from stages of savagery to civilization was much older than Charles Darwin's *Origin of Species* (1859/n.d.). However, once the theory of evolution became the dominant force in explaining biological principles and prehistoric artifacts and fossils were also discovered, the social scientists of the nineteenth century quickly

Peabody Museum, Harvard University

These Andaman Islanders pose with a European, Mr. Honfray, whose height (5 feet 5 inches) serves as an indication of theirs. Presented to the Anthropological Society of Paris by a former governor of the Andaman Islands, the photograph (ca. 1860) appeared in a nineteenth-century volume of racial types entitled *Negroes and Sundries,* part of a set produced by the Museum of Paris (now the Musée de l'Homme).

assimilated their earlier speculations about cultural changes into the evolutionary model. Thus, both biological theory and archaeological research provided powerful stimulating forces to the study of society and culture. The basic argument was that since biological evolution proceeded by a series of stages (from the simple to the complex), the same process would hold for cultures. Thus, the Social Darwinists shared in the basic assumption of unilinear evolution (the idea that all civilizations pass through the same stages of development in the same order); they then sought to apply the ideas of progressive development to social forms and institutions—a primary concern being the development of explanatory schemas on the evolution of marriage and family systems.

A second theme underlying the works of the Social Darwinists was the attitude that regarded civilized man as the antithesis of primitive man; if monogamy is the state of modern man, then polygamy is the state of primitive man. Lowie (1937) believes that the theoretical position of the Social Darwinists was a rebuttal against the theologians who argued that primitive peoples had retrogressed from a higher level of civilization. The evolutionists argued, in rebuttal, that the history of organisms is one of progressive evolution from lower to higher forms. In the nineteenth century, evidence of the "backward" nature, or lower state, of civilization was seen in the newly discovered archaeological artifacts and in the institutions of nineteenth-century primitives—the Australian aborigines, the Indians of the Americas, or the black natives of Africa. Lowie's (1937) quotation from the works of the Darwinist A. Lane-Fox Pitt-Rivers[1] illustrates this:

> . . . the existing races, in their respective stages of progression, may be taken as the bona fide representatives of the races of antiquity. . . . They thus afford us living illustrations of the social customs, the forms of government, laws, and warlike practices, which belong to the ancient races from which they remotely sprang, whose implements, resembling, with but little difference, their own, are now found low down in the soil. . . . (Pitt-Rivers, cited in Lowie, 1937:20–21)

The Social Darwinists differed concerning specific lines of development. Bachofen (1861/1948) argued that there was an historical stage of matriarchy in which women ruled the society, whereas Maine (1861/1960) argued that a matriarchal stage of social evolution never existed. Yet the Social Darwinists generally agreed that the family evolved through certain natural stages. Their general approach was to search the literature—particularly the Bible, the Greek and Roman historians, and the existing cross-cultural literature gathered by rather unscientific and biased missionaries and travelers—in the hope of determining the origin and evolution of marriage, the family, and kinship systems.

The argument among evolutionists on the existence of a matriarchal stage of development went beyond academic historical interest. Ultimately, it centered on the nature of women's roles in nineteenth-century Western European and American societies. The different positions espoused by evolutionists reflected different beliefs on sex-role relationships and the differentiation of labor; these theories had social and political implications for contemporary society. Feminists and socialists argued for the existence of the matriarchal stage to support their belief that nineteenth-century Western culture was exploitative of women. It would be instructive to present brief summaries of these arguments as expressed first in the patriarchal theory of Maine (1861/1960) and then in the matriarchal position of Morgan (1877/1963).

In 1861, Henry Sumner Maine (1822–1888) published *Ancient Law*, in which he presented his patriarchal theory of the family. Maine took issue with the thesis on the historical existence of a matriarchal stage. He rejected the use of non-Western nineteenth-century primitive cultures as sources of data through which we could

---

[1] A. Lane-Fox Pitt-Rivers. 1916. *The Evolution of Culture and Other Essays.* Oxford: Oxford University Press.

trace evolutionary universality. His analysis was limited to classical antiquity. From Greek, Roman, and Hebrew history, Maine concluded that the family's origin was patrilocal, patrilineal, and formally or informally polygymous.

On the basis of the evidence he found in ancient law, Maine advanced the patriarchal theory of society. Basically, this theory states that in classical antiquity society was organized in male-dominated households. The eldest man had supreme power, which extended to life-and-death decisions over his wife, children, and slaves. With changes in the Roman legal system (Justinian law), there was a gradual decline in the authority of the male head, which led to the increased freedom of the sons from the father's influence and, ultimately, to the gradual freedom of women. Maine saw male-centered families as primitive and natural and female-centered families as a more-recent phenomenon.

Maine's primary contribution lies in his analysis of the changing importance of kinship in the social evolution of societies from "status to contract." In primitive society, kinship provided the basic principle of organization. These kinship-dominated societies were characterized by group relations and tradition-determined rights and obligations. Over time, there was a movement to greater urbanization, with an accompanying lessening of the kinship bond. "The contrast may be most forcibly expressed by saying that the unit of an ancient society was the Family, of a modern society the Individual" (Maine, 1861/1960:99). Ancient societies were seen as emphasizing collectivity and were organized around the family. The individual was defined as one whose primary purpose was to support the collectivity and assure its continuity in succeeding generations. The family had collective ownership of property. Societies organized around individuals, and individuals gained power at the expense of the family.

With the decline of familism, the state became stronger. Civil law began to take account of the individual, so the family was no longer considered the basic unit. According to Maine, the growth of power of the state combined with the ascendancy of the ideology of individualism would lead to the further demise of the family.

Maine sums up his position in his famous aphorism that the movement of progressive societies has hitherto been a movement from "status to contract" (Maine, 1861/1960:100). By *status,* Maine means that members of the family have no power to acquire property, or bequeath it, or to enter into contracts in relation to it. By *contract,* he refers to the capacity of the individual to enter into independent agreements with strangers. The individual no longer is legally bound and restricted by the family.

Maine elaborates on the changes in the roles of women as a consequence of this movement from status to contract. In ancient law, a woman was subordinated to her blood relations. In modern jurisprudence, she became subordinated to her husband. Maine believes that initially under Justinian law, women gained personal proprietary independence, but, with the advent of Christianity, there was a noticeable diminishing of women's liberty. Reacting against the perceived excesses of Roman society and favoring asceticism, the new faith strongly restricted the freedom of women and equality within marriage. Ultimately, however, Maine argues that, with the development of the state and the ascendancy of contract-based relations, both sexes will gain greater independence as the ideology of individualism gains in popularity.

In opposition to the patriarchal theory of Maine, Bachofen (1861/1948) and Morgan (1877/1963) formulated theories of evolution that postulated the existence of a matriarchal stage in which women dominated the family and the society. Unlike Maine, Bachofen and particularly Morgan incorporated the study of nineteenth-century primitive peoples into their developing theories. Their evolutionary theory was based on the convergence reported by ethnologists in the existence of matrilineal systems of relationships and matrilocal families among nineteenth-century hunting-and-gathering cultures. This fact, as well as the classical historical documents (for example, the Bible) that reported on the frequency of paternal families among pastoral peoples and in early civilizations, led these scholars to hypothesize that the matriarchal family preceded the patriarchal family.

Lewis Henry Morgan (1818–1881) was an anthropologist who, unlike many of the armchair evolutionists of Europe, conducted field work among the Iroquois and other native American groups. Morgan saw societies moving through fixed series of stages, and he shares with other evolutionary theorists the notion of progress culminating in Western industrial society. Morgan divided all human history into three broad stages of human progress: savagery, barbarism, and civilization. Each stage is characterized by the type of inventions that man uses to gain subsistence. Morgan further argued that the development of technology, government, kinship and family patterns, and other institutions were traced through these stages and their substages. Thus, the three substages of savagery range from the development of a fish subsistence to the knowledge of fire, to the invention of the bow and arrow. The three substages of barbarism proceed from the invention of the art of pottery to the domestication of animals, to the cultivation of maize and plants, to the invention of the process of smelting iron ore and the use of iron tools. Finally, the stage of civilization begins with the invention of a phonetic alphabet and the use of writing and proceeds to the present. A parallel classification is made of marriage and family forms. The family followed the following stages: promiscuity, punalua (group marriage), polygamy, and monogamy.

Richard P. Appelbaum (1970) has noted that Morgan's theory is descriptive rather than explanatory and that the descriptive analysis is frequently erroneous. Subsequent empirical research indicated that many societies do not fit the schema, that Morgan underemphasized cultural diffusion, and that some of the examples cited were incorrect. Marvin Harris (1968) criticizes Morgan for failing to link systematically the stages of kinship with the stages of technology and for not explaining why there should be a particular form of technology associated with a particular form of family system. More fundamentally, Morgan shares the same bias as the other Social Darwinists in believing that the apex of human civilization is found in Western industrial society.

In summary, the evolutionary theory of the Social Darwinists ostensibly dealt with such nonimmediate concerns as the origins and historical development of the family, but underlying their theorizing were implications for the roles of men and women in contemporary nineteenth-century family systems. Indeed, their twentieth-century evolutionary theory counterparts continue to put forth these same arguments—over a century later. The initiative for this rebirth of interest in the evolutionary reconstruction of family forms has been the development of arguments and counterarguments stemming from the concern of the women's movement with origins of patriarchy and male sexual dominance.

However, it was the nineteenth-century founders of communist thought, Karl Marx (1818–1883) and Friedrich Engels (1820–1895), who made gender-role relationships the central and dominating concern of evolutionary theory. Although Engels was strongly influenced by the work of Morgan, he used it to address his primary concern—the social condition of the poor and working classes and the exploitation of men, women, and children.

Evolutionary Theory: The Marxists

During this same period, Karl Marx and Friedrich Engels shared and borrowed some of the evolutionary ideas of the Social Darwinists. They developed their own historical theory of the family. Marx and Engels, like the evolutionists, believed that structural differences among societies were to be accounted for by assuming they existed at different stages in the evolution of human civilization. Unlike their contemporaries, they placed primary emphasis on economics as a causal variable rather than on the ideational variables of art, magic, or religion.

Engels' work, *The Origin of the Family, Private Property and the State* (1884/1972), was profoundly influenced by Morgan's *Ancient Society* (1877/1963), for here was an independent corroboration of the materialistic interpretation of history. Morgan's work seemed to confirm the Marxist principle that social institutions change as a result of specific socioeconomic conditions at certain periods of history. Following Morgan's schema of the three main epochs of human history—savagery, barbarism, and civilization—Engels also borrowed Morgan and Bachofen's theory of the existence of an evolutionary theory linking the particular forms of technology with a particular form of family system.

Engels postulated a primitive natural democracy occurring in the first stage—savagery. Savagery was characterized as a primitive commune with no economic inequalities and no private ownership of properties. The family form was group marriage based on a matriarchy. This was followed by the overthrow of the matriarchally based society when men gained economic control over the means of production during the state of barbarism. Women then became subjugated to the masculine-dominated economic system in civilization. In this conceptualization, a social institution such as the family was seen as almost totally dependent on economic relationships and as a means to combat the evils of prostitution (hetaerism); children and women were subjugated and forced to labor as a result of capitalistic exploitation. Engels argued that rather than monogamy being the apex of marital and family forms, it represented the victory of private property over original naturally developed common ownership, group marriage, and polygymous marital arrangements.

> Thus, monogamy does not by any means make its appearance in history as the reconciliation of man and woman, still less as the highest form of such a reconciliation. On the contrary, it appears as the subjection of one sex by the other, as the proclamation of a conflict between the sexes entirely unknown hitherto in prehistoric times. In an old unpublished manuscript, the work of Marx and myself in 1846, I find the following: "The first division of labour is that between man and woman for child breeding." And today I can add: the development of the antagonism between man and woman in monogamian marriage, and the first class oppression with that of the female sex by the male. Monogamy was a great historical advance, but at the same time it inaugurated, along with slavery and private wealth, that epoch, lasting until today, in which every advance is likewise a relative regression, in which the well-being and development of the one group are attained by the misery and repression of the other. (Engels, 1884/1972:74-75)

Engels goes on to speculate that with the coming of the socialist revolution and the next stage in the evolutionary division of labor, family relationships would be characterized by independence from property rights and women would have equal rights with men in decisions on the persistence and dissolution of their marriage. Shulamith Firestone (1970) has developed a table depicting Engel's evolutionary schema (see Figure 1.1).

Engels' work has attracted the attention of some feminists who see in his analysis of patriarchal marriage and the family a positive statement addressed to the problems of women's liberation. Kate Millett (1970) states that Engels' theory of the existence of ancient matriarchies demonstrates that patriarchy is not inevitable and that the family must be treated as other historical institutions and social phenomena—subject to alteration and processes of evolution and change. Marxist-oriented feminists directly link the women's liberation movement with calls for a socialist revolution. Evelyn Reed,[2] a leading Marxist, writes:

> The renewed interest of women in his book is also a tribute to the value of the author's Marxist method. The outstanding merit of Engels's exposition is that he shows the real historical causes behind the catastrophic downfall of women and

[2] *The Origin of the Family, Private Property and the State* by Friedrich Engels. Introduction by Evelyn Reed. Reprinted by permission of Pathfinder Press, copyright © 1972.

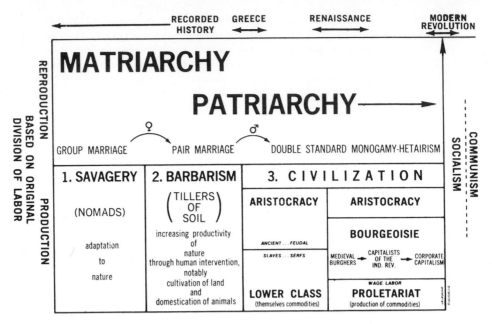

FIGURE 1.1   Shulamith Firestone's schematic presentation of Engel's interdevelopment of matriarchy to patriarchy and the division of labor on a time scale. (Shulamith Firestone. 1970. *The Dialectic of Sex: The Case for Feminist Action.* New York: William Morrow, p. 5. Copyright © 1970 by Shulamith Firestone. Reprinted by permission of William Morrow & Company.)

> thereby illuminates the road ahead for female emancipation. The oppression of women came into existence for the same reasons and through the same forces that brought private property and class society into existence. It did not exist before that. But, as Engels indicates, class society is itself a transitory phenomenon, the product of specific economic conditions at a certain stage of social evolution. It has been—and will be—only a brief interlude in the forward march of humankind. Through further evolution—and socialist revolution—this oppressive system and its degradation of women will be done away with. (Reed in Engels, 1884/1972:22)

Engels' achievement is the exploration of the family as an economic unit and is of great theoretical importance in the study of the sociology of the family. But as Harris (1968) states, insofar as the Marxist orientation constituted a branch of evolutionary thought, it was subjected to many of the same objections raised against the latter.

Evolutionary Theory: Criticism

Evolutionary theory—with its emphasis on large-scale, grand historical theorizing on the origins, evolution, and development of family forms—lost its popularity by the end of the nineteenth century. Evolutionary theorists were criticized on a number of grounds; their concern with establishing evolutionary stages in the family form was rejected because of methodological weaknesses, and their data collection was provided by inexperienced travelers and missionaries with minimal training in the social sciences. For many critics, much of the ancient historical data was worthless.

> Considering how uncertain the information is which people give about the sexual relations of their own neighbours, we must be careful not to accept as trustworthy evidence the statements made by classical writers with reference to more or less

distant tribes of which they evidently possessed very little knowledge. In the very chapter where Pliny states that among the Garamantians men and women lived in promiscuous intercouse he tells us of another African tribe, the Blemmyans, that they were said to have no head and to have the mouth and eyes in the breast. I have never seen this statement quoted in any book on human anatomy, and can see no reason to assume our author was so much better acquainted with the sexual habits of the Garamantians than he was with the personal appearance of the Blemmyans. (Westermarck cited in Bardos, 1964:406–407[3])

Theoretically, the belief in unilinear evolution—that every society develops on a single continuum of evolution—is wrong. There are a great many evolutionary tracks that societies can follow. Evolutionary theory by its very nature tends to be ethnocentric and often racist. The decision as to which factor in society represents the greatest advancement of civilization is subjective; that is, if you measure the apex of civilization by examining technological criteria, Western society obviously ranks on top; however, if you judge advancement by development of kinship classificatory systems, a hunting-and-gathering society (for example, the Arunta of Australia) would rank at the top with Western society pretty low on the continuum. The kinship classificatory system of Western civilization is comparatively undeveloped compared to the Arunta. Not surprisingly, the Social Darwinists measured the advancement of civilization on a unilinear scale based on criteria that placed their own society as the most advanced.

The Social Darwinists made the fatal error of equating contemporary nonliterate cultures with the hypothetical primeval savage. They failed to understand that *all* contemporary peoples have had a prolonged and evolved past. The failure of many of them to have a written record of the past led the Social Darwinists to assume erroneously that they had none. Further, they did not understand that many nonliterate societies de-emphasize changes in the past to stress their continuity with it. This is especially the case in cultures that glorify tradition and reify their sameness with their ancestors. Social Darwinists made ethnocentric and subjective pronouncements. They viewed their own society's art, religion, morals, and values according to their notions of what was good and correct, explaining such "barbaric" practices as polygamy and sexual promiscuity based on their own national and individual norms. They biased their analysis with their own moral feelings on such customs.

Another factor in the decline of comparative analysis was the fact that the Marxists incorporated the evolutionary schema in their own theoretical framework. Contemporary evolutionary anthropologists, such as Leslie White and Marvin Harris, believe that the linkage of Marxism and evolutionism—Engels' *The Origin of the Family, Private Property and the State* being a prime example—gave cause for anti-Marxist–oriented anthropologists to reject the evolutionary schema and the method that it was based on—comparative analysis.

One final factor in the decline of the evolutionary theory was that it was involved with an irrelevant set of questions. What difference does it make which theory you propose on the origin of marriage and family systems or which society represents the apex of civilization and which the nadir if it does not aid in understanding contemporary marriage and family systems? This is especially the case in a world undergoing revolutionary changes and one in which formerly isolated cultures are becoming more and more involved with Western civilization as a result of colonization. Anthropologists—particularly those representing the dominant school in America, the Boasian diffusionists—felt that attempts to theorize about the historical evolutionary process were not as important as examining the influences cultures had on each other. The basic position taken was that societies did not evolve in isolation but rather that they continuously interacted with each other and were constantly in-

---

[3] Edward A. Westermarck. 1922. *The History of Human Marriage*, 5th ed., 3 vols. New York: Macmillan. First published in 1891.

Saudi Women Start to Peek From Behind the Veil

BY ELAINE SCIOLINO

RIYADH, Saudi Arabia, April 8 — While Hend al-Khuthaila was pregnant with her fourth child, she worked full-time as assistant dean of the Women's Center of King Saud University until the day she checked into the hospital to give birth.

Now, as the first woman to become dean of the center, and four months pregnant with her fifth child, the 30-year-old Ph.D. from Syracuse University plans to do the same thing.

Islam, and the particularly strict Saudi interpretation of it, imposes several restrictions on women. Saudi women are not allowed to drive cars, work with men or travel or live abroad without a man who is a member of the family as chaperon. When they leave their homes, they must cover their heads, arms and legs, and the vast majority cover their faces with veils of black gauze or chiffon.

There is a popular perception that all Saudi women stay at home, unseen by the outside world. But Dr. Khuthaila is part of the growing number of Saudi women who are getting educations and going to work. And despite occasional declarations by conservative "ulema" or religious leaders, who rein them in, the trend seems irreversible.

Only 12 years ago, there were no Saudi universities for women. Today, nearly 25 percent of all university students are women, according to Ministry of Higher Education figures.

TELEVISED LECTURES BY MEN

The King Saud University Women's Center, for example, with 500 students and a staff of all women, seems very much like a private convent school. Elderly, bearded guards stand at the gates. Once inside, the students throw off their veils.

Except for the mandatory ankle-length skirts, they can dress anyway they want — even in T-shirts, dangling earrings and lots of makeup. When qualified women are not available to teach, students watch men lecture over television screens, asking questions via classroom telephones.

The students seem to accept their separateness; they say they just want equality. "We fall asleep watching televisions," a graduate student in English literature said. "We have enough money to get the best women professors in the world here."

Veiling themselves in front of a man who is a professor would not do, another student said, because, "How can you see your notebook behind a veil?"

Others want more courses and better schools at home.

Saudi women study medicine alongside men. Last year, pharmacy was added to their university curriculum, and computer science will soon be introduced. But subjects like law, engineering and political science are not offered to women here; only Saudi women abroad can study those subjects.

Although women make up only about 5 percent of the work force — most work as teachers, social workers, doctors and nurses — they are beginning to break into business, journalism, banking and government ministries.

IMPORTANT ROLE SEEN

Some government officials say they believe women can help limit Saudi dependence on foreign workers, as long as their work places can be off-limits to men. In fact, one of the objectives of the new five-year plan is to "identify the areas and bases for employment of women in a manner which would not be contrary to the Moslem faith."

Islam allows women to hold property and money separate from their husbands, and 10 bank branches have opened exclusively for women. At the National Commercial Bank Women's Branch in Riyadh, a staff of 17 women offers services ranging from letters of credit to traveler's checks to 900 women who are customers.

Customers say they find the atmosphere more relaxed than at the men's branch next door.

(continued)

"I get better service here and more respect," said one woman, who removed her black silk aba, designed by Christian Dior, inside the bank. "And it's easier dealing face-to-face with women than behind a veil with men."

Women are investing and running businesses, although most business deals are done over the telephone or by men working as representatives.

Three years ago, Soad al-Dabbagh, a 34-year-old mother of three boys, opened a boutique of original and reproduction Bedouin clothes, jewelry and artifacts in the glittery Akaria Shopping Center in Riyadh. Following the strict Saudi interpretation of Islamic law, she does not sell to customers, but runs the business from a home office.

WOMEN'S EDITORIAL OFFICE

Mrs. Dabbagh wears the colorful, hand-embroidered Bedouin robes sold in her shop, robes that in no way resemble the black aba worn by most Saudi women. She does not cover her face when she goes out, but wears a sheer, gold-trimmed black scarf.

"Covering the face is a tradition borrowed from the Turkish people, not a rule of Islam," she said.

One battle most Saudi women do not seem to be fighting is the battle of the veil. Many say they feel that veiling their heads and faces is preferable to the stares and insults of men.

In many professions, separate staffs of women are slowly being hired. Some ministries have hired women to do research, type reports and handle social welfare cases. Most work in separate, self-contained offices.

One newspaper, Al Riyadh, now has its own women's editorial office, with a woman who is an editor and a staff of 20. They can write about anything but cannot attend events involving men.

"Sure, it annoys you when you can't write about something that interests you,"

said one woman who is a reporter. "But we will achieve our goals in one way or another."

The most commonly heard complaint of Saudi working women is that they are not allowed to drive, a restriction born of Saudi interpretation of Islam that makes Saudi women dependent on their husbands or male relatives or on shuttle buses arranged by their offices. Obviously, women with chauffeurs do not complain.

Islam does not prohibit a woman from driving, only from coming into close contact with a man who is not her husband. One leading Islamic scholar touched off a heated debate in the newspapers two years ago when he suggested that it was worse for a woman to be driven by a foreign chauffeur than to drive herself.

Some women say the separation of men and women in the work force limits the temptations for their husbands. Saudi men are allowed to take up to four wives, but only if they are able to treat all of them with total equality. Few are polygamous.

Most Saudi working women say they do not like the word "feminist" and add that they believe the pace of change for women in the West came too quickly. "A lady is a lady," said Feriyal Jazzar, the director of the Women's Branch Bank. "If you ask for equality, you lose something, and the men will treat you as a man."

Other women say their struggle is a long process. "We don't have as much as we want, but we've made remarkable achievements," said Dr. Khuthaila, the King Saud University Women's Center dean. "We are hoping things will happen more evolutionary than revolutionary. If change happens gradually it will last; if it happens as a result of an explosion, it's easy for a collapse."

SOURCE. Elaine Sciolino. 1985. "Saudi women start to peek from behind the veil." *The New York Times* (Apr. 13). Copyright © 1985 by The New York Times Company. Reprinted by permission.

fluencing each other. Thus, it was felt to be imperative to examine cultures that were being increasingly Westernized. Margaret Mead, in her autobiography, underscores the basic motivation of Boas and his followers:

> . . . the materials on which the new science depends were fast vanishing, and forever. The last primitive peoples were being contacted, missionized, given new tools and new ideas. Their primitive cultures would soon become changed beyond recovery. Among many American Indian groups, the last old women who spoke a language that had developed over thousands of years were already senile and babbling in their cups; the last man who had ever been on a buffalo hunt would soon die. The time to do the work was *now*. (Mead, 1975:138)

Many European and American social scientists of the late nineteenth and early twentieth centuries had a more-immediate concern. They were appalled by the excesses of industrialization and urban society and the calamitous changes in the family system. The study of social change and the family centered on this concern. It is to these concerns and how social scientists analyzed and dealt with them that we address our attention in the following chapter.

Conclusion

The Changing Family: Comparative Perspectives is divided into five main parts. In Part I, Chapters 1 to 3, we examine the main issues in the sociology of the family with particular attention to comparative family systems. These issues influence both the discipline and the very phenomenon they seek to study: the family. An historical account of the development of comparative family analysis is presented and related to the historical developments of Western societies. In addition, we look at the major theoretical orientations used by sociologists to study social change, modernization, and the family.

Part II of our presentation focuses on the family in relation to the community. We apply the theoretical orientation presented in the first three chapters to our later discussions. Chapter 4 is concerned with the family in cities of the Western world, with particular emphasis on the family in England and the United States. Chapter 5 focuses on the experience of immigrant families and their transition to ethnic American families. Chapter 6 looks at poverty conditions cross-culturally and their impact on the family; poverty families in the United States and Latin America are the center of attention here. The concluding chapter of this part aims to increase our understanding of urban family dynamics by seeing how families operate in a non-Western context—sub-Saharan Africa. A family in Lagos, Nigeria, serves as the case in point.

Part III, Chapters 8 to 12, takes an in-depth look at gender roles, courtship, and marital relationships in changing societies. These chapters focus on topics of current interest. Chapter 8 compares biological, religious, and sociological viewpoints to explain male–female differences. The discussion of sexuality and the family includes a discussion of homosexuality; AIDS and its impact on human sexuality concludes our discussion. The next two chapters examine gender-role relationships in the context of dating, cohabitation, courtship, and mate-selection patterns. These are followed by two chapters that are concerned with gender-role relationships in the world of work and the world of the home. Preliterate societies, the Republic of South Africa, the Soviet Union, Sweden, and Israel provide the comparative illustrations in Chapter 11. Chapter 12 deals with the same issues but places particular stress on family patterns in the Western world. It builds on previous chapters and takes an historical approach to a better understanding of contemporary American marital relationships.

Part IV is comprised of three chapters that deal with different aspects of generational relationships within the family. Chapter 13 examines changing fertility patterns, issues regarding abortion, and medical innovations in fertility technology and their respective influences on family dynamics; our comparative illustration deals with India and its population-planning programs. We then shift gears and examine what may be the most crucial stage of the family life cycle—the transition to parenthood. American social-class variations are discussed and analyzed, and changing roles of mothers and fathers also come under scrutiny. Chapters 14 and 15 are centered around the theme of generational relationships as expressed through age-differentiation and age-stratification processes. First, we study childhood and adolescence, then, in Chapter 15, we examine the elderly. The discussion of the relationship of the individual to the family and, in turn, to the community serves as an additional anchoring theme. Contrasts and comparisons between historical preliterate societies and industrial societies in the West are made. Historical changes in the West are also analyzed to help our understanding of contemporary American patterns.

Part V is concerned with families in crisis and change. The emphasis in Chapter 16 is on two of the most dramatic manifestations of family violence—wife battering and child abuse. In our handling of family violence, we emphasize how the structure of the contemporary Western conjugal family system plays a role in the manifestation of violence. The following chapter deals with divorce, single parenthood, teenage motherhood, and remarriage. We begin by examining the situation in Japan and shift our attention to Islamic attitude and behavior toward divorce and contemporary changes in Egypt and Iran are analyzed. This is followed by a detailed investigation of changing divorce patterns in the United States. Such issues as no-fault divorce, changing adjudication decisions on child custody, and the effects of divorce on children are discussed and analyzed. Single-parent households, the problems they face and the solutions to these problems next gain our attention; teenage mothers are looked at as a case in point. We close this chapter with a detailed study of remarriage after divorce.

The concluding chapter of the book differs from the perfunctory summary chapters found in most textbooks. We apply the themes of the entire book to an analysis of a family system that we have only briefly discussed previously—the Chinese family. The usefulness of the presented theories are put to the test by looking at changes in the Chinese family system. The analysis is on modernization processes, the family's relationship with the wider kinship networks and surrounding communities, premarital and marital relationships, divorce, and age- and sex-differentiation and stratification patterns. The subject matter is seen within the framework of one of the most significant and intriguing events of the twentieth century—the social revolution and cultural upheaval in China. However, we emphasize the need for caution in using China as the model for predicting the future of family systems. China demonstrates the complexity that underlies the study of social change and the family and provides a dramatic contrast to the American family.

This book is about families in change. We hope that it makes a contribution to the understanding of this phenomenon.

CHAPTER 2

The Industrial Revolution and the Rise of the Modern Family

A barn raising in Almelund, Minnesota, June 1913. Such activities fostered community solidarity among rural families.

CHAPTER OUTLINE

European societies during the nineteenth century underwent massive changes. The old social order anchored in kinship, the village, the community, religion, and old regimes was attacked and fell to the twin forces of industrialism and revolutionary democracy. The sweeping changes had particular effect on the family. There was a dramatic increase in such conditions as poverty, child labor, desertions, prostitution, illegitimacy, and women abuse. These conditions were particularly evident in the newly emerging industrial cities. The vivid writings of a novelist such as Charles Dickens in *Oliver Twist* and *Hard Times* provide startling portraits of a harsh new way of life.

The Industrial Revolution dramatically changed the nature of economic and social life. The factory system developed, and, with its development, there was a transformation from home industries in rural areas to factories in towns and cities of Europe and America. Rural people were lured by the novelty of city life and the prospects of greater economic opportunity. England became the first and prime example of the new society. In the great midlands, such cities as Birmingham, Leeds, Manchester, and Sheffield emerged. Manchester, which was probably the first industrial city in history, saw its population shoot up from some 70,000 people in 1801 to over 225,000 by 1830 and to slightly over 300,000 by 1850. In these new industrial cities, large amounts of labor, raw materials, and capital were centered.

Neil J. Smelser (1959) describes the effects on the family of the mechanization of spinning and weaving in the cotton industry. The domestic economy of the preindustrial family disappeared. The rural- and village-based family system no longer served as a productive unit; as a productive unit, the cottage industry enabled the family to combine economic activities with the supervision and training of its children. The development of the factory system saw the differentiation of family roles because members of the family performed separate tasks, frequently not even in the same factory or industry. Patriarchal authority was weakened with urbanization. Previously, in rural and village families, fathers reigned supreme; they were knowledgeable in economic skills and were able to train their children. The great diversity of city life rendered this socialization function relatively useless. The rapid change in industrial technology and the innumerable forms of work necessitated a more-formal institutional setting—the school—to help raise the children. In response to the changing family situation, the British passed legislation to aid children. Separated from parental supervision, working children were highly exploited. Laws came into existence to regulate the amount of time children were allowed to work and their working conditions. The law also required that children attend school. These legal changes reflected the change in the family situation in the urban setting; families were no longer available or able to watch constantly over their children.

The separation of work from the home had important implications for family members. Increasingly, the man became the sole provider for the family and the women and children developed a life comprised solely of concerns centered around the family, the home, and the school. Their contacts with the outside world diminished, and they were removed from community involvements. The family's with-

FIGURE 2.1 Poverty in England, ca. 1872: Wentworth Street, Whitechapel, London.

drawal from the community was tinged by its hostile attitude toward the surrounding city. The city was depicted as a sprawling and planless development bereft of meaningful community and neighborhood relationships. The tremendous movement of a large population into the industrial centers provided little opportunity for the family to form deep or lasting ties with neighbors. Instead, the family viewed their neighbors with suspicion and weariness. Exaggerated beliefs developed on the prevalence of urban poverty, crime, and disorganization.

  This chapter deals with the different approaches taken by social scientists in their analysis of the family in the wake of the Industrial Revolution. Throughout the nineteenth and the early twentieth centuries, they voiced concern about the excesses of industrial urban society and the calamitous changes in the family system. Radicals, conservatives, and social reformers called for fundamental changes in the society and in the family and its new way of life. However, by mid-twentieth century, the dominant perspective in sociology, structural functionalism, proclaimed that the family was alive, well, and functioning in modern industrial society.

Nineteenth-Century Critics of the Industrial Revolution

Both radical and conservative critics of the new social order saw the decline in the importance of kinship and community involvements and the changes in the makeup of the nuclear family as more-important areas of investigation than the study of the evolutionary transformations of the family. The radicals, as typified in the writings of Marx and Engels, saw the necessity for the overthrow of the new capitalist-based industrial system to establish equality between the sexes. The conservatives, Frédéric Le Play (1806–1882) being the most important to family study, called for the re-establishment of the old social order. Many of the family issues raised by these ideologically opposed camps are relevant to the analysis of the contemporary family system. It is highly important to see how these theorists examined the pressures on the family created by the social changes that were transforming Western European and American societies.

If we remove the evolutionary trappings from the works of Marx and Engels, especially the Morgan-derived anthropological analyses and speculations on the family in antiquity, we are left with an outstanding critique of mid-nineteenth-century family life. Indeed, this insightful analysis has been most influential in the understanding of later twentieth-century family dynamics.

Marx and Engels examined changes in the nuclear family that were instituted with the rise of industrial and monopolistic capitalism. The new economic system separated work from the home. In the domestic economy of preindustrial Europe, work and family activities were integrated in the household. Husband, wife, and children were all involved in economic production. With the change in the economic order, small landholdings and businesses were lost, and the men became wage earners in factories. As men became dependent on their bosses, the more-fortunate women and children became dependent on their husbands and fathers. The poorest and most unfortunate women and children worked as marginal laborers in the mills, factories, and mines under exploitative conditions for wages that were barely subsistent.

The new economic system was particularly harsh on women. Those who had husbands to provide for them were domestically confined to household tasks and child-care chores. The gradual loss of women's economic independence led to an increased division of labor between men and women and to the subservience of women to men. In the domestic economy of preindustrial society, women had a public role; in the capitalistic industrial society, women had a private role. In the following passage, Engels spells out the implications of the development of the "private" family for women and what is necessary to assure the independence and equality of women:

> . . . her being confined to domestic work now assured supremacy in the house for the man: the woman's housework lost its significance compared with the man's work in obtaining a livelihood; the latter was everything, the former an insignificant contribution. . . . The emancipation of women and their equality with men are impossible and must remain so as long as women are excluded from socially productive work and restricted to housework, which is private. The emancipation of women becomes possible only when women are enabled to take part in production on a large social scale, and when domestic duties require their attention only to a minor degree. (Engels, 1884/1972:152)

In summary, the privatization of the family becomes the key conceptualization in the Marxian analysis of the family. The withdrawal of the family from economic and community activities led to the development of inequality. This inequality was based on the sexual differentiation of labor and the different family roles for men and women. As we will see throughout this book, the study of privatization in the family becomes for us, too, a key conceptualization in the analysis of social change and the family.

Frédéric Le Play, a leading exponent of political conservatism, was profoundly influenced by the effects of the industrial and democratic revolutions on Western society. A devout Catholic, he was appalled by the loss of power and prestige of the family, church, and local community. He strongly reacted against what he saw as the atomizing effects of such forces as technology, industrialization, and the division of labor. He cared less to develop grand evolutionary theories than to react against the growing decline of the extended family and the instability of the nuclear family.

Le Play was a French engineer, administrator, and social reformer. He and his followers, in a half century of unbelievably ambitious work, studied the nature of the family and its relationship to the surrounding community. His magnum opus, *Les Ouvriers Européens (The European Workers)* was published in 1855 and is a comprehensive comparative analysis of more than 300 working-class families who are representative of those who labor in characteristic industries and are from typical localities all over Europe and parts of Asia. Le Play's work was a forerunner of many twentieth-century methodological techniques. He created his own instruments of data collection, which included social surveys, research interviews, family-budget questionnaires, participant-observation methods, and case-history methods. The contemporary American sociologist, Robert A. Nisbet, refers to this work as "the supreme example in the nineteenth century of actual field study of the traditional community, its structure, relation to environment, component elements, and disorganization by the economic and political forces of modern history" (Nisbet, 1966:62).

The European Workers places great stress on the familial form and seeks to demonstrate that the major outlines of any society are set by its underlying type of family. The family types that are characterized by a high degree of stability, commitment to tradition, and security of the individual are delineated. Also dealt with are family systems undergoing disorganization. In the analysis of French families, secularism and individualism are seen as destroying the bases of tradition and community and rupturing the relations between tradition and the family.

Three dominant types of families are recognized by Le Play: (1) the patriarchal, or extended, family; (2) the unstable, or nuclear, family; and (3) the stem family. The patriarchal family is authoritarian and based on tradition and lineage. It is common among pastoral people, such as the Russian peasants and the Slavonic peasants of central Europe. The father has extensive authority over all his unmarried sons and daughters and is the sole owner of the family property. The patriarchal authority of the family occurs where there is a minimum of extended political and social authority. Such a family system is seen as incompatible with political and modern systems.

The unstable family is seen to prevail among working populations who live under the factory system of the West. This type of family was also common during other historical periods of great instability, such as in ancient Athens after its disastrous wars with Sparta and other Greek states and in the later Roman Empire. This family type is seen to be inherently disorganized and is the prime cause of social disorganization. It is strongly individualistic, mobile, and secular. "Where individualism becomes dominant in social relations men rapidly move towards barbarism" (Le Play cited in Zimmerman and Frampton, 1966:14).

The unstable family shows little attachment to family lineage. It has no roots in property and is an unstable structure from generation to generation. It is associated with the pauperization of working-class populations under the new manufacturing regime in the West.

> Under this regime the individual, single or married, finding it no longer necessary to provide for the needs of his relatives, rapidly attains a high position, if he is capable. On the contrary, if he is incapable or unfortunate he is not able to call upon any family help in case of need. Thus, he falls more quickly into a miserable condition. Unhappily, this depraved condition tends to perpetuate itself because parents can no longer contribute further to the establishment of their children, or because the children are not under parental guidance. Thus is formed that peculiar social state which history has not often disclosed before — pauperism. (Le Play cited in Zimmerman and Frampton, 1966:15)

The stem family is seen as the happy compromise between the two other types. It is free of the authoritarianism of the patriarchal family, but it is still rooted in traditionalism. It is stable in structure and committed to perpetuating the family lineage. It, however, joins only one married child to the household; the others are independently established with shares of the inheritance and are free to found their own households or to remain in an unmarried state on the family land. The stem family is seen to arise partly from traditional influences of patriarchal life, but it finally forms itself under the influence of individually owned property. It is found in Scandinavia, Hannover (West Germany), northern Italy, and to some extent in England. This system ensures the continuation of the ancestral household and also encourages individual autonomy, new enterprises, and new personal property. Le Play sees it as combining the best features of the patriarchal system with the individualism of the unstable family form.

> It satisfies both those who are happy in the situation of their birth and those who wish to advance socially or economically. It harmonizes the authority of the father and the liberty of the children. . . . The stem-family satisfies both tendencies and harmonizes two equally imperative needs — the respect for tradition and the yearning for the new. . . . The stem-family, indeed, answered all the legitimate instincts of humanity. This is the reason why public order prevails everywhere it exists in strength. (Le Play cited in Zimmerman and Frampton, 1966:15–16, 20)

Each family type, then, is seen to be related to other types of institutions in the community. Le Play's central concern is the ties uniting the family with other parts of the community — religion, government, education, and economy. His analysis of the family is intertwined with the analysis of the community in which the family finds itself. It is this insightful perspective that has made Le Play's work stand out in the history of family analysis. His conservative orientation, although distasteful to many contemporary social scientists, should not obscure the importance of his empirical findings on the economic basis of family and community life.

The family issues raised by Marx, Engels, and Le Play still are the central core of contemporary analysis of social change and the family. Both the radical perspective and the conservative perspective are highly critical of the emerging family form of the nineteenth century. Marx and Engels refer to it as the monogamous family characterized by the privatization of family life; Le Play refers to it as the unstable family.

Robert A. Nisbet (1966) has provided us with a highly useful comparison of Le Play and Marx, as well as a concise summary of their respective positions. Both were aghast at the bourgeoisie democracy of the nineteenth century. Rather than providing for liberty and prosperity, it was seen as leading to disabling competition and strife. Both sought social orders that would remove the excesses of bourgeoisie democracy and the evils of industrialism. Yet the differences stemming from their opposing ideologies lead to different assessments and conclusions.

> Both Le Play and Marx were sensitive to the institutional component in history, but beyond this generic likeness there is only stark contrast. For Marx the key institution is social class. For Le Play it is kinship: the structure of society varies with the type of family that underlies it. Marx detested private property, Le Play declared it the indispensable basis of social order and freedom. Marx treated religion as something superfluous to an understanding of human behavior and, in its effects, an opiate. For Le Play religion is as essential to man's mental and moral life as the family is to his social organization. For Marx, the whole rural scheme of things is tantamount to idiocy as far as its impact on human thought is concerned. Le Play, for all his conscious acceptance of industry, plainly prefers rural society, seeing in it the haven of security that urban life, by its very nature, must destroy. Marx was socialist; Le Play put socialism, along with mass democracy, secularism, and egalitarianism, among the major evils of his time—all of them unmistakable signs of social degeneration. (Nisbet, 1966:67)

It is the tension between the radical perspective and the conservative perspective that echoes throughout the contemporary analysis of the family in change and takes different forms depending on different substantive issues. But, taken together, these perspectives can be seen as critical perspectives questioning the nature and makeup of contemporary family systems and their relationships with the individuals that compose them and the communities that surround them.

The Ideal Type: Community and the Family

European sociology, which rejected the theoretical assumptions of Social Darwinism by the turn of the twentieth century, developed the ideal type as an alternative procedure to account for and explain historical changes in Western societies—from agriculture-based economies to industrialization-based ones.

The ideal type is a conceptual construct used in the analysis of social phenomena. The techniques for its use were developed by the German sociologist, Max Weber (1949). The ideal type is constructed from observation of the characteristics of the social phenomena under investigation, but it is not intended to correspond exactly to any single case; rather, it designates the hypothetical characteristics of a "pure" or "ideal" case. The ideal type, then, does not imply evaluation or approval of the phenomena being studied. No normative or evaluative connotations are implied—it is an analytically constructed model.

The ideal type does not conform to reality, being an abstraction that hypothesizes certain qualities or characteristics of the social phenomena under study. These qualities or characteristics are believed to be typical of that type of phenomenon, and then the construct proceeds to describe and test hypotheses about actual empirical social phenomena. For example, an ideal type is constructed on the characteristics of cities. No cities would actually conform in an absolute sense to this ideal type, but the construct is useful in that it provides a focus point, a frame of reference, for the study of a given city. Or take the illustration of "the American family." No particular American family can match all the characteristics of a hypothetical construct of the American family, but such a construction can be useful in examining given families in comparison with this construct and in comparison with each other. The ideal type provides a hypothetical model against which real cities or real families can be contrasted, analyzed, and measured. The ideal type facilitates classification and comparison, and actual social phenomena may thus be compared on the basis of actual, as well as hypothesized, characteristics.

Social scientists have found ideal types highly useful as analytical tools. These types make possible a conceptualization of social phenomena and facilitate cross-cultural and historical comparison among them. They aid in locating factors of social change in societies and enable the comparative investigation of institutions, such as the family, over time and space. Yet they have severe limitations. In this chapter, some ideal types of communities will be examined. For the purposes of this book, only a limited number of such conceptualizations will be considered, and they will be analyzed in terms of relevancy in the study of urbanization processes and the family.

The perceived chaotic world of the city was countered by the family turning in onto itself. What Marx described as the privatization of the family reflects this development. A strong emotional transformation characterizes the nineteenth century. The emotional bonds that individuals held for the community, the village, and the extended family were transformed into the development of an exclusive emotional attachment to family members. With the work world seen as hostile and precarious, the family took on an image as a place of refuge. The home was seen as a place that provided security and safety from a cruel, harsh, and unpredictable industrial urban society.

This antiurban state of mind was echoed in the works of contemporary social scientists. The revulsion toward the city and the bemoaning of the loss of an idealized past naturally led sociologists to develop contrasting models of city life versus rural life. The city became identified with social disorganization, alienation, and the loss of community and meaningful relationships. In comparison, the small village and rural community were romanticized for their orderliness, noncompetitiveness, and meaningfulness of personal relationships.

As Robert A. Nisbet (1966) points out, both radicals and conservatives viewed the past with nostalgia and the urban present with distaste. Although the radicals eventually embraced the city, seeing in it the hope for the revolutionary future, they too were aghast at the social conditions existing in the emerging industrial cities of the nineteenth century. Friedrich Engels, a romantic radical, was appalled by the urban prospect:

> We know well enough that [the] isolation of the individual . . . is everywhere the fundamental principle of modern society. But nowhere is this selfish egotism as blatantly evident as in the frantic bustle of the great city. (Engels cited in Nisbet, 1966:29)

One is struck with the similarity of Engels' view with that of the conservative Alexis de Tocqueville (1805–1859), who wrote the following after a visit to Manchester, England:

> From this foul drain the greatest stream of human industry flows out to fertilize the whole world. From this filthy sewer pure gold flows. Here humanity attains the most complete development and its most brutish, here civilization works its miracles and civilized man is turned almost into a savage. (Cited in Nisbet, 1966:29)

Keeping in mind this antiurban bias, let us now look at some of the famous and influential typologies that were developed during this period.

Henry Sumner Maine's (1862/1960) distinction of "status to contract" society was one of the earliest of such typologies. Maine postulated that *status* societies are characterized by group relations that are anchored in tradition. Tradition, in turn, determines the rights and obligations of individuals. The individual's status was fixed by his or her family and kinship system, which served as the foundation of social organization. The movement to *contract* relations was fostered by urbanization, with kinship bonds becoming less strong. With the ascendancy of the state, civil law replaced traditional customs in enforcing and regulating social obedience and social control. Maine argued that with the increased power of the state, the influence of the family over the individual would decline and women's social status, which was extremely low in status communities, would rise and familism would decline. The essence of Maine's argument was that the powers, privileges, and duties that were once vested in the family had shifted to the national state. Concomitantly, people's social relationships, which were based on their status, shifted to individually agreed *contracts*.

Maine's work had a great influence on his nineteenth-century contemporaries. Ferdinand Tönnies (1855–1936), whose *Gemeinschaft und Gesellschaft (Community and Society*, 1963) was originally published in 1887, has been an inspirational source for students of community analysis to the present day. *Gemeinschaft* and *Gesellschaft* are ideal types and refer to the nature of social relationships, basic social groups, and institutions.

Gemeinschaft (community) relationships are intimate, traditional, enduring, and based on informal relations determined by *who* the individual is in the community as opposed to *what* he or she has done — in sociological parlance, ascriptive status rather than achieved status. The culture of the community is homogeneous and the moral custodians are the family and the church. For Tönnies, there are three central aspects of *Gemeinschaft*: kinship, neighborhood, and friendship. These institutions serve as the foundation for social life and activities.

Gesellschaft (society association) refers to the large-scale, contractual, impersonal relationships that Tönnies saw emerging in industrializing and urbanizing Europe in the late nineteenth century. *Gesellschaft* includes business-oriented relations based on rational calculations geared to instrumental ends. Personal relationships are subordinate. In the *Gesellschaft*, family groups and institutions no longer serve as the basis of social life; rather, such societies are organized around work relationships and bureaucratic institutions.

Tönnies was antagonistic to the growth of individualism. He believed that acute individualism led to egotistic, self-willed individuals who sought friends only as means and ends to self-interested gains. He decried the involvement of women in the labor force and feared the loss of their involvement in the family.

> As woman enters into the struggle of earning a living, it is evident that trading and the freedom and independence of the female factory worker as contracting party and possessor of money will develop her rational will, enabling her to think in a calculating way, even though, in the case of factory work, the tasks themselves may not lead in this direction. The woman becomes enlightened, cold-hearted, conscious. Nothing is more foreign and terrible to her original inborn nature, in spite of all later modifications. Possibly nothing is more characteristic and important in the process of formation of the *Gesellschaft* and destruction of *Gemeinschaft*. (Tönnies, 1887/1963:166)

Likewise, he saw the destructive effects of child labor on the family. Basically a conservative, Tönnies cites Karl Marx in documenting the ill effects of child labor. Taken together, these changes are seen as destroying the fabric of traditional society and the solidarity of its people. Old values and attitudes are no longer internalized by the young, and the intertwining rights and obligations that bound the traditional community together are weakened and gradually dissolve. The family itself becomes subordinated to personal interests. "The family becomes an accidental form for the satisfaction of natural needs, neighborhood and friendship are supplanted by special interest groups and conventional society life" (Tönnies, 1887/1963:168).

In summary, Tönnies' depiction of the *Gesellschaft* is strikingly similar to that of Karl Marx. But unlike Marx, who sought future revolutionary changes, Tönnies yearned for the return of the romantic past described in his ideal typification of the *Gemeinschaft*. In Table 2.1, a schematic representation of Tönnies' societal types are delineated.

Emile Durkheim (1855–1917) also distinguished the nature of social relationships with these two contrasting types of social orders. Durkheim's doctoral dissertation, *The Division of Labor in Society*, was published in 1893. He compared societies based on *mechanical solidarity* with societies based on *organic solidarity* in regard to social inte-

TABLE 2.1   Summary of the Contrasts Between *Gemeinschaft* and *Gesellschaft*

	Societal Types	
Social Characteristic	*Gemeinschaft*	*Gesellschaft*
Dominant social relationships	Fellowship Kinship Neighborliness	Exchange Rational calculations
Central institutions	Family law Extended kin group	State Capitalistic economy
The individual in the social order	Self	Person
Characteristic form of wealth	Land	Money
Type of law	Family law	Law of contract
Ordering of institutions	Family life Rural village life Town life	City life Rational life Cosmopolitan life
Type of social control	Concord Folkways and mores Religion	Convention Legislation Public opinion

SOURCE: Don Martindale. 1960. *The Nature and Types of Sociological Theory* 2nd Ed. Cambridge, Mass.: Houghton Mifflin, p. 84. Copyright © 1960 by Don Martindale. Copyright 1981 by Harper & Row, Publishers, Inc. Reprinted by permission.

gration. Mechanical solidarity describes the form of social cohesion that exists in small-scale societies that have a minimal division of labor. The type of relationships that link members of such small, stable communities are characterized as being overlapping and interrelated; they are cohesive because of shared bonds and habits. Social unity, Durkheim said, is mechanical and automatic in that the parts of the society are interchangeable. Close friendship and kinship groups are typical of mechanical solidarity in that they are secured by personal, stable, and emotional attachments.

In contrast, societies based on organic solidarity, which Durkheim believed was emerging in Europe, were founded on increased specialization and the division of labor. Organic solidarity-type relationships are impersonal, transient, fragmented, and rational. The source of societal unity is the interdependence of specialized and highly individualized members and the complementary diversity of their positions and life experiences. In relationships marked by organic solidarity one does not relate as a whole individual, but one relates to those qualities that are relevant to the particular function one is performing in relation to others. Durkheim associated the shift in these two types of solidarities, from mechanical to organic, as resulting from the increased size and density of population, the ease and rapidity of communication, and especially with the increased division of labor. All of these factors are seen to be linked with the rise of industrialization and the growth of cities.

Durkheim mirrors the conservatism of Maine and Tönnies. In *The Division of Labor in Society*—as well as in his other works, notably *Suicide* (1897/1951)—Durkheim argues that the cohesive and stabilizing forces of European society are disintegrating. The destructive forces of industrialization, secularization, and revolution account for the alienation, anomie, and isolation of modern urban life. Indeed, in his *The Elementary Forms of Religious Life* (1912), Durkheim viewed collective consciousness as arising out of the individual's participation in the communal life. The origins of man's conceptualization of the universe and the categories of knowledge, he said, stem from this communal perspective. It is no wonder, then, that Durkheim reflects the concern of his contemporaries, both sociologists and lay people, about the problems inherent in the modern industrial urban society.

In conclusion, the ideal type was developed to contrast the emerging industrial city with the preindustrial rural and village community. This typological approach was tinged with an antiurban bias that distorted both the analyses of these sociologists and the many subsequent analyses of the city. Further, since typologies were too broadly based and too vague, rather than aid in the analysis of urban family-life patterns, they led to obfuscation and distortion. Finally, the typologies failed to deal with the wide range of variations within cities as well as with cross-cultural and historical variations. In the next chapter, our discussion will continue on this theme on the relationship of the family to the city. But now we will pick up on our account of the impact of industrialization on the family by examining American sociology in the late nineteenth and early twentieth centuries.

American Family Sociology: Late Nineteenth and Early Twentieth Centuries

Toward the end of the nineteenth and through the early twentieth centuries, sociology in the United States shifted its emphasis away from the study of evolution to the study of social problems and the advocacy of social reform. The social reform movement's paramount concern was the study of the family in the context of the abuses of rapid industrialization and urbanization. The emphasis switched from the development of theories of family systems to the more urgent concerns of individual families and their members—illegitimacy, prostitution, child abuse, prostitution, and other resultant abuses, which were seen as arising from nongovernmental supervision of industrial and urban institutions. This underlying assumption about the causes of social problems was held by the social reform movement's major advocate, the Chicago School of Sociology, and is reflected in the following quotation from its journal, the *American Journal of Sociology* (founded in 1894): "we understand both the family and the effects of urban and industrial developments; what we must do is solve the resulting problems and strengthen the family" (cited in Adams, 1975:5).

The University of Chicago dominated much of twentieth-century American sociology. The Chicago School of Sociology—under the chair of Robert E. Park and with such important sociologists as Ernest W. Burgess, Ellsworth Faris, E. Franklin Frazier, Louis Wirth, Robert Redfield, W.I. Thomas, and Florian Znaniecki—played a pivotal role in the development of American family sociology and urban sociology. In addition, Chicago was blessed by the presence of such important intellectuals as Thorstein Veblen, John Dewey, and George Herbert Mead. Chicago also saw the blossoming of the social welfare and social reform activities of Jane Addams, Graham Taylor, and other settlement workers. Their work increased the empirical database on city life. The Chicago School served as the intellectual nexus for the study of urban life and dynamics.

Following intellectual biases in sociology and in the larger society, the Chicago School developed a distinct contrast between urban and rural life as well as an implicit antiurban model of city life. They saw traditional patterns of life being broken down by debilitating urban forces, resulting in social disorganization within the family. Another theme picked up by the Chicago School was the loss of family functions as a result of urbanized and industrialized society. Its leading exponents were William F. Ogburn (1886–1959) and Ernest W. Burgess (1886–1965). According to Ogburn, the breakdown of traditional culture saw the development of a new type of family life, one divested of much of its functions—economic, educational, religious, protective, and recreational. This new family emphasized personality functions. Burgess characterized this change as the movement of the family "from institution to companionship." This position on the transformation of family functions was developed and expanded so that it became a major cornerstone in much of structural-functionalist analysis of the family and particularly in the writings of Talcott Parsons.

The Chicago School and Social Disorganization

The typologies of urban–rural societies culminated in the works of the Chicago School and particularly in the writings of Louis Wirth and Robert Redfield. Wirth and Redfield's work can be best understood within the historical context of Chicago during the 1920s and 1930s and the University of Chicago's intellectual activities during this same period.

Chicago epitomizes the phenomenal population growth of American cities. In 1860, its population was 112,000; by the turn of the century (1900), its population was over 1.5 million, and it proceeded to grow at a rate of over 500,000 for each of the next three decades, culminating in a population of over 3.5 million by 1930. As Maurice Stein (1964) has stated, these statistics can give but a suggestion as to what it means in human terms to live in a city whose population swells at such a rapid rate. The unprecedented demands for the development of municipal services—street and transportation systems, sanitary water supplies, garbage disposal and sewage systems, fire and police protection, schools, libraries, parks, playgrounds, and so on—must have been overwhelming. Further complicating the situation was the fact that the new urban population was comprised predominantly of an influx of European immigrants (who had little familiarity with American customs and language) and migrants

Blacks arriving in Chicago during the great rural migration from the South to northern industrial areas, 1910.

Historical Pictures Service, Chicago

from rural America, groups unfamiliar with and unaccustomed to city life and each other.

It is not surprising, given the momentous and unplanned changes taking place in American cities during this period, that social scientists emphasized the negative and opposed the positive qualities of urban life. They focused on social disorganization and its consequences—alienation, anomie, social isolation, juvenile delinquency, crime, mental illness, suicide, child abuse, separation, and divorce—as inherent characteristics of urban life. "Small wonder that the Chicago sociologists focused on the absence of established institutional patterns in so many regions of the city, stressing that the neighborhoods grew and changed so rapidly that sometimes the only constant feature appeared to be mobility . . . *and* why 'disorganization' accompanied 'mobility'" (Stein, 1964:16).

The study of the city flowered at the University of Chicago during the 1920s and 1930s. Under the leadership of Robert E. Park (1864–1944), a community of scholars was established who have had an unprecedented influence on the course of sociology to the present day. Such areas as urban sociology, the family, crime and delinquency, social disorganization, social change, the sociology of occupations, political sociology, and social psychology were developed and shaped by the intellectual activities at Chicago. Among the classical sociological monographs arising out of Chicago during this period and concerned with various aspects of Chicago life are *The Hobo* (Anderson, 1923), *The City* (Park and Burgess, 1925), *The Gang* (Thrasher, 1927), *The Gold Coast and the Slum* (Zorbaugh, 1929), and *The Ghetto* (Wirth, 1938a).

The essay "Urbanism as a Way of Life" (1938b) by Louis Wirth (1897–1952) has become the classic and most influential statement on urbanism in American sociology. Further, his analysis of urban family life has had an equally important influence on the sociology of the family. Wirth was concerned with developing a sociological definition of the city that would focus on those elements of urbanism that mark it as a distinctive mode of human life that is, one that would focus on the human dimension of the city—what it does to people. In addition, his aim was to develop a definition that would transcend a given historical and cultural type of city and that would hold true for all cities, whether they were industrial or nonindustrial, American or foreign, contemporary or historical.

For Wirth, the main concern of the sociologist of the city was to discover the typical forms of social action and organization that characterize the city. Wirth argued that size, density, and heterogeneity were the key elements determining the social organization and behavior in the urban community. The consequences of these three variables are the relative absence of personal relationships; the depersonalization and segmentation of human relations, characterized by anonymity, superficiality, and transitoriness; and the breakdown of social structures and increased mobility, instability, and insecurity. Wirth summarizes his view of the influence of the city on the life of its inhabitants in the following statement: "The distinctive features of the urban mode of life have often been described sociologically as consisting of the substitution of secondary for primary contacts, the weakening of bonds of kinship, and the declining social significance of the family, the disappearance of the neighborhood, and the undermining of the traditional basis of social solidarity" (Wirth, 1938b:21–22). Wirth goes on to describe the impact of the city on the family:

> . . . the low and declining urban reproduction rates suggest that the city is not conducive to the traditional type of family life, including the rearing of children and the maintenance of the home as the locus of a whole round of vital activities. The transfer of industrial, educational, and recreational activities to specialized institutions outside the home has deprived the family of some of its most characteristic historical functions. In cities mothers are more likely to be employed, lodgers are more frequently part of the household, marriage tends to be postponed, and the proportion of single and unattached people is greater. Families are smaller and more frequently without children than in the country. The family as a unit of social

life is emancipated from the larger kinship group characteristic of the country, and the individual members pursue their own diverging interests in their vocational, educational, religious, recreational, and political life. (Wirth, 1938b:22)

Louis Wirth's essay has generated a vast amount of research to test the conclusions drawn from his ideal typification of the city and the urban family. We will discuss this research shortly, but we will first present Redfield's typification of the polar opposite of the urban society — the rural society, or, as Redfield labels it, *folk* society.

The schema of Robert Redfield (1897–1958), the folk–urban typology, is of particular importance to the comparative study of the city and of family life. Redfield was an anthropologist who was strongly influenced by the Chicago School of Robert E. Park and the works of the earlier classical social scientists, Maine, Durkheim, and Tönnies. His employment of the ideal-type approach in his conceptualization of folk societies stands as a polar opposite to Louis Wirth's conceptualization of urban societies. Unlike Wirth's conclusions, which are drawn primarily from an analysis of urban centers in the United States and particularly Chicago, Redfield's conclusions result from extensive field work outside of the United States.

Redfield analyzed the contrasting cultures found in the Yucatán and Guatemala. Among his major works are *The Folk Culture of Yucatán* (1941), *The Primitive World and Its Transformations* (1953), and *The Little Community* (1955).

Redfield comparatively studied contrasting cultures in Central America, ranging from relatively isolated small tribal villages to a large metropolitan city. The typology developed characterized the folk society as small, isolated, nonliterate, and homogeneous and one that had a strong sense of solidarity and intimate communication and stressed the importance of familial relationships and the sacredness of sanctions and institutions. Of paramount interest is Redfield's view that the folk society is a familial society:

> . . . the personal and intimate life of the child in the family is extended, in the folk society, into the social world of the adult and even too into inanimate objects. It is not merely that relations in such a society are personal; it is also that they are familial. The first contact made as the infant becomes a person are with other persons; moreover, each of these first persons, he comes to learn, has a particular kind of relation to him which is associated with that one's genealogical position. The individual finds himself fixed within a constellation of familial relationships. The kinship connections provide a pattern on terms of which, in the ideal folk society, all personal relations are conventionalized and categorized. All relations are personal. But relations are not, in content of specific behavior, the same for everyone. As a mother is different from a father, and a grandson from a nephew, so are these classes of personal relationship, originating in genealogical connection, extended outward into all relationships whatever. In this sense, the folk society is a familial society. (Redfield, 1947:193)

In contrast, Redfield delineates the process of what happens to persons as they live in cities. As communities become less isolated and more heterogeneous, they become more secular and individualistic and more characterized by cultural disorganization. The foundation of the folk society embedded in the family loses strength, with a corresponding decline of patriarchal and matriarchal authority. Traditional customs, which helped anchor legitimate family relations, and extended kinship ties diminish, with a reduction of respect and obligations to extended kin. The sacred religious order gives way to secularized religious practices and the moral order gives way to the legal order.

Underlying all these typologies is an essentially negative view of the city and urban life, particularly in regard to the family. This antiurban bias tends to depict rural life as basically good, clean, and pure as opposed to the city, which is associated with social disorganization, decay, and filth. This emphasis on the negative aspects of city life is not peculiar to social scientists. It pervades the belief system about the city in social philosophy, religion, and popular music, art, and literature (Gist and Fava, 1974:573–595). Morton and Lucia White (1962)—in tracing the intellectual portrait of American cities—conclude that, historically,

> . . . enthusiasm for the American city has not been typical or predominant in our intellectual history. Fear has been the most common reaction. For a variety of reasons our most celebrated thinkers have expressed different degrees of ambivalence and animosity toward the city. . . . We have no persistent or pervasive tradition of romantic attachment to the city in our literature or in our philosophy, nothing like the Greek attachment to the *polis* or the French writer's affection for Paris. (White and White, 1962:1–2)

The fascination with the social disorganization aspects of urban life by these earlier sociologists led them to overlook the role of the city as a positive experience—a social integrator of people and families and with many positive qualities—and also led them to dismiss the social organization aspects of ethnic working-class communities. Further, in their study of the urban poor, particularly the black and Hispanic communities, they developed a conceptualization of the poor that viewed them as socially disorganized, pathological, and suffering from a "culture of poverty," which assured the perpetuation of their poverty-ridden existence.

The works of Wirth, Redfield, and the earlier classical social scientists who developed typologies on the urban–rural dichotomization of society shared a common orientation—a negative view of the city and urban life, particularly in its impact on the family. We will examine the consequences of these biases in the analysis of the poor and ethnic working-class family systems in later chapters. Now we want to switch our attention to the other theme developed by the Chicago School, which concerns the loss of family functions as a result of urbanized and industrialized society. William F. Ogburn sees this loss negatively; Ernest Burgess is more positively disposed. Finally, Talcott Parsons synthesizes these positions and persuasively develops a more-positive, or functional, view that still dominates American sociology and proves to be a pivotal anchoring position of modernization theory and the cross-cultural analysis of the family.

Ogburn's Theory of Social Change and the Family

William F. Ogburn's work has had an important impact on American sociology—the sociology of the family in particular—from the publication in 1922 of *Social Change*, to 1955 when his last major work, *Technology and the Changing Family*, was published with the collaboration of Meyer F. Nimkoff. Ogburn's primary concern was with the processes of social change. His contribution to sociology lies in the distinction he made between *material* culture (technology, factories, machines, transportation, and so forth) and *adaptive* culture (values, ideas, attitudes, customs, and so forth). He argued that the real sources of progressive change were found in material innovations with customs, beliefs, and philosophies adapting themselves to the material substructure. The fact that the adaptive culture follows the material culture led Ogburn to postulate the hypothesis of *culture lag*—changes in the material culture occur and cause changes in the adaptive culture that result in continuous social maladjustment between the two types of culture.

The particular interest of this for students of the family lies in Ogburn's ideas about the processes of social change and the impact of technology, innovations, and ideologies on family systems. Applying this theory to the family, the argument is made that the family system changes as a result of technological changes; the family, then, is an example of adaptive culture. This is the dominant theme of the Ogburn and Nimkoff historical study of the American family: "In this book . . . a single institution has been chosen and upon it are recorded the influences coming from many different inventions and scientific discoveries" (Ogburn and Nimkoff, 1955:iv).

Ogburn and Nimkoff present the argument that inventions and discoveries of modern technological society have led to the decline of the family's economic, educational, recreational, religious, and protective functions. This was in disaccord with the satisfactory adjustment of the family during the earlier history of America, which was dominated by an agricultural economy. In their text, after consultation with 18 prominent American sociologists, a virtual "who's who" of family sociology, they presented a list of the significant changes in the American family systems. This list served as a prime illustration of the effects of cultural lag:

1. Increasing divorce rate
2. Wider diffusion of birth control and decline in family size
3. Decline in authority of husbands and fathers
4. Increase in sexual intercourse apart from marriage
5. Increase in number of wives working for pay
6. Increasing individualism and freedom of family members
7. Increasing transfer of protective functions from family to state
8. Decline of religious behavior in marriage and family

In summarizing the work of Ogburn and Nimkoff, we concur with the assessment of Leslie (1979). Leslie believes that the strength of Ogburn's work does not lie primarily in his theoretical formulations but in his exhaustive descriptions of the changed relations of the family and other institutional structures, which he documented for more than three decades: the increased participation of government, economic enterprises, education, and so on, in the once private domain of the family.

The major theoretical criticism of Ogburn's works lies in his oversimplification of the notions of material and adaptive cultures, his overemphasis on resistances to changes in the area of adaptive culture, and his underemphasis on the resistances in the area of material culture. Sociologists of the family have particularly criticized his work because it views the family as a passive recipient adapting to changes in the materialistic culture, which is viewed as the active causal agent. They believe[1] that the family may itself be a causal faction in the rate and growth of materialistic culture. One final point—Ogburn and Nimkoff's position on the loss of family functions has become a primary investigatory concern in the study of the family and social change.

Ernest W. Burgess and Symbolic Interactionism

At the same time that the Chicago School was making its influence felt in American sociology, another approach was developing that focused on the examination of the internal relationships of family members. This new orientation centered on the organization of roles in family life; for example: What is the role of the father or mother in the family structure? Two major conceptual frameworks developed during this period—symbolic interactionism and structural functionalism. Symbolic interactionism dominated much of early twentieth-century sociology, with structural functionalism serving a similar role in the period after World War II.

Symbolic interactionism, as applied to the study of the family, is a social-psychological perspective that emphasizes the various forms of family interactional patterns: courtship, the honeymoon period, child-rearing practices, divorce and separation, the role of the elderly, and so on. Charles Horton Cooley, George Herbert Mead, W.I. Thomas, and especially Ernest W. Burgess (who spoke of the family as "a unity of interacting personalities") developed this perspective. Symbolic interactionism

---

[1] See in particular William J. Goode's 1963 study, *World Revolution and Family Patterns.*

made important methodological contributions to the study of the family, including the social survey, interview and questionnaire schedules, and participant observation.

The focus of symbolic interactionism is on the study of the family as a small-scale social phenomenon. It became almost completely devoted to the study of the American middle-class family structure. Symbolic interactionists were not as involved with the impact of larger societal institutions and processes on the family. Ernest W. Burgess (1886–1965), however, does pick up on the work of his colleague, William F. Ogburn, to explain the shifting of traditional functions of the family to outside agencies. Industrialization and urbanization are seen as primarily responsible for this shift. Burgess observes that the economic, educational, recreational, health-protection, and religious functions of the family were being transformed to other institutions. The family was left with the functions of achieving the happiness and the personal growth of its members. The family now rested on "mutual affection, the sympathetic understanding, and comradeship of its members" (Burgess and Locke, 1945:vii).

This shift in family functions led to Burgess' famous classification of family types as moving from "institution to companionship." According to this conceptualization, the institutional family is one in which the unity is determined entirely by traditional rules and regulations, specified duties and obligations, and other historical social pressures impinging on family members. The extended patriarchal type of family most closely approximates the institutional family. It is authoritarian and autocratic; it demands the complete subordination of each family member and his or her spouse and children to the authority of the husband or eldest male (the patriarch). The emphasis is on compliance with duty and the following of tradition. Marriages are arranged with an emphasis on prudence, economic and social status, and the subordination of the married couple to the extended family group.

The companionate or democratic family is the recently emerging family type. It has moved away from an institutional character towards a "unity which develops out of mutual affection and intimate association of husband and wife and parents and children" (Burgess and Locke, 1945:27). This type of family includes affection as a basis for its existence, equal status and authority between the spouses, egalitarian decision making, and the sharing of common interests and activities, coexisting with divisions of labor and individuality of interests. According to Burgess, the institutional family is sustained by external community pressures and involvements; the companionate family, on the other hand, is sustained by the emotional attachments among its members.

Talcott Parsons and the Isolated Nuclear Family

Beginning in the late 1930s and accelerating after World War II, the importance of the Chicago School in American sociology greatly diminished, though many of its conceptual viewpoints either merged with or influenced newer perspectives. By the 1950s, the dominant school was structural functionalism, under the intellectual leadership of Talcott Parsons (1902–1980), who was one of the most predominant and influential sociologists of the twentieth century. Arguing from a structural functionalist model, Parsons proclaimed a theory of the American family that has generated extensive research both in the United States and elsewhere on the characteristics of the family system in cities. According to Parsons, the isolation of the nuclear family "is the most distinctive feature of the American kinship system and underlies most of its peculiar functional and dynamic problems" (1943:28). The normal American household consists of a husband, wife, and children economically independent of their extended family and frequently located at considerable geographical distance from it.

Parsons views American society as having been greatly changed by industrialization and urbanization. In particular, he believes it has become highly "differentiated," with the family system's previous educational, religious, political, and economic functions being taken over by other institutions in the society. By differentiation, Parsons means that functions performed earlier by one institution in the society are now distributed among several institutions. Thus, schools, churches, peer groups, political parties, voluntary associations, and formal occupational groups have assumed functions once reserved for the family. Unlike the social disorganization, anomic, and alienating assessments—made by such theorists as William F. Ogburn and Louis Wirth, among others—on the negative impact of industrialization on the family, Talcott Parsons sees the family as becoming a more-specialized group, concentrating its functions on the socialization of children and providing emotional support and affection for family members. To a large extent, Parsons brings into his schema the "institution to companionship" view proposed earlier by Ernest Burgess that, as we noted, sees the family as a "unity which develops out of mutual affection and intimate association of husband and wife and parents and children" (Burgess and Locke, 1945:27).

Parsons further suggests that the isolated nuclear family may be ideally suited to meet the demands of occupational and geographical mobility that is inherent in industrial urban society. Unencumbered by obligatory extended kinship bonds, the nuclear family is best able to move where the jobs are and better able to take advantage of occupational opportunities. In contrast, the traditional extended-family system bond of extensive, obligatory economic and residential rights and duties is seen to be dysfunctional for industrial society. (The classical Parsonian position that there is a close fit between the isolated nuclear family and the industrialized system is essentially similar to that of Goode, who emphasized the fit between the conjugal family and industrial societies.)

Arguing against the social-disorganization thesis on the breakdown of the contemporary family, Parsons (1955) finds support for the importance of the nuclear family in the high rates of marriage and remarriage after divorce, the increase in the birthrate after World War II, and the increase in the building of single-family homes (particularly in suburbia) during this time period. All these trends provide evidence of the continuing visibility, *not* social disorganization, of the family and *increased* vitality of the nuclear family bond. Thus, a specialized family system functionally meets the affectional and personality needs of its members; it may be admirably fitted to a family system that is a relatively isolated and self-sustaining economic unit of mother, father, and children, living without other relatives in the home and without close obligations and ties to relatives who live nearby.

> . . . the family has become *a more specialized agency than before*, probably more specialized than it has been in any previously known society. This represents a decline of *certain* features which traditionally have been associated with families, but whether it represents a "decline of the family" in a more general sense is another matter; we think not. We think the trend of the evidence points to the beginning of the relative stabilization of a new type of family structure, in a new relation to a general social structure, one in which the family is more specialized than before, but not in any general sense less important, because the society is dependent *more* exclusively on it for the performance of its vital functions. (Parsons and Bales, 1955:9)

In summary, Parsons emphasizes the importance of the nuclear family—in the absence of extended kinship ties—in that it meets two major societal needs: the socialization of children and the satisfaction of the affectional and emotional demands of husbands, wives, and their children. Further, the isolated nuclear family, which is not handicapped by conflicting obligations to extended relatives, can best take advantage of occupational opportunities and is best able to cope with the demands of modern industrial urban life.

In Chapter 4, we critically examine Parsons' ideas on the isolated nuclear family in

A large American family: the Cooper family, vicinity of Ames, Iowa, 1942.

the city, conducting our investigation within the context of research that questions the Chicago School assumption that the city is antithetical to family life in general, and to extended kinship ties in particular. This research also argues against Parsons' position that the isolated nuclear family may be uniquely suited to meet the needs of an industrial urban society. We discuss the accumulated research that postulates the existence of viable kinship ties among many urban dwellers and examine the research on kinship family ties in the context of both geographical and social mobility. But, before we return to the urban family issues generated by Parsons' schema, we first pick up on a dominant theme in this first part of the book, and that is the nature of cross-cultural social change and the family. Our discussion in the next chapter centers on an examination of modernization theory with particular emphasis on the work of William J. Goode, who extends Parsons' concept of the isolated nuclear family to a belief that, cross-culturally, families are moving to various forms of the "conjugal" family.

Conclusion

This chapter was concerned with the historical development of sociological interest in the study of social change and the family that was precipitated by the Industrial Revolution of the nineteenth century. Toward the end of that century and into the early twentieth century, the sociology of the family was dominated by the issues of social reform, which was an outgrowth of what was viewed as the excesses of industrial and urban society and the calamitous changes in the family system. We highlighted our discussion by comparing the conservative perspective of Frédéric Le Play with the radical perspective of Marx and Engels. We indicated how these two schools developed alternative and opposing viewpoints and solutions to their common perception of the evils of the emerging family form — Le Play's unstable family and Marx's and Engels' privatized family. Both schools were highly critical of the emerging family form, its treatment of family members, and its relationship to the surrounding community.

A particular concern of sociologists was the impact of the emerging urban industrial city on the family. The ideal type was an analytical technique that was developed to contrast the different forms of social and family life that existed in rural areas compared to urban areas. We sought to demonstrate that there was an ideological bias underlying these typologies that was both antiurban and anti-urban family. We implied (and will later develop this viewpoint) that these biases distorted the analysis of both the city and the family as it was developing in urban industrial societies.

In the last topic of the chapter, we noted that American sociologists turned to the study of internal family dynamics, paying little attention to the broader issues of social change during the first 50 years of the twentieth century. Yet a significant segment of American sociology continued to wrestle with the themes and issues raised by conservatives and radicals in the nineteenth century. The theories of William F. Ogburn and Earnest W. Burgess (with Harvey J. Locke) were discussed for their contemporary significance.

Another notable exception was the Chicago School, which focused on urban structures and dynamics. We discussed the ideal typologies of urban–rural families of nineteenth-century theorists and the position of the Chicago School sociologist Louis Wirth, emphasizing the social disorganization of families in the city. The structural functionalist Talcott Parsons reworked these themes in his conceptualization of the isolated nuclear family and its functionality to urban industrial society.

However, until the end of World War II, American sociology was characterized by almost no interest in large-scale comparative analysis. The interests and concerns of the Chicago School and the symbolic interactionists were picked up and developed by the dominating perspective of the postwar era, that of structural functionalism. An offshoot of structural functionalism, "modernization theory," attempted to re-establish the importance of cross-cultural and historical analyses of social change and the family. The most significant contribution of this theory was the work of William J. Goode and his thesis of the worldwide movement of the family from the consanguineal form to the conjugal one. In the following chapter, we devote attention to a critique of structural functionalism and modernization theory and the analysis of comparative family systems. We return to themes on the family in the community and in the city in Part II.

CHAPTER 3

Modernization and the Family in World Perspective

Pritam Singh Bindra at home with his wife Tejinder Kaur, and their son Bhavjot, and daughter Manmeet, in their Queens, New York apartment.

CHAPTER OUTLINE

Since the mid-nineteenth century, there has been a vacillation of interest in cross-cultural family research. It reached a peak during the second half of the nineteenth century, a drop during the first half of the twentieth century, and a return to comparative study since World War II. The rebirth of interest in comparative studies has two prime sources. The first is an intellectual rebellion against the limitation of the rigorous empirical methods emphasized during the early twentieth century. The development of this methodology, frequently statistical in nature, was used to investigate small-scale social phenomena and paid little attention to social change and its consequences for the family. American sociologists limited their analysis to their own society, ignored other societies and cultures, and left comparative analysis to the other social sciences, particularly anthropology.

The second factor that stimulated comparative analysis was the revived interest in social change. The postwar period was marked by rapid dissolution of the colonial empires of the Western industrial societies and the concomitant transformation of what Westerners called "underdeveloped and backward" societies. In addition, Western societies were also undergoing processes of social change. What was becoming particularly clear was that "scientific" sociological study of the family was not able to come to grips with the dominant social issues and problems of contemporary times.

The sociology of the family was dominated by two conceptual frameworks, symbolic interactionism and structural functionalism. Symbolic interactionism has not been involved with the study of social change; it has, by and large, focused on internal family dynamics as opposed to the family in relation to other institutions in a given society. Structural functionalism, on the other hand—and particularly its offshoot, modernization theory—have been involved in this endeavor, as well as in cross-cultural and historical analyses of social change and the family. However, as we will demonstrate, their frame of reference is inadequate to study family change.

As we discussed in our presentation of the ideas of Talcott Parsons, structural functionalism is concerned with the family's changing functions in light of industrialization and urbanization. It views every society as a system made up of subsystems, which are often called "institutions," and the major ones are the family, religion, economy, politics, and education. These institutions are intertwined so that change in one institution, such as the economy, invariably affects other institutions, such as the family and education. Change results as the society seeks to restore its equilibrium in the light of institutional changes. Structural functionalism has an implicit evolutionary theme integrated into its concern with functional changes.

In this chapter, we investigate some of the factors that help to account for the current interest in cross-cultural study of the family. We look at the dominant perspective, modernization theory, and at its strengths and weaknesses. Modernization theory combines the conceptual orientation from both Social Darwinism and structural functionalism to elaborate the theoretical relationship between societal development and family change. We then present a theoretical critique of modernization theory and provide a comprehensive analysis and assessment of that perspective's strengths, weaknesses, and limitations. We highlight theoretical developments that have extended, modified, and changed the way we think of the family and modernization in nonindustrial and industrial societies and in capitalist and socialist ones as well. Through this analysis, we seek to demonstrate the complexity of family change in a rapidly changing and increasingly industrial and urban world.

Structural Functionalism, Modernization Theory, and Family Change

The structural-functionalist perspective tends to see society as an organism that strains toward maintaining itself in some form of balance—it is an equilibrium model. The concern is with the functional connections among the various parts of a system, whether the society or the family. For example, it views the family as a social system. Its constituent parts, husband-father, wife-mother, and children, are bound together by interaction and interdependence. It is concerned with whether any given part is either functional or dysfunctional to the family; that is, whether it adds or detracts from the system's operation. Stability and order are implicitly viewed as being natural and normal. Conflict and disorder are seen as being deviant phenomena and as evidence that the system is not working properly.

The inherent problem of structural functionalism is in its handling of social change, which stems from its emphasis on consensus and cooperation, its failure to acknowledge the possibility of conflicting interests of constituent elements in a social system, and its reification of the status quo. The structural-functionalist perspective does not lend itself readily to explain or describe the phenomenon of social change. When the system, whether it is a society or the family, is reified and seen as being in a state of equilibrium, we can only emphasize slow, orderly change. Conflict and rapid social change are regarded as pathological trends and the only source of change is by outside agents. Structural functionalism, although in the forefront of cross-cultural family study, has not been able to handle satisfactorily the problem of social change because of its emphasis on studying societies in the ahistorical present and then making cross-cultural historical comparisons, much in the same manner as the Social Darwinists.

Modernization theories were developed from a combination of conceptualizations derived from evolutionary theory and structural functionalism. Modernization theories have been widely used in sociology since World War II. However, the basic conceptual problems of both evolutionary theory and structural functionalism in their handling of social change have also led to similar problems in the development of adequate conceptual tools by the proponents of modernization theory.

The concept of modernization and the theories stemming from it have been the dominating perspective in the analysis of global social change and the family. *Modernization* is usually used as a term in reference to processes of change in societies that are characterized by advanced industrial technology. Social scientists have attempted to make the development of Western European and American technological society the model for the comparative analysis of developing countries. Daniel Lerner, in his influential study, *The Passing of Traditional Society: Modernizing the Middle East*, presents a model of universal process that all developing societies must pass through to become modernized.

> The Western model of modernization exhibits certain components and sequences whose relevance is global. . . . The model evolved in the West is an historical fact. That the same model reappears in virtually all modernizing societies on all continents of the world, regardless of variations in race, color, creed, will be shown. . . . (Lerner, 1958:46).

Marion J. Levy, Jr., defines modernization in relation to technology: "I would consider any society the more modernized the greater the ratio of inanimate power sources and the greater extent to which human efforts are multiplied by the use of tools" (Levy, 1967:190). Levy's definition emphasizes that the transformation of the world by technology is the principal cause of everything connected with modernization. Other theorists expand on this meaning and link the term with a wide range of concomitant institutions in the political, economic, social, and individual spheres. Neil J. Smelser indicates that modernization includes more than technological development:

> The term "modernization"—a conceptual cousin of the term "economic development," but more comprehensive in scope   refers to the fact that technological, economic, and ecological changes ramify through the whole social and cultural fabric. In an emerging nation, we may expect profound changes (1) in the *political* sphere as simple tribal or village authority systems give way to systems of suffrage, political parties, representation, and civil service bureaucracies; (2) in the *educational* sphere, as the society strives to reduce illiteracy, and increase economically productive skills; (3) in the *religious* sphere, as secularized belief systems begin to replace traditionalistic religions; (4) in the *familial* sphere, as extended kinship units lose their pervasiveness; (5) in the *stratificational* sphere, as geographical and social mobility tends to loosen fixed, ascriptive hierarchical systems. (Smelser, 1973:748)

The main tie between modernization theory and structural functionalism is the key concept of structural differentiation. Smelser (1973) explains structural differentiation as the manner in which, after industrialization, family functions lose some of their former importance in matters of training and economic production and schools and economic organizations begin to fill these functions. As the family ceases to be an economic unit of production, family members may leave the household to seek employment in the outside labor market. With the decline of the family's function in the economic sphere, the family (particularly in the figure of the father) loses its economic-training function, which further leads to a decline in general paternal authority. The family's activities become more concentrated on emotional gratification and socialization, with the mother developing more-intense emotional relationships with children because of the absence of the father in the job market. Smelser concludes that

> . . . modernization tends to foster the rise of a family unit that is formed on emotional attraction and built on a limited sexual-emotional basis. The family has been removed from other major social spheres except for the segmental, external ties of individual family members. The family, being thus isolated and specialized, impinges less on these other social spheres, nepotism as a basis for recruitment into other social roles tends to become at most corrupt and at least suspect, whereas in traditional society it was the legitimate basis for recruitment into roles. Finally, within the family the complex and multi-functional relations of family members to one another tend to be pared down to more exclusively emotional ties. (Smelser, 1973:752)

The Conceptualizations of Structural Functionalism

Through what structural functionalists have called the process of structural differentiation, the family has lost a number of functions to outside agencies. These agencies include the schools, the industrial sector, the political parties, and the judicial courts. The structural functionalists, notably Talcott Parsons, have long argued that the increased privatism of the contemporary family has led it to retain and even expand on two functions: the maintenance and stabilization of adult personalities and the socialization of children.

A typical American family of the 1950s bowling together.

© Clemens Kelischer

    . . . what has recently been happening to the American family constitutes part of one of these stages of a process of differentiation. This process has involved a further step in the reduction of the importance in our society of kinship units other than the nuclear family. It has also resulted in the transfer of a variety of functions from the nuclear family to other structures of the society, notably the occupationally organized sectors of it. This means that the family has become a *more specialized agency than before*, probably more specialized than it has been in any previously known society.

    . . . We therefore suggest that the basic and irreducible functions of the family are two; first the primary socialization of children so that they can truly become members of the society into which they have been born; second, the stabilization of the adult personalities of the population of the society. (Parsons and Bales, 1955:9, 16).

    Structural functionalism has developed an analytical schema for the study of the interrelationships of husband – wife – parents – children in the contemporary family.

Although the functionalists, particularly their leading spokesperson, Talcott Parsons, do not directly discuss the dichotomization of the public and private spheres of work and the household, they do analyze and support this dichotomization in the conceptualization of role differentiation. *Role differentiation* in this context refers to the process in which economic production and activities are removed from the kinship household; further, it postulates that a division of labor between husband and wife is necessary for the optimum functioning of the family system within an industrial economic/social order. The analysis of husband–wife relationships stresses the necessity for the husband to be involved with the outside world, whereas the wife's world is restricted to the home. The segregation of activities is also carried over to interpersonal relationships. The wife's role must be as an affectional and emotional support to her husband and her children; her interests must be subordinated to those of her husband. The husband, as wage earner, provides the instrumental leadership that permits the family to function in its dealings with the outside world.

A most influential work in the sociology of the family that has presented this position is the structural-functionalist monograph by Talcott Parsons and Robert Bales (written in collaboration with James Olds, Morris Zelditch, Jr., and Philip E. Slater), *Family, Socialization and Interaction Process* (1955). This book attempts to analyze the structure and function of the American family by conceptualizing the family as a small group and maintaining that the family can be viewed as a social system with the constituent parts—husband, wife, and children—bound together by cooperative interaction and interdependence. The roles of the family are seen to be differentiated on the basis of age and sex, which correspond to two theoretical axes differentiated by the degree of power and the salience of instrumental–expressive behavior. This is presented schematically in Figure 3.1.

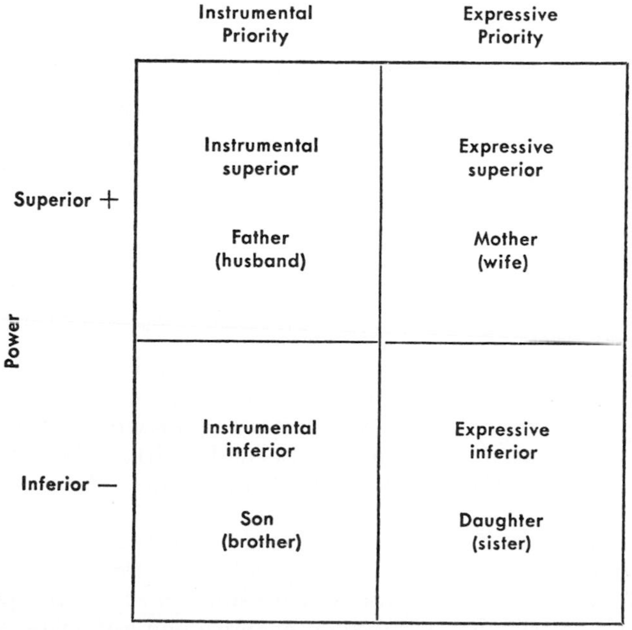

FIGURE 3.1 Talcott Parsons' basic role structure of the nuclear family. (Talcott Parsons and Robert F. Bales. 1955. *Family, Socialization and Interaction Process.* New York: The Free Press, p. 46. Copyright © 1955 by The Free Press. Reprinted with permission of Macmillan Publishing Co.)

The two axes of differentiation result in four basic role positions, a high power–instrumental leader (father), a high power–expressive leader (mother), a low power–instrumental follower (son), and a low power–expressive follower (daughter).

"The great advantage of the family is that these four roles are filled, on the average, by people whose ages and sexes fit especially well the functional requirements of a small group. Hence, the family is a stronger, longer-lasting, and more efficient small group than any other" (Zelditch, 1964:63).

Instrumental activity is primarily oriented toward maintaining the relations of the system with those outside the system: external activities that emphasize occupational, educational, and political behavior. Although each member of the family can participate in these activities, the primary responsibility for instrumental activities lies in the male role. Expressive functions are concerned with the internal affairs of the system —oriented toward maintaining relationships and activities within the system itself. Activities include the bearing and socializing of children and the caring for the religious concerns of the family members. The family system is seen as striving to maintain an equilibrium between these two types of activity.

Parsons and Bales (1955) believe that the basis for this role differentiation and allocation lies in the bearing and early nursing of the child by the mother, which establishes a strong relationship between them. The fundamental importance of this relationship leads Zelditch to state that "the mother's expressive role in the family is largely not problematical" (Zelditch in Parsons and Bales, 1955:314). The father, unable to compete with the mother for this type of relationship with the child, turns instead to instrumental activities. Zelditch argues that the two parents are necessary not only to provide food and shelter for their children but also eventually to loosen the dependency tie between mother and child. This is accomplished through the necessary allocation of disciplinary authority as well as relatively neutral, nonexpressive judgments of the husband-father.

Parsons and Bales believe that the primary importance of the occupational–instrumental role of the male is a boundary role, one in which the society unequivocally designates the husband-father as the instrumental leader of the family system; the status of the family and the lifestyle it leads is largely dependent on the level of job and subsequent income the husband-father earns (Parsons and Bales, 1955:13). The roles played in the family structure are seen to be complementary: the wife's role anchored in the internal affairs of the family, as wife, mother, and manager of the household; the husband's role anchored in the external affairs of the family, as income-earner in the job market, which also provides the status for the family with the outside world.

William J. Goode's *World Revolution and Family Patterns*

The dominant theme emphasized by sociologists who studied the family both in the nineteenth and the twentieth centuries was that industrialization and urbanization radically transformed the family from an extended, authoritarian, stable rural form into a nuclear, more-egalitarian, and relatively isolated and unstable one. Goode picked up on this by extending the analysis to a worldwide historical survey of family systems.

The major work coming out of modernization theory, which centers on the family in change, is William J. Goode's *World Revolution and Family Patterns* (1963). This work has had a profound impact on the comparative study of social change and the family. Goode's major contribution is the comprehensive and systematic gathering and analyses of cross-cultural and historical data to attack the notion of unifactoral hypotheses, which viewed family systems as dependent variables affected by such phenomena as industrial and economic development. Goode concluded that changes in industrialization and the family are parallel processes, both being influenced by changing social and personal ideologies—the ideologies of economic progress, the conjugal family, and egalitarianism. Finally, Goode proposes that in the "world revolution" toward industrialization and urbanization, there is a convergence of diverse types of extended family forms to some type of conjugal family system.

Goode's conceptualization of modernization processes and the classification of societies and family systems stems from an implicit linear developmental orientation that sees societies moving from traditional systems to modern systems and the family moving from extended kinship family systems to the conjugal family form. Thus, at the same time that Goode criticizes unifactoral hypotheses of social change, he himself has developed a unilinear evolutionary schema.

Goode takes issue with theories that view change in family patterns as a simple function of industrialization. Rather, he sees modernization represented by ideological value changes as being partially independent of industrialization as well as having important impacts on both the family system and industrialization itself. Following a structural-functionalist framework, Goode is critical of the position that the conjugal family emerges only after a society is exposed to industrialization. This position ignores the theoretical "fit" (empirical harmony) between the conjugal family and the modern industrial system. For example, the independence of the conjugal family from extended kinship ties permits the family to move where the jobs are. The increased emotional component of the conjugal family relationship provides a source of psychological strength in the face of pressures from the industrial order and the absence of extended kin relations. This seeming "fit" is not seen as obscuring either the importance of ideological factors or the fact that the family itself may be an independent factor influencing the industrialization process.

Goode believes that the ideology of economic progress and technological development, as well as the ideology of the conjugal family, occurred in non-Western societies prior to industrialization and family changes. The significance of the ideology of economic progress lies in its stress on societal industrial growth and change and its relegation of the issue of tradition and custom to a lower level of importance. The ideology of the conjugal family asserts the worth of the individual over lineage, and personal welfare over family continuity. A third ideology is that of egalitarianism between the sexes. The emphasis is on the uniqueness of each individual within the family, with lesser importance given to sex status and seniority. This ideology reduces the sex-status and age inequalities of families and also undermines the traditional subordination of the young to the old.

All three modernization ideologies aim directly or indirectly at ending the dominance of the extended family system over the conjugal family and, in particular, over the young and women. Further, all three ideologies minimize the traditions of societies and assert the equality of the individual over class, caste, or sex barriers.

Goode's theoretical position centers around two major functional fits. The first is that between the desire of the individual to maximize his or her need for equality and individualism and the type of family system that can best satisfy those needs, as well as the type of family system that can best serve the needs of an industrial and technological social order.

Goode argues that the ideology of the conjugal family system, which emphasizes the relationship of husband and wife and their children and de-emphasizes the obligatory relationship with extended kinship systems, is best able to maximize the values of individualism and egalitarianism. The extended family system tends to subordinate the individual to the family group—family continuity is more important than individual welfare and desires—whereas the ideology of the conjugal family asserts the equality of individuals over sex, kinship, caste, and class barriers.

> The ideology of the conjugal family proclaims the right of the individual to choose his or her own spouse, place to live, and even which kin obligations to accept, as against the acceptance of others' decisions. It asserts the worth of the *individual* as

against the inherited elements of wealth or ethnic group. The *individual* is to be evaluated, not his lineage. A strong theme of "democracy" runs through this ideology. It encourages love, which in every major civilization has been given a prominent place in fantasy, poetry, art, and legend as a wonderful, perhaps even exalted, experience, even when its reality was guarded against. Finally, it asserts that if one's family life is unpleasant, one has the right to change it . (Goode, 1963:19[1])

The second functional fit is between the family system and industrialization. Goode states that the ideology of the conjugal family and industrialization fit each other through the sharing of common ideas and values intrinsic within both systems. In addition, he argues that these shared ideas and values are necessary for the development of both types of systems. The conjugal family system is closely tied with the ideology of economic progress and technological development, which stresses industrial expansion and the freedom of economic activity that is demanded in a rapidly changing industrializing economy.

Goode (1963, 1964) assembles a massive amount of comparative data, both historical and cross-cultural (the West, Arabic Islam, sub-Saharan Africa, India, China, and Japan) to test these hypotheses. The conclusion reached is that *all* the family systems examined are moving towards some form of conjugal family system. The trends and changes that are occurring take on the following characteristics.

1. *Free choice in mate selection.* In extended-family systems, marriages are arranged by family elders, frequently without the couple meeting prior to the actual marriage. This is to minimize the development of potentially conflicting emotional and obligatory ties between spouses and to maintain control over the future generational development of the extended kinship system. Marriages today, Goode concludes, are being based on love; dowry and brideprice arrangements are disappearing.

2. *Emphasis on individual welfare as opposed to family continuity.* The authority of parents over children and husbands over wives is diminishing, and greater sexual equality is becoming manifest in changes in legal systems regarding such matters as divorce and inheritance. Further evidence is the weakening of sex, kinship, class, and caste barriers and the assertion of the equality of individuals in various substantive legal actions.

3. *Greater emphasis on the conjugal role relationship.* Husbands and wives are moving more and more in the direction of setting up their own independent households (neolocal residences) as opposed to living within the confines of either the husband's family's residence (patrilocality) or the wife's family's residence (matrilocality), thus diminishing the everyday interaction control of either extended family system. Another development that tends to support the independence of the conjugal family system is the development of bilineal descent systems (tracing lineage equally through both family lines) in contrast to a unilineage descent system (either patrilineal or matrilineal). Goode shows that the development of a bilineal descent system results in the loss of power for both unilineage systems and changes the nature of extended kinship ties to one based on affection and choice rather than on obligation. Thus, neolocality and bilineality aid in the development of relative freedom of the conjugal-family system from the extended-family system and prevent the continuation or the development of powerful unilineage systems that dominate the husband – wife marital relationship.

---

[1] Reprinted with permission of Macmillan Publishing Co., from *World Revolution and Family Patterns* by William J. Goode. Copyright © 1963 by The Free Press, a division of Macmillan Publishing Co.

Goode observes that, whenever a country moves toward industrialization, there is some concomitant change in the family system toward some type of conjugal system. He suggests that the family system may hinder or facilitate industrialization in important ways. He argues that the development of Western economic and technological systems would have been severely handicapped if Western family systems "had been patriarchal and polygynous, with a full development of arranged child marriages and a harem system" (Goode, 1963:23).

In his chapters on China and Japan and in a later work (1964), Goode compares the Chinese and Japanese family systems during the late nineteenth and early twentieth centuries to illustrate the importance of family patterns in facilitating or hindering industrial social change. In Japan, patterns of inheritance, attitudes toward nepotism, narrow patterns of social mobility within the merchant class, and a feudalistic loyalty of individuals to their extended families and — in turn — the feudalistic loyalty of the extended families to the state imperial system all assured the rapid industrialization of the society; in China, patterns of inheritance — equal inheritance as opposed to the Japanese system of the eldest inheriting all — prevented the accumulation of family capital. The Chinese, unlike the Japanese, accorded a low social rank to the merchant status. Thus, when wealth was gained, individuals sought to achieve prestige and power by becoming members of the gentry; this prevented the steady accumulation of financial and technical expertise. Finally, the relationship of the family to the state was familistic not feudalistic; that is, an individual owed loyalty to both the extended family and the state personified in the emperor. However, in the case of conflict between the two, the individual's first loyalty was to the family. Goode concluded that these different family systems played an important part in the industrial achievement of Japan and the lack of such achievement in China.

Goode believes that this analysis emphasizes the independent effect of family variables. But, more important, he is demonstrating that family patterns cannot be solely predicted from a knowledge of economic or technological facts alone. The analysis further demonstrates that even when the family is confronted by antithetical forces it does have the capability of resistance and thus it must be taken into account in any work on societal social change. Finally, his stress on the commonality of ideological factors in both industrialization and the conjugal family demonstrates the inadequacy of unilateral causality, which exists in the evolutionary theories of Social Darwinism and Marxism:

> To be avoided are all theories that turn out to be only unifactorial hypotheses, suggesting that all change and all causal relations flow from some single, global factor, such as race, environment, technology, or industrialism. In the past these seemed plausible only because analysts who proposed them usually included within such global variables almost everything that needed to be explained. (Goode, 1964:116)

In summarizing Goode's work, we see that the basis of his argument revolves around the legitimacy of extended-family systems in terms of their domination over the individual and the belief that the conjugal-family system maximizes the ideology of equality and individuality. This desire for egalitarianism results in a power conflict between the individual and the traditional extended-family systems. Further, the ideology of the conjugal family links up with the ideology of economic progress associated with industrial and economic development. The ideology of economic progress runs counter to the ideology of traditionalism, which emphasizes the continuity of historical traditional patterns. Both ideologies operate to foster change in the society and affect one another. At the end of his seminal work (1963), Goode gives his own evaluation of the changes that are occurring. Although he is aware of the dysfunctions these changes may have — particularly to the elders of extended kinship systems — Goode welcomes them.

> . . . I welcome the great changes now taking place, and not because it might be a
> more efficient instrument of industrialization, for that is irrelevant in my personal
> schema. Rather, I see in it and in the industrial system that accompanies it the hope
> of greater freedom: from the domination of elders, from caste and racial restriction,
> from class rigidities. Freedom is *for* something as well: the unleashing of personal
> potentials, the right to love, to equality within the family, to the establishment of a
> new marriage when the old has failed. I see the world revolution in family patterns
> as part of a still more important revolution that is sweeping the world in our time,
> the aspiration on the part of billions of people to have the right for the first time to
> choose for themselves—an aspiration that has toppled governments both old and
> new, and created new societies and social movements. (Goode, 1963:380)

Goode's great work stimulated a large amount of empirical studies in social change
and the family. Soon after the publication of his monograph, a series of comparative
studies, both cross-cultural and historical, presented evidence contrary to his hypothesis that there was a worldwide trend toward the conjugal-family system. In recent
years, new developments in the analysis of modernization processes and in the sociological study of the family have pinpointed limitations in modernization theory and
begun to show how these limitations can lead to distortions in the comparative
analysis of social change and the family.

Modernization Theory and the Family in Comparative Perspective: Assessments and Developments

Modernization theory's reliance on an evolutionary model grounded in the notion of
progress leads implicitly to the idea that progress is a more-valued phenomenon than
traditional stability and that modern societies—that is, Western industrial societies
—are somewhat superior to traditional nonindustrial societies. This has resulted in a
de-emphasis on problems in modern industrial societies and an emphasis on the
dysfunctional characteristics of traditional societies in regard to industrialization. In
this section, we address ourselves to modernization theory's comparative analysis of
the family and also look at the critical arguments made against this position. In the
following section, we turn our attention to how this perspective views the family in
modern America; here, too, the discussion will be followed by a critique of that
position.

There has been widespread dissatisfaction with these assumptions of modernization theory that dominated comparative sociology in the 1950s and 1960s. Wilbert E.
Moore (1964) has stated that the three-stage model—tradition, transition, and
modernity—has inherent problems. By focusing on societies in transition, the theory
implies a static traditional stage with a social structure persisting in equilibrium
without change, as well as a modern society that is also static and unchanging. Moore
argues that "change is an intrinsic characteristic of all societies and the historic paths
to the present inevitably and significantly affect the continuing paths to the future"
(1964:884). He also states that, owing to temporal myopia and the lack of historical
perspective, the fact is overlooked that most of the world has been under some form
of Western influence for extended periods of time (for example, over 400 years in
Latin America and parts of Africa). This has resulted in a great intermixture of
cultural forms and social organizations that have affected the modernization processes of all the world's societies.

The Winter 1973 issue of *Daedalus*, titled "Post-Traditional Societies" by S.N.
Eisenstadt to emphasize the continuity and reconstruction of tradition, was devoted to
this topic. The general argument made by the contributors to the issue was the need
to look at developing, modernizing, and modern societies in term of processes of

Indians in Flushing Blend Two Cultures

As others who have left India to live in the United States, Pritam Singh Bindra struggles to maintain the old traditions in a new land.

Each morning, he awakens an hour before sunrise, puts on a business suit and turban and enters the prayer room that he built in the den of his Long Island home.

With a Sikh holy book at his side, he recites centuries-old prayers that greet the rising sun—prayers he once recited in the Punjab, which he left 12 years ago, at the age of 27.

After the service, he embarks on the American ritual of fighting rush-hour traffic to Manhattan, where he works as an engineer for the American Telephone and Telegraph Company.

Mr. Bindra came to the United States in the wake of a 1965 Congressional act that raised the Indian immigration quota, from 100 to 20,000 a year.

According to the latest census, there were 361,544 Indians living in the United States in 1980, with more than 82,000 in the New York metropolitan area. In contrast, 3,000 Indians were reported living in the United States in 1950.

With the Indian population in America having grown so large and having established itself as a viable ethnic community, pressures to assimilate have diminished. Still, Indians find themselves in conflict between the ways of their adopted homeland and a way of life they left behind.

Before 1965, an Indian who came to America had no choice but to assimilate, said Dr. Badya Nath Varma, a sociology professor at City College. "When I came to this country in 1948, there was only one Indian spice shop in all of New York City, and it was owned by a non-Indian," he said. "There were two restaurants that served Indian food."

STORES PROLIFERATE IN FLUSHING

Today, the impact of Indian immigration is becoming increasingly apparent.

Flushing, Queens, has been transformed into a center of Indian life. Indian retail stores are proliferating, selling Indian foods and spices, Indian video cassettes and records, Indian cosmetics and saris to a clientele still faithful to the products they knew in India.

Indian temples and smaller, secluded ashrams also dot the area. At 45-57 Bowne Street stands the Flushing Hindu temple, with its domes, sculptured animals and other architectural flourishes of southern India. Frescoes inside tell the stories of ancient gods, and ornate sculptures, carved by Indian artisans called salpis, are the gods themselves.

Ceremonial fires are lighted by Hindu priests. The greatest ceremony of the year honors Ganesh, an elephant idol made of polished granite, which is the temple's main deity.

Nearby, on the corner of Roosevelt Avenue and Parsons Boulevard, is the Gurudwara, the temple where Mr. Bindra and other Sikhs go to pray and share langer, the communal feast that is a 500-year-old tradition. Sikhs come from Jersey City and Stamford, Conn., to be together and sing holy songs to their one god.

This is not an insular neighborhood, however. American values and customs do encroach—through schools, jobs and television—forcing Indians to make adjustments between two worlds.

"There are wide disparities between family life and outside life," said Navina Acharya, a 19-year-old Columbia University student born in Bangalore who lives in Queens. "Sometimes it's hard to reconcile the two."

The Bindra household, in Rockville Centre, reflects the extent to which Indian families maintain their cultural values. To step inside their house can be like stepping into a faraway land.

CURRY, CARDAMOM, CORIANDER

Tejinder Kaur Bindra, Mr. Bindra's wife by an arranged marriage, is a woman of custom. After 12 years in America, she still bakes bread on a karahi, a cast-iron wok used in India, and during mealtime, her kitchen fills with the scents of curry, cardamom and coriander. She wears

(continued)

colorful silk saris, finding them more comfortable than American fashions.

The Bindras' son, Bhavjot, whom his classmates call B. J., is American-born and calls himself a 7-year-old baseball fanatic. But he, too, is obliged to learn the traditions. Each day he recites his prayers in fluent Punjabi, which his family speaks at home. His younger sister, Manmeet, is less than a year old and will learn to say her prayers in time.

Because the Bindras are Sikhs, they have a great deal of custom to uphold. Cutting hair is considered a sacrilege. Mr. Bindra's beard, which he rolls underneath his chin and braids to a fine mat, reaches almost to his belly when unraveled.

"When we came to America, we had no pressure to remain as we are," Mrs. Bindra said. "If we wanted to change, we could have. If we wanted to cut our hair, we could have. No one could have stopped us."

Bhavjot, who is in the third grade, does not have his hair cut either. He wears a patka, a kerchief worn over the skull and wrapped around a bun of hair. He once stood in front of his class to explain his religion.

"I told the class it's part of my religion," he said of his patka and long hair. "I said that my mother and father come from another country.

"They asked me: 'What country? What religion?' I explained it all to them. Nobody bothers me now."

But not all children have Bhavjot's ability to maintain their equilibrium in the face of two divergent cultures.

"There is a real sense of conflict," said Dr. Parmatma Saran, a sociology professor at Baruch College. "Young kids who came when they were very young or who were born here are sensitive to the Indian way of life. But they are at a loss to understand why parents expect so much from them when they are, after all, American."

"Parents, because of fear of losing their cultural identity, seem to have become more conservative," said Jagat Motwani, a social worker who has studied Indian immigration. "Struggling through their own identity crises, the shaken parents tend to 'overdose' their children with Indian values and try to bias them against American values.

"But Indians misunderstand American culture. The American parent doesn't like that their child gets pregnant out of wedlock. No parent likes that their child engages in premarital sex. Indians think that Americans tolerate everything."

According to Mr. Motwani, a cultural divide may exist in the conflicting questions of American dating and Indian-style arranged marriages.

AWARE OF PARENTAL OBJECTIONS

To a couple such as the Bindras, it does not seem odd they were married after two very brief encounters. Throughout India, dating remains an un-Indian activity; parents choose their children's mates, and children accept their parents' judgments.

But in America, children of Indian immigrants are often made painfully aware of parental objections to Western-style marriages.

"Indian kids aren't allowed to date or go out," said Pragna Shere, 16, a student at Martin Van Buren High School in Queens Village. "We see people going out around us, and we feel, 'Why can't we do that?'"

Hemu Shere, 21, Pragna's older sister, said:

"A lot of Indian parents don't want their children to date. They really don't want to look bad in their community. Other Indians will say the parents didn't bring the daughter up right. When children do date, the parents are always the last to find out."

Miss Shere said she was the last of her family in America to face an arranged marriage.

"If I don't find someone within a year, I'll probably get an arranged marriage. I don't know to whom. I only have one more year of college left, and it's expected of me to settle down. My father will probably take out a matrimonial ad."

Megha Bhouraskar, a 23-year-old law student, said she spent her teenage years rebelling against the values of her parents:

"Sixteen-year-olds don't know which way they're going culturewise. Indians being as conservative as they are, it's important for them to rebel a little, to experience a little of what's non-Indian. If I had always done what was expected of me or done only what the Indian community would approve

(continued)

of, I wouldn't be doing the right things for myself now."

She said she had turned more conservative with age and was more open to her Indian background.

Being an Indian growing up in America means being a combination of two things.

"Some try to be ultra-Indian, some try to be ultra-American," Miss Acharya, the Columbia student, said. "Most of us are somewhere in between. Most kids I see go to the Police concert on Friday night and to the temple with their parents on Sunday."

Adults, too, find ways to adjust.

For a pharmacist living in Flushing called Appaji, adjusting is a matter of giving and taking.

"I have been in America for 10 years," he said. "I take the best in the American system, and what I give best, the American system knows how to take."

SOURCE. 1983. "Indians in Flushing blend 2 cultures." *The New York Times* (Dec. 18). Copyright 1983 by The New York Times Company. Reprinted by permission.

(Neg. No. 33643) American Museum of Natural History

A young girl, native of New Guinea, holds young pandanus trees which she has collected for visiting scientists from the American Museum of Natural History. Her reward adorns her neck: a necklace of flashbulbs received in payment for collecting the plants.

change. They argued that we should not be concerned with elements of congruence and uniformity that would eventuate into a world of similar modern societies. They held that this belief—that these modern societies would resemble each other to the extent that earlier cultural identities and traditions would be virtually absent—was wrong.

The dominant theme of this *Daedalus* issue was (1) that tradition is not a static and unchanging entity with no changes occurring in the given traditional society, and (2) that it is wrong to assume that tradition and modernity are conflicting alternative polarities. S.J. Tambiah (1973) addresses himself to the first point. He states that this concept of tradition is applied in an uncritical ahistorical sense and erroneously denotes a collective heritage that is virtually unchanged from the past.

> By conceiving of tradition in this way, two things tend to be forgotten: that the past was, perhaps, as open and dynamic to the actors of that time as our age appears to us; and that the norms, rules, and orientations of the past were not necessarily as consistent, unified, and coherent as we tend to imagine. (Tambiah, 1973:55)

Similarly, J.C. Hersterman (1973) argues that tradition itself is full of paradox. It has to do with the way in which a society deals with fundamental questions, including the meaning of life and death, and, therefore, there can be no final formulations that are totally inflexible.

The second theme was that tradition and modernity do not necessarily have to be exclusive and conflicting categories. On examination of given societies, the contributors reached similar conclusions. They found that in many societies, such as India and Japan, tradition and modernity are inseparable. In these societies, there exists an interactive relationship between modernity and traditional culture that permeates the emerging social and political structures and exercises influence on these societies' economic development and family arrangements.

If we accept the findings of the critics of modernization theory, how can we explain why the theory of the incompatibility of tradition and modernity was voiced in the first place? Or, why was it held that traditional societies were basically static and nonchanging? The explanation lies in large part in Western ethnocentrism. Constantina Safilios-Rothschild (1970) argues that the conceptualization of "modern man" and the "modern attitude" are specifically defined with the contemporary, middle-class American as a model. This conceptualization was broadened to assume that all modern people will become the same regardless of the society of origin or their cultural heritage. It would logically follow, then, that non-Western "traditional" societies and Western "modern" societies are polar opposites in a linear theory of social change and that the content of tradition—institutions and value systems—would be impediments to changes and obstacles to modernization.

Safilios-Rothschild follows Joseph R. Gusfield (1967) in arguing that modernity may be differentially expressed from society to society as a particular blend of tradition and modern ideas, values, and behaviors. In Gusfield's (1967) influential paper he outlines six fallacies relating to the misplaced polarities of tradition and modernity:

1. Fallacy: Traditional culture is a consistent body of norms and values.
2. Fallacy: Traditional society is a homogeneous social structure.
3. Fallacy: Old traditions are displaced by new changes.
4. Fallacy: Traditional and modern forms are always in conflict.
5. Fallacy: Tradition and modernity are mutually exclusive systems.
6. Fallacy: Modernizing processes weaken traditions.

Gusfield argues that tradition becomes an ideology, a program of action that provides a justificatory base for present behavior. He notes that a desire for the preservation of tradition and the desire to modernize do not necessarily have to be in conflict. Modernity depends on and is often supported by traditional ideology: "In this process, tradition may be changed, stretched, and modified, but a unified and nationalized society makes great use of the traditional in its search for a consensual base to political authority and economic development" (Gusfield, 1967:360). Gusfield concludes that the treating of tradition and modernity as conflicting opposites itself leads to the development of an antitraditional ideology, which is manifested in the denying of the necessary and usable ways in which the past may serve as a support to the present and the future.

A basic problem, then, of modernization theory is the tendency to view traditional society and modern society as static entities. It focuses solely on the transitional stage of a traditional society modernizing in terms of process. Traditional society is conceived as a relatively stable social order that does not change over long stretches of historical time periods. Further, modern industrial societies are seen as the end product of societal evolutionary development and this has led to a tendency to overlook and discount changes in modern societies as minor readjustments in the social order. We can readily visualize the intellectual predecessors of this orientation in Social Darwinism, which believed that non-Western stone-using, hunting-and-gathering societies were social fossils from the Neolithic or Paleolithic periods and that Western industrial society was the apex and culmination of human civilization. Although modernization theory was more sophisticated—both theoretically and methodologically—than Social Darwinism and was quite critical of such simplistic unilinear evolutionary schemas, vestiges of the earlier position remained partly as a result of the continuation of Western ethnocentric biases.

This manifests itself in the model used by modernization theorists in which modern industrial man and society are based on the Western archetype. It led to the conclusion that human beings who did not share Western ideologies and value systems were antithetical to modernization and their traditional societies were opposed to modernization. Myron Weiner (1966) suggests that the problem of conceptualization of traditional societies as static entities opposed to modernization and the development of industrial and economic systems stems from a confusion between traditionalism and tradition.

> Tradition refers to the beliefs and practices handed down from the past; as we reinterpret our past, our traditions change. In contrast, traditionalism glorifies past beliefs and practices as immutable. Traditionalists see tradition as static; they urge that men do things only as they have been done before. This distinction between tradition and traditionalism calls attention to a fundamental issue in development: How do people see their past? Are the values and practices of the past to be preserved or adapted? . . . When people are attached to the past in such a way that they will not adopt new practices that modify past behavior, we are confronted with an ideology of traditionalism. Traditionalism, by virtue of its hostility to innovation, is clearly antithetical to the development of modernization; traditions, which are constantly subject to reinterpretation and modification, constitute no such barrier. (Weiner, 1966:7)

Interestingly, both Weiner and William J. Goode illustrate this difference between traditionalism and tradition in their respective discussions on the differences between nineteenth-century China and Meiji Japan. Goode's discussion of the differential relationship of the family systems in China and Japan makes it evident that the family system in China was a hindrance to rapid industrialization, whereas the family system in Japan aided in the industrialization of that country. Weiner states that, "while the Japanese sought to reinterpret their past so as to make it congruent with their efforts to modernize, many Chinese leaders were hostile to innovations that violated previous practices" (Weiner, 1966:7). In Japan, *tradition* was subject to reinterpretation and modification and thus constituted no barrier to industrialization; in China, *traditionalism* was hostile to innovation and was opposed to the development of modernization.

Unfortunately, Goode does not systematically develop the idea that tradition and modernity may *not* be conflicting and polar opposites. This is partly attributable to his conceptual model of modernization (evolutionism and structural functionalism) and to his substantive hypothesis that the family is evolving worldwide to some form of conjugal-family system. Recently, many others (Moore, 1964; Bendix, 1967; Gusfield, 1967) have reached the similar conclusion that tradition and modernity can be inseparable; modernity can be incorporated into the traditional order, and the traditional culture can permeate and have an impact on the individual, social, economic, and political spheres of modernization. Indeed, as we saw, an entire issue of *Daedalus* (Winter 1973) was devoted to this question.

One of the most exciting developments in the analysis of modernization processes is the attempt to delineate different forms of modernization that are characteristic of advanced industrial societies (the Soviet Union, Eastern and Western Europe, and the United States) and the Third World (the less-modernized societies of Asia, Africa, and Latin America). Two monographs stand out in their sociological insight into modernization: Szymon Chodak's *Societal Development: Five Approaches with Conclusions from Comparative Analysis* (1973) and Peter L. Berger, Brigitte Berger, and Hansfried Kellner's *The Homeless Mind: Modernization and Consciousness* (1973). Chodak's work is a macrolevel analysis of societal development and modernization. Berger and his associates are concerned with the utilization of the "social construction of reality" thesis developed earlier (Berger and Luckmann, 1966) to examine the modernization processes and the way individuals see themselves and their roles in life. They attempt to "link the structures of consciousness to particular institutions and processes" (Berger et al., 1973:16). We first discuss Chodak's schema and then link it with that developed by Berger and his associates. Finally, we tie them together to examine their implications for the study of modernization and the family and how they relate to Goode's *World Revolution and Family Patterns* (1963).

© Jason Laure

A Moroccan wedding in the Muslim tradition involves elaborate ceremonies and celebrations, especially in the traditional adornment and presentation of the bride.

Szymon Chodak's Conceptualization of Modernization

Syzmon Chodak (1973), building on the accumulating body of empirical studies and theories on modernization, develops a fourfold classification of modernization. Chodak observes that modernization can either be based on industrialization or on cultural contact with other societies; further, it can advance either through government organization of the economy and social structure or without direct governmental aid. Chodak's classification schema is depicted in Table 3.1.

Modernization based on industrialization occurred spontaneously in Western Europe, England, and the United States. Modernization based on industrialization was organized by the governments of the Soviet Union and Eastern European communist societies. Both forms of industrial modernization created new material conditions and produced a new social division of labor and the exchange of services. Developing concomitantly with industrialization were new roles, organizations, and systems of activities (social and political) that were complementary and interdependent.

Modernization based on cultural contact occurred through the imposition of Western ideologies on nonindustrial Third World countries that were colonized by Western societies. Chodak calls this form of modernization "acculturative" modernization. African societies are examples of this type of society. The prime example of modernization based on cultural contact, but organized by the indigenous government, is China. Chodak calls this form of modernization "induced" modernization.

Chodak compares industrial modernization with accultural and induced modernization and finds that in Third World societies the latter types of modernization are characterized by the absence of industrialization. These societies aim at the transformation of their social structures through the education system and the propounding of new norms and values. "While industrialization in Europe gave birth to modernization, in Africa and Asia the present modernization processes may—though not in all cases—create favorable conditions for the industrialization that will come" (Chodak, 1973:259). Accultural modernization, which was typical of the African colonial systems, emerged from a direct confrontation and superimposition between European colonial culture and the traditional African culture. This created a new semi-developmental buffer culture that was marginal to both and that promoted duality in norms, patterns of behavior, attitudes, and structural affiliations (Chodak, 1973:263). Colin Turnbull (1962) describes his experiences with one individual who led a dual existence in two cultural worlds:

> In Accra I stayed in the town household of a Kwahu family, their home residence being between Accra and Kumasi, in the depths of the countryside. In his country home the family head was a chief—"*Kwame*," or "He who was born on Saturday." In his Accra house the chief became Harold, a prosperous merchant and a politician. His town house was large and rambling, on two floors. He occupied the upper floor with his wife by Christian marriage and their small children. It was a magnificent apartment, with every possible luxury—including a well stocked cocktail cabi-

TABLE 3.1   The Forms of Modernization

Modernization	Spontaneous	Organized by Government
Based on industrialization	Industrial modernization in capitalist societies	Industrial modernization in communist societies
Based on cultural contact	Acculturative modernization	Induced modernization

SOURCE: Szymon Chodak. 1973. *Societal Development: Five Approaches with Conclusions from Comparative Analysis.* New York: Oxford University Press, p. 268. Copyright © 1973 by Oxford University Press. Reprinted by permission.

net, for the one tradition that dies the hardest is the tradition of hospitality. In this apartment lived a happy, settled, thoroughly westernized family. But downstairs lived his other family, the family of Kwame as opposed to that of Harold—all his nephews and other appendages of his extended Kwame family which, as Kwame, he felt obliged to support, even in Accra.

It was like going from one world to another, and I lived a completely double life with ease and pleasure in that household. Upstairs we drank whisky, danced the cha-cha and the mambo, ate bacon and eggs for breakfast and drank tea at teatime. From upstairs, we sallied forth for evenings at the various smart night clubs (evening dress compulsory), or to elegant private dinner parties. But downstairs I ate *fufu* (a kind of unsweetened dough made from manioc flour, from which one tears pieces to dip in a sauce) with my fingers, drank palm wine, danced Abalabi, and learned what real family life is like. (Turnbull, 1962:32[2])

But Chodak sees the acculturative process as a process of alienation. He reports that Colin Turnbull calls these individuals alienated, whereas Franz Fanon (1968), in his book *The Wretched of the Earth,* sees them as men and women with a black skin and a white mask. Chodak views the acculturated alienated individual as being transformed into a "superior inferior" (Chodak, 1973:265). Although such alienated individuals acquire the habits of the European colonizers and are told that they are superior to nonacculturated individuals, they are at the same time treated as inferiors by Europeans. Chodak provides a powerful illustration of this situation in the writings of an African, Robert Mueme Mbate, who, as he searches for his identity, asks: "Who am I?"

I am not a Mkamba, yet I am Mkamba, I was born of Kamba parents. In my veins there flows Kamba blood. . . . I know a number of Kamba customs, but what I know is so little that I am ashamed. . . . Can I claim to be a European? A black European? Now wait a minute! In my veins, there flows Kamba blood. My skin is black like a Mkamba's. . . . And when I eat European food my stomach rebels. It wants most of all the Kamba dish—*isye*—maize with beans and green vegetables. . . .

I speak the English language. I write in English. I even dress like English people. In my best clothes, I look like an Englishman. I struggle hard to learn the manners of the English people. . . . I fall short of European customs and culture. When they say, "Don't be silly," I feel I have been insulted. Yet it's not so. When a daughter kisses her father, my blood says, "Oh no!" It is odd to me. . . .

When I was a young boy, I was "Kambanized." I learned how to make bows and arrows, the Kamba traditional weapons. . . . I don't know how to dance the traditional Kamba dances. I went to school too early to learn them. At school I learned English and Scottish dances. Yet I don't know why the English and Scottish dances are danced. . . .

What then, am I? A conglomeration of indigeneous and borrowed ideas and ideals. As such, I must find my footing in the whole nation, and indeed in the whole human race. I am not a Mkamba, yet a Mkamba, in whose veins Kamba blood flows. (Mbate cited in Chodak, 1973:266[3])

Finally, Chodak perceives the process of acculturative modernization as a process of detribalization; a process in which there is a gradual substitution of traditional roles with an ascriptive allocation of roles and positions based on individual achievements within a new social and political organization of the society.

The third form of modernization is induced modernization, which consists of introducing Western patterns of government and administration, education systems, and value orientations to the still-nonindustrialized country:

[2] From *The Lonely African* by Colin M. Turnbull. Copyright © 1962 by Colin M. Turnbull. Reprinted by permission of Simon & Schuster, a Division of Gulf & Western Corporation.
[3] Robert Mueme Mbate. 1969. "Identity." *Bursara* (Nairobi) 2:31–34.

I call it induced modernization because the changes and transformations—particularly in the sphere of social relations—which are involved, and which are usually government-initiated, lead to the acceptance in the new society of the norms, values, and organizations of the industrial societies. Thus this is a process induced by the existence of industrial societies elsewhere in the world. (Chodak, 1973:267)

Chodak identifies induced modernization as a process of nation building and the generation of national identities. Its primary aim is the transformation of the societal population into a new, national entity while retaining significant parts of the traditional culture (norms, symbols, patterns of behavior, and aspects of the social structure) and trying to integrate these parts into the new social order. The process of induced modernization is not seen as a procedure by which there is growing mass participation in the decision-making processes of the new states, but rather as one in which the government and the ruling political party are the chief organizers and implementers. The process of induced modernization, then, aims at the development of what Chodak calls a "stratified supratribal national society" that is superimposed on the traditional tribal structure.

Berger, Berger, and Kellner's *The Homeless Mind*

This theme is continued and expanded in *The Homeless Mind: Modernization and Consciousness* (1973). In this work, the argument is made that the process of modernization and the institutions that accompany it have had a negative impact on human consciousness of reality not only in the non-Western Third World but also in the industrialized world, especially in the United States. The modernization process, which was supposed to free individuals, is seen instead as increasing feelings of helplessness, frustration, and alienation that beset individuals with threats of meaninglessness. Berger and his associates examine the processes of modernization in the Third World and its effect on traditional ways of life, kinship patterns, and "social constructions of reality" and find them being changed. In industrial societies, they see the development of processes of "demodernization" being manifested in various forms of counterculture movements.

Modernization is seen to consist of the growth and diffusion of a set of institutions (bureaucracy, technological economy, political systems, and social and cultural pluralism) that stem from the transformation of the economy by technological innovations. Modernization has helped lead the individual away from the domination of the extended family, clan, and tribe and has given the individual the opportunity to pursue previously unheard of choices and options. Both geographical mobility (the movement from the small rural community to the larger urban community) and social and occupational mobility have freed the individual from these previously dominating institutions.

As is readily apparent, this position parallels that of William J. Goode, who welcomed these changes in that they provided men and women the potential for greater individual freedom and the "unleashing of personal potentials, the right to love, to equality within the family, to the establishment of a new marriage when the old had failed . . . the right for the first time *to choose* for themselves . . . " (Goode, 1963:380). However, Berger and his associates (1973) go beyond Goode and see that modernization has, in fact, not led to freedom and the maximization of individual potentialities but, instead, has led to a condition of "homelessness" and to feelings of helplessness, frustration, and alienation. The focus of *The Homeless Mind* is to determine the factors in modernization that have had this effect on individuals.

Although Berger and his associates' examination of the modernization processes in the Third World does not explicitly make the distinction between Chodak's accultur-

In Kenya, Tribe Wins a Legal Bout with Modern World

BY DAVID ZUCCHINO

NAIROBI—The body of S.M. Otieno still lies on ice in the Nairobi mortuary, a full 62 days after his death. From the moment he died of a heart attack at age 55 on Dec. 20, the legal struggle for possession of his body has pitted Kenya's past against its future.

In life, Otieno embodied Western values. He was an urbane lawyer fond of quoting Shakespeare and watching "Perry Mason" video reruns. He sent his children abroad to college, telling them that the ways of their Luo tribe were "primitive."

In death, Otieno has become a symbol of an enduring tribalism that still governs every aspect of life for most Kenyans. Kenya's highest court has ruled that Otieno, who called himself a Kenyan rather than a Luo tribesman, must be buried under Luo tribal law.

The death and final disposition of Otieno is an allegory for post-colonial Kenya. It seems to say that the tribe, and not the nation, is paramount in matters of life and death.

Both Otieno's widow and his tribe had claimed his body. The Luo demanded that Otieno be buried under tribal law, and they predicted catastrophes if he were not. Otieno's brother, Joash Ochieng Ougo, testified that the demons of his brother's soul would haunt him the rest of his life unless Otieno were buried under Luo soil.

Otieno's widow, a member of the rival Kikuyu tribe, vowed to bury her husband near their suburban Nairobi home under Christian and Kenyan laws. Virginia Wambui, the epitome of the educated and privileged African woman, openly scorned the Luo belief in demons and ghosts.

The week after Otieno died, both the Luo and Wambui had scheduled separate funerals for the same day on gravesites 200 miles apart. Both were canceled for lack of a corpse.

Later, Wambui—who goes by her Kikuyu name—reportedly warned morgue officials that the tribe was planning to steal the body. She forbade Otieno's brother to enter her home and called police to keep out the rest of the Luo clan.

The Luo finally won in court on Wednesday, and so now a man who rejected his tribe must be buried by it. And his widow, a leading Kenya feminist who despises the Luo treatment of women, will need a Luo blessing to visit her husband's grave, if the appeal she has filed is unsuccessful.

During 17 rancorous days in court that produced 45 hours of remarkable testimony, all of Kenya watched, fascinated.

Two dozen witnesses were called. There was a gravedigger, a witch doctor, a philosopher and the chief of the Umira Kager clan of the Luo tribe. Anthropological and sociological texts were quoted at length. The two opposing lawyers quoted liberally from the Bible, citing passages on death and the afterlife.

There was testimony about precisely what Otieno had said at his father's Luo funeral. Witnesses spoke of spitting on graves, of curses by the dead, of feeding corpses to jackals, and of Otieno's fondness for pubs.

FRONT-PAGE NEWS

The dispute was front-page news for weeks; Nairobi's three newspapers published extra editions to satisfy an insatiable public curiosity.

The city's main courthouse overflowed with spectators, and hundreds more spilled into the streets outside. When the Luo won, riot police had to hold off swarms of tribesmen headed for the mortuary to haul away Otieno's corpse.

The entire nation seemed obsessed by what the outcome of the trial told the world about Kenya. Was it truely a modern nation, or still an awkward pastiche of about 40 tribes?

Otieno paid homage to Kenya, not the Luo. He rejected his father's surname and moved to Nairobi, far from the Luo enclave on the eastern shores of Lake Victoria. He allowed his sons to be circumcised, in defiance of Luo custom. He refused to

(continued)

teach his nine children the Luo language.

Worst of all, in the eyes of the Luo, Otieno married outside the tribe. In 1963, the year of Kenya's independence, he and Wambui became one of the nation's first intertribal couples. Such unions are still rare, despite government encouragement and an official policy that says tribalism barely exists.

Otieno could not have made a more contentious choice of a wife. The Kikuyu and the Luo, Kenya's two largest tribes, have a long history of enmity and mistrust. Marriage between the two tribes is considered anathema by both peoples.

Jomo Kenyatta, Kenya's founding father and its first president, was a Kikuyu. Through him, the Kikuyu prospered in business and government in the capital.

In 1968, a Luo-dominated political party was outlawed by Kenyatta. When a Luo leader named Tom Mboya was assassinated the next year, the Luo blamed Kenyatta. The president's motorcade was stoned on his next visit to Luo territory. His bodyguards fired into the crowds, killing 11 Luo.

In court the last two months, the Luo's simmering resentment seemed to well up at the mere sight of Wambui, who comes from a prominent Kikuyu family. Luo tribal elders glared at her as she entered court each day.

RESENTMENT

Wambui represents everything the Luo, and many other African men, resent in a woman. She is college-educated, outspoken and wealthy. Her father was a leader of Kenyan independence, her brother a High Court judge and another brother a foreign minister. She is an independent and thoroughly modern African woman.

When the U.N. international women's conference was held in Nairobi in 1985, Wambui was its treasurer. In 1969, she became the first woman from Nairobi's suburbs to run for parliament. She lost.

The Luo, like many African tribes, consider women chattel. Wives must obey their husbands, raise children, work the fields. They have no say in their husbands' estates or wills. Their fathers help choose their husbands, requiring a bride price that is normally paid in cattle.

Whether Otieno had paid a bride price for Wambui, in fact, was a central question of the trial. Witnesses called by Wambui's attorney said he had not. They said Otieno considered bride prices archaic and preferred a "Christian household." That, along with the couple's union under the Kenya civil Marriage Act, was proof that the marriage was not subject to Luo customs, the attorney argued.

Even so, High Court Judge S.E.O. Bosire cited other factors in ruling for the Luo. He seemed particularly annoyed at the testimony of Wambui and two of her sons, who denigrated Luo customs.

One son, an economics student at Paterson State College in Wayne, N.J., called the Luo "uncivilized" and "lazy." Other witnesses for Wambui ridiculed the Luo's *tero buru* burial rituals, which are designed to drive out demons.

The testimony drew angry rumbles from the Luo elders in the courtroom, and even the judge, who is not Luo, seemed offended. He said in his ruling: "She [Wambui] cannot now complain that the [Luo] people are uncivilized or have a lifestyle quite different from her concept of civilization, because they did not force her to be married into their clan."

SUBSERVIENCE

In essence, the judge ruled, Wambui was considered Luo because she had married a Luo. He thus held up the Kenya custom of a woman's subservience to male tribal identity.

Wambui and her attorney, John Khaminwa, sought to prove that Otieno wanted nothing to do with Luo customs.

In a single sentence, Khaminwa summed up the dead lawyer's Western ways: "S.M. Otieno loved contemporary music, quoted from Shakespeare and enjoyed going to a pub for his beer, whiskey or gin."

He also spoke for Kenya's increasingly Westernized urban middle class—a segment of Kenyan society that considers tribal customs unbecoming to a modern African nation.

"There has emerged a new class,"

(continued)

Khaminwa said, "of civil servants, professionals and managers on a larger scale than ever before, who have their own tastes which are completely different from those found in the rural communities. They are quite modern and Westernized, and their lives are consistent with the contemporary world."

On the day Otieno died, his widow was certainly alert to the Luo custom that often permits tribesmen to haul away the possessions of a deceased member. She had her servants roll up the rugs and hide Otieno's videocassette recorder.

"She even locked the toilets," Ougo, the brother, complained to the judge.

The attorney for the Luo clan, Richard Otieno Kwach — himself a Luo — portrayed Wambui as a scheming woman who abandoned her own tribe and then sought to force her dead husband to abandon his.

"She is hellbent on creating chaos in the [Luo] tribe," Kwach told the court.

By marrying a Luo, Wambui became a Luo, Kwach said. As such, she is required to obey Luo traditions — regardless of Kenya law, he said. (Kenya law states that burials are "to be guided" by customary law, except when it is "repugnant to justice and morality.")

CALAMITIES

The Luo attribute all manner of calamities — from drownings to fires — to the demons released by a tribesman who is not properly buried under tribal law. Bodies must be placed quickly into the hands of elders. Last summer, after 13 Luo drowned in Lake Victoria, Luo elders rushed to the lake during a storm to retrieve the bodies. Thirty-one of them drowned, too.

When Wambui's attorney portrayed such practices as heathen, the Luo lawyer suddenly burst out in court: "My clients are not a group of cannibals!"

Kwach paused and went on: "They merely want to carry out a time-honored custom which we believe in."

He pointed out acidly that the Kikuyu had their own peculiar burial customs. If a Kikuyu man died in his hut, Kwach told the judge, his body was left inside for hyenas to eat.

"Those are the Kikuyu," Kwach said drily.

Of the Luo customs, Kwach said: "Customs have causes. Customary law is the law of Kenya."

To the laughter of Luo and Kikuyu alike, he added: "Even the English have customs."

In the end, those arguments seemed to prevail on Judge Bosire. He noted in his ruling that Otieno had observed Luo custom in attending the tribal funerals of his father and two other Luos. Witnesses said Otieno did not object to the practices at the time.

The judge said he had been "impressed a lot" by the testimony of a 74-year-old gravedigger, Albert Ongango. The elderly man testified from his hospital bed that Otieno, at the funeral of a Luo friend, cried out to him at the graveside:

"Albert, Albert . . . prepare a grave for me next to that of my father!"

As for Wambui, the judge said simply: "She chose to be married to the deceased, a Luo by birth, knowing him to be such."

On Wednesday, however, Justice Bosire granted the widow an injuction prohibiting the Luo from removing Otieno's body pending the outcome of her appeal of the decision favoring the Luo.

The Umira Kager clan brushed it aside. They were confident that their victory would be upheld.

The Luo elders are still making plans to bury Otieno at his ancestral farm near Lake Victoria. It would be one of the biggest funerals in the history of Luo land.

Luo guests were expected from all over the lakeside district. Though Otieno had scorned them in life, he had become in death Kenya's most talked-about Luo.

Strict Luo burial customs will be observed, the elders have said, and the demons of the soul of S.M. Otieno shall be put to rest. His widow will not be invited.

SOURCE. David Zucchino. 1987. "In Kenya, tribe wins a legal bout with modern world." Reprinted with permission from *The Philadelphia Inquirer* (Feb. 20).

ated modernization and induced modernization, it reaches a similar conclusion by emphasizing that these forms of modernization are experienced in terms of cultural contact and imposition. They extend the argument by noting that even when modern technology is encountered, most people in the Third World are related to it in terms of low-skill labor without experiencing the ideologies of modernity. "What frequently happens in such cases is that there are very destructive effects on traditional patterns of life *without* any significant modernization of consciousness in terms of positively identifiable themes" (Berger et al., 1973:121). They illustrate this very persuasively by looking at how mining in South Africa has had the immediate consequences of weakening village life and its traditional cultural patterns. Men are separated from their families and their traditional way of life and are placed in an industrial life-world that is amorphous and composed of uprooted individuals.

> In such a situation the structures of modernity (in terms of institutions, patterns of everyday life, cognitive and normative themes and anything else one may wish to name) must necessarily appear to the individual as an alien, powerful and, in the main, coercive force that completely uproots his life and the lives of those he most cares about. In such a situation, there is little if any direct identification with modernity. (Berger et al., 1973:122[4])

The development of an identification with modernization can only begin to occur when individuals begin to settle into a new life and if and when they are joined by their families. Berger and his associates also observe that initially only a small number of individuals adapt to modernization. These people—who are labeled modern types—are seen to have been marginal to the life of the traditional community. These are the people to whom Chodak refers in his concept of acculturated modernization and who Colin Turnbull calls "the lonely African."

In their examination of what Chodak has called induced modernization, Berger and his associates view this phenomenon as representing a later stage of the modernization process occurring in the Third World. The earlier stages occur when both the modern state and the modern economy impose themselves as alien realities on traditional social situations, and it is in this earlier stage that the acculturated modern man is found. In the later stage—particularly when the Third World society achieves political independence (in Africa or Asia) or gains a revolutionary government (in Latin America or Asia)—the state itself is presented as a mobilizing agent for development. This makes it easier for various people and groups, particularly the acculturated modern type, to identify with what Chodak has called the "supratribal national society" rather than with the traditional tribal structure, as well as to identify with the state rather than with a particular economic system. Further, the state becomes the vehicle for accomplishment of the social ambitions of these people, especially for those who are involved with the governmental bureaucracy, which becomes the ladder for the attainment of status, privilege, and power. Berger and his associates explain this phenomenon in the following passage:

> [It] is probably because the bureaucracy is able to accommodate itself to traditional patterns of social relations more easily than an increasingly technological economy can. Even a very modern bureaucratic structure can establish working relations with traditional power structures far better than a modern economic enterprise can with traditional patterns of production. Traditional patterns can actually be incorporated into the workings of the bureaucracy, as the importance of family, clan and tribal loyalties in the politics of Third World states clearly indicates. (Berger et al., 1973:127–128)

[4] From *The Homeless Mind: Modernization and Consciousness* by Peter L. Berger, Brigitte Berger, and Hansfried Kellner. Copyright © 1973 by Peter Berger, Brigitte Berger and Hansfried Kellner. Reprinted by permission of Random House, Inc. and Penguin Books Ltd.

This insight is broadened with the authors' understanding that bureaucracy in the Third World is frequently tied up with ideologies of nationalism and socialism. The aim of the state government is to make the governmental system combine the benefits of modernity within the traditional tribal community and offer the individual meaning and solidarity. Here Berger and his associates integrate the idea that modernity and tradition do not have to be polar opposites since they see that the goal of socialism and state nationalism is to provide an answer to the problems of modernization.

> . . . we repeatedly emphasized that the dichotomization of private and public life is one of the crucial social characteristics of modernity. Modernization in contemporary Third World societies imposes this same dichotomization, and in most instances it is felt to be an extremely difficult and often repugnant ordeal, which gives birth to profound threats of anomie. Socialism presents itself as a solution to this problem. It promises to reintegrate the individual in all-embracing structures of solidarity. *If modernization can be described as a spreading condition of homelessness, then socialism can be understood as the promise of a new home.* (Berger et al., 1973:138)

The goal of the socialist Third World society is to offer both modernity and traditional community and thus reverse the alienating, fragmenting, and disintegrating processes relating to the destruction of tribal and communal solidarities. The ambition of the Third World is the combination of development and modernization of society with the protection of traditional symbols and patterns of life. This is an extremely difficult task because, as we have seen, modernization brings with it reclassification schemas of social relationships based on economic status, occupation, and supratribal relationships rather than on social relationships based on tribal and kinship criteria. Thus, nationalism is seen as being both a liberator and an oppressor: liberating individuals from colonialization and from the controls of family, clan, and tribe, and oppressing individuals in the quest for modernization and the development of technological and bureaucratic institutions.

In the advanced industrial nations, Berger and his associates see modernization as leading to a variety of discontentments stemming from the technologized economy, the bureaucratization of major institutions, and the "pluralization of social worlds," resulting in a condition that they label as "homelessness."

These authors develop the argument that technology's primary consequence has been in the separation of work from private life. This condition has also had an impact on the individual's "levels of consciousness." Technological production, they say, is characterized by anonymous impersonal social relations where individuals interact with each other in terms of the functions they perform in their structured work tasks and where there is no need to be aware of each other's uniqueness as individuals. The consequence of this is that "the individual now becomes capable of experiencing himself in a double way; as a unique individual rich in concrete qualities and as an anonymous functionary" (Berger et al., 1973:34). The implication of this dichotomization of self is that it is only in their private lives that individuals can express elements of their subjective identity, which is denied them in their work situation. However, people are unable to find ample satisfaction in their private lives because their private lives tend to be composed of weak institutions, a prime illustration being the family.

The reason for this is that the nature of modern industrial society is characterized by a "plurality of life-worlds"—modern life is segmented (pluralized) to a high degree, and the different sectors of everyday life that an individual experiences are not related and may represent vastly different worlds of meaning and experience. In contrast, according to these authors, traditional society is characterized by a life-world that is relatively unified, with a high degree of integration existing among the various groups in which the individual participates. Thus, individuals do not experience the sense of segmentation of modern life and do not have the feeling that a particular social situation took them out of their common life-world, whether they are involved with their family, religious groups, or work groups.

The pluralization of life-worlds is distinguished by the dichotomy of private and public spheres; furthermore, pluralization can take place *within* these spheres. Berger and his associates examine the family to show the effect of pluralization within the private sphere:

> . . . the private sphere itself is not immune to pluralization. It is indeed true that the modern individual typically tries to arrange this sphere in such a way that by contrast to his bewildering involvement with the worlds of public institutions, this private world will provide for him an order of integrative and sustaining meanings. In other words, the individual attempts to construct a "home world" which will serve as the meaningful center of his life in society. Such an enterprise is hazardous and precarious. Marriages between people of different backgrounds involve complicated negotiations between the meanings of discrepant worlds. Children habitually and disturbingly emigrate from the world of their parents. Alternate and often repulsive worlds impinge upon private life in the form of neighbors and other unwelcome intruders, and indeed it is also possible that the individual, dissatisfied for whatever reason with the organization of his private life, may himself seek out plurality in other private contacts. This quest for more satisfactory private meanings may range from extramarital affairs to experiments with exotic religious sects. (Berger et al., 1973:66–67)

INDIA ABROAD

CLASSIFIED

MATRIMONIAL

Matrimonial — Female

New York based physician sister invites correspondence from professionals for very attractive, vegetarian Rajput Doctor sister 23, merit scholar intern Lady Hardinge Delhi, family of physicians. No bars. Reply biodata, photograph.

N

Gujarati Charotar Patel parents invite correspondence from professionals for daughter, U.S. educated, citizen, professionally employed, 24, 5'1". Please correspond with returnable photograph and biodata to:

N

Proposal invited from compatible, handsome professional for beautiful, talented, Bengali Hindu girl, 25, US raised, BS, professional, employed. No bars.

E

Match for convent educated, pretty, smart, Gujarati girl, 27 yrs, 5', B.A., L.L.B., from Bombay, currently visiting USA.

E

Punjabi Brahmin parents invite correspondence for their highly cultured and extremely beautiful, US citizen daughter, 5'2", 32 years, physician, innocent divorcee. Boy must be Punjabi, broadminded and highly educated from respectable family.

N

Matrimonial—Female (Contd.)

Well placed Indian parents invite correspondence for their attractive 25 year old daughter, U.S. citizen, completing graduate school, has infant daughter. No bars.

N

33 years, 157 cms., divorced issueless Punjabi, M.Sc., Ph.D. girl looking for suitable match, Green Card holder. MW

Aiyangar groom for graduate bank employed girl, 29 years, Bombay based. Contact brother: F0158 N

Bengali Kayastha teacher English in India 25, beautiful, smart. C

Brother invites correspondence from Gujarati issueless professional for attractive sister, graduate, 35, divorced. Biodata and photo must. N

Brother invites correspondence from well-settled professionals for 29 yrs. old girl (MBBS, MD, MRCS), 5'6", cultured, charming, fair, currently living in U.K. Brother in States. N

Brother invites correspondence from Rajput professionals for beautiful, well educated sister, 23, in India. Send returnable photographs/details. N

Brother invites correspondence from professionals, medical doctor preferred, for Jat Sikh medico girl, 5'4", MBBS, presently in India. Brothers doctor and engineer settled in California. N

Brother invites correspondence from well settled, professional, Gujarati gentlemen, 43-48 for attractive, intelligent, talented sister, 43, 5'3", B.Arch., visiting U.S.A. soon. Send recent photographs and all pertinent details to: E

Brother invites correspondence from Ramgarhia Gursikh professionals for sister 31, 5'2", teacher, U.K. educated. N

Brother seeks correspondence from non-Harida Iyer men for sister 30, tall, slim, smart, postgraduate, teacher in India. E

Charotar Patel family invites correspondence from educated professional for educated girl, U.S. citizen, tall and beautiful. Reply with details and photograph. MW

Matrimonial—Male

Correspondence invited from educated, cultured, good looking girls, 22-27, for tall, Gujarati Charotar Patel, immigrant Doctor, 29, of excellent family background, completing residency. Parents well settled in Gujarat. Please send details with returnable photograph. N

Correspondence invited for two immigrant Patel brothers. Contact:

Correspondence invited by divorced professional of Indian background, 54, 5'6", $44K income, many interests.

Educated Gujarati recently divorced, 42 years old, well settled Engineer, 5'9", no children invites correspondence for matrimonial relationship. Returnable photo must be. N

Engineer, B.Tech./CS, MSCS, 27, 5'6", 130, Green Card holder, seeks match. No bar. N

Family invites correspondence from cultured Patel girl for well settled, 30, innocently divorced. N

For 41 years old Punjabi man, M.A., LL.B., bank officer. W

Forty year old male Satsangi invites correspondence from female Satsangi for meaningful relationship. Reply: N

Good looking Gujarati Hindu, MS, MBA, mid 30, seek never married girl. N

Gujarati Brahmin, veg., non smoker, non drinker, 6', 175 lbs., Green Card, well established, self employed, 33 yrs., divorced no children, invites biodata and returnable photographs from sincere, fun loving, non professional, unmarried Gujarati girls with high moral values. N

Gujarati Jain immigrant, 38, divorced, well settled. Call: E

Gujarati Jain businessman, B.Com., LL.B., M.B.A., 28, 5'7", invites correspondence from Gujarati educated girls, photos must. Call. N

Handsome Hindu professional, MS, MBA, seek match in 30. No divorcees. No bar. N

Handsome doctorate Engineer seeks pretty, spiritually inclined, never married professional. N

Handsome, educated Punjabi Brahmin businessman, 35, never married, well placed family. No divorces. Photograph, biodata. E

Handsome, fair, M.B.A., Maharashtrian businessman, Green Card holder, intelligent, compassionate, 34 yrs., tall, looking for beautiful, tall, fair, M.D. or dental doctor girls from excellent family background in U.S. or India. Please write with full particulars and current returnable photograph is a must. Reply:

Matrimonial—Male (Contd.)

Parents seek suitable match for their son 25, handsome, business executive. Returnable photograph with biodata. E

Physician brother invites correspondence from beautiful professionals for handsome, 5'7", 25 year old brother, MS Electrical Engineering, USA, currently doing Ph.D. computers, student visa, well connected Punjabi Brahmin family. Call: or send returnable photograph to: E

Physician, well settled, early 40's seek correspondence from attractive, cultured, educated, homeloving girls under 35. Religion no bars. Reply photo/biodata. M 0117, IA N

Professional match for Doctorate Economist, 45, handsome, tall, Bengali. C

Professional, late fifties, seeks understanding, caring, unencumbered, slim, South Indian lady with character. 45-54. Send photo: M0166 N

Proposals invited from fair and attractive girls/parents with Green Card and US higher education (Doctor, Engineer, MBA, CPA, etc.) for Keralite Marthomite boy aged 30, 5'6", 160 lbs. with BSBA, MBA and MAC degrees from US university. Call: N

Punjabi professional, handsome, cultured, 30, 5'7", well placed Chemical Engineer, immigrant, seeks an attractive, caring match. Details (picture appreciated) to: E

Refined match for an accomplished, ambitious, handsome Indian Christian man, 29, 5'10", Engineer, MBA - no bars. Reply with photo:

Responses invited for son 26, 5'9", Comp. Engr. from Vaishnav/Jain Gujarati graduates. (312) MW

Seek suitable bride for 33 yrs., Gujarati Jain, 5'4", 120 lbs., businessman in L.A., Green Card holder. N

Sincere professional match for 32 yr., 5'4½", 1st year resident physician. Sikh gentleman with no religion/caste bars. N

Modern classified matrimonial ads in *India Abroad*.

In summary, these authors put forth the argument that marriage—which was seen as providing a meaningful world for its participants—is, in fact, unable to overcome the homelessness resulting from the pluralization of life-worlds in modern society. This conclusion is diametrically opposite to that reached by William J. Goode. Where Goode welcomes the changes and is optimistic about the actualization of individualism and egalitarianism, Berger and his associates are quite pessimistic. In their delineation of the public and private life, they hit at a key variable in explaining much of the tensions surrounding the contemporary American family system.

In essence, we are in agreement with this latter position. The dichotomization of public and private spheres of activities is a main characteristic of contemporary Western family systems. It is this dichotomization that provides the key to the analysis of social change and the family. Much of cross-cultural and historical analysis of family change has ignored this characteristic. Influenced by modernization theory, scholars have overemphasized the need to investigate structural changes in the family. These theorists have built up the case that the distinctive feature of modern society is the predominance of the nuclear family and the prevalence of the large patriarchal extended kin group of traditional societies from the historical past of Western Europe and America.

Interestingly, William J. Goode (1963) debunks the myth that the "classical family of Western nostalgia" was the large extended family living happily in the large rambling house on the farm. But, in his emphasis on the close "fit" between industrialization and the conjugal family and on the retarding effects of the extended family with industrialization, his argument takes a different twist; it centers on changes in the structural nature of the family and limits the analysis of changes to the family's involvement in the community. His argument, then, becomes one aspect of the theme that industrialization means the end of the viable extended family and the development of the conjugal family, which has severed meaningful involvements with other kin.

Recently, family historians have taken issue with the conclusion that the history of the Western family is a movement from the consanguineal system to the conjugal one. And, in their historical analysis of the Western family form, they reach strikingly similar conclusions to cross-cultural comparative sociologists, such as Peter L. Berger, and to the conclusions of Karl Marx and Friedrich Engels on the privatization of the family. In the next chapter, we turn our attention to these new developments and examine these research findings and conclusions. This is part of our larger discussion of the family in the community context. We conclude this chapter with an examination of the critics of Talcott Parsons and structural-functional conceptualizations of the contemporary American family.

Critics of Structural Functionalism's Conceptualizations of the American Family

Critics of the contemporary American family take issue with the structural-functionalist belief that it is the optimum family system for solving the needs for intimacy, individualism, and egalitarianism. Such critics as Arlene S. and Jerome H. Skolnick (1971/1977) believe that supporters of the conjugal family have overlooked problems inherent within the family because of the limitations of structural-functionalist-based modernization theory. They argue that modernization theory tends to view industrial society as a static entity, representing the final stage in industrial history. The critics believe that the sociological study of the family in industrial society can be strengthened by extending the line of inquiry to a new stage of development—postindustrial or postmodern society. They see that a better understanding of the

Social Ills of Modernity Catching Up with Japan

BY STEVE LOHR

TOKYO, May 3 — Foreigners have long marveled at Japan's ability to acquire appurtenances of modernity, like computer-age industries, while seeming to keep underlying social patterns unaffected. But today, two generations after World War II, traditional values are significantly changing in this nation of 118 million people.

The shifts, whose signs and strains are becoming increasingly evident, are documented in surveys of public attitudes, in statistics that track social behavior, in books and in the comments of educators, corporate executives, housewives, doctors and others.

For example, the suicide rate among Japanese men in their 40's and 50's, normally years of stability and professional recognition, is rising sharply. In 1983 they accounted for 41 percent of total suicides in Japan, which reached a postwar peak of 25,202. More and more Japanese executives are suffering from depression, doctors report.

DIVORCE RATE IS RISING

The divorce rate, though one-fifth that in the United States, is rising. The Health and Welfare Ministry reported over the weekend that the number of single-parent families sharply increased over the last five years, mainly because of the rising divorce rate. It said there were 718,100 families, or about 2 percent of all households, that were headed by the mother alone, a rise of 13.3 percent in five years.

Young people are less enamored with the notion of lifetime employment at one company, the centerpiece of Japan's widely admired labor-management system.

"For people in their 20's and 30's, loyalty to the company is zero," said Kenichi Ohmae, a management consultant in Tokyo.

THE PROBLEM OF "ME-ISM"

"More than a decade ago, people in America started talking about me-ism," said Michio Nagai, a former Minister of Education, who is a professor at Sophia University. "Now, for the first time since World War II, this has become a problem in Japan, too."

Dr. Teruo Konishi, head of the mental health department at the Matsushita Health Service Center in Osaka, said that although depression among older managers had become more prevalent in the last four years, fewer younger people were coming in with work-related emotional troubles.

"Japanese people are changing, becoming more like Americans," Dr. Konishi said. "The young employees don't care so much any more about their relations with their superiors at work. They are not so worried if there is some minor conflict."

BYPRODUCT OF PROGRESS

To a degree, the problems that are causing concern in some quarters are merely byproducts of social and technological progress that are welcomed by others. The divorce rate, for example, is climbing partly because women have made modest but steady gains in the job market, achieving some measure of economic freedom.

Thanks to its industrial ascent, Japan is no longer a center of cheap-labor sweatshops, and the five-day workweek has arrived. Leisure time — how to spend and enjoy it — has become the focus of public attention. Jogging and aerobic dancing are the rage, and "shape up" is a phrase that has entered the Japanese vernacular.

Rising national wealth, equitably distributed, has meant that Japan is a middle-class society in which more and more people have the means and the time to pursue personal interests.

Just what the greater emphasis on individual concerns will mean for Japan is uncertain. For example, Japan's traditional group-oriented values — particularly workers' spirit of self-sacrifice and unswerving loyalty to their company — are credited with contributing greatly to the nation's postwar economic success.

AFFLUENCE AND WESTERN VALUES

Affluence and the influence of Western

(continued)

values are the reasons most often cited for the changes in attitudes.

Although these two forces have been evident in Japan since the late 1960's, Japanese say the recent difference is that the trends are accelerating. The shifts in attitude seem to be particularly pronounced in people raised after World War II, under the social changes and cultural diversity introduced by the American occupation.

Ken Hayashibara, president of Hayashibara Biochemical Laboratories in Okayama, said:

"If the person is over 40 years old, I tell him he should do something because it is first good for Japan, good for the company, good for his family and finally good for him. If the person is under 40, I tell him he should do it because first it is good for him, good for his family, good for the company and finally good for Japan."

For the most part, attitudes have changed more than working habits. The Japanese still work longer hours than people in the other developed nations.

Industrial workers in Japan in 1982 worked an average of 2,136 hours including overtime, according to the Labor Ministry. Their counterparts in the United States worked 1,851 hours, in France 1,707 hours and in West Germany 1,682 hours.

A recent survey by the Labor Ministry found 30 percent of Japanese salaried workers spend less than three waking hours a day at home with their families on weekdays.

Apparently, the Japanese are working as hard as ever, but feeling worse about it.

This is one explanation for the rising incidence of depression and suicide among middle-aged men.

PRESSURES IN THE HOME

According to Dr. Hisakazu Fujii, an Osaka psychiatrist, the prevalence of depression among middle-aged corporate managers is partly caused by Japan's lifetime employment and seniority system.

In many cases additional pressure comes from home, especially from wives increasingly dissatisfied with being little more than housekeepers.

The changed attitude of women is reflected in Japan's divorce rate, which has doubled in the last decade. Many experts say the rate is kept artificially low because financial settlements for women are so low, less than $4,500 on average.

Miserable marriages are abundant, according to *Wives in the Autumn of Life*, a book by Shigeo Saito that documents the private lives of women married to graduates of prestigious universities who become Japan's elite bureaucrats, bankers and corporate executives. The book has become a bestseller since it was published in 1982.

For the women Mr. Saito interviewed, mostly in their 30's and 40's, there is no longer any pretense of finding happiness in sacrificing themselves for their husband's career.

SOURCE. Steve Lohr. 1984. "Social ills of modernity catching up with Japan." *The New York Times* (May 9). Copyright © 1984 by The New York Times Company. Reprinted by permission.

conjugal family can be accomplished by studying it as a social problem, viewing the problems of the conjugal family as arising out of its very nature and structure.

Skolnick and Skolnick (1971/1977) and Skolnick (1973/1978) observe that Talcott Parsons and William J. Goode in his *World Revolution and Family Patterns* (1963) do recognize that tensions and points of strain in the conjugal-family system can have negative effects on family members. However, they believe that Goode's structural-functionalist orientation tends to prevent him from giving full systematic treatment to the implications of these tensions and strains. They assert that the structural-functionalist perspective sees society as being in a state of equilibrium, with individuals integrated into society through various social roles and with the family serving as the basis of this integration. What structural functionalism does not see is that these tensions and points of strain may be much more serious in nature and represent fatal flaws and contradictions that question the viability of modern family arrangements and the supportive social system (Skolnick, 1973:125–126).

Critics of the conjugal family condemn the emphasis on privatization and female domesticity. One such critic, Michael Gordon (1972), states that although industrialization has created the possibility of the emancipation of women from the larger extended family, it has substituted the increased domestic burdens inherent in the conjugal-family system. Gordon emphasizes what Goode suggests: The division of labor necessitated by the economic system has subjugated women to the household and its domestic-task drudgeries. The reality, then, has not been emancipation but continued subservience. Gordon argues that economic analysis would suggest the greater efficiency of communal work, as opposed to the duplicated individual work of such tasks as child care, meal preparation, and clothes washing, as one structural improvement over the conjugal-family system.

Skolnick (1973/1978) amplifies on Goode's observation that strains in the male role result in an industrial system that is based on competition and achievement. Thus men have not totally benefited from the freedom from kinship-determined occupational succession, which was characteristic of traditional society. The demand for excellence in the modern technological system places great psychological demands on the individual in that it demands an unremitting discipline. Lower-skilled jobs are psychologically burdensome because they provide little pleasure; higher-skilled jobs—professional, managerial, and creative positions—demand high standards of excellence in areas that in many cases are unspecified and result in pressures to perform to unattainable levels.

Kenneth Keniston (1965) has observed that the family is the primary area in which feelings can be fully expressed; it is the individual's emotional center. Men find the world of work demands highly cognitive, unemotional, and analytical behavior. The home-centered family provides the opportunity for them to express sentiment, tenderness, and emotionality. Life is thus compartmentalized; "the feeling, support, sensitivity, expressiveness, and exclusive love of the family contrast with impersonality, neutrality, cognition, achievement and accomplishment of work" (Keniston, 1965:279). A tension can develop—or, at best, a delicate balance may exist—between the man's occupational and domestic commitments, and he can often find himself solely deriving satisfaction from his work (careerism) or his home (familism).

The privacy and domesticity of women leave them solely responsible for the raising of children. Although this allows a certain independence, it also cuts them off from outside help, supports, involvements, and activities. It is only through the accomplishments of her husband or children that the housewife can vicariously derive satisfactions from the world of work.

A common theme running through the criticisms of the conjugal family revolves around the belief that its privatization and isolation have prevented it from achieving for its members the very intimacy and psychological gratification that it was designed to foster. In two widely read and influential books, *The Uncommited: Alienated Youth in American Society* (1965) and *Young Radicals: Notes on Committed Youth* (1968), Kenneth Keniston develops the argument that the isolation of the family fosters childhood dependency and handicaps the development of autonomy and maturity: "Our middle-class families, despite their goodness of fit with many aspects of American society, involve inherent conflicts in the roles of mother and father, and produce deep discontinuities between childhood and adulthood" (Keniston, 1965:309).

Philip Slater, who was strongly influenced by structural functionalism, breaks with that perspective in his provocative analysis of American culture in *The Pursuit of Loneliness* (1970). This book, written at the height of the antiwar period and of the youth counterculture movement, is highly critical of privatization and the separation of home and work. He sees the emotional dependency of the young on their middle-class suburban parents as leading to their alienation and the inability for affective emotional expressiveness.

These arguments parallel those of the radical psychologists such as David Cooper and R.D. Laing. Cooper, in his *The Death of the Family* (1970), states that "The family form of social existence that characterizes all our institutions essentially destroys autonomous initiative by its defining nonrecognition of what I have called the proper dialectic of solitude and being with other people" (1970:140). Laing (1969) emphasized the repressive nature of the private family and its denial of internal conflicts to itself and to its neighbors.

> So we are a happy family and we have no
> secrets from one another.
> *If* we are unhappy/we have to keep it a secret/
> and we are unhappy that we have to keep it a secret
> and unhappy *that* we have to keep secret/the fact/that we
> *have* to keep it a secret
> and that we *are* keeping all that secret.
> But since we are a happy family you can see
> this difficulty does not arise. (Laing, 1969:100)

Skolnick and Skolnick (1971) examine the dysfunctionality of the conjugal family for children and youth in their discussion of the "politics of child rearing." They emphasize the complete subjugation of children not only in terms of their political rights but also in how they can be psychologically emulsified by their total dependence on the conjugal family. To illustrate, they report on a number of recent theories regarding childhood schizophrenia. The structural organization of the conjugal family, in which the child is relatively isolated from other personal and emotional contacts, may be a conducive setting for driving children crazy.

> In the isolation of the nuclear family, the parent can easily deny some aspect of reality, usually the parent's behavior or motives, thus causing the child to doubt his own perceptions. For example, the parent may act very angry or sexy, yet deny he or she is doing so. (Skolnick and Skolnick, 1971:306)

In assessing the position of the structural functionalists as compared to that of the critics of the contemporary private family, it is apparent that ideological biases distort the respective analyses. The structural functionalists, working off an equilibrium and organismic model, tend to view society as an organism that strains toward maintaining itself in some form of balance. The various parts of the system, in this case the members of the family, are seen to act in a cooperative and coordinating fashion. Stabilty and order are implicitly viewed as being natural and normal.

The critics of the contemporary family — be they conservatives who abhor modernity and its consequences for the family or radicals who take an essentially negative view of psychological dynamics and processes in the family — let their respective biases distort their analyses. Both groups see the loss of autonomy and individuality as inherently being a loss for young people in the private family. One group, the conservatives, call for the re-establishment of some traditional order, the other group calls for the establishment of a new form of intimate public community without private families.

Essentially, in evaluating the perspectives put forward in the last two chapters, we become cognizant of a twentieth-century replay of the ideological positions and arguments put forth by the Social Darwinists, the conservatives, and the radicals. In our earlier discussions of nineteenth-century theories of social change and the family, we examined the moral valuations inherent in these orientations. Structural functionalism can be seen as the twentieth-century counterpart of Social Darwinism — echoing the position of conservatives like Frédéric Le Play — whereas the radical positions set forth by the psychologists R.D. Laing and David Cooper, and to some extent by the more-vehement critics of structural functionalism, share a similar perspective to that put forth by Marx and Engels.

One final word would be appropriate here. Since the mid-1960s, there has been a major revolution in the American family. Dramatic changes — first in women's roles and more recently in men's roles — make many of the assumptions of structural functionalism and its "Father Knows Best" 1950s model of the American family obsolete. The notion of husbands being the instrumental leaders, the "breadwinners" of the family, while wives serve as the expressive leaders, the "breadbakers," and children take subordinate roles and are predominantly "breadeaters," sounds antiquated and untrue. Yet this model has dominated American family sociology and much of the way many of us still think of the family. The balance of this book is devoted to a more-realistic examination of the American family and its cross-cultural counterparts.

Conclusion

In this chapter, we examined the post–World War II nature of interest in comparative family sociology. We began with an examination of the basic premises of structural functionalism, the theoretical perspective most influential in the comparative analysis of social change and the family. We argued that an inherent problem of structural functionalism is its basic assumption that social change is an "abnormal" phenomenon and detrimental to the functioning of the social system. This approach tends to reify the given social system, whether it is of the society or the family, and thus overlooks the inequalities that may exist within it.

Given the limitations of structural functionalism, it is somewhat surprising that it has been so dominant in American sociology. It has been incorporated with evolutionary theory into modernization theory. A main component of modernization theory is the construct of structural differentiation. This construct has been open to criticism for its tendency to view society as a mechanistic equilibrating system. In addition, modernization theory's use of Social Darwinist evolutionary theory has led to the biased viewpoint that Western industrial societies are superior to non-Western nonindustrial societies and to the de-emphasis of the problems of Western societies.

The most significant and important representation of modernization theory in the comparative analysis of social change and the family is William J. Goode's *World Revolution and Family Patterns* (1963). Goode's study is of pivotal importance in that it is the culminating work on both the strengths of modernization theory and its weaknesses in the analysis of family systems.

Goode's major contribution to the comparative analysis of the family is the comprehensive and systematic analysis of cross-cultural and historical data that attacks the unifactoral hypotheses of industrialization and the family. These hypotheses see the family as a dependent variable changing as a result of industrial processes. Goode emphasized the interaction of family and industrial processes of change, which are both influenced by ideological changes and, in turn, are influenced by them. Finally, Goode proposed that in the "world revolution" toward industrialization and urbanization, there is a convergence of diverse types of extended-family forms with some type of conjugal-family system.

We argued that Goode's theory suffers from the limitations of modernization theory. Modernization theory has a conservative bias developed out of the use of an equilibrium model that tends to de-emphasize conflict and social change. The framework was seen to suffer from a simplified conceptualization of traditional and modern societies, seeing them primarily as static entities. Traditional societies were viewed as being antithetical with modernization processes. This is a gross distortion; it has been combated with a new emphasis on the positive, nonproblematic nature of modernizing nonindustrial societies.

Further, the biases and inadequacies of structural-functionalist–based modernization theory were seen to be derived from its implicit reification of the societal social order or system and a de-emphasis of the individual. In contrast, we presented the orientation of Szymon Chodak and Peter L. Berger and his associates. Chodak delineates different forms of modernization that are characteristic of advanced industrial societies and the less-developed societies found in Asia, Africa, and Latin America. Berger is concerned with the manner in which modernization processes affect the way individuals see themselves and their roles in life. Both viewpoints examine society and the individual in terms of processes of change as opposed to being static entities. Both also view society as composed of "active" human beings who are conscious of their world and who take an active part in constructing their social reality and social world.

In Part II, we investigate changes in the family's relationship with the larger community, emphasizing that the modernization of the family can best be understood in terms of changes in nuclear-family values and orientations. As we will see, although the historical evidence seems to indicate that the nuclear family has been prevalent in the West for the last 300 years, there has been a fundamental change in the family's involvement with the world of work and with the community.

In Chapter 4, we focus on Western communities, with particular attention to the family in American cities. This is followed in Chapter 5 by an examination of ethnic family-group variations within the community setting. Chapter 6 is devoted to the impact of modernization processes and structures on poverty families, and it examines social policy implications for families living in economically deprived communities. Chapter 7 is a comparative examination of the family in African cities, thus rounding out our comparative analysis of the family in the community. Subsequent chapters investigate how these changes in the texture of private family life and the family's involvement in work and the community affect the relationships of family members with each other.

PART II

The Family in the Community: Comparative Perspectives

The Family in the City: The Western Experience

One of the pleasures of urban life, for those who can afford it, is eating in luxurious restaurants.

CHAPTER OUTLINE

Sociologists studying historical changes and cross-cultural variations in family institutions have employed various methods of comparative analysis. Social scientists of the nineteenth century used the evolutionary-progress conception of Charles Darwin. This approach was largely discarded by the turn of the twentieth century for numerous reasons: ethnocentric value judgments, biased and distorted methodological techniques, and erroneous theoretical assumptions headed the list. A contemporary offshoot of Social Darwinist evolutionism is modernization theory.

Another major approach favored by social scientists was the comparison of rural agricultural communities with urban industrial communities by using typologies, or ideal types, of communities. As we demonstrated, this approach was a direct outgrowth of the antiurban bias of sociologists of the nineteenth and early twentieth centuries. Their ideological biases were coupled with a strong distaste for emerging urban family forms. Ultimately, their values distorted their analysis of the phenomenon that they sought to investigate—the family in the city.

We begin the chapter with an extensive examination of the recent research by family historians who have taken issue with the conclusion that the history of the Western family was a movement from the consanguineal system to the conjugal one.

Social History, Modernization Theory, and Family Change

In the last 20 years, social historians have begun gathering evidence that seriously questions the assumptions that the emergence of the nuclear family in the Western world is a recent phenomenon. Research on the historical European and American family system has convinced most social scientists that modernization theory, which postulates the historical existence of the large extended patriarchal family and its transformation into the nuclear family, is wrong. Now social scientists are reaching relative agreement that the nuclear family has predominated in Western societies for the last 300 years.

Most interestingly, their historical investigation of the size and composition of the family has led them to a new research focus, one that is virtually the same as that expressed by Peter L. Berger and his associates in *The Homeless Mind: Modernization and Consciousness* (1973). Family historians also emphasize changes in Western society, a society that has seen the development of private life and the private sphere. The great public institutions of the society, including work and the community, are seen as being separated from the private sphere of social life, particularly the most important one—the family. It is observed that this development is in striking contrast to the family's historical position in the nonindustrial and early industrial past. Historically, the family has served as the very foundation of social life and the center of the institutional order. There was no segregation between the family and the totality of the institutions in the society. It is precisely this change in the texture of private family life and the family's involvement in work and the community that is seen as the outstanding feature of the contemporary family. It is this change, rather than the transformation from the consanguineal extended-family system to the nuclear conjugal-family system, that is the distinguishable characteristic of the modern family.

We now briefly discuss the research findings that questioned the hypothesis that the Western trend was from the consanguineal to the conjugal family. Particular attention is given to the emerging position that believes that the general concern over structural and size changes was misspent and that the new research concern should be with the examination of the familial texture of the nuclear family and its relationship to social, economic, and political changes in Western societies during the last 300 years.

We begin our analysis by looking at the important contributions of Peter Laslett and the Cambridge Group for the Study of Population and Social Structure. Their concern has been in examining household size and composition and internal family relationships. They have employed a technique of data analysis which has been given the name *family reconstitution*. Essentially, this technique uses demographic data culled from records of births, deaths, marriages, wills, and land transfers to establish lineages and relationships. The aim is to reconstruct family and household patterns of ordinary people who have directly passed down little information of their way of life. Although data on the wealthy and wellborn have been more readily available, family reconstitution is one way of retrieving information on people whose everyday life has heretofore been hidden from history.

Peter Laslett in *The World We Have Lost: England Before the Industrial Revolution* (1965) contrasts the small-scale, primarily rural and familial society of seventeenth-century England with the large-scale, industrial and urban English society of contemporary times. Laslett utilizes the family-reconstitution technique in examining the household size of preindustrial England. Parish registers provided him with data on household size in rural English villages. His findings indicate that, although many English households contained servants, there was a general absence of extended kin; this data led him to conclude that the nuclear family was predominant in preindustrial England and to question the thesis that emphasizes the connection between industrialization and the small nuclear family.

Based on this conclusion, Laslett and the Cambridge Group used the family-reconstitution technique and examined historical census data from a number of societies. Laslett posited a series of questions and dictated the methodological format based on census lists to provide comparative evidence on changes in household size and organization. The resultant volume, *Household and Family in Past Time* (1972), consists of 22 articles written by different scholars who utilized Laslett's theoretical and methodological research design and who presented their findings at a conference that Laslett organized in 1969. These papers are concerned with the size and structure of domestic groupings over the last three centuries in England, France, Serbia, Japan, and the United States.

According to Laslett, research findings reveal that, except for Japan and possibly Serbia (part of present-day Yugoslavia), household size has not varied to a great extent in the last 300 years. The extended-family system is found not to be particularly prevalent. Households contain nuclear families, with the poor serving as servants of the rich. Laslett reaches the conclusion that these findings support his earlier one that the small nuclear family was an essential part of these societies long before industrialization.

Studies of colonial American family life have provided additional evidence of the prevalence of the nuclear family in Western history. Philip J. Greven, Jr.'s (1970) analysis of colonial Andover, Massachusetts, documents that newly married couples were expected to set up their own households. Greven examined four generations of settlers in Andover, using family-reconstitution techniques. His findings reveal the control parents had over children through their control and ownership of the farming land. Although patriarchal control was reinforced through inheritance patterns and the availability of land, Greven documents how children prevailed and how the nuclear family predominated family life.

John Demos (1970) found the family-reconstitution technique instrumental in his study of Plymouth Colony, the settlement founded by the Pilgrims in the seventeenth century. Demos examined official records of the colony and the content of wills and physical artifacts—which included houses, furniture, tools, utensils, clothing, and the like—to reconstruct family patterns. He sought to relate demographic and psychological approaches to demonstrate that the extended-family system was by and large absent in the colonial era.

Demos analyzed the structure of the household and the relations between households and the larger community. He found that households were composed of nuclear families and the basic structure of the family and the roles and responsibilities of family members were essentially the same as the American pattern of the 1960s: Husbands were the dominating individuals in the family; women were given considerable authority in their own sphere of concern; and children were expected to take on adult responsibilities and activities by the age of 6 or 7—much earlier than in contemporary society.

The distinguishing feature of life in Plymouth Colony was the prevalence of nonkin-related members of households. The presence of these individuals in the household is explained by a different conceptualization of the role of the family in relation to the community than the one we have today. Demos uses a structural-functionalist perspective and develops the point that the range of functions performed by the family contrast strikingly with contemporary patterns. He sees the family being charged with social responsibilities that have subsequently been taken over by institutions specifically designed for this purpose:

> The Old Colony family was, first of all, a "business"—an absolutely central agency of economic production and exchange. Each household was more or less self-sufficient; and its various members were inextricably united in the work of providing for their fundamental material wants. Work, indeed, was a wholly natural extension of family life and merged imperceptibly with all of its other activities.
>
> The family was also a "school." "Parents and masters" were charged by law to attend to the education of all the children in their immediate care—"at least to be able duely to read the Scriptures." Most people had little chance for any other sort of education, though "common schools" were just beginning to appear by the end of the Old Colony period.
>
> The family was a "vocational institute." However deficient it may have been in transmitting the formal knowledge and skills associated with literacy, it clearly served to prepare its young for effective, independent performance in the larger economic system. For the great majority of persons—the majority who became farmers—the process was instinctive and almost unconscious. But it applied with equal force (and greater visibility) to the various trades and crafts of the time. The ordinary setting for an apprenticeship was, of course, a domestic one.
>
> The family was a "church." To say this is not to slight the central importance of churches in the usual sense. Here, indeed, the family's role was partial and subsidiary. Nonetheless the obligation of "family worship" seems to have been widely assumed. Daily prayers and personal meditation formed an indispensable adjunct to the more formal devotions of a whole community.
>
> The family was a "house of correction." Idle and even criminal persons were "sentenced" by the Court to live as servants in the families of more reputable citizens. The household seemed a natural setting both for imposing discipline and for encouraging some degree of character reformation.
>
> The family was a "welfare institution"; in fact, it provided several different kinds of welfare service. It was occasionally a "hospital"—at least insofar as certain men

thought to have special medical knowledge would receive sick persons into their homes for day-to-day care and treatment. It was an "orphanage"—in that children whose parents had died were straightaway transferred into another household (often that of a relative). It was an "old people's home"—since the aged and infirm, no longer able to care for themselves, were usually incorporated into the households of their grown children. And it was a "poorhouse" too—for analogous, and obvious, reasons. (Demos, 1970:183–184[1])

According to Demos, the family in America has increasingly contracted and withdrawn from social responsibilities. The central theme is the gradual surrender to other institutions of functions that once lay very much within the realm of family responsibility. The result was that the family became more isolated and detached from the community as a whole. Replacing the declining social functions, it now took on more-important psychological functions for its members. The inseparable and indistinguishable facets of social life—family and community, private life and public life—were cleaved.

Thus, although Demos differs from Goode in his stress on the historical prevalence of the nuclear family in the West, he shares Goode's viewpoint (and that of other modernization theorists) on the predominant characteristics of the contemporary family. These characteristics include the decline in the functions of the family and the severing of the family's ties with the community, which has led to the development of the private family. This family form has turned inward; the home is seen as a private retreat. The emotional intensity of the ties between family members has heightened as the ties with the community have lessened.

The Family-Reconstitution Technique: An Assessment

The study of ordinary families through the use of family-reconstitution techniques has provided social science with fascinating information on the historical Western family. Taken together, these historical studies have led to the questioning of the thesis of the emergence of the nuclear family tied to recent industrialization processes. The extended-family historians generated much controversy in social science. It stems in part from their overemphasis on structural changes in the size and composition of the family and their neglect of the emotional arrangement of the family. And, when they do look at the emotional texture of the family, they do so from an inadequate base: census data and household size. Critics question how we can infer emotional qualities of family life from the analysis of birth, death, and marriage records, or from household size and composition, or from the physical layout of the household. Let us examine these criticisms in more detail and then examine the new approach being put forth by social scientists interested in family change.

Peter Laslett and the Cambridge Group's conclusions have been open to criticism on both methodological and theoretical grounds. In a stinging critical review of the *Household and Family in Past Time* (1972), Lutz K. Berkner (1975) questions the almost complete dependence on census data in making household analysis. Berkner argues that this source of data severely limits the kinds of analysis that can be made and the conclusions one can reach. He believes that the available cross-cultural data used is woefully deficient, incomplete, and noncomparable. Berkner seriously questions Laslett's decision of refusing to allow his contributors the right to consider family ideals of norms as part of the field of inquiry. He further decries the failure of the articles to differentiate household structures of different social classes

---

[1] From *A Little Commonwealth: Family Life in Plymouth Colony* by John Demos. Copyright 1970 by Oxford University Press, Inc. Reprinted by permission.

within a given society. These researchers should have distinguished between the wealthier households, which had servants, and the households of poorer families, whose children were forced to leave to serve richer families. This leads Berkner to conclude that, because of these severe theoretical and methodological deficiencies, we can discard much of the Cambridge Group's conclusions.

Christopher Lasch (1975a, 1975b, 1975c), in his caustic reviews of Peter Laslett and the Cambridge Group, believes that their 15 years of laborious investigations into the structure of the household have only established the unimportance of the question to which they have devoted much of their attention. He criticizes the "empty" findings of those who seek answers by looking at census data and exclude from analysis the emotional nature of the family. The position taken is that sociologists cannot describe the family solely in terms of size or structure alone; they must take into account the emotional dynamics of family life. Further, changes in the emotional character of the family must be seen in relation to the changes in the economic, social, and political activities occurring in given societies.

The argument against Demos (see, for example, Rothman, 1971; Henretta, 1971) takes a similar stance. When Demos limits his analysis to examine the physical setting of colonial life in his chapters on the housing, furnishings, and clothing of the colonists, he is remarkably successful. However, when he attributes the crowded conditions of the household to fostering frustrations and aggression in child-rearing practices, he outstrips scientific plausibility. The physical characteristics of the household could have achieved the opposite results; for example, they could have developed closeness among siblings. Further, the aggressive behavior of childhood, which is seen to culminate in a large number of court cases, can be explained by other factors in the community. David Rothman (1971) observes the following.

> Many historians have experienced that middle-of-the-night panic when contemplating how thin a line sometimes separates their work from fiction. But on this score the study of childhood seems especially nerve-racking, threatening to turn us all into novelists. (Rothman, 1971:181)

In summary, family historians have established the fact that the nuclear family has been prevalent for the last 300 years. These findings have convinced sociologists that it was wrong to identify the distinctive feature of the modern family as its structural isolation from the larger extended-kinship structure. The new position that has emerged believes that the modernization of the family can best be understood in terms of changes in nuclear-family values and orientations and in the changing involvement of the family with work and the community.

Tamara K. Hareven (1971), picking up on John Demos' findings on the family's relationship to the community, has observed that the modernization of the family can be better estimated in terms of household membership. Modernization involves the gradual withdrawal of nonkin-related individuals from the household. As we have seen, extended kin were never present in significant numbers in the household. Family historians have provided the evidence on the relative nonimportance of extended kin in everyday household activities. They have also revealed the importance of nonkin-related individuals in the household. The involvement of the latter in the household reflect the different conceptualizations of the ideology of the nuclear family over the last 300 years. It is the implications of this fact that should have been studied but were not.

Unfortunately, too often family historians got caught up in asking structural questions on the size and composition of families within households in their attempt to investigate the thesis on the transformation of the Western family from extended to nuclear. They further confused the issue by failing to distinguish between household composition and family composition. They did not give proper attention to the fact that members of the same family may not live in the same household, nor are households restricted to only family members. The absence of extended kin in the household led them to dismiss the thesis of structural changes in the family, but they ignored the involvement of nuclear families with extended kin outside the household. Nuclear families were intertwined with a network of relatives, all residing in the same community. Further, although extended kin did not reside in the household, this did not mean that the nuclear family was not involved with them or that they had no influence on them. In summary, although the majority of households studied historically were composed of nuclear families, they did not conform to the characteristics of the conjugal family described in modernization studies by sociologists such as William J. Goode. The historical Western European and American nuclear family was not a conjugal family. It was not intimate and did not encourage domesticity or privacy. It was neither detached from the community nor highly mobile, either socially or geographically. The overemphasis on family-structure variables, that is, from extended family to nuclear family, obfuscated the variations in orientations and values of the historical nuclear family.

Why did this transformation take place? Why did the personal life in the eighteenth and nineteenth centuries move toward privatization and domesticity? Why is the significance in the change of the historical family seem not so much in terms of size and composition of the household but in the detachment of the nuclear family from the outside world? Why did the family develop an ideology that saw it as the center for emotional support and gratification? What were the implications of these changes for the family, for the husband, for the wife, and for the children? How successful has the family been in becoming a private institution? We have only briefly sketched out some of the answers so far. The answers to these historical questions on the Western family will be examined in greater detail in this and ensuing chapters.

The City and Urban Kinship Patterns

How has urban industrial society altered kinship solidarity? In the previous section, we observed that Peter Laslett and others concerned with household structure thought that they found the answer in its composition of kin and nonkin. But, as we pointed out, household composition does not tell us about the nature of relations with kin. Tamara Hareven (1978), in her critique of the historians' concentration on the household, restricted the definition of the functions of the family and overlooked functions of extended-family members who resided outside the household. This misguided emphasis, in turn, inadvertently reinforced the myth of the "isolated nuclear family" in modern urban society.

The contention put forward by sociologists such as Talcott Parsons and William Goode was that the family had to change to meet the needs of the industrial system, which required a mobile labor force that was detached from rigid rules and economically irrational demands of extended kin. The isolated nuclear (conjugal) family was viewed as the functionally ideal institution to meet the labor demands of modern industry.

Recent historical studies have convincingly refuted the claim that industrialization destroyed the three-generation family and the assumption concerning Goode's notion of the "fit" between the nuclear family and the industrial family. One of the earliest of these studies was done by Neil Smelser in 1959. In that work, Smelser investigated the recruitment of workers into the textile mills during the early stages of the Industrial Revolution. He found that textile mills recruited entire family groups who served as work units. Fathers not only contracted for their children but also collected their wages and disciplined them within the factory. A reciprocal relationship developed between the family and the factory: The entire family was dependent on the factory as the employer at the same time that the employer depended on the recruitment of family groups to maintain a continuous labor supply. Smelser, however, concluded that the family worked together only during the early stages of the Industrial Revolution. He believed that, by 1830, industrial specialization that included the development of new machinery led to the dissolution of the family as a work unit.

In a later study, Michael Anderson (1971) discovered that among textile workers in mid-nineteenth-century Preston—an industrial city in Lancashire, England—recruitment of family units into the textile industry still occurred. Especially intriguing is Anderson's finding that there was a higher incidence of three-generation families (involving older, often widowed parents) in Preston than in the surrounding rural countryside. He argued that these people were important economic assets, assisting in such matters as child care, that allowed the mother to do industrial work. Anderson stressed the survival of vital kinship ties and the continuity of kinship roles in migration and adaptation to industrial life, seeing these ties as viable because of the reciprocal services performed by the three-generational family members.

Tamara Hareven's research on workers at the Amoskeag mill in Manchester, New Hampshire, during the opening years of the twentieth century extends the period that reciprocal extended nuclear-family ties predominated. She states that extended nuclear-family ties were not only important at the onset of industrialization, but also were very useful in the subsequent adaptation of migrants to the industrial setting. In Amoskeag, the largest textile mill in the world at the time, kinship provided an important element in the recruitment of workers from Canada and in the organization of mill work itself. The French-Canadian immigrants initially carried over kinship ties and traditional practices of kin assistance in Manchester and subsequently adapted them and continue to provide aid and assistance to each other during periods of need. Hareven concludes that geographical migration did not sever kinship links:

> Geographic distance did not disrupt basic modes of kin cooperation, but rather revised and diversified priorities and modes of interaction. Under certain conditions, migration strengthened kinship ties and imposed new functions upon them, as changing conditions dictated. Kin affiliation in the new setting not only facilitated migration to and settlement in Manchester but also served as reminders and reinforcers of obligations to premigration communities. (1978:160)

Studies of long-distance overseas migration during the mass-immigration period in America that extended from 1880 to 1920 also reveal that relatives on both sides of the Atlantic maintained ties and transmitted aid and assistance. We examine these immigrant family groups in the following chapter. But, for now, let us turn our attention to the post–World War II research that has documented the persistence of kinship interaction and mutual support in contemporary American society outside the confines of the nuclear family. In the remainder of this chapter, we examine research that questions the assumption that the city is antithetical to family life. This theme is also continued in the other chapters in Part II.

The Rediscovery of the Urban Family

Since 1950, a mass of empirical data has accumulated that questions the basic assumptions of theorists such as Louis Wirth[2] and Talcott Parsons.[3] These studies have shown that viable relationships exist among relatives and that they constitute a family's most important social contacts; they also demonstrate that relationships with

---

[2] "The family as a unit of social life is emancipated from the larger kinship group characteristic of the country, and the individual members pursue their own diverging interests in their vocational, educational, religious, recreational and political life" (Wirth, 1938:21).

[3] The isolation of the nuclear family "is the most distinctive feature of the American kinship system and underlies most of its peculiar functional and dynamic problems" (Parsons, 1943:28).

kin are a major source of recreational and leisure activities and that there is a considerable interchange of mutual aid among related families. The studies directly contradict the prevalent notions about the social isolation of the urban nuclear family and the underlying theme of social disorganization as a characteristic of urban life that leads to the disintegration of families and the alienation and anomie of individual city dwellers.

These studies of urban family relations in New Haven (Sussman, 1953), East Lansing (Stone, 1954; Smith, Form, and Stone, 1954), Detroit (Axelrod, 1956), Los Angeles (Greer, 1956), San Francisco (Bell and Boat, 1957), Philadelphia (Blumberg and Bell, 1959), Cleveland (Sussman, 1959), and Buffalo (Litwak, 1959–1960, 1960a, 1960b) all provided evidence of the significant role played by extended kin in contemporary American families. Sussman and Burchinal (1962) summarized this relevant research and concluded that the urban nuclear family must be seen within the context of an interrelated kinship structure that provides services and aid in a reciprocal-exchange system. They schematically summarize this research on the functional interrelationship of nuclear families in Figure 4.1. They find that the major forms of help and service include the following: help during illness, financial aid, child care, personal and business advice, and valuable gifts. Social activities were found to be the principal functions of the interrelated family network — major forms being interfamily visits; joint participation activities; and participation in ceremonial activities, such as weddings and funerals, which are significant demonstrations of family unity. These findings led Sussman to conclude the following in an earlier paper.

> The answer to the question "The Isolated Nuclear Family, 1959: Fact or Fiction?" is, mostly fiction. It is suggested that kin ties, particularly intergenerational ones, have far more significance than we have been led to believe in the life processes of the urban family. While these kin ties by no means replicate the 1890 model, the 1959 neolocal nuclear family is not completely atomistic but closely integrated within a network of mutual assistance and activity which can be described as an interdependent kin family system. (Sussman, 1959:340)

Sussman (1953, 1959), Litwak (1960a, 1960b), and Sussman and Burchinal (1962) provide a theoretical explanation accounting for the existence of viable kinship relations in urban centers when the early theorists hypothesized that they did not exist. Whereas Parsons (1943) suggests that the isolated nuclear family is ideally suited to the demands of occupational and geographical mobility, which are an inherent part of urban industrial society, these researchers suggest that it may not be the most functional family type. They hypothesize that the modified extended family may be more functional than the isolated nuclear one.

Litwak (1959–1960, 1960a, 1960b) found that an extended-family kinship structure existed in a modern urban center — Buffalo, New York. This extended-family structure differed from the classical extended family in that there was no authoritarian leader and it was not dependent on geographic mobility or occupational similarity to assure its viability. This modified extended-family structure consisted of a series of nuclear families joined together on an egalitarian basis for mutual aid. It differed from the isolated nuclear family in that considerable mutual aid is assumed to exist among these family members, and thus the family does not face the world as an isolated unit.

The question naturally arises as to how these later findings reporting on the viability of extended-kinship relationships can be reconciled with the earlier sociological accounts reporting the existence of isolated nuclear families and the absence of viable kinship networks.[4] Key (1961) suggested that the hypothesis on the disintegra-

---

[4] The ensuing discussion follows an earlier presentation of this argument by Hutter (1970).

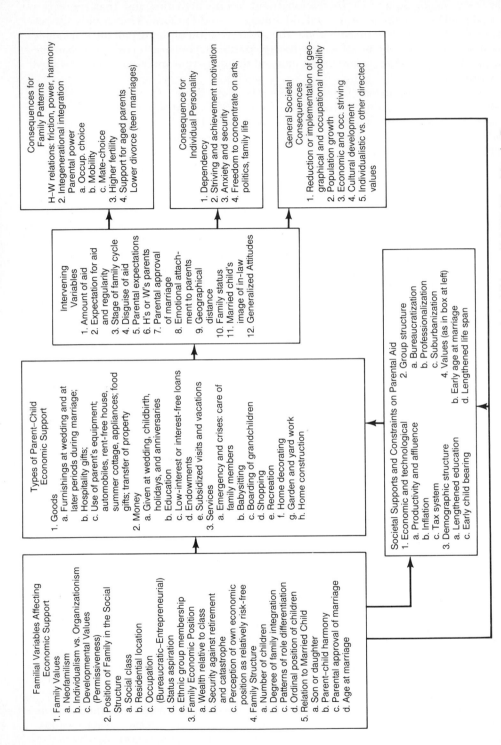

FIGURE 4.1 Functional analysis of parental aid to married children. (SOURCE: Marvin B. Sussman and Lee Burchinal. 1962. "Kin family network: Unheralded structure in current conceptualizations of family functioning." *Marriage and Family Living* 24:233.) Copyright 1962 by the National Council on Family Relations, 1910 West County Road B, Suite 147, St. Paul, Minnesota 55113. Reprinted by permission.

tion of the extended family was focused on the experiences of immigrant groups coming to the city during the period of urbanization in Western society before these immigrants had the opportunity to establish families. In addition, this period of industrialization was characterized by rapid change and great geographical mobility from rural areas to newly urbanized ones. The events that occurred in many American cities, such as Chicago, during the first 30 years of the twentieth century dramatically illustrate this point.

It is our contention that the earlier theorists, particularly Wirth and Parsons, confounded the effects of differential socialization experiences on intergenerational families when they examined the relationship between industrialization and kinship solidarity; that is, when they looked at that relationship, they did not control for the "transformation of identity" of family members as a result of their differential socialization experiences. This belief is shared by Peter L. Berger (1963), who notes that kinship ties are weakened by social mobility *when* social mobility has consequences in terms of the reinterpretation of our lives. Berger argues that individuals reinterpret their relationship to the people and events that used to be closest to them because their self-image changes as they move up the occupational and ethnic assimilation ladder. "Even Mama, who used to be the orb around which the universe revolved, has become a silly old Italian woman one must pacify occasionally with the fraudulent display of an old self that no longer exists" (Berger, 1963:60).

During this earlier stage of industrialization and urbanization, then, social mobility was accompanied by differential socialization experiences that accounted for the "transformation of identity" of the younger family members and the resultant weakening of kinship ties. This period of rapid social change — great geographical mobility from rural areas to newly urbanized ones and, in the United States, a great influx of Europeans emigrating from their homelands — caused great social and cultural mobility and separation among intergenerational families. Today, following Litwak (1960b), we contend that in the Unites States social-class differences based on cultural diversity are moderate and shrinking. They are not growing larger. Litwak argues that social-class similarities are sufficiently large to provide cross-class identification by extended-family members. He maintains that among white Americanized groups, especially those of the middle class, upward mobility does not involve radical shifts in socialization and, therefore, does not constitute a real barrier to extended-family communication. Here, then, is one key intervening variable between social mobility and kinship solidarity — transformation of identity caused by differential socialization experiences. It is because differential socialization experiences have been largely absent in urban America in the last 25 years that helps to account for the appearance of the modified extended family.

In summary, some would argue that the discovery of the viability of extended-kinship ties, albeit modified, may be a post – World War II phenomenon and may or may not have existed prior to that time. Recently, however, family historians have presented evidence that extended-kinship ties may have existed during the latter part of the nineteenth century and the first half of the twentieth century. They believe that the conceptual straitjacket of the ideal typology led sociologists to concentrate their attention solely on examining the social disorganization of the city and the isolation of the nuclear family.

They argue that an important factor in the failure of sociologists to see the viability of urban kinship relationships stems from the oversimplification of the ideal typology, which contrasts urban and rural life and modern city families and traditional rural families. Sociologists failed to recognize the urban manifestations of extended-kinship involvements. They failed to see that all too frequently traditional family systems also served as agents of modernization through example as well as by offering direct assistance to geographically mobile families. Tamara K. Hareven (1975), in her study of the industrial town of Manchester, New Hampshire, from the end of the nineteenth century through the first quarter of the twentieth, found that kin served as conveyers of individuals from preindustrial to industrial settings. They did not "hold down individuals" nor did they delay their mobility. Her research reveals that the kinship patterns of immigrant groups may be representative of a modern adaptation to new conditions. Kin relationships changed and were modified so that they could function within the industrial system, but such relationships were quite different from what they had been in their rural origins. Her findings led her to conclude that the ideal typology, with its either/or assumptions, might be a simplification of the historical process.

A further limiting aspect of the ideal typology was its failure to take into consideration differences in class and ethnicity. As we will soon see, the working-class family still served as a basic economic unit. It had a strong influence on the work and occupational careers of its individual members. Working-class and ethnic families banded together in their attempt to overcome their poor economic circumstances. The middle-class family with its values of privacy and individualism best approximates the ideal typology of the urban family, but the working class developed their own "modern" and urban attitudinal value system to allow them to cope with the vicissitudes of urban industrial life. Thus, within the same historical period there was a myriad of urban adaptation processes. Herbert Gans (1962b) has represented the first and most important statement of this argument.

Urbanism and Suburbanism as Ways of Life

Herbert Gans (1962b) takes issue with the dominant sociological conceptualizations concerning cities and urban life held by the Chicago School, as well as with the definitive summary statement in Louis Wirth's "Urbanism as a Way of Life." Gans makes the following points: (1) Wirth's urbanites do not represent a picture of urban men and women but rather depict the depersonalized and atomized members of mass society—they are representative of society, not of the city; (2) residents of the outer city tend to exhibit lifestyles more characteristic of surburbia than of the inner city; and (3) Wirth's description of the urban way of life fits best the transient areas of the inner city—here too it is best to view the inner city as providing a diversity of ways of life rather than a single way of life. Of immediate interest is Gans' argument that there are at least five urban ways of life that characterize the inner city (downtown) and vary depending on the basis of social class and the stages in the family life cycle. Gans uses the following classifications:

1. Cosmopolites
2. The unmarried or childless
3. Ethnic villages
4. The deprived
5. The trapped and downwardly mobile

The cosmopolites place a high value on the cultural facilities located in the center of the city and tend to be composed of artistically inclined persons, such as writers, artists, intellectuals, and professionals. A large proportion of inner-city dwellers are unmarried or, if married, childless. This group is composed of the affluent and the powerful members of the city. The less-affluent cosmopolites may move to suburban areas to raise their children while attempting to maintain kinship and primary-group relationships and resist the encroachment of other ethnic or racial groups.

The deprived population find themselves in the city out of no choice of their own. This group is composed of the very poor, the emotionally disturbed or otherwise handicapped, broken families, and—in significant number—the nonwhite poor who are forced to live in dilapidated housing and blighted neighborhoods because of discrimination and an economic housing marketplace that relegated them to the worst areas of the city.

The fifth and final group are composed of trapped people who stay behind in the city as a result of downward mobility, who cannot afford to move out of a neighborhood when it changes, and who cannot economically compete for good housing. Aged persons living on fixed incomes and families that do not have a stable economic income fall into this category.

The first two groups described—the cosmopolites and the unmarried or childless —and the last two groups—the deprived and the trapped—share a common residential characteristic—they live in transitional areas of the inner city. These areas are heterogeneous in population because they are either inhabited by transient types who do not require homogeneous neighborhood relations (the cosmopolites and the unmarried or childless groups) or by deprived or trapped people who are forced to live in transitory heterogeneous neighborhoods. The relationships these two groups have with their communities is the same—segmented role relationships that are necessary for obtaining local services and are characterized by anonymity, impersonality, and superficiality. However, these segmented role relationships have different consequences for the two groups. The cosmopolites and the unmarried and childless groups live in their neighborhoods by choice and frequently have positive psychological experiences; the deprived and trapped groups are forced to live in such communities and may suffer psychological damage resulting from their forced isolation.

Gans (1962b) does not address himself to Parsons' conceptualization of the isolated nuclear family, although it may fit to some degree the cosmopolites and the married childless or the affluent with young children, all of whom are found among the first two inner-city types. These individuals positively benefit from the occupational opportunities of urban industrial society and are not handicapped by economically detrimental obligatory ties with extended kin. The economically deprived and trapped groups share the negative impact of isolation from relatives; their isolated family system takes on all the negative characteristics of the family unit described by the social disorganization and alienation theories of urban life, which we have already discussed.

Gans goes on to describe a sixth urban way of life that is characteristic of individuals and families who live in the outer city and the suburbs. He describes the relationship between neighbors as *quasi primary*, "Whatever the intensity or frequency of these relationships, the interaction is more intimate than a secondary contact, but more guarded than a primary one" (Gans, 1962b:634). Although Gans does not describe the relationship these people have with their extended kin, we may conjecture (based on previously mentioned studies) that their relationship shares many of the characteristics of the modified extended family. Families residing in outer city and suburban communities tend to live in single-family dwellings and they are younger, more of them are married, they have higher incomes, and they hold more white-collar positions than their inner-city counterparts.

Urban Villagers and Closed Communities

Among the five inner-city resident groups, the ethnic working-class villages are the most highly integrated and tend to resemble small-town homogeneous communities more than they resemble Wirth's depiction of urbanism. Far from being depersonalized, isolated, and socially disorganized, urban villagers put an emphasis "on kinship and the primary group, the lack of anonymity and secondary-group contacts, the weakness of formal organization, and the suspicion of anything and anyone outside their neighborhood" (Gans, 1962b:630).

John Mogey (1964), in his essay "Family and Community in Urban-Industrial Societies," draws on the descriptive writings about urban villages in England, France, and the United States and develops a theoretical dichotomy between *open* and *closed*

In a City of Singles, Many Look to Be Couples

BOSTON, Sept. 1 (AP)—Boston is home to nearly half a million single men and women. And despite dating services for Jews, Christians, entrepreneurs, advanced degree holders and computer zealots, untold numbers of these single people still yearn for the other half of a couple.

"I never hear anyone say how great it is to be single anymore," says Jane Carpineto, a social worker who has taught "Spouse Hunting: The How-To of the Mating Game" to hundreds of single people at the Boston Adult Education Center. "Urban life is so anonymous, everybody is dying to know how to meet somebody."

With scores of colleges and universities in the area, eligible people seem to abound: strolling on the banks of the Charles River near Harvard University, shopping at the trendy boutiques on Newbury Street, dancing at the clubs and discos near Kenmore Square.

But Mrs. Carpineto and other experts on the single life say looks are deceiving: Boston is full of lonely men and women hoping for a relationship.

"There was a time when everybody wanted to be single, but that has shifted," says William Novak, the author of *The Great American Man Shortage*. "Now most single people want to be in a committed relationship.

"People aren't meeting each other anywhere," he says. "It's not just Boston, but the city does seem to be the center of dating services."

PAGES OF PERSONAL ADS

Mr. Novak's wife, Linda, runs New Possibilities, a dating service in the suburb of Newton. "Boston is loaded with well-educated, upwardly mobile professionals looking for their equivalents or better," she says. "They start here as students, they go to graduate school and then they hang around. They become very involved in their other, working lives and feel it's really hard to let something as ambiguous as love happen when everything else in life is so controllable."

Every month six pages of personal advertisements appear in *Boston Magazine*, the bible of the young, urban professional crowd, or "yuppies."

"Beautiful sensitive professional F, 29, 5-5, 130, graduate student, jogger, cross-country skier, oenologist, loves music, dining, books, Trivial Pursuit, photography, sports cars, picnics, parties, quiet evenings, seeks a sincere, mature, professional B, W or J male, 30-40, for wining, dining, conversation and seeing the NH foliage in my new sports car," said a typical ad.

Every week *The Boston Phoenix*, catering to the city's students and young professionals, runs hundreds of classifieds placed by an army of purportedly warm, sensitive professionals eagerly seeking the same.

Evening and adult education centers in the city offer a number of specialized classes: "Single Again," "Dating After 40" and "How to Find a Mate in Boston" at the Boston Family Institute in Brookline; "Dealing With the Opposite Sex," "Finding Your Mate" and "Love and the Single Life" at the Cambridge Center for Adult Education.

In her "Spouse Hunting" class, Mrs. Carpineto, married for 14 years to a man she met in school, asks her students to describe in detail the perfect mate. But she finds they are so unrealistic in some cases, it is no wonder they are single.

"There is a lot of emphasis on money these days," she says. "It's amazing. Women who are very successful, who come in dressed to the nines, want to marry someone who makes more than they do. That cuts out a huge percentage of the available men."

Mrs. Carpineto advises her students to try anything in search of a mate, including dating services, personal ads and singles clubs.

"If you put some energy into it, and really hustle for it, you can find someone," she says. "I've been accused of taking the romance out of it by being calculating and cold. But if you believe love happens when you look into someone's eyes, you'll find out later why divorce happens."

Mrs. Carpineto and the Novaks say some of the problem is the shortage of men in Boston. The 1980 census reported 216,907 single men and 250,394 single women in Boston, a surplus of about 33,400 women.

SOURCE. Associated Press. 1984. "In a city of singles, many look to be couples." *The New York Times* (Sept. 2). Reprinted by permission of the Associated Press.

Urban villagers on a special occasion: a wedding in one of the Puerto Rican neighborhoods of New York City.

communities. The closed community is the urban village, characterized as one in which schemes of intense interfamilial cooperation exist, and that is cohesive, homogeneous in cultural values, and closed against outsiders. The open community, on the other hand, is similar to Gans' depiction of the urban way of life of the cosmopolites, the unmarried, and the married without children. In these communities, people have voluntary attachments to a variety of associations and secondary groups. Families who live in these communities interact with individuals from other areas as well as from their own.

An open community has an in-and-out migration of population, whereas the closed community is characterized by relatively little mobility. The closed community or urban village has families who are acquainted with each other and have extensive ties with neighbors; in the open community, each family lives in relative anonymity and few personal relationships exist among members of the community.

Mogey states that the conjugal family is not prevalent in the closed community. No isolated nuclear family structure exists since it requires an open community structure, with secondary group relationships predominating over primary ones. Family mobility is also seen as leading to the abandonment of segregated family-role patterns.

Young and Willmott (1957/1962) in their study of the working-class community of Bethnel Green in east London report that the extensive family ties, far from having disappeared, were still very much prevalent. They provide an interesting illustration of the extensiveness of family relations in Bethnel Green — the report by one of their children who was attending a local school. The child came back from school one day and reported the following.

> The teacher asked us to draw pictures of our family. I did one of you and Mummy and Mickey and me, but isn't it funny, the others were putting in their Nannas and aunties, and uncles and all such sorts of people like that. (Young and Willmott, 1957/1962:14)

A similar observation is made by Gans (1962a). He reports that the Italian-Americans residing in the working-class community on the West End of Boston have a family system that shares some of the characteristics of the modified extended family and the classical extended family. Although each of the households is nuclear — composed of husband, wife, and children — there are extended-family ties.

> But although households are nuclear or expanded, the family itself is still closer to the extended type. It is not an economic unity, however, for there are few opportunities for people to work together in commercial or manufacturing activities. The extended family actually functions best as a social circle, in which relatives who share the same interests and who are otherwise compatible enjoy each other's company. Members of the family circle also offer advice and other help on everyday problems. There are some limits to this aid, however, especially if the individual being helped does not reciprocate. (Gans, 1962a:46)

Mogey describes the impact of the closed community on marital roles as one characterized by husbands and wives each performing a separate set of tasks. The wife is in charge of household tasks and child raising, the husband is primarily responsible for being the breadwinner. Leisure-time activities are similarly segregated. In times of emergency, aid for either the husband or wife is provided by same-sex relatives. Within families with segregation-role patterns, mother–daughter relations tend to be stronger than father–son relations. This is particularly true when the husband has moved his residence at the time of marriage to the street of the wife's mother. Both Gans (1962a) as well as Young and Willmott (1957/1962) report that a particularly strong relationship exists between married daughter and mother:

> Marriage divides the sexes into their distinctive roles, and so strengthens the relationship between the daughter and the mother who has been through it before. The old proverb applies:
>
> > My son's a man till he gets him a wife,
> > My daughter's a daughter all her life.
>
> The daughter continues to live near her mother. She is a member of her extended family. She receives advice and support from her in the great personal crisis and on the small domestic occasions. They share so much and give such help to each other because, in their women's world, they have the same functions of caring for home and bringing up children. (Young and Willmott, 1957/1962:61)

Of particular importance to the Italian-Americans of Boston are the peer-group relations with friends and kin of the same generation. Social gatherings of married adults do not revolve around occupational roles as they do among the middle class, but rather among the same-age kin and longstanding friends. Social gatherings tend to occur regularly — for example, once a week to play cards — and usually with the same people. These activities as well as major family events, such as christenings, graduations, and weddings, are all sex segregated — men staying in one group, the women in another.

The working-class families are an adult-oriented family system. Children do not have center stage as they do among families of the middle class and upper-middle class. Gans reports that in the West End of Boston, the child is expected to develop and behave in ways satisfying to adults. Little girls are expected to assist their mother with household tasks by the age of 7 or 8; little boys are treated in a similar way as their fathers are, free to go and come as they please but staying out of trouble. Thus, the children tend to develop a world for themselves that is relatively separate from their parents and in which the parents take little part:

> . . . parent–child relationships are segregated almost as much as male–female ones. The child will report on his peer group activities at home, but they are of

relatively little interest to parents in an adult-centered family. If the child performs well at school or at play, parents will praise him for it. But they are unlikely to attend his performance in a school program or a baseball game in person. This is his life, not theirs. (Gans, 1962a:56–57)

Of considerable interest are the studies that report the effects of social and geographical mobility—from the inner city's ethnic villages to the outer city and the suburbs—on the family's way of life. Earlier, we suggested that Gans' description of middle-class families residing in these areas fits to some degree the characteristics of the modified extended-family type. Now, we would like to turn our attention to a more-detailed look at the family life of working-class and middle-class residents in this geographical area.

The Suburban Family

Young and Willmott (1957/1962) contrasted the working-class urban village of Bethnel Green in east London with the upwardly aspiring working-class suburban community of Greenleigh, located outside London. They found that the migrants from Bethnel Green did not leave because of weaker kinship attachments. Rather, they left for two main reasons: first was the attraction of a house with its modern conveniences as opposed to the antiquated, crowded flats that pervade Bethnel Green; second was that Greenleigh was generally thought to be "better for the kiddies." These migrants left their extended kin in Bethnel Green with regret. However, these people were not deserting family so much as acting for it, on behalf of their children rather than the older generation.

The effect of moving to Greenleigh was a significant drop in the frequency of visiting relatives in Bethnel Green, despite the close proximity of the two areas. Life in Greenleigh became much different than life in east London. In day-to-day affairs, the neighbors rarely took the place of kin. Even when neighbors were willing to assist, people were apparently reluctant to depend on or confide in them. For the transplanted Bethnel Greeners, their neighbors were no longer relatives with whom they could share the intimacies of daily life. This had a particularly strong impact on wives, who were no longer in daily contact with their mothers and sisters; their new neighbors were strangers and were treated with reserve. The neighbors did not make up for kin. The effect on the family was that the home and the family of marriage became the focus of a couple's life far more completely than in Bethnel Green.

Young and Willmott (1957/1962) conjecture that, since Greenleigh was a newly developed community populated by upwardly aspiring working-class couples, they neither shared longtime residence with their neighbors nor had kin ties to serve as bridges between themselves and the community. Young and Willmott believed that it would not have mattered quite so much in their neighborhood relationships if the migrant couples from Bethnel Green had moved into an established community. Such a community would have already been crisscrossed with ties of kinship and friendship; thus, one friend made would have been an introduction to several more.

Two research papers by Irving Tallman (1969; Tallman and Morgner, 1976) examined the effect of the move of working-class couples from inner-city communities in Minneapolis-St. Paul to a suburban community outside the Twin Cities. This research was concerned with what effect social and geographical mobility had on couples who had lived in urban villages and who were intimately tied to networks of social relationships composed of childhood friends and relatives. It found that, despite the considerable amount of neighborhood contacts established by these couples after they moved to the suburban community, the wives experienced a considerable amount of dissatisfaction and personal unhappiness and feelings of anomie and personal disintegration. They believed that this resulted from the loss of contacts with their relatives and longstanding childhood friends in the city and the failure of the couple to reorganize their conjugal relationship; that is, the emotional and psychological supports that the wife received from her relationships with her relatives and friends were severed by the move to the suburbs and this required fundamental changes in the husband–wife relationship to make up for this loss. The working-class wife who was very dependent on extranuclear family, primary-group relations was not able to make adequate adaptations to the suburban move.

> The disruption of friendship and kinship ties may not only be personally disintegrating for the wife but may also demand fundamental changes in role allocations within the family. Suburban wives may be more dependent upon their husbands for a variety of services previously provided by members of tightknit networks. In addition, the ecology of the suburbs makes it necessary for the women to interact with strangers and to represent the family in community relations. Such a reorganization can increase the strain within the nuclear family and take on the social-psychological dimensions of a crisis in which new and untried roles and role expectations are required to meet the changing situation. (Tallman, 1969:67)

Tallman's work suggests, then, that the movement from working-class urban villages of the inner city to outer city and suburban open communities necessitates fundamental reorganization of conjugal and community roles of working-class couples to the middle-class type that emphasizes the importance of the conjugal-role relationship. To support this contention, research indicates that the anomie and alienation characteristic of working-class couples does not exist to the same extent with middle-class families in suburban communities.

The study by Wendell Bell (1958) of 100 middle-class couples residing in two adjacent Chicago suburbs provides a vivid contrast to the working-class couples' experiences. Bell tested the hypothesis that the move to the suburbs expressed an attempt to find a location in which to conduct family life that is more suitable than that offered by inner cities; that is *familism*—spending the time, money, and energy of the nuclear conjugal family—was chosen as an important element of the couples' way of life.

© Joel Gordon

A family enjoys the pleasures of suburban living: a family bike outing.

Bell devoted his concern to probing the reasons that the couples moved to the suburbs. Four-fifths of them gave reasons that had to do with better conditions for their children, a finding similar to Young and Willmott's (1957/1962) Greenleigh couples. Three-fourths of the respondents gave reasons that were classified as "enjoying life more." This classification was composed of such responses as being able to have friendlier neighbors, greater participation in the community, and easier living at a slower pace than in the city. A third major theme was classifed as "the-people-like-ourselves" motive. These couples wanted to live in a neighborhood where people were the same age and had the same marital, financial, educational, occupational, and ethnic status as themselves.

It is important to note that the latter two themes, "enjoying life more" and "the people like ourselves," were not given by the working-class couples of Young and Willmott's study of Greenleigh. The different social-class compositions of these two suburban populations account for these differences; only one-third of Bell's couples were identified as blue collar, whereas all of Young and Willmott's couples fell into that category. It is particularly relevant in Bell's finding that only 14 percent gave as the reason for their moving to the suburbs more space inside the home; this was the major factor for the Greenleighers. Finally, the fact that the Greenleighers all had moved from the closed community of Bethnel Green, as opposed to Bell's couples who moved from transitional inner-city neighborhoods or from the outer city, may account for the differences in their attitudes toward the suburban community and their neighbors.

A most important variation in these two groups of people is the overwhelming familistic orientation of the Chicago suburban couples. This familism, as it enters into the suburban move, largely emphasizes the conjugal-family system. This is indicated by the fact that only a small percentage of the respondents moved to be closer to relatives. In fact, in vivid contrast to the working-class couples described by Young and Willmott (1957/1962) and by Tallman (1969), several of the middle-class couples moved to get away from their relatives, a condition they considered desirable. In conclusion, Bell's (1958) findings support his hypothesis that the suburbanite couples have chosen familism as an important element in their life styles and, in addition, have a desire for community participation and involvement in neighborhood affairs. Both factors are absent as motivators for the blue-collar families of Greenleigh and the Twin Cities and may be the crucial reasons for the instability and unhappiness of the transplanted urban villagers.

In contrast to the adult-centered life of the urban villagers and the transplanted couples in the outer city and suburbs is the child-centered orientation of their middle-class counterparts. Wendell Bell has indicated the importance of familism and the involvement of parents with their children, as opposed to their extended family; a similar finding has been made by John Seeley and his collaborators (1956) in their study of an upper-middle-class, outer-city suburban community in Toronto. Seeley reports that the focus in these families is on the children; close, continuous attention is given to them. Tied with this is the extensive involvement of the couple with each other, a condition that is not present to the same degree in working-class couples of the city and suburbs. The Crestwood Heights suburban couple of Toronto is characterized by intense interaction and exchange by all family members, the family is viewed as a refuge from the trials and tribulations of the outside world. The dominant theme is home-centeredness; family members are expected to ask for and achieve psychic gratifications from each other.

Willmott and Young (1960) report a similar pattern in a predominantly middle-class suburban community (Woodford) in England. The young middle-class couples see little of their relatives and do not depend to any great extent on the extended family for regular help or companionship. Instead, they create social networks with people of their own age in the community. However, Willmott and Young believe that, although they have a larger circle of friends outside the family than do the urban villagers of Bethnel Green, their social relationships are not as closely knit nor are their loyalties as strong. The "friendliness" does not have the same characteristics in the two districts. In Bethnel Green, people are seen to take each other for granted based on long-term friendship ties; in Woodford, relations are not so easygoing. This results in sociality becoming a sort of how-to-win-friends-and-influence-people contest, with a great amount of superficiality and noncommitment—and with people leaving out some part of their inner self in the process. This corroborates Gans' (1962b) observation that the common element in the ways of life of the outer city and suburban family is quasi-primary relationships that are more intense and occur with greater frequency than secondary contacts, but that are more guarded and less intimate than primary relationships. Gist and Fava (1974) have concluded that the vast literature on suburban family relationships makes similar observations. Finally, as with the research on suburban couples in America, Willmott and Young find that the area for intense emotional relationships for their English suburbanites lies not in contacts with friends, neighbors, or relatives, but within the nuclear family. The conjugal role organization of these families is home-centered; couples share in many household tasks, including the raising of the children.

The Dispersal of Kin

Claude Fischer, a sociologist at the University of California, Berkeley, has conducted an important research study (1982a, 1982b) that provides us with up-to-date information regarding kinship involvements in today's automobile society. Fischer investigated kinship patterns of almost 1,000 adults living in northern California in 1977. He was concerned with the geographical distribution of relatives deemed active and important in those individuals' lives; the respondents' social characteristics associated with their various patterns of spatial distribution; the nature of the interaction patterns that they had with kin who lived outside the household; and what factor distance had in shaping the interaction patterns.

Fischer described the social networks of "modern" California kinship as being geographically dispersed. Individuals were not necessarily isolated from kin, but dispersed kin were infrequently used as helpers. The type of specified aid included borrowing money, considering opinions for decisions, talking about personal matters, and joining in social activities. Those relations that were most viable with ongoing exchanges were most likely to be with parents, siblings, and children. Extended-kinship ties were not actively utilized. This dispersal of kin was greater for educated and urban individuals than for their opposites, and these educated individuals were least dependent on kin.

Fischer reasons that educated people lived further away from relatives as a consequence of a number of interrelated processes. These people may be participating in a continental job market that demands that they be highly mobile. (For example, college and university teachers often find that jobs in their areas of specialization are not regionally located but may be found throughout the country.) The likelihood of their living near kin is further diminished by the fact that these kin may also be well educated, so that even if they remain geographically stable, their kin may be mobile. A third possibility is that the value system of the educated may place relatively little value on maintaining kinship ties (a "modernity" ideology). Finally, they may be better able to keep in touch with and call on their kin than the less educated. In such circumstances, there may also be greater reliance on the telephone and mail to keep contact with kin.

Urban residents were also likely to have less kin living in close geographical proximity. Fischer believes that migrants to large cities, particularly in the West, may be transplanted easterners who have moved large distances. Another explanation is that people who reside in metropolitan areas are likely to have alternative opportunities for social affiliations—business associates, activities, and social worlds that would permit them to disregard nearby kin. Finally, urban residents, like their well-educated counterparts, may exhibit a "modernity" ideology that places less emphasis on kinship.

Overall, Fischer believes that modern American patterns of kinship may be limited to involvements and commitments with parents and siblings (family of orientation) and with children (family of procreation) than with other relatives. The ties with parents, siblings, and children may thus survive distance and competing social involvements with nonkin, whereas other kin ties may not survive. The result is a family form that is neither the isolated nuclear family nor the extended family. Fischer states that "modern extended kin networks are distinctive in being spatially elongated, in losing out to nonkin relations in certain regards, and perhaps in being more functionally specialized" (1982a:366).

Fischer concludes his work by asking how his findings might be explained. He outlines three fruitful areas for speculation: industrialization, culture, and technology. He does not feel that contemporary geographical dispersion patterns are a result of industrial or factory work; rather, they may have been generated more by office work and white-collar occupations. He reasons that, during the rise and establishment of the industrial order, work and extended kinship may have been intertwined as scholars such as Michael Anderson and Tamara Hareven have argued. But during the period of growth in white-collar and professional work, there may have been little necessity to connect work and extended kinship. "Such jobs — in law, medicine, corporate management, academia, specialized accounting, etc. — have national job markets, tend to be insulated from nepotism and cronyism more than is factory work (although not as much as we think), tend to be filled through 'weak tie' networks . . . , and have as entry requirements educational credentials which can often be most advantageously gotten by leaving home" (Fischer, 1982a:362).

The second area of speculation may be in terms of ideological changes regarding kinship structures and involvements. The emerging view may be toward tolerance, or even preference, for spatial dispersion of kin. The well-educated and the urban respondents conform to this belief in their expression of opinion that living close to relatives or seeing them frequently is not very important to them. But Fischer believes that this cultural value alone is insufficient explanation and, rather, it is more likely that it was stimulated by structural changes in the society.

Some of these structural changes that Fischer deems to have facilitated the geographical dispersal of kin may be the advent of rapid mass communication and transportation; that is, the telegraph and telephone, and trains, planes, automobiles, and so forth may be as important to dispersion as is industrialization, since these means of communication/transportation make possible dispersion *without* isolation. Fischer cites an interesting study of rural France by Eugen Weber (1976), entitled *Peasants into Frenchmen*, to indicate how transportation changes can impact on kinship ties. Weber, in his chapter "Roads, Roads, and Still More Roads," discusses how previously isolated back-country regions were opened up by roads, rail lines, bicycle paths and the like. These conduits to the outside world removed the necessity for the rural French people to remain in the village for either a day or a lifetime. It, of course, also removed the mandatory requirement for the individual to participate in extended-kinship networks.

Fischer concludes by bemoaning the lack of attention given to this topic by historians and sociologists and the potential significance that mass communication and transportation may have to understanding contemporary family-kinship patterns.

> It may be that, in our effort to understand the nature of "modern" as opposed to "traditional" social and personal life, of which spatially dispersed kinship networks are but one element, we have been too mesmerized by the dramatic sight of the "satanic mills," gargantuan dynamos, and seemingly endless assembly lines to give due notice also to the car keys in our pockets and the telephones on our nightstands. These mundane symbols represent dramatic changes in the material "givens" of

social life, changes that alter the context within which people negotiate and manage their personal relations, including their kin ties. (Fischer, 1982a:369)

Conclusion

We opened this chapter with an extensive examination of the recent research by family historians, who have taken issue with the conclusion that the history of the Western family was a movement from the consanguineal system to the conjugal one. Family historians have emphasized that changes in Western society resulted in the development of distinct public and private spheres. The result has been the gradual separation of the public institutions of work and the community from the private sphere of the family.

During the early stages of the Industrial Revolution and through much of the nineteenth century, there was some intertwining of work, the family, and kinship relations. However, what was undergoing major change was the texture of nuclear-family life. We emphasized the position that the modernization of the family can best be understood in terms of changes in nuclear family values and orientations. Thus, although the historical evidence seems to indicate that the nuclear family has been prevalent in the West for the last 300 years, there has been a fundamental change in the family's involvement with the world of work and the community. This change drew our attention.

We then compared and contrasted the different ways of family life of urban and suburban families. Our particular focus was on working-class families of the urban villages (closed communities) and the middle-class families of the outer city and suburbs (open communities). In addition, we looked at the impact of the movement to open communities by both middle-class and working-class couples. We were concerned with the variations in these two classes in regard to their relationships with their communities and extended kin and the internal family relations of husband, wife, and children. We concluded the comparison by examining the latest changes in family life and involvement with kin of well-educated urban families living in a prime example of modern technological society, northern California.

In light of the previous discussions of the ideal typologies of urban–rural families and the position of Wirth, Parsons, and Goode on the relative isolation of the nuclear family system in urban industrial societies, we saw that the issue is much more complicated than it was made out to be by these earlier theoretical schools of thought. Urban villagers have a family life that is a combination of traditional extended-kinship ties and modified extended-kinship ties, whereas the middle-class family system tends to have way of life that is a combination of relative nuclear-family isolation (with emphasis on the conjugal-role relationship) and modified extended-family form (which allows the conjugal family to take advantage of the extended family for mutual aid without giving up structural independence). Following Claude S. Fischer, we speculate that in today's automobile society comprised of well-educated urban families, there may be a greater reliance on nonkin involvements, with kinship ties restricted to members of the families of orientation and of procreation.

In the following chapter, we extend our analysis of divergent family forms by looking at the processes of assimilation and pluralism of American immigrant family groups. In Chapter 6, we turn our attention to poverty family systems that are located in industrial and nonindustrial societies' cities. In Chapter 7, we examine in some detail the ways of life of family systems in urban centers that are located in African countries, to shed additional light on the relationship of the family to the city. By using this comparative approach, we are best able to grasp the complexity of relationships in family systems undergoing processes of change in contemporary communities of the world.

CHAPTER 5

From Immigrant Family to Ethnic American Family

Mulberry Street, New York City, in 1900: home to thousands of Italian immigrants to America.

CHAPTER OUTLINE

In previous chapters, and notably in Chapter 4, we observed that most sociological research on the family has historically held to the belief that industrialization and urbanization have transformed the family in Western society. This position was taken to the extreme by sociologists who argued that industrialization and urbanization disrupted the traditional family patterns to the extent that extended-family ties had virtually disappeared and the isolated nuclear family emerged in its place. This position particularly categorized sociologists of the Chicago School, such as Robert Park and Louis Wirth, who were guided by an orientation that argued that industrial development and urban life brought about social disorganization and caused the disintegration of the family unit.

The functionalists such as Talcott Parsons and William J. Goode—while disagreeing with the notion of social breakdown and the declining social significance of the family—argued that the "isolated nuclear" family (Parson's term) and the "conjugal" family (Goode's term) "fit" the functional requirements of industrial urban society. In our discussion of working-class families in urban centers, we observed that more-recent sociological studies have refuted the claim that industrialization destroyed the extended family and the assumption concerning the "fit" between the nuclear family and industrial urban society. In examining the working class, we saw how urban villagers have a family life that is a combination of traditional extended-kinship ties and modified extended-kinship ties. In the middle-class family system, there tends to be a family system that is a combination of relative nuclear-family isolation, with emphasis on the conjugal role relationship, and the modified extended-family form, which allows the conjugal family to take advantage of the extended family for mutual aid without giving up its interpersonal and structural independence.

In this chapter, we extend the analysis on the effects of modern industrial urban society on family systems by focusing on ethnic families in America. We begin with an historical overview of the "new" immigration in the late nineteenth and early twentieth centuries of eastern and southern Europeans and their family experiences in urban America. By so doing, we see how these ethnic families adapted to the United States and how their current ethnic-family patterns emerged. To highlight our discussion of the "new" immigrant family, we look at Jewish-Americans and Italian-Americans. To round out our presentation, we also study two other prominent American ethnic groups, Japanese-Americans and Mexican-Americans.

Immigration: The Melting Pot and Cultural Pluralism

The period of time from 1880 to 1924, when immigration laws placed severe limitation on movement into the United States, witnessed a massive exodus of people from southern and eastern Europe. This "new" immigration was from countries like Austria-Hungary, Greece, Italy, Poland, Rumania, Russia, and Serbia (now a part of Yugoslavia). Immigrants from these countries were joined by others from China and Japan, Mexico, French Canada, and the West Indies. In contrast, the peoples of the "old" immigration, those who arrived between 1820 (when federal statistics of origin were first recorded) and 1880, were made up almost entirely of northwest Europeans who came from countries such as England, Ireland, Scotland. France, Germany, Norway and Sweden.

Immigration in the three decades before the Civil War totaled five million. Between 1860 and 1890 that number doubled, and between 1890 and the beginning of World War I in 1914 it tripled. The peak years of immigration were in the early twentieth century, with over a million people entering annually in 1905, 1906, 1907, 1910, 1913, and 1914. The main explanation for this massive movement of people to the United States was that the countries of origin of the "new" immigrants were experiencing population explosions and dislocations. By the latter part of the nineteenth century, the pressures of overpopulation, combined with the prospects of economic opportunity in the United States and the availability of rapid-transportation systems that included railroads and steamships, set the wheels of world migration moving. Maldwyn Allen Jones, whose study *American Immigration* (1960) has been a standard work on the subject, comments on the shared motives of the culturally diversified immigrants for coming to America.

> The motives for immigration . . . have been always a mixture of yearning—for riches, for land, for change, for tranquillity, for freedom, and for something not definable in words. . . . The experiences of different immigrant groups . . . reveal a fundamental uniformity. Whenever they came, the fact that they had been uprooted from their old surroundings meant that they faced the necessity of coming to terms with an unfamiliar environment and a new status. The story of American immigration is one of millions of enterprising, courageous folk, most of them humble, nearly all of them unknown by name to history. Coming from a great variety of backgrounds, they nonetheless resembled one another in their willingness to look beyond the horizon and in their readiness to pull up stakes in order to seek a new life. (Jones, 1960:4–5)

There was a great deal of variation in immigrant family migration arrangements. Some immigrant groups from Scandinavian societies and Germany came as nuclear families responding to America's need to settle and farm the vast lands of midwestern America. For these groups, settlement often meant the almost complete reconstitution of Old World rural village life and family patterns to rural America (Hareven and Modell, 1980). One extreme example of this practice was the Hutterites, a German religious group that lived in Russia and migrated to the United States in the late nineteenth century. They settled in isolated rural agricultural sections in order to maintain their distinctive family patterns, which included early marriage, exceptionally high fertility, and near-universal remarriage after widowhood. The Hutterite community was a highly cooperative economy ruled by a family patriarch that operated through kinship affiliations created by the high fertility and strict laws of intermarriage. This isolated group could and has maintained itself until today because of its ability to find marriage partners within the group.

As agricultural opportunities in rural America declined and the demand for skilled and especially unskilled urban workers grew, young unattached males became the mainstay of the the migration population. The ethnic historian Thomas J. Archdeacon (1983) reports that in the decades between 1840 and 1899, males constituted 58 to 61 percent of the arrivals. By contrast, the importance of single males accounts for the statistic that 70 percent of the newcomers between 1900 and 1909 and 66 percent of those between 1910 and 1914 were males. Data on immigration and emigration compiled annually by the U.S. Commissioner of Immigration, presented in Table 5.1, reveal that the proportion of males to females did not take place evenly across the immigrant nationalities. Jews displayed the best balance with an almost fifty–fifty split; southern Italians, on the other hand, had more than three times as many males as females. The sex ratio among the Greeks was the most extreme, indicating that for every Greek female there were eleven Greek men. Commenting on these statistics, Tamara Hareven and John Modell (1980) observe that this obviously set limits on the possibility of Greek family life during this time period.

Slovak Museum and Archives, Middletown, PA

"When this picture was taken I was nine years old and my father was in America. Once he was there for six months and another time for two years when my mother had to send him money for passage home. I do not know how my mother was able to do it; run our farm, raise all the children properly, travel to Bardejov to buy seeds she would sell. Often she walked from Velky Saris to Presov carrying milk and butter to sell in the marketplace. Poor Mom, she had so much spunk and drive. I remember going with her to Poland to sell leather boots which Father, a boot maker, made (no nails). I am the tall one in back and now the only one left. I was seventeen when I came to America." Steve Timcak, 91 years old, Fresno, CA, commenting on this photo of his family taken in 1913, in Slovakia (now part of Czechoslovakia).

TABLE 5.1   Family Characteristics of Major Immigrant Groups, 1909–1914

Group	Estimated Percent of Departures of Male Arrivals Within Period	Number of Males per 1,000 Females	Percentage Under Age 14	Percentage Married Males Ages 14–44	Estimated Percent of Departures of Female Arrivals	Number of Married Males per 1,000 Married Females
Czechs	5	1,329	19	36	10	1,453
English	6	1,358	16	35	13	1,157
Finnish	7	1,812	8	25	15	1,882
Germans	7	1,318	18	35	16	1,312
Greeks	16	11,696	4	29	12	8,643
Hebrews	2	1,172	25	36	3	1,258
Hungarians (Magyars)	22	1,406	16	63	38	1,968
Italians, South	17	3,200	12	46	15	3,181
Poles	13	1,876	10	38	16	2,695
Slovaks	19	1,622	12	55	27	2,659

Note: Median annual observation except for estimated departure rate.
SOURCE: U.S. Bureau of Immigration and Naturalization. 1910–1914. *Annual Reports, 1910–1914.* Washington, D.C.

The ultimate success of an immigrant group depended in large part on its ability to re-establish a normal pattern of family life in America. This initially proved quite difficult. Common themes in the popular literature of that time were stories of wives forgotten in the old country and of families torn asunder by the clash of the old ways of life with the new. The editorial columns of the immigrant press frequently reported on the life struggles of its readers. Many newspapers had "advice" columns with the editors serving as lay clergy, social workers, friends, and relatives to those who had nowhere else to turn. The "Bintel Brief" ("Bundle of Letters") of the *Jewish Daily Forward* has become the most famous of these advice columns. Through it, readers wrote of their marital and family problems, the impact of poverty on their lives, religious conflicts in terms of attitudes and behavior, and other life concerns. The two letters reprinted from *A Bintel Brief,* edited by Isaac Metzker (1971), are illustrative.

Urban Communities and Immigrant-Family Systems

Immigrants from southern and eastern Europe concentrated in the industrial cities of the Northeast and the Midwest because it was in these urban areas where job opportunities were plentiful and chances of success were greatest. By 1920, almost 60 percent of the population of cities of more than 100,000 inhabitants were first- or second-generation ethnic Americans (Seller, 1977). The immigrants settled in ethnic enclaves that people referred to as "Little Italys," "Polonias," "Little Syrias," and "Jewtowns." Each enclave reflected its distinctive ethnic flavor with its own church, stores, newspapers, clothing, and gestural and language conventions. The Chicago newspaper journalist Mike Royko, reminiscing on his own Slavic community back-

A Bintel Brief

ISAAC METZKER (ED.)

1906

Worthy Mr. Editor,

I was married six years ago in Russia. My husband had not yet been called up for the military service, and I married him because he was an only son and I knew he would not be taken as a soldier. But that year all originally exempted men were taken in our village. He had no desire to serve Czar Nickolai and since I didn't want that either, I sold everything I could and sent him to London. From there he went to America.

At first he wrote to me that it was hard for him to find work, so he couldn't send me anything to live on. I suffered terribly. I couldn't go to work because I was pregnant. And the harder my struggles became, the sadder were the letters from my husband. I suffered from hunger and cold, but what could I do when he was worse off than I?

Then his letters became fewer. Weeks and months passed without a word.

In time I went to the rabbi of our town and begged him to have pity on a deserted wife. I asked him to write to a New York rabbi to find out what had happened to my husband. All kinds of thoughts ran through my mind, because in a big city like New York anything can happen. I imagined perhaps he was sick, maybe even dead.

A month later an answer came to the rabbi. They had found out where my husband was but didn't want to talk with him until I could come to America.

My relatives from several towns collected enough money for my passage and I came to New York, to the rabbi. They tricked my husband into coming there too. Till the day I die I'll never forget the expression on my husband's face when he unexpectedly saw me and the baby.

I was speechless. The rabbi questioned him for me, sternly, like a judge, and asked him where he worked and how much he earned. My husband answered that he was a carpenter and made twelve dollars a week.

"Do you have a wife, or are you single?" the rabbi asked. My husband trembled as he answered, "I have committed a crime," and he began to wipe his eyes with a handkerchief. And soon a detective appeared in the rabbi's house and arrested my husband, and the next day the story appeared in the Jewish newspapers. Then some good women who had pity on me helped me. They found a job for me, took me to lectures and theaters. I began to read books I had never realized existed.

In time I adjusted to life here. I am not lonely, and life for me and my child is quite good. I want to add here, too, that my husband's wife came to me, fell at my feet and cried, but my own problems are enough for me.

But in time my conscience began to bother me. I began to think of my husband, suffering behind bars in his dark cell. In dreams I see his present wife, who certainly loves him, and her little boy living in dire need without their breadwinner. I now feel differently about the whole thing and I have sympathy for my husband. I am even prepared, when he gets out of jail, to wish him luck with his new life partner, but he will probably be embittered toward me. I have terrible pangs of conscience and I don't know what I can do. I hope you will print my letter, and answer me.

Cordially,

Z.B.

ANSWER:

In the answer to this letter, the woman is comforted and praised for her decency, her sympathy for her husband and his second wife. Also it is noted that when the husband is released he will surely have no complaints against her, since he is the guilty one in the circumstances, not she.

(continued)

1910

Worthy Editor,

My husband, ———— [here the name was given], deserted me and our three small children, leaving us in desperate need. I was left without a bit of bread for the children, with debts in the grocery store and the butcher's, and last month's rent unpaid.

I am not complaining so much about his abandoning me as about the grief and suffering of our little children, who beg for food, which I cannot give them. I am young and healthy. I am able and willing to work in order to support my children, but unfortunately I am tied down because my baby is only six months old. I looked for an institution which would take care of my baby, but my friends advise against it.

The local Jewish Welfare Agencies are allowing me and my children to die of hunger, and this is because my "faithful" husband brought me over from Canada just four months ago and therefore I do not yet deserve to eat our bread.

It breaks my heart but I have come to the conclusion that in order to save my innocent children from hunger and cold I have to give them away.

I will sell my beautiful children to people who will give them a home. I will sell them, not for money, but for bread, for a secure home where they will have enough food and warm clothing for the winter.

I, the unhappy young mother, am willing to sign a contract, with my heart's blood, stating that the children belong to the good people who will treat them tenderly. Those who are willing and able to give my children a good home can apply to me.

Respectfully,

Mrs. P.*
Chicago

ANSWER:

What kind of society are we living in that forces a mother to such desperate straits that there is no other way out than to sell her three children for a piece of bread? Isn't this enough to kindle a hellish fire of hatred in every human heart for such a system?

The first to be damned is the heartless father, but who knows what's wrong with him? Perhaps he, too, is unhappy. We hope, though, that this letter will reach him and he will return to aid them.

We also ask our friends and readers to take an interest in this unfortunate woman and to help her so that she herself can be a mother to her children.

*The full name and address are given.

SOURCE. Isaac Metzker (ed.). 1971. Excerpts from *A Bintel Brief*. Translation copyright © 1971 by Isaac Metzker. New York: Ballantine Books, pp. 50–52, 104–105. Reprinted by permission of *Doubleday Publishing*, a division of Bantam, Doubleday, Dell Publishing Group.

---

ground, recalls that you could always tell where you were "by the odors of the food stores and the open kitchen windows, the sound of the foreign or familiar language, and by whether a stranger hit you in the head with a rock" (cited in Seller, 1977:112).

Yancey, Ericksen, and Juliani (1976) explain that the establishment of immigrant "ghettos" reflects a stage in the development of American cities because there was a great need for occupational concentration as a result of the expansion of the industrial economy. Low-paid industrial immigrant workers were forced by economic pressures to live close to their places of work. The particular choice of residence and occupation was strongly influenced by the presence of friends and relatives in a process that has been called chain migration. *Chain migration* refers to the connections made between individuals in countries of origin and destination in the process of international migration and to the process in which choices of residence and occupation were influenced by friends and relatives.

Networks of friends and relatives established in America maintained their European kinship and friendship ties and transmitted assistance across the Atlantic. Relatives acted as recruitment, migration, and housing resources, helping each other to shift from the often-rural European work background to urban industrial work. A number of social historians (Anderson, 1971; Hareven, 1975; Yans-McLaughlin, 1971) have observed that nineteenth-century, as well as twentieth-century, migrants chose their residential and occupational destinations in large part because of the presence of kin-group members in the new area.

Chain migration can be seen as facilitating transition and settlement. It assured a continuity in kin contacts, and made mutual assistance in cases of personal and family crises an important factor in the adjustment to the new American environment. Workers often migrated into the new industrial urban centers, keeping intact or reforming much of their kinship ties and family traditions. As previously mentioned, a prevalent practice was for unmarried sons and daughters of working age, or young childless married couples, to migrate first. After establishing themselves by finding jobs and housing, they would send for other family members. Through their contacts at work or in the community, they would assist their newly arrived relatives or friends with obtaining jobs and housing.

The fact that so many individuals came to America alone, accounts for the fact that turn-of-the-century urban households of immigrants often included people other than the nuclear family. These people were not kinship-related but were strangers, boarders, and lodgers who for various reasons came to America alone and for a period of time lived with fellow immigrants. This practice of taking in boarders and lodgers proved extremely valuable in allowing new migrants and immigrants to adapt to urban living (Hareven, 1983).

The family can be seen as being an important intermediary in recruitment of workers to the new industrial society. Family patterns and values often carried over to the urban setting and provided the individual with a feeling of continuity between the rural background and the new industrial city. Immigrants tended to migrate in groups; often entire rural communities reconstituted themselves in ethnic enclaves. They helped recruit other family members and countrymen into the industrial work force. Migration to industrial communities, then, did not break up traditional kinship ties; rather, the family used these ties to facilitate its own transition into industrial life. Tamara Hareven (1983), after examining the historical evidence, concludes that it is grossly incorrect to assume that industrialization broke up traditional kinship ties and destroyed the interdependence of the family and the community.

What is of particular interest to us here is that these findings on the viability of kinship involvements of urban immigrants in the early twentieth century provide additional and earlier historical support to the post–World War II studies by Litwak, Sussman, and others (who questioned the sociological assumption by the Chicago School that the city is antithetical to family life) and to the assumptions by functionalists such as Talcott Parsons and William Goode (who postulated that the isolated nuclear family or conjugal family best "fit" the needs of urban industrial society).

Poverty and Immigrant Families

Our discussion until now has not focused on the severe problems that confronted the immigrant families in America. We do not want to mislead the reader in thinking that all went smoothly for immigrant families; that was far from the case. The huge influx of immigrants to the American cities gave new meaning and visibility to urban poverty. Ghetto housing was appalling; ill-conceived and inadequate buildings were cheaply and quickly built to meet immediate needs, which soon outgrew them. People lived in overcrowded, dirty, unsanitary, poorly ventilated, and badly heated apartment buildings that were still expensive because of the demand. Boarders and lodgers were numerous and helped provide some of the needed money to pay the rent. It was not uncommon for beds to be occupied around the clock, with day-shift workers using them at night and night-shift workers using them during the day.

The horrible living conditions were dramatically exposed in the muckraking works of novelists such as Upton Sinclair, whose famous novel *The Jungle* exposed the grinding poverty of the Slavic communities in Chicago located within the stench of the blood and entrails of cattle being slaughtered in the neighborhood stockyards, and in the journalistic accounts of newsmen such as Lincoln Steffens, whose book *The Shame of the Cities* refers to the ghetto slums as literally looking like hell. The journalist Jacob Riis, himself an immigrant from Denmark, wrote and photographed the urban poverty of New York's ghetto life in his classic work, *How the Other Half Lives*. His graphic descriptions of the barren and filthy firetraps of New York's tenements startled the nation. The following passage from his book is typical of what life was like in one of these buildings:

> —Cherry Street. Be a little careful please. The hall is dark and you might stumble over the children. . . . Not that it would hurt them; kicks and cuffs are their daily diet. They have little else. Here where the hall turns and dives into utter darkness is a step, and another, another. A flight of stairs. You can feel your way, if you cannot see it. Close? Yes! What would you have? All the fresh air that ever enters these stairs comes from the hall-door that is forever slamming, and from the windows of dark bedrooms that in turn receive from the stairs their sole supply of the elements God meant to be free, but man deals out with such niggardly hand. . . . The sinks are in the hallway, that all the tenants may have access—and all be poisoned alike by their summer stenches. . . . Hear the pumps squeak! It is the lullaby of tenement house babies. In summer, when a thousand thirsty throats pant for a cooling drink in this block, it is worked in vain. But the saloon, whose open door you passed in the hall, is always there. The smell of it has followed you up. Here is a door. Listen! That short hacking cough, that tiny, helpless wail—what do they mean? They mean . . . a sadly familiar story—before the day is at an end. The child is dying with measles. With half a chance it might have lived; but it had none. That dark bedroom killed it. (Riis, 1890/1957:33–34)

A series of photographs documenting the assimilation of an immigrant family: (left) The Gustozzo (Justave) family at Ellis Island in 1905; (middle) the Justave family in Scranton, PA in 1927; and (right) again in 1954.

In the late nineteenth and early twentieth centuries, as a result of the public outcry generated by the exposures by social-minded individuals such as Sinclair, Steffens, and Riis, and tragedies such as the Triangle Shirtwaist Factory fire (which claimed the lives of one hundred and forty-six people), reforms were directed to change the living and working environments of immigrants. These movements included tenement-house reforms, workmen's compensation, abolition of child labor, and protection of women and children in industry.

However, the pervasive poverty in rapidly growing industrial cities led many to the erroneous conclusion that it was an immigrant phenomenon. This led to the development of a wide number of social programs aimed directly in changing the immigrant families themselves. Social reformers created both private and public welfare agencies to help alleviate the problems of the sick, the poor, and the delinquent or criminal. Immigrant families and especially their children became the major targets for discipline and reformation and programs were designed to intervene in the affairs of immigrant families. The concern was to Americanize them into what they saw as the great American melting pot, where the cultural variations of the given immigrant group would be altered to the standard American way of life.

The settlement house, a private social-welfare agency, is a typical example of how some of these practices became articulated. The term *settlement* meant giving the immigrant newcomers the wherewithal to survive in a modern industrial city. Located right in the heart of the immigrant communities, it sought to help the immigrant families cope with poverty and improve their living standards. Settlement-house workers tried to teach English, American social customs, and — when necessary — the rudiments of household management, health care, and sanitation. They encouraged family-member involvement in work and household roles that often conformed to their own middle-class standards of family morality. When successful, as in the case of Jane Addams of Chicago's Hull House, they integrated their work without undermining the immigrants' native culture. Unfortunately, much too frequently, workers saw as their primary task the eradication of "non-American" cultural points of view and family traditions regarding marital roles and parent–child relationships.

Education and Immigrant Families

Education was seen as the key institution to eradicate immigrant cultures and achieve Americanization. For example, in the years before World War I, Henry Ford required all of his foreign workers to attend English school. For a five-year period, 1915–1920, the Federal Bureau of Education subsidized a Division of Immigrant Education, which encouraged school districts throughout the nation to establish special Americanization programs. The response was favorable, and many state governments provided funds for the education of immigrants. During this period and continuing afterward, numerous public-school systems instituted night classes in which foreign students could learn English and gain knowledge of American government to acquire citizenship (Archdeacon, 1983).

For the Americanization of immigrant children, the school system became the primary vehicle to help accomplish this task. Education meant more than simply teaching proper English and the three "Rs" of reading, 'riting, and 'rithmetic; it also meant socializing children to American ways of life, habits of cleanliness, good housekeeping, nutrition, and social graces. Children were also graded on their level of acculturation to American values, as measured by behavior in school. State legislation was passed, making compulsory-attendance laws more stringent to help insure that children were adequately exposed to the assimilative influences of the schools.

Settlement-house workers also played a role here by assisting in the supervision of school attendance and observance of child-labor laws.

To illustrate how conflict or cooperation could arise between an immigrant-family culture and an Americanizing institution such as the school system, let us briefly examine the experience of the Italian immigrant family and the Jewish immigrant family with the school system in the early twentieth century. Such an analysis can also emphasize the point that immigrant-family cultures were not alike and that immigrant groups often experienced different occupational and educational opportunities in America. A comparison of the profoundly different experiences of Italian and Jewish children in schools will document this. Different cultural and economic factors played a decisive role in their respective educational success and failure in the first half of the twentieth century.

The children of immigrant Jews from eastern Europe were very successful in American schools. There are several possible explanations for this. First, while they did experience considerable discrimination, the Jews were not treated as a separate caste group as blacks were; they were able to pursue, for the most part, whatever economic activities they chose. Second, they came to America with exceptionally strong backgrounds in skilled trades and entrepreneurial activity (67.1 percent in skilled occupations for the 11 years between 1899 and 1910, compared to 20.4 percent for northern Italians and less for southern Italians) and established traditions of literacy (Hogan, 1983). Third, soon after they arrived in America, they were able to establish themselves in the skilled trades and manufacturing in a rapidly expanding economy. Fourth, they were able to take advantage of the educational opportunities offered them in urban centers. Finally, on graduation from high school and college, there were job opportunities in chosen occupations. David Hogan (1983), in commenting on Jewish educational success, observes that it was not merely the product of a Jewish commitment to education: "Jewish traditions of literacy and scholastic application resulted in classroom achievement because the structural conditions—the opportunities, the educational facilities, and a record of economic success—sponsored expectations that academic success would result in occupational success" (1983:44–45).

In contrast, Italian students were viewed by school personnel as more difficult to discipline and irresponsible than their Jewish counterparts when they both were newly arrived immigrants during the turn of the century. Truancy was not uncommon; many of the children were not in school because they were working. There was an appreciably higher number of Italian children in the work force than any other ethnic group. Attendance in secondary school or college was rare. In general, Italian children were viewed as difficult to discipline, slow to learn academic skills, and more concerned with outside jobs than with the classroom (Berrol, 1975).

The explanation that is frequently offered for this behavior pattern stems from the significance attached to work by the students' parents and the disdain placed by them on the value of education. Richard Gambino (1974), in his *Blood of My Blood*, states that the "contadino," the Italian peasant, viewed being educated in terms of proper behavior with the elders and did not refer to formal schooling. According to Leonard Covello (1967) in his comprehensive study *The Social Background of the Italo-American School Child*, there were many aspects of southern Italian cultural patterns and structural factors that contributed to the Italian child's resistance to American education. In southern Italy and Sicily, schooling had very little relationship to material success and this view carried over to America. And, indeed, as Stephen Steinberg (1981) observes, this attitude toward education also reflected conditions of Italian life in this country. Their chances of reaching college were slim, and the likelihood of occupational and status achievement was not dependent on their school performance. Steinberg notes the parallel view in the poor black men of Eliot Liebow's (1966)

Tally's Corner, who also adjusted their aspirations and strategies to what they believed they could realistically hope to achieve.

Covello refers to the importance of family ties and the associated belief that education was an indoctrination process into an alien culture that would destroy family unity and break down accepted social patterns, creating a generation gulf. This belief was interlocked with the one that saw the parents as the prime socializing agents for future occupational involvement. Finally, the expectation was that children from the age of 12 had responsibility to contribute to the economic needs of the household. (The late nineteenth-century American middle-class invention of adolescence as a stage in the life cycle was not shared by the poorer Italians.) Little benefit was seen for staying in school beyond the age of 12 for girls in particular, and somewhat less so for boys. This attitude put them in direct conflict with compulsory education laws.

The totality of this belief system and the consequent behavior of the Italian student was reinforced by teachers in the school system. In contrast to the Jewish student, who was usually placed in the higher-ranked academic curriculum track, the Italian student was tracked in either lower-ranked academic programs or nonacademic programs that included general, vocational, and commercial tracks. The result was that school officials had low expectations regarding the Italian student and, while they may not have explicitly prevented Italian students from achieving success in school, they did relatively nothing to encourage it (Berrol, 1975). The result was that a self-fulfilling prophecy began to operate, making it easier for Jewish children to succeed in school and more difficult for Italian students. It was only after World War II, when the occupational structure and opportunities began to change, did we get an appreciable change in the educational achievement rate of Italian youngsters.

The Chicago School and Ethnic-Family Systems

To set the historical stage for this discussion, I would like to remind the reader that sociology at the University of Chicago during the first four decades of the twentieth century was strongly influenced by the prevailing sentiments on the state of the family in the city. That sentiment emphasized anomie, social isolation, mental illness and suicide, and family-disorganization patterns that exhibited child abuse, separation, and divorce. The Chicago School focused on the absence of established institutional patterns and saw neighborhoods growing and changing so rapidly that social disorganization seemed to be a constant feature of city life.

The Chicago School, reflecting the prevailing social ethos of that period, saw the immigrant as a key component of urban social disorganization and individual deviance and pathology. It failed to recognize fully that these social problems were the inevitable and inherent costs of the emerging urban American society. Instead, seeking simpler and more-visible answers, mass immigration was seen to exacerbate the urban condition and was the prime cause of all that was wrong with the city.

Richard N. Juliani (1980), in his comprehensive analysis of the attitudes of the Chicago School regarding the immigrant community, clearly points out that Chicago School sociologists adopted this predominant American ideological perspective and emphasized the pathological aspects of immigrant experiences, making adjustment and acculturation the key problems for research and theory. Sociologists became preoccupied with the issue of assimilation and the processes by which the immigrant would become completely integrated into the new urban society. Lingering old-world ethnicity was seen negatively as a factor that would retard this integration and the concern was now on those social processes that would erase it. The sociological focus was on the cultural transformation of immigrants and their descendants into the social fabric of the American metropolis.

The thrust of the study of urban ethnic groups by the Chicago School was on the problems of individual assimilation and the dissolution of the ethnic community and family. See, in particular, Thomas and Znaniecki's *The Polish Peasant in Europe and America* (5 vols., 1918–1920), Louis Wirth's *The Ghetto* (1938), and Harvey Zorbaugh's *The Gold Coast and the Slum* (1929). They misunderstood immigrant traditional-family patterns because they were looking at city life solely in terms of deviance. For example, Thomas and Znaniecki, in trying to explain the high delinquency rate of Polish youth in early twentieth-century Chicago, place the blame entirely on the family and the community and fail to note the larger social issues: "There is a large proportion of immigrant children—particularly in large cities—whose home and community conditions are such that their behavior is never socially regulated, no life-organization worthy of the name is ever imposed on them" (cited in Hareven and Modell, 1980:352).

Their approach reflects the antiurban bias of much of early sociology both in the United States and in Europe. Reading passages in *The Polish Peasant in Europe and America*, we see a repeat of the conservative arguments of sociologists such as Le Play and Tonnies, who stressed the disintegration of the family and the individual. Thomas and Znaniecki state that position this way:

> Formerly the individual counted mainly as a member of the family, now he counts by himself, and still more than formerly. The family ceases to be necessary at all. The unequal rate at which the process of individualization and the modification of traditional attitudes takes place in different family members leads often to a disintegration of both the familial and the personal life. (Cited in Hareven and Modell, 1980:353)

Thomas and Znaniecki also shared the view of those social reformers who felt that the quick Americanization of immigrant children was the only means for their salvation. The immigrant family was seen as a handicap that inhibited that smooth transition; therefore, social agencies had the right to intervene in the private affairs of the immigrant family to enable the children and other family members to "make it" in American society.

Hareven and Modell (1980), in their review of ethnic-family patterns in the *Harvard Encyclopedia of American Ethnic Groups*, observe the similarity of this position with that taken by the culture of poverty thesis that fails to stress adaptations to poverty informed within culturally determined preferences. For example, the Moynihan Report on the black family in the mid-1960s posited that structural weaknesses in the black family system were among the important causes of black urban poverty. This family "pathology," which included father-absent households and "welfare mothers," was considered as an immoral family arrangement and therefore governmental social agencies had the right to intervene in their family dynamics. Hareven and Modell observe that "recent scholarship, however, has been more inclined than either Thomas and Znaniecki or Moynihan to stress that even superficial deviant family behaviors contain large adaptive elements, and express group values" (1980:353).

The Chicago School sociologists recognized that the different immigrant groups shared a common problem of assimilating and acculturating into American society. The sociologist Everett V. Stonequist (1937) captured the dilemma of the individual trying to adapt within the two worlds of the immigrant community and the larger American society in his phrase the "marginal man." Robert E. Park, the head of the University of Chicago's sociology department, stressed the necessity of understanding the immigrant community and its impact on the individual and the family. He referred to the city as being composed of "a mosaic of segregated peoples" (1928/1952:100).

For Park, the city or any given human community is specified by territory occupied by inhabitants that are distributed over and confined in it. The problems of social disorganization and social control are a central orienting feature of Park's work. The city is organized territorially as a constellation of diverse areas. The key analytical concept in understanding the make-up of urban communities is the "natural areas" of the city, the building blocks of the city.

> The urban community turns out, upon closer scrutiny, to be a mosaic of minor communities, many of them strikingly different one from another, but all more or less typical. Every city has its central business district; the focal point of the whole urban complex. Every city, every great city, has its more or less exclusive residential areas or suburbs; its areas of light and of heavy industry, satellite cities, and casual labor market, where men are recruited for rough work on distant frontiers, in the

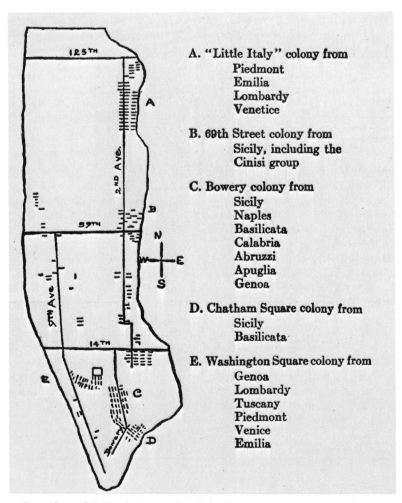

A. "Little Italy" colony from
  Piedmont
  Emilia
  Lombardy
  Venetice

B. 69th Street colony from
  Sicily, including the
  Cinisi group

C. Bowery colony from
  Sicily
  Naples
  Basilicata
  Calabria
  Abruzzi
  Apuglia
  Genoa

D. Chatham Square colony from
  Sicily
  Basilicata

E. Washington Square colony from
  Genoa
  Lombardy
  Tuscany
  Piedmont
  Venice
  Emilia

P. Hollembeak, American Museum of Natural History

Location of Italian ethnic villages in New York City, with sources of emigration from Italy (from *Old World Traits Transplanted* by Robert E. Park and Herbert A. Miller).

mines and in the forests, in the building of railways or in the borings and excavations for the vast structure of our modern cities. Every American city has its slums; its ghettos; its immigrant colonies, regions which maintain more or less alien and exotic cultures. Nearly every large city has its bohemias and hobohemias, where life is freer, more adventurous and lonely than it is elsewhere. These are the so-called natural areas of the city." (Park, 1952/1926:196)

Natural areas are seen to be formed because of "natural" or ecological forces largely determined by economic factors. Natural areas select and segregate people whose needs and problems are congruent with local institutional facilities. He views the immigrant community in his classic 1916 essay "The City: Suggestions for the Investigation of Human Behavior in the Urban Environment" as follows:

> . . . the isolation of the immigrant and racial colonies of the so-called ghettos and areas of population segregation tend to preserve and, where there is racial prejudice, to intensify the intimacies and solidarity of the local and neighborhood groups. Where individuals of the same race or of the same vocation live together in segregated groups, neighborhood sentiment tends to fuse together with racial antagonisms and class interests. (1967/1916:9–10)

Park's portrait of the immigrant community of the 1910s and 1920s is similar to the description of the urban villages of the 1950s and 1960s described by sociologists such as Young and Willmott (1957) in their account of East London's Bethnel Green and Herbert Gans (1962a) in his analysis of the Italian-American West End of Boston. But Park, who died in 1944, would have been surprised to see that these types of communities persisted after World War II and continue into the present, where they have been the locale for the articulation of forms of working-class ethnic revivalism, the "new ethnicity." For, according to Park, the solidarity of such communities would not last more than a single generation and the future for that community would be devastated as the more-successful members of the second and subsequent generations moved out and assimilated into the larger social order. They would have left the immigrant community to the unsuccessful, the socially disorganized, and the original aging migrants.

For Park, then, urban neighborhoods manage to retain their identity over time only occasionally and, at best, with great difficulty. The increasing proliferation of transportation and communication facilities in the city stimulates population mobility, and thus tends "to break up the tensions, interest, and sentiments which gave neighborhoods their individual character" (1967/1916:8). Often, stabilizing influences strong enough to isolate neighborhoods from the rest of the city and its disruptive forces are exerted by race, language, and belief. Yet such culturally isolated colonies as the ghetto, the "Black Belt," or "Little Sicily" cannot maintain a perpetual hold on their inhabitants. Processes of selection recruit the intelligent, specially skilled, and ambitious residents of the culturally segregated areas and deposit them in other, less-isolated places. As a consequence of the birth, persistence, and dissolution of neighborhoods and other natural areas, the growth of the city may be conceived as a kind of social metabolism. In the same manner, the forces that destroy the neighborhood in the urban community also destroy other primary groupings, such as the family and ethnic identities. "The growth of cities has been accompanied by the substitution of indirect, 'secondary' for direct, face-to-face 'primary' relations in the association of individuals in the community," states Park (1967/1916:23). This, of course, is the same theme picked up by Park's younger colleague and former graduate student, Louis Wirth (1938b), in his essay "Urbanism as a Way of Life."

Given this orientation, it is not surprising to see Park so intellectually inclined to see assimilation of ethnic groups as being inevitable. With Herbert A. Miller, a professor of sociology at Ohio State University, (and possibly W.I. Thomas), Park in

Old World Traits Transplanted (1925) concludes the analysis of the Americanization process by specifying the conditions with which an immigrant group could maintain a separate group identity. "[T]here are apparently only three grounds on the basis of one or more of which an immigrant group could remain culturally separate for an indefinite time: (1) the ability to perpetuate in the new generations the traditional memories of the group without loss; (2) the ability to create values superior to those of America, and the maintenance of separation in order not to sink to the cultural level of America; or (3) an ineradicable prejudice on one or both sides" (Park and Miller, 1925:301–302). But Park's entire orientation leads to the inevitable conclusion that assimilation is the logical and preferred consequence of immigration.

> Assimilation is thus as inevitable as it is desirable; it is impossible for the immigrants we receive to remain permanently in separate groups. Through point after point of contact, as they find situations in America intelligible to them in the light of old knowledge and experience, they identify themselves with us. We can delay or hasten this development. We cannot stop it. If we give them freedom to make their own connections between old and new experiences, if we help them to find points of contact, then we hasten their assimilation. This is a process of growth as against the "ordering and forbidding" policy and the demand that the assimilation of the immigrant shall be "sudden, complete, and bitter." And this is the complete democratic process, for we cannot have a political democracy unless we have a social democracy also. (Park and Miller, 1925:308)

The New Ethnicity and Ethnic Families

In the late 1960s and 1970s, there was great attention in the popular media, as well as by social scientists, on the increased ethnic consciousness among numerous urban Catholic working-class groups. They were categorized as "white ethnics" and their vocal advocacy of their ethnic identity became labeled as the "new ethnicity." Some saw this ethnic revival as a backlash to the increased militancy of blacks and Hispanics and to the antiwar movement of the affluent children of white liberals, politicians, and intellectuals. Michael Novak, a Slovak-American, interpreted the ethnic revival not as part of the assimilation process but as evidence of "unmeltable ethnics." He sees two basic elements in the "new ethnicity"—a sensitivity to ethnic pluralism that is combined with a respect for the cultural differences among ethnic groups and a self-conscious involvement and examination of our own cultural heritage.

Given the prediction of Robert E. Park and the Chicago School in the 1920s on the inevitable Americanization and assimilation of immigrant groups and their cultures, how can we understand the resurgence of ethnicity in the 1960s that continues to the present time? The important essay "Emergent Ethnicity: A Review and Reformulation" by William L. Yancey, Eugene P. Ericksen, and Richard N. Juliani (1976) argues that ethnic-group behavior and identity are contingent in significant ways on a number of interrelated societal conditions that include occupation, residence, and institutional affiliation that were tied to the changing technology of industrial production and transportation of late nineteenth-century and early twentieth-century American cities.

> . . . [E]thnicity, defined in terms of frequent patterns of association and identification with common origins . . . , is crystallized under conditions which reinforce the maintenance of kinship and friendship networks. These are common occupational positions, residential stability and concentration, and dependence on common institutions and services. These conditions are directly dependent on the ecological

structure of cities, which is in turn directly affected by the processes of industrialization. (Yancey, Ericksen, and Juliani, 1976:392)

Prior to the 50-year dramatic growth period—1876–1925—of the industrial urban centers of the United States, the "old" immigrants had a geographically dispersed residential pattern. The "new" immigrants were bunched together because of concentrated large-scale urban employment and the need for low-cost housing near the place of employment. When immigrants arrived, they were drawn to the urban areas of economic expansion, and the migration chain—the subsequent arrival of relatives and friends—continued the concentrated settlement pattern.

What distinguishes the work of Yancey, Ericksen, and Juliani (1976) from the earlier work of Park is their ability to integrate an economic causal model with one that allows for the utilization of cultural and symbolic factors. Park saw the gradual disappearance of the culture of the old immigrant group as the Americanization process proceeded. Park's urban theoretical model was essentially one that viewed social disorganization as an urban way of life and placed too great an emphasis on spatial patterings based on an economically determined urban ecology. It did not give sufficient attention to the nature of social-interactional patterns that were developing in the city. Overwhelmed by a secondary-group orientation toward city life, it did not see the emergent primariness of urban communities. It also did not see that urban social relations, like any other set of human interactions, are in a continual state of change, transition, or process.

What Park did not foresee was the emergence of new ethnic cultures with institutional, structural, and community supports for the subsequent generations of these immigrant groups. The thesis developed by Yancey and his associates is that the ethnic communities and the cultures that make up what is popularly called the "new ethnicity" become elaborated and developed out of the American urban experience and not the largely rural European background of the original immigrant generation; that is, rather than emphasize the transplanted cultural heritage as the principal antecedent and defining characteristic of ethnic groups, Yancey, Ericksen, and Juliani suggest that the development and persistence of ethnicity is dependent on structural conditions characterizing American cities and positions of groups in American social structure. The expression of ethnicity is more the expression of structural conditions in American society than the influence of the cultural heritage of ethnic groups. They therefore conclude that

> examination of ethnic experience should use the urban American-ethnic community, rather than the place of origin, as the principal criterion of ethnic group membership. . . . Ethnicity may have relatively little to do with Europe, Asia or Africa, but much more to do with the exigencies of survival and the structure of opportunity in this country. In short, the so-called "foreign heritage" of ethnic groups is taking shape in this country. (Yancey, Ericksen, and Juliani, 1976:400)

It is our view that the above quotation overstates their case. It would be more correct to see the expression of ethnicity as a consequence of the interaction of American structural conditions *and* the influence of the cultural heritage of ethnic groups. Yet these authors are on target in observing that ethnicity was elaborated and reinforced through systemic isolation of ethnic groups that historically occurred in the United States in residential segregation and occupational stratification. These factors allowed for the emergence of ethnic-group consciousness. This is particularly true of working-class ethnic groups. The concluding section of this chapter discusses a phenomenon called symbolic ethnicity, intermarriage, and ethnic-family patterns of the educated and more-affluent middle and upper classes who may not live in homogeneous urban villages.

Symbolic Ethnicity, Intermarriage, and Ethnic-Family Groups

In their important article, Yancey, Ericksen, and Juliani (1976) observe that communication and participation in ethnic organizations on a cosmopolitan level can reinforce ethnic identity even among residentially dispersed groups. This "situational" ethnicity may be characterized by such things as "church and synagogue attendance, marching in a Saint Patrick's or Columbus Day parade, voting for a political candidate of a similar ethnicity, or supporting a political cause associated with the country of origin, such as the emigration of Russian Jews to Israel or the reunification of Ireland" (Yancey, Ericksen, and Juliani, 1976:399).

Herbert Gans' article (1982/1979) "Symbolic Ethnicity: The Future of Ethnic Groups and Cultures in America" observes the same phenomenon but reaches a different conclusion. His essay can be seen as tying together a number of loose sociological ends and, to a large extent, bringing back the basic assimilationist view of Park and the Chicago School, but with greater sensitivity to symbolic as well as territorial communities and their meaning to the descendants of the early twentieth-century immigration groups.

Gans in this piece and in his earlier important work, *The Urban Villagers* (1962), emphasizes the importance of controlling for social class in the examination of ethnicity in the community context. *The Urban Villagers* sees a working-class culture as compared to an "Italian-American" culture per se as being an important determinant of individual behavior and social organization. Likewise, in the "Symbolic Ethnicity" article he raises this theme. He sees the rise of the "new ethnicity" primarily as a working-class phenomenon that uses ethnicity and ethnic organization on behalf of mobilizing working-class interests. His discussion of symbolic ethnicity is largely in terms of third- and fourth-generation upwardly mobile ethnics, with American Jewry being the case in point. It is defined largely in nostalgic cultural terms with a situational manifestation of ethnic identification.

> Symbolic ethnicity . . . is characterized by a nostalgic allegiance to the culture of the immigrant generation, or that of the old country; love for and a pride in a tradition that can be felt without having to be incorporated in everyday behavior. The feeling can be directed at a generalized tradition, or at specific ones: a desire for the cohesive extended immigrant family, or for the obedience of children to parental authority, or the unambiguous orthodoxy of immigrant religion, or the old-fashioned despotic benevolence of the machine politician. People may even sincerely desire to "return" to these imagined pasts, which are conveniently cleansed of the complexities that accompanied them in the real past, but while they may soon realize that they cannot go back, they do not surrender the wish. Or else they displace that wish on churches, schools, and the mass media, asking them to recreate a tradition, or rather, to create a symbolic tradition, even while their familial, occupational, religious and political lives are pragmatic responses to the imperatives of their roles and positions in local and national hierarchical social structures. (Gans, 1982 1979:501)

Gans concludes that, in the long run, acculturation and assimilation as secular trends will culminate in the eventual absorption of the given ethnic group into the larger culture and general population. These ethnics, while they retain some form of their religious heritage, will find their secular heritage to be only a dim memory and will have only the minutest traces of their national origins.

One of the arenas in which symbolic ethnicity may come into play is interethnic and interfaith marriage. Norvell D. Glenn (1982), in a study of patterns and recent trends in interfaith marriage in the United States, estimates that about 15 to 20 percent of today's marriages are between spouses with different religious preferences, such as

Protestant, Catholic, and Jewish. This is a substantial increase in the intermarriage rate since 1957. The apparent change in the willingness of people to marry persons of a different religion and to change their own religion to that of their spouse led Glenn to speculate that "marriage in the United States has become very largely a secular institution, with religious institutions exerting only weak influences on marital choice" (1982:564).

The high interfaith-marriage rate has been a cause of much debate among religious leaders of the major American religious groups. For example, members of 28 major Jewish groups—including the rabbinical associations for the Orthodox, Conservative, Reformed, and Reconstructionist branches of Judaism, along with such secular Jewish groups like B'nai B'rith International, Hadassah, and the American Jewish Committee—met in 1983 at a conference entitled the "National Conference on Jewish Population Growth" (Brozan, 1983). At the conference, they reported that with a current birthrate of 1.6 children per couple, American Jews had a lower birthrate than the population at large, for which the birthrate was 2.2. This—combined with a number of accelerating trends that include increasing intermarriage, delayed marriage and childbirth, and rising divorce rates—led them to forecast that by the year 2000, the Jewish population in this country, now 5.5 million, may shrink by 25 percent.

The theme of the conference was to develop a list of programs that would encourage the growth of Jewish families. These programs included establishment of Jewish day-care services with scholarship aid; provisions for mortgage assistance, in which organizations would subsidize mortgages on homes for large families; development of family-centered activities programs; and the establishment of Jewish dating services. Two years earlier, in 1981, the synagogue branch of Reform Judaism started a vigorous program to invite conversions by non-Jewish partners in interfaith marriages and by those Americans who express no religious preference (Briggs, 1981). The emphasis placed by Reform Judaism on conversion was largely in response to the above-mentioned factors and particularly to the alarm felt to the rising intermarriage rate between Jews and non-Jews. Surveys have shown that one-third of the nation's Jews marry outside their faith and that their non-Jewish spouses have often faced difficulties in being accepted into a synagogue. The program planned by the Union of American Hebrew Congregations, an organization of 735 Reform synagogues, was to develop a more-hospitable climate for non-Jewish marriage partners and children of interfaith marriages in the synagogue and to provide information for those who seek religious identity and involvement.

David M. Heer (1980), commenting on interethnic marriage, states that it has had an impact on the distinctive features of the given ethnic groups. He notes that a high proportion of Americans now have ancestors of so many different national backgrounds that in a 1969 Current Population Survey, 50 percent of the adult respondents no longer considered themselves belonging to any particular ethnic group. Finally, he observes that, while interethnic marriages may continue, this does not mean that the cultures are in a process of dissolution. Thus, Italian festas are still being held and lox and bagels are still being eaten, but in what may be the ultimate symbolic ethnicity, the people who are culturally consuming may not be members of that ethnic group! "The distinctive elements of each European culture are being preserved in the United States by those people who appreciate them, who may or may not be those for whom the features form part of an ancestral heritage" (1980:520).

In trying to reconcile the different scholarly beliefs with Gans' beliefs on the future trends of American ethnicity and ethnic-family dynamics, it is important to distinguish between the "new ethnicity" as articulated among working-class ethnics and the ethnic expressiveness of upwardly mobile middle- to upper-middle and upper-class ethnics. Further, ethnic-group variations should be studied. More specifically, in a 1964 article, Andrew Greeley raised five key problems that would aid in the study of ethnic groups. They are particularly relevant to the study of the new ethnicity.

1. Under what circumstances does ethnicity provide a means of self-identification?
2. To what extent do ethnic groups continue to function as interest groups?
3. To what extent do ethnic groups provide differential norms and values?
4. If ethnic groups do these first three things, do they also determine the choice of associates, particularly in primary-group roles?
5. What is the interrelation between ethnicity and religion? (Greeley, 1964:110–111)

The family served as the center of social interaction and socialization. Just as the family played an essential role in organizing social life in the old-world setting, it did the same in the new world. However, the family is but one of the many institutions (including the school, church, mass media, and occupational settings) that has affect on individuals. Present ethnic-family patterns can be seen as a result of interaction of cultural tradition with continuous American experience contingencies. The result is that ethnic families are not the equivalent of immigrant families; they have undergone significant changes through the generations. Ethnic-family variations are a consequence of cultural background, recency of migration, residency and geographical locale, socioeconomic status, educational achievement, upward mobility, and political and religious ties. The nature of the response of the given ethnic group and the nature of its adaptation reflect the interaction of these factors. Ethnic families have been affected by social change and have, in turn, affected it. In sum, contemporary ethnic groups have been actively involved in delineating their particular family patterns; they have not been the passive recipients of a one-way Americanization process.

The Japanese-American Family

The year 1853 is a milestone in Japanese and American relations for, in that year, Commodore Perry sailed into Tokyo Bay and ended more than 200 years of self-imposed governmental isolation of Japan in which foreign visitors were prohibited and Japanese were not allowed to leave their country. Beginning in 1868, the Japanese began emigrating, first as laborers and eventually as permanent settlers to the United States. They shared the same motives for movement to America as other immigrant groups: better jobs, better lives, and an escape from harsh living conditions in Japan. Movement was slow at first; U.S. Census records indicate that only 55 came to the United States in 1870, and 2,039 in 1890. The period after that witnessed a much greater number of immigrants—reaching 24,326 in 1900, 72,157 in 1910, and 111,010 in 1920 (Parillo, 1985).

During the period beginning in 1890, a significant number of the immigrants were young single men—like their Italian, Slav, and Greek counterparts—who came with the hope to earn sufficient money to return to their homeland and buy land or a small business. They settled in the Pacific states and, meeting discrimination in more-economically remunerative occupations, they found jobs in domestic service, farm labor, and contract gardening.

The fact that single men initially sought to return to Japan is reflected in the great imbalance in the ratio of the males and females who came to America. In 1900, out of the total Japanese population of 24,326 there were only 985 females. Although an unknown number of Japanese males returned to Japan, a larger number stayed and make a permanent home in America. This change is reflected in the sex ratio during succeeding decades with the arrival of additional females. In 1910, the number of females was 9,087, and by 1920 there were 22,193 out of the total population of 111,010 (Gee, 1978).

The increase in the number of women came about from either the single young

Intermarriage: Jewish Children Subject of Study

BY NADINE BROZAN

What happens to the beliefs, practices and relationships of children born to Jews married to non-Jews? According to a study issued last week by the American Jewish Committee, they tend to define their Judaism as a belief in a religion but do not feel strongly linked to other Jews in ethnic or cultural ways. Although they may identify themselves as Jews, according to the study made public at a news conference, they rarely if ever attend synagogue services and are not distressed by the prospect that their own children may marry non-Jews.

The implications of intermarriage for the future of American Jewry are an increasingly troublesome concern to Jewish leaders as it becomes more commonplace in this country. According to a present estimate, 40 percent of the 5.5 million American Jews marry outside their faith and the offspring of such marriages number 400,000 to 600,000. Reflecting this, the Reform branch of Judaism has broadened its definition of a Jew from an individual with a Jewish mother—the traditional criterion—to one with a Jewish parent and is encouraging conversion.

The study, conducted last year by Dr. Egon Mayer, professor of sociology at Brooklyn College, surveyed 117 children, aged 16 to 46, of 70 couples who had participated in an earlier American Jewish Committee study on intermarriage.

THE MOST VITAL FACTOR

The conversion of the non-Jewish parent was found to be the most vital factor in the preservation of a Jewish heritage. Significant differences were found between those children whose non-Jewish parent had converted (36 percent of the respondents) and those whose non-Jewish parent had not (64 percent). The survey did not include a control group of children of Jewish parents as a basis for comparison.

The overwhelming majority of children (84 percent) of marriages that included a convert identified themselves as being Jewish, compared with 24 percent of those of marriages in which the non-Jewish partner did not adopt Judaism. But the responses to the survey questionnaire indicated that for children of intermarriage Judaism is a religion, not an ethnic identity, and as a religion it is observed through study and celebration at home more often than through synagogue worship. Though 86 percent of the conversionary couples had joined synagogues, only 36 percent of their children did so.

Only 25 percent of the children of conversionary marriages and 10 percent of those of mixed marriages said they considered ethnic ties "very important," with greater numbers in both groups categorizing them as "somewhat important."

Yehuda Rosenman, director of the American Jewish Committee's William Petschek National Jewish Family Center, the sponsor of the study, said: "Jews may always have ranked low in terms of synagogue attendance, but they have always remained Jewish because they considered themselves to be part of a people. They have never distinguished between their religion and their peoplehood to transmit their heritage."

A majority of the respondents said they would not be upset to see their children marry non-Jews and very few said they would attempt to deter them.

males returning to Japan for brides or the already-married males sending for their wives and children. Another method was the "picture-bride" practice that grew out of the traditional Japanese practice of arranged marriage (see the discussion of this practice in Chapter 9). Through agreed-on "go-betweens," pictures were exchanged between potential spouses and their families. Apart from the fact that the couple neither met during the course of the negotiations nor were present at the actual marriage ceremony, the marriage was socially and legally recognized in Japan. A Japanese woman on her way to meet her unseen husband in an unknown America conveys her thoughts in the following passage:

> On the way from Kobe to Yokohama, gazing upon the rising majestic Mount Fuji in a cloudless sky aboard the ship, I made a resolve. For a woman who was going to a strange society and relying upon an unknown husband whom she had married through photographs, my heart had to be as beautiful as Mount Fuji. I resolved that the heart of a Japanese woman had to be sublime, like that soaring majestic figure eternally constant through wind and rain, heat, and cold. I never forgot that resolve on the ship, enabling me to overcome sadness and suffering. (Cited in Gee, 1978:56–57)

This practice was denounced as "immoral" by American immigration exclusionists and was terminated after 1921 (Gee, 1978). Yet, as Kikumura and Kitano (1981) emphasize, the picture-bride and other practices bringing the Japanese women to America were crucial in shaping the Japanese immigrant experience and moving it toward a more "normal" family life. For, by having a family, the Japanese were able to make a stronger commitment to remaining in and adapting to their new country. This is especially the case for a people who believe that "no matter what possessions a man may have, he is not a success unless he is married and has a family . . . to fail in this is to fail in life" (cited in Gee, 1978:55).

The Japanese were industrious and knowledgeable in cultivation. Despite discrimination, they acquired farms of their own. Often this was on marginal land, arid and abandoned, and only coaxed into productivity with prodigious labor. Both the husband and wife worked long hours in fields or shops. One woman who was a picture-bride recounts her experience and provides a vivid picture of the laborious nature of agricultural work:

> At the beginning I worked with my husband picking potatoes or onions and putting them in sacks. Working with rough-and-tumble men, I became weary to the bones; waking up in the mornings I could not bend over the wash basin.
> Sunlight came out about 4:00 A.M. during the summer in the Yakima Valley (Washington). I arose at 4:30. After cooking breakfast, I went out to the fields. There was no electric stove or gas like now. I took over one hour to cook, burning kindling wood.
> As soon as I came home, I first put on the fire, took off my hat, and then I washed my hands. After cooking both breakfast and lunch, I went to the fields. (Cited in Gee, 1978:58)

Similarly, urban work also proved very difficult, as indicated in this account of a woman who operated a laundry with her husband. After working the entire day, she reports:

> . . . I started at 5:00 P.M. to prepare supper for five or six persons, and then I began my evening work. The difficult ironing remained. Women's blouses in those days were made from silk or lace, with collars and long sleeves and lots of frills.
> I could only finish two in one hour, ironing them with great care. Hence, I worked usually until 12 to 1 A.M. But it was not just me—all women who worked in the laundry business probably did the same thing. (Gee, 1978:58)

The economic competitiveness of the Japanese, particularly in agriculture, led to discriminatory legislation by the California state government. In 1913, the California Alien Land Act was enacted to prevent the Japanese and other Asian immigrants from owning or leasing land. Under the United States Naturalization Act of 1790, then still in effect, citizenship was available to any white alien who was not a slave. This act was modified in 1868, after the Civil War, to extend citizenship to persons of African descent. The foreign-born who were neither white nor black therefore could not become citizens. However, since Japanese children who were born in America were automatically U.S. citizens, this law was somewhat circumvented by the Japanese holding land in their children's names. In reaction, California in 1920 passed a law prohibiting first-generation immigrants (*Issei* Japanese) from being guardians of their native-born children's property. The Supreme Court upheld this law in 1923, and similar legislation was swiftly passed in New Mexico, Arizona, Louisiana, Montana, Idaho, and Oregon (Parillo, 1984).

Patterns of discrimination against the Japanese continued with the *Nisei*, or the second generation, who were American-born children of the *Issei*. While the *Nisei* had a distinct advantage over their parents—American citizenship—this did not help them when Japan declared war against the United States in 1941. On February 19, 1942—two months after the attack on Pearl Harbor—110,000 Japanese, many of them second- and third-generation Americans, were removed from their homes and placed in concentration camps (euphemistically called relocation centers). There were a number of factors that led to the forced expulsion of Japanese-Americans from the West Coast. Part of it is explained in terms of the war hysteria of the time, but probably a more-perfidious and accurate assessment was that it was the logical culmination of the history of American discriminatory practices against the Japanese and a convenient way for white businessmen and farmers to end the competition of Japanese enterprises.

The effect on family life in the internment camps was profound. Family life was disrupted; old people and children were disoriented; and farms, shops, household property, and skills were lost. The authority of the parents was undermined. Husbands-fathers could no longer act as primary providers and wives-mothers could not function in their household roles. Children ate in mess halls, and dormitory living was prevalent. The atmosphere was one of boredom and stagnation. The consequence was that gambling became prevalent, and often family quarrels escalated into violence (Kitano, 1980).

In spite of these early discriminatory and prejudicial historical experiences, by the 1970s Japanese-Americans were considered one of America's most "successful" minorities. Kikumura and Kitano (1981) attribute this to (1) the economic mobility of the family; (2) the compatibility of American and Japanese values, particularly the emphasis on politeness, diligence, long-term goals, respect for authority and parental wishes, keeping up appearances, social sensitivity, and suppression of desires and emotional feelings; and (3) the wartime evacuation that broke up the ghettos and the subsequent scattering of many of the young into parts of the country that did not have a Japanese population. The last factor "exposed them to American ways, dissolved old institutions and structures, and reordered the family structure by putting more power into the hands of the *Nisei*" (Kikumura and Kitano, 1981:45).

Contemporary Japanese-American Family Patterns

Kikumura and Kitano (1981), commenting on the contemporary Japanese-American family, see it as containing features of Japanese and American cultures. The process of acculturation still contains salient features regarding family solidarity and the retention of certain Japanese values. Using 1970 census data, they found that 86 percent of the families included both husband and wife, which was the same rate for the country as a whole. The percentage of children under six (27 percent) was also at the national norm. The size of the nuclear family was slightly above the national

George Kiriyama/Japanese Historical Society of Southern California

First annual third-generation picnic of Japanese Americans, California.

average (3.7 to 3.5 persons) as was the extended family (16 to 12 persons). This similar pattern to that of Americans as a whole reflects a high degree of acculturation.

In an interesting study comparing *Nisei* and *Sansei* (third-generation Japanese-American) kinship interaction in Hawaii, Colleen Leahy Johnson (1977) reports a persistence and even an increase in kinship solidarity and sociability among the younger generation. This occurs despite their social mobility and increased assimilation into institutions outside the family. She attributes this to the Japanese-American kinship system that operates on a more-obligatory basis than the optional basis characterized by the American kinship system in general. An exchange system is seen to operate that encourages indebtedness and takes place in an interdependent kinship network with an obligatory pattern of interaction. This differs from the option model of the modified extended family characterized by the white ethnic families of northeastern cities.

Kitano (1980), in an essay on the Japanese in the *Harvard Encyclopedia of American Ethnic Groups*, reports that the rise in the intermarriage rate is one dramatic change that is occurring in family patterns. Antimiscegenation laws prohibiting Japanese from marrying Caucasians were in effect in many states until they were declared unconstitutional in the late 1960s. In part, this kept the intermarriage rate down through the 1950s. However, since then the rate has risen quite rapidly. For example, Kitano reports that in 1972, 49 percent of Japanese-American marriages were to non-Japanese. Similarly high figures were obtained in data surveys from San Francisco, Fresno, and Honolulu. Kitano sees that "these changes in marital patterns reflect increased opportunity for social contact, a weakening of the traditional Japanese family, acculturation, upward social mobility, and changing attitudes toward the Japanese" (1980:570). He predicts that the trend toward more interethnic marriages will continue.

Similarly, Darryl Montero (1981) reported similar trends in his study of changing patterns of assimilation over three generations of Japanese-Americans. Montero studied data derived from a sample of 2,304 *Nisei* and 802 *Sansei* and earlier collected data on the *Issei*. He examined four basic indicators of assimilation: visiting patterns with relatives, ethnicity of two closest friends, ethnicity of favorite organization, and ethnicity of spouse. These indicators were used to answer the broader question of whether socioeconomic mobility led to cultural, structural, and marital assimilation.

He found that, with socioeconomic success measured in terms of education and occupation, there was greater assimilation among those who made it than those who did not. Economic success also was seen to encourage movement from "little Tokyos" and "Japan-towns" into the surrounding suburbs with the consequent splintering of community ties. Further, for those who lived in non-Japanese communities, they formed friendships and professional acquaintances among Caucasians that had important implications for racial intermarriage.

Montero examines the view that Japanese ethnic identity may be breaking apart in favor of an Asian-American ethnic identity. He sees some evidence for this in studies that report on Japanese-Americans marrying members of other Asian groups. Also, there is some collective political movement of Asian-Americans, there are changes occurring in their historical attitudes to each other, and there is a greater number of Asians in metropolitan areas. However, Montero's data on the intermarriage patterns of the *Nisei* and *Sansei* do not confirm this Asian identity viewpoint. The overwhelming number of these second- and third-generation Japanese-Americans who intermarry marry Caucasians. Ninety-two percent of the intermarried *Nisei* married Caucasians; the comparable figures for intermarried *Sansei* are 78 percent marrying Caucasians, 19 percent marrying other Asians, and 3 percent marrying other ethnic groups.

The more-salient finding for Montero is that 40 percent of the *Sansei* intermarried, compared to only 10 percent of the older-generation *Nisei*. He observes that the remarkable strides in socioeconomic advancement by the *Nisei* and *Sansei* are accompanied by an accelerated role of assimilation that may contribute to the demise of some of the traditional Japanese values that accounted for that success in the first place. This, in turn, may foster a leveling off of future socioeconomic achievement. Montero ends his paper by wondering about what the consequences of future high intermarriage rates may mean for Japanese-American family patterns in particular and what similarly high intermarriage patterns may mean to other ethnic groups as well.

> Given the dramatically increasing trend of outmarriage among the *Sansei*, with its concomitant erosion of ethnic ties and affiliation, we are justified in wondering whether a Japanese-American ethnic community can be maintained into the next generation — the *Yonsei*. If it cannot, the survival of other distinct ethnic groups may be similarly uncertain as their members advance socioeconomically. (Montero, 1981:837–838)

The Mexican-American Family

Mexican-Americans have a unique place in American immigration history. They can be considered in terms of being a native American group as well as an immigrant group. Their historical immigration patterns have shown great variation. Within the last 50 years there has been a major change from being a major ethnic group with the largest rural population to one that is strongly urbanized, with 85 percent being city dwellers (Cortes, 1980). Further, while about 83 percent of the 8.7 million Mexican-Americans still live in the southwestern states, an increasing number have migrated to urban areas throughout the United States; for example, Los Angeles has more

"The Ultimate Assimilation"
Asian Intermarriage, Once Taboo, is on the Rise

BY BARBARA KANTROWITZ ET AL.

Tokyo-born Emiko Greenidge speaks only Japanese to her 9-month-old daughter, Ashley Nagako Greenidge. Her husband, Ron, tells the baby stories in his best Brooklyn accent. Despite the bilingual baby talk, there's no language gap in their Los Angeles home. Ashley's vocabulary consists of just one word—"da"—and, says her mother, "I think 'da' is universal."

Forget the ancient wisdom about East and West: Today, the twain do meet—and fall in love. Between 1970 and 1980, the number of Asian-Americans marrying non-Asians nearly doubled, from 118,144 to 235,707. Intermarriage will probably increase even more in the next few decades as the number of native-born Asian-Americans grows. Intermarriage is more common among second- and third-generation Asian-Americans; they are likely to be better educated and have higher-paying jobs than their immigrant parents or grandparents. Even now, recent studies show that more than half of all Japanese-Americans, 40 percent of Chinese and 30 percent of Koreans marry outside of their ethnic groups. "It's an indication of acceptance by the larger society," says Betty Lee Sung, a professor of Asian studies at the City University of New York who is writing a book on Chinese intermarriage. Marriage to a non-Asian, says Sung, is "the ultimate assimilation."

A generation ago, such interracial unions were rare and controversial. Frank Rathbone courted Wu Shih-san in World War II China; he was a GI, and she was a student. After their marriage he brought her home to New York to meet his parents. The elder Rathbones at first refused to let the newlyweds stay in their house; after newspaper articles headlined the young couple's plight, the parents relented. There were more rough moments. People used to stare at them when they walked down the street. One son got in a fight at school after a classmate made racist remarks. Mrs. Rathbone says she tried not to let the pain show: "I held it all inside."

Cross-cultural couples have it a little easier in the 1980s. Newlyweds Randy Bowman, 32, and Dorothy Han, 26, are both musicians in Boston. Han was born in this country and considers herself more American than Chinese. The couple never thinks of their marriage as interracial. And, adds Bowman, in the world of the concert hall "no one cares what you look like as long as you can play." But other couples find there are problems. Sung says that among the husbands and wives she has interviewed, familial objections are the biggest hurdle. Asian parents fear that their culture will disappear if their children intermarry. To many Chinese families, "it's the worst thing that could happen," says Sung. "The parents disown their children. They are terribly, terribly hurt."

There are obstacles on the other side of the aisle as well. When one of Charles Halevi's relatives found out that his wife, Jean Ikezoe-Halevi, 33, a third-generation Japanese-American, was pregnant, she asked if he was worried that his children might not look like him. "I told her then I would be fortunate," says Charles, a Chicago writer, "because the children would look like the woman I loved enough to marry."

Sometimes, the birth of children brings families back together. John Chan, a 26-year-old gas-station owner in Los Angeles, says his parents put pressure on him to marry a Chinese woman. But 3½ years ago, he married his blond, blue-eyed high-school sweetheart, Laura, 25. They produced twin sons who will carry on the family name. John Chan says his family loves Laura now, despite initial reservations. "That's because I had twin boys," jokes Laura. "If I'd had twin girls, I think I'd be kicked out of the whole family." If the children had been girls, John concedes, his parents "might have taken that opportunity to tell me that I should have married a Chinese girl."

CULTURAL TIES

An appreciation of each other's cultures helps smooth the way for a relationship,

(continued)

mixed couples say. Philip Chiang's parents fled from Shanghai to Japan at the end of World War II. His father, a diplomat, enrolled Philip in an American school in Tokyo. "I had an American education, kind of a Japanese upbringing and a Chinese heritage," says Chiang, 38. He moved with his family to San Francisco when he was a teenager and now runs several family restaurants in Los Angeles. For the last four years he has been living with Annie O'Neill, 34, a New York-born actress. "Philip is the most American guy I know," says O'Neill, who feels at home with Chiang's Asian background as well. The couple have traveled to Asia together several times and share a love of Japanese food. Chiang feels the senior members of his family disapprove of intermarriage; the only exception is an aunt who has been married to an American for many years. That uncle studied ancient Chinese history, says Chiang, "so he's almost like a Chinese." Chiang feels that a little bit of effort goes a long way. "One of the persons

in this relationship has to bend. I think it's the non-Asian or the Caucasian that has to have the affinity for the mate's culture."

With U.S.-born Asian-Americans, those cultural differences blur. Jennifer Jong, 25, and Jim Sandling, 27, recently bought an apartment in Manhattan after living together for more than two years. Jong is a fourth-generation Californian; Sandling grew up in Michigan. "The values our families instilled in us," says Jong, "were pretty similar—the importance of the work ethic and education, family values and personal values." Still, Jong says, many of her colleagues at work didn't think the blond guy in the photo on her desk could be her boyfriend. "For a long time," she says, "everyone thought the picture was from GQ."

SOURCE. Barbara Kantrowitz et al. 1986. "'The ultimate assimilation': Asian intermarriage, once taboo, is on the rise." *Newsweek* (Nov. 24):80. Copyright 1986 Newsweek, Inc. All rights reserved. Reprinted by permission.

than a million Mexican-American residents. As Carlos E. Cortes (1980:697) has observed: "The shifts from regional to national minority, from farm to city, and from field to factory have set in motion a series of other changes whose consequences are still unfolding." Here we focus our attention on the impact of these changes on family life.

Initially, Mexican-Americans were created through conquest and annexation rather than through immigration. The Mexicans were here when what is now Texas, New Mexico, Arizona, California, and parts of Colorado, Nevada, Utah, and Wyoming were acquired by the United States through the war of separation of Texas from Mexico, the United States–Mexican War, and the Gadsden Purchase during the period between 1845 and 1854. This annexed regional minority experienced a diminishing influence in the economy of the southwestern states throughout the nineteenth century. Queen and his associates (Queen, Habenstein, and Quadagno, 1985) make the point that as slavery is a key element in understanding the black American experience, so too is the labor utilization of Mexican-Americans and Mexicans in understanding the Mexican-American experience. This historical experience has influenced their contemporary social position and, to a lesser extent, their family patterns.

In Texas, first cattle ranching, then land ownership, and then cotton farming determined economic superiority and the Mexican-Americans became a subjugated, exploitable minority group. What land they owned was obtained both legally and illegally during this time. Anglo-dominated agricultural production became large-scale and labor intensive. Mexican-Americans were relegated to serve as cheap labor and to compete economically with job-starved Mexican nationals who were willing to work for even lower wages. The immigration policy allowed for the crossing back and forth over the border of Mexican migrants and this further undermined the economic position of Mexican-Americans.

A Mexican-American family-owned bakery.

In New Mexico, their situation was somewhat better. When they were in the demographic majority through the 1860s, they dominated the economy and controlled the territorial legislature. However, with the expansion of the railroads, the depletion of grazing lands, the development of industrial mining, and the consequent movement into New Mexico of Anglos or Anglo-Americans (white persons of non-Hispanic descent), the balance of power gradually shifted. Still, by the turn of the century, they retained some economic and political power. However, many Mexican-Americans were forced to become part of the unskilled labor force.

In southern and central California, powerful *rancheros* dominated the economy at the time of annexation. However, the Gold Rush of 1849 brought more and more Anglos into both the northern and the southern parts of the state. Prejudice reinforced by legislative actions biased against Mexican-Americans resulted in the loss of most of the old Mexican land grants. By 1900, their political and economic power plummeted throughout the Southwest, with only New Mexico being the notable exception.

The dominant Anglos gained economic and political control of the Southwest, and their ethnic stereotypes prevailed. Mexican-Americans became characterized as an inferior people whose religion, language, and culture were seen as antithetical to the "American" way of life. The resultant consequences of being relegated to manual labor, poverty, and subjugation only served to reinforce the stereotype of Mexican-Americans as ignorant, shiftless people.

The United States shares a 2,000-mile boundary with Mexico. Two rivers, most notably the Rio Grande, and open land separate the two countries. Mexican immigration into the United States during the second half of the nineteenth century was relatively modest compared to what it is in the twentieth century. The total number of native-born and foreign-born Mexican people in the United States was estimated at being between 381,000 and 562,000 in 1900 (Cortes, 1980).

Social, political, and economic factors in both countries led to a substantial rise in the number of immigrants from Mexico to the United States in the first three decades of the twentieth century. Political upheavals, social unrest, and poverty in Mexico, combined with the growth of the American Southwest, accounted for the movement of more than 500,000 legal immigrants in the 1920s alone. Dinnerstein and Reimers (1975) observe that Mexican laborers provided more than 60 percent of the common-labor force in the railroad-track gangs, the mines of Arizona and New Mexico, the fruit and truck crops of Texas and California, and the packing plants on the West Coast. They also dominated the sugar-beet farming industry that extended from Colorado to Montana, Michigan, and Ohio. The use of these laborers coincided with the rapid growth of the Southwest and with the changes in the immigration laws that severely restricted the immigration of Chinese and Japanese laborers at the beginning of the century and European immigration in the mid-1920s.

Mexican immigration began to decline in 1928 and remained low through the Depression and the coming of World War II. Indeed, during the 1930s, many Mexicans either returned home voluntarily or were pressured to do so by communities where there were high rates of unemployment. During the war, labor shortages encouraged American industry to welcome Mexican workers. Mexicans with permanent visas continued to grow in the 1940s, expanded rapidly in the 1950s, and exceeded 30,000 in every year from 1960 to the end of the 1970s (Cortes, 1980). In addition, countless numbers of Mexicans have entered the United States illegally throughout the twentieth century. The estimate of the number of illegal aliens is between 3.5 to 6 million (Parrillo, 1985). The 1986 Immigration Reform and Control Act was passed to regulate better the number of legal immigrants and to end the illegal status of those who entered the United States surreptitiously. An amnesty program has been put into effect that confers legality to all illegal immigrants who have been living in the United States on a continuous basis before January 1, 1982. However, problems in the operation of the amnesty program may cause difficulty for many Mexican and Mexican-American families.

Contemporary Mexican-American Family Patterns

We recognize that there is no such thing as *the* Mexican-American family, and that there are social-class variations and historical-experience variations in relation to when these people settled in the United States. Yet a distinct set of values centering on the family and not on the individual has been an overriding cultural feature. The *familia* is the center of Mexican-American culture and is seen as the single most important social unit (Queen et al., 1985). Traditionally, it has been an extended family containing not only parents and children but also grandparents, uncles, aunts, and cousins. Migration patterns usually require the relocation of both the nuclear family and the consanguineal one.

Familism, incorporated in a theme of family honor and unity, is seen to persist even in today's ethnic enclaves, or *barrios. Barrios* are the equivalent of the urban villages that we have seen characterized the urbanization patterns of such "new" immigration groups as the Italians, Poles, and eastern European Jews in the Northeast and Midwest. An example of the persistence of traditional cultural family values can be seen in the changes that have affected *compadrazqo* (godparentage), a special form of ritual kinship that promotes continuing close relationships among extended families.

The *compadrazqo* is designed to generate social and interpersonal cohesion and, at the same time, to reduce the potential extrafamilial conflict that might arise in a highly family-centered society. Mutual patterns of obligations are expected to develop between *compadres* (people or groups). In the event of trouble or difficulty, *compadres* are expected to offer help and advice. Cortes (1980) has observed that the

Immigrants Face New Amnesty Fear: Split Families

BY FAWN VRAZO

MISSION, Texas—It was an ambitious family-improvement plan, but a workable one, provided that everyone was willing to make a few sacrifices.

Estella Villerreal, an illegal immigrant and homemaker who lives in a small yellow house set in the middle of the hot, humid farm fields of south Texas, agreed to take in her 41-year-old brother, Florencio Reyna, after he crossed illegally from Mexico into the United States.

Reyna agreed to share a cramped bedroom with his two little nephews—he would sleep during the day, the boys at night. During the night, Reyna would pack onions in a warehouse in nearby McAllen. He would earn enough for his room and board and have enough left over to send $60 to $100 a month to his wife and daughter in Mexico.

Eventually, they would join him in the United States.

It was a plan well on the way to succeeding, until the Immigration Reform and Control Act of 1986 got in the way. In Villerreal's words, it made the whole thing "blow up."

Like many Mexican immigrants these days, she and her brother are finding that the new law's sweet offer of amnesty to illegal aliens carries an unexpectedly bitter aftertaste. Immigrant rights groups and lawmakers are calling it the "family unity" problem: Some family members can qualify for amnesty, others cannot.

Simply put, many close-knit families stand to be split apart.

Villerreal is likely to qualify for legalization because she can document that she has been in the States continuously since before the law's required date of Jan. 1, 1982. But Reyna can only document having been in this country continuously since 1983. This means he probably will not qualify, and Reyna is thinking he will have to go back.

For a culture that treasures the extended family, the options in such cases are painful: breaking up the family, or trying to survive together while one or more of them remains in the shadowy world of the illegal alien.

Although Immigration and Naturalization Service officials have promised to use fairness and discretion in deciding the cases of nuclear families who face separation under the new law, there is wide skepticism among immigration rights groups that the INS will indeed look the other way when its agents run across anyone who fails to qualify under the act.

The new law itself makes no special provisions for keeping together families who apply for amnesty, although it allows for the waiving of some provisions in the interest of family unity.

"If they do not qualify, we have no choice under the law," INS Commissioner Alan C. Nelson testified at a Senate subcommittee hearing earlier this month. He added later in the hearing: "We will do what we can. We will look at individual cases."

Few people—including many illegal immigrants—believe that the INS will begin actively seeking out and deporting aliens who do not qualify for legalization. After all, millions of illegal immigrants have been living in the United States for years without being bothered by the INS.

But it will be difficult for them to find jobs now that employers are required to ask all workers for documents showing they can legally work in the United States.

This can produce hardship for Mexican families. Some family members will be eligible for legalization "but dependent on the income of those who will have to be going back," said Benigno Pena of the South Texas Immigration Council, a nonprofit counseling organization.

Psychologically and economically, Pena said, Mexican families "are very dependent [on each other], very closely knit together, brothers and sisters and uncles and aunts."

U.S. Rep. Edward R. Roybal (D., Calif.) has proposed legislation that would waive the five-year residency requirement for the

(continued)

spouses and minor children of adults who qualify for amnesty.

But Roybal and leaders of immigrant rights groups believe that it is futile to seek the same exceptions for other family members—brothers, sisters, grown children, mothers, fathers, grandmothers or aunts.

"I have to operate in an atmosphere that is not conducive to an all-inclusive request," Roybal said in an interview last week. "It's going to be difficult to get the immediate family united."

Others, including former INS Commissioner Leonel Castillo, now a leader of the immigrant rights community in Houston, worry that an all-inclusive amnesty policy for illegal immigrant families would create great bitterness among other immigrants who have waited for years to bring their own relatives legally into America through the INS preference system.

That system holds some relief for families applying for amnesty under the new immigration law. For instance, a man or woman who wins permanent residency under the law (a process that will take a minimum of 18 months) may then seek residency for a spouse or unmarried son or daughter. And once an applicant is granted U.S. citizenship (a process that takes at least 6½ years), he or she can petition the INS on behalf of a spouse, children or other relatives, including brothers and sisters.

Waits for approval, though, can be stunningly long—particularly for Mexicans, the most backlogged immigrant group. A new Mexican-American citizen applying for residency for a brother or a sister would have to wait a minimum of 11 years for approval because of the backlog of requests. A Mexican permanent resident would have to wait at least 10 years before winning residency for a son, daughter or spouse.

Castillo and Professor Jose Cuellar of Stanford University's Center for Chicano Research doubt that many illegal Mexican immigrants will choose to move back to Mexico while they wait for the distant day when a relative can petition to bring them back in.

Instead, predicts Castillo, many immigrants who fail to win amnesty on their own will stay in the United States, where they will live "an underclass existence. . . . They won't find work here, but the underclass in the U.S. is a lot better than going home."

Cuellar is among immigration experts who believe that the new immigration law falls especially hard on Mexican families, who typically come to America not all together but person by person over the generations. In many cases, the '82 cutoff will sever that human chain.

Traditionally, said Cuellar, "one person comes first, a son comes, or his brother comes, then two more brothers come, then his sister comes. Now they have three brothers and a sister living in an area where they already have a couple of cousins and a couple of nephews. . . . Very few come without relatives that haven't themselves had relatives here for generations."

"It's a long tradition of relationships, very thick," Cuellar said, and the new law does not take that into account.

In south Texas, a half-Mexican, half-American land where the Burger Kings accept pesos and the Whataburger chain advertises that it is open *24 horas*, the dilemma is clear in the stories that the immigrants tell.

Virginia Rosales, a 44-year-old onion picker who lives in Alton, Texas, is worried about her daughter. Standing in line recently under the crushing sun while waiting for a cheese giveaway at City Hall, Rosales, a legal resident, said that 21-year-old Marta Alicia came illegally to the States in 1978—well before the required 1982 date.

The problem is that Marta has worked only for her mother, babysitting for her younger brother and sister while Rosales worked in the fields. Rosales worries that the INS will be very skeptical when Marta offers this thin evidence—work for her mother—as her proof that she has been in the States since before 1982. And without legalization, the mother wonders, how will Marta find a real job?

"All my people live here," Rosales said through an interpreter. "It will be very, very hard" for Marta to go back to Mexico if she is denied amnesty.

Farm worker Marco Antonio Vasquez is

(continued)

worried about his wife, Petra. She has been raising their two small children at home. Because she hasn't been working, he fears that she doesn't have enough documentation to prove that she has been in the States since before 1982.

His sister, Criselda Vasquez de Salgado, has been working in the fields, but she says she doesn't have pay receipts to prove it. Neither does she have rent receipts, because she had been living in a relative's house.

"I don't know what we can do," says Marco Vasquez, who himself faces possible disqualification as a "public charge" because he has periodically accepted food stamps. "They can't send [my wife] to Mexico," he says through an interpreter. "They can't send her—our children were born here."

But the INS indeed can deport illegal aliens even if they are the parents of children born in the United States.

SOURCE. Fawn Vrazo. 1987. "Immigrants face new amnesty fear: Split families." *The Philadelphia Inquirer* (May 31). Reprinted by permission of *The Philadelphia Inquirer* May 31, 1987.

practices of the traditional family and the *compadrazqo* have been declining in the face of the pressures of the more-militant young Mexican-Americans (Chicanos). Similarly, these practices are in decline throughout Latin America and in many Mediterranean nations; however, they still maintain a viable force in the *barrios*, even where the dynamics of urban life strain traditional practices. Cortes explains: "Although these traditional structures and practices have eroded among all immigrant groups, it is likely that they have survived more widely among Mexican-Americans because of their historical isolation, residential segregation, continuing immigration, geographical proximity to Mexico, and deep commitment to these social institutions" (1980:714).

Ruth Horowitz's (1983) monograph *Honor and the American Dream* is an excellent study of an inner-city Chicano community in Chicago. (She refers to all people of Mexican ancestry in the United States as Chicanos and therefore her use of this term differs from the political implications noted previously.) She finds support for Cortes' belief that *compadres* serve, in part, to maintain cultural continuity. In addition, the naming of friends as *compadres* not only strengthens the relationships with each other, but also "the mutual obligations further strengthen the relationship of the entire expanded family unit both as a symbol of their cohesiveness and because they need each other" (Horowitz, 1983:56). Horowitz observes that the exchange of economic and personal services is frequently needed since these families rarely turn to outside agencies such as public welfare or public employment. This help is regarded as a failure of a family's solidarity and social worth. In addition, *compadres* and relatives provide emotional and social support.

> Having a large, close family that can be augmented by *compadres* who can and will readily help in time of need is very highly valued. Being seen as a cohesive family transcends economic success. In such a family on 32nd Street and in other Chicano communities, members lend each other money, locate a car mechanic, and help out in innumerable other situations. "We can hardly keep track of all the money that goes around between us anymore. We just assume it's about equal," a young couple declared while discussing the state of their finances and their family's aid. (Horowitz, 1983:57)

Horowitz goes on to observe that the strong network of intergenerational ties among the families fosters the continuation of traditional gender-role relationships in the family. Horowitz sees the articulation of gender–family role relationships in terms of male domination, virginity, motherhood, and respect. Manhood is defined in terms of independence, personal strength, situational control, and dominance over wives and daughters. Great importance is given to a daughter's identity as a virgin. Tension is seen in the more-assimilated young woman's attempt for autonomy over parental control regarding dating and freedom to do things unsupervised, and the parents' desire to assure that such activities are not perceived as the activities of nonvirgins. Motherhood is the culturally acceptable identity; the role of independent career woman is not. Women's identities are anchored in their familial roles as wives, sisters, and mothers. Respect, another symbol of family life, refers to systems of chivalry and etiquette that formalize social interaction both in the family and in the community. Formal rules delineate ways of acting; for example, swearing in front of females is strictly forbidden, older people must be greeted with courtesy, and insolence or rudeness is not tolerated within the home.

Horowitz believes that these symbols of family life, taken together, provide order and stability for everyday social interactions in the context of an urban community that is highly industrialized and educated. Yet the changing nature of urban life results in many circumstances that prove problematic for the traditional culture. Horowitz focuses on the ambiguity and conflict that are found in the expectations concerning gender-role behavior and child–parent relationships particularly faced by youths. "Youths are caught between the traditional model of social relationships and the urban Chicago reality: the streets, the school, the media, and the job scene. With the freedom they take or are given, the youths are faced with many dilemmas as they venture beyond the confines of the communal and familial order" (Horowitz, 1983:76).

Similarly, Lea Ybarra (1982) has investigated changes in Mexican-American family life in Fresno, California. Her study of 100 married couples found that marital-role relations ranged from a patriarchal pattern to a completely egalitarian one. However, the most prevalent pattern was one in which the husband and wife shared in decisions. The factor that appeared to have the strongest impact on whether household chores and child care would be shared between spouses was whether or not the wife was employed outside the home. These families demonstrated a more-egalitarian family pattern relative to decision making, sharing of household tasks, and caring of children. Further, in her investigation of other studies of Mexican-American families in different regions of the United States, Ybarra found that egalitarianism was the predominant conjugal-role relationship. Similarly, Staples and Mirande (1980) found that "virtually every systematic study of conjugal roles in the Chicano family has found egalitarianism to be the predominant pattern across socioeconomic groups, educational levels, urban–rural residence, and region of the country." Such findings led Ybarra to question previously accepted assumptions on the nature of Mexican-American family life that more often than not viewed it negatively, especially compared to "mainstream" American family life.

Ybarra touches on an important critique that has been made of the biases inherent in many of these studies. Staples and Mirande (1980) have observed that much of the research has a pejorative view of the Mexican-American family. This research, based on psychoanalytical assumptions, examines *machismo* (masculine patriarchal authority) as the key variable in explaining the dynamics of both family life and culture, seeing *machismo* as a compensation for powerlessness resulting from feelings of inadequacy, inferiority, and rejection of authority. However, beginning with the influential studies by Miguel Montiel (1970, 1972), "the social science myth of the Mexican-American family" has been exposed.

This myth developed a pathological view of Mexican-American culture in terms of three characteristics: fatalism; patriarchy; and familism, or strong orientation to kin. *Machismo* was not equated with honor, respect, and dignity; it was defined in terms of power, control, and violence (Staples and Mirande, 1980). Murillo (1971:101) has redefined *machismo* in positive terms: "An important part of the [father's] concept of machismo . . . is that [of] using his authority within the family in a just and fair manner." Similarly, the family is depicted in terms of its warmth and nurturance and providing emotional security and a sense of belonging to family members. This pattern continues through generations and "the mother continues to be close and warm, serving and nurturing even when her children are grown, married, and having children of their own'' (Murillo, 1971:104).

In summary, this overview of the Mexican-American family has sought to demonstrate that the understanding of this ethnic group has been distorted by both social and intellectual biases. Ruth Horowitz has observed that the understanding of Mexican-American family structure and dynamics must be viewed in the context of community involvement. The economic hardships often faced by Mexican-Americans, whether in the urban *barrios* or in agricultural regions where they make up a large percentage of the migrant labor force, plays a crucial role in the articulation of patterns of adaptation and survival of the family. In recent years, the Chicano movement has resulted in an attempt to overcome economic discrimination and subordination while maintaining familial cultural values. As Ruth Horowitz observes of the Mexican-American family system (which, in principle, also holds true for the other groups that make up America's ethnic heritage):

> Some aspects of culture, such as the expanded family network, will survive, even if their content alters slightly by ecological or class changes. Not only do Mexican-Americans have a low divorce rate compared with other ethnic groups, regardless of the length of United States residency and location, but the expanded family network remains the valued and predominant family form. Some traditions may persist much longer than any class-based theory would hypothesize, while other symbols, values, and norms may change as community members achieve greater economic stability and begin to spread through the city and into the suburbs. The United States as a melting pot may not only be unachievable but undesirable. Why should everyone be the same? (Horowitz, 1983:235)

Conclusion

This chapter examined ethnic-family variations within the community setting. We utilized a social-historical context with a focus on immigration patterns and the sociological response and analysis of those patterns. Our discussion began with an historical overview of the "new" immigration of the late nineteenth and early twentieth centuries. The setting was New York City and Chicago, and the particular concern was on family dynamics of Italian and Jewish immigrants. The social-disorganization biases of the Chicago School of sociology were shown to have distorted and underemphasized the integrative effects of the family and community institutions in the assimilation patterns of these immigrant groups.

We followed the emerging patterns of these two southern and eastern European peoples as they moved from immigrant-family status to ethnic-family status. We saw that both Italian-Americans and Jewish-Americans have undergone significant cultural changes as they experienced America in the twentieth century. The resultant ethnic-family variations were seen as a consequence of cultural background; recency of migration; residency and geographical locale; socioeconomic status; educational achievement; upward mobility; and political, social, and religious factors. We emphasized how ethnic families not only have been affected by social change but also have affected it. The result is that, for these two groups of hyphenated Americans, the resultant family patterns have been a consequence of their active participation in the Americanization process—acting on it as well as being affected by it.

Similarly, when we switched our focus to the Japanese-American and the Mexican-American experiences, we found further evidence of the active role that these ethnic groups have had in determining their family structure and cultural dynamics. The changing assimilation patterns of these two ethnic groups was discussed within the specific social-historical contexts of their respective experiences in the United States. Prejudices and biases — along with social, political, cultural, and economic discrimination patterns and processes by local, state, and federal government agencies — were seen to have affected these ethnic groups. Their adaptation to both formal and informal discriminatory policies and practices was discussed and analyzed.

In the following chapter, we continue our study of the diversity of the American family experience within the community context by examining families living under poverty conditions. In addition, we broaden our understanding of the impact of poverty on family dynamics by opening with a cross-cultural examination of poverty and family systems in Latin America.

CHAPTER 6

Poverty Families in Communities

Earl Dotter/Archive

Disabled miner and family in Eastern Kentucky coal camp.

CHAPTER OUTLINE

In the preceding chapters of Part II, we discussed how the sociological model of the city, which stresses the social-disorganizational qualities of city life and its negative implications for the family, has influenced sociologists in their descriptive analysis of the city. In particular, the dichotomization of rural and urban life through the use of various ideal-type conceptual constructs has led many sociologists to stress the positive qualities of rural life and to develop nostalgic views of the rural-family system. Conversely, the model of urban life has been essentially negative, focusing on the social disorganization of the city and its consequences—alienation, anomie, social isolation, family isolation, juvenile deliquency, crime, child abuse, separation, and divorce.

In our examination of the family in American cities (and the working-class families of Bethnel Green, London), in African cities, and in immigrant families and their ethnic descendants, we see that the previously held position was an oversimplification of reality. In particular, studies of working-class urban villagers—both in the United States and in England—who resided in closed communities are seen to have an urban way of life. These studies emphasized the importance of neighborhood ties and relationships with relatives, friends, and neighbors in the tightly knit community. These communities were relatively homogeneous and, as far as possible, excluded outsiders from involvement in the community. (As an aside, it is important to note that the contemporary controversies centering around the issues of school busing and community control of schools may be seen as a manifestation of this closed-community solidarity ethos of these urban villagers. Although racial undertones are also present, it would be an oversimplification to analyze this conflict solely in racial terms.)

We also examined the validity of the social-disorganization model in our study of immigrant and later ethnic-family systems. Unlike the predicted model developed by the Chicago School and by Louis Wirth, these centers were and are characterized by social organization and viable family structures.

Although the model of Wirth and other proponents of the social-disorganization school has lost validity for its oversimplifications and distortions in depicting a debilitating urban way of life for all city dwellers, the model has continued to be used in the analysis of the poverty classes. In addition, both in anthropology and in sociology, a viewpoint has been developed that stems from this position and stresses the development of a *culture of poverty* by those individuals and families who live in poverty conditions. This culture exhibits all the negative qualities associated with social disorganization. This viewpoint argues that there exists a culture among the poor that transcends given societies and exists in the slums, ghettos, and squatter settlements of the United States, Latin America, Africa, and Asia—wherever a capitalistic economy exists. The people and families who exhibit this culture of poverty tend to share similar attitudinal and behavioral patterns relating to the family, work, and the given society. In this chapter, we investigate the poverty family in light of the social policy implications of the contemporary social-disorganizational framework—the culture of poverty. Our focus is on the poor of the United States and of Latin America.

Squatter Settlements and Poverty Families

The geographer Brian J.L. Berry (1973) points out that it is in the Third World societies of Latin America, Africa, and Asia where the major thrust of urban growth is occurring. While the industrialized societies of the world have increased in urban population from 198 million to approximately 546 million in the last 50 years, the urban population of Third World societies has increased from 69 million to 464 million. Although the Third World accounted for only 25 percent of the world's urban population in 1920, it is estimated that it accounted for 51 percent in 1980.

It is important that we emphasize a major variation in the urban growth patterns of Third World societies and industrial societies. The rapid urbanization of the industrial societies of western Europe and North America occurred at the time when these societies had the highest level of economic development. In contrast, the contemporary accelerated growth occurring in the Third World is taking place in the countries with the lowest level of economic development. Berry (1973:74) also notes that this urban growth is occurring in countries with the lowest life expectancy at birth, nutrition, energy consumption, and education. In addition, Third World urbanization, although it involves greater numbers of people than it did for the industrial societies, is characterized by less industrialization. One consequence of this is that many of the population are unemployed or finding marginal employment in the cities.

A further striking variation in the Third World urbanization patterns is the development of peripheral settlements, squatter settlements, around a city; they serve in transforming rural societies into urban societies and account for a substantial percentage of the urban population. The squatter settlements are shantytowns that have sprung up around large cities, largely because of the inability of the governments in those cities to provide adequate housing for the overwhelming influx of migrants. The residents are migrants from rural areas who have banded together and have established squatter settlements by constructing their own houses on land, both publicly and privately owned, usually against the armed opposition of the government. Often these settlements, as in Latin America, disregard urban planning and building regulations; nevertheless, they provide "uniquely satisfactory opportunities for low income settlers" in that they are built according to the needs of the inhabitants in terms of social and economic urban changes (Turner, 1970:10).

John F.C. Turner (1969) cites a United Nations report estimating that during the 1960s, over 200 million people migrated into the Third World cities of Asia, Africa, and Latin America. "One-and-a-half million people, over one third of the population of Mexico City, live in the 'colonias proletarias'—known originally as 'barrios paradaidaristas' or 'parachutists' neighborhoods; nearly half of Ankara's [Turkey] population of 1,500,000 live in the 'gecekondu'—the squatter settlements whose name describes an overnight house-builder; the area of the 'villes extracoutumiers' of Kinshasa is greater than that of the city itself" (Turner, 1969:507). The housing problem of these newcomers is not unique to the Third World; in France, the *bidonvilles* ("tin-can towns") surrounding Paris house over 100,000 North African and Portuguese migrants in flimsy wood-and-cement dwellings and in abandoned buses.

Turner points out that squatter settlements vary greatly in terms of permanency and security of tenure settlement and in the financial and social resources of its inhabitants. A correlation exists between the conditions of the settlement with the wealth and income levels of a given society's population. The *bustee* settlements of

Old Delhi, India, are among the poorest, whereas the *cuevas barriada* of Lima, Peru, has residents whose income approaches that of the average working-class level. Settlements such as those in Peru are seen to be transitory phenomena that will eventually evolve into working-class suburban areas; however, their present state is merely at, or a little above, the poverty level. William Mangin presents a vivid picture of the *barriadas* around Lima:

> At worst a "barriada" is a crowded, helter-skelter hodgepodge of inadequate straw houses with no water supply and no provision for sewage disposal; parts of many are like this. Most do not have a rough plan, and most inhabitants convert their original houses to more substantial structures as soon as they can. Construction activity usually involving family, neighbors, and friends is a constant feature of "barriada" life and, although water and sewage usually remain critical problems, a livable situation is reached with respect to them.
> For most of the migrants the "barriada" represents a definite improvement in terms of housing and general income, and Lima represents an improvement over the semi-feudal life of the Indian, "Cholo," or lower-class mestizo. (Mangin, 1960:911–917)

The people who inhabit the barriada are portrayed in the following manner:

> The early stereotype held by most middle- and upper-class Peruvians of the barriada dwellers as illiterate, nonproductive, lawless, recent communistic Indian migrants is still held by many—but is giving way among young architects, politicians, academics, and anthropologists to an equally false picture. Perhaps as an antidote to the first, it paints them as happy, contented, literate, productive, adjusted, politically conservative—forever patriotic citizens. They are, in fact, about like the vast majority of Peruvians, moderately to desperately poor, cynical *and* trusting of politicians, bishops, outside agitators, and their own local leaders. They are alternately hopeful and despairing about the future of their children and themselves. They love and resent their children and their parents. They are, in short, human beings. (Mangin, 1968:56)

Life in the squatter settlements has been portrayed in two predominant conceptualizations. The first and more-prevalent emphasizes the chaotic and socially disorganized aspects of the settlement; marital breakdowns, anomie, alienation, poverty, and misery are the lot of the migrant population. The second position takes an opposite stance; it argues that the settlement is able to maintain community organization and family continuity and that the residents have the general ability to adjust to the somewhat overwhelming demands of the potentially debilitating consequences of urban poverty.

As we have discussed, the social-disorganization approach stems from the intellectual tradition in the social sciences that has developed an ideal-type dichotomization of rural and urban life. The ideal typification of rural life stresses the group solidarity and the primacy of personal relationships anchored by familial and kinship bonds. The typification of urban life, on the other hand, sees the development of secondary relationships based on a pragmatic philosophy of looking out for oneself; the absence of viable family and neighborhood relationships, which ultimately lead to social and personal disorganization; the breakdown of personal integration; and crime, delinquency, and individual isolation.

In a powerful and moving autobiographical account, Carolina Marie de Jesus (1962) reports on the impact of extreme poverty on people's lives in the *favela* (squatter settlement) that is an integral part of one of the most beautiful cities in the world—São Paulo, Brazil. She describes the life of quiet desperation; a life without rest or relaxation. The daily search of garbage, for either junk that might have some resale value or even food, and its often dire consequences is recounted in this poignant passage.

Yesterday I ate that macaroni from the garbage with fear of death, because in 1953 I sold scrap over there in Zinho [a section of São Paulo, Brazil]. There was a pretty little black boy. He also went to sell scrap in Zinho. He was young and said that those who should look for paper were the old. One day I was collecting scrap when I stopped at Bom Jardim Avenue. Someone had thrown meat into the garbage, and he was picking out the pieces. He told me:

"Take some, Carolina. It's still fit to eat."

He gave me some, and so as not to hurt his feelings, I accepted. I tried to convince him not to eat that meat, or the hard bread gnawed by the rats. He told me no, because it was two days since he had eaten. He made a fire and roasted the meat. His hunger was so great that he couldn't wait for the meat to cook. He heated it and ate. So as not to remember that scene, I left thinking: I'm going to pretend I wasn't there. This can't be real in a rich country like mine. I was disgusted with that Social Service that had been created to readjust the maladjusted, but took no notice of we marginal people. I sold the scrap at Zinho and returned to São Paulo's back yard, the favela.

The next day I found that little black boy dead. His toes were spread apart. The space must have been eight inches between them. He had blown up as if made out of rubber. His toes looked like a fan. He had no documents. He was buried like any other "Joe." Nobody tried to find out his name. The marginal people don't have names. . . .

The children eat a lot of bread. They like soft bread but when they don't have it, they eat hard bread.

Hard is the bread that we eat. Hard is the bed on which we sleep. Hard is the life of the *favelade.*.

Oh, São Paulo! A queen that vainly shows her skyscrapers that are her crown of gold. All dressed up in velvet and silk but with cheap stockings underneath—the favela. (Carolina Maria de Jesus, 1962:41,42)

The problems of urban life may be seen to fall most heavily on those who do not have the financial resources to cope with the monetary demands of urban life and who do not have the personal contacts to provide them with aid in times of need. The social group that is at the greatest disadvantage is the poverty class. We examine the poverty classes in this chapter, focusing on the family structure of these people. Following Rodman (1971), we believe that the study of poverty families' behavior and values is important in that they provide information on a people's culture. The family represents the major organizational group in which adaptations are made to poverty conditions; thus it provides a convenient analytical unit in which to examine the ways of life of people living in poverty.

An additional factor that supports our contention of looking at the family in poverty is that the family has been the focal point for much of the intellectual discussion on the consequences of poverty on individuals, and it has also served as the center of social-policy programs aimed at helping the poor. A notable, and somewhat notorious, illustration is the controversy surrounding a policy document of the U.S. Government, *The Negro Family: The Case for National Action* (U.S. Department of Labor, 1965)—known as the Moynihan report. The framework for our discussion is the contemporary social-disorganizational position—the culture of poverty—which stresses cultural or subcultural developments in poverty families that prevent them from taking advantage of occupational opportunities—if and when they occur. The opposing position stresses the conditions under poverty to which poor families must adapt and that account for the different behavioral forms such families take in contrast to the more affluent families in society. As we will see, the intellectual stance that is advocated, culture or conditions, not only has implications for the analysis of poverty families but also plays a strong role in determining the nature and extent of governmental policies relating to the poor. We illustrate our discussion by exploring

Residents of a Lima Shantytown Improve Their Lot

BY H. G. BISSINGER

LIMA, Peru—Adela Huaman needed only one word to describe all that was here when she came to this pocket of Lima called Villa El Salvador 10 years ago: *Desert.*

For the Huaman family—living in a home made of straw, shivering against the winds that blew from the foothills each night—there was nothing else except an endless vista of sand. The family had no electricity, no running water.

"We suffered very much at the beginning," said the 31-year-old mother of eight. "Sometimes I thought I could not stand it. I thought of leaving. Some people could not take it and left."

Hers is a common saga for hundreds of thousands who, in the perception that the capital holds jobs and hope, have come to Lima and have been forced to make do in the desert settlements that ring the city. Their communities are called *pueblos jovenes*, which means "young towns." Most people refer to them as shantytowns.

There are hundreds of them, some as small as a collection of 40 shacks, others as big as small cities. In conditions that are empty and invariably impoverished, they are home to an estimated one-third of Lima's four million residents.

For Huaman, however, life in the *pueblo joven* of Villa El Salvador took on a rare twist: It changed for the better.

Since its inception 15 years ago, the residents of Villa El Salvador have fought to improve the quality of life there, refusing to cave in to physical surroundings that make any kind of viable life seem unattainable.

Among Lima's *pueblos jovenes*, it is considered the best example of what can be done through solidarity and commitment— and virtually everything accomplished there has been done without any financial support of the government.

"Villa El Salvador is a model," said Mario Zolezzi, Lima's secretary of urban development. "In other places, because of poverty, they live from day to day. In Villa El Salvador, they always have plans for the future."

The efforts of the community of 300,000, which is considered a separate political district of Lima and has its own elected mayor, have not gone unnoticed outside Peru.

Villa El Salvador has been nominated for the Nobel Peace Prize this year. In February 1985, Pope John Paul II made a visit during a Latin American tour, and he was so stirred by what he saw as he stood before one million people on a patch of sand that he threw away his prepared remarks and told the residents he knew of their "hunger for God and hunger for bread."

Lima as a whole is not as well off. In total, 45 percent of Lima's residents have running water, compared with 80 percent in Villa El Salvador. Twenty percent of Lima's residents live without electricity; only 5 percent of Villa El Salvador's do.

"I feel happy," said Huaman, who now lives in a home built of brick. "Now everything here is organized."

Massive poverty still exists here. Mayor Michel Azcueta said 70 percent of the town's work force is either unemployed or underemployed. The annual per capita income is about $670.

The streets, nothing more than sandy strips between rows of brick houses in varying states of completion, are littered with garbage. As children played soccer with a small gray ball, they had to dodge mangy dogs roaming for food.

Nonetheless, the advances made by the community have been remarkable, and many residents give credit to Azcueta, who came here in 1971 to start an educational program.

He helped organize one of the community's first projects: the construction of eight schools. And every night after work, the soft-spoken Azcueta recalled, residents donned hard hats with kerosene lamps and built hundreds of wells. Later, the government supplied utility poles and the residents supplied the money to buy electrical wires to connect the town to the city's power system.

(continued)

Villa El Salvador also was helped in its early stages by the attitude of the Peruvian government, then under military rule. Instead of forcing the residents of Villa El Salvador to leave land on which they had no legal claim, the government—perhaps fearing an uprising—sanctioned their presence. In 1981, after Peru had returned to a democracy, President Fernando Belaunde Terry made all the existing *pueblos jovenes* in Lima legal entities.

"It took us seven years to have light and water," said Azcueta, 39, who was born and educated in Spain and has a doctorate in education. "There are other shantytowns much older that don't even have that now."

Overall, Azcueta said, the community has established nine medical centers, 34 schools, 150 nurseries, 22 markets and a sports complex. Communal kitchens to feed the needy have been established.

As he stood on a hill overlooking the area, Azcueta could see what many consider the most impressive accomplishment of all: the eucalyptus trees.

More than 1,000 of them zigzag across the landscape, providing rows of green amid the desert's barren brown. Trees, fruit, corn and grass for cattle are being cultivated under a program that started in 1980 and utilizes the community's sewage wastes for irrigation and fertilization.

Azcueta downplays his role in the community's growth. "There has always been an atmosphere of happiness in Villa El Salvador even when there was no water or light," he says.

Elda Munive came here with her husband and children a dozen years ago. It was "hard at first," she recalled, but little by little, improvements were made. Like many of the town's residents, the Munives built their modest three-room brick home piece by piece with whatever money they managed to save.

"We have started Villa El Salvador," Munive said, "and we have to stay."

SOURCE. H. G. Bissinger. 1986. "Residents of a Lima shantytown improve their lot." *The Philadelphia Inquirer* (Aug. 9). Reprinted by permission of *The Philadelphia Inquirer* Aug. 9, 1986.

how these opposing positions have been utilized in the study of the poverty classes and family systems in the United States and in Latin America.

Oscar Lewis and the Culture of Poverty

Oscar Lewis' studies of the poor in Mexico, Puerto Rico, and New York have appeared in a series of anthropological monographs that have stimulated a vast amount of interest in both academic and public circles. His biographical analysis and sympathetic portrayal of different families are organized around a conceptual framework that he called the culture of poverty.

In *La Vida: A Puerto Rican Family in the Culture Of Poverty—San Juan and New York*, Lewis presents a benumbing and almost overwhelming portrayal of three generations of a Puerto Rican family in the slums of San Juan and New York. He portrays through a family biographical framework (much of which is told in the tape-recorded words of the subjects themselves), "the life histories of the individuals . . . reveal[ing] a picture of family disruption, violence, brutality, cheapness of life, lack of love, lack of education, lack of medical facilities—in short, a picture of incredible deprivation, the effects of which cannot be wiped out in a single generation" (O. Lewis, 1966:xiv). Lewis believes that the study of specific families can best help us understand the relationship between societal institutions and the individual. Through intensive analysis of family systems, the interrelationship between culture and personality becomes meaningful with "whole-family studies bridg[ing] the gap between the conceptual extremes of culture at one pole and the individual at the other" (O. Lewis, 1966:xx).

Lewis contends that people who live in capitalistic societies under the poverty

Homeless children spending the night on Copacabana Beach,
Rio de Janeiro, Brazil.

conditions of slums, ghettos, and squatter settlements develop similar family structures, interpersonal relationships, and value systems that transcend national boundaries. The culture of poverty is seen to flourish in societies that have the following
characteristics: high rate of unemployment and underemployment, low wages for
manual labor, stress on the importance of accumulated wealth and property, and an
interpretation that attributes the lack of the accumulation of wealth by the poverty
people residing in these societies as a result of their personal inadequacies and
inferiorities. In these societies, a virtually autonomous subculture exists among the
poor, one which is self-perpetuating and self-defeating. Oscar Lewis sees the culture
of poverty developing from families adapting to societal conditions. These adaptations represent an effort to cope with the feelings of hopelessness and despair that
arise from their realization that achieving success in terms of the prevailing values
and goals is improbable. This hopelessness and despair, this sense of resignation and
fatalism, involves an inability to put off the satisfaction of immediate desires to plan
for the future. A self-perpetuating cycle develops: Low educational motivation leads
to inadequate job preparation that, in turn, perpetuates unemployment, poverty, and
despair.

The culture of poverty, however, is not only an adaptation to a set of objective conditions of the larger society. Once it comes into existence it tends to perpetuate itself from generation to generation because of its effect on the children. By the time slum children are age six or seven they have usually absorbed the basic values and attitudes of their subculture and are not psychologically geared to take full advantage of changing conditions or increased opportunities which may occur in their lifetime. (Lewis, 1966:xiv)

Oscar Lewis points out that in African towns, where a tribal heritage is still strong and village relationships carry over into the towns, the culture of poverty does not appear. The tribe and ethnic group organize the social life of the impoverished migrant town dweller. In a similar way, the caste and clan system of India provides members of the lower impoverished castes a sense of identity and belonging that integrates them into the larger society. The Jews of Eastern Europe are seen as another exception. Although poor, they escaped from many of the traits of the culture of poverty because of their traditions of literacy and learning and the strong communal solidarity centered around their religion, rabbis, and the proliferation of voluntary associations. The fourth exception is speculative and relates to socialism, particularly in Cuba. Although poverty conditions still exist, Oscar Lewis reports little evidence of the despair, apathy, and hopelessness that are characteristic of urban slum dwellers in capitalistic societies. He attributes this to the people's optimism about a better life in the future, the highly organized structure of the community, and a concomitant new sense of power and importance. "They were armed and were given a doctrine which glorified the lower class as the hope of humanity" (O. Lewis, 1966:xlix). A final exception is that of preliterate people living at subsistence levels who suffer from dire poverty and the absence of technology. These people do not exhibit the culture of poverty because of strong communal organization that centers around the tribal band and band chiefs, tribal councils, and local self-government.

Oscar Lewis's (1966) studies identify over 70 traits that characterize the culture of poverty. They are grouped by him into four major categories: the relationship between the subculture and the larger society; the nature of the ghetto, slum, or squatter settlement community; the nature of the family; and the attitudes, values, and character structure of the individual.

1. *The relationship between the subculture and the larger society.* Lewis believes that one of the most crucial characteristics of the culture of poverty is the disengagement and nonintegration of the poor in the major institutions of the larger society. Poverty, segregation and discrimination, fear, suspicion, and apathy are all factors accounting for this lack of effective participation, especially in the larger economic system. Low wages, chronic unemployment, and underemployment lead to low incomes, little savings, the use of the services of exploitative money lenders, the payment of high prices for used furniture and secondhand clothing, and the overpayment for smaller quantities of food staples. There is a low level of literacy and education among the poor that further aggravates the situation.

Although exposed to middle-class values, poor people, on the whole, do not live by them. For example, although many will claim that marriage by law, by the church, or by both is ideal, few will marry. For those with few job prospects, no property, and with little expectation for improvement in the future, a consensual marriage or free union makes good sense and avoids the legal expenses and difficulties involved in marriage and divorce. Women will often turn down marital offers because they feel that it will unnecessarily tie them down to men who are immature, difficult, and generally unreliable. As with the men, the women feel that a consensual union gives them greater freedom and flexibility. By not giving the fathers of their children legal status as husbands, the women have a stronger claim on the children and also maintain exclusive rights to their own property.

2. *The nature of the ghetto, slum, or squatter settlement community.* Poor housing conditions, crowding, and gregariousness characterize the slum community. More important, however, is the minimum of organization beyond the nuclear and extended family. Oscar Lewis (1966) observes that most preliterate people have achieved a higher level of sociocultural organization than the urban slum dweller.

3. *The nature of the family.* The family in the culture of poverty is characterized by the absence of the middle-class trait that cherishes childhood as a specially prolonged and protected stage in the life cycle. In the culture of poverty there is, for example, an early initiation into sex. Free unions or consensual marriages are common, and there is a relatively high incidence of the abandonment of wives and children by men. With the instability of consensual marriage, the family tends to be mother-centered and tied more closely with the mother's extended family of orientation. The female-centered household is given to authoritarianism. Although there is lip service given to family solidarity, it is rarely achieved because of intense sibling rivalry for the limited supply of goods and maternal affection.

4. *The attitudes, values, and character structure of the individual.* Individuals who grow up in the culture of poverty have strong feelings of fatalism, helplessness, dependence, and inferiority. Oscar Lewis (1966) points out that these characteristics are common among black Americans who have the additional disadvantage of racial discrimination; they are also prominent in slum dwellers in Mexico City and San Juan who are not segregated or subject to discrimination as distinct ethnic or racial groups. He lists other traits including a high incidence of weak ego structure; confusion of sexual identification, which reflects maternal deprivation; a strong present-time orientation, with relatively little disposition to delay gratification or plan for the future; and a high tolerance for psychological pathology of all kinds. Finally, there is a widespread belief in male superiority and, among men, a strong preoccupation with machismo (masculinity).

Critique of the Culture of Poverty: The Analysis of Squatter Settlements

The urban anthropologist William Mangin (1970), reviewing the literature on squatter settlements in Peru, Turkey, Athens, Hong Kong, and Brazil, reports that they are characterized by an absence of the culture of poverty. He further points out that the poor of a given country have more in common with their compatriots in that country than with the poor in other societies. For example, the poor of Mexico and Puerto Rico are seen to have more in common with the general population of their respective countries than they do with the poor of France or Pakistan: "In terms of cultural views of the world, ideal family and kinship patterns, aspirations, values, and even body movements and language habits, the poor of a country have more in common with the rest of their country (or culture) than they have with the poor of another country (or culture)" (Mangin, 1970:xvii).

Oscar Lewis' culture of poverty position is similar to the social-disorganization view that sees the impact of urbanization in terms of depersonalization and anomie with the poverty community almost totally devoid of community and associational life. However, as Charles Valentine has pointed out (1968), Lewis himself contradicts this position in his description of La Esmeralda:

> The setting for the story of the Ries family is La Esmeralda, an old and colorful slum in San Juan, built on a steep embankment between the city's ancient fort walls and

the sea. Squeezed into an area not more than five city blocks long and a few hundred yards wide are 900 houses inhabited by 3,600 people. . . .

Seen from the walls above, the slum looks almost prosperous. This is because all the houses have roofs of new green tar paper. . . .

Even though La Esmeralda is only ten minutes away from the heart of San Juan, it is physically and socially marginal to the city. The wall above it stands as a kind of symbol separating it from the city. La Esmeralda forms *a little community of its own* [italics added] with a cemetery, a church, a small dispensary and maternity clinic, and one elementary school. There are many small stores, bars and taverns. . . .

To the people of Greater San Juan, La Esmeralda has a bad reputa- tion . . . today the residents of La Esmeralda think of it as a relatively elegant healthful place, with its beautiful view of the sea, its paved streets, its new roofs, the absence of mosquitoes, the low rentals and its nearness to their places of work.

. . . the general mood of the people of La Esmeralda is one of gaiety and exuberance. They seem outgoing, friendly and expressive, with relatively little distrust of outsiders. They live amid constant noise from radios, juke boxes, and television sets, and spend a great deal of time in the stores and bars, where they drink and play dominoes. (O. Lewis, 1966:xxxii–xxxiii)

Among the town dwellers in sub-Saharan African cities, there is the continued presence of traditional networks of social relations, which have facilitated the adop- tion and assimilation of migrants into city life. The voluntary associations found in African cities, combined with the persistence of extended kinship relationships, assures the continuity of rural ways in the city and has resulted in the strengthening of tribal consciousness in the new urban environment.

Janet L. Abu-Lughod's (1961) analysis of Cairo, Egypt, and Edward M. Bruner's (1963) study of Medan, Sumatra, Indonesia, contradicted the social-disorganization position on the existence of anonymity, alienation, and absence of primary relation- ships. Bruner's study concluded that the Medan migrants were part of a single kinship community. Every person in the kinship community was bound by multiple ties in a wide-ranging kinship network that once established, structures all subsequent interactions, including those with voluntary associations. He believed that the Batak clan groups of Medan are similar to the clan associations of the overseas Chinese, to the tribal associations of West Africa, and to the *Zaibatsu* of industrial Japan. Further, he hypothesized that future research on peasant communities in societies undergoing rapid cultural change and urbanization will "disclose not only the maintenance of existing kinship ties, but also the development of novel and stable recombinations based upon traditional structural principles" (Bruner, 1963:134).

Charles A. Valentine (1968), who has written a much-cited critique on the culture of poverty, argues that the essence of that position is the comparison of the lifeways of groups who live by a distinctive poverty culture consisting largely of negative qualities, lacks and absences — group disintegration, personal disintegration, and lack of purposeful action — in contrast to that of the more-affluent segments of the population, who exhibit positive qualities. It is further argued that the poor maintain a self-perpetuating and self-defeating way of life.

Valentine poses an alternative interpretation by suggesting that the destructive nature of the social life of these poverty-level people is determined by the structure of the society as a whole, as well as by forces beyond the control of poor people; that is, the variations in lifestyles of the poor are not shaped by a distinct culture. Rather, they are influenced by the actual conditions of life under poverty that is inconsistent with the fulfillment of the cultural design. Mangin (1970) reaches a similar conclu- sion. He criticizes the view of the cyclical nature of the culture of poverty — the passing down of the patterns from one generation to the next. Mangin believes that it is necessary to emphasize the fact that peasant communities are part of the larger society and that decisions made by the more-powerful elements of the society relating to the peasant community are more important in maintaining their economic depression than are any questionable social and personality attributes of the poor. "It is to the advantage of commercial interests and the middle classes, as well as to some peasant leaders and professional leaders of the poor, to maintain social systems with large numbers of peasants and poor people on the bottom rungs" (Mangin, 1970:xxviii).

Valentine (1968) applies this perspective to the family and argues that varieties in family patterns of the poor can be seen as adaptations to the externally imposed conditions of poverty. More specifically, consensual unions and female-centered or mother-centered households may be regarded as flexible adaptations to the uncertainty and fluctuations of economic circumstances. Thus, alternative family structures are developed as necessities to cope with poverty conditions and should be seen as positive contributions to the health and well-being of family members. The following family adaptations are viewed by Valentine as responses to economic deprivation:

> Separation by mutual consent, sometimes including considerations of alternative means of support for mother and children.
> Informal and extralegal but effective adoption which shifts dependents to households better able to support them.
> Attenuated affinity, in which kin ties and support sources established through the marital union continue to function in the absence of the husband.
> Reunion, planned or otherwise, after temporary separation.
> Support of fatherless families through other lines of kinship connection. (Valentine, 1968:267)

For children, socialization occurs in a wider network of relatives, adults, and peers rather than being concentrated in the nuclear family. Valentine asserts that this may contribute to healthy early maturity, including development of numerous supportive relationships and sources of emotional security.

In a similar vein, Hyman Rodman (1965) states that it would be more appropriate to interpret the behavior of poverty families (he uses the term, lower-class families) as *solutions to problems* they face—owing to life under poverty conditions—than as *problems*. In an insightful illustration, Rodman points out that the characteristics attributed to the poor—*promiscuous* sexual relationships, *illegitimate* children, *desertion* by husbands and fathers, *unmarried* mothers—use middle-class–biased terminology and distortions that tend to emphasize a social-disorganization model of family behavior. Rodman emphasizes that these italicized concepts are not utilized by the poor and that it is misleading to describe their behavior in this manner. Since such words as *promiscuity, illegitimacy,* and *desertion* have middle-class meanings and judgmental implications, Rodman believes that it is necessary to analyze and describe the family patterns of the poor by paying more attention to the language and description that the poor employ in analyzing their own behavior. By doing this, social scientists can avoid "the major middle-class conception of lower-class families—viewing certain patterns as problems, when in reality they can easily be viewed as solutions" (Rodman, 1965:225).

Rodman (1971) completed an ethnographic and explanatory description of lower-class family behavior and attitudes in Coconut Village, a small rural village in northeastern Trinidad. He documents how the use of the conceptualizations of the people themselves aids his own sociological analysis. Rodman focuses on lower-class family behavior and attitudes and the impact that poverty has on culture and family organization. Of particular interest to us is Rodman's concern with the validity of the culture of poverty theory to explain family patterns.

Rodman finds three types of marital or quasimarital relationships—friending, living, and married—in Trinidad. The three types vary in the degree of acceptance of marital responsibility, especially on the part of the man. During friending, which involves the least responsibility and occurs most frequently, the marital pair do not live together in the same household. In this form of relationship, the woman is supposed to make herself sexually available to the man at his leisure, and the man is supposed to provide support for the woman and any children they may have. Children ordinarily live with the mother, although they may live with the father if it is more convenient. Rodman reports that most friending relationships eventually dissolve, but a substantial number evolve into a living relationship. During living, the marital pair live together but are not legally married. The living relationship is seen to combine the advantages of common residence characteristic of legal marriage, without its legal responsibility but with the limited responsibility of friending.

Rodman reports that the living relationship is more common among the lower classes than marriage and usually precedes marriage when and if it occurs. This marital relationship is socially acceptable and has a reciprocal base with the husband contributing to the household and the wife carrying out the household chores of cooking, cleaning, and washing.

The married relationship, to all extents and purposes, is similar to a living relationship, but there is a church wedding and legal ties between the man and woman. The legal advantage of the marital relationship is that the woman is entitled to financial support from her husband; in a living relationship, only the man's children are eligible for such support. The marriage relationship occurs less frequently than the living among the lower class and is seen to reflect the reluctance to take on responsibility.

Rodman believes that the reluctance to take on the responsibility of marriage is closely related to the generally cautious attitude of both sexes in placing trust and confidence in the other, as well as to a shared feeling that any marital relationship is a temporary one. These attitudes reflect the relation of family life to the structure of the larger society, particularly to its economy. The lower-class families of Coconut Village suffer from economic deprivation. The land is poor and the meager crops that are produced are difficult to market because of inadequate transportation systems. Consequently, wage earning is necessary to supplement and, in most cases, to provide a more-reliable income base for the family. Unfortunately, wage earnings are unreliable: The lower-class man involved in wage labor finds much unemployment, underemployment, poorly paid employment, and unskilled employment. Since the man's role as wage earner and income provider is central to the family relationship, his status within the family is determined by his economic success. If the man is responsible for the financial support of his wife and children and his economic circumstances are so precarious, it becomes more understandable why men are reluctant to take on the additional responsibilities of marriage. The consequences for the man when he is unable satisfactorily to complete his duties as a wage earner are the loss of status, esteem, income power, and position in the community and in the family. It is this economic factor that explains the greater frequency of friending relationships than living relationships, living relationships than marriages. These variations provide the individual with different patterns to permit some semblance of family life in the face of economic uncertainties.

These three forms of marital and quasimarital relationships are seen by Rodman as being functional for the lower-class family since they provide solutions to social, economic, and legal problems. In response to the culture of poverty argument, Rodman suggests that members of the lower class stretch the values of the society to fit their circumstances—they do not develop a distinct culture of poverty. They do not abandon the values of legal marriage and legitimate children but stretch these values to allow for other marital systems (for example, friending and living), which allow for the existence of nonlegal unions and illegitimate children. By not rejecting the general value systems of the society (its culture), the poor are able to add additional value choices to their cultural base, which thus help them to adjust to their deprived circumstances. The following passage summarizes Rodman's perspective:

The theories we have presented put a new perspective upon lower-class family life and values. As the middle-class critic sees lower-class life it is characterized by "promiscuous" sexual relationships, "illegal" marital unions, "illegitimate" children, "unmarried" mothers, "deserting" husbands and fathers, and "abandoned" children. These are typically viewed in a gross manner as, simply, *problems* of the lower class. According to our perspective it makes better sense to see them as *solutions* of the lower class to problems that they face in the social, economic, and perhaps legal and political spheres of life. This means that the typical member of the lower class is faced with a chronic economic problem that spawns a series of related problems. Part of the solution to these problems is to be found in the nature of lower-class family life and values. By permitting certain practices (e.g., marital shifting and child-shifting) and by developing certain relationships (e.g., *friending, living*) the lower-class person is able to solve some of the problems that he faces because of his deprived position in society. (Rodman, 1971:197)

The Culture of Poverty in the United States: The Moynihan Report

The Moynihan report, *The Negro Family: The Case for National Action*, is a document prepared in 1965 by the Office of Planning and Research of the U.S. Department of Labor under the supervision of the Assistant Secretary of Labor, Daniel Patrick Moynihan. The report is an illustration of the use of the culture of poverty position and, as we will see, has important social-policy implications. The report is loaded with such terms as *tangle of pathology, broken families, illegitimacy,* and *social disorganization* to describe the family structure of blacks living in poverty. These terms are commonly associated with the culture of poverty orientation, which we described previously. The implications of the report are that it is necessary to change the culture of poor black families if the government expects them to improve their economic position. The focus of social-policy legislation that follows from this position is concerned with psychiatric treatment, social-welfare reforms, dissemination of information relating to birth control and family planning, and other individual-oriented programs. Alternative policy would see the need to create jobs, to train individuals to fill these jobs, and to institute reform designed to reduce the large economic distribution inequalities in the United States. Although the report was published in 1965 and has been severely criticized for its biases and distortions, it still reflects a viewpoint that is held by many laypersons, social scientists, and legislators in the United States. This is especially important in that such a position has led to the wastage of public monies and has diverted maximum effort away from the task at hand—the ending of poverty and its concomitant evils in the United States.

The dominant thesis of the Moynihan report is stated dramatically:

> At the heart of the deterioration of the fabric of Negro society is the deterioration of the Negro family.
> It is the fundamental source of the weakness of the Negro community at the present time.
> The white family has achieved a high degree of stability and is maintaining that stability. . . .
> *By contrast, the family structure of lower-class Negroes is highly unstable, and in many urban centers is approaching complete breakdown.* [Printed in boldface.] (U.S. Department of Labor, 1965:5)

Although the Moynihan report discusses discrimination and unemployment and sees them as being contributory causes of the difficulties of poverty in black family systems, the report places its primary emphasis on the demographic data culled from census and governmental reports on households—*dissolved* marriages, *broken* families, *illegitimacy*, welfare rates, Aid to Families with Dependent Children figures, and delinquency and crime rates. From these sources, Moynihan develops a social-disorganization thesis with a lower-class subculture that is characterized by matriarchy, emasculated males, educational failure, delinquency, crime, and drug addiction.

Rainwater and Yancey (1967) note that the report is neither a scholarly article prepared for a professional journal nor a simple governmental position paper. It is a hybrid, presenting certain social science information to advocate a social-policy position that follows the guidelines of the culture of poverty argument and postulates the existence of a self-perpetuating cycle of poverty anchored by the family system. The policy implications follow directly from this position:

> The harsh fact is that as a group, at the present time, in terms of ability to win out in the competitions of American life, they [the Negro people] are not equal to most of those groups with which they will be competing . . . the circumstances of the Negro American community in recent years has probably been getting *worse, not better*. . . .
>
> The fundamental problem, in which this most clearly is the case, is that of family structure . . . the Negro family in the urban ghettos is crumbling . . . for vast numbers of the unskilled, poorly educated, city working class the fabric of conventional social relationships has all but disintegrated. . . . So long as this situation persists, the cycle of poverty and disadvantage will continue to repeat itself.
>
> . . . a national effort towards the problems of Negro Americans must be directed towards the question of family structure. The object should be to strengthen the Negro family so as to enable it to raise and support its members as do other families. After that, how this group of Americans chooses to run its affairs, take advantage of its opportunities or fail to do so, is none of the nation's business. (U.S. Department of Labor, 1965: Preface, 47–48)

The controversy surrounding the report lies in its support of the culture of poverty position in its stress on the cultural deprivations of the black family that have impeded it from taking advantage of the opportunities the United States offers. Further, although briefly stating that the socioeconomic system played a role in the deterioration of the Negro community, the Moynihan report emphasizes the dysfunctional characteristics of a black matriarchal family structure. The report argues that female-headed families constitute a problem for the black family.

> In essence, the Negro community has been forced into a matriarchal structure which, because it is so out of line with the rest of the American society, seriously retards the progress of the group as a whole, and imposes a crushing burden on the Negro male and, in consequence, on a great many Negro women as well. (U.S. Department of Labor, 1965:29)

It is vital to consider in detail the basis of the culture of poverty criticism of the black matriarchal family structure and its alleged consequences. In addition, it is necessary to determine the extent that black families are headed by women and its implications for the family members. At the onset, a conceptual clarification must be made. The term *matriarchy* refers to a family authority system controlled by females, whereas a female-headed household refers to a household where no male head is present. It does not necessarily follow that a census-defined female-headed household is a matriarchy. Thus, it is a gross oversimplification simply to equate the two, which is what Moynihan does without any further basis of information; that is, Moynihan does not justify his use of social statistics as indicators of cultural patterns. Although census figures give us a demographic picture of statistical shape, they tell us nothing directly about either the structure or process in a cultural system or about the variety of cultural designs underlying it.

Consider, for example, a demographic pattern in which at any time there are many households without an observable resident adult male heading the domestic menage. This picture may reflect a system of plural marriage in which co-wives reside separately and husbands live with one wife at a time, as in the case of polygynous societies in numerous parts of the world. It may reflect a community organization in which all adult males reside together and apart from their wives and children, as in much of the Southwest Pacific. It may be associated with a traditional family form in which male support for the household comes from kinsmen by blood, with no such social position as resident husband, as among the Nayar of South India. It may be found in societies where males are migrant laborers for periods of years while their spouses and offspring remain in the home community, as in many colonial areas. Or it may reflect a variety of systems in which multiple consensual unions involve males in various standardized obligations to women and children, not including cohabitation, as reported from Caribbean societies. *Thus the census taker's finding by itself has no definite cultural significance but may turn out, with further investigation, to have many different meanings.* [Italics added.] (Valentine, 1968:6–7)

In addition to the unwarranted suppositions drawn from the statistical data in regard to cultural patterns, the Moynihan report also distorts that data. The report has been criticized quite heavily on methodological procedures. Rainwater and Yancey (1967) note the following major methodological criticisms:

1. The data were oversimplified. Moynihan failed to include data that tended to contradict his hypothesis and the data that were reported did not lead to such semantically loaded conclusions as "rapid deterioration" and "alarming rate of illegitimacy."
2. The thesis did not consider the effects of economic position and the differences between social classes; controlling for these variables washes out the racial differences. Blacks and whites of the same economic class have virtually the same type of family structure.
3. The report downplayed the great range and variability in the black family and family behavior, including the great diversity of low-income families.

To illustrate these criticisms, let us look at the third point in more detail. The report states that demographic data indicate that black families are more likely to be characterized as having a female head than white families, 21 percent to 9 percent, respectively. However, the report virtually ignores the fact that the overwhelming majority of black families, over 70 percent, were headed by both a husband and a wife. This point must be stressed: When less than 30 percent of black families are headed by women, it is erroneous to talk about *the* black family. As Hylan Lewis (1965) points out, when the great diversity, range, and variability of black families are overlooked, "there is danger that the depreciated, and probably more dramatic and threatening, characteristics of a small segment of the population may be imputed to an entire population" (H. Lewis, 1965:315). For another thing, even if there is a greater predominance of female-headed families among blacks, the question remains whether this condition is pathological.

Robert Staples (1971) argues that, regardless of the role of black women in the family, it is necessary to stress that the female role evolved out of the struggle for black survival. The position is similar to that of Rodman (1965, 1971), who views the behavioral adaptations of poverty people as solutions to the problems of economic deprivation. Andrew Billingsley (1969) has shown that many families in the black inner-city ghettos have demonstrated an impressive capacity to adapt to the social, cultural, and economic deprivations fostered in them by the larger society and have developed strong family relationships. Finally, Rainwater (1966) contradicts the notion that female-centered households are dysfunctional; in research of poverty families, Rainwater finds an *adaptive* urban matricentric family form (among others) that successfully copes with the problems of poverty. Carol B. Stack offers additional support to this position.

Carol B. Stack's *All Our Kin* (1974) is an anthropological study of a poor black community, which she called The Flats, that is located in a midwestern city called Jackson Harbor. She examines how families cope with poverty by adapting domestic networks to link people who are not necessarily related. Stack emphasizes that a census-defined, female-headed, single-parent household does not indicate separatedness or isolation. A cooperative-support network exists that is composed of both relatives and fictive kin, who are treated as kin by family members and are given such kinship terms as sister, aunt, and uncle. These people unite for mutual aid and to meet daily needs.

> Black families living in The Flats need a steady source of cooperative support to survive. They share with one another because of the urgency of their needs. Alliances between individuals are created around the clock as kin and friends exchange and give and obligate one another. They trade food stamps, rent money, a TV, hats, dice, a car, a nickel here, a cigarette there, food, milk, grits, and children.
>   . . . Without the help of kin, fluctuations in the meager flow of available goods could easily destroy a family's ability to survive. . . . Kin and close friends who fall into similar economic crises know that they may share the food, dwelling, and even the few scarce luxuries of those individuals in their kin network. Despite the relatively high cost of rent and food in urban black communities, the collective power within kin-based exchange networks keeps people from going hungry. (Stack, 1974:32–33)

Stack stresses that social scientists who employ such culture of poverty terms as *pathology* and *social disorganization* fail to understand the adaptive forms of familial and quasifamilial relationships and structures that have developed in these economically deprived communities. Further, they are not aware how resilient urban black families are to the socioeconomic conditions of poverty, the inexorable unemployment, and the limited access to scarce economic opportunities of single-parent mothers and their children who receive welfare under such programs as Aid to Families with Dependent Children (AFDC). Stack points out that these structural adaptations do not lock people into a cycle of poverty or prevent them from marrying or removing themselves from the networks. But her study does indicate that the very success of these cooperative networks force women to think twice about marriage:

> Forms of social control both within the kin network and in the larger society work against successful marriages in The Flats. In fact, couples rarely chance marriage unless a man has a job; often the job is temporary, low paying, insecure, and the worker gets laid off whenever he is not needed. Women come to realize that welfare benefits and ties within kin networks provide greater security for social mobility. A woman may be immediately cut off the welfare roles when a husband returns home from prison, the army, or if she gets married. Thus, the society's welfare system collaborates in weakening the position of the black male. (Stack, 1974:113)

In summary, Stack's work graphically reveals how viable family structures develop to handle chronic poverty and governmental programs that reinforce welfare dependency and unemployment.

As for the Moynihan report overall, most social scientists conclude that it was more of a polemical document with social-policy implications than a scientific one. Gans (1967a) believes that the focus on family problems leads to a clamor for pseudopsychiatric programs as well as to a wave of social and psychiatric solutions that are intended to change the alleged dysfunctional black female-headed family to an alleged functional white middle-class type of family. Gans argues that the knowledge of the black poverty family is relatively weak, whereas there is much greater certainty of the primacy of economic deprivation. He concludes that "it would thus be tragic if the findings were used to justify demands for Negro self-improvement or the development of a middle-class family structure before further programs to bring about real equality are set up" (Gans, 1967a:456). Gans feels that too much attention is devoted to the disabilities and that insufficient attention is given to the causes. He advocates that instead of psychiatric solutions the following types of programs should be instituted: the establishment of jobs, the development of income maintenance programs, the building of housing outside ghetto areas, and the desegregation of existing housing.

His position is an illustration of the situational approach. This orientation argues that although the behavior of poverty families is different than the middle-class pattern, both groups have a similar culture. The behavior is viewed as an adaptation to poverty conditions. This is a direct rebuke of the culture of poverty position. In a different paper, Gans (1967b) views the poor as an economically and politically deprived group whose attitudes and behavior are seen as adaptations, just as the behavior and attitudes of the affluent are adaptations to their social situation. Similarly, Elliot Liebow (1967), in his ethnographic study *Tally's Corner: A Study of Negro Street Corner Men*, stresses the point that although each generation may provide role models for each succeeding one, of greater importance is that the similarities between generations "do not result from 'cultural transmission' but from the fact that the son goes out and independently experiences the same failures, in the same areas, and for much the same reasons as his father" (Liebow, 1967:223). Liebow, in his study of lower-class black men in Washington, D.C., found no evidence indicating deviation from white middle-class norms nor did he find that family role deviancy is perpetuated intergenerationally. Liebow concludes that there is a direct relationship between socioeconomic discrimination and family instability.

William Ryan (1971) argues that the culture of poverty position and such manifestations of it as the Moynihan report blame the victim for being poor; the reform is still to be of the lower classes, the poor, with some saying that they should reform themselves and others saying that the rich and more-affluent classes should help. As Charles A. Valentine (1968) has argued, few say that the more-powerful, the influential controlling classes of the culture, should change or that the total social structure needs changing. Instead, they place the burden for reform on the poor and are primarily concerned with doing away with a culture and not with poverty.

Our position is that the culture of poverty perspective that focuses on family structure is too narrow. It does not matter whether we evaluate family structure as pathological (a problem) or as a positive functional adjustment (a solution); the real issue is the causes and consequences of racial, economic, political, and social inequality. The following statement by Leonard Reissman (1972), although concerned with the black poverty family, can be generalized to all families who live under the wretched conditions of poverty:

> It must certainly be the case that, if blacks did not suffer from inequalities and were economically secure, then the type of family they have would not bother anyone; at the most, the nature of the concern would be of an entirely different order than it is now. By the same reasoning, I must assume that the efforts to change the matriarchy, and thus to cure the pathology, are not likely to make much difference in the conditions of blacks if the causes and consequences of their inequality are left untouched. Rather, I am convinced that if the causes and consequences of inequality are removed, then the structure of the Negro family will become much less important as an issue for reformers. (Reissman, 1972:94)

White Families in Poverty

We believe that it would be instructive to discuss the characteristics of poor *white* families living in poverty. All too frequently, sociology textbooks focus solely on poor black families in America and disregard the plight of their white counterparts. In addition, discussions of the American white family in these textbooks virtually ignore the existence of poor white families and tend implicitly to juxtapose in the reader's mind poverty and social minorities.

Robert Coles (1968) describes the situation of poor white families in Appalachia and notes their adaptation to poverty is similar to the adaptation made by persons living in the racial ghettos of urban American and the squatter settlements of the Third World. He sees the behavior of the poor as symptoms of a dysfunctional cultural system rather than as reasonable responses to poverty conditions. The following statement summarizes Coles' position:

> Appalachia is full of ironies, but nothing is more ironic than the fact that America's oldest ethnic group, its white Anglo-Saxon Protestants, live there in poverty as desperate as that experienced by any other impoverished people. It took courage and enterprise to settle the region—and now the region's people are called inert, apathetic, and unresourceful. The region has experienced the severest kind of unemployment as a result of technological change, and yet side by side one sees an almost primitive economy. If ever there was a section of America that needed planned capital investment, federally sustained—as indeed this country has done in other regions of the world with its money—then indeed Appalachia is that reason.
>
> In my experience the people of Appalachia do not fit the usual sociological and anthropological descriptions applied to them. By that I mean that their apparent inertia and apathy are reasonable responses to a lack of opportunity and a lack of employment. Given jobs, real jobs, jobs that are not substitutes for work, Appalachian men and women work well and hard. They also can be open, friendly, and generous—even to an outsider like me. What they do not want is a kind of patronizing and condescending sympathy. They are proud and stubborn people who want from this country a share of its wealth. Given that, I don't think we would have any "psychological problems" with the region's citizens. (Coles, 1968:27)

An interesting monograph is that of Joseph T. Howell (1973), *Hard Living on Clay Street*. Howell's book concerns his participant-observation field study of poor white families living in a blue-collar suburb of Washington, D.C. The families, who lived on Clay Street, were southern migrants who moved to Washington from farms in North Carolina and the mountains of West Virginia. The men had service-oriented jobs: painters, plasterers, plumbers, repairmen, auto mechanics, truck drivers, and so on. Stereotypically, they were called rednecks, lower class, irresponsible, and white trash.

Howell (1973:263–352) distinguishes between two opposing lifestyles, which represent two ends of a continuum of family life on Clay Street—hard living and settled living—by delineating seven general areas of attitudes and behavior:

1. *Heavy drinking.* Heavy drinking occurred quite frequently in hard-living families and occurred only occasionally, if at all, among settled families.
2. *Marital stability.* Hard-living families were married more than once, with their current marriages being precarious. Settled families had long-term stable marriages.
3. *Toughness.* Profanity, talk of violence, and general attitudes of "toughness" were commonplace among both husbands and wives, whereas the settled-living families had a moderate approach to life.
4. *Political alienation.* Clay Street's hard-living families rarely voted or held strong political beliefs. This was based on their view that government was unresponsive, corrupt, and irrelevant to their needs. In contrast, despite their feelings of frustration, the settled-living families voted as political conservatives and felt that it was worthwhile to fight for and preserve the society.
5. *Rootlessness.* The hard-living families were more mobile; they rented their houses, moved frequently, and had a general attitude that they had no roots in the community or elsewhere. The settled families owned their homes, lived in the same home for a period of time, and felt ties to the community.
6. *Present-time orientation.* Hard-living families were preoccupied with surviving from

day to day and gave little thought to the future. The settled families of Clay Street, by virtue of the fact that they could save a little money, expressed greater concern about the community and their family's future.

7. *Individualism.* Hard-living families valued independence and self-reliance, calling themselves loners. They had little involvement with or use for clubs or organizations, and they liked to work alone. The settled families, on the other hand, participated in community life and in groups and rarely had the same feelings of individualism.

Howell believes that the degree of marital stability was a key indication of involvement in either of the two lifestyles. Howell quotes a local police officer to illustrate this:

> Well, there are basically two types of folks in this community: middle class and what you might call lower class. The middle-class folks, the working people, they never cause no trouble—law abiding, upright, quiet. Now the lower class, they are different. We're all the time getting calls when husbands and wives get into fights, husband leaves, wife leaves, that sort of thing. (Howell, 1973:274)

The hard-living families of Clay Street were characterized by family instability. Howell reports that practically every hard-living family member had been married more than once, with many having common-law consensual marriages. A striking characteristic of the Clay Street marriages was the changing nature of the marriage relationship: many marriages were on shaky ground and apparently stable couples would suddenly break up, their marriage dissolved. The causes of marital dissolution varied—adulterous affairs, drinking, unemployment were the most frequently cited causes. The couples viewed divorce as an eventual consequence of marriage; remarriage was also seen as an integral part of the hard life. Howell quotes a frequent philosophical attitude regarding marriage: "Divorce is simply part of life, that's just the way things are" (Howell, 1973:290). Their ambivalence toward marriage is illustrated by a quote from a male resident of Clay Street:

> Well it's too bad. Sure, I want my marriage to work out. But it didn't. And it doesn't for most folks around here. The way I see it, it's inherited. My grandaddy, he had it. He was married several times. My dad and mom, hell, they had it. And my children, they are going to have it, too. Divorces, separations, broken marriages. Hell, that's just the way life is. It just runs in the family. It's inherited. (Howell, 1973:292)

The frequency of divorces and other forms of marital instability had ramifications not only for the couple but also for their involvement with each of their extended families. Howell reports that the residents of Clay Street rarely saw their relatives, including such close ones as sisters and brothers. Many did not know whether these relatives were alive or not. The absence of ties with relatives is partially explained by the fact that the husbands and wives were themselves from broken homes. Further, the ones who moved from the South or from the Appalachian Mountains to Clay Street described themselves as black sheep compared to the rest of their family. The general pattern, according to Howell, was for the families to scatter, with some remaining on the farm; some settling in the Washington, D.C., area; some going to industrial northern cities or moving out West; or some just disappearing. The result was that, although many of the hard-living families of Clay Street had nostalgia for their rural homes, there was no "home" for them to return to and there were very few close relatives who stayed there. The result was a feeling of rootlessness.

Most husbands and wives fought, and both tried to maintain an image of toughness and independence. These attitudes reflect the difficult marital experiences of the couple. One hard-living wife experienced an early marriage, divorce, the birth of six children and the death of two of the children, poverty, poor health, and her current husband's alcoholism and violence. She explains her attitudes this way: "Take me, . . . If I wasn't a fighter I'd never of made it, not to say that I've made it now" (Howell, 1973:303). Yet underneath that tough image, Howell reports that most hard-living families of Clay Street were compassionate and sensitive and demonstrated compassion and affection for each other and their children.

Howell concludes that simplistic social-psychological and social and cultural causal theories do not provide an adequate explanation of these families. He argues that providing social-psychological reasons for a particular individual's behavior—coming from a broken home, alcoholism prevalent, and so on—obscures the structural and cultural forces that influence an individual's and a family's behavior patterns. Howell also condemns sweeping societal generalities to explain the behavior of the poor. He rejects simplistic structural arguments and culture of poverty theories that see the main reason for "reckless" and "unstable" behavior as a result of self-perpetuating family instability. In his concluding cautionary statement he argues a point that is important for all of us to keep in mind in our own personal analysis and depiction of poverty families:

> June [a Clay Streeter] put it better than anyone else: "You can call us what you want to, but folks around here, hell, we're just plain folks. We got problems like everybody else. Maybe the difference is we don't try to shove 'em all into some closet. That's 'cause we ain't too proud to admit we're just folks." Above all else, the people on Clay Street were "just folks," and their humanity expressed itself in every aspect of their lives. (Howell, 1973:359–360)

Black Families in Poverty

The great social-class diversity of black American families has long been noted by social scientists. The majority of black families have both parents present (60 percent) and over 80 percent of adult black males work and support their households. One-third of all black families have incomes above the American median, and in this group 90 percent have two parents present. Furthermore, black working-class families have long been characterized as belonging to more organizations, having greater church participation, and holding a higher status within their own community than their white counterparts (Willie, 1981). Yet there are significant differences between black families and white families in the United States. These include a larger proportion of black families than families of other races having children present and a large and continually growing number of single-parent households maintained by women. Further, blacks marry later and are more likely to divorce and separate, have fewer intact marriages, and are less likely to remarry after divorce (Glick, 1984). As we have indicated, these prevailing black family variations have been interpreted, in part, as adaptations to the special circumstances in which blacks find themselves and, in part, to certain differential values attributable to these circumstantial variations. In this section, we examine and try to shed light on the contemporary state of affairs of black families living under poverty conditions.

To try to explain the growing class diversity within the black community, black social scientists have developed a number of views and diverging opinions that have led to considerable debate. In his 1978 book *The Declining Significance of Race*, William J. Wilson argued that racial distinction is not as important a factor in determining the economic opportunities of blacks as is their social class. Wilson does not claim that racism has completely vanished, but rather he contends that economic and class differences have become more important now than race for determining access to positions of power and privilege and for entering middle-class and upper-

Peter Howe/Camera Press from Topham/The Topham/The Image Works

The shack people: A family sits out on the porch of its home in Plains, Georgia, 1979. Poverty-level families often live in appalling, overcrowded conditions, fourteen to a shack with no water or electricity. (Plains is also the home of former President Jimmy Carter.)

status groups. Through affirmative-action programs, qualified blacks meeting the educational criteria are able to take advantage of new opportunities for better-paying white-collar jobs found in the expanding government and private corporate sectors. Unfortunately, blacks in the underclasses continue to be subordinated; relegated to low-paying service, unskilled-labor, and farm jobs; and trapped in poverty.

Wilson feels that present trends offer little hope unless there is recognition of the dependency nature of welfare and until there is recognition of the need to provide skills and education to the urban poor. If this is not done, society cannot effectively attack the problem of inequality. Wilson believes that the Moynihan report mistook a social-class problem for a problem of black culture. The problem for Wilson, then, is no longer race but the existence of an extremely poorly equipped and disadvantaged underclass that makes up about one-third of the black population and a sizable number of whites, Hispano-Americans, and native Americans as well.

> Underclass whites, Hispano-Americans, and native Americans are all victims . . . of class subordination under advanced capitalism. . . . And since 1970 both poor whites and nonwhites have evidenced very little progress in their elevation from the ranks of the underclass. In the final analysis, therefore, the challenge of economic dislocation in modern industrial society calls for public policy programs to attack inequality on a broad class front, policy programs—in other words—that go beyond the limits of ethnic and racial discrimination by directly confronting the pervasive and destructive features of class subordination. (Wilson, 1978:154)

Other black sociologists do not agree with Wilson. One of his most vocal opponents is Charles V. Willie, whose *Caste and Class Controversy* (1979) and *A New Look in Black*

Families (1981) maintain that economics is but one facet of the larger society and should therefore not be considered in isolation. Willie argues that white racism permeates society, affecting all social institutions and controlling entry to all desirable positions in education, employment, housing, and social status. Willie points out that — while they have moved up on many social indicators of social position, including education (from 79 percent of whites' educational achievement in 1940 to 94 percent in 1975) — blacks have not caught up in income. To help prove his point, Willie matches blacks and whites by education, occupation, and other traits, and finds that blacks received 15 to 20 percent less income than their white counterparts. Further, Willie asserts that blacks, while gaining middle-class status, often become psychologically chained in a white world that permits only token entry and retains actual power, control, and wealth.

Wilson's thesis of a social-class split within the black community is still subject to much debate. Andrew Cherlin (1981), after a thorough analysis of census and other sources of statistical data, observes that it does appear to fit with the post–World War II trends in black family life. Cherlin found that single-parent black families began to occur on a much larger scale within the last 50 years than in the post–Civil War period, and this trend accelerated in the 1960s and 1970s. Further, the difference between blacks and whites grew larger as well. In 1960, 21 percent of black families were maintained by a woman compared to 8 percent for white families. By 1979, the figure grew to 41 percent and 12 percent respectively (Cherlin, 1981:104). Cherlin concludes that today's female-headed, lower-class black family represents a relatively recent type of family structure.

Cherlin also reports that — whereas whites used to wait longer to marry than blacks — ever since 1950 blacks have been marrying at a later age than whites, having a higher divorce rate than whites at all class levels, and taking longer to remarry or never marrying (1981:94–95, 99, 107). Among the black lower classes the trend not to remarry has accelerated over whites in the same class. Illegitimacy rates are also differentially higher. In 1978, one out of every 12 unmarried black women of child-bearing age had a child, compared to one out of every 72 unmarried white women (Cherlin, 1981:95–96). Cherlin graphically depicts the divergence in the marital status of black and white 25- to 44-year-old women from 1950 to 1979 in Figure 6.1. He observes that "the proportion of these women who were single has more than doubled for blacks but has hardly changed for whites during this 29-year period. The census data suggest that during the postwar period some aspects of the living arrangements and marital experiences of blacks and whites have diverged sharply. Taken together, later marriage, a higher rate of separation and divorce, and more time spent in the separated and divorced statuses meant that relatively fewer black people were currently married" (Cherlin, 1981:99).

What accounts for these differences? Why has there been such a divergent typical family pattern of blacks and whites in the past 25 years? Cherlin rejects answers that seek explanations in terms of the presumed still-felt long-lasting effects of slavery on black family life; rather, bolstered by the statistical evidence that the contemporary divergence goes no further back than the depression of the 1930s and has accelerated since 1960, he argues that the causes lie in part in the contemporary diverse economic experiences of blacks and whites in today's urban society. This view parallels Wilson's.

A possible additional explanation is that it is a consequence of economic situations tied to governmental welfare policies. This viewpoint was developed by Charles Murray (1984) in his controversial book *Losing Ground*. Murray states that the greater availability and increased benefits of public-assistance programs since the mid-1960s have encouraged or enabled more single-parent families to exist. Coming under particular attack are such programs as Aid to Families with Dependent Chil-

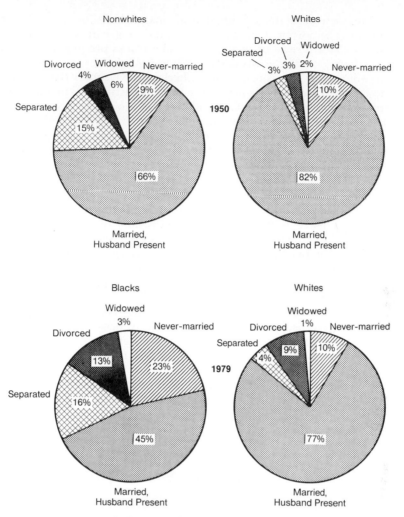

FIGURE 6.1   Current marital status of women aged 25 to 44, by race or color, 1950 and 1979 (Cherlin, 1981. *Marriage, Divorce, Remarriage,* p. 98. Cambridge, Mass.: Harvard University Press. Reprinted by permission.).

dren and food stamps. However, Cherlin believes that the empirical evidence indicates, at most, that increased welfare benefits may have a modest effect on the proportion of single-parent families.

The development of alternative support networks composed of both kin and nonkin neighbors in poverty communities as a rational adaptive response to economic deprivation that prevents lower-class men and women from marrying and living together is also cited by Cherlin as a possible explanation. He refers to the research of Carol Stack (1974) and others [see Billingsley (1969) and Hill (1972)] who found that most residents in a low-income black neighborhood participated in a complex social network that exchanged mutual support. Cherlin believes that the functionality of such networks, and particularly networks composed of kin, may have contributed to a situation where marriage is of less central importance to the lives of these poor families than it is to the population at large.

This view takes the position that for many blacks, ties to a network of kin may be the more-important family bond over the long run. Often, the extended-kin networks characteristic of many low-income blacks provide a dependable, stable, and functioning family environment. While household compositions may change, the network tends to remain intact. Cherlin (1981) notes that census figures are not designed to identify this network support structure of kin and others who reside in different households and share and exchange goods, services, and emotional support. Instead, census figures define a family as two or more individuals related by blood or marriage who reside in the same household. Census figures taken by themselves can give the mistaken impression that most single parents and their children belong to unstable families without any social supports.

Yet Cherlin cautions that we should not overestimate the strengths of these kinds of family structures. For they, themselves, are not immune to problems; they tend to foster group loyalty that may mitigate against the goals of individuals. For instance, they may make it difficult for one individual to accumulate sufficient capital to advance his or her own standard of living because of obligations to share gains with others in the network. The combined resources of the support network, then, may not eliminate the economic hardships of the single female parent and her children. Evidence indicates that financial difficulties are typically severe for single mothers as compared to single fathers.

In summary, the statistical evidence and academic research studies all point to the fact that there is a sharp divergence in recent decades between blacks and whites in the typical patterns of marriage. This divergence is centralized in the black underclass. And, as Cherlin points out, this is a relatively recent phenomenon that is characterized by a family structure composed of a strong network of kin, but fragile ties between fathers and mothers. The consequence of this development may be ominous, for "the emerging family system among lower-class blacks suggests that some are becoming even less integrated into the mainstream of American life than ever before" (Cherlin, 1981:112).

Twenty Years After the Moynihan Report: The Feminization and Childization of Poverty

On the twentieth anniversary after writing *The Negro Family: The Case for National Action*, Daniel Patrick Moynihan, now the senior senator from New York, reported on the current state of American families with particular concern with families living under poverty. This report was in the form of three lectures, the 1985 Godkin Lectures at Harvard University, and later was published as a book, *Family and Nation* (1986). Moynihan carefully avoids identifying the feminization of poverty (single-parent households headed by a female) and the childization of poverty (the rapidly increasing number of children living in poverty) as largely limited to black families; instead, he focuses on the intensification of problems faced by poverty families since 1965.

In 1984, Moynihan reports, more than half of poor families were single-parent families and the great majority of those were headed by women. More than three-fourths of all the poor were either adult women or children under the age of 18. Children, who represented less than 27 percent of the population, comprised 40 percent of the poor. They had displaced the elderly as the poorest age group and were the only age group overrepresented in the poverty population. Further, and most disturbingly, Moynihan points out that single-parent families are increasing rapidly in all segments of the population. In the next 20 years, Moynihan projects, the number of female-headed families will increase at more than five times the rate of husband–wife families.

Births, Marriage and Jobs: Statistics of Black Family Life

WILLIAM RASPBERRY

CHICAGO — William Julius Wilson, ever the patient professor, will lead you through his fascinating little charts, trying to get you to recall what all of us used to know but what has somehow slipped our minds.

The subject is the dismaying increase in single-parent households among blacks, and he'd like you to understand how it came to be. He'll grant the possibility that both the "new morality" and the unanticipated influence of welfare may be a part of the explanation. But those are by no means the whole explanation.

Look at his charts. In 1954, the ratio of "marriageable" (meaning "employed") 18- and 19-year-old men to women of the same age was roughly the same among blacks and whites, with black men slightly more likely to be working. The trend continued through 1960 — 50 "marriageable" black men for every 100 black women of the same age; 48 "marriageable" white men for every 100 white women of the same age.

Then the two curves began to separate. By the late '70s, the ratio was 63 marriageable white men per 100 women; 40 per 100 for blacks. The same trend occurred for the 20-to-24 age group, with the trend lines separating markedly in the late '60s.

Wilson's conclusion: The shrinking pool of marriageable black men seems a likely explanation for at least some of the increase in out-of-wedlock births and single-parent households among blacks.

"The interesting thing," says the University of Chicago sociologist, "is that we used to know this. Back in the 1960s, Pat Moynihan, Kenneth Clark and Bayard Rustin, among others, were making the connection between black male joblessness and the breakdown of black families. Now we seem to have lost sight of that relationship, placing much more emphasis on the role of welfare."

Charles Murray (*Losing Ground*) has succeeded in convincing a lot of us that welfare, serving as a father-substitute, is a major reason for the increase in single-parent households among blacks.

Wilson's 1978 book, *The Declining Significance of Race*, was frequently interpreted — incorrectly — as a statement that race was no longer an important factor in the income and employment disparities between blacks and whites. He doesn't want to be misunderstood this time.

"We [Wilson and his graduate student, Kathryn M. Neckerman, co-authors of a monograph on Poverty and Family Structure] are not making a single-minded argument. But this male marriageable pool index has to be a part of the explanation. It may be the major explanation. Certainly there's no reason why the welfare connection should receive more attention than the joblessness connection, which has been pushed to the back burner.

"As a matter of fact, the marriageable pool index has an advantage over other measures because, if it is true that most of the black men who are undercounted in the census are jobless, then that proportion is automatically included in the index, which also covers the higher incarceration and mortality rates for black males."

The 49-year-old professor makes another point that tends to get lost. The fertility rate for black women — including out-of-wedlock births — has declined in the last decade or so. "The problem," he says, "is that these women just aren't getting married."

And one result is a major increase in black poverty, female-headed households being the single largest category of poor families.

Virtually everyone acknowledges that these problems are particularly devastating for blacks. But the Wilson-Neckerman index suggests that we've been looking in the wrong direction for remedies.

We have been looking for moral, cultural and policy explanations of single parenting and delayed marriage among young blacks (who, at an earlier time would have put heavy emphasis on "legitimizing" their out-of-wedlock children).

For Wilson, a major part of the explanation is obvious: The young women don't get married because the marriageable men aren't there.

SOURCE. William Raspberry. 1986. "Birth, marriage and jobs: Statistics of black family life." *The Courier-Post* (May 12). Reprinted by permission of the Washington Post Writers Group.

Moynihan calls attention to the accelerated trend toward family disorganization among blacks living under poverty conditions that he first investigated in the 1965 Moynihan report. Armed with statistics and academic citations, some of which we cited earlier, Moynihan states that there has been a startling increase in the proportion of children living under poverty conditions in single-parent families headed by females for both whites and blacks. But the gap between them has widened. In 1984, 59 percent of all black family groups were in single-parent situations, compared to the near 20 percent among whites. This is a three-to-one ratio. The ratio was somewhat less than two-to-one in 1950 and somewhat more in 1960.

Although this trend holds true for all races in America, the problem is particularly ominous for blacks. From 1960 to 1982, the number of children under the age of three living in single-parent families has doubled. However, the doubling has resulted in a relatively small increase in the percentage of white children (15 percent from 7 percent) living with one parent as compared to the 30 percent increase among black children (60 percent from 30 percent). Often, it is these children who are most likely to feel the ramifications of poverty.

The role of governmental welfare programs in inhibiting or fostering the rise in the number of American families living in poverty comes under Moynihan's scrutiny. He is very critical of Charles Murray (1984), who argues in his book *Losing Ground* that these programs may have increased the poverty. Moynihan takes issue with Murray's contention that it has become "socially acceptable" in poor communities to live off welfare. Murray's thesis, which has its share of supporters in the Reagan administration, is that government programs themselves brought about the present "alarming rate of family disintegration." Moynihan counters by asking, "How does Mr. Murray know? The answer is that he does not know. He may be right. But he has not proven anything" (1986:129).

Moynihan argues that there is no evidence that welfare "breaks up families." Indeed, he effectively dismisses fashionable attacks on welfare programs as the source of family disintegration. For example, he presents evidence that the accelerated development of single-parent, female-headed households was occurring prior to government actions. Moynihan utilizes research on differences in welfare-benefit levels by states to young unwed mothers to develop his position that welfare does not appear to be the primary cause of variations in family structures. To illustrate, in a state such as Minnesota, with high welfare benefits, divorce rates and unmarried births are low. On the other hand, a state such as Mississippi has reverse patterns.

The adjacent states of Arizona and New Mexico provide another case in point. Arizona—during a 15-year period, 1967 to 1982—chose not to participate in Medicaid, a federally financed health-care system for the dependent; New Mexico did participate. Moynihan reasons that if welfare does break up families, the availability of Medicaid would be an added incentive in that it provides for complete medical insurance. Yet Moynihan finds no significant difference in the increased rate of AFDC families in these two similar states. He asks rhetorically, "Where, then, is the Great Society effect on welfare dependency?" (1986:141).

Moynihan points out that some social welfare policies have been very successful, particularly in regard to the elderly: Only about 3 percent of elderly Americans are poor. But, in contrast, programs for children have been less successful. Among preschool children, the comparative figure is 18 percent. Two out of every five Americans living in poverty are children and the rate of poverty among the very young in the United States is nearly six times as great as among the very old. He strongly believes that family change, not welfare programs, is the source of poverty. He does observe that some welfare programs appear not to be work-incentive and instead are work-disincentive and associated with the receipt of public welfare, but these are of only marginal significance.

However, Moynihan has no alternative explanation to Murray and others on why there is a rising trend toward family instability. "[W]e do not know the processes of social change well enough to be able confidently to predict them, far less to affect them," he asserts (1986:163). Nor does he provide us with any comprehensive panacea to solve the problem of family poverty. Instead, he urges that government initiatives of all kinds be reviewed for their potential impact on families. He outlines a potentially constructive number of identifiable family – child issues that he hopes both conservatives and liberals can agree on. These include the following:

1. *Re-enlarge personal and dependent tax exemptions.* Moynihan observes that in 1948 the tax laws allowed a personal exemption of $600 for each family member. Today, the personal exemption is $1,090. This current exemption figure has not risen at the same rate of inflation and family income since 1948. If it had, the current exemption figure should be about $5,600. As a consequence, 1948 families earning 10 percent above the poverty line were exempt from income taxes while today families well below the poverty line are taxed.
2. *Index welfare aid for children.* Since 1965, federal entitlement programs for veterans, the aged, the disabled, and the retired have been indexed against price inflation. The entitlements of children have not been indexed.
3. *Establish a national benefit standard for child-welfare aid.* Currently, there is no national benefit standard; each state continues to administer welfare aid with wide variations in benefits. A standardized rate would be beneficial to millions of children.
4. *Identify and support programs that work.* Moynihan provides two examples of such programs. Head Start, the early-childhood enrichment program, has been very successful in saving millions of dollars. Supported Work is another successful program that had led welfare recipients into regular jobs.
5. *Protect children, and their children, from teenage pregnancy and abortion.* Moynihan calls for the development of constructive education and other public programs.

Given the fact that there are a multitude of factors associated with living under poverty conditions that affect increases in illegitimacy, single-parent families, and other profound changes in the family, Moynihan's call for such social policy incentives is most welcome. They could provide help to many American families living under poverty conditions in contemporary affluent America.

In summary, Moynihan restates his 1965 call for a national family policy that would promote the stability and well-being of the American family. While he does not provide any quick answers, Moynihan has achieved his major goal of raising the level of public discourse on the family crisis. Further, he has successfully overcome his 1965 position that placed the onus of responsibility for poverty from those families living under poverty to the nature of government and its family policies. He correctly observes that, while many Americans believe it is not government's business to interfere in family matters, there is no way that government cannot influence a family's well-being. The government simply does things that affect people. For that reason, Moynihan's closing remarks are most appropriate: "A commonplace of political rhetoric has it that the quality of a civilization may be measured by how it cares for its elderly. Just as surely, the future of a society may be forecast by how it cares for its young" (1986:194).

Conclusion

In this chapter, we devoted our attention to poverty families in both industrial and nonindustrial Western societies. Two theoretical orientations dominate the analysis of poverty families, and both have different consequences for social policies affecting the poor.

The cultural position (the culture of poverty) emphasizes the cultural dynamics of

Slipping into Poverty: Hard Times for Women in '80s

BY MARY JANE FINE

The worst moments, during a period rife with bad moments, come late in the month, when the food stamps are gone, and late at night, when her daughters are asleep. In those bleak hours, Mary Louise Smith juggles the mathematics of her life and invariably arrives at the same answer: insufficient funds.

Since August, when she went on welfare, Smith's checks have arrived predictably on the first of each month and around the 13th, bisecting the months into a sad parody of good times and bad.

Early in the month, her cupboard is stocked with snacks—cookies, bananas, apples, potato chips—and she serves her daughters dinners with salad and two vegetables. By mid-month, the cupboard is bare, and dinner is downgraded to hot dogs and beans or potato soup, which both girls detest.

"They always say, 'Mom, this is for poor people. We're not poor,'" says Smith, 41, of the city's Kensington section. "But after the first week of the month, that's it."

Being poor—she calculates her present income to be $348 a month plus $177 worth of food stamps—is relatively new for Smith, whose solidly blue-collar background did not prepare her for such circumstances. Her plight, however, is achingly familiar to thousands of other women in Pennsylvania and around the country, who increasingly find themselves slipping below the federal poverty line, which is an income of $8,850 for a family of three.

Termed the "feminization of poverty," the situation, by all accounts, has been on the rise over the last 15 years. Poverty, say those familiar with the situation, is "only a divorce away" for many women—those who are college-educated and upper-middle-class as well as the persistently poor.

A Census Bureau report released in August showed a decrease in the overall poverty rate from 15.2 percent in 1983 to 14.4 percent in 1984, but for women and children, the economic picture drawn by city and federal census data remains disturbing:

- Over the last 15 years, the number of female-headed households below the poverty line has increased dramatically. In 1970, there were less than two million poor households with female heads; by 1984, the number had shot up to 3.5 million.
- Currently, two out of three adults living below the poverty level are women.
- In 1982, half of all female-headed families had incomes under $11,480, while those of married couples averaged $26,000.
- In Philadelphia, a recent survey indicated that among the homeless, the percentage of women climbed from 20 percent to 30 percent in the last year.
- Fifty-three percent of the city's female-headed households live in poverty.

During a period generally marked by economic prosperity, the plight of such women cannot be blamed on hard times. Rather, experts cite numerous factors in addition to the rising divorce rate—including unwed motherhood, inequities in the workplace and the lack of affordable child care—to explain the growing phenomenon.

"One of the major reasons why women are slipping below the poverty level is that when a male breadwinner leaves, a family is extremely vulnerable," says Lori Rubenstein of Women's Agenda, a statewide organization of women's advocacy groups, in Philadelphia. "And the problem is that women never catch up."

Census Bureau statistician Steven Rudolph, who is based in Washington, says that despite a large decline in the number of children in the United States between 1966 and 1985, the number of poor children nationally actually rose—from 12,146,000 in 1966 to 13,274,000 in 1985.

The poverty rate would have dropped "if not for the increase in female-headed households," he says.

"There's been a shift in the mix of children from the Ozzie and Harriet, David and Ricky family to female-headed

(continued)

households," Rudolph says. "And they have a higher level of poor kids."

Five years ago, after nearly 20 years of marriage, Mary Louise Smith and her husband separated. Since then, she has quit one job for a better-paying one, lost that job to a layoff, received unemployment compensation and, out of options when that ended, applied for welfare.

Her altered life nags at her on the nights when she sits up, scribbling budget calculations on scraps of paper. "I think how I was married all those years and had it good and just took it for granted," she says. "They say God only gives you what you can bear. But sometimes I say, 'Lord, check on my record up there. I've had enough.'"

In 1964, when she and her husband bought a home in Kensington, his income as a textile worker was about $16,000, she estimated. Smith didn't work outside the home until their oldest daughter entered kindergarten 11 years ago.

Her job, running a machine that wound fabric onto cones in the same factory where her husband worked, paid a fraction of his salary. The work, a night shift, was tedious and involved heavy lifting. At the time, however, her paycheck was considered an extra, a supplement to the family income.

By September 1984, when she was laid off from another job, earning $6.36 an hour wrapping bubble gum, she was separated, living in a rented house and the sole support of her two children.

She limped along on unemployment payments until those ceased in July, and she began receiving AFDC (Aid to Families with Dependent Children) benefits and food stamps.

By the third week of the month, feeling miserly and mean, Smith sat down with her daughters—ages 16 and 7—for a family cost-cutting conference where the distinctions between wants and needs undergo intense scrutiny.

Among the budget parings: using teabags twice, restricting the use of the electric hair dryer and curling iron (15 minutes to dry, 10 to curl), putting batteries in the radio rather than plugging it in, turning off all upstairs lights.

Such skimping reduced Smith's electric bill from $88 in October to $55 in November, and she is making ends meet, she says, "just barely."

A 10-year study by California sociologist Lenore Weitzman indicated that men fared much better financially than their spouses when they divorced. One year after a divorce, the standard of living for men goes up by an average of 42 percent, while that of women goes down by an average of 73 percent.

And the long-range prospects continue to be better for men than women. Women still earn only 62 cents for every dollar earned by men—better than 59 cents in 1981 but down from 64 cents in 1955.

Because women often do not begin work until their children are grown or their marriages end, they frequently find themselves lacking the skills needed for higher-paying positions. The unemployment rate for single women maintaining families also is high—10.4 percent in 1984 compared with the overall rate for men and women of 7.6 percent. In addition, women tend to suffer from the last-hired, first-fired syndrome.

Smith says she has made exhaustive attempts to find work. Often, "I would come home [from job applications] and sit staring at the four walls and go stir-crazy. I want to work."

Toward that end, she enrolled in Women at Work, a program designed to help low-income women enter the job market. Funded by the Public Welfare Foundation in Washington, the program began in January 1984, an outgrowth of the Community Women's Education Project in Kensington.

"We wrote the proposal based on the feminization of poverty," says Marilyn Wood, the program's assistant director. "The courses are based on [women] understanding their situation sociologically. It's a phenomenon happening to lots and lots of people. Hopefully, instead of feeling like failures, they'll feel a little more angry and try to move beyond the situation."

Smith is studying math, English and sociology in addition to practical-application courses, such as computer skills.

"The usual philosophy of programs like this is to give women a skill and place them

(continued)

in a job quickly," Wood explains. "But if they go in at entry-level, they wind up making less. It just takes one small crisis, and they're bumped back into the poverty cycle.

"We try to take a long view. It takes people a long time to get into the situation, and it's going to take a long time to get out."

When Aida Mendez reflects on the before-and-after of things, her face takes on a faraway expression.

Seven years ago, with her husband fresh out of the Navy and working as a deputy sheriff, they owned a three-bedroom house in Orlando, Fla. "A nice kitchen," she says dreamily. "New stove, new refrigerator. A family room, central air. A washer and dryer. A garage. It was a corner lot with trees and bushes. We had all trees in the back yard. A big, big yard. Grapefruit trees in the back yard. I would pick them and give them away to friends. . . ."

Five years ago, she returned home to Philadelphia—divorced. Now, she and her children share a two-bedroom house on Water Street where the rent is $275 a month, more than half of the $428 she receives monthly from AFDC.

Mendez, 29, finds the comparison painful.

"I know what it's like to be doing OK," she says, "to have a house and to have a car and all those things I don't have now."

Mendez had a job as a clerk-stenographer not long after returning to Philadelphia, but she quit to have a baby, a boy now 2. Six months ago, she had another child, a daughter. The babies and her 11-year-old daughter live with her; her 9-year-old son recently went to live with his father in Florida.

"If I had any kind of person to care for the children, I would have gone back to work," says Mendez.

The difficulty of finding affordable or subsidized child care keeps many women at home, with welfare their only available source of income. A survey done by Choice Inc., which operates a child-care referral service, counted 73,471 working women with children under 6 and only 40,885 licensed child-care slots in the five-county area.

"The number of subsidized spots is simply not enough for the number of people eligible," says Mary Ann Measure of Choice Inc. "The southeast region is very underserved."

Measure said the state enacted a $6 million increase in its child-care budget for 1985–1986, but the money is earmarked for a variety of purposes, and it is unclear to what extent day care will be expanded.

U.S. Rep. Bob Edgar (D., Pa.), a member of the Congressional Caucus for Women's Issues, has said that 36 percent of unemployed mothers with family incomes below $15,000 reported to the Census Bureau that they would work if adequate day care were available.

"I really think there's still the myth that people who are poor want to be poor and if they'd just go out and get a job, they'd be all right," says Lori Rubenstein of Women's Agenda. "That's a model that works for men but not for women, because they have child-care problems."

Aida Mendez, attracted by the offer of free child care, also enrolled in the Women at Work program, where she is learning computer skills. She is excited by her job prospects.

"I think the worst thing . . . is just being on welfare," she says. "I like working more than anything else. I hate having to go to the [welfare] office and talk to the caseworkers and prove this and prove that. I find it degrading. I can't wait to get off it."

This was not supposed to happen to Diane Haughwout.

She grew up in middle-class comfort, earned a bachelor's degree in English, married twice—first a college professor, then an architect—stayed home to rear her son and daughter and later taught English.

At the moment, Haughwout is out of work, collecting $150 a week in unemployment benefits, renting a house in Hershey and wondering how long it will take to regain her footing.

"Some of us have lived the Cinderella syndrome," she says bitterly. "We went to college and got our nice degrees. It rounded us out. Big deal. We came out and were a big asset to our husbands. We could talk about Picasso and look good on his arm. I think it's time women get practical

(continued)

and take their heads out of the clouds.

"I've had people say to me, 'You actually stand in line at the unemployment office?' and I say, 'You'd be surprised who's standing in that line.' . . . " The plunge from life in the upper-middle class to life on the economic edge is painful but not uncommon, say those familiar with the phenomenon.

The once-well-off woman "probably suffers most of all," says Linda Crosson, a counselor at the Single Parents and Homemakers Program in the Harrisburg area. "She can literally go from having much to having next to nothing."

Speaking last month at a national conference of the National Displaced Homemakers Network in Washington, Marna S. Tucker of the National Women's Law Center gave a speech titled, "Women, Divorce and the Legal System: Equality Came Too Soon."

No-fault divorce and recent property-distribution laws, intended to equalize men's and women's positions after divorce, have actually hurt women, Tucker concluded. Research shows, she said, "that what seemed like good sense and enlightened progress was more like wishful thinking."

No-fault laws were designed to reduce hostility in the courtrooms, Tucker said, but have also "removed the leverage" for attorneys to obtain good economic settlements in the wake of adultery or desertion. Tucker also found fault with the awarding of rehabilitative alimony— temporary support given while a woman acquires the skills to support herself.

"The danger here," she said, "is that women have been declared equal when, in fact, their earning power is significantly lower across the board."

Diane Haughwout did not ask for alimony after her second divorce three years ago because, at the time, she "had an excellent salary." She had developed a program for the Navy, teaching English as a second language, but when her seven-month contract ran out, the program fell victim to budget cuts.

Since then, she has held several jobs, but "nothing I can live on." Her ex-husband, who is retired, provides some money for the children from his Social Security, but it is insufficient to send their 17-year-old daughter to college.

Because Haughwout's career has been sporadic, fitted in between the years she willingly and happily stayed home with her children, finding a job is especially difficult.

"You take a resume like that into an employer and, as I've learned, they use that resume as a negative: You don't have this, you don't have that," she says, "instead of seeing what you can do."

Additionally, at 41, she is "finding it a whole lot different than finding work in my 20s."

Much of the time, Haughwout is able to keep things in perspective, focusing on her strengths and talents, spending time with her children, drawing on the experiences of others in similar straits and telling herself that the future holds promise. But occasionally, her optimism falters.

"The fear is sometimes immobilizing," she says. "I feel I'm sitting on the brink of something new, and I'm scared."

In November of 1984, while a resident of Wesley House, a shelter for the homeless in Chester, Doreatha McGurn gave birth to her fourth child. She was on welfare at the time, receiving $504 a month in AFDC plus $190 worth of food stamps.

Recently, McGurn accepted a job with Wesley House, with take-home pay that will amount to $285 every two weeks—not much better than welfare after calculating her expenses.

Either way, she says, "it's hard."

McGurn grew up in Chester, one of the nation's most economically depressed cities. McGurn, like about 60 percent of Chester's residents, is black, a group long overrepresented in poverty statistics.

Since 1973, black families have increasingly fallen into poverty—up from one in four to one in three today. Of all black children, half grow up in poverty. Among black female-headed families, 68 percent are poor—a major factor in the feminization of poverty.

McGurn's father, a steelworker, died when she was 12, leaving her and six siblings to be reared on their mother's

(continued)

meager income as a domestic in nearby Swarthmore and Media.

At 16, she got a job as a teacher's aide to help the family. She later worked as a nurse's aide, an inhalation therapist and an assembly-line worker.

She first went on welfare in 1971, when her first child was born. She remained on welfare, she says, because Chester's job market dried up.

"There's just nothing here for nobody," she says. "Chester's went down a lot. A whole lot." Her employment at Wesley House will be her first job in 15 years.

On Oct. 12 of last year, Marie Beaver celebrated her 21st wedding anniversary in San Antonio, Texas. On Oct. 15, her husband asked for a divorce. Two months later, she came home to Springfield, Delaware County, and the room she slept in when she was 17.

"I asked my father if I could move in with him," says Beaver, 45. "How was I going to make it on my own?"

Beaver's son, Christopher, 12, came home with her. Her 21-year-old daughter stayed in Texas with her father and his new girlfriend. At the time of the divorce, Beaver's husband was unemployed, so no alimony was awarded, but he does send $200 a month in child support for Christopher.

According to the Legal Defense and Education Fund for the National Organization for Women, an estimated $3 billion a year in child support awards are never paid. The average court-ordered child support payment due in 1983 was $2,290—more than twice the average yearly amount actually paid, $1,330.

In an effort to correct that situation, Congress last year passed the Child Support Enforcement Amendments, requiring states to develop workable tracking systems for delinquent parents. The law requires withholding payment from a parent's wages if it is more than a month overdue.

Pennsylvania adopted its plan at the end of October, so its effectiveness remains untested, "but it certainly does give us broader ways of getting at folks," says Lori Rubenstein of Women's Agenda.

Unwilling to rely on child support, or strain the resources of her widowed father, Beaver enrolled in New Beginnings, a displaced-homemakers program, three days after her divorce became final. Through the program, she got a trainee's job as a customer-service representative for a Wayne bank.

Two nights a week, as part of the program, she takes courses at Delaware County Community College, hoping that scholastic achievement eventually will pay off in career advancement. She remains upset that her daughter recently dropped out of college, unwilling to heed her mother's advice about the importance of education.

"If ever she needed examples without being told, it was in her own family," Beaver says.

SOURCE. Mary Jane Fine. 1985. "Slipping into poverty: Hard times for women in '80s." *The Philadelphia Inquirer* (Dec. 22). Reprinted by permission of *The Philadelphia Inquirer* Dec. 22, 1986.

---

poverty and is seen to have long-range effects on individuals' and families' behavior and values. This position argues that, although social conditions may be or may have been the underlying cause of poverty, emergent cultural conditions may lead to the development of self-perpetuating cultural patterns that are inimical to movement out of poverty. A self-perpetuating cycle is seen to come into play—broken families and low educational motivation lead to inadequate job preparation, which, in turn, perpetuates poverty, unemployment, despair and broken families.

The second position, the situational approach, hypothesizes that although the behavior of poverty families is different than the middle-class pattern, the values of culture of the poverty group are basically the same. The behavior of poverty families is seen as adaptations and solutions to poverty conditions. The cultural similarity among generations is seen to result from the perpetuation of poverty conditions—no jobs, discrimination, inadequate housing, and so on—rather than the cultural transmission of a poverty culture.

The chapter concluded with a discussion of the widening difference between the proportion of white and black families found in poverty and the proportion maintained by women. The social-policy programs and their implications were examined. The recent work by Daniel Patrick Moynihan was used as a focal point for our discussion of the complexity and severity of the problem for contemporary American society and its families.

In the following chapter, we broaden our discussion of the family in the community by looking at a non-Western setting, black families in sub-Saharan African cities. That discussion provides further evidence to invalidate the social-disorganization thesis. As we will see, families in these cities are not characterized by alienation, anomie, family disorganization, or other forms of disorganization. For the vast majority of African city dwellers, the ties between the extended family and those between city and rural village were maintained and, instead of isolation and detribalization, comprehensive associational structures were developed for the purpose of mutual aid and to provide the necessary transitional supports for the new urban residents.

By comparatively examining a diverse number of poverty families representing different races and different societal cultures, we reach a similar position with that of the situationalists. Our position is that the culture of poverty perspective tends to put the blame of poverty on the very victims of poverty—the poverty families, themselves. It downplays the societal factors and the debilitating consequences of inequality. We share the viewpoint of men like Leonard Reissman who have argued that the removal of the causes and consequences of inequality will also remove the "tangle of pathology" of poor people: If we want to change poverty families, we must end poverty.

CHAPTER 7

The Family in the City: The African Experience

Marc Riboud/Magnum

A contemporary street scene in Lagos, Nigeria. Observe the juxtaposition of African and European dress.

CHAPTER OUTLINE

In Part I, we examined various theories in sociology that were concerned with comparative cross-cultural analysis. The most influential was structural functionalism, which was limited by a theoretical bias that led it to underestimate the importance of social change. This bias stemmed from the emphasis of structural functionalism on an organismic model of consensus and cooperation and on its failure to acknowledge the possibility of conflicting interests among the constituent elements in a social system. In anthropology, this theoretical position is labeled social anthropology. Like structural functionalism, social anthropology presents rather static models of society and tends to ignore change, even as it is occurring. Traditionally, social anthropologists in their study of nonliterate tribal or ethnic peoples have tended to view their cultures as static entities and have, by and large, ignored the impact of colonial regimes on them.[1] Instead, they have preferred to focus on the historical past prior to colonialism rather than on the transitional colonial era and the postcolonial present. This is evident by the limited number of studies that exist on tribal (ethnic) peoples outside their tribal (ethnic) communities. Peter C.W. Gutkind states that although contemporary social anthropologists are turning to urban studies, the previous generation of fieldworkers, as the noted social anthropologist, Max Gluckman, has pointed out, were "reared on the rural tradition of the tribe" (Gutkind, 1969:215). This attitude is reflected in the following report by British anthropologist Audrey Richards:

> In 1931 I first left the underpopulated bush inhabited by the Bemba of northeastern Rhodesia to study the men and women of this tribe who had migrated to the copper mining towns of the south. My conduct was then thought rather unusual in a social anthropologist. I was even told by one of my professors not to meddle with these modern urban problems, but to stick to "really scientific work" in an unspoilt tribe! (Audrey Richards cited in Gutkind, 1969:215)

Tied to this concern for study in the untampered past was an avoidance of both national political issues and the economic, political, and social forces accompanying colonialism. William Mangin (1970) believes that the dislike of anthropologists for the study of acculturation and the involvement of "their" people with cities and with national and international politics is shared by sociologists in their small-town and rural bias and their dislike of cities. Both orientations are part of the overall antiurban sentiments of intellectuals, artists, politicians, and lay people of Western industrial societies. In recent years, however, an increasing number of anthropologists have turned from this traditional position and have concerned themselves with the transitions and changes in non-Western preliterate societies. Of particular interest to us is the accumulating research in urban anthropology that is concerned with the

---

[1] The term "tribe" or "tribal" was used by social scientists prior to the 1980s. The term "ethnic" or "ethnic group" is now preferred. Given the historical emphasis of this chapter, both sets of terms are used where most appropriate.

FIGURE 7.1 Western, middle, eastern, and southern regions of sub-Saharan Africa (Thomas J. Goliber. 1985. "Sub-Saharan Africa: Population Pressures on Development." *Population Bulletin,* vol. 40, no. 1, p. 2).

migration of peoples into the cities of colonial and postcolonial societies as well as their various adaptations and modifications of traditional family, religious, and political institutions and their emerging new patterns of life.

In this chapter, we look at migrants to African cities south of the Sahara (black Africa; see Fig. 7-1) to shed comparative light on urban ways of life. We must warn the reader that the peoples and family patterns of sub-Saharan Africa vary a great deal and, by necessity, there will be a glossing over of these differences. Our main concern is to look at the profound effect urbanization has had on the family and to compare the adjustments, modifications, and new emerging patterns of these peoples with those that have occurred in Western industrial cities, particularly in the United States. In addition, we will be able to explore the validity of urban–rural ideal typologies and the isolated-nuclear-family theories of Louis Wirth and Talcott Parsons.

We limit our attention to sub-Saharan African cities, but we do not claim to provide a complete, comprehensive treatise on the family systems in this area owing to space limitations. Further, we wish to point out the great differences that exist in the different regions of tropical Africa. East, Central, and South Africa are characterized by extreme racial intolerance. The various policies of apartheid have generated fear and hatred. Colin M. Turnbull (1962) observes that this has occurred in those regions where Europeans decided to settle and where they appropriated the tribal lands of the Africans. Ultimately, in all but the Republic of South Africa, the Europeans were forced out, leaving a feeling of hatred and dislike. In West Africa, the situation was different, and this difference must be underlined. The Europeans did not have the desire to set up permanent residence; the malaria problem partly accounted for this attitude. Further, there was less hostility between the African and the European because the European chose to live in the towns and cities of West Africa, did not take over the tribal lands, and did not have the vast private farming estates characteristic of the other regions of sub-Saharan Africa. Turnbull (1962) believes that the Africans developed less antagonism toward European-dominated towns and cities because of these factors and owing to the greater economic opportunity and political equality of West Africa. Further, there were greater educational opportunities for the West African. The segregation occurring in these towns tended to be more social than racial, in contrast to the rigid segregated districts of cities in South Africa.

In the course of our discussion, we make note of these distinctions. For now, we want to alert the reader to their existence and to point out that in sub-Saharan cities and family life there are differences that exist based on these regional variations, as well as on ethnic and social-class criteria.

Sub-Saharan African Cities

African cities, especially the main cities in each country, are the centers of modernization. These cities, which anthropologists have labeled *primate* cities, are the intellectual and social capitals, the seats of government and political activity, and the economic capitals of their respective countries. The geographer William A. Hance (1970) observes that the most notable characteristic of many African cities is the rapid fading away of modernity as we leave these urban centers.

Sub-Saharan African cities are growing at a phenomenal rate, as shown in Table 7.1. According to 1982 U.N. population assessments, the overall urban population of the 42 countries in this vast area grew from 21 million in 1950 to 93 million in 1980. This represents an increase of 450 percent in just 30 years. The United Nations estimates that for the 30-year period from 1980 to 2010 there will be a further increase of 475 percent (Goliber, 1985). The proportion of urban dwellers will rise from the estimated 24 percent in 1980 to 45 percent in 2010.

Rapid urbanization is associated with many negative consequences. Delegates to the Second African Population Conference, convened in Tanzania by the Economic Commission for Africa in January 1984, summarized the current situation:

> The major cities in Africa [are] plagued by the adverse effects of rapid growth — urban sprawl, unemployment, delinquency, inadequate social services, traffic congestion and poor housing. Undoubtedly these features and the rapid rate of urban population [will] from now till the end of the century have serious implications for food, housing, education, health services, job opportunities and social amenities in the urban areas and the nation[s] as a whole. (Economic Commission for Africa, 1984:11)

Nigeria is typical of this phenomenal urban growth pattern. The U.N. estimates that the total number of urban dwellers in 2010 will be more than 94.1 million, which is a number greater than the total population of Nigeria in 1984. In 1950, the urban population was 2.4 million and, in 1980, it rose 480 percent to 16.4 million people.

TABLE 7.1　Urbanization in Sub-Saharan Africa: 1960–1982

| | Urban Population | | Average Annual Growth Rate (percent) | Number of Cities Over 500,000 Persons | | Percentage of Urban Population in Largest City |
| | As Percentage of Total Population | | | | | |
Country	1960	1982	1970–1982	1960	1980	1980
WESTERN AFRICA						
Benin	10	15	4.4	0	1	63
Burkina Faso	5	11	6.0	0	0	41
Ghana	23	37	5.0	0	2	35
Guinea	10	20	5.2	0	1	80
Ivory Coast	19	42	8.2	0	1	34
Liberia	21	34	5.7	0	0	—
Mali	11	19	4.7	0	0	24
Mauritania	3	26	8.1	0	0	39
Niger	6	14	7.2	0	0	31
Nigeria	13	21	4.9	2	9	17
Senegal	23	34	3.7	0	1	65
Sierra Leone	13	23	3.9	0	0	47
Togo	10	21	6.6	0	0	60
EASTERN AFRICA						
Burundi	2	2	2.5	0	0	—
Ethiopia	6	15	5.6	0	1	37
Kenya	7	15	7.3	0	1	57
Madagascar	11	20	5.2	0	1	36
Malawi	4	10	6.4	0	0	19
Mozambique	4	9	8.1	0	1	83
Rwanda	2	5	6.4	0	0	—
Somalia	17	32	5.4	0	0	34
Sudan	10	23	5.8	0	1	31
Tanzania	5	13	8.5	0	1	50
Uganda	5	9	3.4	0	1	52
Zambia	23	45	6.5	0	1	35
Zimbabwe	13	24	6.0	0	1	50
MIDDLE AFRICA						
Angola	10	22	5.8	0	1	64
Cameroon	14	37	8.0	0	1	21
Central African Republic	23	37	4.5	0	0	36
Chad	7	19	6.4	0	0	39
Congo	30	46	4.4	0	0	56
Zaire	16	38	7.6	1	2	28
SOUTHERN AFRICA						
South Africa	47	50	3.2	4	7	13

SOURCE:　World Bank. 1984. From *World Development Report 1984*. Copyright © 1984 by The International Bank for Reconstruction and Development / The World Bank. Reprinted by permission of Oxford University Press, Inc. Table 22, p. 260.

In Nigeria, as elsewhere in sub-Saharan cities, the urban explosion is the result of a desire for paid employment, which for those fortunate to obtain jobs is many times higher than in rural areas. Cities are also the center for such important social services as schools, health facilities, potable water, and entertainment. For those migrants who do not benefit fully from city life, the hope is that their children will have opportunities not available to them in the countryside. As Thomas J. Goliber of the

Population Reference Bureau points out: "Despite the squalor of huge garbage piles, abandoned automobiles, open sewers, shanty housing, air pollution, noise, and physical danger, urban centers still offer a glimmer of hope for a better life" (1985:28.) And, as we will see, the family system is an integral factor in obtaining that objective.

African cities can be classified according to size and age as well as political, economic, tribal, social, and cultural functions. The most widely used system is one that classifies cities as to whether they were founded by Africans (indigenous cities) or by Europeans (expatriate cities). The anthropologist Aidan Southall (1961) refers to the indigenous cities as Type A towns. These are old-established, slowly growing African towns whose social structure is basically traditional. Type B towns are of European creation, are comprised of rapidly expanding populations, and are mostly found in the industrialized areas that have the largest white populations.

Southall (1961:1–13) delineates the characteristics of Type A and Type B towns. Type A towns are composed of homogeneous indigenous populations. Although subsistence agriculture still plays a part in the economic life of the towns—with residents moving to the surrounding countryside for daily farm work and returning to the town in the evening—the dominant occupations tend to be clerical and commercial rather than industrial. Variations in social status are based on economic position, distance from rural origins, and length of time one has lived in the city. Kinship and tribal structures are not as extensive as in the rural areas, but they do exist and are sufficiently flexible to permit tribal and kinship concentrations.

In contrast, Type B towns are composed of an immigrant African population whose ties are severed from their rural origins. During the colonial period, the administrative control of the town was exercised by the white colonizers. The emerging independent African nations are developing managerial, entrepreneurial, landlord, and professional skills since they were little developed during the colonial period and the immediate preindependence period [when Southall wrote his essay (1961)]. Of economic and political importance to urban Africans are trade unions, political parties, and tribal welfare associations. In relation to the Type A town situation, there is little kinship and tribal concentration. Further, regional diversities of culture and social structure are minimized, with emphasis being placed on the problems and solutions to the new urban condition.

The distribution of indigenous (Type A) and expatriate (Type B) towns and cities are mapped by Hance in Figure 7.2. Spatially, the Type A urban areas are centered around marketplaces, which are in open areas devoid of houses. Frequently, the quarters surrounding the market in North Africa take on the appearance of a rural village populated on the basis of tribal or religious affiliation, whereas they are likely to be of more homogeneous character in sub-Saharan Africa. The markets are devoted to the sale of farm produce and handcrafted items. In the towns that have fallen under modern influences, industrial crafts, mechanical and electrical repair shops, plumbing supplies, and so on are present.

The Type B expatriate towns and cities differ in almost every respect from the indigenous towns. Founded by Europeans, these colonial urban centers take on European architectural and street-layout styles and patterns. Populations are diverse, with Indians, Pakistanis, Syrians, Lebanese, and other minorities residing exclusively in these European-oriented towns, as opposed to the indigenous ones. During the colonial period, the indigenous African population was separated and segregated in surrounding suburban areas called *bidonvilles* ("tin-can towns"). The indigenous Africans migrated into the city to work and then returned to their rather squalid shantytowns at night. This is the reverse of the American industrial city pattern. With independence, the more squalid of these communities have been replaced by low-cost housing in many sub-Saharan countries, but there is still a great need for adequate housing for these people. The amount of residential segregation has varied—from the extreme government policy of apartheid in the Republic of South Africa (where sections of the major cities are composed exclusively of African, European, Indian, and Coloured, that is, mixed-race, populations) to the mixed residential patterns of a city in West Africa such as Lagos, Nigeria. However, as A.L. Epstein (1969) states, the tendency for Africans to be housed in strict segregation was almost universal in preindependent countries. The anthropologist V.G. Pons' description of Stanleyville (now Kisangani), Belgian Congo (now Zaire), is typical:

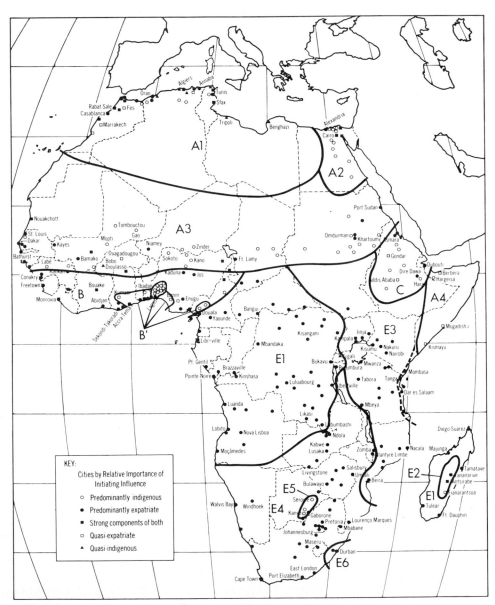

FIGURE 7.2   Selected towns and cities of Africa mapped according to the relative importance of indigenous and expatriate influence and tentative urban cultural regions. See key. (William A. Hance. 1970. *Population, Migration and Urbanization in Africa.* New York: Columbia University Press, pp. 246–247. Copyright © 1970 by Columbia University Press. Reprinted by permission.)

The physical layout of the town could be seen as both an expression and a symbol of the relations between Africans and Europeans. European residential areas were situated close to, and tended to run into, the area of administrative offices, hotels, shops and other service establishments, while African residential areas were strictly demarcated and well removed from the town centre. (V.G. Pons cited in Epstein, 1969:249)

Type A Indigenous Towns

In this section, we first discuss the family and kinship systems existing in the traditional indigenous Type A towns south of the Sahara, using the towns of the Yoruba in western Nigeria as the illustrative case. We then discuss and compare these towns with the family and kinship systems in the expatriate Type B towns that have developed as a result of direct European contact.

Yoruba, Nigeria

The anthropologist William Bascom (1968) describes the old historical Yoruba cities. These were based largely on agriculture and the populace were mainly farmers. The inhabitants commuted, not from the suburbs into the work places of the city, but

---

Regions delineated in Figure 7.2:

A. Areas of Strong Muslim Influence
  A1. North Africa, indigenous influence Arab-Berber; modern influence predominantly French in the Maghreb, Italian in Libya, Spanish in northern Morocco, Ceuta, and Melilla.
  A2. Egypt. Considerable European influence in modern cities.
  A3. Sudan belt. Emirate cities, old caravan centers; Arab and some Egyptian influence in east; modern influence French and British.
  A4. Somalia and East Coast. Arab influence strong.
B. Western Africa
  B. Modern cities predominate; French and British influence most important.
  B'. Subregions where indigenous cities are best represented.
C. Ethiopia. Mainly indigenous; Muslim and Italian influence in Eritrea; Italian influence in Addis Ababa, Gondar.
E. Middle, eastern, and southern Africa. European influence predominant in most areas.
  E1. Middle Africa. French, Belgian, and Portuguese influence dominant. On Madagascar (now the Malagasy Republic) French influence predominant in newer towns, some Arab influence at Majunga.
  E2. Merina and Betsileo towns of Malagasy Highlands; important French influence in new sections.
  E3. Eastern Africa. Modern influence primarily British; important Indian components in most towns; Arab influence on coast and islands.
  E4. Central and South Africa. Influence predominantly British; Afrikaner initiative in some South African towns.
  E5. Botswana. Agrotowns of Tswana.
  E6. Natal. Mainly British towns, strong Indian component.

Marilyn Silverstone/Magnum

A bush market at Yankasari, outside Kano, Nigeria
(ca. 1950). Women of the Housas ethnic group are selling
their agricultural products. "Bush" is a pejorative term
for rural and unsophisticated.

rather from their city homes to the belt of farms that surrounded each Yoruba city.
Kinship was the principal factor in, and primary determinant of, behavior in every
aspect of community life and, most important — since farming itself was organized
around family and kinship — these institutions set the way of life in both city and
countryside.

Bascom describes the large number of urban centers that existed in western Nigeria prior to the slave-trade wars of the first half of the nineteenth century. A large
number of these towns were destroyed or abandoned during this period. He quotes
Bowen, the first American missionary in Nigeria, who traveled through much of the
Yoruba country in 1849–1856:

> I have counted the sites of eighteen desolated towns within a distance of sixty miles
> between Badagry and Abbeokuta [*sic*] — the legitimate result of the slave trade. The
> whole of Yoruba country is full of depopulated towns, some of which were even

larger than Abbeokuta is at present. Of all the places visited . . . only Ishakki (Shaki), Igboho, Ikishi (Kishi) and a few villages remain. Ijenna (Ijana) was destroyed only a few weeks after my arrival in the country. Other and still larger towns in the same region have lately fallen. At one of these, Oke-Oddan, the Dahomey army killed and captured 20,000 people on which occasion the king presented Domingo, the Brazillian slaver, with 600 slaves. The whole number of people destroyed in this section of the country, within the last fifty years, can be not less than five hundred thousand. (Bascom, 1968:84)

Today, these traditional cities continue to exist without industrialization. Farming, specialized production in wood carving, metalwork, brass casting, weaving and dyeing, the trade of domestic products, and so forth are the cornerstones of the Yoruba town economy. The local retail trade has remained primarily in the hands of women, who tend to specialize in yams, corn, chickens, and other such commodities. They, like the artisans, are organized into guilds. The foundation of group activities is lineage, which involves reciprocal social and economic obligations. Thus, there is little loneliness and insecurity. Yoruba society is pecuniary and highly competitive. Therefore, economic failure can lead to frustration, aggression, or suicide, but such outcomes are minimized because of social and economic lineage support.

Bascom contrasts this description of the Yoruba way of life with that of Louis Wirth, who argued that the bonds of kinship, neighborliness, and sentiments stemming from a common folk tradition would be absent or, at best, very weak in the city. Such is not the case in the Yoruba cities. Bascom (1968:90–91) emphasizes the fact that Yoruba cities, unlike Wirth's ideal-type city, are not characterized by the substitution of formal control mechanisms for bonds of solidarity. Instead, formal control mechanisms were developed as mechanisms of political control on a secondary, suprakinship level, transcending the primary groups, such as lineages. Kinship bonds were not weakened by urban life or, on a higher level, by the political control of city governments. Lineage *was* the basis of both urban and rural political structure.

Bascom concludes that in these indigenous cities the majority of the residents marry, raise their children, and live with their families throughout most of their lives. They die and are buried within the city and with their own lineage. Ties with family and lineage are not broken or even suspended by urban life. The authority of the family, lineage, and the chiefdom are maintained in the cities through the family and lineage and through the town chiefs and heads of the Yoruba states. As a result, there are low rates of illegitimacy, juvenile delinquency, and crime in comparison to the newer African cities and to the cities of Europe and America.

Finally, Bascom notes the effects of European influence during the present century. Both the old residents of Yoruba cities and the new migrants from rural areas are forced to adapt to European acculturation. Yoruba religion was also undermined and its sanctions of behavior were sapped by Christian and Muslim missions and by schools and government. With the destruction of old belief systems and the substitution of Western concepts of individual salvation and individual responsibility, there has been a concomitant undermining of the traditional respect for elders, lineage responsibilities, and the strength of lineage controls. Bascom predicts that with the increasing industrialization and urbanization in Nigeria "although African cultural features will be retained, . . . the new and old cities of Africa will tend to approximate each other and the cities of Europe and America in their sociological characteristics" (Bascom, 1968:93).

We examine the transitions occurring in family life in indigenous Type A towns by reviewing in some detail the impact of family change in the increasingly industrial city of Lagos, which has its origins as a Yoruba town. We then contrast the events occurring in these types of urban areas with those cities of Africa that are of European origin and influence in regard to family and kinship patterns.

Lagos, Nigeria

In the study of family and kinship ties in indigenous Type A urban areas, a landmark research monograph was written by Peter Marris (1961), *Family and Social Change in an African City: A Study of Rehousing in Lagos.* Marris' aim was to replicate Michael Young and Peter Willmott's (1957) study of working-class families of Bethnel Green in east London, England, and the effect of the move to a suburban housing development, Greenleigh, located outside of London. As you recall from our discussion in an earlier chapter, Young and Willmott found that Bethnel Green working-class families were characterized by widespread cohesive kin groups embedded in a closed community with a strong sense of homogeneity and togetherness. The immediate effect of the move to Greenleigh was the loss of this sense of community, restrictions in contact with neighbors and friends, and a withdrawal of the husband and wife into their households—home-centeredness,

Lagos, Nigeria, the African city studied by Marris, is a city with a strong Yoruba traditional history that is being subjected to the demands of modernization and industrialization. Marris was fortunate in finding a parallel situation to that which occurred in east London; the central district of Lagos, which was inhabited by extended-family systems, was undergoing a slum-clearance disruption. Marris was concerned with comparing the family life in the central area before people were forced to move with the life of those living in the newly established rehousing estate. He was also interested in people's assessments of life in the central district before they moved. Finally, he wished to compare his findings with those of Young and Willmott's London study.

Marris describes the traditional Yoruba family as residing in a family compound based on a lineage that traced its descent from the same male ancestor. The characteristic pattern of residence consisted of a group of sons and grandsons—with their wives, children, and descendants—of the man who established the compound. Although they resided in the same compound, the members of it did not form a single economic unit; rather, each married man with his wives and unmarried children and any other kin for whom he was responsible (for example, a widowed mother or unmarried brother) formed a separate household. Each household would become an independent economic unit centered around the farmland the man owned. In cases where the man had more than one wife, each wife and their respective children would form a subsidiary household within the larger one, with the mother as the focal point of the children's ties, loyalties, and affections. This, then, was the smallest family unit in the Yoruba pattern of kinship—the mother and her children. The mother and her children formed part of the husband's household; the husband's household, in turn, was incorporated with several that resided within the same compound under the dominance of a single senior male; and these lineages, in turn, were part of a larger and more-comprehensive lineage residing in separate dwellings. Ultimately, the whole lineage became part of still-larger social groupings, with members recognizing the bonds of distant kinship with each other (Marris, 1961:12–16). The following account illustrates this traditional family compound arrangement that—although changing more in Lagos as a result of industrialization than in other parts of the Yoruba country—still had a profound influence on its members.

> This house was built by a wealthy trader about a hundred years ago. It fronted on to a narrow lane, the walls patched with corrugated iron, the windows boarded with cream and black shutters, grimed with age. Inside the door on the right, a passage extended past two rooms to an open yard, where chickens and guinea fowls clattered in their pens. A second passage facing the entrance led past three more rooms to a larger yard at the back of the house, where the households cooked, washed and kept their stores. Sheds lined two sides of the yard, and lavatories were built into a corner. Inside the passage a narrow staircase gave access to the upper floor: the

three lower steps were of concrete, the remainder thin wooden slats, worn away by years of use. At the head of the stairs was a landing with a gable window, where in the rainy season basins were spread to catch the leaks. On either side were sets of rooms, low-pitched under the iron sheeting of the roof. The walls and ceilings were of uneven, cream-painted boarding, and there was a gap between wall and floor, through which appeared the supporting poles of the eaves. On this floor were six more rooms, beside two small anterooms through which they were reached. Altogether, the house contained eleven rooms, each occupied by a separate household.

As with many of the old houses of Lagos, it seemed shabby and neglected. The furniture of each room was bare and functional—a bed, a few wooden stools or folding chairs, a cupboard, a pile of trunks and boxes, mats thrown on the floor. In the passage hung a mirror and a wall clock, no longer working. The only decorations were the calendars of commercial firms—the playfully exotic landscapes with which airlines like to match the months, or Coca Cola girls with their insatiable thirsts—and large wall almanacs put out by Lagos publishers, with inset photographs of chiefs and leading politicians. But in spite of their apparent indifference to appearances, the family was deeply attached to their home.

The most senior member of the house, a vigorous woman in her seventies, was the only surviving child of the original owner. She spent most of her day in a corner of the passage which flanked the front of the building, where every visitor would pause to pay her their respects. Here she presided over the affairs of the house. She shared a room and parlour with her eldest son, his wife and the wife's twelve-year-old niece, who helped with the housework. Two other rooms were occupied by women of her generation; the widow of one of her brothers, with her daughter and grandchildren, and the widow of a half brother with three grandchildren. Most of the rest of the house was taken up by six of her nephews, with their wives and children, and usually one or two young girls of the wives' families. Lastly, one room was used by the granddaughter of one of her brothers, who was separated from her husband. In all, these ten households contained eighteen men and women, and sixteen children. The head of each was a child (or his widow), grandchild or great-grandchild of the original owner of the house. In this sense, they lived as a traditional Yoruba family But there were many other grandsons and great-grandsons who, because of their work, or simply because there was no place for them, lived elsewhere, either with other relatives or in rooms they had rented. (Marris, 1961:17–19)

In summary, the traditional Yoruba extended family was composed of individuals with strong obligations to give economic assistance to kin while maintaining their social ties within the customary residential unit of a compound based on lineage. The extended family recognized the authority of a single head, usually the senior male member, and concomitantly the status of each family member was defined by his seniority. Finally, family relationships emphasized the importance and predominance of the family group over the individual.

The large family compound described is becoming more and more scarce with fewer houses in Lagos under common family ownership or entirely occupied by an extended family. The separate household has replaced the compound as the predominant unit of residence. However, the vast majority of the residents of the central district of Lagos interviewed by Marris still have strong family ties with their kin. And despite the predictions of such sociologists as Louis Wirth and Talcott Parsons, "the households are not isolated; their connections branch out into the neighborhood, and their lives are still centered on the affairs of their family group" (Marris, 1961:27). Friendship and kinship networks are maintained by daily meetings, which serve as communicative interchanges to pass on family news and to discuss family problems. Assistance patterns continue, with regular sums of money given for the support of kinfolk; the feeling is that the needs of relatives assume first obligatory priority. Individuals, rather than being primarily responsible and having first loyalties to themselves or to their conjugal nuclear families, see their prime responsibility to their extended family. Marris observed that the extended family also serves as the basis for some of the voluntary associations individuals join to further their economic interests.

Of the families studied by Marris, two-thirds of them were Muslim, one-third Christian. Of the 126 marriages studied, 118 had a customary marriage solemnized by the consent of the bride's family, the bridegroom usually providing an agreed-on monetary sum and ritual gifts. Although traditionally these marriages are arranged between the kinsfolk of the couple, eight of sixteen men sampled chose their wives themselves. Of the remaining eight marriages, seven were performed in church and one was a civil ceremony. The significance of this is that to be married in church places one under the rights and penalties derived from English custom rather than Nigerian custom.

Two-thirds of the householders in central Lagos were Muslim and half had more than one wife. Polygyny was also found in the Christian households but to a lesser degree. Polygyny is correlated with wealth and social status, and most important, more children are beneficial for the extended family system (Marris, 1961:47–49). There are also practical and moral advantages associated with polygyny. The Yoruba consider it wrong to have sexual relationships with pregnant women and women who are breast feeding.

In the polygynous household, the senior wife enjoys a privileged position and has authority over the junior wives, especially in allocating heavy housework. The junior wives, in turn, can benefit from this arrangement since the household can provide aid to them in times of need, for example, sickness. However, Marris observes that most women in Lagos do not prefer polygyny and that polygyny is particularly vulnerable to the precarious economic circumstances of the husband.

The disappearance of the extended-family traditional compound has led to the weakening of the extended-kinship control of the husband's family over the wife. This, combined with the fact that most marriages are no longer arranged by the couple's kinfolk, has led to greater freedom of the wife from the husband's lineage and at the same time has lessened the extended family's support, especially if some misfortune befalls the husband. Marris believes that the weakening of the traditional sanctions has also made divorce more prevalent than previously. This has led women to secure an independent income to replace the dependency on their husband's extended family—nine out of ten wives work in some kind of trade.

The greater independence of the wife has had an effect on the raising of children. In the traditional family compound, children were raised by all members of the lineage. Although kinfolk still care for each other's sons and daughters, the breakdown of the compounds has led to a lessening of this everyday contact. Grandparents still have grandchildren residing with them to help with the household chores, since failure of the parents to respond to such a request is a serious breach of familial respect. Although there is an increase in the number of women who set up economically independent households from their husbands and the extended family of their husbands, and although there is an increase in the divorce rate, children who live with only one parent may still see the other parent very often. The pattern emerging is one in which, despite the breakdown of extended-family solidarity, there are various accommodations made to maintain intimate and continuous relationships of children with their larger families.

Marris sees an evolution of the family resulting from the new urban patterns. There has been a gradual weakening of the extended-family system and an increase in the independence of wives from family control and the control of their husbands. New patterns of marriage and kinship are beginning to be formed with the outcome still in doubt.

> In this discussion of some Lagos families, I have tried to bring out a theme which seems especially relevant to the evolution of urban patterns of life. In any society, people look for secure affection above all to their family relationships, and find

there also much practical help. Without this fundamental assurance, they tend to lack confidence in other social roles. The stability of family relationships is therefore very important, but the emphasis varies according to whether ties of marriage or ties of blood command the strongest loyalties. Traditionally, in Nigerian societies, the households of husbands and wives were subordinate to a wider family grouping. But as this subordination was not questioned, and the family group shared a common dwelling, obligations of marriage and of kinship could, at least in principle, be reconciled within the values of the culture. In Lagos, as households tend more and more to live apart, the group reasserts its common interests by frequent meetings both formal and informal, by the acceptance of mutual obligations, and by caring for each other's children. But this pattern of family affairs does not seem to have reasserted so effectively the authority of the group over relationships between husband and wife, nor is the group so responsible for the women who have married into it. If wives have more freedom from the control of their husbands' family, they cannot at the same time depend on them so much. But they cannot instead depend more on their husbands, unless he can both ensure her welfare and reconcile his obligations to her with those to his kin. She, for her part, may put more trust in an economic independence and the support her own family can give her. So the dispersal of the family group is not necessarily compensated by the strengthening of ties of marriage. In a time of rapid social change, people may rely less on any relationship, and as this also affects the care of children, the next generation may grow up without the experience of secure attachments, and so be less able to form them.

The reconciliation of ties of marriage and kinship seems a crucial issue in the evolution of Lagos family life. (Marris, 1961:65)

In contrast to family life in Lagos, a study of the rehousing estate outside the city highlights and accentuates the social dynamics of family processes and the dissolution of extended family ties. Here, families see less of their relatives and the characteristic qualities of these relationships also change. Although in central Lagos the communal family compound is gradually disappearing, there remains strong vestiges of the extended family. In the rehousing development, extended-family ties are disappearing; individuals find it more difficult to visit their relatives and to fulfill their familial obligations:

We used to see them almost every day when we were in Lagos, sometimes two or three times. But they don't come because of the transport, and they think this place is far.

The slum clearance has scattered us. Apart from those of the same father and mother, I don't see my family again. All other family is scattered, some at Shomolu, some Agage, some of them have gone to the bush of their villages. I've not been able to see some of my family for two years, and I don't even know where they are.

I don't see my sister at all unless I force myself there. If you don't go to see them they don't come. Sometimes I visit them four times before they come — they don't like this side. They have to change bus six times.

When I was in Lagos they were with me. We lived in the same street. Old wife's family, new wife's family, we see each other every day. In Lagos you see everybody nearly every day. Do you see any of my family visiting me here?

On Saturday I made 5s gain, and I ran to see my mother. I've not seen her since Saturday, and God knows when I shall see her again. She wept when I was to leave, because she didn't want to leave me, and she is afraid to come here. When I was in Lagos there was not a day I don't see her. (Marris, 1961:110–111)

Marris asserts that for some of the young married couples moving to the rehousing estate was a welcome occurrence as they became more independent from extended kin. Three main reasons were delineated: (1) they were able to free themselves from the controls of their elders; (2) they were free from the quarrels between wives and mothers, which divided their loyalties; and (3) they were free from the continual demands of extended kin for monetary aid. [The reader will be aware of the motivational similarities of these people with those of middle-class Americans who moved from the city to outer city and suburban areas in the United States (Bell, 1958).] The Nigerians who welcomed this change tended to be Christian rather than Muslim, Ibo rather than Yoruba. Marris suggests that their occupations — many were civil servants provided with governmental security and prospective old-age pensions — allowed them to be less dependent on their extended kin and thus helped them to repudiate the traditional kinship obligations.

However, the more-traditionally oriented Yoruba who were forced to migrate to the rehousing development found their family life in turmoil — a similar reaction of the transplanted working-class Bethnel Greeners who were forced to move to Greenleigh. The increased costs of living in the rehousing estate led to the withdrawal of financial aid to their kinfolk and a decrease in their visits to them. The slum clearance scattered the family group. It may have pleased a few non-Yorubas, but for the Yorubas to be out of reach of their relatives was distressing. It was particularly disruptive for the elderly who had lived on family property and had been cared for by relatives and now found themselves isolated from them:

> There's plenty of breeze and it's quiet here," said an old woman, who had been moved from her uncle's house. "But this seems to be a sort of hidden place — some of my family have never been able to find me here. And if you think of going to see them, you have to think of transport. . . . There's a proverb says there's no good in a fine house when there's no happiness. It's by the grace of God that you find me still alive. I've tasted nothing since morning, and I'm not fasting yet. The money I'd have spent on food has all gone on light. I handed over six and threepence this morning." (Marris, 1961:112–113)

In the end, the isolation of the estate led to an impoverished social life and disruption of the family, and it did not increase the self-sufficiency of the husband and wife. The greater expenses of suburban life led many husbands to send their wives to their families and distribute their children among relatives who could care for them. Further, the increased emotional dependence and intimacy necessary to cope with the loss of supportive extended-kinship relations did not develop, leading to additional feelings of dependency. [Again, the reader is alerted to a similar phenomenon occurring among blue-collar suburban wives in the United States, who developed feelings of alienation and anomie as a result of the severing of their ties with their extended kin (Tallman, 1969; Tallman and Morgner, 1970).]

Marris ends his discussion with the plea that future city planners take into account the social and psychological needs of the populace. Drastic dislocations mean disruptions not only in economic activities but also in social lives; although good housing is a necessity, it must be provided without causing major disruptions in people's lives.

> There is a danger that their family life will be improverished as much as their livelihood, and in turn create new hardships as they are forced to abandon obligations to their kin. Good housing is very much needed in Lagos, and a nation naturally desires a fine appearance for its capital city. But unless these aims can be reconciled with the needs and resources of the people who must be displaced, the harm done will be disproportionate to the achievement. (Marris, 1961:115)

Despite the extreme dislocations of families resulting from the slum clearance of central Lagos, the overall picture of family life in the indigenous towns of western Africa continues to show the vitality of the extended-family system. These family systems continue to exist because they serve useful purposes for their members. Joan Aldous (1968), reviewing existing research up to 1962, reports that extended-family and kinship ties are important in meeting economic, religious, legal, and recreational needs because of the absence of such services by the central government. As long as substitute institutions do not develop to satisfy the demands of the populace, the vitality of the extended-family and kinship ties will play an important role in the urbanization of African cities. The continued viability of the extended-family system runs counter to the theoretical positions of such sociologists as Louis Wirth and Talcott Parsons, who suggested that the extended family would disappear in the urban milieu.

We now turn our attention to exploring changes in the urban way of life existing in the European-influenced expatriate cities of Africa, especially in regard to family and kinship patterns.

Type B Expatriate Towns

The expatriate towns and cities are a result of colonialism and economic interests requiring administrative centers. Nairobi, which is now the largest city in East Africa, began as a construction camp for the Uganda railway in 1899 (Little, 1973). The capital of Uganda, Kampala, and the capital of Tanzania, Dar es Salaam, were founded by the British and Germans, respectively. Europeans in West Africa established port cities at Accra, Ghana; Freetown, Sierra Leone; Dakar, Senegal; and Lagos, Nigeria. Other urban centers developed as communication centers; as collection points for locally produced commodities, like cocoa and groundnuts; and for their convenience to the mining centers of gold, diamonds, iron ore, and tin.

The colonial period was marked by the forced movement of workers from ethnic areas to areas where their labor was needed for agriculture, mining, and construction:

B. Campbell/Sygma

The modern market economy of Kano, Nigeria, exists in the shops and on the street, shown by this typical confrontation between a woman selling canned goods and a customer looking for a better price.

> The Belgians used forced labor to build the Congo-Ocean railway, which was completed in 1934 at a cost of over 15,000 African lives. The British also used, until the 1920s, a system of compulsory service known as the "Kasanvu System." (Palen, 1975:372–373)

Although the forced-labor systems are disappearing in the newly independent African states, the large-scale migration continues. Kenneth Little (1973) points out that the city sets the pace for the wider society, that city growth in Africa is proceeding at a more rapid rate than in other regions of the world, and that it exceeds the city growth of the Western industrial nations, including the United States, during their own periods of fastest urban growth.

> For example, of the original port towns on the west coast of Africa, Lagos had a population of 126,000 in 1930 and had more than doubled to 364,000 by 1960. (A recent estimate . . . puts the population of greater Lagos in 1963 at 1.2 million.) Accra had only 40,000 inhabitants in 1930, had doubled in population by 1950, and had a population approaching a half million by 1960. Similarly, in the Francophone countries, there was an increase of 100 per cent in the populations of the principal towns of Senegal between 1942 and 1952, while those of the Ivory Coast grew by 109 per cent during the same decade, and those in the Cameroons by 250 per cent between 1936 and 1952. In what is now Zaire, Kinshasa (formerly Leopoldville) was a large country town of 34,000 in 1930, but in 20 years it had a population of 402,000. On the other side of Africa, Nairobi doubled in size during the 1940–50 decade and rose from 119,000 inhabitants in 1948 to about half a million in 1969, while Dar es Salaam grew from 69,000 in 1948 to 128,700 in 1957, and to 272,500 in 1967. Also, not only have existing towns swelled in size, but in some cases entirely new urban centres and agglomerations have come into being. For example, Enugu, now one of the largest cities of eastern Nigeria, was founded in 1914 on an empty site, had a population of some 10,000 by 1921, which rose to 138,457 by 1963; while the population of Port Harcourt—another "new" town—grew to 208,237 by 1969. [Little, 1973:12–13 (sources omitted)]

It is no wonder, then, that social scientists, like William J. Goode (1963), observe that in the modern world it does not seem possible to distinguish clearly between urbanization and modernization and their effects on the individual, the family, and kinship and tribal groups. It is now time to examine these effects on the newly emerging urban centers of sub-Saharan Africa.

William A. Hance (1970) examines the differences between urban growth in Africa and in the West during a comparable period. Of note is the contrast in the greater rates of growth of the major cities of Africa with those in the West and the fact that the growth of urbanization in Africa is not accompanied by a comparable change in the rural areas. This has led to a greater dichotomy between the rural and urban areas that is reflected in individual behavior, social values, and economically—a factor which has reduced the tempo of economic life. This is in contrast to the Western pattern, which is characterized by the Protestant ethic and its emphasis on hard work, achievement, and success. Hance takes note of the dual existence of tribal and Western structures in many African cities, a phenomenon that has not had an equivalent counterpart in Western industrial cities and one that is worthy of a longer look. This theme on the duality of value systems of African urbanites will be followed up later in our discussion.

Research on black Africans migrating to urban areas indicates that the social structure that emerges is not a simple modification and adaptation of rural life structures. Peter C.W. Gutkind (1969) views urbanism in Africa as a distinct way of life, with urban institutions exerting strong pressures on individuals and groups to adopt an urban model—"we are dealing with townsmen in town and not tribesmen in town" (Gutkind, 1969:217). The urbanization of sub-Saharan Africa has had a profound effect on the family life of the rural African. Although, as Goode (1963) has discussed, there is great danger in oversimplification and generalization of the sub-Saharan family system, an overall pattern does emerge: extensive extended-kinship ties are articulated within the tribal system.

Goode (1963), while cautioning the reader on the variability of family systems, does outline some of the main African family patterns. Of particular importance is the high emotional significance of the son–mother relationship. Tied in with this is the importance of legitimate descendants and the focus on the birth and possession of children. Almost all kinship systems are unilinear, the tracing of descent through one lineage. Polyandry, the marriage of one female to two or more males, is quite rare. Polygyny, the marriage of one male to two or more females, has greater appeal in Africa than in any other part of the world. However, it is more common as an ideal (in 88 percent of the 154 African societies studied by Goode) than an actuality. Most African men have only one wife (Goode, 1963:168).

In polygynous families, the most common living arrangement is setting up separate households for each wife and her children. Goode sees the importance of the mother–son relationship stemming in part from the existence of polygynous households and the fairly high percentage of children growing up in them. The son's emotional dependence on his own mother is heightened by the separate household existence of other mothers and other sons in the same family. In addition to her emotional support of her son, the mother provides assistance to the son in matters of advice, analysis, and teaching techniques. The second factor in explaining the importance of the mother–son relationship is the importance of the mother as seen in the reciprocal exchanging of bride prices by which two extended families or lineages are gradually united over time. "Marriage was not generally an event but a *process*, in which visiting, services, and gifts were exchanged over a period of time, as the marriage relationship was gradually strengthened, and each spouse was more fully accepted by his affinal relatives" (Goode, 1963:177–178). This factor, tied in with the high value placed on children and lineage possession of children, contributes to the importance of the relationship. Together, these all reinforce the importance of kinship in the tribal community, within which the primary bond of association is kinship descent.

The movement to the European-founded expatriate cities was stimulated by the industrial economy of the colonizing countries. The Western market economy was extended into these African urban areas and brought the indigenous African into a wider social system than the tribe. Industrialization and urbanization led to a greater specialization of institutions and gave rise to a new series of social groupings, networks, and relationships that transcended those based on family, kinship, and tribe. However, it would be erroneous to assume that these processes of modernization simply supplemented the traditional tribal arrangement; in many cases they were adapted to them. Viewed in this light, modifications of the traditional institutions — combined with Western industrialization, technology, and economic and social values and practices — gave rise to an emerging social structure that, although in the process of change, still maintained cultural continuity with the past.

Gutkind (1969) describes two formative processes that influenced the individual's life in the city: (1) tribal and ethnic identities in the urban context, and (2) a distinctive urban lifestyle based on economic and political processes. Combined, these processes lead both to the development of new relationships that are components of the restructuring of traditional tribal roles and to the development of new roles derived from the industrial system.

The families Gutkind studied in Kampala, Uganda, constantly moved back and forth from the world of associations based on kin and ethnic similarity and familiarity, to participation in groupings that cut right across such associations, particularly in economic and political activity and leisure pursuits. There is a constant convergence and separation of these two networks, and the conditions that produce them are mutually dependent and compatible. Together they contribute to the social and economic stability of urban family life. Family life, kin ties, and neighborhood associations or groups of friends are explicitly designed to assist and meet the social and psychological needs of their members and they act to support, protect, and guide their members. The complementary network of relations extends from the urban neighborhood community and is determined by economic and political processes based on the broader urban, national, and international marketplace. The result is an intertwining of these two processes in relation to individuals and families:

> Above all, in the local community, decisions which affect its life are taken by members who are known to one another. Not so in the larger social field of urban life, the structure of which is largely determined by agents external to it. Thus, while the social-psychological processes give the African urban family the opportunity to adjust to a new social environment, the urban institutions provide the same family with the opportunities of educational and economic mobility. But in either world African residents in towns are not merely rural residents transplanted who seek a conscious modification of rural ideas and habits suitable under new conditions. Rather, where for example tribalism prevails, or tribal settlements come into being, the reason is that this form of association is as purposeful a part of urbanism and a style of life as it is for a New Yorker not to know his neighbor. Both styles of life are not incompatible with their opposites, i.e., the increasing importance of nontribal and nonethnic-based associations in Africa, or the neighborhood associations aiming at a development of neighborliness and face-to-face contact in a New York City housing development. (Gutkind, 1969:218–219)

African migrant laborers finding themselves in a strange new urban area look to fellow tribal members already residing in the town to provide intimate and protective forms of association. Kinship and tribal affiliation serve as the linkage from the rural village to life in the city. Tribal membership gives newcomers an immediate identification, furnishes the normative guidelines on how to behave, and gives them community supports with ties to people like themselves. The African who comes to the city does not come as a stranger. The situation of the migrant to Dar es Salaam, Tanzania, is typical:

> It would be difficult to find a single African who arrived in Dar es Salaam knowing not a soul. . . . Almost every African who decided to come [there] comes to a known address, where lives a known relation; this relation will meet him, take him in and feed him and show him the ropes, help him seek a job . . . until he considers himself able to launch out for himself and take a room of his own. (J.A.K. Leslie cited in Epstein, 1969:256)

The urban dweller tends, therefore, to be involved in a complex network of relationships based on tribal affiliation, which includes neighbors, friends, and fellow workers as well as kin. Tribal association can be seen as an adaptive device that eases the adjustments of migrants to the urban area. Thus, although urbanization is supposed to weaken traditional bonds, in the urban area it has strengthened rather than weakened tribal ties. Further, it gives migrants a new conception of their tribal culture that transcends the particular tribal community from which they came.

However, African urbanists [for example, Epstein (1969) and Southall (1961)] state that *supertribalism* is quite different in the urban setting than tribalism in the rural areas. In the city, tribalism's main function is to classify Africans of heterogeneous tribal origins and to provide a limited number of meaningful social categories that serve as the basis for new groupings so that the new demands of city life may be met. "This form of urban tribalism is a category of interaction within a wider system, not the corporate and largely closed structure of social relationships provided by a tribe in its traditional areas" (Southall, 1961:3). A.L. Epstein (1969) observes that there are various forms of organizations that have their basis in urban tribalism. These organizations range from those that have institutionalized tribal eldership and head-manship to oversee various forms of social activity (for example, arranging funerals, parties, and marriages; or serving as arbitrators in disputes, which is characteristic in Dar es Salaam, the Copperbelt, and Freetown); to associations that are no longer dominated by the conservative elders but rather by upwardly aspiring younger men looking for prestige and status; to pantribal federations of the Kenya Luo or some of the Nigerian groups, which developed the infrastructure for nationalist movements and competitive political parties; and to those tribal associations that approximate exclusive social clubs (Epstein, 1969:257).

Aidan Southall (1961) describes the various applications and outcomes of supertri-balism in urban areas, especially as it affects kinship and family relationships. He reports that urban conditions have led to the diminished importance of the finer points of distinction in kinship systems and to the use of common denominators that are acceptable to all for intertribal dealings. But there has been little development of local kin groups; most urban dwellers still maintain strong rural ties, with the inten-tion of eventually returning to their tribal homes in their old age. Life in the city is seen as an economic necessity and, although it may satisfy their financial ambitions and needs, their ultimate goal is to return home. Economic development, then, strengthens the tribal structure.

Southall delineates three phases in tribal associations. First, recently arrived mi-grants are not interested in the formation of affective tribal associations; rather, they are concerned with the ways that kinship and tribal bonds can be of mutual aid situationally. Second, the ethnic associations are formed for general welfare pur-poses. Third, Africans begin to move beyond a tribal basis to form associations for common interests and to express their similar achieved status. This cuts across tribal lines. Thus, Southall sees tribal bonds developing new patterns; hampering and inappropriate close-knit traditional situations are being replaced by new ones that stress interpersonal relationships and associational organizations appropriate for urban life.

> Evidence from the Copperbelt, from Dar es Salaam, and from Sierra Leone shows how tribal headmen or representatives have been important in the early stages of urban settlement but later were eclipsed. On the Copperbelt the formal way in is through tribal elders, but in Salisbury through friendly societies, usually of twenty to thirty tribesmen, which also act as burial societies. Immigrants later tend to join groups with a more specific focus, such as friendship at work or common religion. Similarly, immigrants to Freetown come under the patronage of tribal headmen or notables and join voluntary associations with special interests later, entry to certain élite associations being the most difficult of all. Tribal associations are reported from East, West, and Central Africa. They mark a stage in which immigrant workers have become sufficiently used to town life to be able to organize themselves effectively in that context, yet on the basis of interest fundamentally centered in the countryside, indicating that they reject any irrevocable commitment to the town. (Southall, 1961:37)

In examining the relationship of kinship and tribalism to the individual and family, Southall emphasizes the need to distinguish between the experience of West Africa and the other regions of sub-Saharan Africa. As we described earlier, the West African family is firmly established in both Type A and Type B cities, with a minimal break between family life in town and that in the rural areas. However, the propor-tionately smaller migrant population in the cities is characterized by similar charac-teristics as the more prevalent migrant population in the European-founded towns and cities of East, Central, and South Africa. Southall describes the conditions of migrant labor in East and Central Africa as having a "disproportion of the sexes, high mobility, lack of family life, and failure to achieve full integration in an urban existence" (1961:41). The disproportionate number of males and females varied by geographical area and by governmental policy. John J. Palen (1975) notes that the situation was reasonable in West Africa, where there was a ratio of 95 women to 100 men. However, in Central Africa it was only 85 women to 100 men; in parts of East Africa 55 to 75 women per 100 men was prevalent. The situation was aggravated to a larger extreme in South Africa, where government policy prevented workers from bringing their wives to the cities with them.

Goode (1963) reports that in Salisbury (Zimbabwe), the much greater number of men to women, seven to one, prevented most men from ever marrying as long as they remained in the city. Further, the women available for marriage found that prostitution provided more lucrative rewards than marriage. The result was an almost complete breakdown of stable family patterns and the substitution of prostitution, temporary sexual liaisons, and illegitimacy for legalized family arrangements. In these European-dominated cities, urbanization had led to the separation of the individual from his family and lineage, with the consequent weakening of the family as an institution and the increase of extramarital relations and of illegitimate children, who were raised in poorly constructed housing with inadequate care and supervision. These processes are similar to those described by Louis Wirth in his examination of Chicago in the 1920s and 1930s. These disorganization patterns, rather than being indigenous to Africa, are the result of European colonial policies and, with the removal of the colonial governments, there has been a reestablishment of families and lineages and a subsequent decline in illegitimacy, juvenile delinquency, and crime similar to the pattern of urbanism found in the Type A traditional African city. The roles of the tribal associations have been partially responsible for this organizational stability. An additional organizational structure, which in some cases emerged out of the tribal association and in other cases was independent of it, is the voluntary organization.

Voluntary Associations

Little (1965) believes that voluntary associations of men and women, institutions based on common economic and social interest, are of great importance in urban areas. They are seen to facilitate a transition from the rural village to the city, with its highly differentiated social system anchored by occupation-derived achieved statuses rather than by traditional-based ascribed statuses. The voluntary association assists the individual in adapting to urban life — to the behavioral patterns, the acquisition of technical skills, and the development of new social relationships. The voluntary association helps rural migrants to adjust to the town and to becoming members of a multitribal metropolitan community. By aiding in the establishment and validation of new urban values and norms, the voluntary associations develop controls over the behaviors of their members and ultimately aid in the development of an overall system of relationships based on law and order for the heterogeneous populations of these towns and cities. This is particularly important because it provides a substitute for the traditional institutions of lineage and kinship that have not been established in the city or that need to be modified because of their dysfunctionality.

Little argues that the voluntary associations are particularly important because there are few agreed-on patterns and moral standards in the urban family for such concerns as the bringing up of children and marriage. The voluntary associations have developed policies of their own. For example, they all strongly support marriage as an institution; many forbid their members to divorce. Many of the associations condemn adultery and promiscuity, and treat abortion as a crime. Social control is obtained through formal controls such as legislation, or in informal ways, such as the following song, cited by Michael P. Banton, that was sung to a chief's wife when she was estranged from her husband:

> Oh Bom Posse, Oh Bom Posse, patience in marriage is a good thing,
> Which God has given you,
> When you grow old you will see how good is this thing,
> Which God has given you.
> (Banton cited in Little, 1965:101)

Or in the following song used as a weapon of ridicule to ensure conformity:

> The shame of it, Ai Kamara, the shame of it!
> Ai Kamara bore a child:
> He had no sooner grown up than she made him her husband.
> Ah friends, let us come together
> And consider if this is what is done in Temne-land?
> (Banton cited in Little, 1965:98)

Finally, in addition to the functions of family and kinship groups, tribal associations and voluntary associations are the sources of the emerging literature of indigenous African writers in soap-opera novelistic contexts as well as Dear Abby-type syndicated columns, published in indigenous newspapers, and providing suggested guidelines to reconcile the rural village tribal customs to the emerging norms demanded in city life. William Mangin (1970) cites the "Tell me, Josephine" column in East and South Africa. Two letters are presented; the first one tries to reconcile the conflict of a man and a wife; the second discusses the choice between loyalty to a mother's brother and a man's obligations to pay a matrimonial bride price. Mangin observes that Josephine's answers attempt "to bridge the gap but always on the side of adapting the traditional to modernization, westernization, and the new marketplace" (Mangin, 1970:xv):

> [1.] Q. During the course of my marriage I find my wife belongs to a tribe which is maternal. When we divorce or one of us dies, our children will belong to her brothers. I rushed into marriage without learning of this custom.
> I am afraid that if we divorce, I shall go to my village quite old and helpless while my wife's brothers will get every help possible from my children. So where should I get children to support me? My tribe does not do this. I find some difficulty in divorcing her now, before the children come, because I love her very much and she does the same to me. But what about this awful custom? When I mention my fears she tries to bluff me by saying her brothers will let me get my children, but I don't believe it. What have you to say before I sadly act?
> A. That it would be foolish to break up a happy marriage for fear of an old custom that may no longer be practiced when you are old. Do not think of divorce, many people live happily together all their lives. Also, you may die before your wife. If you are good to your children they will not desert you in your old age. Twenty years from now, these customs may have died out completely.
> [2.] Q. My uncle who is a charcoal-burner was taken to Native Court and told to pay 15 pounds for damaging two virgins.
> He has written to me that according to our custom I must get money for him, and send it quickly to the Northern Province or he will go to prison. This will take all my savings which I had planned to use for marriage in two years. So must I send him the money?
> A. If you wish to keep tribal custom, then you are obliged to help your uncle.
> If you do not care about tribal custom any more and do not intend to visit your family in the rural areas again, then no one can make you pay. Only you can decide.
> I presume that according to the same custom you will inherit your uncle's property when he dies. (Josephine cited in Mangin, 1970:xv–xvi)

The Urban Elite

Our concluding discussion considers the urban elite, who, although not a numerically significant number, are of vital importance to the independent sub-Saharan African states. Also the family system of these urban elite may provide clues to the eventual direction in which African family and kinship patterns may move.

P.C. Lloyd (1969) states that the leaders of the precolonial African societies were the tribal chiefs and priests. During colonialism, they served as the link between the Europeans and the indigenous people. Eventually, the Western-educated Africans, who led the nationalist movements, arose and achieved control of the newly independent African states. These individuals displaced the traditional elite and now serve as the mediators between Western and traditional African value systems. Lloyd discusses the various elite groups that have emerged and contrasts them in terms of their origins in a particular European colonial government and in the postindependence period. For our purposes, we will ignore these distinctions and treat these elite groups as a single phenomenon, focusing our attention on the overall marital, family, and kinship patterns.

The marital roles that have emerged find women in a rather egalitarian relationship, much to the dismay of traditionalist males. This particularly occurs when the educated wife is employed outside the home. The husband–wife relationship also features a segregated role pattern, with separate domestic activities and separate occupational spheres of activity and responsibility, Lloyd notes that the pattern is quite different from the Western one, where there is a greater sharing of roles and activities. The segregated role pattern is more similar to the working-class pattern in the West. It is derived from two sources: (1) the traditional marital relationship in African societies that emphasizes the separate social networks of husband and wife, and (2) the continuation of the strong ties that men retain with their own parents and kin:

> Many educated husbands still say that their mothers are more important in their lives than their wives; one can always get another wife, never another mother. Men will first discuss matters such as building a new house or changing jobs with parents or brothers. Tension between the husband's mother and his wife, if the former lives with her son, seems to be even more acute in Africa than in the England of the music-hall jokes. (Lloyd, 1969:178–179)

The continuation of ties with one's own kin is frequently incompatible with loyalty to one's wife. The wife's response is to seek and maintain the more-egalitarian form of marital relationship and to emphasize the segregation of marital roles.

The children of the elite are raised within the nuclear family with the aid of a few domestic servants, a vivid contrast to the involvement of extended kin in the raising of children in the Yoruba family compound. Child-rearing practices for elite children are more tolerant of aggressive play, and the child is encouraged to realize his or her own potential. In contrast, the traditional pattern emphasizes that the child follow parental expectations and discourages fighting among children. Cooperation among children is encouraged as it diminishes the possibility of quarrels and tensions between co-wives residing in physical proximity to each other.

In examining the relationship between individuals and their kin, Lloyd acknowledges the tensions arising out of the different interpretations of a person's traditional ways and values. However, the relationships between the residents of the towns and their rural counterparts continue, as do the viability of extended-kinship ties. Lloyd sees the expectations of the extended family for individuals as spurring them on to achieve economic success. Further, individuals may be judged by their success rather than by their censure of the elders in the extended-family group. He concludes that the assertion that the extended family is an impediment to the modernizing process needs considerable qualification when applied to the African situation.

Kinship Interaction in Nigerian Cities: Recent Findings

In two recent articles in a special issue of the *Journal of Comparative Family Studies*, the respective authors shed light on contemporary developments in the nature of kinship interactions in urban Nigeria. Let us examine each in turn.

In the paper by E. Adewalde Oke (1986), a sociologist at the University of Ibadan in Nigeria, the argument put forth is that, although industrialization and urbanization affect the structure and functions of the extended family, the extended-kin group remains a dynamic and viable force. It maintains its importance by being highly flexible and adaptive in terms of the relationships between family and kinship structures and political and economic needs. Strains on the traditional extended family include the peer group, various religious sects, social clubs, unionism, politics, and ideology. These groups often demand loyalty to them as opposed to continued loyalty to the family. Yet the family continues to play an important role in the lives of its urban members. Frequently, the family sponsors the training of and securing of accommodations and work for the migrant family member. It also provides financial and moral help and mutual support among family members whenever needed.

The family member is able to balance potentially conflicting loyalties by being highly pragmatic. Kinship interaction is manipulated and varies with both situational and individual needs. The degree of interaction or involvement is influenced by the extent that the family member views the Nigerian kin system and interacting with other family members as necessary and important for sustaining the solidarity or continuity of the unit. Oke outlines five interaction strategies that are utilized by family members. The first, avoidance, is a common practice among upwardly mobile individuals who wish to minimize kinship responsibilities. For these individuals, it is only when there is a need to assert political power or economic aid is required that efforts are made to coordinate family and professional responsibilities. One informant, who studied at an overseas university, married a foreign woman, and is now head of a unit in the civil service epitomizes this pattern:

> I have not disclosed my residential address to any of them (kin group), except my immediate brothers/sisters. If you do, they keep on coming every day. If I spend all my salary on them, I'd still be in debt and they'll still complain — I have never been home (his village home) since my homecoming or my arrival — And you know what, they are trying to get me a wife, despite the fact that I went home with my wife. (Quoted in Oke, 1986:191)

The second strategy is selective interaction. The urban Nigerians who exhibit this pattern interact only with those members of the kin group who are also living in the city and who share a similar social status. They participate with these family members in joint activities and provide mutual assistance. They avoid associating with kin who are considered liabilities or potential embarrassments.

Inconsistency/flexibility is the third interaction pattern. This pattern is demonstrated by individuals who use the kin system to achieve social mobility and, once that is achieved, they minimize their family relations. Oke tells of a man, Mr. Bayo, who received a doctoral degree from an overseas university and upon his return became a university lecturer. He did not interact with his family or identify with his native village. He avoided participating in monthly family meetings, although he continued to pay his monthly dues. However, when he decided to run for political office, he became an active family member, socializing with members of his kin group both in the city and at home in the village. On losing the election, he reverted back to his noncontact patterns. Now, once again, he is thinking to run for political office and he has started to participate actively with his kin. Oke observes that, "The point of Mr. Bayo's case is that the degree or form of interaction with the kin group can vary with the situation and the individual's needs. Family needs do not necessarily supersede individual needs" (1986:192).

The fourth pattern is close interaction. Here, the individual is strongly committed to the extended family. The extended-family–oriented member often travels long distances to maintain contact with the family and social mobility does not diminish his commitment to the family. The following case study is provided:

> Mr. Taiwo has just returned from a successful overseas adventure. He works as a personnel manager in a large firm in the city. He lives in a duplex owned by his company in a respected section of the city. Mr. Taiwo is married to a Nigerian woman from a major city. They met at an overseas university. Mr. Taiwo partici-pates actively in all social activities by his kin group in the city and attends every family meeting in his village, a distance of several hundred kilometers. His residence is now filled with relatives from his village. Some are attending school; some are working. Seemingly, he is able to maintain these numerous relatives in a peaceful environment. But upon closer notice, it is evident that he is unable to keep the peace. His home is often noisy, quarreling and untidy. Moreover, the situation is causing some problems between Mr. Taiwo and his wife. With Mr. Taiwo, the family (extended) comes first; and he has decided to meet all its demands. (Oke, 1986:193)

Oke believes that often these types of marriages end in divorce. The scenario follows this pattern. The urban wife often encourages her son not to respect the patriarchal family's authority. In turn, the husband's kin group instigates and initiates the push for divorce and remarriage, often to an uneducated woman from the patrilocal village. This woman would not question the extended kin's authority. Oke observes that men who fall into the close interaction pattern are usually not as successful as professionals or businessmen. The desire to sustain family supremacy prevents this. Those who are successful come from kin groups that have wealth or power to support them and their number is minimal.

The fifth pattern is relatively complex and refers to the extension of kinship ties to nonmembers (fictive kin). These fictive kin are usually people who are of the same social-class background or professional group. Kinship terminology is indiscrimi-nately used by these people to refer to each other as "uncle," "aunt," "niece,""nephew," and even "brother/sister" regardless of actual consanguineous relationship. The fictive kin perform many of the actual kin functions and are seen as a threat to the future of the extended family. They also do not make what may be thought of as unreasonable demands on the individual, nor are they burdensome.

In summary, Oke emphasizes the flexibility and adaptability of traditional African family structure to explain its continued persistence in the industrial urban setting of contemporary Nigeria. Further, "Reconsideration of the adaptability, versatility and utility of the extended family will contribute to knowledge of social interaction, particularly the interrelations between the individual and the kinship group" (Oke, 1986:194).

The second study that has relevance for us here is a comparison of three Nigerian ethnic groups — the Yoruba, the Igbo, and Ibibio — to the processes of industrializa-tion. The author, Sheilah Clarke Ekong (1986), a member of the department of sociology and anthropology at the University of Ife in Nigeria, argues that the historical development of kinship in Nigeria has necessitated the development of alternative approaches to industrialization than those found in the Western model. The result has been alternative patterns to the Western one regarding urbanization and the transition to nuclear families.

Ekong is of the opinion that industrialization occurred differently among three Nigerian ethnic groups. She refers to the variations as examples of differential "ethnic industrialization." According to this concept, industrialization is achieved through the utilization of the indigenous skills and customs, including those pertinent to the family and kinship, of the respective ethnic group. The Yoruba, Igbo, and the Ibibio ethnic groups are examined in regard to their kinship patterns, the resources available to them, and their traditional occupations. These are seen as determining factors in their orientation to industry.

The Yoruba, as we noted earlier, have a tradition of nonindustrial urban residence while working in adjacent rural areas. Men are urban-based farmers and women are traders and retailers. The Yoruba are the most industrialized, and their industrial development has been predominantly urban-based. The Yoruba have experienced little disorganization in the transition to urban industrialization, despite the fact that the emigration of young men in particular has altered the character of not only the traditional rural areas but also the urban areas. The most pervasive reinforcing factor in maintaining kinship solidarity and meeting family obligations is the corporate descent group. Joint ownership and interest in both rural and urban land and residential housing is transmitted between generations. This ensures that landed property remains in the family.

Yoruba industrialization is primarily confined to small-scale family companies such as service-repair industries, motor dealerships, and long-distance urban transportation systems. These family industries have provided the impetus for the expansion of an entrepreneurial class among the Yorurba. It has allowed them to take advantage of urban land holdings and to manage and dispose of them to the benefit of the economic corporate group—the family. Ekong states that "adapting commercial ventures to pre-existing kinship structures maintains continuity in kinship patterns. The Yoruba kinship system, therefore, has not hampered the processes of industrialization because no change is necessary in the orientation toward kinship and its consequent obligations" (Ekong, 1986:200).

The Igbo are less industrialized than the Yoruba. They traditionally have been a rural people with agriculture as the basis of their economy. Their philosophy encourages individual effort within a communal context and individual achievement with the necessity to maintain kinship obligation. They have not adapted their kinship pattern to industrialization or urbanization. In the urban areas that they have settled in, they have developed a reputation of being excessively clannish or tribalistic. Their industrialization tends to utilize their indigenous skills and materials in the making of tools, iron, and brass work. These manufactured products are attributed to and demonstrate the expressive bond between kinsmen in passing down "family craft skills."

The third ethnic group studied, the Ibibio, have a very elaborate kinship structure and network that has remained virtually stable over the years. The Ibibio have a transitional economy based on subsistence farming and a philosophy that is inconsistent with productivity. The Nigerian state that they reside in has quite limited industrial development, and they have continued their primary occupation of farming in government-run plantations. Ekong believes that "although eventually the Ibibio may follow a path toward greater industrialization, the strength of their kin ties and primary group relationships, a philosophy that does not emphasize productivity, and an erroneous understanding of industrialized societies make industrialization at this time difficult and limited" (1986:203).

In assessing Nigeria's industrialization process, Ekong believes that the concept of ethnic industrialization is useful in understanding how various ethnic groups direct their economic activities to certain types of industry in accord with their own social, cultural, and historical development. She argues for the Nigerian development of national agriculture and industry based on the use of local products and structured to be consistent with the cycle of indigenous farming and consistent with established kinship systems. Further, she observes that the disorganization that is seen to accompany industrialization has been minimal in Nigeria because the kinship structure accommodates to the processes of industrialization and urbanization.

Conclusion

In this chapter, we examined the city in West Africa and sub-Saharan Africa and its relationship to urban family systems. Our discussion sought to test the basic hypothesis of the urban sociologists who see family life in the city as gradually diminishing in importance, particularly causing the dissolution of the extended-family system and the substitution of the isolated nuclear-family type. William J. Goode shared this position: "If the new African nations follow the paths of many other emerging nations, the next decade will witness an accentuated move away from tribal family patterns, and toward a conjugal system" (1963:201–202).

In examining the evidence, we found that in the traditional African cities, for example those found in the Yoruba of West Africa, the fundamental family pattern took on the pattern of the extended family. This runs contrary to the position of such social scientists as Louis Wirth and Talcott Parsons, who believed that the extended-family form would be nonexistent in cities, whether industrialized or not. When, in turn, we examined family, kinship, and ethnic relationships in the more-industrialized European-founded towns, family-based networks still remained visible and still provided needed resources for the populace. Then we turned our attention to the urban elite, those who would most likely follow the Western model, and discovered a continued existence of extended kin ties. In addition, the nuclear family arrangement was characterized by a greater egalitarianism and independence of husband and wife than in their Western counterparts. This was a departure from what we would have expected from the dominant theoretical positions of the sociologists of the urban family. Finally, recent research provided further indication that the flexibility and adaptability of traditional African family structure explains its continued persistence in urban centers in Nigeria. This research also revealed that ethnic variations must be accounted for in explaining the diversity of kinship structures and processes as well as the extent and nature of industrialization in these cities.

The existence of extended-family relationships, of ethnic associations, and of voluntary associations all suggest that differential adaptations are possible when confronted with urbanization processes. Further, it is vital to understand the cultural context of the populace under study to predict in what manner urbanism as a way of life will evolve.

PART III

Gender Roles, Courtship, and Marital Relationships

CHAPTER 8

Gender Roles and Sexuality

An unmarried girl and boy in the Telefolmin region of New Guinea (ca. 1958). The boy wears the standard head ornament of his tribe.

E. T. Gilliard, Courtesy Dept. Library Services, American Museum of Natural History

CHAPTER OUTLINE

The social sciences make an important distinction between sex and gender. Sex refers to biologically determined differences between males and females, which is most evident in male genitalia and female genitalia. Maleness and femaleness are determined by biology. Gender refers to social and cultural definitions of masculinity and femininity based on biological differentiation. Gender involves socially learned patterns of behavior and psychological and emotional expressions and attitudes that socially distinguish males from females. Ideas about masculinity and femininity are culturally derived and provide the basis for differing self-images and identities of men and women.

Given this distinction between sex and gender, the term used to refer to the social behavior of men and women should be *gender roles*, not *sex roles*. However, in popular usage, sex roles is often used in place of the more-accurate gender roles. Keep in mind that the term *sex* refers to an ascribed status, in that a person is born either a male or a female. The term *gender* refers to an individual's psychological, social, and cultural attributes, and thus is an achieved status.

Are gender-role differences innate? The dominant view in most societies is that the learned gender identities are expressions of what is "natural." People tend to assume that acting masculine or feminine is the result of an innate biologically determined process rather than the result of socialization and social-learning experiences. Proponents of both the biological and the social-learning views have sought evidence from religion, the biological sciences, and the social sciences to support their respective positions. Whereas most religions tend to support the biological view, both biology and the social sciences provide evidence suggesting that what is "natural" about gender roles expresses both innate and learned characteristics.

In this chapter, we review the biological and religious views on gender roles and examine them in light of sociological viewpoints and the cross-cultural evidence. We indicate how patriarchy, the main ideological justification for the sexual division of males and females, manifests itself. Also in this chapter there is an historical analysis of sexuality, including homosexuality within the context of cross-cultural family systems and structures. A section includes an analysis of the gay community in contemporary America. Subsequent chapters in Part III are devoted to discussions of love; courtship; premarital relationships; mate selection; the sexual division of labor, especially how it is articulated within the family; and marital intimacy.

Biology and Gender Roles

Supporters of the belief that the basic differences between males and females are biologically determined have sought evidence from two sources: studies of other animal species including nonhuman primates—monkeys and apes—and studies of the physiological differences between men and women. We will examine each in turn.[1]

[1] The ensuing discussion follows an earlier presentation of this argument by Hutter (1982).

Ethology is the scientific study of animal behavior. Ethologists have observed that there are sexual differences in behavior throughout much of the nonhuman animal world. Evidence indicates that these differences are biologically determined — that in a given species, members of the same sex behave in much the same way and perform the same tasks and activities. Popularized versions of these ideas, such as those developed by Desmond Morris in *The Human Zoo* (1970) or Lionel Tiger and Robin Fox in *The Imperial Animal* (1971), generalize from the behavior of nonhuman primates to that of humans. They maintain that in all primate species, including *Homo sapiens*, there are fundamental differences between males and females. They try to explain human male dominance and the traditional sexual division of labor in all human societies on the basis of inherent male or female capacities. They even have extended their analysis to explain other human phenomena, such as war and territoriality, through evolutionary comparisons with other species. A more-sophisticated treatment of this same theme is found in the field of sociobiology, the study of the genetic basis for social behavior (Wilson, 1975, 1978).

Sociobiologists believe that much of human social behavior has a genetic basis. Patterns of social organization — such as family systems, organized aggression, male dominance, defense of territory, fear of strangers, incest taboo, and even religion — are seen to be rooted in the genetic structure of our species. The emphasis in sociobiology is on the inborn structure of social traits.

Opponents of this view use two types of arguments to criticize it. First, they note that sociobiologists have overlooked studies showing the importance role learning plays among nonhuman primates in their acquisition of social- and sexual-behavior patterns (Montague, 1973). Second, critics of sociobiology observe that those who generalize from animal behavior to human behavior fail to take into account fundamental differences between human and nonhuman primates, such as the human use of a complex language system. Even though they freely acknowledge the biological basis for sex differences, these critics claim that, among humans, social and cultural factors overwhelmingly account for the variety in the roles and attitudes of the two sexes. Human expressions of maleness and femaleness, they argue, although influenced by biology, are not determined by it; rather, gender identities acquired through social learning provide the guidelines for appropriate gender-role behavior and expression.

While not denying the impact of social and cultural influences on gender roles and sex-linked behavior, some investigators maintain that genetic and physiological differences between the sexes also influence (but do not predetermine) what types of things members of each sex can do and learn and the ease with which they do so (Rossi, 1977). According to this view, the study of gender roles should take into account well-established biological and physiological differences between the sexes in such traits as size and muscle development (both usually greater in males); physiological and mental development (males ahead in some areas, females in others); longevity (females live longer than men and have a lower death rate at all ages); and susceptibility to disease and physical disorders (generally greater in males). For instance, some diseases that primarily affect males have a genetic basis and are related directly to the male sex chromosomes (XY), which differ from the female sex chromosomes (XX). Among these sex-linked ailments are color-vision defects, blood-clotting disorders (hemophilia), deficiencies in immunity, and baldness.

While many differences between males and females have a biological basis, other physical conditions may be tied to cultural influences and variations in environment and activity. Men react differently to psychological stress than women; each sex develops severe, but dissimilar, symptoms. Changing cultural standards and patterns of social behavior have had a pronounced effect on other traits that formerly were thought to be sex-linked. For example, the rising incidence of lung cancer among women — a disease historically associated primarily with men — can be traced directly to changes in social behavior and custom, not biology; women now smoke as freely as men.

In sum, differing learned behaviors and activities do contribute to the relative prevalence of certain diseases and disorders in each sex. But, as has been pointed out, not all male–female differences in disease and susceptibility can be attributed to these factors. In addition to genetically linked defects, differences in some basic physiological processes—such as metabolic rates and adult secretion of gonadal hormones—may make males more vulnerable than females to certain physical problems.

Most sociologists believe the way people are socialized has a greater effect than biological factors on their gender identities. Cross-cultural and historical research offers support for this view, revealing that different societies allocate different tasks and duties in men and women and that males and females have culturally patterned conceptions of themselves and of each other.

Religious Views On Patriarchy and Gender Roles

Many religions have given overt expression to the view that men are superior to women. For example, the Judeo-Christian story of Creation presents a God-ordained sex-role hierarchy, with man created in the image of God and woman created as a subsequent and secondary act. This account has been used as the theological justification that man is superior to woman, who was created to assist and help man and bear his children. This kind of legitimation of male superiority is called a patriarchal ideology.

> For a man indeed ought to have his head veiled, forasmuch as he is the image and glory of God; but the woman is the glory of the man: for neither was the man created for the woman but the woman for the man: for this house ought the woman to have a sign of authority on her head. (1 Cor. 11:3–10)

Patriarchy has been the basis on which tasks, rights, and roles are allotted to the sexes, usually with the woman's position subjugated and inferior to the man's. Patriarchy also voices the belief that a woman's "proper" place is within the home and her role devoted to domestic activities—housework and the bearing and raising of children. As societies have developed industrially and technologically and have moved further and further away from cultural patterns where tasks are distributed on the basis of physiological factors, patriarchal ideas are increasingly open to challenge. It is necessary to understand the multifaceted nature of patriarchy to understand sex-role relationships.

A patriarchal ideology has two components; the first emphasizes the dominance of males over females, the second the subjugation of younger males by older ones. The first component is of concern here; the second is examined in the chapters devoted to generational relationships.

The institution of patriarchy is anchored in an ideology of male supremacy and it is reinforced by traditional socialization practices that implement it in matters of status, role, and temperament. Patriarchy has been deeply entrenched in political, social, and economic institutions. Kate Millett (1970) persuasively argues that patriarchy must be viewed in political terms as the domination of males over females. The term *sexual politics* is used by Millett to emphasize the power-structured basis of the male–female relationship and the arrangements whereby one group of persons, females, is controlled by another, males. This relationship is legitimated through the socialization of both sexes to the patriarchal ideology, for example, temperament, which involves the formation of self-concepts and is stereotyped along sex lines. Aggressiveness, force, intelligence, and efficacy are seen as "masculine" traits; passiv-

Women — the Stronger Sex Due to Lifestyle, Experts Say

BY ELLEN HALE

BALTIMORE— The dramatic changes in women's lifestyles, changes that have taken them out of the house and put them in the workplace in unprecedented numbers, also are taking their toll on women's health by exposing them to environmental risks only men used to face.

But if more and more women are choosing to live like men, they are not dying like them. The risk factors that endanger a man's life are not nearly as likely to threaten a woman's, new studies show.

In fact, even as more women enter the professional arena and take on tasks once considered male territory, the historical life-span gap between the two sexes continues to grow in favor of the female, and women now outlive men by a greater margin than ever.

The main reason, say experts, is that women inherently are biologically superior to men, with a natural protection against many diseases and illnesses that nature does not extend to men. It is this biological shield, probably most active during a woman's childbearing years, that makes her far less susceptible than men to the major causes of death: accidents, heart disease and cancer.

For some time, population experts and health researchers have wondered how employed women would stack up to men in health, and whether the difference in life-span between the sexes has been a result of differing lifestyles. Women, it was suspected, were more protected from external and environmental risk factors because they lived less stressful and less dangerous lives.

"We wondered: Would women be sicker, would they die sooner, if they had been as involved in the workplace earlier?" said Dorothy P. Rice, director of the National Center for Health Statistics.

Recent changes in traditional sex roles might suggest the answer would be yes, but the latest statistics from Rice's agency and from studies around the country show no such change. "There seems to be no real change in health status," said Rice. "The mortality advantages of women extend to every age phase of their lives."

As women shed their traditional female roles, they are encountering new health problems, however. For example, lung cancer rates among females are skyrocketing as women in growing numbers take up the traditional male practice of smoking cigarettes. Similarly, as women become more sexually active and at earlier ages, they increase their risks of getting certain diseases, cervical cancer in particular.

Several new studies also show that women who shun the traditional family role and put off having children completely or until later years apparently lose some of their superior defense mechanisms and face greater chances of developing other kinds of diseases.

In spite of all this, though, women still live longer and are at appreciably lower risk of developing many, if not most, diseases. Experts met here recently, in the first conference of its kind, to discuss the changing risk of disease in women. Some of the findings they reported:

- Heart disease, while still the major killer of women, is 46 percent more common in men. And as with men, its incidence is decreasing among women despite the fact that more women are entering the work force and should, theoretically, be facing the same stresses men do. The famous Framingham project in Massachusetts followed working women and housewives over time and found that "working women did not have significantly higher rates of coronary heart disease than did housewives," reported Suzanne G. Haynes, an epidemiologist from the University of North Carolina.
- Diabetes, a common chronic disease, was long considered to be more prevalent among women, making it one of the few diseases that was. Now, however, researchers say it appears this "excess" is either nonexistent or is greatly

(continued)

exaggerated. In fact, the diabetes death rate in men has increased much more rapidly than it has in women, reported Dr. Elizabeth Barrett-Connor of the University of California in San Diego. The risk is worse for obese men than it is for obese women, and diabetic women live longer with the disease than do diabetic men.

• Stress either is overrated as a disease factor or it is simply handled more easily by women than by men. Women have lower blood pressure than men through two-thirds of their lives, a benefit most specialists credit to women's inherent protective mechanisms. And the fact that working women still spend more time at household work than do working men is another indication that they must be able to handle stress better. Said Estelle Ramey, a prominent Washington physiologist: "Measuring the stress of a working woman who is bringing up a husband and children is very difficult to do."

Some experts attribute these advantages to what they call the "inactivation" of the X chromosome. Females are born with two sets of X chromosomes, while males have one X and one Y, and the extra X chromosome gives females more flexibility in responding to environmental risk factors, said Dr. Leon Gordis, head of the epidemiology department at Johns Hopkins University here.

If something goes wrong with one of the X chromosomes, there's a backup ready to pick up the slack, he explained.

The lack of this inborn genetic advantage in males is apparent in the fact that boy babies have far more infections than do girl babies, and that female fetuses have a 25 percent higher survival rate than do male fetuses.

In addition, more and more studies are indicating that the male sex hormone testosterone plays an important, and destructive, role in the health of men. The "take-charge" hormone, as physiologist Ramey calls it, apparently affects blood platelet formation in a way that increases a man's risk of developing coronary artery disease. Studies of eunuchs and of castrated animals, for example, reveal that they have much healthier platelet formation and longer and healthier life spans as well.

But all this is not to say that women are not facing significant changing or increasing health risks as they make sweeping changes in their lifestyles. In addition, they lose much of their natural protection once the childbearing years are over. In addition, recent studies of women who postpone having children or who never have them show that they have a two to three times greater chance of developing breast or ovarian cancer.

SOURCE. Ellen Hale. 1981. "Women—the stronger sex due to lifestyle, experts say." *The Courier-Post* (Nov. 2). Copyright 1981, Gannett News Service. Reprinted with permission.

---

ity, ignorance, docility, and ineffectuality are "feminine" traits. Sex roles are associated with temperament. Millett observes that "sex role assigns domestic service and attendance upon infants to the female, the rest of human achievement, interest, and ambition to the male" (Millett, 1970:26). Socialization practices are biased towards male superiority and male superior status. Women are viewed as inferior. Millett sees these three facets—status, temperament, and role—in terms of political, psychological, and sociological components. Each is interdependent and, in totality, they serve to support the patriarchal ideology.

The patriarchal ideology has dominated the Greco-Roman, Semitic, Indian, Chinese, and Japanese civilizations. It has also been the predominant pattern in Western Christian civilization. The European sociologist Evelyne Sullerot (1971) believes that the basis for the patriarchal pattern stems from the reproductive function of women, which serves as the justification for women's existence and the reason for their subordination. Sullerot sees patriarchal rule as a coherent system linked by four

Geoffrey Biddle/Archive

Contemporary Orthodox Judaism exhibits a strong patriarchal influence in the synagogue and at ceremonial events such as weddings, where females are segregated from males behind screens.

elements—attitudes toward fertility and adultery, domestic confinement, property, and civic rights. She proceeds to show how these four types of restriction on women are elaborated in patriarchal civilizations.[2]

1. *Fertility and adultery.* Sullerot observes that the primary function of the woman was "as a breeding machine to perpetuate the male line of the husband, the tribe, and the race" (1971:20). The entire rationale for the woman's existence was her ability to produce children, particularly male children. Failure to do so resulted in severe punishment. The Manu code of India stated that if a wife had no children after 8 years of marriage, she would be banished; if all her children were dead, she could be dismissed after 10 years; and if she only had produced girls, she could be repudiated after 11 years. Similarly, the Mosaic law of the Biblical Israelites allowed a husband to repudiate his infertile wife and to father children with servants. The story of Abraham and Sarah is illustrative.

Female adultery was prohibited and punishments were extremely severe. Female adultery represented an attack against male dominance and the assertion of female individuality and free will. This was seen as a threat to the patriarchal system. Potentially, it was destructive to the patriarchal-based system of property, inheritance, and power. Common to the historical civilizations of Israel, China, India, and Greece was the norm that a husband could put to death his adulterous wife. It was this assault on patriarchy, not simply emotional jealousy, that was the underlying motivation for such extraordinary punishment.

[2] The following discussion follows that of Evelyne Sullerot, 1971, pp. 20–28.

2. *Domestic confinement.* The seclusion and separation of women were practiced to assure masculine dominance and to prevent the possibility of adultery. Their confined world had both actual and symbolic significance. Such confinement symbolized the inferior status of women. Domestic activities were viewed as less important than and subordinate to outside involvements. In traditional India, the Hindu religion conceived of women as strongly erotic and thus a threat to male asceticism and spirituality. Women were physically removed from the outside world. They wore veils and voluminous garments and were never seen by men who were not members of the family. Similar practices existed in China and Japan and in the Muslem Middle East. Only men were allowed access to and involvement with the outside world.

3. *Property.* Stemming from the patriarchal ideology was the practice of excluding women from owning and disposing of property. The prevalent practice in traditional Hindu India was that property acquired by the wife belonged to the husband. Similarly, restrictions on the ownership of property prevailed in Greece, Rome, and in ancient Israel.

4. *Civil rights.* The general pattern was the exclusion of women from civic matters. This included, as is the case in Jewish tradition, the exclusion of women from the majority of religious observations. Islam uses as its justification for the exclusion of women from the city and religion the notion of female impurity and uncleanliness. Oriental religions share a similar philosophy. In ancient China, female infanticide was practiced through child neglect. The birth of a daughter was accompanied by a period of mourning. The low status and power of women are summed up in the following passage from the book *Several Articles Intended for Women*, written in the first century A.D. by a Chinese woman, Pan Hoei Pan:

> Never let us forget that we belong to the lowest form of human life. We must expect only contempt. There will never be disillusionment for a women so long as she remembers that she will always be made to suffer by those with whom she lives. (Cited in Sullerot, 1971:27–28)

Sociological Views: Cross-Cultural Evidence

Cross-cultural and historical research reveals that societies allocate different tasks and duties to men and women. Among other animals the differentiation is biologically determined, and all the animals within a given species behave in the same way and take on the same tasks. Among humans, however, social and cultural factors account for variations in the roles and attitudes of the two sexes. The relationship between man and woman, although influenced by biology, is not determined by it; rather, gender identities acquired through social learning provide guidelines for appropriate behavior and expression.

Biological factors can be seen as having a great influence on gender-role relationships in less-technologically developed societies. Physiological factors, periodic childbearing, and the relative physical strength of men and women play an important part in designating the role allocations within these societies. Clellan S. Ford, the noted anthropologist, argues that, for preindustrial peoples, "the single most important biological fact in determining how men and women live is the differential part they play in reproduction" (1970:28). The woman's life was characterized by an endless cycle of pregnancy, childbearing, and nursing for periods of up to three years. By the time the child was weaned, the mother was likely to be pregnant again. Not until menopause, which frequently coincided with the end of the woman's life, was she free from her reproductive role. In these circumstances, it is not surprising that such activities as hunting, fighting, and building were usually defined as the male's task;

the gathering and preparation of grains and vegetables were female activities, as was the care of the young.

In an early study, George Murdock (1937) provided data on the division of labor by sex, in which 224 preliterate societies divided their labor. Such activities as metalworking, weapon making, boat building, woodworking and stoneworking, hunting and trapping, house building, and clearing land for agriculture were tasks performed by men. Women's activities included grinding of grain; the gathering and cooking of herbs, roots, and seeds as well as fruits, berries, and nuts; basket, hat, and pottery making; and making and repairing clothing. D'Andrade (1966), after reviewing the cross-cultural literature, concluded that a division of labor by sex occurs in all societies. Generally, the male activities are those that involve vigorous physical activity or travel; the female activities are those that are less physically strenuous and require less geographical mobility.

We should not overestimate the importance of biological factors in gender-role relationships. Although physiological factors tend to play a more-influential role in gender-role differentiation in preindustrial societies, that is not to say that biology *determines* these allocations. A classic illustration of the diversity of human behavior is Margaret Mead's (1935/1963) study of sex and temperament in three South Pacific societies.

Each society held a different conception of male and female temperament. The Arapesh were characterized as gentle and home loving, with a belief in temperamental equality between men and women. Both adult men and women subordinated their needs to those of the younger or weaker members of the society. The Mundugumor assumed a natural hostility between members of the same sex and slightly less hostility between the sexes. Both sexes were expected to be tough, aggressive, and competitive. The third society, the Tchambuli, believed that the sexes are temperamentally different, but the gender roles were reversed relative to the Western pattern.

> I found . . . in one [society], both men and women act as we expect women to act — in a mild parental responsive way; in the second, both act as we expect men to act — in a fierce initiative fashion; and in the third, the men act according to our stereotype for women — are catty, wear curls and go shopping, while the women are energetic, managerial, unadorned partners. (Mead, 1963; Preface to the 1950 edition)

Even if we grant the premise that physiological factors are contributing components in the distribution of tasks in preliterate societies, they are not as important in societies that are more technologically developed; that is, as technology develops, we move further away from cultural patterns where tasks are allocated on the basis of physiological justifications. Yet we continue to find the tasks, roles, and rights of men and women to be different. The justification for these differences has been moral and "sacred" arguments, combined with and stemming from the physiological argument.

In recent years, there has been a re-examination of the basis on which tasks and roles are allocated and their concomitant justification. Modernization processes, scientific and technological developments, rapid social change, and the resurrection of such social movements as women's liberation have led to the questioning of traditional gender-role relationship patterns. In an earlier time marked by relative stability, little discussion or argument was made on the appropriateness of socially derived gender identifications and societal notions of masculinity and femininity. The "proper" roles, statuses, and attitudes for men and women were taken for granted. This has changed not only in the industrialized West but also in varying degrees throughout the world. This is a theme that we return to in later chapters.

Zurich Decides Boys Must Learn Homemaking, Too

BY RICHARD MURPHY

ZURICH, Switzerland—One of the cornerstones of Swiss male chauvinism is gradually being chipped away as the country phases out compulsory housekeeping classes for girls only.

Switzerland's largest canton, Zurich, has become the latest to abolish the once-widespread practice of training girls at special schools to become good housewives.

In a Sept. 28 referendum, Zurich voters approved the lifting of a requirement that all schoolgirls complete several weeks of "further education" in housekeeping after they have left school and before they have reached age 20.

Now, boys as well as girls will have to learn some knitting, cooking and needlework as part of their basic education.

Zurich made housekeeping classes— similar to home-economics courses in the United States—compulsory in 1931, and most other cantons had similar laws.

But in 1981, 10 years after Swiss women were granted the right to vote in federal elections, a national referendum enshrined equality for women in the constitution and sounded the death knell for girls-only housekeeping classes.

"It is high time that the obligatory classes disappeared, not only because of the injustice between boys and girls, but above all because of the changed makeup of households," wrote columnist Eva Maria Borer in the weekly *Zuri-Woche.*

She said that many people were living alone and that both partners in many marriages had jobs, rendering obsolete the tradition of training women to run homes for their working husbands.

Education here is run by Switzerland's 26 cantons, the equivalent of states. Three of the cantons—Uri, Obwalden and Schaffhausen—still have the compulsory housekeeping classes for girls.

In Zurich, the compulsory classes for girls will be phased out while regular schools gradually introduce new courses.

Currently, Zurich schoolgirls attend institutions such as the Domestic Economy Further Education School for housekeeping courses lasting three to eight weeks. About 2,500 pupils pass through its doors every year.

"Our school is very progressive," said director Erika Welti.

"We don't just teach them cooking and sewing. They learn nutrition, how to manage a budget, how to shop, how to repair and recycle things, how to unblock drains—everything necessary to create an environment in which human beings will feel well."

The courses already are offered to boys on a voluntary basis, but few attend, Welti said.

On a recent afternoon, 16-year-old girls were learning to bake bread, and their heavy makeup and punk-style clothes clashed with the traditional image of the conservative Swiss hausfrau.

In another classroom, 18-year-olds were learning to set tables for dinner.

"The compulsory classes are a good idea, but boys should have to do them, too," said one 16-year-old girl.

That is roughly what will happen.

Starting next year, students of both sexes will take the same basic housekeeping courses in their regular schools. Local authorities still will be obliged to offer further, voluntary housekeeping classes, and schools such as Welti's will be retained for that purpose.

Beatrice Grotzer, an Education Ministry official, said many Zurich schools began offering coeducational classes in skills such as knitting and crocheting to 8-year-olds last year.

"The classes have certainly become livelier since the boys joined, and there have been some discipline problems, but generally the reaction has been very positive," Grotzer said.

The Zurich newspaper *Tages-Anzeiger* hailed the fact that 69 percent of those voting supported the end of the compulsory classes for girls as welcome recognition that running a home is not purely a job for women.

"The clear 'yes' is also a yes to the legal equality of women," it wrote.

SOURCE. Richard Murphy. 1986. "Zurich decides boys must learn homemaking, too." *The Philadelphia Inquirer* (Oct. 12). Reuters, owner of the copyright. Reprinted by permission.

Sexuality and the Family

Cross-cultural and historical evidence reveals that every society controls the sexual behavior of its members. Further, in comparing sexuality in different parts of the world, we find an amazing variety of intercultural differences of practices, rules, and sentiments. In this section, we try to account for societal variations in sexuality norms and expressiveness through linkage with the manner in which sexuality is controlled.

Every society has a culture of sex, and the sexual sector of culture varies in the same ways as the total culture of which it is a part. The anthropologist William H. Davenport (1977), in his survey of sex in cross-cultural perspective, finds that there are constants within what seems the confusing complexity of variations. He states (1977:162–163) that in every society the culture of sex is anchored in two directions: "In one direction, it is moored to the potentialities and limitations of biological inheritance. In the other direction, it is tied to the internal logic and consistency of the total culture."

What this means is that, although human sexual behavior is directly based on inherited biological factors (genes, bodily organs, hormones, and so forth), every society shapes, structures, and constrains the development and expression of sexuality in all of its members. The difference between sex and sexuality is that the latter is socially structured and regulated. The rules for sexual conduct can only be understood within the broader context of customs and laws embedded within the cultural system and the social fabric of the society. These sexual conduct rules are inextricably linked with rules dealing with generational, gender, marriage, and family roles. Since sexual behavior is embedded within the complex web of societal rules, regulations, sanctions, and taboos, as one sector of culture changes it has implications for other sectors, including sexuality. Within the context of social and cultural change, we examine sexuality and the family.

All societies have developed rules regulating premarital, marital, and extramarital sexual behavior. The reason for sexual regulation lies in two basic facts: Sexual intercourse has the potential for creating a new human being; and a person's desirability as a sex object is a valuable, but scarce and perishable, resource (Davis, 1976). As a consequence of the first fact, sexual norms and reproductive norms become intertwined, and, as a consequence of the second fact, sexual norms become linked with norms governing the distribution of goods and services. Kingsley Davis, in his development of this viewpoint, observes that "sex norms contribute to the replacement of people in society and to the maintenance of an orderly distribution of rights" (1976:225). Further, sex norms are subordinate to the family since they support or interfere with the formation and continuation of families and nonfamilial aspects of sex norms are inherently tied to the economic and political systems of societies. Let us examine these points.

Davis observes that the primacy of marriage and the family in sex regulation has great importance in the elaboration, importance, and universality of such sex mores as the principle of legitimacy (which establishes a family by locating children through fatherhood and sanctioning a mother's childbearing), the incest taboo (which eliminates sexual rivalry from the nuclear family), and the rule that makes coitus a mandatory obligation within marriage. The primacy of the family is also seen to account for the concern regarding premarital sexual activities and relationships and why sex norms are different for men and women. Men usually have greater freedom and latitude since it is women who become pregnant. Variations in the strictness of sex rules are seen to reflect the degree of their potential interference with the primacy of marriage, family formation, and continuance.

Political and economic differentiation is the second factor that explains sex norms. Societies, in addition to assuring orderly biological continuation into the next generation, must see to it that goods and services are generationally transmitted. Sexual access is seen as a good and service that can be politically and economically distributed. The nature of sexual rules is tied to the societal division of labor and "bargaining" regarding sexual favor and distribution is seen as being intrinsically linked with economic exchange. Davis notes that sexual desirability and economic capacity are age-graded and balanced, with youth having greater defined sexual attractiveness and middle or later aged having greater economic and political advantage. Similarly, the sexual division of labor is balanced, with the man's sphere primarily economic and the woman's primarily familial (Davis, 1976).

Following this structural-functionalist argument, Davis observes that—while conflict can arise between the primacy of marriage and family and the economic exchange in elaborating sex rules and regulations—there is often a balance between the two. "The exchange influence prevents familism from turning the society into an economically unproductive breeding system, and yet familism is strong enough to prevent economic domination from subordinating all sex to money, status, and pleasure" (Davis, 1976:228).

Davis' analysis reflects a somewhat sanguine functional view of the inherent equality in the articulation of sexual rules and regulations for people of different social classes and for men and women. It has engendered much criticism among theorists who point out that sexual rules and regulations often reflect the allegiance and domination of economically and politically powerful social-class groups and patriarchal authority figures within family systems. As a consequence, economically and politically disadvantaged groups and youth and women family members in all social classes are subjected to greater sexual restrictions and regulations.

Randall Collins (1971), in his examination of the cross-cultural and historical evidence on sexuality and the sexual division of labor, develops a theory that bases the sexual-stratification system in terms of conflict theory and social exchange. Collins combines Sigmund Freud's proposition that human beings universally exhibit strong sexual and aggressive drives with Max Weber's proposition that humans strive to achieve as much dominance as their resources allow. This leads Collins to the conclusion that women will be the sexual prizes for men, since men are physically larger and stronger, are free from the biological limitations of menstruation and childbirth, and have greater economic advantages.

As evidence of this view that men will be sexual aggressors and women will be their sexual prizes, Collins describes how in some societies females are clearly viewed as sexual property, taken as booty in war, used by fathers in economic bargaining, considered to be owned by husbands, and so on. In our own society, as in virtually all other societies, men act as the sexual aggressors. He lists the following as additional evidence:

> Rape is defined as a crime only as committed by males, and cases of sexual assault by women are virtually unknown; men are the sexual aggressors in free courtship systems; men are much more motivated by sexual interests as a reason for marriage, whereas women emphasize romantic love, intimacy, and affection more highly than men; exclusively male culture has a heavy component of sexual jokes, bragging of sexual conquests, pinups, and pornography, which have little or no equivalent among women; prostitution occurs almost exclusively among women, and male prostitutes are sex objects for male homosexuals, not for women; men are much more likely to masturbate, experience sexual arousal earlier in life, and are generally more active sexually than women. (Collins, 1971:7)

Collins believes that historical changes in the structure of sexual dominance are the result of shifts in resources dealing with political and military force and economic power. These changes are supported by changes in sexual ideologies. The expectation of his conflict model is that, when economic resources and forces are equalized between men and women within a society, sexual conflict and marital bargaining will

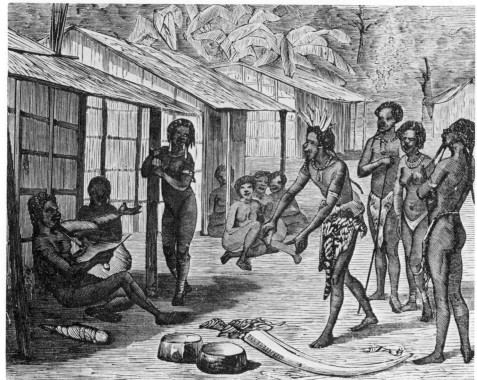

Antman Archives/The Image Works

An ethnic group in what is now Gabon, Africa, participating in a wife-bargaining ritual (nineteenth-century engraving).

be individualized rather than divided across sex lines. Four types of social structures are analyzed in terms of male and female resources, sexual stratification, and dominant sexual ideologies. Let us review them, as outlined by Collins in Table 8.1.

Low-technology tribal societies are more commonly referred to as hunting-and-gathering societies. Their technology produces little or no economic surplus and as a consequence there is little economic, political, or status stratification. Kathleen Gough (1971) reports that these types of societies are found in marginal forest, mountain, arctic, or desert environments. People live at subsistence levels in social bands of about 20 to 200 people. Premarital sexual behavior tends to be unregulated and, for the most part, egalitarian relations exist between women and men. Sexual practices are relatively permissive, with premarital sexual freedom for both males and females. Gough comments that the evolutionary thoughts of Lewis Henry Morgan (1877/1963) and Friedrich Engels (1884/1972) speculated that hunters and gatherers might be representatives of a first state of original promiscuity with people living in communal sexual arrangements. Gough dismisses this evolutionary view by pointing out that hunters and gatherers live in nuclear families rather than in large, extended-kinship groups and certainly not in communal sexual arrangements.

Ford and Beach's (1951) comparative study of sexual behavior found that equally active sexual behavior of men and women occurs in hunting-and-gathering societies. This has led sociologists, such as Betty Yorburg (1974), to speculate that this is attributable to the fact that these societies are poor and families are not greatly differentiated with respect to wealth. As a consequence, the sexual behavior of children and consequent offspring would not be disruptive to the economic future of

TABLE 8.1   Types of Social Structure, Sexual Stratification, and Dominant Ideologies

Social Structure	Male and Female Resources	Sexual Roles	Dominant Ideology
1. Low-technology tribal society	Male: personal force, personal attractiveness. Female: personal attractiveness.	Limited male sexual property; limited female exploitation.	Incest taboos.
2. Fortified households in stratified society	Male: organized force; control of property. Female: upper-class women head lineage during interregnum of male line.	Strongly enforced male sexual property; high female exploitation; women as exchange property in family alliances.	Male honor in controlling female chastity.
3. Private households in market economy, protected by centralized state	Male: control of income and property. Female: personal attractiveness; domestic service; emotional support.	Sexual market of individual bargaining; bilateral sexual property in marriage.	Romantic love ideal in courtship; idealized marriage bond.
4. Advanced market economy	Male: income and property; personal attractiveness; emotional support. Female: income and property; personal attractiveness; emotional support.	Multidimensional sexual market of individual bargaining.	Multiple ideologies.

SOURCE: Randall Collins. 1971. "A conflict theory of sexual stratification." Copyright 1971 by The Society for the Study of Social Problems. Reprinted from *Social Problems* Vol. 19, No. 1, Summer 1971, pp. 3–21 by permission.

the family. Collins concurs in this belief. The lack of surplus combined with little economic and political stratification does not permit dowry or bride-price systems to develop. Further intermarriages are tolerated in that they have little effect on extended-family systems since no families are powerful enough to be highly preferred for political alliances. Daughters are given sexual freedom and are not strongly controlled because they are not used as property in a bargaining system. As a consequence, "it is in low-technology tribal societies that most norms favoring premarital sexual permissiveness are found" (Collins, 1971:11).

The second type of social structure discussed by Collins is the fortified household in stratified society. Collins' classification is similar to Henry Sumner Maine's conceptualization of the "status" society and Ferdinand Tönnies' *Gemeinschaft*. In this type of society, economic and political organization coincides with the family community; force is not monopolized by the state. Work activities are integrated with familial activities, and authority over both is invested in the patriarchal head. In the case of preindustrial Europe, patriarchal households could vary in size, wealth, and power, from the holdings of a king or lord, through the households of merchants and financiers, to knightly manors, and down to the households of minor artisans and peasants. In addition to the subservience of family members to the patriarch, propertyless workmen, laborers, and servants were subservient as well.

This type of society, with its form of social organization, maximizes male sexual dominance and is characterized by the double-standard sexual ideology. These types of societies also include ancient Greek, Roman, and Arab societies. Sharp inequality among households can result in the upper classes practicing polygamy or concubinage and monopolizing more than their share of women. Males assert their rights in sexual property in these types of societies. The sexuality of women is strongly controlled and women are often exchanged on the basis of economic bargaining. Often in such societies, women "are closely guarded so as not to lose their market value" (Collins, 1971:11). This has given rise to customs such as wearing a veil, strict chaperonage, and the institution of the harem.

Similarly, Betty Yorburg observes that in agricultural societies where differences in wealth, power, and prestige between families become more extreme as the economic surplus increases, there is a greater desire by families to regulate premarital sexual behavior and control the sexual activity of women. "The mating of offspring is controlled (by arranged marriage) to increase family power and wealth. The sexual activity of women is more rigorously suppressed (confined, ideally, to procreation), and women come to be regarded, conveniently, as having a weaker sex drive" (Yorburg, 1974:31).

As we observed earlier in this chapter, the patriarchal ideology views sexual property as a form of male honor. Collins observes that in a highly warlike patriarchal society like that of the Bedouin Arabs, the result is an almost-obsessive desire to maintain sexual property and a concern for adultery, and the institution of extreme controls over women. Women's sexuality was thought to be much greater than that of men. They were regarded as sexually amoral, unclean, and lacking in honor. The extreme reflection of this belief was the practice of clitoridectomy. By removing the clitoris, it was felt that temptation was being removed from women.

The rise of the centralized bureaucratized state, accompanied by the expansion of commerce and industry, led to the development of the third form of social structure, the private household in a market economy (Collins, 1971). The separation of the workplace from the home, another characteristic of this society, resulted in the development of the smaller and more-private nuclear family. While men remained heads of households and controlled property, women gained a better bargaining position and were no longer under the control of their patriarchal family. Collins writes that "they become potentially free to negotiate their own sexual relationships, but since their main resource is their sexuality, the emerging free marriage market is organized around male trades of economic and status resources for possession of a woman" (1971:13).

The development of the smaller private household that lacked servants resulted in women being valued for their capabilities in homemaking and in providing emotional support for males along with their sexuality. Fostering this development was the ideology of romantic love, which included a strong element of sexual repression. Collins' argument suggests that the continuation of the double standard and the suppression of women's sexuality was upheld principally by the interests of women in contrast to the male-supported female chastity norm of traditionalistic patriarchal societies. Collins reasons that "the most favorable female strategy, in a situation where men control the economic world, is to maximize her bargaining power by appearing both as attractive and as inaccessible as possible" (1971:15).

An ideal of femininity was developed in which overt sexuality may not be used to attract the male but only indirectly hinted at as a sort of grand prize or ultimate reward, because "sexuality must be reserved as a bargaining resource for the male wealth and income that can only be stably acquired through a marriage contract" (1971:15). Femininity and female chastity are idealized because men and women are bargaining with unequal resources. A negative consequence of this idealization was the reinforcement of patriarchal ideology by the placement of nineteenth-century Victorian women on a pedestal that limited their involvement to the home and further excluded them from the world of work.

The movement to today's advanced market economy has resulted, in Collins' view, in a new shift in sexual-bargaining resources. The relatively high level of affluence, combined with the increased employment opportunities for women, has resulted in greater bargaining options for women. Those freed from economic dependence on males can be less concerned with marriage and more concerned with other kinds of exchanges. For example, dating can take the form of short-run bargaining, in which *both* sexes can trade their sexual attractiveness or social abilities for sexual favors and social involvements. Evidence for that is the rise, especially in the youth culture, of the ideal of male attractiveness.

In sum, Collins' conflict model asserts that political and economic factors play a determining role in influencing both sexual behavior and sexual ideology. The discussion highlights the cross-cultural and historical variations in which the dominant group (predominantly male) oppresses or exploits the other (predominantly female). The contemporary trend, as Collins speculates in his brief discussion of dating patterns, is one in which sexual bargaining between the sexes is beginning to occur on a more-equal-exchange basis.

The following chapter is devoted to an in-depth historical analysis of the intersection of sexual behavior and sexual attitudes by examining changes in love, courtship, and premarital relationships. Before we move on, we would like to comment briefly on the contemporary gay-liberation movement as an extension of our discussion on sexuality and the family.

Homosexuality and the Family

Most societies strongly disapprove of homosexuality, although there is wide variation in its tolerance. Kingsley Davis (1976) attributes disapproval of homosexuality to its incompatibility with the family and the sexual-bargaining system; by this he means that it interferes with the norms and attitudes regarding the reproduction of societal members and the sexual allocation of males and females. He asserts that the negative attitudes toward homosexuality can be seen as part of the broader proscriptions concerning prohibited sexual partners—masturbation involves no partner at all; incest involves a kinsman; adultery involves a partner other than one's spouse; and homosexuality involves a partner of the same sex. In this section, we look at some of the cross-cultural variations in societies' views of homosexuality vis-à-vis the family, but first we briefly survey variations in its cross-cultural and historical prevalence.

Clellan S. Ford and Frank A. Beach (1951), in their pioneer cross-cultural survey, found that in 49 of 76 societies on which reports were available, some form of male homosexuality for some members of the community was approved. In 28 of them, adult homosexual acts were rare, absent, or so secret that they remained unknown. In general, homosexuality was found to be more prevalent among men than women; lesbianism was found to exist in only 17 societies. It is possible that the low rate of reported female homosexuality may be explained by the fact that female behavior may be less visible and less studied by anthropological research, which has been conducted primarily by men.

Barbara Alper/Stock, Boston

A lesbian couple at a Gay Pride march, New York City.

Societies that report male homosexuality as being rare have definite and specific social pressure against the disapproved behavior. This ranges from such lighter sanctions as ridicule among the Mbundu of Angola, Africa, and the condemning to death of male and female violators by the Rwala, a Bedouin tribe of the northern Arabian desert. Of the 49 preliterate societies in which homosexual activities are considered normal and socially acceptable, they tend to be limited to the roles of *berdaches* (transvestite homosexuals) and *shamans* (magicians or priests, in some societies homosexual).

It should be noted that Ford and Beach do not specify the actual incidence of homosexual activities. For example, it can vary from an isolated or occasional incidence of group masturbation among boys to regular anal intercourse by adult men. Nor are they clear on how given societies define homosexuality. Definitions can also vary in terms of type of activity or frequency of a given activity on whether or not it is "homosexual." Further, especially in regard to industrial societies—while laws may be liberal regarding homosexuality—public attitudes, especially among segments of the population, may be much more conservative.

The sexual liberation of the 1970s—which included the much-publicized communal marriage, mate swapping and swinging, and the rise in premarital heterosexual permissiveness and cohabitation, along with the gay-rights movement—has led to speculation that, taken together, these attitudes are symptomatic of a much larger sexual-liberation movement. This more-comprehensive movement, anchored in the belief that human sexuality is learned, calls for a "liberation" of sexuality that transcends the "bias" of heterosexuality and advocates the encompassing of homosexuality into normative sexuality. Both those who advocate this view and those who condemn it see it as seriously undermining heterosexual relationships and ultimately marriage and the family.

However, there is no statistical evidence indicating that there has been a change in the rates of homosexuality of American men and women. In the 1940s, Kinsey found that four percent of men and about a third as many women were predominantly homosexual. According to recent studies by the Institute for Sex Research, the statistics are virtually the same today. The thought that the sexual revolution and the gay movement would have increased the incidence of homosexuality has proved to be wrong. Indeed, we could argue the opposite; that is, the same loosening of the norms governing heterosexuality may reduce homosexuality by permitting easier and earlier heterosexual experience. A cross-cultural illustration to provide support for this argument is the people of Mangaia, one of the Cook Islands in the South Pacific. The Mangaians are very permissive regarding heterosexual activities. They let their children begin sexual experimentation at an early age, including masturbation for both girls and boys. They view sexual exploration as a normal part of childhood. Even though there is little or no social pressure against homosexuality, almost no homosexual behavior is reported. This has led some (Sandler et al., 1980) to speculate that "perhaps the general availability of heterosexual partners, as a result of the high degree of permissiveness toward heterosexuality, explains this low incidence of homosexuality among the people of Mangaia" (1980:28).

While the rate of homosexuality may not have changed in recent years, what has changed is the visibility of homosexuality from a largely private form of sexual activity to one that is more open and public. This change is most typified by the emergence of gay communities in almost every major city in Western Europe and America, a process that had its origins in the mid-nineteenth century. Furthermore, this movement from private to public homosexuality has been instrumental in changing the very way that our culture has conceptualized homosexuality in general and in the conceptualization of homosexual identity in particular. Let us trace this development.

Of particular interest to us is the recent scholarship that examines the cultural conceptualization of sexuality and homosexuality. A very influential study has been Michel Foucault's (1978) *The History of Sexuality, Volume 1: An Introduction*. Foucault sees the modern conceptualization of sexuality as developing as a consequence of the decline of importance of kinship and extended-family ties in controlling individuals. He observes that, beginning in the eighteenth century, there was a shift in emphasis away from marriages that were constructed to control individuals through the continuation and development of kinship and lineage ties. This movement was accelerated during the Industrial Revolution and continued into the Victorian era, and a new control system developed that placed emphasis on marriage and conjugality within a broader context of the control of sexuality and its modes of expression. Foucault writes: "The deployment of alliances (kinship ties) has as one of its chief objectives to reproduce the interplay of relations and maintain the law that governs them; the deployment of sexuality, on the other hand, engenders a continual extension of areas and forms of control. For the first, what is pertinent is the link between partners and definite statutes; the second is concerned with the sensations of the body, the quality of pleasures, and the nature of impressions . . ." (1978:106).

Foucault argues that Victorian society was not, as popularly depicted, a society that denied and suppressed sexual discussion; rather, it was a society that sexualized all social relations and was consumed with the study of sexuality and its control as part of its obligation to assume total responsibility for its citizens' lives and welfare. The study of sexuality becomes incorporated into the world of therapists, psychologists, social scientists, and educators as part of an all-encompassing attempt to shape and influence people not only in terms of their acting in socially, economically, and politically appropriate ways, but also in terms of their views of their bodies, their sex, and their human potentials. Foucault's analysis of sexuality shares a similar orientation to that of his French associate, Jacques Donzelot (1979), and of Christopher Lasch (1977), all of whom call attention to the perceived intrusion of the state and subsidiary medical and social agencies (the "helping" profession) on the family beginning in the nineteenth century and continuing today. We examine this viewpoint later in our discussion of children; for now, let us see its applicability in regard to the conceptualization and policies regarding homosexuality.

In recent years, scholars [see Berube (1981), D'Emilio (1982), Walkowitz (1982), and Weeks (1981)] on gay history have assembled evidence that homosexuality as it is currently conceptualized is of relatively recent origin. John D'Emilio (1983), in his excellent historical study of the formation of the gay community, reminds us that in colonial America there was no concept of "homosexuality." Erotic behavior between individuals of the same sex was viewed as a sporadic and exceptional activity that did not differ essentially from other sexual transgressions such as adultery, bestiality, and fornication. Heterosexuality was assumed to be the natural way of sexuality. Colonial society placed such a great emphasis on the family and on reproduction (the average pregnancy rate for white New England women was eight) to populate the vast American wilderness that "homosexuality" was inconceivable.

It was not until the second half of the nineteenth century, with the advent of full-blown industrial capitalism and the modern city, that gay and lesbian conceptualizations and identities emerged. D'Emilio traces the movement of large populations from kinship-dominated closely knit rural communities into the more-impersonal urban centers. The family, in turn, shifted from a public community institution into a private insular one. For individuals, industrialization and urbanization created the social context for the development of a more-autonomous personal life. Affection, intimacy, and sexuality became more a matter of personal choice than a determination by family members. Homosexually-inclined men and women, who would have been visible and vulnerable in small rural communities, began moving into the city. In this setting, men and women who wished to pursue active and public sexual involvements with others of their own sex felt free to do so and began to fashion from this desire a new sexual identity and way of life (D'Emilio, 1983).

D'Emilio astutely traces the development in urban settings of male homosexual bars, cruising areas, public bathhouses, and parks that enabled men to meet each other at the beginning of the twentieth century. Lesbians, more constrained in terms of both economic dependence on husbands and patriarchal ideologies, developed more-private meeting places that included literary societies, social clubs, faculties of women's colleges, and settlement-house involvements. By the 1920s and 1930s, public institutions such as lesbian bars made an appearance, although they never assumed the size of their male equivalents.

World War II had a similar effect in developing gay male and lesbian community and identity. The war geographically mobilized young people—at the time that their sexual identities were just forming—from the heterosexual settings of their families, communities, and hometowns. D'Emilio asserts that "because the war removed large numbers of men and women from familial—and familiar—environments, it freed homosexual eroticism from some of the structural restraints that made it appear marginal and isolated" (1983:38). This was the case not only for men and women in the sex-segregated armed forces, but also for nonmilitary females who entered the work force to fill America's labor needs. D'Emilio reminds us that this analysis should not let us think that heterosexuality did not continue as the predominant form of sexual expression, but the war did temporarily weaken the patterns of daily life that fostered heterosexuality and inhibited homosexuality. It provided a new situation in which those that were sexually attracted to their own sex but were previously constrained by their circumstances from acting on this attitude could do so. Further, the war reinforced the identities of gays and lesbians and strengthened their ties to homosexuality as a way of life.

By the 1950s, gay urban territories—such as Greenwich Village in New York City and similar enclaves in Chicago, Los Angeles, and San Francisco—were established. Gay and lesbian subcultures also came into existence in smaller cities such as Worcester, Massachusetts; Buffalo, New York; and Des Moines, Iowa. Activist groups such as the Mattachine Society and the Daughters of Bilitis formed to provide a vehicle for self-expression and protection against hostile actions and discrimination in government and the work world. Coinciding with and reinforced by the gay-rights movement, gay communities emerged in the late 1970s and early 1980s; in that short time period they have made a significant impact on urban politics in the United States, with San Francisco being the most notable example.

In San Francisco and elsewhere, gays have moved into centrally located, but run-down, areas and have sought to transform them into hospitable neighborhoods. The most successful attempts have been marginal sections of New York's Greenwich Village and San Francisco's Castro Street area. However, gays have often faced the competition and hostility of other groups for control of the limited supply of cheap and moderate housing. Low-income gays have been the victims of street violence exacerbated by economic conditions and homophobia. In addition, in cities such as San Francisco that are undergoing massive downtown business development and high-cost condominium construction, gays are either being forced out or are depicted as the cause of the evaporation of affordable housing. Rubin notes that in San Francisco, "the specter of 'the homosexual invasion' is a convenient scapegoat which deflects attention from the banks, the planning commission, the political establishment, and the big developers" (1984:296).

John D'Emilio (1983), in his analysis of the emergence of gay and lesbian identity and the creation of their respective communities, observes that structural changes in industrial urban society made possible the emergence of gay and lesbian identity and the creation of their respective communities. Yet, at the same time, the society is unable to accept homosexuality. He asks what accounts for societal heterosexism and homophobia and finds the answer in the contradictory relationship that exists between this form of society and the family. His analysis is provocative.

D'Emilio picks up on the theme shared by many sociologists that industrial capitalism shifted the family away from a productive economic unit into one that emphasized the affective function of the family in terms of the nurturance of children and the emotional happiness of its members. As a consequence, sexuality ceased to be defined primarily in terms of reproduction and instead became defined largely in terms of emotional expressiveness. Indeed, affection, intimacy, and sexuality became more and more a matter of individual choice and no longer were solely defined in terms of the family. This attitudinal and behavioral shift provided the setting and opportunity for people who wished to fashion their notions of sexuality with people of their own sex.

The increased reaction against the development of gay and lesbian identities and their communities stems from recent developments in heterosexual marriage that point to its failure to satisfy the emotional demands and needs of its members.

D'Emilio points out that since the mid-1960s there has been a plummet in birthrates, a continuing decline in average household size, a rise in divorce rates, and an increase in the variety of living arrangements that people are choosing. The reason for these lies in the inherent contradictions of capitalism, which allows for individuals to live outside the family in relative economic independence and at the same time ideologically dictates that men and women marry and have children to assure the perpetuation of the society. As D'Emilio has indicated elsewhere (1983), "[t]hus while capitalism has knocked the material foundation away from family life, lesbians, gay men, and heterosexual feminists have become the scapegoats for the social instability of the system. . . . The elevation of the family to ideological preeminence guarantees that capitalist society will reproduce not just children, but heterosexism and homophobia" (1983:109, 110).

Moral Panics and AIDS

Conflicts between the majority view on the "proper" expressions of sexuality and minority "deviant" expressions often become expressed as *moral panics*. Jeffrey Weeks (1981) coined this term to refer to important and consequential kinds of sex conflict. Moral panics are seen as the "political moment" of sex, in which diffuse attitudes are channeled into specific political actions that bring about social change. Examples include the hysteria regarding prostitution as a form of white slavery in the 1880s; the antihomosexual campaigns that were associated with the anticommunist activities of the U.S. Congress House's Un-American Activities Committee and of the Senate's Joseph McCarthy in the 1950s; and the outcry against child pornography in the late 1970s.

Similarly, the current medical and emotional attention regarding AIDS can be seen in terms of a moral panic. Gayle Rubin (1984), writing at the beginning of the AIDS

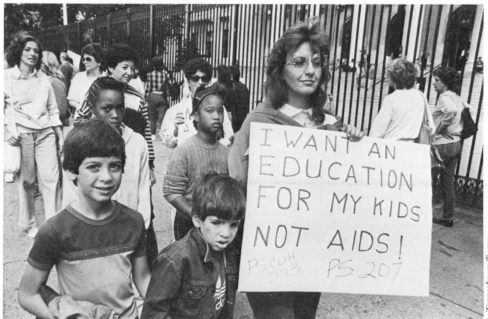

Parents and schoolchildren protest the enrollment in public schools of children who carry the AIDS virus.

phenomenon, has astutely predicted that AIDS will have far-reaching consequences on both homosexuality and heterosexuality. She observed the effect AIDS has on sexual ideology regarding homosexuality at the very time that the taint of mental illness was being removed. "The syndrome, its peculiar qualities, and its transmissibility are being used to reinforce old fears that sexual activity, homosexuality and promiscuity led to disease and death (Rubin, 1984:299). As we now see, her prediction has largely come true.

AIDS—an acronym for acquired immune deficiency syndrome—is a contagious disease that, until mid-1985, was regarded as a disease largely confined to the United States that attacked specific "risk" groups: gays, intravenous drug abusers, and hemophiliacs. Persons stricken with full-blown cases of AIDS are victims of a virus that directly attacks a group of white blood cells that serves as one of the main coordinators of the immune system. As the disease progresses, these defensive cells are almost entirely destroyed. The immune system collapses, and victims fall prey to one infection after another. Ordinarily mild diseases become dangerous, even fatal, and many patients develop rare cancers, severe neurological disorders, and brain damage. There is an AIDS-related complex (ARC) that infects people who have been exposed to the AIDS virus but who have not yet developed the disease. The flu-like symptoms of ARC include swollen lymph glands, fatigue, malaise, fever, night sweats, diarrhea, and gradual loss of weight. In addition, science is finding that there are also human immunodeficiency viruses (HIV) that may eventually cause AIDS in unsuspecting healthy persons.

In June 1987, the Centers for Disease Control (CDC) in Atlanta recorded more than 36,000 cases of AIDS in the United States, with more than 20,000 deaths having occurred. In Africa, the figure is even higher. The World Health Organization (WHO) conservatively estimates that more than 50,000 people have died from the disease. The worst-hit countries all touch on the Great Rift Valley of east central Africa: Zambia, Zaire, Burundi, Rwanda, Uganda, and Tanzania. In the West, the high-risk groups initially were homosexuals and intravenous drug users. In Africa, half of all AIDS patients are women in their childbearing years, and AIDS is spread predominantly through heterosexual relations. Increasingly, more women in the United States are becoming AIDS victims. This fact has led Dr. Alexandra Levine of the University of Southern California to comment: "[AIDS] is not really a disease of homosexuality at all. It is spread by sexual contact of any kind—homosexual or heterosexual. This is a disease of all of us" (quoted in *TIME*, August 5, 1985). A similar belief was also articulated by Dr. Robert Redfield at the U.S. Army's Walter Reed Hospital: "As time goes by, it will be more evident that this is a sexually transmitted disease that is not limited to one sexual practice" (quoted in *Newsweek*, August 12, 1985).

In the April 29, 1985, issue of *Newsweek*, an article appeared under the title "AIDS: A Growing 'Pandemic'." It reported on a conference of more than 2,000 public-health experts from around the world that met in Atlanta for the U.S. Centers for Disease Control's international symposium on the deadly disease. The head of the CDC's task force on the disease, Dr. James Curran, stated that "AIDS is now recognized as a worldwide problem, with cases diagnosed on almost every continent" (quoted in *Newsweek*, April 29, 1985). Participants at the conference were predicting that AIDS threatened the world's general population and may assume the proportions of what epidemiologists call a "pandemic" as opposed to a "mere" epidemic.

AIDS tends to be viewed as a problem of Africa and the United States, but in reality it is a worldwide epidemic. There is no proof that the AIDS epidemic began in Africa any earlier than in the United States (*Newsweek*, November 24, 1986). WHO in October 1987 reported a total of 62,438 cases worldwide but estimated the actual number of cases to be 100,000. A growing number of cases have been reported in Europe, South America, and Asia. WHO believes that as many as 10 million people are infected with the human immunodeficiency virus (HIV), and that 50 to 100 million will be infected by 1991, with more than 3 million potential AIDS cases (*Internal Medicine World Report*, November 1987).

For the general public, the fact that AIDS was largely limited to the gay population led them, at first, to have a detached attitude toward the disease. This lack of concern was seen in the minimal amounts of government medical research money allocated to the study of AIDS. Anti-gay moralists saw AIDS as a fitting punishment for those who violated the "natural" way of sex. The political conservative Patrick J. Buchanan, who is now director of communications at the White House, wrote in May 1983 in his syndicated column that "The poor homosexuals . . . have declared war on nature, and now nature is exacting an awful retribution" (quoted in *Newsweek*, August 12, 1985).

Rubin (1984) reports that homophobic columnists have viewed AIDS as appropriate punishment for violation of the Bible's Levitical codes and that moral conservatives in Reno, Nevada, sought to ban the annual gay rodeo. *The Moral Majority Report* of July, 1983, ran an article with the headline "AIDS: HOMOSEXUAL DISEASES THREATEN AMERICAN FAMILIES." This article was accompanied by a photograph of a white family of husband, wife, son, and daughter wearing surgical masks. Rubin quotes from a passage in a pamphlet by the anti–women's-movement advocate Phyllis Schlafley that the passage of the Equal Rights Amendment would make it illegal for people to protect themselves from AIDS and other diseases associated with homosexuals.

However, as AIDS has continued to spread to many segments of the population — including children and the famous, such as the actor Rock Hudson — there has been an outcry for more research on this disease. As significant as the call for more medical research has been, the hysterical reaction — tinged in part by the moral panic first associated with AIDS and homosexual behavior — has centered on the issue of school-age children with AIDS. As of September, 1985, 165 cases of AIDS were reported among children 12 years of age or younger, according to the Federal Centers for Disease Control. Of that number, 113 of the children have died and the parents or guardians of only about 20 children have requested that their children attend school. There has been a community outcry by parents who do not want their children interacting with these AIDS victims. Their concerns are blown out of proportion to their numbers by the media. The emotional content of the question has led one epidemiologist to speak of an "epidemic of fear." Dr. Jeffrey J. Sacks, the Florida state epidemiologist involved in a Dade County case, believes "AIDS is two epidemics. It's an epidemic of disease and death, but it's also been an epidemic of fear, and that's much harder to treat" (cited in Clendinen, 1985:22).

What has fueled the "epidemic of fear" has been the somewhat contradictory statements of physicians who continually maintain that there is no known instance of casual transmission of AIDS and that children would not be infectious; yet they qualify their medical opinion by saying that they do not know enough about the disease, and often recommend extraordinary precautions when working with AIDS victims.

Newsweek (1985), in a special report, "The Social Fallout from an Epidemic," sees as the immediate outcome a "safe sex" movement and an aura of fear. The article reports on a continuous survey since 1983 by the California Council on Mental Health, in which among gay and bisexual men in a recent six-month period there was a fivefold decrease in multiple sex partners and high-risk sexual activity. In another study conducted for the San Francisco AIDS Foundation, the percentage of respondents with more than one sex partner had declined from 49 percent in 1984 to 36 percent a year later. There has also been a sharp decline in oral and anal intercourse. In many establishments catering to gays, pamphlets and fliers are distributed that urge the use of condoms, reduced promiscuity, or even the elimination of all "exchanges of bodily fluids" (*Newsweek*, August 12, 1985:29).

Newsweek (August 12, 1985) also speculates that the aura of fear will affect heterosexual behavior. The article reports that unmarried heterosexual women may be making behavioral adjustments by thinking twice before having a casual sexual encounter. Supporting this view is the statement by Dr. Donald Francis, a medical epidemiologist at the U.S. Centers for Disease Control, that even if there are only a few cases among heterosexuals, AIDS "will certainly end the sexual revolution. You can take your chances with herpes and hepatitis B, but you can't take your chances with this" (cited in *Newsweek*, August 12, 1985:29).

In addition to affecting sexual behavior, those afflicted with AIDS, and those viewed most susceptible to the disease — homosexual men and women — may involuntarily be tested, treated, and isolated. Stories have been appearing in the media about deceased AIDS victims who have been refused proper burial by funeral parlors. For example, a Massachusetts mother dressed her dead son's body after funeral homes refused to handle the corpse. Fearful members of hospital staffs refuse to care for patients with AIDS and often neglect them. Patients have been discriminated against, including the pastoral care of those on their deathbeds. One particularly insensitive case illustrates this. A chaplain, introducing himself to AIDS patients, stated, "'I understand you're very sick because you've lived a very sinful life and God is punishing you. Without repentence,' the chaplain continued, 'you're going to die a terrible death'" (Ritter, 1985:15F).

Rubin (1984) points out that when the cause of Legionnaire's disease was unknown, there was no comparable moral outcry. Nor was there a call to quarantine members of the American Legion or to close their meeting halls. *Newsweek*, in an article titled "Epidemics: A Paralyzing Effect" (September 23, 1985), similarly points out that society has not dealt well with widespread illness. This includes the bubonic plague, an epidemic known as "the Black Death" that killed about 75 million people in Europe between 1347 and 1351. This plague, which was carried from Asia by infested rats and then fleas, was outrageously blamed on Jews and many thousands were massacred. Large numbers were stoned and burned to death.

An epidemic of syphillis in the sixteenth century was symptomatically evident in victims who had large postules, deterioration of their flesh and bone, and baldness. This led young men to advertise their own freedom from the disease by growing long hair and full beards. The Great London Plague of 1665, a particularly deadly epidemic, led to the wholesale killing of cats and dogs who were erroneously blamed as being the carriers instead of the responsible rats, who were then able to reproduce at will without worrying about their now-dead, dreaded enemies. That plague was also marked by the false belief that those with syphillis would be immune, which led many to voluntarily contract the venereal disease.

More recently, in the twentieth century, the influenza epidemic of 1918–1919 killed as many as 50 million people worldwide. In Philadelphia, a city that was particularly affected, with as many as 4,500 people dying in one week, uniformed nurses on house calls were alternately mobbed by flu victims seeking help or shunned by nonvictim pedestrians. The post–World War II polio epidemic led some towns to take the unwarranted step of spraying deadly DDT to kill flies that might be infected, although there was no evidence that the virus was transmitted by insects. Other cities, like Milwaukee — on the theory that polio was a "summer" disease — delayed school openings and called for a citywide quarantine of children, restricting them to their own backyards.

In summary, as Gayle Rubin points out, it has been the medical misfortune of the gay community to be the population in which the epidemic of the deadly disease AIDS first became widespread and visible. That community should not have to deal with the social consequences of moral panic. She reminds us that "the history of panic that has accompanied new epidemics, and the casualties incurred by their scapegoats, should make everyone pause and consider with extreme scepticism any attempts to justify anti-gay policy initiatives on the basis of AIDS" (Rubin, 1984:300).

Experts Fear Global AIDS Epidemic

BY ELLEN HALE

While AIDS so far has hit the United States harder than any other country, the incidence of the deadly disease is about to explode worldwide. Its spread in Third World countries has health experts terrified.

Because medical care there is primitive, economies poor and living conditions often unsanitary, the countries are prime territory for rapid spread of the lethal virus. And because illiteracy is common, public education will be difficult, the experts fear.

Already, in some capital cities of Africa, one in five persons is a carrier of the virus. That's three times more than in New York, the American city hit worst so far by the disease, where one in 15 residents carry it.

AIDS is knocking at the door of Asian countries that cater to the practice of "sexual tourism," in which people from different countries—many economically well off and well educated—travel to Asia for the express purpose of having sex with young boys or girls.

In Europe, AIDS is just beginning to show up with regularity, but the number of cases is expected to increase tenfold within the next two or three years.

"No area of the world can consider itself immune," says Dr. Jonathan Mann, director of the AIDS program for the World Health Organization (WHO).

WHO estimates that by 1990, between 50 million and 100 million people will be infected by the virus that causes the disease. Present theory—and experts warn it is conservative—holds that 10 to 30 percent of these people will develop AIDS within a few years of being infected.

As of December, 36,210 actual cases of AIDS worldwide had been reported to WHO, and 78 countries had recorded at least one case of it. While most of the cases —more than 27,000—have occurred in the United States, experts believe the disease is on the verge of running amok globally.

AIDS, they predict, will become the major international concern in the next decade, and putting an end to the global plague will call for transcending the political, racial and economic barriers that now exist between countries. "People expect this disease to disappear fast because of the accomplishments of modern medicine—but it won't," says Mann. "It's already spread to two generations, there's really no hope for vaccine, and treatments will be of limited use and have bad side effects.

"We're years away. We're involved in a struggle that will last our lifetime, and beyond."

The World Health agency is trying to organize a global effort to help governments develop AIDS control strategies, to coordinate research on potential treatments or vaccines, to help screen for the disease and to serve as an information clearinghouse. But the project is going to wind up requiring more money than the entire WHO budget, and most experts doubt the agency can come up with the $200 million it needs to operate the AIDS program in 1987, not to mention the estimated $1.5 billion it will take to run it by 1990.

"This kind of program is unprecedented," admits Mann, "but so is the problem."

Indeed, only now is the scope of the AIDS problem being recognized worldwide.

It has taken some time, but Americans are finally shedding their notion that AIDS is a homosexual disease. While it still strikes predominantly among gays in this country, AIDS clearly is slowly and steadily working its way into the heterosexual population.

In African countries, where some two to five million are infected with the virus, it has always been a disease of heterosexuals —proof, experts say, anyone can get AIDS.

"Every sexually active person on the planet is now at risk," says Jon Tinker, president of the nonprofit Panos Institute, which recently issued the most extensive

(continued)

and detailed report yet on the worldwide incidence of AIDS.

The institute contends that the most crucial battle lines in the AIDS epidemic are now in Africa—not the United States —because "the great majority of those already marked for death [from AIDS] live in the Third World."

The AIDS virus, called HIV, for human immunodeficiency virus, can remain in the blood for years and possibly even decades. It then causes visible disease by destroying the body's immune system and making the victim vulnerable to infection from any pathogen he or she encounters. Because it can lie dormant, many people infected by the virus might not know they are carrying it and can spread it to others.

As far as scientists now know, transmission is limited to only three channels: sexual activity; direct contact with blood, such as through transfusion; or by intravenous drug abuse involving dirty needles.

Clearly, experts say, the latter two channels are going to play an increasingly important role. In Africa, for example, vaccinations and other treatments are often administered to lines of patients as doctors use the same needle time and again because of the lack of medical supplies.

But the dangers of worldwide HIV transmission are particularly fearsome should the virus spread among the estimated two million IV drug users in Asia, the Panos Institute warns.

That's because drug addicts spread the disease to their sexual partners; in New York, 10 percent of AIDS cases are among women who are believed to have thus contacted the disease. Some 60 percent of the 250,000 IV drug users in New York City carry the HIV virus.

Thailand has an estimated 500,000 IV drug abusers. It also has a booming sex-trade business, and, according to the Panos researchers, prostitutes overlap greatly with the addict community. If a pool of residents with AIDS develops in Thailand, it could mean the disease will spread throughout the rest of Asia's drug abusers and among the many tourists who visit Thailand for sexual adventure.

"Asia's drug abusers . . . form an AIDS time bomb waiting to go off," says Tinker.

These countries, as well as Africa and Latin America, share a common poverty of health services. They are ill-equipped, if equipped at all, to handle an AIDS epidemic. Nowhere is this lack of resources more painfully highlighted than with the problem of AIDS babies, say experts.

While the United States has reported fewer than 400 cases of AIDS among children and infants, Zambian doctors say their African country may have 6,000 with the virus next year. In Rwanda, one in five AIDS patients is a child.

The youngsters get AIDS—or "slim" disease, as it is called there because it wastes people to death—during or before birth from their infected mothers. Researchers also suspect, but haven't yet proven, that it can be transmitted through breast-feeding. In Africa, breast milk might be the only decent source of nutrition for a child, so a mother has little option.

On one thing most public health workers agree: The barrier to the spread of the AIDS virus in any society is a social one. That means monogamy and lifetime relationships, and no drug abuse.

"But," says WHO's Mann, "there's no society on Earth like this."

SOURCE. Ellen Hale. 1987. "Experts fear global AIDS epidemic." *The Courier-Post* (Jan. 4). Copyright 1987, Gannett News Service. Reprinted with permission.

Conclusion

This chapter introduced the reader to an important theme of this book—patriarchal ideology and its effect on gender-role relationships. Patriarchy legitimates power and authority vested in the hands of men, with the eldest man usually wielding the greatest authority and power. We outlined the major components of patriarchal authority, emphasizing four types of restrictions for women: attitudes toward fertility and adultery, domestic confinement, property, and civil rights.

We began the chapter by observing that sociology makes a distinction between sex — the biological differences between women and men — and gender — the social and cultural definitions of femininity and masculinity. We then observed that two views of the nature of gender behavior have been proposed. The first sees it as innate and biologically determined; the second takes the position that it is acquired through socialization. Ethologists and sociobiologists are of the opinion that human social and gender-role behavior, like that of other animals, is biologically and genetically determined. Critics of sociobiology emphasize the qualitative differences of humans from other animals, particularly in terms of their use of language, and maintain that social learning is the important factor.

Cross-cultural and historical research offers support for the belief of most sociologists that socialization has a greater effect than biology on gender-role behavior. Studies indicate that every culture exhibits different, culturally patterned gender-role behavior and gender identities. Other studies show that in all preindustrial societies, there generally is a division of labor and activities by sex. Most scholars agree that in all societies, biology may influence, but does not determine, differences in gender roles.

Our attention then turned to sexuality and the family. Here again, we saw from the cross-cultural and historical evidence how society, often influenced by patriarchal ideology, controls the sexual behavior of its members. The work of Randall Collins in this area was seen to be particularly important in understanding how political and economic factors play a determining role in influencing both sexual behavior and sexual ideology. The discussion of homosexuality illustrated the importance of social and cultural factors in determining the societal reaction. The chapter concluded with a discussion of AIDS. We tried to demonstrate how the societal reaction to this dreadful disease is influenced and distorted by ideological factors relating to homosexuality. We used the concept of a "moral panic" to frame our argument.

In the following chapter, we comparatively examine how the patriarchal ideology manifests itself in the way we conceptualize love and courtship. We also examine premarital gender-role relationships. That chapter is followed by one on mate-selection processes. The following two chapters then focus on the sexual division of labor. Chapter 11 provides a cross-cultural view of men and women vis-à-vis their marital relationship and their respective involvements in the world of work and in domestic household and child-care activities. This discussion is followed in the concluding chapter of Part III by an historical examination of marital gender-role relationships, focusing on the United States.

CHAPTER 9

Love, Courtship, and Premarital Relationships

Campus conversations, Dean Union College.

Elizabeth Crews/Stock, Boston

CHAPTER OUTLINE

In this chapter, we build on the previous discussion of patriarchal authority and indicate how it has affected love, courtship, and premarital relationships. We begin with a discussion of how the conceptualization of romantic love was elaborated out of the conceptualization of patriarchy. As a consequence, the historical articulation of love, courtship, and premarital relationships took on a still-recognizable character. In addition, the features that mark contemporary dating patterns and cohabitation among the young still exhibit patriarchal overtones.

We begin the chapter with an historical analysis of romantic love and the double standard, examining the Western historical experience of love and courtship and indicating the influence of patriarchal thought. We then proceed to a contemporary look at premarital relationships, focusing on college students. That discussion is followed by an in-depth examination of premarital cohabitation, where unmarried heterosexual couples live together and share the same household. Many sociologists believe that this is becoming a fundamental new state in premarital relationships and has implications for the way we think of marriage.

Romantic Love and the Double Standard

The advent of Christianity in Europe after the fall of Rome witnessed a continuation of the patriarchal ideology. Reacting against the "corruption of Roman morals" and the increased freedom of women in imperial Rome, the Christian Church under the influence of St. Paul developed a very low regard for sexual relations, marriage, and women. Women were hated, feared, and degraded. The following passages from St. Paul illustrate this attitude. The first demonstrates the extent of the depreciation of heterosexual relations; the second enunciates the ideal of sexual abstinence and the subjugation of women.

> To avoid fornication, let every man have his own wife, and let every woman have her own husband. . . . For I would that all men were even as I myself [a bachelor]. . . . I say therefore to the unmarried and widows, it is good for them if they abide as I; but if they cannot contain, let them marry; for it is better to marry than to burn. (1 Cor. 7:2–9)

> For a man indeed ought not to have his head veiled, forasmuch as he is the image and glory of God; but the woman is the glory of the man. For the man is not of the woman; but the woman of the man; for neither was the man created for the woman, but the woman for the man . . . for this house ought the woman to have a sign of authority on her head. (1 Cor. 11:7–10)

During the Middle Ages, Christianity adopted a strong ascetic morality. Sex was inherently evil and shameful. Abstinence was viewed as the ideal, with the proper role of sex being limited to procreation. In the fifth century, St. Jerome expressed this limited view of sex in marriage when he said:

> It is disgraceful to love another man's wife at all, or one's own too much. A wise man ought to love his wife with judgment, not with passion. Let a man govern his voluptuous impulses, and not rush headlong into intercourse. . . . He who too ardently loves his own wife is an adulterer. (Cited in Hunt, 1959:115)

Tied to the ascetic morality was an ambivalent attitude toward women. At one end of the continuum was the depiction of woman as Evil, the temptress Eve, and at the other end was the depiction of woman as Good, Mary, the Virgin Mother of Christ. Women, as the source of sin, were lesser beings who deserved subordination to men. They were not allowed to own or inherit property. However, certain females, nuns, were respected. They were often permitted to exercise vast authority and power within their convents.

Arising out of this dual conceptualization of women were the patterns of chivalry and courtly or romantic love among the nobility of the eleventh century. These sentiments flourished in the world of knights and ladies and were spread by troubadours and poets—finally to become the ideal of the European middle classes. The essence of courtly love was the belief in the distinction between love and lust. Love was seen as a pure and enobling romantic ideal. It was anchored by the belief that one could become obsessed with the beauty and character of another. Romantic or courtly love occurred only outside of marriage. An integral feature was that it was asexual. It idealized a fantasy of unconsummated desire: Lovers were allowed to kiss, touch, fondle, and even lie naked together, but they could not consummate their love. It was thought that to consummate the love was to destroy it.

In contrast to love was the attitude of lust. Lust allowed sexual relations and was confined to marriage. It was viewed as an inferior emotion to romantic love. Morton M. Hunt (1959), who has written a delightful historical account of love in Western society, observes that marriage during the Middle Ages was primarily a business proposition. It involved the joining of lands, loyalties, and the production of heirs and future defenders (Hunt, 1959:137). Romantic love thus offered an alternative to the mundane relationships of marriage. Hunt's presentation of the autobiography of a thirteenth-century knight, Ulrich von Lichtenstein, dramatically illustrates the dynamics of romantic love.

Eventually, the ideal of romantic love with its nonconsummating characteristic was rejected; however, it was of extreme importance in the evolution of gender-role relationships in Western civilization. Prior to its inception, the Middle Ages were distinguished by a pervasive male-dominant/female-subordinate society. Women were treated with hatred and contempt. Hunt (1969) believes that courtly love brought about three major changes in the male–female relationship. First, it introduced tenderness and gentleness into it. It developed an emotional relationship between men and women that eventually played a role in increasing the status of women. Second, it advocated the sexual fidelity of one partner to another, even though marital fidelity developed out of adulterous fidelity. Third, it introduced the revolutionary notion that love must be mutual and must involve respect and admiration. Thus, "the adulterous flirtation and illicit infatuations of the Middle Ages were the very instrument that began to enhance woman's status, and hence eventually to alter marriage" (Hunt, 1959:171–172).

Unfortunately, the dichotomization of love and lust and the "good" and "bad" woman, which was part of courtly love, continued to be manifest in the patriarchal ideology of the double standard. The double standard, which has been the dominating pattern of the gender-role relationship, is based on the notion of female inferiority. Women were divided into two categories: "good" women, who were premaritally chaste and thus were eligible marriage partners, and "bad" women, who were

The Creation of the Romantic Ideal

BY MORTON M. HUNT

When he was a mere lad of five, says Ulrich, he first heard older boys saying that true honor and happiness could come only through serving a noble and lovely woman; he was deeply impressed, and began to shape his childish thoughts in that direction. Even at that tender age it was perfectly clear to him that such service, the keystone of courtly love, could be undertaken only for a woman one could never marry. True love had to be clandestine, bittersweet, and beset by endless difficulties and frustrations; by virtue of all this, it was spiritually uplifting, and made a knight a better man and a greater warrior.

The subject evidently dominated the thoughts of the boy, for by the age of twelve he put away childish things and consciously chose as the lady of his heart a princess. In every way, it was a perfect choice; she was far too highborn for him, considerably older than himself, and, of course, already married. He became a page in her court, and conscientiously cultivated his feelings of love until they commanded his whole being. He adored her in total secrecy, and trembled (inconspicuously) in her presence. When he saw her hands touch the petals of flowers he had secretly placed where she would see them, he was all but in a faint. And when she washed her hands before dinner, young Ulrich would sometimes filch the basin, smuggle it off to his room, and there reverently drink the dirty water.

Five years of this went by; his love affair progressed no further, however, since being totally unworthy of the lady he dared not even tell her of his feelings. At the age of seventeen he therefore took himself off to the court of the Margrave Henry of Austria, to raise his status; there he studied knightly skills for five more years, and at last was made a knight in 1222, during the wedding festival of the Duke of Saxony. By a marvelous coincidence, his ladylove, whom he had not seen but religiously dreamed of during those years, was one of the guests at the wedding, and the very sight of her so moved him that he immediately took a secret vow to devote his newly won knighthood to serving her. This decision filled him with melancholy and with painful longings, a condition which apparently made him very happy.

That summer, feverish and flushed with his infatuation, he roamed the countryside fighting in numerous tourneys and winning many victories, all of which he ascribed to the mighty force of love within him. At last, having compiled an impressive recʌ̕ d, and feeling worthy to offer the lady the tribute of his devotion, he persuaded a niece of his to call on her and privately tell her of his desire to be an acknowledged but distant, respectful admirer of hers; he even got his niece to learn and sing for the Princess a song he had written. (Ulrich was already a competent *Minnesinger*—the German equivalent of the troubadour—as were many young noblemen of breeding.)

The heartless lady, unmoved by his ten years of silent devotion and his recent feats of valor, sent back a cruel and pointed reply: she considered him presumptuous, was scornfully critical of the high-flown language of his quite inappropriate offer, and for good measure, took the trouble to let him know he was too ugly to be considered even in the role of a very distant admirer. For it seems (and the lady was specific) that the unhappy young knight had a harelip. Undaunted—perhaps even inspired by this obvious proof that she had actually noticed him—Ulrich promptly undertook a journey to a famous surgeon and had his lip repaired. Considering the techniques of medieval surgery, this must have been both excruciatingly painful and quite dangerous; indeed, he lay feverish on a sickbed for six weeks. News of this, plus a new song he wrote for her, softened the lady's heart, and she sent word that he might attend a riding party and enjoy the rare privilege of speaking with her for a moment, if the opportunity should arise. And it did, once, when he had the chance to help her down from her horse, and could have uttered a sentence or two of devotion; unfortunately he was tongue-tied by her

(*continued*)

nearness and could say nothing. The lovely lady, considerably put out, whispered to him that he was a fraud, and gracefully indicated her displeasure by ripping out a forelock of his hair as she dismounted.

Not in the least angered by this, Ulrich reappeared the next day, this time found his voice, and humbly begged her to permit him to be her secret knight and to allow him to fight for her and love her. She accepted his service, but under the very minimum conditions, granting him no "favor" whatever—neither embrace, kiss, nor word of promise, and not so much as a ribbon to carry in his bosom. Ulrich, nevertheless, was filled with joy and thankfulness for her kindness, and sailed forth, tilting about the countryside with anyone who would break a lance with him, and composing many a song to his ladylove, which his secretary set down for him since writing was not a knightly accomplishment. The messages and letters that passed between him and the Princess at this time conveyed, in the one direction, his endless, burning, worshipful feelings and, in the other direction, her condescension, coldness, and criticism. But this was exactly what was expected of her in the situation, and he found each new blow a delicious pain; it even sounds somewhat as though a part of his pleasure lay in observing his own noble constancy under duress. If so, he must have had a thoroughly agreeable time for the next three years.

At the end of that period, Ulrich petitioned her forthrightly through a go-between to grant him her love, at least verbally, in return for his faithful adoration and service. The Princess not only sharply rebuked the go-between for Ulrich's unseemly persistency, but expressed her scorn that Ulrich had falsely spoken of losing a finger fighting for love of her. Actually, he had suffered a finger wound which healed, but an incorrect report had reached her. When the go-between related her scornful message, Ulrich paled for a moment, then resolutely drew out a sharp knife and ordered his friend to hack off the finger at one blow. This done, the knight had an artisan make a green velvet case in which the finger was held by gold clasps, and sent her the mounted digit as a keepsake, together with a special poem

about the matter. Deeply impressed by this evidence of her power over him, she returned word that she would look at the finger every day from thenceforth, a message which, incidentally, he received as he did all other communiqués from her— on his knees, with bowed head and folded hands.

Determined now to earn her love by some stupendous feat, Ulrich conceived the scheme of the jousting-trip from Venice to Bohemia in the disguise of Venus. He went to Venice and there had seamstresses make a dozen white gowns to his own measurements; meanwhile he sent off a messenger with the open letter announcing the event. The northward march began on schedule on April 25, and concluded five weeks later, during which time Ulrich shattered an average of eight lances every day, made the notable record already mentioned, and acquired great glory and honor, all in the cause of love and for the sake of the Princess he so faithfully adored.

All this being so, it comes as something of a shock when one reads Ulrich's own statement that in the midst of this triumphal *Venusreise* he stopped off for three days to visit his wife and children. For the fact is that this lovesick Galahad, this kissless wonder, this dauntless knight-errant, had long had a wife to lie with when he had the urge, and a family to live with when he felt lonely. He himself speaks of his affection (but not his love) for his wife; to love her would have been improper and almost unthinkable. Like the other men of his class and time, Ulrich considered marriage a phase of feudal business-management, since it consisted basically of the joining of lands, the cementing of loyalties, and the production of heirs and future defenders. But the purifying, ennobling rapture of love for an ideal woman—what had that to do with details of crops and cattle, fleas and fireplaces, serfs and swamp drainage? Yet, though true love was impossible between husband and wife, without it a man was valueless. Ulrich could therefore unashamedly visit his wife during his grand tour, proud of what he had been doing and certain that if she knew of it, she too was proud, because *Frauendienst* made her husband nobler and finer.*

Having completed his epochal feat of

(*continued*)

love service, Ulrich waited for his reward, and at long last it came: the Princess sent word that he might visit her. Yet he was to expect no warm welcome; she specified that he must come in the disguise of a leper and take his place among lepers who would be visiting her to beg for alms. But of course this monstrous indignity fazed the faithful Ulrich not in the least; nor did he falter when she knowingly let him, disguised in his rags, spend that night in a ditch in the rain; nor was he outraged when the next night he was finally allowed to climb a rope up the castle wall to her chamber, only to find it lit by a hundred tapers and staffed by eight maids-in-waiting who hovered about her where she lay in bed. Though Ulrich pleaded urgently that they all be sent out, she continued to be coyly proper, and when she began to see that this patient fellow really was getting stubborn at last, she told him that to earn the favor he would have to prove his obedience by wading in a near-by lake. She herself assisted him out the window—and then, bending to kiss him, let loose the rope, tumbling Ulrich to the ground, or perhaps into a stinking moat. (It is worth remembering at this point that this painful incident was not recorded by any enemy or satirist of Ulrich, but by himself, his purpose being to make clear the extent of his suffering for love and his fidelity in the face of trials.)

Even such torments cannot go on forever. The cruel Princess next ordered Ulrich to go on a crusade in her service, but when she learned that he joyfully and obediently received the direct command from her, she suddenly relented, bade him rather stay at home near to her, and finally granted him her love. What an outpouring of thankful verse then! What a spate of shattered lances, dented helmets, broken blades, humbled opponents! For having won her love, Ulrich was puissant, magnificent, impregnable; this was the height of his career as a knight. Regrettably, it is not clear in the *Frauendienst* just which of her favors she so tardily vouchsafed after nearly a decade and a half, but in the light of other contemporary documents concerning the customs of courtly love, one can be fairly sure that she permitted him the kiss and the embrace, and perhaps even the right to caress her, naked, in bed; but if she gave him the final reward at all, it was probably on extremely rare occasions. For sexual outlet was not really the point of all this. Ulrich had not been laboring nearly fifteen years for so ordinary a commodity; his real reward had always been in his suffering, striving, and yearning.

SOURCE. Morton M. Hunt. 1959. *The Natural History of Love.* New York: Knopf, pp. 134–139. Reprinted by permission of Morton M. Hunt.

*Ladies, too, were increased in value by being loved. In a fictional counterpart of Ulrich's relations with his wife, a lady in an old Provençal romance, reproached by her husband for having a lover, proudly replies: "My lord, you have no dishonor on that account, for he is a noble baron, upright and expert in arms, namely, Roland, the nephew of King Charles" (*Gesta Karoli Magni and Carcassonam et Narbonam,* p. 139).

available to satisfy men's sexual needs outside of marriage. Men were allowed sexual access to women both in and out of marriage. "Good" women must restrain their sexual activities prior to marriage and in marriage. The double standard had a two-pronged basis: the notion of the lesser sexual interests of women and the idea of women as personal property. The argument was made that a woman was the personal property first of her father and second of her husband, and a woman had no right to give herself to another man without their consent.

In addition to the rights and privileges of men in regard to sexual activities, the double standard was extended to other spheres of life, including religion, politics, and economics. In all spheres, women had subordinated duties and obligations. Moreover, the placing of women on a pedestal (derived from romantic love ideology) further discriminated against them. Although supposedly protected from the harsh "realities" of the outside world, women were actually placed in a position of subservience and dependency. By viewing women as "delicate flowers" who must be

Historical Pictures Service, Chicago

Love in the age of the troubador.

protected and sheltered, men effectively removed women from those spheres in the outside world that would have made the equality of women possible.

We return to these themes in later chapters. Here, let us take an historical look at how patriarchal ideology influenced the way we conceptualize love and practice courtship. This discussion is followed by a contemporary examination of the double standard in its effects on premarital dating, courtship, and cohabitation. Our focus is on the American scene, with emphasis on college students.

Love and Courtship in Comparative Perspective

> Love and Marriage,
> Love and Marriage,
> Go together like a horse and carriage,
> This I tell you brother,
> You can't have one,
> No, You can't have one,
> Without the other.[1]

The above lyrics from a popular song of the 1950s reflect a prevalent contemporary view of the inseparability of love and marriage. Historically, until very recently,

[1] "Love and Marriage" lyrics by Sammy Cahn; music by Jimmy Van Heusen. Copyright © 1955, Barton Music Corporation.

however, it was not true. In this chapter, we discuss the relationship of these two phenomena within the context of an examination of courtship and mate-selection processes. To frame our analysis, we work off the basic ideas of what has become known as the sentiments approach in family history (Anderson, 1980).

A few general remarks on the sentiments approach are desirable before we proceed more directly in our analysis of courtship systems and processes. The pivotal works in this area are Phillipe Ariés' *Centuries of Childhood* (1962), Edward Shorter's *The Making of the Modern Family* (1975), J.L. Flandrin's *Families in Former Times* (1979), and Lawrence Stone's *Family, Sex and Marriage in England 1500–1800* (1977). We will have more to say on Ariés' and Shorter's works in later chapters. Here, let us limit our attention to Stone and Flandrin within the context of courtship systems and processes.

We begin our account by examining the influential work of Lawrence Stone (1977), who hypothesizes that the most important cultural change in the history of early modern Europe, and perhaps within the last thousand years of European history, was the rise of *affective individualism*. Stone discusses this conceptualization through an historical construction of three family types (the open lineage family, 1450–1630; the restricted patriarchal nuclear family, 1550–1700; and the closed domesticated nuclear family, 1640–1800) to explain change between 1500 and 1800. Anchoring his analysis is the sociological thesis that an inward-turning nuclear family gradually replaced the extended-kinship networks.

Stone's central argument is that family relationships are markedly different over the last 400 years. Similarly, Flandrin makes the point that the very concept of "family" has historically undergone major changes. The premodern English and French concept of the family reflected notions of kinship and co-residence. It referred both to sets of kinsfolk who did not live together and to all people who lived within a household and were not necessarily linked by ties of blood and marriage. Flandrin (1979:5) observes that this was still the case in the second half of the eighteenth century in both France and England, "that the members of the family were held to include both the kinsfolk residing in the house and the domestic servants, insofar as they were all subject to the same head of the family."

In the sixteenth century and extending into much later periods in many geographical areas and among certain social-class groups, the family is seen as being patriarchal and authoritarian, and demanding deference. Husbands had virtually absolute power and control over wives and children. This held true not only in economic terms but also in moral matters. Enforcement included the right as well as the duty to use physical force on those who disobeyed. Both women and children were relegated to subordinate legal positions that were based on the economic and political control of the husbands and fathers. Children were legally subordinate to their fathers to the extent that they could not enter into contracts until into their twenties (if even then). Similarly, children's rights either in law or in practice to select their own spouses were often strictly circumscribed (Anderson, 1980).

The "open lineage" family patterns are seen by Stone as a reflection of the overall patterns of people of premodern Europe who were typically violent, distrustful, and suspicious. People are characterized as having a markedly low level of affection and emotional interaction. The society is depicted as one in which everyone found it difficult to establish any emotional ties and there was a lack of warmth and tolerance in interpersonal relations. Privacy in this period is nonexistent. Concurring with Stone, Flandrin—basing his analysis on a study of confessors' manuals—finds no evidence of a duty to love either spouse or children. The prominent emphasis is on respect, deference, and obligation. Affection and sentimental attachments are treated with suspicion and seen as likely to lead to disorder.

This family system, with its emphasis on broad kinship ties and emotionally remote relations within the nuclear unit, changed in the mid-sixteenth century when the upper and middle strata of English society began to substitute loyalty to the state for loyalty to the broader kinship group that comprised the lineage. The resultant family form, the restricted patriarchal nuclear family, reconceptualized the family to its nuclear core while maintaining paternal authority. The result was a contradictory system that began to emphasize affectional ties between husband and wife, and between parents and children, within a nuclear family environment that continued to stress patriarchal obedience. In essence, Stone follows the recent historical interpretation that sees patriarchal authority within the nuclear family as being reinforced by the demands of the state and the church in the sixteenth and seventeenth centuries.

The final type of family, the closed domesticated nuclear family, rests on the belief in affective individualism. Stone observes that the change occurred first among the upper bourgeoisie and the affluent landowners. The emphasis in the nuclear family moved from absolute patriarchal authority to affectional ties. Children were seen as neutral and plastic beings who could best be molded by nurture and kindness. Prior affection was now an essential ingredient to a marriage, and young people were increasingly given the freedom to choose their own mates instead of having them selected by parents. Traditional patriarchy was replaced by romantic love, companionate marriage, and an affectionate and permissive mode of child rearing.

The various factors to which Stone attributes these eighteenth-century changes include Renaissance ideas about education, Reformation ideas of holy matrimony, and emerging ideas about liberty and the importance of the individual. The result was the rise of a more-affectionate and more-individualistic family type that is the direct antecedent of the contemporary conjugal family in both structure and emotional content. How this change in the closed domesticated nuclear family influenced changes in courtship processes concerns us here.

Stone views the period from 1660 to 1800 as one in which there was a shift in beliefs in how to assure that the interests of "holy matrimony" would best be served. By 1660, the belief moved from the previously held view of absolute parental decision making to the emerging opinion that children of both sexes should have the right of veto over a future spouse chosen for them by their parents. By 1800, the more-radical view that children themselves should make their own choices prevailed. Accompanying this shift was the parallel one that moved the primary motive for marriage away from extended-kinship interest toward personal affection. Stone believes that the overall change to allow children much greater say in their choice of a spouse was a reflection of a new consciousness and a new recognition of the need for personal autonomy and for the individual pursuit of happiness.

There are three sociological conditions that are seen by Stone as essential for the development of relatively free mate selection. The first is the increased independence of the nuclear family from extended-kinship bonds. The second is the development of close parent–child bonds so that parents are assured that their values are shared by their children and that their children would make appropriate mate-selection choices. The third is the development of settings that would allow members of both sexes the opportunity to develop their own "courting rituals of conversation, dancing, etc." (Stone, 1977:184). In the next section, we examine how courtship rituals and institutions were articulated in nineteenth-century America and how they reflected the ideology that Stone has called affective individualism.

Courtship and Love in America

The historian Carl Degler (1980) reflects the current consensus among social historians that the modern American family emerged in the approximate 50-year period from the Revolution to 1830. During that period, the family is seen to have changed not only in structure but also in internal dynamics. The four predominant characteristics of that family form as outlined by Degler embrace themes already discussed here. Marriage becomes based on affection and mutual respect, low fertility, child-centeredness, and, most important, what Degler calls the "doctrine of the two spheres."

Degler's analysis emphasizes the importance of the doctrine of the two spheres or separate spheres in the articulation of husband and wife roles. Essentially, this doctrine held that the primary role of the wife was child care and the maintenance of the household while the husband's was work outside the home. The very real potential of this doctrine is the belief that, while the wife may be the moral superior in the relationship, the source of legal and social power rests with the husband. The consequence is the subordination of women's roles to their husbands. To deal with that subordination, women are seen to have carved out a source of power based on the emerging importance of mutual affection, love, and sexuality as integral components of modern marriage. The following discussion examines this development within an analysis of courtship processes.

Degler, influenced by such social historians as Lawrence Stone (1977) and Philip Greven (1970), developed his argument that prior to the American Revolution, fathers were not adverse to use "economic blackmail" to assure that their children married whom they wanted. For example, as Greven has observed in his historical analysis of four generations in colonial Wendover, Massachusetts, the threat of withholding of land from their sons increased the influence of Puritan fathers over their sons during the 1700s. By the eighteenth century, however, there was a notable weakening of parental control over the marital choice and this form of coercion was less likely to occur. Degler traces similar historical developments in the freedom of mate-selection choices for both sons and daughters in other sections of preindependent America. The overall pattern is that by the beginning of the nineteenth century, parental control over the choice of marriage partners of their children was limited to a nonbinding veto much as it essentially is today (Degler, 1980).

The reasons for this change in the courtship decision-making process came as a consequence of the emerging belief that marriage should be based on personal happiness and the affection of the partners for each other. This attitude stems from the equating of marriage for love with individualism. "Love as the basis for marrying was the purest form of individualism; it subordinated all familial, social, or group considerations to personal preference" (Degler, 1980:15). Further, the growing acceptance of affection as the primary ground for marriage became an essential factor in the change in women's roles and a potential source of power and autonomy within the family. This was of particular importance, because women in the nineteenth century had declining power or influence in the economic sphere.

> [M]ost relationships between people involve the exercise of power, and cetainly the relationship of marriage is no exception. Yet once affection is a basis of marriage, the marital relation becomes significantly different from other relationships between superiors and inferiors. To begin with, unlike any other subordinate, such as a slave or an employee, a young woman contemplating marriage did have some choice as to who her new master would be. Clearly unsatisfactory possibilities could be ruled out completely, and from acquaintance at courtship, she had an opportunity to learn who were the undesirable partners. After the marriage, the woman also had an advantage that few slaves or employees enjoyed in dealing with their masters or employers. She was able to appeal to her husband's affection for her, and she, in turn, could use that affection in extracting concessions that a slave or an employee could not. In short, by the very nature of the relation, a woman in the family of affection had more power or influence than any other subordinate one can think of. (Degler, 1980:18)

Similarly, the expression of sexuality both within and outside of the courtship process took on a power component. Nancy Cott (1978), in an insightful article, sees that the Victorian notion of the "passionlessness" of women served to improve their status. The downplaying of sexuality was seen as a means of limiting male domination. At the same time sexuality was replaced by an emphasis on moral and spiritual superiority over males. "The belief that women lacked carnal motivation was the cornerstone of the argument for women's moral superiority, used to enhance women's status and widen their opportunities in the nineteenth century" (Cott, 1978:173).

Ellen K. Rothman—in a delightful as well as insightful comprehensive history of courtship in America, *Hands and Hearts* (1984)—explains the interweaving of sexuality and courtship through an examination of three periods. Her account is drawn heavily from the analysis of unpublished courtship correspondence of 350 native-born, Northeastern, middle-class Protestants. Rothman acknowledges the limitation of this source of data in that it excludes large segments of the population—such as blacks, immigrants, and the poor—from her analysis. However, given that caveat, it is still of interest to see the courtship processes of that segment of American society to see what light it may shed on contemporary courtship and marriage practices.

Young males and females in the first period, 1770–1840—we are told—enjoyed a good deal of autonomy in regard to their dating. Places to get together included schools and churches, fields and factories, and dances and parties. Gender roles reflected a division of labor and did not, as yet, reflect the future development of the two spheres of work and home. Bundling, an eighteenth-century precursor to pre-marital sex in which couples would sleep together, albeit with their clothes on, was a common practice that allowed them to get to know each other better. Historians see it as a compromise between persistent parental control and the pressures of their children to subvert traditional family authority. A song written during that time period leads Rothman to conjecture that bundling may have been a practice that mothers and daughters favored because it was a ritual over which their sex had control.

> Some maidens say, if through the nation,
> Bundling should quite go out of fashion,
> Courtship would lose its sweets, and they
> Could have no fun till wedding day.
> It shan't be so, they rage and storm,
> And courtship girls in clusters swarm,
> And fly and bus, like angry bees,
> And vow they'll bundle when they please.
> Some mothers too, will plead their cause
> And give their daughters great applause,
> And tell them, 'tis no sin nor shame,
> For we, your mothers, did the same.
> (Cited in Rothman, 1984:47)

The second period, 1830–1880, was so marked by the doctrine of the two spheres in almost all areas of life that Alexis de Tocqueville made a point to comment on this in his first visit to America in 1831 that "constant care" was taken to "trace two clearly distinct lines of action for the two sexes . . . in two paths that are always different" (quoted in Rothman, 1984:91). Clearly demarcated boundaries for men and women were developed in the community, the home, and in the world of work. Of equal importance was the commonly held view that women, while intellectually inferior to men, were their superior in terms of moral sensibilities. This definition of gender differences became the cultural context for the articulation of courtship processes and the transition into marriage during this period.

The essence of maleness was defined in terms of their occupational involvement and the pursuit of worldly and material success. Women, on the other hand, were defined in terms of home—wife and mother—involvement and moral virtue. Ralph Waldo Emerson, the spokesman of New England transcendentalism, captures that

Historical Pictures Service, Chicago

Flirtation and courtship in the nineteenth century.

sentiment as "Man's sphere is out of doors and among men—woman's is in the house—Man seeks for power and influence—woman for order and beauty—Man is just—woman is kind" (cited in Rothman, 1984:92).

Rothman believes that this idealization of masculine and feminine behavior affected courtship to the extent that romantic love took on greater importance as the criterion for marriage than ever before. Further, romantic love as a basis for marriage must go beyond transient passions but must serve as a base for sympathy and shared interests. It was vital that such a marital relationship be grounded on mutuality, commonality, and sympathy in order to overcome the gulf between men and women that resulted from their division in two different spheres. "The increasing isolation of married women in the home and the involvement of married men in the world made it imperative that lovers sympathize with each other; they must have a mutuality of tastes and interests because they might have little else to share" (Rothman, 1984:107).

Candor became a dominant value in mid-nineteenth-century courtship ritual. It was seen as a vital link between people whose involvements were in two disparate worlds. Rothman observes that men were in constant struggle between the dominant masculine ideology of self-control and the felt necessity for self-exposure and intimacy in courtship. When it did occur, candor produced an intimate environment that was in direct contrast to the emotional reserve they experienced with other people. Further, courtship intimacy led to other changes; marriages took on a more-companionate perspective and parent–child relationships—with particular emphasis on mother–child involvements—became a central focus of family life.

Candor also affected attitudes and behavior regarding sexual intimacy during courtship. Repeatedly, Rothman found in her examination of the correspondence of young people that erotic play, in both fantasy and reality, was a common component of mid-nineteenth-century courtship. Letters between separated lovers evoked the past and anticipated the future with images of sexual imagery. The following letter is illustrative:

> O happy hours when I may *once more* encircle within these arms the dearest object of my love—when I shall again feel the pressure of that "aching head" which will delight to recline upon my bosom, when I may *again* press to my heart which palpitates with the purest affection the loved one who has so long shared its undivided devotion. (Cited in Rothman, 1984:122–123)

However, the achievement of candor and intimacy that was so necessary for the success of courtship and subsequent marriage and family patterns was severely handicapped by the continued prominence of the doctrine of the two spheres, which advocated the separation of male and female worlds. The third period, 1870–1920, was characterized by the beginning of the reaction against this doctrine and its offshoot, the doctrine of "female influence." This doctrine advocated the innate moral superiority of women while at the same time argued that women's place was at home. The doctrine of female influence soon fell under attack; for example, the women's suffrage movement pointed out the hypocrisy in the view that women did not need the vote because their innate superiority gave them so much influence over their enfranchised husbands and sons.

Yet the doctrine of female influence was part of the more-encompassing doctrine of the two spheres. The consequence of these doctrines continued to foster obstacles to friendship between the sexes, often resulting in a reliance on friendships with their own sex. Further, it severely handicapped the development of emotional bonds within courtship. In the next section, we see how these historical changes in courtship affected the dating and courtship processes of middle-class Americans after 1930.

The Double Standard and Premarital Relationships

In the United States, individual motives, particularly love, play an important role in the decision-making process related to whom we should marry. Yet falling in love is usually limited to someone who is socially approved by parents and peers; that is, through informal long-term socialization and through informal pressures, marriage is usually restricted to partners who share similar backgrounds, social class, religion, race, and education. We now discuss an additional factor that helps explain American dating, courtship, and mate-selection processes—the double standard.

The double standard is usually associated with sexual behavior. It allows greater freedom for men to have premarital and extramarital sexual experiences than for women. It originates in ancient Hebrew, Greek, Roman, and early Christian doctrines. Ira Reiss, who has done extensive analyses of premarital sexual standards and behavior, observes that the basis of the double standard involves the notion of female inferiority. Reiss (1960) argues that the double standard is not solely restricted to sexual behavior. The double standard allows men preferential rights and duties in a variety of roles. By and large, the more-challenging, the more-satisfying, and the more-valued positions are awarded to men and not to women.

> It is not just a question of different roles—anyone looking fairly at the division of roles will see that women's roles are given low status as compared to men's roles. The particular role does not matter; whatever a woman does is valued less and whatever a man does is valued more, e.g., if men herd then herding is highly valued—if women herd it is not. (Reiss, 1960:92–93)

In later chapters, we examine in more depth the origins of the double standard and its implications for gender-role relationships in the family and in other spheres. Now we investigate its impact on mate-selection processes.

For Amish, Now is Marrying Season

BY BARBARA LITTLE

LANCASTER—Brides-to-be are beginning to think of the new white cap and apron they will wear on their wedding day. And the future bridegrooms are preparing to travel from farm to farm in their buggies to invite the wedding guests.

The mothers of the brides are thinking of the sumptuous feasts they will prepare for the big day with the assistance of their relatives and friends.

Tuesdays and Thursdays in November are being set aside by the various families for the weddings of their sons and daughters. And young couples with such names such as Stoltzfus and King and Beiler and Fisher are beginning to appear at the marriage-license bureau in the Lancaster County Courthouse.

The Amish marrying season is at hand. Traditionally, the Amish marry during November, when the harvesting is done and it is a time for thanksgiving.

Perhaps 100 or more Amish couples will apply for marriage licenses this year, and most will marry on a Tuesday or Thursday in November. It may be, however, that there are not enough wedding days to accommodate all of the couples and some may marry at the beginning of December.

In keeping with Amish practices, they will have their intentions announced two or three weeks ahead of the wedding date by the deacon during a worship service.

The Amish wedding, an occasion for worship and feasting, is held at the home of the bride and may be attended by 350 or more guests. Some of the guests will travel as many as 10 miles in their buggies to reach the bride's home by 8:30 A.M.

Most of the preparations have been done the day before, with relatives and friends assisting the bride's mother in the cooking. And in keeping with the spirit of the Amish, the women will pitch in to help

serve the meal—at noon and in the evening—on the wedding day.

Feasting follows the morning service, with the newlyweds sitting at a big table with other young people who have recently been married or are soon to be married.

The wedding ceremony is a simple one without flowers or ring. It is part of a worship service that may last from 8:30 A.M. to noon.

For the worship service, plain wooden benches have been placed in every nook of the bride's home and are used to capacity by the guests and the wedding party.

Conducted in German, the traditional worship service opens with the singing of Gregorian hymns and is followed by silent prayer. Included is a testimony by the minister and a sermon by the bishop, who presides at the nuptials.

When it is time for the nuptials, the bride and bridegroom, who have been sitting with the rest of the people, step forward and stand before the bishop. Each is attended by a young man and a young woman.

After they are married, the bride and bridegroom return to their benches and the bishop continues the worship service.

Traditionally, the bride and bridegroom return to their respective homes after the daylong festivities and then begin a series of weekend visits to the homes of those who were invited to the wedding.

They will then receive gifts of kitchen utensils and other items for the home into which they will move in the spring. Amish parents generally help the young couple buy their own farm.

SOURCE. Barbara Little. 1986. "For Amish, now is marrying season." *The Philadelphia Inquirer* (Oct. 30). Reprinted by permission of *The Philadelphia Inquirer* Oct. 30, 1986.

The double standard has had a pervasive effect on mate-selection processes. As Willard Waller (1938) has pointed out in his classic study of the family, double-standard–based courtship practices can be analyzed in terms of bargaining and exploitive behavior that denigrates both men* and women. The stigma attached to being an unwed nonvirgin combined with the desire of women to marry, partly because of the lack of meaningful alternative options in the work sphere, promoted an atmosphere in courtship that was destructive for both sexes. In return for sexual "favors," women bargained for an ultimate marriage contract. But paradoxically, the loss of virginity lessened her marital desirability and eligibility (a man's wish to marry a virgin). The result was a frustrating relationship where there was a constant give-and-take revolving around sexual permissiveness and marital commitment. Ira Reiss (1960) has stated that the double standard results in a net of contradictory and unfulfilled desires:

> Many women very strongly resent this contradictory virginity-attitude on the part of men. These women feel it most unfair for a man to date a girl, try to seduce her, and then if he succeeds, condemn her and cross her off his marriage-possibility list. Many girls find themselves upset when they become fond of a particular boy and would like to be more sexually intimate with him, but must keep restricting their advances for fear of losing his respect. . . .
>
> Many girls who tease are merely playing the man's game. If men are so interested in sex, but dislike girls who "go too far," the logical thing to do, these girls feel, is to play up their sexual attributes to attract men and then restrict sexual behavior. The double-standard male creates his own "enemies" — he makes women use sex as a weapon instead of an expression of affection; in this case, the weapon is in the form of the tease. This sort of situation leads to the anomalous case of a female who, on the surface, seems highly-sexed but who internally may be quite frigid — a sweet "sexy" virgin whose dual nature may well cause her much internal conflict. Such a virgin is similar to wax fruit — in both cases the appearance may be appetizing but the object is incapable of fulfilling its promise. (Reiss, 1960:106)

Bernard Farber (1964) has observed that mate-selection processes used to be characterized by a series of stages that culminated in marriage — dating, keeping company, going steady, a private agreement to be married, announcement of the engagement, and finally marriage. This pattern can be seen as a reflection of the double standard, which placed a great deal of emphasis on "approved" sexuality confined to marriage and women's confinement to marriage as the only career possibility. Today, this pattern is changing. The increased independence of women and their greater involvement in institutions other than the family, work, politics, religion, and education have provided them with career alternatives. Further, technological developments in controlling impregnation (the pill, the loop) combined with less-stringent norms about sexual permissiveness for both sexes have changed the courtship process. Farber points out that such a term as keeping company is no longer in the courtship vocabulary. As for the term going steady, it now mainly refers to a person with whom one is currently involved. Since Farber wrote his monograph, such terms as dating and courtship have become antiquated. Farber concludes that with the whole system of courtship, which was based on the double standard, there was an ever-narrowing field of eligible spouses. This has given way to a series of personal "involvements," one of which may result in marriage (Farber, 1964:161).

Michal M. McCall (1966) has analyzed this new courtship pattern. Sexual exploitation is not associated with it. In this new relationship, there is an emphasis on intimacy and exclusiveness with a personal commitment. This commitment includes sexual intimacy. Most men no longer expect women to be virgins at the time of their first marriage. The relationship is more egalitarian and can be terminated by either partner if it turns out to be unsatisfactory. In this relationship, exploitation refers to the possible impregnation of the woman and the failure of the man to marry her. Analogous to the earlier pattern, where there was a legitimate expectation that marriage followed sexual intimacy, today's pattern has a legitimate expectation that marriage follows impregnation. The relationship of the couple is intensely personal. Given the greater equality of women, there is a greater tendency for either the man or woman to break the relationship and seek to form a new one. This is attributed to the fact that the notion of the "one and only love" (a main component of romantic love) is no longer as viable as before. It also helps explain why contemporary premarital relationships are less stable and enduring.

From Dating and Rating to Cohabitation

We expand the above discussion by examining changes in premarital relationships in the United States during the past 50 years. We begin with Willard Waller's (1937) famous study of the dating and rating complex that existed at Pennsylvania State University in the later 1920s and early 1930s. We end with an analysis of nonmarital cohabitation.

Waller (1937) distinguished courtship from dating. Dating refers to the pursuit of sexual pleasure as an aim in itself; courtship involves interaction with a person who is seen as a possible marriage partner. Hedonistic considerations count for less than in dating, and the person's family and class background count for much more. Waller describes the dating process within the context of the fraternity system then in existence at Penn State. Half the male students lived in fraternities. These students were a homogeneous group predominantly from the lower-middle class. For these men, the dating system was highly competitive and based on a scale reflecting campus values. Males were rated highest if they were members of the better fraternities, were prominent in activities, had a large supply of spending money, were well dressed, were good dancers, and had access to an automobile. Girls were rated on their appearance, their popularity, their ability to dance well, and who they dated.

An integral aspect of the dating system was the boys' open antagonism toward the girls, the exploitative nature of their relationships, and what Waller calls "thrill seeking." The "thrills" varied by sex; men sought sexual gratification while women sought to enhance their prestige by going out with the more-desirable men and gaining financial benefit, such as free admission to amusements, restaurants, theaters, and the like. This resulted in dating becoming a bargaining relationship with exploitative and antagonistic overtones. Waller illustrates this point by citing a woman student informant:

> A fundamental antagonism exists on this campus between the men and women students. There is an undercurrent of feeling among the men that the school really belongs to them, and that the coed is a sort of legalized transgressor on their territory. A typical procedure of the college man is to give a coed a terrific rush, and then either drop her suddenly without any explanation whatsoever, or tell her that "Mary Jane Whosis, the girl he is engaged to at home, is coming up for Senior Ball," or something of that sort. . . .
>
> Against this sort of attitude the coeds build up a defense mechanism which usually takes the form of cynicism. "They're out for what they can get? That's fine. So are we." Everything is just one grand, big joke. Many of the girls really fight against liking a boy and try very hard to maintain this cynical attitude. One way in which they do this is the use of ridicule. Many coeds put on an act for their girlfriends after a date, mimicking certain characteristic actions of the boy she has been out with, and making a joke of the things he has said to her. Often the less a girl feels like doing this, the worse she will make it. It is her way of convincing herself that her armor of cynicism is as strong as ever. (Waller, 1938:252–253)

Waller attributes the development of the dating and rating system to the disappearance of community controls over the younger generation. Their loss is seen in the decline of the primary group community and in the reduction of such adult supervised activities as school and church socials. "From the sociological viewpoint, this represented social disorganization, a decay of older forms, a replacement of socially agreed-upon definitions of situations by hedonistic, individualistic definitions" (Waller, 1938:223). In short, Waller saw the dating and rating process being dominated by a desire for fun and amusement that was expressed in a system of exploitativeness, antagonism, and bargaining.

Waller saw dating becoming separated from courtship. The implications of Waller's study are that the gender-role antagonisms generated by the dating system are carried over to courtship and lead to undesirable emotional tensions in this relationship and in marriage. Waller developed the conceptualization of the "principle of least interest" to summarize this point. He believed that courtship grew out of dating as one or both partners became emotionally involved. But unequal emotional involvement could lead to the person with "least interest" exploiting the other, thus repeating the debilitating dating relationship:

> Exploitation of sorts usually follows the realization that the other person is more deeply involved than oneself. So much almost any reasonably sophisticated person understands. The clever person, in my observation usually a woman, knows how to go on from that point. A girl may pretend to be extremely involved, to be the person wholly dominated by the relationship; this she does in order to lead the young man to fasten his emotions and to prepare the way for the conventional denouement of marriage, for, in the end, while protesting her love, she makes herself unattainable except in marriage; this is certainly not an unusual feminine tactic and is executed with a subtlety which makes the man's crude attempts at guile seem sophomoric. (1938:276–277)

Waller sees love and marriage emerging out of courtship. Love is depicted as an outgrowth of the initial desire of one partner to get the other partner emotionally involved in the relationship. However, individuals, without being aware of it, may develop an idealized image of the other that takes on an irrational character, and thus they get caught up in an emotional surge that culminates in marriage. The consequences are that the couple must reorient their early stages of marital adjustment to a relationship based on the reality of each other, not on their idealizations of each other. For many, this becomes an impossible task, culminating in a marital relationship that is characterized by conflict and, in many cases, divorce.

Attempts to replicate Waller's finding of the existence of a "rating and dating complex" have not been successful. Christopher Lasch (1977a), in a review of the studies of the 1940s and 1950s, finds many flaws in their methodologies, particularly in the way they operationalized Waller's concept of rating and dating. Michael Gordon (1978) and Richard R. Clayton (1979), in their respective reviews of studies done in the 1950s, 1960s, and 1970s, report that personality factors may play a more-influential role than Waller's rating criteria in dating relationships. Gordon further develops the view that these more recent studies may reflect historical changes that have occurred in the attitudes and values that govern premarital heterosexual relationships, as well as the greater possibility that marriage may take place either during or immediately after college. Another factor that is emerging in the nature of premarital relationships is the dramatic increase in the number of college students who are now cohabitating. Cohabitation represents a significant movement away from the situation in which the dating relationship—according to Waller—was a means to an end, to a relationship that is an end in and of itself and characterized by personal involvements and commitments. Let us now turn our attention to this emerging new trend in premarital relationships.

Researchers [see Gordon (1978) and Leslie (1979) for reviews of these studies] have observed that there is a movement away from pairing off in casual dating patterns to more-informal group activities among high school and college students. Exclusive dating begins at a later age and is more clearly associated with greater emotional involvements and commitments. Further, a more-innovative development is occurring: the increasing number of nonmarried couples beginning to live together in a marriage-like situation. This development, nonmarital cohabitation, is characterized by greater informality, spontaneity, and intimacy outside the parameters of traditional dating and courtship relationships.

The research of Rebecca S. Vreeland (1972a, 1972b) studied dating patterns among male Harvard University students during the 1960s and early 1970s. She identified four dating patterns among the class of 1964. The *instrumental* pattern most clearly approximated Waller's rating and dating complex. The emphasis was on sexual exploitation and the enhancement of one's social reputation. Harvard students would take their dates to football games, dances, nightclubs, and so on, where they could be highly visible and "show off." In the second pattern, the *traditional* relationship, dating was ultimately designed to find a suitable wife. Women who ranked high by virtue of their good reputation, sexual inhibition, family background, and social status were the most sought after. In the *companion* pattern, the emphasis was on informal couple activities. The goal was to find someone with whom to share intimacies and engage in private activities. The fourth and last pattern that Vreeland thinks may be more typical of elite colleges was *intellectual* dating. Here, the emphasis was to find a woman who was the man's intellectual equal and with whom he would be able to share discussions and concerns.

Vreeland compared these patterns of the 1964 class with those of their 1970 counterparts. The companion pattern and the intellectual pattern still persisted. The former, while emphasizing friendship, broadened its activities to include recreational and social involvements. The latter became a defensive mechanism for intellectually gifted but socially inadequate men more than a means to form a mature relationship. The greatest changes occurred in the instrumental and the traditional dating patterns. The instrumental relationship became characterized by less emphasis placed on sexual exploitation and a greater concern placed on political activities, drug taking, and shared lovemaking. Men in the traditional dating pattern were now more concerned with finding women who were "liberated" and nonconventional, and who shared their rejection of traditional social patterns, than in becoming involved with socially acceptable women. Vreeland believes that these trends indicate that dating has become less formal and less exploitative. "Students in search of their own humanity have begun to treat their dates as persons and potential friends rather than as competitors or candidates for marriage" (Vreeland, 1972a:66).

Recent studies of dating indicate additional changes in the traditional practice. The traditional "date" required it to be arranged ahead of time, with the male calling or inviting the female to accompany him. He would pick her up and take her to a place of his choosing with her agreement and he was expected to pay for all the expenses. Roger Libby (1977) reports that today, young people congregate in groups and pair off while retaining allegiance to the group. Knox and Wilson (1981), in a study of 334 East Carolina University students, were interested in how students met, where they went, and what they did on dates. They found that many students met their date through a friend's introduction. People also met at parties and work. Surprisingly, the classroom was the least likely place for students to meet. Attending a public event — such as a movie, a football game, or a party — and then returning back to the man's or woman's room was a common form of dating activity. Michael Gordon (1981) also finds that a typical date involves spending the evening with a number of people, with pairing off occurring later in the evening. He also reports that females are more likely to initiate a date than their historical counterparts. In all, dating was seen to be less concerned with establishing and maintaining popularity, less gender-role–stereotyped, and less formal than the college students studied by Willard Waller in the 1930s.

Knox and Wilson (1981), in their survey of college students, inquired on matters of sexual values and encouragement or discouragement of sexual intimacy. By the third date, after some initial reluctance by females, kissing was acceptable to all. Men were also more willing to engage in heavy petting and sexual intercourse earlier in the dating sequence than females. Sexual intimacy was tied to emotional involvement, particularly in the case of females.

The above-mentioned studies reveal significant changes in heterosexual premarital relationships. The other change is the movement toward nonmarital heterosexual cohabitation, particularly among college students. Eleanor D. Macklin (1978), after reviewing the abundant research evidence, opens her discussion with the following statement: "Nonmarital cohabitation is fast becoming a part of the dominant culture in this country and it seems likely that in time to come a majority of persons will experience this lifestyle at some point in their life cycle" (1978:1). She estimates that about 25 percent of the undergraduate college population have engaged in living together under marriage-like conditions. In the years since her study, cohabitation has become even more commonplace. Before we begin our analysis of this phenomenon in the contemporary American middle class, a brief examination of its historical and cross-cultural existence is appropriate to set the discussion in perspective.

Cohabitation: A Brief Cross-Cultural View

Cohabitation is not a phenomenon unique to contemporary America. Miriam E. Berger (1971) cites cross-cultural evidence to document its existence in non-Western societies. Traditionally, among the Peruvian Indians of Vicos in the Andes, cohabitation was an integral form of courtship. The Andese parents made cohabiting arrangements for their children to test the work capabilities of the girl and the couple's compatibility. In modern Vicos, the young are free to choose their own partners — with romantic love playing an important role — yet the men still value the traditional virtues of responsibility, hard work, household skills, and the willingness of the women to help in the fields. Trial marriage is still practiced. It lasts an average of about 15 months and 83 percent of these arrangements are finalized in marriage. M.E. Berger notes that this practice seems to aid in the transition from adolescence to adulthood by virtue of the partners acquiring the social and sexual advantages of adulthood without assuming the full responsibilities of marriage.

Precedent also exists in Western Europe. M.E. Berger discusses the old Teutonic custom of trial rights, which is still practiced in the traditional community of Staphorst, the Netherlands. With parental acknowledgment, a man can spend three nights a week with his girlfriend. The hope is that the woman will become pregnant, for no marriage can take place if she is barren.

Jan Trost (1975, 1978) has observed that Germany, Sweden, Norway, Denmark, and Ireland have long traditions of cohabitation. However, attitudes toward cohabitation do undergo modification from time to time and are reflected in the cohabiting rate. Trost observes that the rate of cohabiting is also related to the marriage rate. During the period of 1970 to 1974, the number of lasting nonmarried cohabiting Swedish couples doubled (from 6.5 percent to 12 percent). Concomitantly, the number of marriages decreased steadily from 61,000 marriages in 1966 to 38,125 in 1973. Trost argues that cohabitation is a kind of test or trial marriage to see if the couple are compatible or to be sure that the woman can conceive. He believes, if this view is correct, that the marriage rate in Sweden should eventually increase. Trost also thinks that cohabitation will also have an effect on future divorce rates. "The situation will arise that many marriages between two partners not fitting together will never be formed, those marriages being formed will be happier and thus the divorce rate, *ceteris paribus,* will be lower" (1975:682).

Trost also observed that the incidence of cohabitation is related to political pressure and social policy. Scandinavian countries have liberalized their social policies and societal sanctions against cohabitation. As a result, there is less fear of social stigma and a resultant high cohabitation rate. In contrast, Trost cites the situation in

Mexico. In 1950, 20 percent of the couples living together were unmarried. Trost believes that this figure may have declined in recent years as a result of governmental pressure to get unmarried couples married officially and legalize their relationship. Through the efforts of a wife of a Mexican president, the Mexican government has sponsored "Wedding Days." These governmental proclamations have been promoted since 1955 and an estimated 240,000 couples have legalized their cohabitation by getting married.

Cohabitation: An American Perspective

Nonmarital cohabitation has been a topic of debate through most of the twentieth century in the United States. Miriam E. Berger (1971), in her historical account, mentions the controversy surrounding the beliefs of Ben B. Lindsay in the 1920s in his call for "companionate" marriage and the tumult surrounding the opinions of the philosopher Bertrand Russell. Russell advocated trial marriages for university students and believed that students could more easily combine work and sex "in a quasi-permanent relationship, than in the scramble and excitement of parties and drunken orgies" that prevailed during the 1920s Prohibition era (Russell cited in M.E. Berger, 1971:39). Russell's beliefs aroused a storm of controversy when he was appointed to a professorship in New York.

In the 1960s Margaret Mead (1966) recommended a two-step marriage. The first step, "individual" marriage, provided for a simplified marriage ceremony, limited economic responsibility of each partner to the other, easy divorce, and no children. "Parental" marriage, the second step, would be undertaken only by those couples who wished to share a lifetime involvement in a marital relationship that would include children. Such a marriage would be more formalized with divorce more difficult to obtain. Mead argued that for too many young people their desire for sexual relationships led them into making premature decisions on marriage and parenthood and often led to unhappiness and divorce. Similar proposals have been voiced and have had wide publicity. These include Vance Packard's (1968) call for a two-year marriage confirmation period, after which the marriage could be finalized or dissolved, and the much-publicized ideas of Robert H. Rimmer (1966) in *The Harrad Experiment*. Rimmer advocated a trial marriage period with group marriage overtones. His novel depicted Harrad as an institution where college-aged couples would live together under the benevolent guidance of a husband-and-wife team of sociologist and marriage counselor. This couple would require their students to become well versed in the subjects of marriage, love, sex, contraception, moral values, and philosophy. Rimmer's belief was that through a structured, socially approved form of premarital experimentation more viable and stronger marital and parental relationships would ultimately be developed.

These intellectual discourses on the desirability of nonmarital cohabitation reached behavioral fruition in the experiences of a significant number of college students by the late 1960s and increasing numbers through the 1970s and into the 1980s. Paul C. Glick and Graham B. Spanier (1980), on the basis of national data from the Census Bureau's *Current Population Survey* (1975, 1977, and 1978), report that there has been a profound increase in unmarried cohabitation in the last 20 years. Further, there has been an accelerated rate increase since 1970 as shown in Figure 9.1. Using data derived from the June 1975 *Current Population Survey*, Glick and Spanier report that 1.8 percent of all couples living together then were unmarried. This was approximately 886,000 unmarried couples. In comparison, unpublished data from a survey only three years later showed that an estimated 1.1 million couples, or 2.3 percent, were living in the same household and were not married to each other. Commenting on these and other statistics they observe the following:

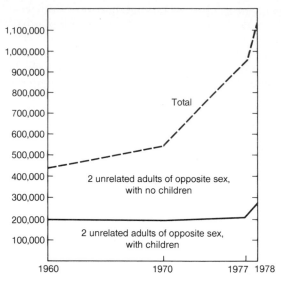

FIGURE 9.1 Unmarried couples living together
in the United States, 1960—1978.
(SOURCE: Paul C. Glick and Graham B. Spanier.
1980. "Married and unmarried cohabitation in the
United States." *Journal of Marriage and the Family*
42 (Feb.):20. Copyright © 1980 by the National
Council on Family Relations 1910 West
County Road B, Suite 147, St. Paul,
Minnesota 55113. Reprinted by permission.)

> Rarely does social change occur with such rapidity. Indeed, there have been few
> developments relating to marriage and family life which have been as dramatic as
> the rapid increase in unmarried cohabitation. (Glick and Spanier, 1980:20)

These authors believe that the explanation for this increase is that young Americans are finding this emerging lifestyle attractive and that their parents are voicing
little objection as long as the relationship does not end in childbearing and the couple
is economically independent. To support this explanation, Glick and Spanier compared unmarried couples with married couples in which the women were under 35
years of age. One observed difference was that the unmarried partners were more
likely to be college educated. Both were also more likely to be in the labor force than
their like-aged married counterparts. Further, in the situations where neither the
man nor woman was employed among the unmarried couples (12 percent), it seemed
likely that the couples were either students living on money given them by their
parents or young, poor couples living on welfare payments. The authors conclude by
speculating on the future.

> The rapid increase in the number of adults who choose to live with an unrelated
> person of the opposite sex has been showing no signs of diminishing. . . . Increased
> freedom in adult behavior, less pressure to marry at traditionally normative young
> ages, and greater acceptance of unmarried cohabitation as a lifestyle are evidently
> providing a context in which this way of living is becoming increasingly accepted as
> an alternative to marriage or as a temporary arrangement preceding or following
> marriage. (Glick and Spanier, 1980:30)

Glick and Spanier, working primarily with quantitative data, are somewhat limited in their analysis of the qualitative nature of the relationship of the cohabiting couple and the internal dynamics of the relationship and their consequent effects. Eleanor D. Macklin's (1978) review essay complements the work of Glick and Spanier. Macklin was one of the first researchers (1972) to report on the rising incidence of nonmarital cohabitation on college campuses. In her 1978 article, "Nonmarital Heterosexual Cohabitation," she systematically analyzes the growing number of studies about this phenomenon. The balance of our discussion will examine her conclusions.

Macklin argues that it is inaccurate to talk about *the* cohabitation relationship. She asserts that there are at least five types, which significantly vary, and that at this time there is insufficient data to say what proportion of cohabiting couples fall into each category. The following are the five types:

1. *Temporary casual convenience* . . . where two persons share the same living quarters because it is expedient to do so;
2. *The affectionate dating-going together* type of relationship where the couple stays together because they enjoy being with one another and will continue as long as both prefer to do so;
3. *The trial marriage* type, which includes the "engaged to be engaged" and partners who are consciously testing the relationship before making a permanent commitment;
4. *The temporary alternative to marriage,* where the individuals are committed to staying together, but are waiting until it is more convenient to marry; and
5. *The permanent alternative to marriage,* where couples live together in a long-term committed relationship similar to marriage, but without the traditional religious or legal sanctions. (Macklin, 1978:3)

With that cautionary note, Macklin compares cohabiting and noncohabiting couples in terms of their degree of commitment, division of labor, satisfaction, and sexual exclusivity. Because of the lack of systematic differentiation of the five types of cohabitation, Macklin limits her analysis to a comparison of a composite type of cohabitation with unmarried couples not cohabiting and married couples. Reviewed studies report that nonmarried cohabitants indicate significantly less commitment to continuing the relationship than do married couples. In comparison to engaged couples, the unmarried cohabitants express the same degree of commitment to each other but are less committed to the idea of marriage. Finally, research evidence reveals that the amount of exploitation in the relationship is uncertain. There is some evidence to suggest that women who tend to have a higher degree of commitment to the relationship than their male partners may be more vulnerable to exploitation.

Macklin reports a surprising finding: The division of labor of the cohabiting pair is traditional. Researchers expected that the couple's innovative lifestyle and their relatively liberal attitudes would be evidenced in a shared division of labor. Macklin observes that the cohabiting couple tend to share the same attitudes and behavioral patterns of their more-conventional counterparts. Macklin, citing one researcher, makes the following conjecture: "The many years of subtle socialization and role scripting, and the fact that role adaptation requires constant negotiation and accommodation, serve to maintain more conventional modes of behavior, even in what on the surface would appear to be nontraditional relationships" (1978:5).

The satisfaction of the cohabiting couple with each other did not seem to be significantly different from other couples. Finally, most cohabiting couples believe in sexual exclusivity and voluntarily restrict their sexual activities to their partner.

Macklin then discusses the internal dynamics of the cohabiting couple. She states that the decision to cohabit is a gradual one as opposed to a planned, considered decision. Usually, couples tend to drift together over a period of time after sleeping with each other and gradually moving their possessions to one household. In some cases, external events — such as the end of the semester, graduation, and housing or other economic needs — become a determining factor. The evidence on the length of the cohabiting relationship or how many relationships end in marriage is incomplete. Longitudinal studies, which would follow cohabiting couples over a period of time, have not been done. We are left with studies that have provisional dimension with no systematic follow-up. This limitation also affects the information that we have on how cohabitations end and their resultant effects on the cohabitants. Macklin hypothesizes that their readjustment in the postseparation period may be faster and less traumatic than if they were married and then separated or divorced. She attributes this to two factors: Friends and relatives may place less social pressure on them to maintain an unhappy cohabiting relationship, and litigation is usually not involved when they break up. The lessened social stigma and reduced visibility of ending their living-together arrangement should result in a lessened feeling of guilt and sense of failure.

One of the popular arguments in favor of cohabitation is that it has positive effects on the participants' personal growth and the quality of later marriage, and serves as an effective screening device that will eventually reduce the society's divorce rate. Macklin examines each of these arguments. She reports that there is no evidence to support the belief that cohabitation leads to enhanced personal growth more than any other form of premarital relationship. The lack of evidence reflects the fact that no studies directly test this belief. However, research findings do reveal that the vast majority of cohabitants indicate that this experience was very positive and that "they would elect to cohabit again if they 'had their lives to live over' and would not wish to marry without having lived with the partner first" (Macklin, 1978:6). There also is a gap in the literature about the opinions of individuals who had unsatisfactory cohabiting experiences and their assessments of it in terms of their personal growth.

In examining the effects of cohabitation on the quality of future marriages, Macklin observes that there is little systematic evidence to prove or disprove the popularly held belief that it leads to successful or different types of marriages. However, Macklin does speculate that the transition into marriage would most likely result in easier relationships with relatives and fewer problems with social institutions, and might increase the likelihood of traditional forms of gender-role behavior, possessiveness, and reduced autonomy.

The impact of cohabitation on marriage and divorce rates also receives Macklin's scrutiny. Unlike Jan Trost (1975), who believes that cohabitation has an effect on marriage and divorce rates in the Scandinavian countries, Macklin argues that there should be no substantial decrease in overall marriage rates in the United States owing to the strong social supports for marriage. Rather, cohabitation will remain a part of the courtship phase for most people and will eventually culminate in marriage. The effects of cohabitation on the divorce rate are less certain, according to Macklin. She speculates that with the long life span, changing views of marriage, and yet-to-emerge lifestyle options, it seems doubtful that whether a couple cohabited or not will have significance regarding their decision to divorce.

Macklin concludes by examining the implications of nonmarital heterosexual cohabitation for the society. Among her observations, she notes the need to change legal statutes and practices that view living together as man and wife without being legally wed a crime (in 20 states in 1976) and having sexual relations without being married a crime (in 16 states in 1976). Changes also have to be made in the financial obligations of the man and woman to each other if and when they decide to separate. The Lee Marvin/Michelle Marvin legal case is illustrative of this problem. In that case, the courts examined the question of the legality of agreements between unmarried partners regarding income and property. (They concluded that such agreements are legal but ignored the issue of whether a partner is entitled to support after separation.) Also, the rights of children born to unmarried couples have to be clarified, as do the respective parental custody rights.

The essay ends with a call for new research to answer the questions suggested by the review. Macklin urges that future research include longitudinal studies on non-college and older populations. Finally, she sounds a different note: She questions the wisdom of placing too much emphasis on the legal status of heterosexual relationships. Instead, she calls for more emphasis on the study of relationships, regardless of whether the couple is legally wed or not.

> Knowing that an individual is living with someone to whom she/he is not married tells us little about either the relationship or the person. Rather than focus on the specific legal status of a given relationship, investigators should be concerned with how the particular individuals define their own relationship, their degree of commitment to and investment in that relationship, the quality of the interaction, the emotional maturity and interpersonal skills of the individuals involved. If the focus of research were more on the dynamics of intimate relationships and on the skills needed to function effectively within them, and less on the structural quality of relationships, . . . would be more rapid. (Macklin, 1978:11)

The trend toward cohabitation dramatically increased between 1970 and 1980. The Census Bureau (U.S. Department of Commerce, 1981) found that the number of unmarried women and men living together in a single household had tripled — from 523,000 to 1,560,000. By 1982, only two years later, the Census Bureau (U.S. Department of Commerce, 1983) increased its estimate to 1.86 million unmarried-couple households. Given the fact that census figures often underestimate the actual occurrence, this reported rise is certainly spectacular and indicates the pervasiveness of the sexual revolution ideology that sprang up in the late 1960s.

Graham Spanier (1983), in his analysis of the Census Bureau's 1981 report, found that about four percent of all couples cohabited. Of these couples, three in ten had one or more children present in the household. Most of the increase in unmarried cohabitation has occurred among relatively young adults. Spanier also believes that a significant number of these unmarried couples reflect the continuing high divorce rate and a trend in the direction of postponement of remarriage following divorce. The rapid rise in the number and extent of cohabiting unmarried couples leads Spanier to conclude that "it is incumbent on demographers and other social scientists to examine this living arrangement less as an alternative 'lifestyle' and more as a normative phenomenon" (1983:287).

The extent to which premarital cohabitation has become institutionalized in our society has been suggested in a recent article by Patricia A. Gwartney-Gibbs (1986). The researcher examined marriage-license application data from a representative American county — Lane County, Oregon. She ingeniously compared data gathered from two years, 1970 and 1980, to answer the question, To what extent do couples who marry cohabit prior to marriage? Marriage applicants who reported identical home addresses were considered premarital cohabitants. The data findings indicate that the rise in premarital cohabitation, from 13 percent to 53 percent, reflected the national trend. Another important finding was that cohabiting couples postponed marriage longer than noncohabiting couples. The average age at first marriage for cohabiting brides and grooms was 1.1 and 1.4 years later, respectively, than noncohabitants. Gwartney-Gibbs conjectures that the extensiveness of cohabitation in this county suggests that social norms regarding premarital sexual relations have relaxed substantially during this 10-year period. She echoes the opinion of other investigators that "premarital cohabitation may indeed become institutionalized as a new step between dating and marriage for many couples" (Gwartney-Gibbs, 1986:433).

However, the Census Bureau and the studies by Glick and Spanier, Spanier, and Gwartney-Gibbs worked primarily with quantitative data. These studies are somewhat limited in their analysis of the qualitative nature of the relationships of cohabiting couples. Extensive qualitative research study is still needed. The works by Macklin (1981) and Cherlin (1981) provide a framework for some of the concerns and questions that must be addressed.

In 1981, Macklin reported on the cohabitation of college students. She notes that there are a number of advantages and disadvantages. Among the advantages of cohabitation are allowing the couple to develop sexual experience, love, caring, sharing, and understanding, without the bonds of commitment or permanence. This allows the two people to develop a close and intimate relationship while maintaining their independence. On the practical side, it can reduce housing costs and living-arrangement problems.

The negative factors associated with cohabitation are seen by Macklin to fall into four major categories: emotional problems, sexual problems, problems related to the living arrangements, and problems with parents. The emotional problems include feelings of being used or jealousy about the partner's involvement with others. Cohabiting individuals often develop feelings of guilt about beginning, maintaining, or ending the relationship. A feeling of temporariness often leads to feelings of nonbelonging. Sexual problems include discomfort during intercourse, lack of orgasm, impotence, and fear of pregnancy. Lack of money or privacy, inadequate space, and conflicts with other housemates are included under the living-arrangement category. Cohabiting individuals fear that parents will discover the situation and find it difficult in keeping the situation a secret from parents.

Andrew Cherlin (1981) believes that cohabitation seems to be a new stage of intimacy that precedes or follows marriage. He states that "the evidence . . . suggests that for most young adults, cohabitation is not a lifelong alternative to marriage but rather a stage of intimacy that precedes (or sometimes follows) marriage. Young adults appear to be cohabiting as a way of finding a compatible partner whom they often marry" (1981:13). According to this view, cohabitation has become a way of finding a compatible partner, rather than a permanent way of life for most people. In any case, cohabitation has significantly impacted on the nature of premarital relationships and certainly reflects changes in the way we think of marriage itself.

Conclusion

This chapter continued the investigation of patriarchal ideology and its effect on gender-role relationships. Here, the context of our discussion was on premarital relations. The double standard that epitomizes the patriarchal ideology was studied. We discussed how it became an integral part of the Westernized idea of romantic love. (In Chapter 16, we discuss the opposite side of romantic love—the belief in witches.) An historical analysis of the origins of romantic love was presented and detailed in our historical examination of courtship practices. We moved into the contemporary period by examining the movement of dating practices from the "rating and dating" methods of the 1930s to the more-intimate patterns of today. The chapter concluded with a discussion of premarital heterosexual cohabitation and its implications for gender-role relationships.

In the next chapter, we compare differences in mate-selection processes and examine how they are influenced by the pervasiveness of patriarchal ideology.

CHAPTER 10

Mate Selection

Richard Kalvar/Magnum

At this arranged wedding banquet in Tokyo, the matchmaker (left) and his wife are in attendance with the bride and groom.

CHAPTER OUTLINE

In earlier chapters, we discussed an important structural change occurring in family systems—the movement toward the conjugal family. The conjugal family emphasizes the importance of the marital relationship and the ties of parents with children. In contrast, the consanguineal family stresses the extended-kinship relationship based on a common ancestry. In this family form, the emphasis is on the reciprocal ties and obligations of individuals with their extended kin. The importance of the conjugal (marital) relationship is de-emphasized, whereas the individual's involvement with the consanguineal (blood) family is emphasized.

A most dramatic piece of evidence of the movement toward the conjugal family system is in the areas of premarital sex, conceptions of love, and mate selection. In many societies, men and women were not expected to choose the person they would marry; marriages were arranged by their parents and kinsmen. The freedom to choose one's spouse is an emerging phenomenon. In this chapter, we investigate the whys and wherefores of arranged marriages and nonarranged marriages. We examine the factors that accounted for the prevalence of arranged marriages and the various forms these marital arrangements took. Of considerable interest is the relationship of modernization processes with marital-arrangement patterns and the contemporary modification of these patterns. Changing conceptualizations regarding premarital sex and love and the relationship of these to marital-selection arrangements attract our attention. The consequences of the changes in attitudes and behavior regarding sex, love, and marriage for the individual, the family, and the society are investigated and analyzed. We conclude by looking at singlehood as an alternative to marriage.

Mate Selection: Free Choice or Arranged?

Who do people marry? One way this question can be answered is to look at how spouses are chosen. William N. Stephens (1963) states that, when persons have freedom to choose their spouses, individual motives account for marital decisions. These can include romantic love, sexual desire, loneliness, desire for children, and the feeling of the attainment of adulthood. In some societies, individual motives are allowed to be the determinants in selection of spouses. However, the majority of the world's societies chose to have family elders arrange the marriage of the potential couple. Frequently, this occurred without the consent of the prospective marital couple and in some societies, like Hindu India, China, and Japan, the couple did not meet until the marriage day. In these societies, individual motives, like romantic love, were not supposed to be factors in mate selection. For example, in classical China or Tokugawa Japan, love was viewed as a tragedy and at best as irrelevant to the family. The criteria for the selection of a spouse revolved around such matters as the size of the bride price or dowry, the reputation of the respective kin groups, and traditional, customary, and obligatory marital arrangements.

Stephens (1963) (see Table 10.1) is concerned with the frequency, distribution, and forms of mate choice and the factors that account for them. He delineates four forms of social mate choice: (1) arranged marriage; (2) free choice of mate, subject to parental approval; (3) free choice of mate, not subject to parental approval; and (4) societies in which both arranged marriage and free choice of mate are practiced. Stephens compared data from 40 societies. These data were based on interviews with ethnographers familiar with a particular village or other subcommunity in a variety of traditional, feudal, and modern industrial societies. Stephens found that those societies that had extended-family systems or unilineal kin groups tended to give the heads of these families either the entire responsibility for arranging the marriage of their children or did not allow children to choose for themselves without reserving the right to veto that choice. Further, those societies that were characterized by a nuclear conjugal-family system and bilineal kin groups were exclusive in that they were the only ones that allowed free choice of mate with parental approval not being necessary. Stephens concludes that "the form of mate choice is in part a function of extended kinship: when large kin groups are strong and important, then marriage tends to be a kin-group affair—it is taken out of the hands of the potential bride and groom" (Stephens, 1963:198).

This strong relationship between types of family organization, extended or nuclear, and the form of mate choice is consistent with our earlier discussion of conjugal and consanguineal systems. The conjugal-family system, which takes the nuclear form, emphasizes strong husband–wife and parent–child ties. As William J. Goode (1963) has noted, the *ideology* of the conjugal family emphasizes the independence of the marital couple from extensive obligatory ties with extended consanguineal kin. It stresses individual choice in mate selection that is guided by romantic love and sexual attraction. On marriage, the couple set up their own independent household (neolocal residence), which symbolically and actually demonstrates their commitment to the development of strong conjugal ties and the desire to sever potentially dominating ties with either kin groups.

The consanguineal family, on the other hand, is a quite different form of family organization. Here, the stress is on the maintenance of extended blood relationships. On marriage, a couple may move into or near the household of either the husband's or wife's family (patrilocal or matrilocal residence). Children are socialized into the larger extended kinship group. The consequent strong blood ties of unilineal members of the consanguineal-family system thus account for the greater need and desire to control the mate choice of their members.

Marriage Regulations

There is a striking increase in the number of societies that now allow individuals to marry through free choice in contrast to their former predominant practice by which family elders arranged the marriage. The choice of eligible mates for their children was governed by two conflicting types of marital regulations. The first, *endogamy*, refers to the requirement that an individual marry someone within a particular group. This group could be a kinship group, a clan, a religious organization, or any other social category. The second, *exogamy*, refers to the requirement that an individual marry someone outside a particular group.

Exogamous rules usually coincide with incest taboos—the prohibition of sexual intercourse between certain blood relations, for example, between father and daughter, mother and son, or brother and sister. Exogamous rules are primarily kinship-based and generally prohibit sexual activities and marriage among people who are closely related. Frequently, exogamous rules are extended to apply to larger social

TABLE 10.1   Mate Choice Compared with Presence of Unilineal-Kin Groups and Extended-Family Households

Form of Mate Choice	Society	Unilineal-Kin Groups Present	Extended-Family Households the Norm
Free mate choice, parents' approval not necessary	Ifugao	no	no
	Jamaica	no	no
	Kaingang	no	no
	Barranquitas (Puerto Rico)	no	no
	San Pedro la Laguna (Guatemala)	no	?
	United States (modern)	no	no
Free mate choice, parents' approval necessary	Colonial America	no	?
	Hopi	yes	yes
	Iban	no	yes
	Peyrane (France)	no	no
	Samoa	no	yes
	Trobriands	yes	no
Both arranged marriage and free mate choice practiced	Alor	yes	no
	Fiji	yes	yes
	Kaska	yes	no
	Kurtachi	yes	no
	Kwoma	yes	no
	Lepcha	yes	yes
	Murngin	yes	no
	Navaho	yes	no
	Ojibwa	yes	no
	Tikopia	yes	no
	Tepoztlan	no	?
	Wogeo	yes	no
Arranged marriage	Anglo-Saxons	no	?
	Ashanti	yes	no
	Cheyenne	yes	no
	China (Taitou)	yes	yes
	Hindu India (Rajputs)	yes	yes
	Ireland (County Clare)	no	yes
	Hebrews (Old Testament)	yes	?
	Japan	no	yes
	Kipsigis	yes	no
	Muria	yes	?
	Mundugumor	yes	no
	Papago	yes	yes
	Pukapuka	yes	no
	Siwai	yes	no
	Subanum	no	no
	Tibet	yes	yes

SOURCE: William N. Stephens. 1963. *The Family in Cross-Cultural Perspective*, New York: Holt, Rinehart & Winston, p. 199.

units. In classical China, a man was not permitted to marry a woman who had the same surname, even though they were not kinship-related. Certain societies prohibit the marriage of members of the same village or the same tribe. Yonina Talmon (1964) reports that children raised in the same peer group on a collective settlement (kibbutz) in Israel are informally pressured against intrakibbutz marriage. She suggests that the excessive familiarity of young people socialized together prevents them from falling in love.

There are numerous theories of incest and exogamy. This is a much-discussed topic in the social sciences with many explanations proposed through the years. The explanations seem to fall into two main categories: First, there are theories that revolve around biologic, genetic, and psychological factors to explain individual motivations; second, there are theories that deal with mate-selection patterns in terms of their effect on intragroup or intergroup solidarity with macrolevel analysis of the society.

Falling into the first category are such theories as (1) a horror instinct against incest, (2) Freudian psychoanalytical theory, and (3) genetic influences on the incest taboo. The first theory, horror instinct against incest, postulates that individuals have an instinctive horror of having sexual relations with close kin. To avoid such an occurrence, incest taboos were created to provide further social pressure against the commitment of such a "horror." This theory is somewhat contradictory in that if there was an instinctual dread of incest, there would be no need for the creation of incest taboos socializing individuals against it. This theory has been generally discarded.

The Freudian psychological theory in regard to the incest taboo was developed out of Sophocles' tragedy, *Oedipus Rex*. Oedipus, the son, unknowingly slays his father and marries his mother. On becoming aware of his actions, he blinds himself. Freud stressed the universal tendency of children to have a strong sexual attraction to the parent of the opposite sex. Incest taboos arise as a reaction to incestuous wishes and are a rejection of the forbidden and frightening sexual attraction of the opposite-sex parent. The Freudian theory is weak in that it does not explain the extension of incest taboos beyond the immediate family.

The genetic theory postulates that incest taboos were developed to prevent the potentially harmful effects of inbreeding, that is, madness, hemophilia, and so on. The theory emphasizes the real and imagined deleterious effects of inbreeding and ignores the positive ones; for example, the inbreeding of cattle to develop a superior strain of usable beef. Further, although there is some genetic evidence of the negative consequences of inbreeding, the theory assumes a level of biologic sophistication and knowledge that goes beyond that exhibited by most persons in most societies. An extreme example is the Arunta of Australia who were unaware of the role of the father in procreation.

There are several theories that focus on societal factors in regard to the incest taboo. George Murdock (1949) used psychological behavior theory, Freudian psychoanalytic theory, and previously developed theories in anthropology and sociology to construct his theory of the incest taboo. His ideas were enhanced by his use of his own cross-cultural data from 250 societies. He argues that the origins of the incest taboo arise out of the unwillingness of parents and siblings to satisfy personally the child's sexual desire. Further, the family, which provides important societal needs (economic cooperation, reproduction, education, and socialization), wishes to avoid anything that weakens it. It is thought that weakening the family would, in turn, weaken the larger social system. Conflict within the family resulting from sexual competition and jealousy would be highly disruptive. Thus, "the reduction of sexual rivalry between parents and children and between siblings consolidates the family as a cooperative social group, promotes the efficiency of its societal services, and thus strengthens the society as a whole" (Murdock, 1949:295).

Murdock then argued that the extension of the incest taboo to more distant and remote relatives beyond the nuclear family can be explained by the behavioristic psychology concept of stimulus generalization. According to this principle, any response evoked by one stimulus will tend to be elicited by other stimuli in direct proportion to their similarity to the original stimuli. Murdock sees that secondary or remote relatives who resemble a sexually tabooed member of the nuclear family will have the avoidance behavior extended to them. His illustration is that of a mother's sister (ego's aunt), who may possess similar features and other physical traits of the mother. This relative will be perceived as similar to the mother and thus will be sexually avoided. He states that there is a prevalence of applying the same kinship term to the two women in many societies (both referred to by the term, mother) and ego exhibits similar patterned behavior towards both.

Murdock does not answer the question on why the marital restrictions and taboos are extended further in many societies. The theory of reciprocity by Claude Lévi-Strauss seeks to answer this question. Lévi-Strauss (1957) believes that the prohibition of incest is one of the rules related to reciprocity. The marriage between individuals belonging to different nuclear families may be viewed as an exchange between two families, one providing the husband, the other providing the wife. The newly formed nuclear family is conceived of as a social organization that links several families in a chain of reciprocal exchanges. The cultural development of a society is seen to be dependent on the development of a more complex culture than can be developed by any given family. Cultural development is enhanced by the linking of families into wider social organizations through reciprocal social bonds.

To illustrate this, Lévi-Strauss utilizes the following model. The prohibition of incest is a rule of reciprocity when it means that a family must give up a daughter or sister if its neighboring family will also do so. Marriage is viewed as an exchange between families in which, at one point in time, a given family gives up a daughter and at another point accepts one. Thus, there is a perpetual mutual obligation to supply women in marriage. If one looks at a hypothetical situation in which one family has a monopoly on desirable women, whereas the other family in the group has none available, a potential climate of hostility and tension can arise. Reciprocity thus serves to assure a more-balanced state. This illustrative model assumes that women are treated as property and that there is a scarcity of women for marriage. It is based on an assumption of male polygyny and on the greater attractiveness and desirability of certain women. More important, the principle of reciprocity in regard to marriage is seen by Lévi-Strauss as assuring the occurrence of social exchange and the establishment of alliances between families. The incest taboo serves as the basis for the development of groups larger than the nuclear family and is a key organizing factory in society. The family, then, is vital to society as it establishes broader social relationships through the patterned exchange of sexual relationships.

Rules of endogamy run counter to the rules of exogamy, or totem prohibition. To repeat, endogamous rules require a person to marry someone within a given social grouping. These social groups can range from the extended-kinship system, the tribe, community, social class, race, or nationality. Linton C. Freeman (1974), following the analysis of George Murdock, sees the basis for endogamous rules stemming from ethnocentrism, or group conceit, which is common to all social groups. Freeman observes that, almost universally, outsiders are suspect; people tend to distrust or to dislike people who are different from themselves. People discriminate on the basis of race, creed, and cultural backgrounds. Conversely, they accept members of their own family and community more readily since they share a common background and heritage. In sex relations and mate selection, ethnocentrism is expressed by prohibiting marriage with outsiders through specified rules of endogamy. In the United States, endogamous rules are exhibited through pressures for individuals to marry someone of the same race, social class, ethnic group, religion, and age.

TABLE 10.2 Marital Selection Typology

| | Preferential Mating | |
| | Highly Specified Preferences Leading to Narrow Field of Eligibles | Little Specification of Preferred Mate Leading to Wide Field of Eligibles |
Degree of Arrangement of the Marriage		
High: Parents or others select one's spouse	Yaruros	Feudal Japan
Low: Principal selects own spouse	Hottentots	Middle-class United States

SOURCE: Linton C. Freeman. 1974. "Marriage without love: Mate-selection in non-Western societies," in Robert F. Winch aand Graham B. Spanier (eds.), *Selected Studies in Marriage and the Family,* 4th ed. New York: Holt, Rinehart & Winston, p. 366.

Together, exogamy and endogamy are seen by Freeman as delineating a "field of eligible mates" (Freeman, 1974:355). This field of eligible or approved marital partners can be large or small, depending on the relative strengths of the two complementary tendencies of endogamy and exogamy. Together, they are seen to make up the rules for preferential mating. In addition to preferential mating, a second principle is seen to underlie the process of mate selection: marriage arrangement. Marriage arrangement is defined by Freeman as referring to the degree to which persons other than the prospective bride and groom participate in the process of selection; for example, whether or not parents are involved in the mate-selection process. Here, again, a wide range of societal patterns exist, ranging from families having little involvement in the selection of a spouse to societies where families select the individual's spouse with little or no involvement by that individual in the decision-making process. Using these two principles—preferential mating and marriage arrangement—Freeman in Table 10.2 goes on to analyze four cultures that vary according to the interplay of these principles.[1]

The Yaruros of Venezuela are a nomadic tribe of fishermen and hunters who inhabit a vast plain southeast of the Andes. They have few material possessions: some baskets and pots and some hunting equipment. There is a strict division of labor in the tribe, with men doing all the hunting and fishing and women gathering plants, herbs, and roots. Young crocodiles are the basic staple in their diet, along with crocodile eggs, turtles, turtle eggs, and various plants and herbs. Clothing is sparse in this hot and dry climate, with temperatures climbing well above 100 degrees during the day. Men wear a simple loincloth; women a more-elaborately fashioned foliated girdle.

Yaruro society is divided into two halves. This division serves as the basis of kinship, with each tribal member belonging to one or the other moiety. Descent is matrilineal; one inherits moiety from one's mother. Marriage is both arranged and highly specified. One must marry into the opposite moiety and, more specifically, one must marry a cross-cousin; that is, a man must marry the daughter of his mother's brother or the daughter of his father's sister. An incest taboo exists against marriage to his sisters, his mother, and his mother's sisters or their daughters. His mother's sisters are called by the same classificatory term as his own mother. The taboo also exists for the daughters of his father's brother, since they belong to the same moiety as he does.

The marriage to an eligible cross-cousin is arranged by the shaman, or religious leader, on consultation with one of the boy's uncles who, in turn, selects one of his daughters. The boy then moves into his uncle's household and is obliged to work and hunt with his uncles. In effect, he takes the place of his uncle's sons who, in turn when

[1] The following discussion is based on Linton C. Freeman's (1974) analysis.

they marry, move into the camp of their fathers-in-law. These marriage practices are seen to be necessary to maintain tribal solidarity.

> Yaruro marriage practices, therefore, typify a procedure which serves to delimit an extremely narrow field of eligibles. Taken together, the incest taboos and the attitudes of ethnocentrism restrict the field of eligibles for the typical Yaruro man to one of his cross-cousins. Such an arrangement solves the problems raised by poor communication and sparse population. It affords access to a potential mate in the immediate vicinity but requires that the mate be obtained from another camp. This promotes interaction between camps and tends to maintain interfamilial solidarity. (Freeman, 1974:360)

The Hottentots of southwest Africa are a group of seminomadic herders who live on a great grassy plateau. Their economy is based on hunting and herding, with milk and meat constituting the basic part of their diet. The Hottentots, who number about 20,000 are divided into 12 tribes. Each tribe is comprised of a number of clans— groups of persons united by a common ancestor. The clan is the organizational unit of Hottentot society; the members of each clan form a single community.

Dwellings in a community are arranged according to age seniority. Like many preliterate societies, the Hottentots place great value on age, and the eldest male member serves as the clan chief. The clan, however, is governed by a council of peers, consisting of the older men of the clan. They direct the clan's activities, settle quarrels, and punish minor offenders.

The Hottentots allow polygyny, but the practice tends to be restricted to those who can afford it; the wealthier men take more than one wife. Each wife lives in a separate dwelling with her children. They own their dwellings and have their own herds of animals. Women control the distribution of household provisions. They are involved in milking the animals, gathering edible plants, cooking, making clothing and pottery, and maintaining the houses. The herds are tended by young boys or servants. Hunting is the primary responsibility of adult males.

Prior to becoming eligible for marriage, Hottentot boys and girls must pass through a series of rites at puberty. Each boy must also demonstrate his proficiency as a hunter by killing some big-game animal. Upon reaching adulthood, the young are allowed considerable sexual freedom. However, like the Yaruros, cross-cousin marriage is required. But, unlike the Yaruros, the Hottentots are free to choose for themselves which cross-cousin to marry.

The process of choosing a marriage partner is set by established ritual. When the male youth has chosen from eligible cross-cousins, he informs his parents, who, in turn, send emissaries to the girl's parents to seek permission for their son to marry her. The tradition dictates that they refuse. The youth then elicits the support of the girl. At night, after everyone is asleep, he goes to her house and lies down beside her. Tradition dictates her actions; she gets up and moves to another side of the house. The next night he returns and if he finds her on the same side as she was originally and she stays, the marriage is consummated.

The couple live with the bride's family for a one-year period or until the first child is born. They then set up permanent residence in the camp of the groom's parents.

For the Hottentots, the field of eligibles is narrowly defined, limited to cross-cousins; but, unlike the Yaruros, individuals are allowed to choose their own spouses. Freeman concludes that

> the field of eligibles for the Hottentots is established on the basis of kinship. Incest prohibitions are strong—they are extended to include every member of a person's clan—everyone in his local encampment. The Hottentots camp in clan groups like the Yaruros, and most interpersonal contacts are with kinsmen. And like the Yaruros, isolation and ethnocentrism force them to seek a spouse from a neighboring encampment. In both cases the person sought is a cross-cousin. But here the resem-

blance ends. For while Yaruro custom dictates that the choice among cross-cousins be made by the uncle, the Hottentots allow the persons marrying to make their own choice. (Freeman, 1974:365)

Freeman next looks at feudalistic Japan (Tokugawa Japan) in the eighteenth century, which illustrates a society that permits a wide variety of marital eligibles, but the actual choice is determined by the family, not the marrying person.

Feudal Japan was divided into local small duchies, each ruled by a lord and supported by an army of knights (samurai). Governing the society was a hereditary military leader, with the emperor having little importance. As in most feudal societies, there was a clearly delineated social-class system, with each class restricted to designated dwellings, styles of clothing, food, and so on.

The family in feudal Japan was at the heart of an individual's activities. The family was ruled by a patriarch with the assistance of a family council, which included most of the mature males and the old women in the family. The extended family included the patriarch's wife, all his sons and their wives and children, his unmarried daughters, younger brothers and their wives and children, and finally the servants. As head of the family, the patriarch's approval was required for marriages and divorces, for adoptions, and for the expulsion of recalcitrant members. He was responsible for the family's fulfillment of its obligations to the state. Professor Kawishima, a Japanese social scientist, observes the following:

> As a means of emphasizing through external impressions the mental attitude of filial obedience, the head of a family (generally the father) enjoys markedly privileged treatment in everyday life. The family head does not do with his own hands even trifling things — or rather is prohibited from doing such things because it is thought to compromise his authority. He must be served in everything by his wife, children or others subject to his patriarchal power. For instance, he should get his wife or servant to hand him anything which is right under his nose. The family head must be better fed and must not eat the same things as other members of his family (especially children), for it impairs his authority as such. When entering or leaving his house, he should be treated with special ceremony. In his house the head's room must be one fit for his authority. In all other trifles of everyday life the head of a family should enjoy special treatment becoming his position as absolute ruler. A parent's, especially a father's, position is majestic and supreme. (Kawashima cited in Mace and Mace, 1960:35)

The power of the patriarch was exercised in the name of the preservation and perpetuation of the lineage and the enhancement of family status. The independence of the individual was strongly de-emphasized. The stress was on the importance of familial obligations and responsibilities as a member of the family and of the immediate community. Within the family, a rigid hierarchy existed that delineated social roles and responsibilities. David and Vera Mace (1960) illustrate this by noting that a rigid ordering of rank is exhibited in the sequence in which family members take turns in using the bathtub. The sequence reflects the rank order in the family and where the person stands in the official family hierarchy. The father has the first turn, followed by the eldest son and all other sons, according to birth order; then, the mother is followed by the daughters in birth order; finally, the servants take their turn.

The practice of subsuming individuality to the family system was most evident in socialization practices and in mate selection. Children were socialized relative to their position in the family hierarchy. Robert N. Bellah (1957) points out that the socialization of sons differed depending on whether they would inherit the property or not. The oldest son, who most likely would inherit, was trained to be responsible and cautious, befitting his prospective responsibilities. Younger sons were encouraged to be more independent and show initiative and cleverness, which would aid them in the outside world. Girls were raised with the expectation that they would marry and join their husband's family. Their training emphasized the fact that they would represent their family in the appropriate manner in their husband's household. Thus, children were socialized relative to their social positions in the family hierarchy. An intricate system of duties and obligations was taught, emphasizing an individual's position within the family and the position of the family in the larger society. Individuality was submerged in the family system.

> Ideally, by the time they reached adulthood the Japanese had learned to view each other, not as individuals at all, but almost completely as stereotypes. If two people were members of the same family they treated each other in terms of their relationship. They met neither as personalities nor as persons, but only as representatives of particular relationships. All fathers treated, and were treated by, their sons in much the same way. Their interaction was based upon their kinship, not upon personal feelings. (Freeman, 1974:362)

With the great emphasis on family lineage and its perpetuation, it is not surprising to learn that marriages were arranged by the family. The marriage gained its importance in the fact that it established a reciprocal bond between the two families and in that it could enhance the prestige and security of each of the families. The concerns and choices of the young people were inconsequential in light of this feudalistic family model.

Marriages were arranged through the services of a family friend, who acted as a go-between. After consideration and negotiation about the respective worth of the families, the marriage ceremony occurred. As was frequently the case, the young couple did not meet until the wedding ceremony.

The feudalistic Japanese family dominated the mate-selection process. Although there was a wide choice of eligible marriage partners, the children were neither consulted nor involved in the decision-making process. This pattern is a logical development, given the importance of the extended kinship in Japanese society.

In the United States, individual motives play an important role in deciding the question of whom one should marry. The common assumption is that two people marry on the basis of love. However, the determination of eligible love-mates is influenced by the principle of preferential mating. Incest taboos preclude the eligibility of immediate kin. Frequently, the incest taboos extend to the first-cousin relationship, but there are no clan or other kinship structure restrictions.

Rules of endogamy are expressed in ethnocentric beliefs that define "suitable" marriage partners to people of the same social class, religion, ethnic group, and race. The field of "suitable" partners is further limited to people of the same age group and to people who live nearby in the same neighborhood or community. Until recently, ethnocentric biases were supported by legal statutes in the most dramatic case—racial intermarriage. As late as 1967, almost 20 states still had antimiscegenation statutes, with penalties up to 10 years imprisonment and fines up to $1,000. In that year, the Supreme Court declared that such laws were unconstitutional.

Although there has been some trend away from ethnocentric restrictions, the general pattern continues to be the marriage of people who share similar backgrounds, values, attitudes, and interests. Informal ethnocentric pressures, which still characterize American mate-selection processes, help account for the fact that marriages outside these norms tend to have greater difficulty and more frequently end in divorce. The result is that although the field of eligibles can be the entire unwed opposite-sex population, it is in fact significantly narrower because of these endogamous practices.

The choosing of one's spouse is ideally depicted as being solely within the province of the individual. Parents, friends, and others are normally not supposed to interfere in the mate-selection process. In addition, it is felt that such interference is not

Stock, Boston

Choosing a wedding ring.

effective and can even backfire. For example, *The Fantasticks,* a long-running contemporary play, uses this normative guideline as the central theme: Two fathers scheme to keep their respective children apart in the hope that such interference will have the opposite effect and bring them together. In many cases, parents are not informed or consulted by children about their prospective spouse either prior to or after the wedding.

Although their formal input in the marital decision-making process is diminished, the parents have a strong indirect influence in the mate-selection process. By residing in selected areas and sending their children to selected schools, parents restrict the options of young people in forming friendships. Further, through parties and selective invitation lists and verbalizing their own ethnocentric biases, parents influence their children. By influencing the informal social contacts of their children, the parents indirectly control the mate-selection process. As William J. Goode states, "Since youngsters fall in love with whom they associate, control over informal relationships also controls substantially the focus of affection" (Goode, 1959:46).

The following passage from Peter L. Berger's *Invitation to Sociology: A Humanistic Perspective* nicely summarizes our discussion on American mate-selection processes:

> In Western countries, and especially in America, it is assumed that men and women marry because they are in love. There is a broadly based popular mythology about the character of love as a violent, irresistible emotion that strikes where it will, a mystery that is the goal of most young people and often of the not-so-young as well. As soon as one investigates, however, which people actually marry each other, one finds that the lightening-shaft of Cupid seems to be guided rather strongly within very definite channels of class, income, education, racial and religious background. . . . The suspicion begins to dawn on one that, most of the time, it is not so much the emotion of love that creates a certain kind of relationship, but that carefully predefined and often planned relationships eventually generate the desired emotion. In other words, when certain conditions are met or have been constructed, one allows oneself "to fall in love." (Berger, 1963:35)

Why Marriages Are Arranged: Love and Marriage

We now turn our attention to a more-systematic analysis of the factors that account for the widespread prevalence of arranged marriages. Of particular interest is the role of love in the arrangement of marriages.

In his essay "The Theoretical Importance of Love," William J. Goode (1959) has delineated the reasons why marriages are arranged. Goode argues that allowing individuals the freedom to marry on the basis of individual motives, particularly love, can be potentially disruptive to the larger stratification system. Unless love is controlled and channeled in some nonthreatening manner, it could lead to marriages that ultimately could weaken stratification and lineage patterns. Goode argues that, when marriage involves the linking of two kinship groups and when kinship serves as the basis of societal organization, mate choice has important consequences for the social structure. Thus, when marriage affects the ownership of property and the exercise of influence, the issue of mate selection and love have been considered "too important to be left to the children" (Goode, 1959:43).

Goode states that, "Kinfolk or immediate family can disregard the question of who marries whom, only if a marriage is not seen as a link between kin lines, only if no property, power, lineage honor, totemic relationships, and the like are believed to flow from the kin lines through the spouses to their offspring" (1959:42). As we saw in our discussion of the Yaruro, the Hottentot, and feudalistic Japan, societies that emphasize kinship find it necessary to control marriages. Incidentally, the American upper classes also desire to control marital-selection processes as a large amount of wealth is involved.

Goode, then, distinguishes among several methods for controlling the selection of marital partners. First, it is controlled by child marriage, where, as in India, the young bride moves to the household of her husband and the marriage is not consummated until a much later date. This practice precludes the possibility of the child falling in love and also limits the resources for the opposition to the marriage. Second, mate selection is controlled by kinship rules, which define a relatively small number of eligible spouses. The Yaruros and Hottentots illustrate this type of selection by limiting the field of eligibles to cross-cousins. Third, mate selection is controlled by socially and physically isolating young people from potential mates. This makes it easier for parents to arrange the marriage of their children in that there is little likelihood that these children would have developed love attachments to conflict with their parents' wishes. In feudal Japan, the social contacts between members of the opposite sex were limited and were highly ritualized. They were permitted only in the presence of elders. This had the effect of minimizing informal and intimate social interaction. Fourth, love relationships are controlled by strict chaperonage by duennas or close relatives. Here again, young people are not permitted to be alone together or in intimate interaction. Finally, although formally allowing individuals to choose their own marriage partners, parents control the field of eligibles through the influence of the informal contacts of young people. As we stated, this is done through living in selected neighborhoods, restricting guest lists to parties and informal gatherings, and making the children aware of their parents' ethnocentric biases relating to race, religion, ethnicity, social class, and so on. This pattern, as we have seen, is characteristic of the United States.

Bernard Farber (1964) takes a different theoretical approach than Goode in his analysis of mate-selection processes. Whereas Goode stresses the restrictions placed on mate selection to maintain the social-stratification system, Farber stresses the importance of rules regarding mate selection in terms of preserving family culture. Family culture is seen to have as its constituent elements the norms and values that people hold regarding courtship, marriage, divorce, kinship identity and obligations, socialization of children, residence, and household maintenance. Farber argues that exogamous rules may lead to individuals marrying outside of their family group; potentially the possibility does exist that one will marry someone with different norms and values and open the family system to external influences that can be damaging to the continuity of the culture of the particular family group. The choice of marriage partner, then, is controlled by the family of orientation to assure transmission of the family culture to future generations.

> Thus, at the point of marriage of the child both parental families are in danger of having their culture interrupted in transmission by the introduction of possibly contradictory values from the other family. Restrictions in the society on mate selection would delimit the direction of change in family cultures from one generation to the next. If certain families will permit marriage only with other families very similar to themselves in norms and values, then a general continuity of the cultures of both families can be expected. (Farber, 1964:63–64)

In summary, where societies emphasize the importance of kinship lineage and its preservation—and support this by establishing strong ties between family interests and economic and social interests—marriages are arranged by the couple's respective consanguineal families. On the other hand, where societies emphasize the importance of the conjugal relationship between husband and wife and de-emphasize their obligations and responsibilities to the extended-family system, the choice of marriage partners is more or less left up to the individuals involved.

Modernization and Arranged Marriages

The concern here is to examine the effect of modernization processes, industrialization, urbanization, and the ideologies of egalitarianism and individualism on traditional contractual marriage-arrangement procedures. One question that we seek to answer is whether there is an emerging pattern toward romantic love as a prime criterion in the mate-selection process. We begin our investigation by examining the findings of George Theodorson (1968), who investigated the impact of Westernizing influences on the attitudes toward romanticism and contractual marriage arrangements in three non-Western societies: Chinese Singapore, Burma, and India. We then examine, in some detail, changes that are occurring in contemporary Japan. This should provide an interesting comparison with the earlier discussion of marriage in feudal Japan.

Computer Joins Ancient Rite of Matchmaking

BY MARK FINEMAN

NEW DELHI, India—For two hours each day in a downtown New Delhi district where ox carts and rickshaws still vie for space, a powerful American-built computer is quietly playing the ancient role of an Indian grandmother.

Dutifully, it scans its memory banks for the details and desires of thousands of lonely and frustrated Indian young people.

"Should your partner be a vegetarian?"

"What caste should your partner belong to?"

"Should your partner be an extrovert? A thinker? Emotional? Disciplined?"

"What complexion should your partner have? Black? Dark? Wheatish? Fair?"

And each day, the Burroughs 6900 series computer spews out a digital printout, a listing of hundreds of possible matches for marriage.

Now, along with fast-food restaurants and video libraries, computer matchmaking has finally arrived in India—where, for centuries, marriages have been arranged along strict economic and social caste lines by wizened old grandmothers, often at birth, usually after consultation with astrologers and almost never with an eye toward whether the couple in question is even remotely in love.

Perhaps it was only natural in this fast-modernizing nation, now governed by a prime minister who owns a home computer, that the institution of marriage would be included in the latest round of India's budding high-tech revolution.

At least that's how Raj Sawhney views his new venture—India's first computerized matrimonial service, called Partners, which opened its doors in the nation's capital earlier this month. Already, Sawhney said, he has 3,000 names in his data base.

"All we are is a modern system for the arranged marriage," said Sawhney, 38, an Indian accountant who worked for a computer firm in Montreal for five years. "Of course, we will always have a large number of professional village matchmakers in the country, but they are dealing with the lower class. We are focusing on the middle and upper class.

"And the Indian grandmother as an institution will always be there. We just want to plug into her system."

Specifically, Sawhney and his computer expert, Sugata Mitra, have designed—with the help of a computer—a two-foot-long data form with 31 questions relating to the physical, emotional, linguistic, educational, social and religious traits of the prospective bride or groom, and 31 more about their desired mate.

The questions reflect many of the social prejudices that persist in modern India.

Although the Hindu religion's distinctions of social castes—predetermined roles that many Hindus believe are fixed for life—were officially outlawed by the Indian government more than 20 years ago, few marriages even today take place between couples of different castes. So Sawhney's form asks not only the applicant's caste, but his subsect as well. There is also a blank space for a client's astrological sign.

There is no blank in the form, however, for an applicant's expectations of dowry—an Indian tradition in which the bride's family showers gifts and money on the parents of the groom.

The dowry practice has turned insidious in India's increasingly materialistic large cities in recent years. Young brides are often harassed by their new in-laws for more money after marriage, and, in hundreds of cases each year, the brides are actually killed by their in-laws to make way for a second marriage—and a second dowry.

"We left dowry out because officially it is illegal," Sawhney said. "But the questions about monthly income and family income will give clients some clues. We have to be pragmatic, but we let the families sort out the dowry issue on their own after we supply them with their lists of matches."

All Partners does, according to Sawhney, is supply—for a fee of 150 rupees (about $12)—three computerized lists of possible matches over a period of three months. The firm guarantees a minimum of three and maximum of 10 names and addresses of well-matched prospects, or the client's money will be refunded.

(continued)

"After that, it's up to the grandmothers," said Mitra, Sawhney's programmer, who said he had to "think like a grandmother" for several months while he designed the company's matchmaking software.

Sawhney and Mitra both emphasize that Partners is not a dating service. "Everybody realizes in India that nobody is going to do business running a dating service," Mitra said. "Here, marriage simply doesn't take place as a result of dating. In fact, even our marriage lists are being read by the parents and grandparents—not the boys and girls. We are still too conservative a society to tolerate dating."

Partners has had its hurdles. The first has been simply making the service known in a city where fewer than 5 percent of the residents have a television set. Most of New Delhi's large English-language newspapers will not accept Partners' advertising—not because the service is controversial, but because it competes directly with the newspapers themselves.

Every Sunday, the three largest New Delhi-based dailies together carry more than 1,500 "matrimonial" advertisements—classified come-ons for prospective mates placed by parents and grandparents trying to marry off their children.

Typical of the small-type ads that fill three full pages of each Sunday newspaper every week is one that detailed a prospective groom's race, caste, income and demands: "Beautiful, fair, slim, educated girl wanted for slim, 27-year-old, 173 cms respectable Punjabi Khatri project engineer. 2,500 [rupees] per month salary—plus perks." The salary would be about 215 U.S. dollars.

"The newspaper ad men all told us that if they accepted our ads for Partners it would put them out of business," Sawhney said.

Instead, Sawhney has arranged for his computer forms, titled "India's first super matchmaker," to be placed in video lending libraries, trendy restaurants and shops throughout northern India. This method, he said, attracted the first of his more than 3,000 customers.

Sawhney predicted that his service, which he says is more discreet than "some nosy grandmother snooping around the house," eventually would catch on big because of the increase in computer awareness in India since Prime Minister Rajiv Gandhi came to power stressing high technology.

"There is a computer wave in the country now," Sawhney said. "So it's only logical that in India, marriage, too, will be swept up in it."

SOURCE. Mark Fineman. 1985. "Computer joins ancient rite of matchmaking: Report on arranging marriages in India." *The Philadelphia Inquirer* (June 6). Reprinted by permission of *The Philadelphia Inquirer* June 6, 1985.

Theodorson believes that contemporary attitudes toward romanticism and marriage in non-Western societies can best be analyzed by looking at the relationship between contractualism (arranged marriage) and cultural change. Theodorson observes that the degree of contractualism was different in the three societies of China, Burma, and India. In China and India, arranged marriages were commonplace; a high degree of contractualism existed. The criteria for the selection of suitable marriage partners were based on economic and social (for example, caste in India) considerations. Child marriages and the separation of the bride and groom until the marriage ceremony prevented romantic love from being a factor in mate selection. The prime responsibility and obligations of sons were to their extended families, not to their wives.

By contrast, traditional Burmese culture was characterized by arranged marriages but usually with the child's consent. Romantic love, although not a widespread pattern, did occur and was a factor in the mate-selection process. Unlike India and Japan, Burma allowed its young people some opportunity to meet in supervised social gatherings. Children could initiate the contractual arranged-marriage process by informing their parents of their desire to marry. It must be emphasized that the marriage was contractual and that the contacts between the young were restricted and were supervised. Dowries were paid by the groom's family to the bride's parents.

The second analytical variable is the degree of cultural change. The Burmese were the least changed by Western influences. India experienced major changes in attitudes in regard to divorce, widow remarriage, intercaste marriage, and equality of the sexes. However, the Singapore Chinese experienced the greatest change in traditional patterns regarding the consanguineal-family system. Theodorson attributes this change to three factors. First, the Singapore Chinese were immigrants from rural farming Chinese provinces to a highly urbanized society. Second, there was a confusion of dialects, subdialects, and sub-subdialects among the Singapore Chinese, a result of their diverse provincial backgrounds. And third, the separation from the ancestral home heightened family mobility.

Theodorson developed five indices to test the hypothesis that the impact of industrialization, urbanization, and Western education would lead to the development of a romantic-love orientation toward mate selection. He tested his hypothesis with a large sample of college students from India (1,038 men and 202 women), Burma (249 men and 237 women), and Singapore (510 men and 287 women). For comparative purposes, he examined the findings from American students (748 men and 576 women) with those of his non-Western groups.

He concludes that "Despite the impact of industrialization, urbanization, and Western education, despite changes in specific traditional family norms and despite the sexual frustration which results from delayed marriage combined with premarital sexual taboos, Indian, Burmese, and Singapore Chinese respondents have maintained a contractualistic value-orientation toward marriage and basically have not accepted the ideals of the romantic orientation" (Theodorson, 1968:130).

However, Theodorson's finding of the differential degrees of contractualism of the three non-Western groups is of considerable importance. The Chinese, who traditionally had elaborate contractual-marriage procedures, had the greatest amount of cultural change. The result was that they accepted the ideals of the romantic orientation more so than the Burmese, who have a tradition of acceptance (albeit limited) of the romantic orientation. The Indians, despite many cultural changes, still express the most contractualistic value-orientations.

Dowry: The Price of a Life (and a Death)

The above subheading is taken from a subheading in the introductory chapter of Robin Morgan's (1984) comprehensive collection of articles by leading feminists from 70 countries, *Sisterhood is Global: The International Women's Movement Anthology*. Morgan writes that the "woman as property" concept is epitomized by the dowry. The dowry is a form of payment in money or goods from the groom's family to the bride's and in essence represents a payment for a woman. In some societies, a bride's family makes payment to the groom's, ostensibly to enhance her marriageability and to provide property for her. Morgan observes that the payment is almost never controlled by the woman herself; instead, it binds the bride to a marriage that she may never have wished to enter in the first place and prevents her from leaving.

George Murdock (1949), in his comprehensive cross-cultural survey of marriage and family practices, observed that payments for a bride can be seen as a compensation for the loss of work represented by the loss of a daughter. The practice occurs most frequently when the rules of residence for the new couple are patrilocal, especially when the bride is removed from her local community. In Murdock's (1957) *World Ethnographic Sample*, about 70 percent of the societies included have some form of marriage payment. By far the most common is the bride-price, in which the groom's family transfers some property to the bride's family.

Beyond its economic value, the dowry serves as a symbol of the commitments of the families to one another. It gives the family a vested interest in the stability of the marriage since the bride's family is more likely to adjust to the loss of the girl if it is accompanied by a gain in wealth and less likely to look forward to a cancellation of the dowry agreement. In marriage situations where there is a dowry, economic considerations take precedence over romantic or emotional criteria both in the selection of mates and in the maintenance of marriage. For that reason, "[r]eturn of the dowry is one of the most frequent reasons families on either side oppose divorce" (Morgan, 1984:11).

Murdock asserts that the bride price "seldom if ever is regarded as a price paid for a chattel, or as comparable to the sum paid for a slave" (1949:21). Yet we must emphasize that there is an economic component to both consanguineal and conjugal families. Indeed, the very term *family* comes from the latin *familia*, a term that referred to household property. This property included both people — wives, children, as well as slaves — and objects — fields, house, furnishings, and so forth. Given the economic reality that underlies dowry systems, it should not be surprising to find incidents of dramatic abuse.

The practice of dowry still exists in most parts of the world. In some countries, custom and even statute still require it. In other societies, even when legislation prohibits it, loopholes are often found to get around the law, or the practice takes on a contemporary guise. For example, in Kenya, such customs as the paying of a bride-price still continue to exist. The payment is determined by the girl's level of education and her ability to produce or earn money. Directly contradicting Murdock, Rose Adhiambo Arungo-Olende contends that "Today, bride-price makes the intended bride look like a chattel for sale" (1984:397). She observes that women never have a say on the subject of bride-price. In fact, there are cases in which the bride has to assist her husband financially in completing the payment of the dowry by the groom's family. The dowry can often leave the newly married couple in economic ruin, struggling to set up their new home in the face of the dowry's burden.

Similarly, in Lebanon, education and work have contributed to women's economic independence. The percentage of women in the labor force has increased from 17 percent in 1972 to 25 percent in 1981. In addition to the traditional careers of teaching, nursing, and secretarial work, women have been entering the professions of medicine, engineering, architecture, pharmacy, and law (Ghurayyib, 1984). However, women's gains are still modified by traditional-family practices. The family structure of both Christians and Muslims still adheres to tribal laws and clan loyalties that seek to perpetuate family control. The extended-family system remains the bastion of entrenched traditions which stand against change and women's rights. Notions of women's inferiority and subservience are still articulated. A woman who has achieved economic independence often finds herself "using her job as bait for attracting suitors, thus continuing the dowry tradition" (Ghurayyib, 1984:422). Bowing to family pressure and public opinion and the fear of living alone, women often accept compromises and sacrifice their ambitions.

Horrible cases of murders or forced suicides, "dowry deaths" in India in the early 1980s, have caught the attention of the media and have publicized the pervasiveness of continued abuses of the dowry system. To fully understand why these occurrences happened, it is necessary to provide some background. Traditionally, only sons inherited property, because they were the ones that perpetuated the patrilineal family system. To make the marriage of their daughters more enticing, families gave large dowries to the grooms' families. India has passed legislation that has sought to eliminate this form of gender discrimination. For example, laws pertaining to inheritance now give daughters equal rights with sons. Antidowry legislation was passed in 1961.

Unfortunately, families have virtually ignored the laws that attempt to change the system. Young women, whether they are illiterate, poor, and reside in rural areas or are educated and live in the more progressive cities, do not actively oppose the dowry system for fear that they will not marry. Nor do they actively claim their inheritance rights out of respect for tradition and to protect the economic interests and viability of their natal families. Similar to the situations in Lebanon and Kenya, the dowry system has taken on a modern form. A well-educated male of a higher-caste group can command considerable dowry payment (as much as $10,000 in some cases) from a prospective bride's parents. His parents view such payment as a proper reimbursement for their son's educational expenses. The bride's family sees it important to marry her well even if the economic sacrifice is severe (O'Kelly and Carney, 1986).

O'Kelly and Carney (1986), in their review of Hindu men and women, observe that the family is patriarchal, patrilineal, and patrilocal. Men control the chief resources and family authority and inheritance is transferred to the sons. Daughters serve temporarily in their natal family and then move to the household of their husband's family. Their children are raised as members of the husband's lineage. As a consequence, male children are preferred because they will serve their consanguineal family for their entire lives. Sons also bring wealth into their families through their wives' dowries. The birth of a son is viewed as a blessing; that of a daughter may be an occasion for sorrow and grief. As we discussed previously, female infanticide was a not unfamiliar occurrence in India's past and it continues today in the form of more-subtle practices, such as medical neglect.

Ursula Sharma (1980), in a study of two villages in northern India, observes that the dowry represents a payment to the groom's family; it is not a source of personal security for the bride. To back up her belief, she provides as evidence the numerous numbers of murders or forced suicides of brides because of familial dissatisfaction with the value of the dowry. Robin Morgan (1984) states that the 1975 Report from the Indian Commission on the Status of Women reacted to the growing commercial intensity of the dowry system and the growth of violence against brides. It declared that the dowry system was one of the gravest problems affecting women in India. By 1980–1981, there were 394 cases of brides burned to death in Delhi. Indian women's groups claim that this figure represents only a very small percentage of the actual cases that occur in Delhi and elsewhere. They believe that the police register only one out of every 100 cases of dowry murder or attempted murder and that for each of these cases six go unreported.

The increase in "dowry deaths" is a contemporary phenomenon. As we mentioned, the institution of dowry began in India largely because, under Hindu law, parental property was not allowed to be shared by female children. In compensation, parents would give their daughter a gift at the time of her marriage. In time, bridegrooms and their families made handing over the gift as dowry an institutionalized demand. Especially for younger Indians who covet a lifestyle and whose incomes do not allow them to achieve it, dowry has become a means of bridging the gap. Morgan observes that the threat of dowry death has become a form of extortion. The husband and his family can harass, beat, or torture a bride to extract more money from her family. In the extreme case, the bride is murdered. Her death is made to appear accidental (for example, dousing the woman with kerosene and setting her afire and claiming that it was a cooking accident) or as a suicide. The bride's parents are reluctant to prosecute for lack of evidence, for belief that others would think they had reneged on the dowry, or if they have other daughters for fear that they will not be able to marry them off.

The incidences of dowry murder became so great that massive antidowry demonstrations have been a major focus of the Indian women's movement. The feminist journal *Manushi* has reported in both its Hindu and English versions on hundreds of attempted and committed dowry murders and has brought this to the attention of the Western press. We are reprinting one such article here. Morgan concludes her denunciation of dowry with the following statement:

Only by such indigenous women's activism will practices like these—whether so dramatically posed as in India or subtly preserved through "trousseau" commercialism and symbolic "giving the bride away" in the West—be eradicated, and with that eradication come the end of transacted love, and of women's marital servitude. (Morgan, 1984:12)

Mate Selection in Contemporary Japan

Contemporary Japanese society has emerged out of a feudal past that emphasized an elaborate formal hierarchical and authoritarian structure. As we saw earlier, marital arrangements were determined by the respective family heads in the name of the preservation of lineage and the enhancement of family status. The marrying individuals had little or no say in the determination of their prospective marriage partners. Robert O. Blood, Jr. (1967), in a comprehensive analysis of Japanese marital arrangement patterns, observes that a revolutionary transition is occurring in contemporary Japan. There is a movement toward greater equality between parents and children and between men and women. This change is reflected in the appearance of a new system of mate selection parallel to the older system. Further, the old system of marriage arrangement is gradually being transformed.

Blood presents the following illustrative case of a Japanese colleague's father on "what marriage was like in the old days" (Blood, 1967:4).

In those days (the 1850s), marriage was a contract between families, not between individuals. My grandparents carefully investigated my mother's family background before choosing her to be my father's wife. They wanted to be sure that her background was of the same rank, was of good financial reputation, and had no hereditary diseases that might be transmitted to later generations of Kondos. After they decided she was suitable, they went around and got the approval of all their close relatives before entering into negotiations with the other family, using a relative as a go-between. The wedding was followed by a series of drinking parties lasting several days, first at the groom's home and then at the bride's home. The women attended these festivities, but only the men did any drinking. Every year after that, the two families got together at every festive occasion.

My father and mother were from villages ten miles apart in an age when sedan chairs were the only means of transportation. They never met until the wedding ceremony. My own marriage was unusual in that my wife and I didn't meet even then. I was away from home at the Imperial University and studying hard for the civil service exam. Since I was the eldest son, my parents were anxious to have me get married. My father's uncle and my mother's uncle were good friends and made the arrangements on behalf of the two families. My wife was 17 years old at the time of the wedding, and I was 27. She had seen my picture, but I had never seen hers—I was too busy to be disturbed. The wedding was unusual because I was presented by proxy. After the ceremony, the main relatives on both sides brought my wife to Tokyo to meet me, completed the formalities, and then left us to begin living together. In those days, love affairs were unheard of except in the lower class. (Blood, 1967:4)

Blood contrasts two major forms of marriage arrangement in Japan, the love match and the arranged marriage. Since the mid-nineteenth century, arranged marriages were negotiated through the *nakodo* ("go-between"). By using a go-between, families avoided direct dealings with each other and the possibility of losing face in the event that one family would reject the arrangement. It also protected the family who broke off the negotiation from any negative consequences of offending a family that, by virtue of its social status, was important to them.

In India, a Judge Avenges a Social Evil

BY MARK FINEMAN

NEW DELHI, India—About half past 12 on a sleepy, sweltering Friday afternoon a few weeks back, S. M. Aggarwal, a veteran judge of the Indian courts, evened the score for the murder of a pregnant bride and made history.

Courtroom 36 was packed that afternoon, and, as Aggarwal prepared to pronounce sentence for a crime he now calls the most ruthless and sickening he has ever dealt with, a silence fell over the humid little room.

The judge leaned forward to stare coldly at the stately, gray-haired woman in a bright sari of the finest silk and her two well-dressed sons sitting beside her in the front row. Then, matter-of-factly, the judge spoke.

"Kindly recall that fateful night and what happened that night," he told the family in English, pausing just long enough to initial the sentence decree on his desk. "I have made up my mind to award the death sentence to each of you—all three of you. You will be hung by the neck until dead."

Screams broke the silence. Some shouted or wept, while others simply gaped, dumbfounded. Even the bailiff's jaw dropped. Aggarwal had broken new ground in India's struggle against one of its most barbaric social evils—bride-burning.

For the first time in history, an Indian court had awarded the death penalty to one of the scores of middle-class families that each year become so consumed with greed and status that they are driven to murder.

The grisly crime of bride-burning—or dowry death, as it also is known—is a relatively contemporary one, but it is rooted in the ancient marriage custom that requires a bride's parents to give substantial sums of money and household goods as dowry to the groom's parents.

The amount of dowry usually is fixed at betrothal, when the parents arrange their children's marriage. But in recent years, widespread unemployment and the increasingly seductive pull of consumerism in Indian society have led more and more grooms and their families to demand additional dowry several months after the marriage has taken place.

Typically, the husband and his family begin by ordering the bride to go back to her parents and fetch more money. If her family is too poor or refuses to pay, the in-laws intensify their harassment, sometimes to the point of physical abuse. Often, that mental and physical abuse, combined with the taboo that bars a woman from moving back into her parents' home for any reason after marriage, pushes the young bride to kill herself.

In many other cases, however—nearly 100 of them last year in New Delhi alone—the woman's new in-laws do the job for her. By killing their daughter-in-law, they pave the way for a second marriage and a second dowry.

But the crime must look like an accident. In a country where most women cook on kerosene stoves, wearing flowing saris, deaths by burning are not uncommon—and so the method of killing is often that of burning. In addition, because women often cook alone in the kitchen, the lack of witnesses is credible.

Although there are several laws against bride-burning, against aiding and abetting suicide and even against the payment of dowry in the first place, they are next to impossible to enforce, according to lawyers, judges and social workers. Invariably, the only witnesses to the crimes are the accomplices, members of the immediate family. Beyond that, authorities say, the family involved often buys the silence of the police officers investigating the crime

Thus, with no effective deterrent, dowry-related crimes have increased astronomically in the last several years.

Before Aggarwal's ruling on May 27 hit the front pages of the newspapers here, the frequency of bride-burnings in the capital was setting a record. Since the onset in April of the brutal summer heat—a searing 100-degree-plus season that frays emotions and magnifies tensions—an average of two women were being burned to death each day, according to city police records.

(continued)

On the day of Aggarwal's ruling, three were burned; the following week, a dozen died. But as word of the ruling spread this month, the deaths have all but stopped. For the first time in modern history, 10 days passed without a single bride being burned; in the last week, there have been only a handful of burning deaths, all of which the police say were accidental.

"In my opinion, people just needed some time to think about the consequence of this ruling," Aggarwal said during a recent interview, adding that it was partly the disturbing frequency of the crime that led him to impose the death sentences.

Aggarwal is not alone in his concern. His decision has been lauded by New Delhi judges, lawyers, social workers and media, and it culminates more than a year of sometimes violent protests by groups of concerned citizens. New Delhi's lieutenant governor last week announced that separate courts would be set up in the city just to try dowry crimes.

Prime Minister Indira Gandhi herself, although she has not yet commented directly on Aggarwal's decision, often has lashed out against the crime of bride-burning.

"I believe very strongly that the death penalty is a real deterrent," Aggarwal said. "True, it must be used only in the rarest of cases. But, look at what has happened here. I might have saved thousands of brides from their deaths by this one case."

Aggarwal described the case of *People vs. Shakuntala Kumar, Subhash Kumar and Lakshman Kumar* as "a pure and simple case of murder motivated solely for monetary gain."

"It was preplanned—meticulously planned—and ruthlessly executed by taking all precautions that no one would be able to save this woman," the judge said. "I say it was diabolical and barbaric. They were not only killing an innocent young woman in this case, but a pregnant woman at that. They were putting to death a fully grown yet unborn child whose birth would take place in less than a week's time.

"When you see such a thing, it is revolting to the very soul."

Aggarwal said that the case of the murder of Calcutta-born Sudha Kumar, 21

years old—while a classic illustration of how and why bride-burnings occur—was exceptional in that there was proof. There were dozens of neighborhood witnesses to much of the crime and concrete evidence of collusion on the part of the police officer and the doctor who investigated the murder.

According to testimony given during the year-long trial—by neighbors, medical experts and police investigators involved in the case—Sudha Kumar's murder was a premeditated conspiracy hatched and executed by her husband, Lakshman, and her in-laws nine months and 15 days after the couple married.

At the wedding, Sudha's brothers had paid the Kumar family 23,000 rupees in cash (about $2,300) and had given them a wardrobe of new saris and suits, as well as a full array of kitchenware. Sudha's father had died when she was a child, and her lower-middle-class family had to sell several of its possessions to afford the dowry.

Two months later, Lakshman and his mother, Shakuntala, 50, demanded more. They told Sudha to go to her brothers, both steel brokers in Calcutta, and convince them to give an additional 10,000 rupees, plus a refrigerator and a motor scooter. But Sudha's's family had no more to give, and sent her back empty-handed to her in-laws.

Soon after, the harassment began. Sudha was shunned at family functions. She was constantly insulted in public by her husband, mother-in-law and brother-in-law, Subhash. Finally, on Dec. 1, 1980, the Kumar family "felt they were running out of time and this was the most suitable time to execute their plan," Aggarwal recalled.

"The child would be born in just a few days. A child would be an obstacle to a second marriage and second dowry for Lakshman. So with preplanned and barbaric precision, they poured four to five liters of kerosene oil on Sudha, set her on fire and locked her in the family's enclosed back yard."

The entire neighborhood heard Sudha shrieking for help. Neighbors rushed to the Kumars' comfortable middle-class home, where four of them broke down the front door and saw Lakshman and his mother

(continued)

looking out the back window as Subhash used his body to hold the door to the back yard shut.

When the neighbors reached the yard, they found Sudha "engulfed in an inferno of death," according to Aggarwal. "She was desperately pulling at her burning clothes, tearing off her sari and even her undergarments." When finally the neighbors doused the flames and led the girl through the front door of the house and into a waiting ambulance, Sudha shouted four times to the large crowd of neighbors that had gathered:

"Ke enona mare jayar chhin liya hai"—These people have stolen my jewelry. "Mite ka tel dalkar jalara hin"— Then they set me on fire.

Burned over 70 percent of her body, Sudha Kumar lived for nine hours. Not once during that time did the police subinspector assigned to the case ask her about the kerosene-soaked clothes he had found burned in the yard or about her exclamations to the neighbors.

Instead, he submitted a statement purporting to be Sudha's dying declaration, stating that she was burned accidentally while boiling milk on a stove in the back yard. The officer contended that the statement was signed with Sudha's thumbprint, despite the fact that the skin on all of her fingers had been burned off.

"Obviously the police officer was in collusion with the doctor, and both of them were in collusion with the family," Aggarwal said, adding that he had ordered a thorough investigation into the apparent police cover-up.

"Sudha simply could not have made this dying declaration. It was forged, fabricated and concocted by the police officer and the doctor for some ulterior motives. And all I can say is, when the police officers and doctors take part in this whole dowry-death

scheme, it shows a breakdown in the entire system.

Aggarwal knows that, in the long run, his recent ruling will do little to change that system. "It will take time and a huge effort," he said. "We must first ensure that only senior police officers will be assigned to investigate these bride-burnings, and we must spread the word throughout this city that the friends and neighbors of women in this situation can play an active role either in preventing this or at least ensuring that offenders are punished."

Even on that level, though, the judge's ruling already seems to have had an impact, at least in one community here. Just a week after the ruling was published, neighbors in the middle-class Kirshna Nagar section formed an angry mob outside the home of Anil Khurana, whose wife, Padmawati, had been burned to death less than a month after their wedding on May 4.

Having witnessed a series of violent arguments between the girl and her in-laws, the neighbors were convinced that her death was not accidental. With family members, the neighbors went to the local police station and took the woman's body. For an entire afternoon, they paraded her charred remains in front of Khurana's home, demanding that police investigate the case.

The next day, the investigators discovered that both of Padmawati's legs had been broken and that her neck had been snapped before she was burned. Khurana, his mother and his brother are now charged with murder and are awaiting trial in the same prison in which Lakshman Kumar and his family await the outcome of appeals of their death sentences.

SOURCE. Mark Fineman. 1983. "In India, a judge avenges a social evil." *Philadelphia Inquirer* (June 27). Reprinted by permission of *The Philadelphia Inquirer* June 27, 1983.

The *nakodo* had three basic functions: introduce the participants, negotiate the conditions, and perform a ceremonial function at the wedding. The *nakodo*'s task was to assess the compatibility of the respective families in terms of lineage and socioeconomic status. In addition, a woman's physical appearance was important as was the fact of her proper instruction in marital and family affairs. If all proved satisfactory, a *miai* ("formal introductory meeting") was arranged for the prospective partners and their parents. Blood notes that although the meeting attempts to introduce the young people to each other in an informal manner and encourages them to converse, the underlying motive for the meeting makes such interaction difficult. The tension of the situation, a marital eligibility trial, makes conversation stiff and awkward if it occurs at all. He observes that *miai*s are standard fare for slapstick movies in Japan. David and Vera Mace discuss the *miai* in the following passage:

> The atmosphere was very formal, and there was much bowing. Politeness forbade any mention being made of the object of the meeting, and the boy and girl had little chance to talk with each other. Even when attempts were made to get them to talk, these were not generally successful. "Some young couples are so shy that they keep silent from beginning to end. The matchmaker tries to make them talk but usually fails. Then when a daughter who has kept her eyes cast down on the tatami throughout the interview is later asked by her family how she likes the man, she says she cannot say because she didn't see him!" (Mace and Mace, 1960:144)

The arranged marriage was made with the sole aim of assuring the continuation of the family line. Although love might be expected to occur over time, the extended-family household de-emphasized the husband–wife relationship. Households consisted of three generations, with the emphasis on strong ties between mother and son. For the husband, sexual satisfaction and affection were more usually obtained through a concubine or mistress than through the relationship he had with his wife.

Arranged marriage still occurs in contemporary Japan, but its character has changed. Blood states that *miai kekkon* ("interview marriage") is no longer arranged by parents on behalf of unknowing children but rather by matchmakers on the behalf of the participating families. " 'Arrangement' now means primarily the formal introduction of potential marriage partners to each other and secondarily the follow-up message-carrying which cements a promising relationship" (Blood, 1967:12). The prospective husband and wife preview each other through personal and family credentials and photographs provided by the matchmaker. This provides the young people a chance to reject one another prior to the arrangement of a *miai*.

If the impressions after meeting at the *miai* are favorable, the couple is allowed to meet informally in limited contact for a period of up to six months. R.P. Dore (1965), who has written an interesting monograph entitled *City Life in Japan: A Study of a Tokyo Ward*, reports that it is not uncommon for the young couple to go to the cinema after the *miai* and to court each other for some weeks or months afterward. The continued involvement of the courting couple with each other provides the indication that the marriage is acceptable and usually, in less than six months after the *miai*, the marriage takes place within the guidelines of the traditional marriage ceremony and the exchange of betrothal gifts.

Blood (1967) believes that his findings indicate that the main function of the formal introduction was to allow the prospective couple the opportunity to meet and assess their interest in one another. It was not to arrange the marriage. Hardly more than 10 percent of the *miai*s led to marriage. Further, this modern version of the marriage arrangement usually occurs among young people who fail to contract a successful love match. They also tend to be confined to the "old-fashioned" (less-educated, less-emancipated) segments of the younger generation.

By contrast, the love match is defined as the falling in love of the man and woman prior to getting engaged. The love-match couples do not date much more than the arranged-marriage couples. The difference is that their relationship developed into love. It must be remembered that traditionally Japan has been a sex-segregated society and potentially eligible partners had little opportunity for informal socialization. Blood reports that almost 75 percent of the love-match couples met at work. The scarcity of coeducational colleges and congregational churches and the nonprevalence of using the homes of friends and relatives for informal meetings account for the importance of the place of work for the meeting of eligible singles.

The criteria for the selection of a spouse are different for the love-match couples and the arranged-marriage group. The traditional emphasis in arranged marriages is the wife's ability to fit into the husband's family, provided that the family background and status qualifications are met. In the self-selection process of love-match individuals, the emphasis is on personal qualifications. Those who are introduced through the *miai* stress the husband's income and the wife's health and housekeeping ability. Couples who meet through their own initiative emphasize the importance of love.

Blood (1967) then raises the question: Which of these two patterns of mate selection, the modernized version of arranged marriage or the love match, is superior in terms of the ultimate happiness of the couple and the stability of the marriage? This is a somewhat inappropriate question since, where marriages are arranged, the happiness of the spouses is not the primary purpose of the marriage. Yet Blood's answer is interesting. He found that the happiest arranged marriages were those in which the couple dated for an extended period of time after the formal introduction at the *miai*. These couples had the opportunity to get to know each other and to start developing a love relationship. The happiest love-match couples were those whose parents were enthusiastic about the pending marriage. When the parents viewed the love match negatively, the consequent marriage ran into the greatest difficulty. In general, Blood believes that those marriages that combined affectional involvement and parental approval tended to be the most successful. The combining of the positive sentiments of both generations, the parents and the children, gave the greatest assurance of the eventual happiness of the marrying couple.

In a recent book, Jane Condon (1985), a writer for *Life* and *People* magazines, interviewed a number of Japanese women about their lives, thoughts, and beliefs. What they had to say about mate selection and marriage is fascinating. Condon reports that contact between single men and women is still much more limited than in the West. Further, the Japanese tend to be shy, particularly in public places and especially with the opposite sex.

Another factor that limits the contact of singles is that, for economic and traditional reasons, most live at home with their parents until they marry. Housing is relatively scarce and expensive. In addition, customs that advocate dependency particularly for the female are still popular. Indeed, single women who live apart from their families are often stigmatized as being too independent or tainted by the opportunity to engage in sex without parental knowledge. Condon observes that some job notices specify that women not living with parents or relatives need not apply for them. As a consequence of all these factors, while some singles meet at school or at work, date, fall in love, and marry, for many others arranged marriage, or *omiai* (literally, "look" or "meet"), still serves as a safety net for those wishing to marry.

Condon reports that estimates of the percentage of *omiai* marriages range from as low as 25 percent to as high as 60 percent. The great fluctuation is that many arranged meetings turn into a love marriage and are counted as such. One woman comments:

> To my mind, *omiai* is just a first clue for *ren'ai* [love marriage] really. After our first meeting, we went to movies and restaurants a lot together. Then the *nakodo* began pressing us to make a decision. So two months later we held our engagement ceremony. (Quoted in Condon, 1985:27)

The Japanese term for this new type of marriage is *omiai/ren'ai*, because the young people fall in love after they meet. Condon contrasts the differences in the courtship pattern of a a contemporary *omiai* with the courtship pattern of a love marriage. She describes the first speaker, Noriko Aoki, and her husband as an upwardly mobile, prosperous young couple (the Japanese equivalent of American Yuppies). The second woman, Miwako Yamakawa, a friend of Noriko Aoki, comes from an aristocratic background, worked before marriage, and describes the days and the events leading up to her marriage.

Noriko Aoki states that prior to the *omiai* ceremony, through the offices of a matchmaker, families exchange photographs and documents that provide social background and personal interest information about the prospective couple. In some cases, private detectives are employed by families to assure that the future spouses have not had previous lovers or there there are no criminals in the family. Neighbors may be interviewed to comment on the type of people they are, and indeed, such interviews are considered to be a normal occurrence when people marry through arrangements. Noriko Aoki's *omiai* was successful, and she was married after a two-month engagement.

Like Noriko Aoki, Miwako Yamakawa was college-educated. The death of her mother and the lack of extended-family support forced her to support herself after graduation. She met her future husband through her married sister who knew him in Houston, Texas. After a brief dating period they became engaged. Her father believed that changing attitudes and values no longer required the approval of relatives for marriage. Miwako Yamakawa's fiancé was college-educated, as were his parents and siblings. They, too, believed that a love marriage was proper. Yamakawa comments on her married life:

> So we encountered no opposition to our marriage. Now I'm very happy to have married him. My husband and I agree that my most important job is to keep the house clean. I take care of the home, which means taking care of my daughter, too. My husband goes out any time he likes, but he thinks that his wife should always be home. I think he's right. You see, if a mother goes outside for a walk, there might be a phone call or a problem, and she wouldn't be there. I want to be home when my daughter comes home from school, and her school advised me to do so. I stay home because I don't want to disturb any other member of the family. (Quoted in Condon, 1985:36–37)

Condon (1985) observes that although most young people prefer love matches, a potential difficulty is their future relations with their in-laws. In Japan there is a much greater chance for discord than in America, since parents have a strong say in their children's married life. Further, Japanese women are becoming less and less subservient to their in-laws. A popular post-World War II saying is, "Since the war, women and nylons have become stronger" (Condon, 1985:37). The result is often conflict between daughters-in-law and in-laws that reflects different generational expectations, as well as different expectations between the sexes.

In another insightful interview, Condon uses the experience of a young Japanese woman to highlight some of these difficulties. Miki Suzuki spent her senior year at a midwestern American high school and is now employed in Japan as a full-time professional translator working on magazines. Like Miki, her fiancé graduated from Keto, one of Japan's elite universities. After much soul-searching Miki Suzuki decided not to marry. Her story dramatizes some of the difficulties confronting young people who wish to marry on the basis of love.

Essentially, Miki Suzuki's prospective in-laws asked her parents to financially contribute to the setting-up of the newlyweds' household. Failure to comply would indicate a lack of commitment to the marriage and result in a termination of the engagement. Further, they wanted Miki Suzuki to forego her career as a translator and immediately have children. Suzuki comments:

> I couldn't believe it! His mother [stated that] all his family really wants in a wife for him (the fiancé) is a healthy, obedient girl who could produce a baby boy — that is, a family heir! And listen to this. During the first year that he is away they insist that I move from my home in Tokyo to Osaka to live with them, so they can train me! Train me? These people are really old-fashioned. Their ideas seem to come from a time before *Meiji*. They are positively feudal. (Quoted in Condon, 1985:39)

Ultimately, even the fear of her in-laws' continued interference and influence over her fiancé could not offset her fear of humiliation if she ended the engagement. Condon did not feel it was her place to tell Miki that it was worth the risk to endure "the potential short-term embarrassment of not having the wedding compared to a lifetime spent with an unpleasant mother-in-law and a spineless husband" (1985:42). Despite her serious misgivings, Miki Suzuki, a woman torn between traditional and modern views of marriage and family, was married. Condon, who could not attend the wedding because of other obligations, concludes:

> Eight days later, I was in the United States visiting my family, and I felt a sad twinge as I imagined Miki in her kabuki-white makeup, elaborate hairpiece, and elegant kimono standing at the Shinto shrine sipping sake from nuptial cups with her husband-to-be. It was supposed to be the day little girls dream of. I wondered how she felt. (Condon, 1985:42).

Institutional Matchmakers: A Comparison of Contemporary Japan and America

In traditional Japan, the matchmaker (*nakodo*) provided an invaluable service for families in arranging the marriage of their children. The *nakodo* served as a go-between negotiating the delicate relations between families and providing a face-saving service in case the negotiations failed. Today, the Japanese matchmaker's primary function is to introduce young people formally and give them the opportunity to get to know each other rather than actually to arrange a marriage. Blood (1967) found that almost 90 percent of the formal introductions did not culminate in marriage. Further, despite the pressure of families on young people to marry as soon as possible, the remaining 10 percent who did eventually marry did so only after a considerable period of time and a considerable number of dates.

In a later book, Blood (1972) observes that urbanization and mobility have made it more difficult for Japanese families to find potential partners for their children. This has produced a gradual shift away from the personalized matchmakers toward municipal governmental sponsorship of matchmaking agencies. Marriage consultation centers in urban areas provide an inexpensive public service to individuals in search of marriage partners. He reports that the Tokyo center in the early 1960s arranged 1,000 marriages a year through its facilities. One problem was that twice as many women applied as men; the result was that men were more likely to find partners than women. An additional form of matchmaking agency was established by the segregated women's colleges in Japan for their alumnae. The general belief was that such alumnae would become "submissive" wives and this image attracted large numbers of men from the largely segregated men's prestige universities.

Blood (1972) observes that analogous institutional matchmaking agencies are to be found in the United States. Here, they take the form of computer centers or dating services, singles or date bars, summer resorts, and holiday cruises. Additional mating institutions include matrimonial bureaus, lonely hearts clubs, encounter groups, classified ads, and sexual liberation groups.

The American matchmaking institutions are somewhat different from the Japanese ones. Blood points out that the American pattern emphasizes personal qualities of the prospective partner, a natural consequence of the American system of self-selection. In Japan, the emphasis is on objective family-background criteria, an outgrowth of traditional kin-selected arranged marriages. In America, the couple arrange their own dates through correspondence or by phone; in Japan, the agencies set up formal introductory meetings at their establishments that are presided over by a staff counselor. However, as in Japan, more women in America avail themselves of these institutional matchmaking agencies then men. Again, this reflects the double-standard ethos that allows women less initiative than men in personally soliciting dates.

The mass media in America have found that stories on such matchmaking institutions as computer dating services and singles bars sell newspapers, and the tendency is to publicize them beyond their actual importance. Starr and Carns (1973) in an article titled "Singles in the City" make this point. They report on a sample of 70 never-married male and female college graduates in Chicago. These people did not find singles bars the best place for making friends or for meeting persons of the opposite sex. Singles bars were seen to lack the spontaneity required for making contacts. Further, these people found that apartment dwellings and their neighborhoods were also unsatisfactory in this regard. The home and neighborhood were seen as havens for privacy in which the person did not have either the desire or the time to interact informally with neighbors.

The work setting was most frequently mentioned as the place for developing personal associations. Starr and Carns report that a two-stage process operates in the relationship between work and dating. Most graduates form friendships on the job. But they do not date their work associates since they desire to avoid intimacy with those with whom they must interact regardless of whether a personal relationship succeeds or not. Rather, they use work friends to arrange dates through a friend-of-a-friend pattern.

The authors conclude that the popular image of the swinging singles developed and nurtured by the media is patently false. Singles bars and their ilk do not attract people looking for meaningful relationships. Further, singles do not lead lives of hedonistic abandonment. "They are people coping with the same problems we all face: finding a place to live, searching for satisfaction from their jobs and seeking friends, dates and ultimately mates in an environment for which they have been ill-prepared and which does not easily lend itself to the formation of stable human relationships" (Starr and Carns, 1973:161). In response to the lack of institutional supports found in the city environment, these people look to the world of work, much as their Japanese counterparts do, to provide them with opportunities to meet and to form friendships.

A final word on the computerized dating service may be of interest. It is a mushrooming business. Individuals fill out lengthy questionnaires dealing with family background (for example, religion, race, social class, and so forth), interests, and attitudes. Men and women are then matched on the basis of similar backgrounds and likes and dislikes. By and large, the computer is a gimmick since matchings can occur by other sorting techniques. Its basic function is a legitimizing one, giving "scientific" credibility to the sorting procedure. The computer simply sorts punched cards, coded with biographical information, and pairs individuals on the basis of "compatible" areas of interests, attitudes, and desires.

The entire procedure rests on the quality of the questionnaire data. In-depth, detailed questionnaires, if properly utilized, can match individuals on common interests, attitudes, and backgrounds. Such match-ups do not necessarily guarantee that the two people will be attracted to each other.

> The most obvious weakness of the system, however, is its inability to gauge attraction. At its scientific best it can only weigh a certain limited range of psychological and physical factors and conclude that two people are *compatible*. Frequently this means nothing whatsoever in terms of human relationships. How little compatibility may count was shown by this letter addressed to another dating outfit:
> "Your computer was right. Mitzi W. and I like all the same things. We like the same food, we both like the opera. Mitzi likes bike riding and so do I. I like dogs, and so does Mitzi. Actually, there was only one thing we didn't like—each other." (Goodwin, 1973:87)

Computer dating services and other formalized introduction agencies can provide a service for those people who cannot or will not find dates or prospective marital partners on their own. Although many find the use of such agencies repugnant and artificial, they can be helpful to others. As they are currently operated, the initiative to develop the relationship rests solely on the participants. Thus the individual decision-making process on the compatibility and attraction of the matched individual still remains a personal matter. Unfortunately, a significant number of these "mating trade" organizations have been guilty of exploitation. The charges against them run from the charging of exorbitant fees to fraudulently based "computer" match-ups. Some have exploited the weaknesses and desires of their clientele. If the abuses of the system can be minimized, perhaps through effective governmental legislation, these agencies can provide a service for those so inclined to use them.

Major characteristics of singles bars include the predominant sexual undertones of interaction, the underlying competitive aspects of that interaction, and a preoccupation with first impressions and appearance. Natalie Allon and Joan Fishel (1981) observe that in eight singles bars in Manhattan, participants were constantly monitoring their appearance and comparing it to others in attendance. Games of staring and touching were played. Women would try to establish eye contact with men who they wanted to meet but left it up to the men to initiate the relationship. Touching was used frequently to initiate conversation, signal approval, or as a gesture of affection, and often took on sexual connotations. Gender-role stereotypes were much in evidence—men would light women's cigarettes, buy them drinks, offer them bar stools, and so forth. Men were expected to be the initiators of interaction and of asking for phone numbers.

A twin phenomenon of alienation and sociability was observed by the researchers. The atmosphere seemed strained and forced, with participants acting defensively and on guard and not naturally. Allon and Fishel noted that in their interviews, participants often expressed surprise with how differently people who they met in singles bars acted on a date:

Life at a singles bar.

Mary Ellen Mark/Archive

> Everyone knows why you're here; you want to meet people. But at the same time no one wants to seem overanxious. You have to be very cool about it, and the tougher you act the cooler people will think you are [man].

> I do want to meet new men to go out with, but I don't want them to think I'm hard up for a date. I try not to seem too excited if a guy asks for my number or asks to take me out. . . . Guys can be real smart asses, especially if they think you really want them [woman]. (Allon and Fishel, 1981:119)

Pepper Schwartz and Janet Lever (1976) summarize the alienating nature of singles bars in the title of their article "Fear and Loathing at a College Mixer." In their study of college mixers at Yale University where women from Vassar, Smith, and Mt. Holyoke "mixed" with Yale men at Saturday parties, Schwartz and Lever found that underlying the social activities were interaction processes that impacted on participants' concepts of self and identity. This was a consequence of a structural setting where strangers met with the express purpose of evaluating each other. They observe the following:

> Rather than seeing the event as "pure fun," to the contrary, the participants feel the tension and anxiety associated with a situation where high personal stakes are involved. Interactions with the opposite sex occur in a predominantly conflict-ridden context where mutual satisfaction rarely occurs. Noncooperative strategies to protect face are accepted as rational by nearly everyone, and the "battle of the sexes" becomes more than a metaphor. (Schwartz and Lever, 1976:430)

Another means of getting people together has taken the form of video tapings. A dating service videotapes an interview and casual conversation with a client, which is then placed in a file along with a personal profile and a photograph. Other clients then select from this video file people whom they would like to meet. On mutual agreement after seeing each other's video, arrangements are then made for the male and female to meet.

Video dating organizations are popular in many countries, including England and Japan, as well as in many cities and states in America. For example, as early as 1974, one agency in Japan had a roster of 4,500 clients and about 100 couples a month met through this modern-day *nakodo* (*Newsweek*, 1974). A reporter for *The New York Times* reports on her own investigation of a video dating service in Parsippany, New Jersey:

> "Hello, I'm number 043 and I'm the spontaneous type."

> Number 137 (the writer) then looks at others:

> "Hi, I'm 005 and I like to party," said the young man on the screen. He had longish curly hair, big eyes and a thick moustache. "I like to play chess," he added. "I like to do things on the spur of the moment, I'm an optimist."

> "Too young," stated 137.

> Then, "I'm 053," he said, scratching a bald spot in the middle of his head, "I make lists. I tear them up. I live in a cave. And I'm very pleasant in the morning."

> "Not him either," said 137.

> "I'm number 061," said the next man. "I'm basically a nice guy." He had straight hair, an inviting smile and deep-set eyes.

> "Him," said 137, "I'd love to meet him." (Kleiman, *The New York Times*, March 7, 1976)

The Meet Market

BY DAVID O'REILLY

Don't be nervous. Don't by shy. Just step on the rubber mat outside the supermarket door and . . . *errrnh* . . . Presto! You're part of the fun. "Hi," shouts Beth Minker over the rock music. She's an account executive for radio station WKXW-FM in Trenton, which is broadcasting live from the checkout counters, and she wants to know your first name so she can write it on a name tag and—*slap*—stick it on your chest.

Welcome to the Plainsboro Thriftway, a supermarket not far from Princeton, where Thursday night is "singles night," and where thousands of young professionals, teeny-boppers, widows, widowers, divorcees and would-be philanderers come to cruise the aisles in search of . . . "LARGE CANTALOUPES, 69¢ each," says a sign in the window. "SWEET, PLUMP, N.J. BLUEBERRIES, 89¢ a pint," says another.

But there is more than the promise of sweet plumpness here—and at supermarkets in Dresher, in Cherry Hill, in Rhode Island, in New York and in Washington, D.C.—on a singles night. There is the promise—oh, can it be?—of romance.

Supermarkets have discovered there are a lot of single men and women eager to find one another, and some are cashing in on all those lonely hearts with high-glitz extravaganzas that would make most singles bars look like a church tea.

Here at the Thriftway, everybody gets a name tag on Thursday nights. Sure, sure. You really just came to get some cat food, but hey! Fun's fun, right? And if you meet somebody. . . .

"She's *fresh*. . . . She's so eck-*sight*-ing, . . . " throbs the rock music, at about 88 decibels. Some teenagers are laughing in the frozen-food aisle, and—can you *believe* it? —Minker says you *just* missed the excitement. The song "Locomotion" came on, and a dozen people formed a conga line and danced in step from the produce section to the meat aisle.

"You wanna meet anybody in town, you'll meet 'em here sooner or later," said divorced-and-looking Richard Gerber, 43, who wore a gray pin-stripe suit. He's "in commercial real estate."

"We just literally walked in," said Gigi, who wore a name tag and carried a box of disposable diapers. But, she said "I'm single. Really. I have to take these to work tomorrow for a product sample." No, no, no, she insisted. She didn't come here because it was singles night. She was just wearing the name tag "because I couldn't get in the door without it."

WKXW was meantime laboring to yank in more shoppers. "Yeah, we're givin' away that Dr. Pepper inflatable raft, and that black-and-white TV, and that trip to California," disk jockey Steve McKay told listeners. "So come on down to the Thriftway on Sutter's Mill Road. . . . "

"Are you having fun?" McKay asked a shopper named Nancy.

"Oh, I'm having a blast," she said into the microphone. And what kind of guy was she looking for? "Well . . . nice," she said, pensively. "And good-looking. And a nice personality."

The trick, of course, is to look cool. Paul was nonchalantly pushing a cart containing just a six-pack of Coke. Nettie was wearing shorts and pushing a bag of plums up and down the aisles. And Jerry, who looked like a 30-year-old surfer with brass-colored hair, had a six-pack of toilet paper, a box of frozen waffles, a jar of Mrs. Butterworth's pancake syrup, a box of frozen pizzas and a jar of salted peanuts, suggesting he was in need of a home-cooked meal.

So, um, how does this work? Do you signal your interest by reaching into somebody's shopping cart and squeezing his buns?

"I think you try to be as casual as possible," said John Zygmaniak, 22, an electrical engineer from Princeton Meadows. He wore a shirt with the top two buttons undone, and a gold chain around his neck. It was his first time here. "It's a nice atmosphere. You can just be yourself —say hello and introduce yourself. You don't have to be nervous."

(continued)

People have been flirting in supermarkets for decades. "Every night is singles night here," said Charlie Cushman, manager of the Safeway supermarket in the Georgetown district of Washington.

It is the busiest Safeway in America, popular with college students and embassies, according to Cushman, who says several marriages have developed out of conversations begun in his store. But dancing? Radio stations? Name tags? "Nahh," said Cushman. "Our customers do it on their own."

But not at the Price Chopper supermarkets in upstate New York. Last November, the chain, which has 58 supermarkets in four states, took the simple concept of flirting in the aisles and went wild with it. "We began with radio stations and giveaways," said Joanne Gage, manager of consumer affairs.

"But since then, we've had aerobic dancing in the aisles, fashion consultants who give shoppers advice on hair and makeup, fountains of nonalcoholic wine." One store even began playing a version of the TV show *The Dating Game*, she said. Another had an astrologer in to tell shoppers their love horoscopes, and so many shoppers waited in line that he worked for an hour after the store closed. "People come in droves," said Gage. "Sometimes you can forget you're in the business of selling groceries."

Or consider the Star Market in East Providence, R.I. It hands out name tags to singles-night shoppers, but with a twist: Each shopper gets a name tag bearing the name of one partner in a famous romance: Napoleon or Romeo or Adam for a male shopper, and Josephine, Juliet or Eve for a female shopper. Romeo then pushes his cart around the store until he finds Juliet, and the two can then claim a prize. Reports out of East Providence indicate that the store is filled with the sounds of squealing shoppers as they find their "mates."

Pete Endrigian, owner of the Dresher Plaza Shop 'n Bag, says that he knows of 15 couples who met at Wednesday singles nights in his supermarket, including a couple in their 60s. "We grossed an additional $5,000 our first night," he said, "but whether or not people buy doesn't bother me. People are getting to know the store and they don't have to go to singles bars."

Singles nights are said to have begun locally at the Cherry Hill Shop 'n Bag, where store owners Len and Judy Brown made Tuesday singles night beginning in February, complete with the name tags, radio station WMGK-FM (102.9) broadcasting live from the aisles and drawings for a free night (for two, natch) at Trump's Castle in Atlantic City.

Al Fingerman, a Pennsauken publicist whose clients include the Browns and their nine local Shop 'n Bags, says he had never heard of the Price Chopper gimmicks when he dreamed up singles night. His inspiration, he said, came in Florida. "I was in a supermarket Jan. 4," said Fingerman. "And I accidentally bumped into a guy making a play for this girl. Then they were behind me at the checkout counter, talking and laughing, and I thought, 'Isn't that cute?' "

Fingerman mentioned them to his wife when he got home, and then his wheels began to turn. Why not do singles nights at a Shop 'n Bag? The store's owners loved the idea—they had met at a farm market 25 years before—and so it began. Fingerman says the number of customers has increased 85 percent on Tuesday nights.

Things were pretty pokey at the Cherry Hill store on a recent Tuesday night, however. The store had quietly suspended singles nights for the summer, according to the night manager, and intends to resume them in the fall.

A few "lookers" had come anyway, unaware that singles night had been canceled, and they expressed disappointment at the lack of excitement. "Yeah, I had to get milk, so I figured what the heck," said a 17-year-old girl who lives in Cherry Hill.

"We don't normally shop here," explained her girlfriend. "We just thought we'd check it out." But things were slow. Dead, in fact. So they decided to cruise elsewhere. "Maybe the Echelon Mall," said the 17-year-old.

Marge Willard thought things were slow, too. "I've never been here before, but I heard about it," said Willard, who gave her

(continued)

age as 53. Willard, who is single, said she had heard about the Shop 'n Bag singles nights on the radio. She said she was interested in finding someone "a little taller" than herself "with a sense of humor and a nice personality."

The Plainsboro Thriftway won't be doing any more singles nights until September, either, because of renovations and an expansion. But the energy and excitement the other night were still undiminished at 10 P.M. "We try to create a party atmosphere," explained McKay, the disk jockey. "And a lot of people come here because they know what's happening. They'll say 'no, no' when we offer them a name tag, but three hours later they're still here."

"Oh, you people are way ahead of us," said Joan Lapin, 62, who had just flown in from her home in San Francisco. Her 38-year-old daughter, Ruth, had picked her up at the airport "and we didn't even go home yet. We came right here. I never even unpacked," said Lapin who, like her

daughter, is single. "It shouldn't just be for young people, should it?"

Store manager Henry Shields said he knew of at least one couple who met at a previous singles night here. Despite all the excitement, few if any of the shoppers at Thriftway left with anything more thrilling than breakfast cereal.

Shortly after 10 P.M., Norm, a tall, good-looking man in his mid-20s, was passing through the checkout counter. The radio station had ceased its live broadcast, others had won the trip to California and the TV and the Dr. Pepper inflatable raft, and the crowd was thinning out.

He had spent about two hours here, with his arms folded shyly across his chest, but he was leaving now with a half-gallon of strawberry ice cream and a bouquet of flowers.

Did these mean he had met someone?

"Oh, no," he said. "They're just for my apartment."

SOURCE. David O'Reilly. 1986. "The meet market." *The Philadelphia Inquirer* (Aug. 5). Reprinted by permission of *The Philadelphia Inquirer* Aug. 5, 1986.

Classified advertisements have become an increasingly popular way for people to meet others. In a recent study by Bolig, Stein, and McKenry (1984), the authors found that both men and women who place ads in singles magazines hope to find respondents who are physically attractive and have desirable personalities. The ad-placers view themselves as offering attractiveness, intelligence, good education, and stable careers. Here again, the use of this impersonal form of contact can be seen as indicating the difficulty that many people feel in finding ways to meet others.

Singlehood as an Alternative to Marriage

In the concluding section of this chapter, we turn our attention to a group of people who find singlehood a positive alternative to marriage. The demographer Paul Glick (1984) notes that the largest proportion of singles in the United States are those who never married. Since 1970, there has been a dramatic increase in the percentage of men and women between the ages of 20 and 24 who are single. In 1970, 55 percent of the males and 36 percent of the females in this age range were single; just ten years later, these percentages jumped to 69 percent and 50 percent, respectively. The never-married represent over 19 million men and over 15 million women over the age of 18. Together, they represent nearly one-quarter (24.5 percent) of our population (Statistical Abstract of the United States, 1984).

The number of separated and divorced singles is also rising. There are more than 4.5 million divorced men and nearly 7 million divorced women who are "single" again. As a group, the divorced represent nearly 5.9 percent of our population. The final category of singles is the widowed. There are 1,860,000 widowed men and

Peter Southwick/Stock, Boston

Cooking for oneself is part of the single life.

10,795,000 widowed women in America. As a group, the widowed represent 2.4 percent of our population. Taken together, the total number of single people in the United States is nearly one-third (32.8 percent) of our adult population over the age of 18 (Statistical Abstract of the United States, 1984). Our discussion here focuses on those singles who either voluntarily or involuntarily have accepted singlehood as an alternative to marriage.

The reasons why many choose singlehood include the increased acceptance of sex outside of marriage; a rejection by many women of the patriarchal constraints of marriage, which places them in unequal and subservient roles; and a rejection by members of both sexes that the institutions of marriage and parenthood are absolutely mandatory to lead the "good" life. In any case, an increasing number of people are not only delaying marriage but also are choosing not to marry at all. Peter J. Stein (1981b), one of the leading researchers on singles, predicts that the number of individuals who will never marry will be twice as great for this generation (8 to 9 percent) than the previous generation. Three years later, the noted demographer Paul Glick (1984) raises that estimate to 10 to 12 percent of young adults in the 1980s who will remain single, and these will be mostly by choice.

One important demographic statistic that has been an important factor in the rise in the number of singles, particularly women, has been what demographers have called the "marriage squeeze." Demographers have observed that between 1946 and 1957, each year's number of new babies was larger than the previous year. Since most women marry men who are several years older than themselves, women who were born during this period who were looking to marry older men find that they far outnumbered the available pool. This caused a large number of women to postpone marriage or put it off entirely. Andrew Cherlin (1981) has observed that "women tended to delay marriage more than men did in the 1960s and 1970s" and those that did marry lived in areas of the country with a more-favorable sex ratio (1981:58–59).

Newsweek—in a June 2, 1986 cover story (Salholz et al., 1986)—reports on an unpublished demographic study "Marriage Patterns in the United States" by Neil G. Bennett, Patricia H. Craig, and David E. Bloom that had received much media attention. Extrapolating from marriage-squeeze statistics, these researchers state that college-educated women who are still single at the age of 35 have only a 5 percent chance of ever getting married. *Newsweek* states that "Within days, *that* study, as it came to be known, set off a profound crisis of confidence among America's growing ranks of single women" (Salholz et al., 1986:55). Being single was redefined from being a voluntary option to a statistical mandate.

In January 1987, a new Census Bureau study (*Time*, 1987; Webb, 1987) reported that college-educated single women have nearly 2–1 odds that they will get married, not the 1–5 chance of the Bennett, Craig, and Bloom survey. Further, it stated that women who go to college are more likely to get married than those who have only a high school diploma. This is a significant change from past years, when getting a college degree often meant giving up marriage. The Census Bureau said its analysis of marriage, birth, and education rates indicated that a 30-year-old unmarried woman in 1985 who graduated from high school stood a 47 to 56 percent chance of getting married by the time she turned 65. The comparable rates for the same woman if she spent four years in college were even higher—58 to 66 percent.

Jeanne E. Moorman of the Census Bureau was critical of the highly publicized Bennett, Craig, and Bloom study that received cover-story treatment in *Newsweek* and other publications. She argues that the study assumed that a woman who has not married within a narrow range of years had dealt herself out of the matrimonial pool. According to Moorman, college women "are spreading out their marriages over a longer period" (quoted in *Time*, March 26, 1987).

Nevertheless, as *Newsweek* did point out, the Bennett, Craig, and Bloom study reflects the impact of the marriage squeeze on "baby-boomer" women who have not as yet married. Further, the voluntary decision of many women not to marry is a reflection of the changing roles of women in our society and is not a consequence of the marriage squeeze. The acceptability of careers for women no longer requires them to have husbands for economic security and the sexual revolution no longer requires women to marry for sex.

Newsweek believes that singlehood is one manifestation of the struggle of men and women to reach a new gender-role accommodation. "Even though men say they respect women's career aspirations, many openly long for full-time wives and mothers. For professional women, the challenge is to remain independent without sacrificing companionship" (Salholz et al., 1986:56).

The stereotypes regarding singles range from the lusty swingers to the lonely losers. Peter J. Stein (1981b), addressing himself to these stereotypes, counters with a typology of singlehood. This typology contrasts four types of singles: (1) voluntary temporary singles; (2) voluntary stable singles; (3) involuntary temporary singles; and (4) involuntary stable singles. It would be instructive to look at Table 10.3 to see how these types of singles differ.

Being single is neither totally good nor totally bad; rather, there are both advantages and disadvantages. The benefits of deciding to remain single include freedom

TABLE 10.3   Typology of Singlehood

	Voluntary	Involuntary
Temporary	Never-married and formerly married who are postponing marriage by not currently seeking mates, but who are not opposed to the idea of marriage	Those who have been actively seeking mates for shorter or longer periods of time, but have not yet found mates Those who were not interested in marriage or remarriage for some period of time but are now actively seeking mates
Stable	Those choosing to be single (never-marrieds and formerly marrieds) Those who for various reasons oppose the idea of marriage Religionaries	Never-marrieds and formerly marrieds who wanted to marry or remarry, have not found a mate, and have more or less accepted being single as a probable life state

SOURCE: Peter J. Stein. 1981. "Understanding single adulthood." In Peter J. Stein (ed.), *Single Life: Unmarried Adults in Social Context*. New York: St. Martin's Press, p. 11. Copyright 1981. Used with permission.

to have a variety of interpersonal relationships or not interact with others and less restrictions on having different sexual partners. Being single also gives one more mobility to move and this could be a benefit for career advancement. Responsibilities to others are much more limited; often one is responsible only for oneself. This would allow more-spontaneous activities and greater freedom to go out and travel. The disadvantages of being single include not fitting into a society that defines marriage as normative. Being single may be viewed as deviant and can cast aspersions on an individual's character. For example, business and corporation personnel managers may be of the opinion that unmarried persons are "less stable" or "emotionally immature" and unwilling to take on "responsibilities." As a consequence, they may not be as eager to promote and advance such individuals.

Stein (1975) observes that the attitudes toward singlehood often are a reflection of attitudes toward marriage. In his early study, Stein found that singles believed marriage inhibited personal growth, provided inadequate emotional support, and promoted an unwelcome dependency on one's spouse. These singles believed that singlehood gave them greater freedom and greater opportunity to meet new people and experience more and better sexual encounters. The women interviewed felt that the psychological autonomy that they felt would be impossible within the context of marriage.

The greatest difficulty that these singles encountered was confronting a couple-oriented society. Married people tend to think in terms of couples. In the typical situation where people get together as married couples, married people felt that if they invited singles to their home, they must match them up. Stein's respondents report that they have few married couples as friends, and the circle of their friendships is generally restricted to other single people. To ward off feelings of loneliness, singles believe that they must have networks of friends who can provide them with their basic needs and satisfactions of intimacy, sharing, and continuity.

In this account of singles and in later works (1976, 1981b), Stein delineates the pros and cons of being single in terms of the "pushes and pulls toward marriage and singlehood" (see Table 10.4). Pushes represent negative factors and pulls represent attractions. The strength of these pushes and pulls is seen to vary according to a

TABLE 10.4   Pushes and Pulls Toward Marriage and Singlehood

Marriage	
Pushes (negatives in present situations)	Pulls (attractions in potential situations)
Pressure from parents	Approval of parents
Desire to leave home	Desire for children and own family
Fear of independence	Example of peers
Loneliness and isolation	Romanticization of marriage
No knowledge or perception of alternatives	Physical attraction
Cultural and social discrimination against singles	Love, emotional attachment
	Security, social status, social prestige
	Legitimation of sexual experiences
	Socialization
	Job availability, wage structure, and promotions
	Social policies favoring the married and the responses of social institutions

Singlehood	
Pushes (to leave permanent relationships)	Pulls (to remain single or return to singlehood)
Lack of friends, isolation, loneliness	Career opportunities and development
Restricted availability of new experiences	Availability of sexual experiences

Suffocating one-to-one relationship, feeling
   trapped
	Exciting lifestyle, variety of experiences,
	   freedom to change

Obstacles to self-development	Psychological and social autonomy, self-sufficiency
Boredom, unhappiness, and anger	Support structures: sustaining friendships,
Poor communication with mate	women's and men's groups, political groups,
Sexual frustration	therapeutic groups, collegial groups

SOURCE: Peter J. Stein. 1976. *Single.* Englewood, Cliffs, N.J.: Prentice-Hall.

number of other variables that include stage of the life cycle, nature and extent of involvement with parents and family, availability of friends and peers, perception of choice, and sexual identity.

In conclusion, the increase in the number of young adults who are postponing marriage or who will never marry reflects important social developments that include the following:

1. The increase in the number of women enrolled in colleges and in graduate and professional schools;
2. Expanding employment and career opportunities for women;
3. The impact of the women's movement;
4. The excess of young women at the currently "most marriageable" age, resulting in a marriage squeeze;
5. A shift in attitudes about the desirability of marriage among both college and noncollege youth;
6. The increasing divorce rate, which has led many people to question the traditional appeal of marriage and family life; and
7. The increasing availability and acceptability of birth-control methods. (Stein, 1981a:5–6)

What is striking about the rise in the number of singles is the fact that more and more people remaining single may reflect a change in the contemporary attitudes toward marriage and the family. In order to understand this phenomenon fully, we now turn our attention to the understanding of the patterns and structures of marriage and the family.

Conclusion

In this chapter, we looked at different marital-arrangement structures in different societies. We examined the social factors that account for the wide prevalence of arranged marriages in many of these societies and the reasons that a relatively small proportion of societies allow for free choice of spouse. A predominant correlation exists between types of marital arrangements and types of family systems. Generally, where a consanguineal-family form exists—one that emphasizes the rights, obligations, and duties of family members to the larger extended family—there is a tendency for such families to control the marriages of their members. On the other hand, where a conjugal-family form exists, there is a greater emphasis on individual motivations and, consequently, a greater freedom is allowed family members in choosing their partners.

Of particular interest to us was the effect of modernization on traditional arranged-marriage structures. The emerging pattern is the breaking down of arranged marriages and the development of free-choice systems based in large part on romantic love. We took a longer look at the mate-selection procedures of Japan and the United States. Japan is a society that historically has controlled the marriages of its youth; the United States has emphasized the importance of individual decision making. Our analysis has indicated that both societies are moving along the same path; both are emphasizing the free-choice system.

We looked at the emerging phenomenon of computer dating services. Arising out of the needs of an increasingly urbanized society, these agencies seek to be the contemporary counterparts of traditional matchmakers. Their limitations are insurmountable to a society that views romance as the cornerstone of marriage; although they can match people's interests, they cannot guarantee that the one ingredient deemed essential for marriage will surface in the relationship—love.

We concluded the chapter by discussing singlehood as an alternative to marriage. We examined the factors that have caused the increase in the number of people in America who have chosen this lifestyle over marriage. In light of the prevailing sentiment that marriage is the "only way to go," those who voluntarily choose singlehood represent a perspective that casts a different light on this assumption.

CHAPTER 11

Gender Roles in Changing Societies

Both men and women are found in the medical profession in the Soviet Union. In this Soviet photo of a medical family we see Sozhida Zufarova from Uzbekistan and her husband Orifzhon Zufarov, who have been married for forty years. They have eight sons and four daughters. Ten of their children have become doctors, and the two youngest are in medical school. In all there are seventeen certified doctors in the Zufarov family, including in-laws.

CHAPTER OUTLINE

In Chapter 8, we pointed out that sex-linked factors based on physiology as well as patriarchal ideology served as the philosophical and moral justification for discriminatory gender-role differentiation. We observed that variations on the patriarchal theme predominated in Greco-Roman, Semitic, Indian, Chinese, Japanese, and Western Christian civilizations. We also mentioned that in recent years there has been a reevaluation of patriarchal ideology. Modernization processes, scientific and technological developments, rapid social change, and ideological revolutions have led to questioning of the ways that tasks and roles are allocated on the basis of sex. Traditional gender-role – relationship patterns and their ideological justification have been undergoing scrutiny and change. In the past, societies marked by relative stability, socially derived gender identifications, and role allocations were nondebatable and were taken for granted. In a rapidly changing world, this is no longer the case.

We begin now by turning our attention to societies with different economic systems and examine the relationship between patriarchy and values about the sexes in work and in the family. First, we look at agricultural societies. Some of them are patriarchal, some are not. However, those in non-Western societies that are not based on patriarchy were forced to adopt such an ideology through the policies of European colonial administrators. These agricultural societies provide interesting illustrations of how patriarchy influences men and women.

Then, we explore gender-role relationships in highly industrialized societies. The focus will be on the relationship between the sexes, particularly as it revolves around the areas of work and the family. This relationship is examined by looking at societies that have officially espoused an antipatriarchal ideology: the Soviet Union, Sweden, and Israel. The Soviet Union has a government that uses Marxist principles in its policies regarding the status of the sexes. The major goal of these policies has been to bring about equality of women and men in all spheres of life. Both Sweden and Israel have developed highly elaborate social-welfare systems. They, too, share a desire for equality of the sexes. Unlike the Soviet Union, they start from different ideological points of view that stem from their different philosophical positions and their different societal circumstances. Yet they are striving to change the patriarchal ideology and practices still inherent in their societies. Further, because all these countries have attempted to bring about equality of the sexes, they should provide a useful perspective for looking at future problems and their possible solutions that countries such as the United States may face as they seek to change the formal and traditional barriers to women's full participation in society.

Gender Roles in Male and Female Farming Systems

Anthropologists distinguish between two types of agricultural system: shifting agriculture and plowing agriculture. *Shifting agriculture* is practiced by clearing an area of trees and brush, burning them, and planting seeds. Rainfall waters the growing crops and the ripened foods are harvested. The cleared fields are used for two or three years and, when the soil becomes depleted, they are abandoned and allowed to lie fallow. The people then move on to cultivate a new area that has been cleared, and the cycle is repeated. The technology is rather simple: digging sticks serve as the most common agricultural implement.

Plow agriculture uses either the plow and fertilizers or irrigation works in permanently cultivating the land. Domestic animals are raised on those parts of the land that are not being cultivated. This is a more-advanced technological form of agriculture and is the most widespread form of farming found throughout the world today. Shifting agriculture was found most frequently in Africa, the Pacific, and the Americas.

Ester Boserup (1970), a researcher and consultant with the United Nations and other international organizations, refers to shifting agriculture as the female farming system and plow agriculture as the male farming system. Using Africa as an illustration of a shifting agricultural culture, Boserup observes that this farming system dominated the whole of the Congo region, large parts of southeast and East Africa, and parts of West Africa. Men and young boys helped to fell trees and hoe the land in

R. H. Beck (Neg. No. 117456), American Museum of Natural History

In shifting agricultural societies the women work at maintaining the food crops. Suvia, New Guinea, 1929.

preparation for the planting of the crops. The bulk of the work with the field crops, including sowing, weeding, and harvesting, was done by women. Before European colonization and involvement, the men devoted their time to hunting and warfare.

Closely tied to the female farming system, shifting agriculture, is a widespread pattern of polygamy that is closely related to economic conditions (Boserup, 1970:37–51). In such farming communities, the more wives a man has, the more land he can cultivate. This adds to his wealth and prestige. In the typical polygamous-marriage arrangement, a husband has two or three wives, each residing in a separate household, cultivating her own land and feeding her own children. The economic advantage of having multiple wives leads to an increase in the status of women. This is evident in the payment of a bride-price to the prospective wife's family by the bridegroom. Women have relatively high status, enjoy considerable freedom, and have some economic independence derived from the sale of some of their own crops.

The ability to sell one's own crops is an important aspect of the female farming system. The regions in Africa where women dominate the food trade of rural and urban markets are usually those regions that are characterized by a tradition of female farming. Such agricultural products as fruits, vegetables, milk, eggs, and poultry are sold by the women. Boserup (1970:93) reports that marketing is done by two-thirds of adult women in the Yoruba region of Nigeria and by 70 percent of adult women in the towns of Ghana. Associations of women traders are formed and wield considerable power. Boserup points out that the cultural tradition of female farming and involvement in traditional market trade accounts more for her relatively high status and placement in the modern trade sector of contemporary independent African states than does the stage of modernization achieved by any given country.

Although shifting cultivation is quite prevalent in Africa, it is not exclusively found there. It also occurs in Latin American communities and in regions of India and Laos. Here, too, agricultural work is solely within the province of women. Boserup notes that the lazy-man label applied to African males by Europeans is also applied to the males of shifting agricultural communities by both Europeans and by the people of the plowing agricultural communities.

> Thus, the Vietnamese find that the Laotians, with shifting cultivation and female farming, are lazy farmers, and the Indians have a similar opinion of the tribes of Manipur (in northeast India) which likewise practice shifting cultivation and female farming. They are said to take it for granted that women should work and it is quite usual to hear that men wile away their time doing nothing very much. (Boserup, 1970:24)

The value judgment implied in such lazy-men labels reflects an ethnocentric bias by those who do not believe or practice this form of agricultural system. The gender-role allocations reflect not a lazy attitude but, rather, a distinctive form of economic enterprise.

According to Boserup, in regions that practice plow agriculture, the division of labor between the sexes is quite different than that in shifting agricultural societies. The agricultural labor force is primarily composed of men, with women being almost completely excluded from field work. Most of the techniques associated with plow agriculture, for example, sowing the land by using draft animals, are done by the men. Women are confined to domestic duties and the care of some of the animals. It is for this reason that Boserup labels plow agriculture as the male farming system (1970:16).

Associated with the male farming system is the low status and treatment of women. Whereas in female farming systems men pay a bride-price to the prospective wife's family, in societies where plow culture predominates, a dowry is usually paid by the girl's family. With the lessened economic importance of women, there is a concomitantly lower number of polygamous marriages. Where polygamy does occur in plowing cultures, particularly in Asia, it is not closely related to economic conditions associated with agriculture. A further factor contributing to the low status of women is their almost complete economic dependence on their husbands.

Women's low status may be seen as a result of their low economic value. In contrast to a shifting cultivation system where women have high status and economic value, in a plowing cultivation system, women's primary status is in their reproductive role — particularly giving birth to sons, who are considered to be more valuable than daughters.

The low economic value of women is attributed to the fact that female births are not welcome. In some extreme cases, China and India being prime illustrations, female infanticide was practiced. In northern Indian communities where women did little work in agriculture, parents bemoaned the birth of daughters, who were considered economic burdens and would eventually cost their parents a dowry. It therefore became customary to limit the number of surviving daughters through infanticide. Although this practice has virtually disappeared, vestiges of it still remain in a more-subtle form: Boys are treated better than girls in matters of nutrition, clothing, and medical care. The result is a much higher mortality rate for female children than for male children. Thus, although female infanticide is no longer prevalent, the neglect of female children continues. Boserup illustrates this with a quote from a study done by an Indian social scientist in a district in central India that had a deficit of women:

> The Rajputs always preferred male children. . . . Female infanticide, therefore, was a tolerated practise. . . . Although in the past 80 years the proportion of the females to males has steadily risen, yet there was always a shortage of women in the region. . . . When interrogated about the possibility of existence of female infanticide, the villagers emphatically deny its existence. . . . It was admitted on all hands that if a female child fell ill, then the care taken was very cursory and if she died there was little sorrow. In fact, in a nearby village a cultivator had twelve children — six sons and six daughters. All the daughters fell ill from time to time and died. The sons also fell ill but they survived. The villagers know that it was by omissions that these children had died. Perhaps there has been a transition from violence to nonviolence in keeping with the spirit of the times. (K.S. Bhatnagar cited in Boserup, 1970:49).

Not only were women barred from field work in plow agriculture, they were also barred from public life. The loss of economic function was replaced by a rise in the sexual value of women. The result was a practice of guarding women. This was evident in the physical isolation of women from the outside world and their virtual segregation in the household. In Muslim societies, the wearing of the veil symbolized this segregation; in northern India, Hindus adopted the Muslim practice of female isolation. Their custom *purdah*, which literally means a curtain, segregated women from all outside contact. Women were locked up out of sight in the *zenana*, or women's private quarters of the household.

> Women were shut away in crowded, airless and isolated rooms at the back of the house, or screened in by shuttered divides through which only faint glimpses could be obtained of the life outside. These rooms were usually overcrowded, poorly lit and ventilated — the barest and ugliest in the whole house. Under such crowded conditions, shut away from all cultural life, with no stimulation from outside, how could women preserve a sense of beauty? It grew to be an envied boast for a Hindu woman to be able to assert that not even the eye of the sun had ever beheld her face. (Freida Hauswirth, cited in Mace and Mace, 1960:68).

David and Vera Mace (1960) report that estimates place the number of women in *purdah* at the close of the eighteenth century at 40 million. As late as 1930, the number of women restricted to their households was estimated at between 11 and 17 million.

The phenomenon of the seclusion of women from the outside world and the restriction of their appearance in public is associated with plow cultivation and is virtually unknown in regions of shifting cultivation where women are involved in agricultural work (Boserup, 1970:25–27). To illustrate, the seclusion of women was more prevalent among rich families than poor families in northern India. The reason was that poor women were involved in agricultural work and this economic necessity helped to break the custom. Similarly, in Pakistan, a Muslim society, the wearing of the *burqa*, or veil, was and is a more-common sight in Pakistani cities than in villages. The *burqa* envelops women from head to foot in a cloaklike garment. It even covers the face, leaving only holes or an open mesh through which the women can see. However, in the villages, where 85 percent of the people live, women do not wear the *burqa* or observe *purdah*. The reason for this is that they have to work in the fields. The *burqa* would be too restricting and *purdah* would be economically unfeasible (Aziz-Ahmed, 1967:48).

In general, then, the movement from shifting agriculture to plow agriculture is accompanied by a rigid gender-role differentiation, with women becoming more isolated and confined to the domestic sphere and more dependent on the male. In shifting cultivation, where women are involved in economic production, they are highly valued as both workers and mothers. In plow cultivation, where women take little part in field work, they are valued less and their value tends to be restricted to their reproductive role of bearing sons.

Gender Roles, Agriculture, and Modernization: Africa

The coming of the European colonizers to Africa initially benefited women in societies that were based on shifting agriculture. The foreign powers ended intertribal warfare and built roads. This gave women greater geographical mobility and increased their trading profit. Missionaries and colonial government policies alleviated some of the harsher treatment of women—they suppressed the slave trade, reduced the husbands' power of life and death over their wives, and rescued women who were abandoned after giving birth to accursed twins (Van Allen, 1974:61).

As time passed, however, the colonial imposition had detrimental impact on women. Foreign powers did not recognize or approve of the practice of women being primarily responsible for the cultivation of crops. Europeans had little sympathy with the role allocations of shifting agriculture. They came from plow cultivation societies where men were primarily responsible for agricultural cultivation. They viewed men in shifting agricultural societies as lazy and, with the decline in the importance of tree felling and hunting and the prevention of intertribal warfare, there was little work remaining for the men to do. A self-fulfilling prophecy thus operated—men are lazy because they do not do anything, and they do not do anything because the Europeans were instrumental in the decline of the male-role tasks.

A dramatic change in the relative status of men and women occurred through the colonial imposition of modern agricultural techniques. Europeans saw a need to introduce modern commercial agriculture and its accompanying technology. The crops produced were designed for export to European markets. The Europeans were ethnocentrically biased against women's involvement in agricultural work. They believed that cultivation was a job for men and that men could be better farmers than women. This bias led the colonial male technical experts to train only men in the new farming techniques. Female cultivators were neglected and ignored.

As a result of these practices, the women were at a distinct disadvantage. Whereas the men were cultivating crops by applying modern methods and equipment, the women were confined to using the traditional methods of cultivation—hoes and digging sticks. The inevitable result was that cash crops became a completely male enterprise. The men were able to expand their production; women who produced the food crops for the family had no cash income for improving their farming techniques. The result was an inevitable decline in the status of women and the enhancement of the status of men. Men were involved with modern technology; women with traditional drudgery. "In short, by their discriminatory policy in education and training the Europeans created a productivity gap between male and female farmers, and subsequently this gap seemed to justify their prejudice against female farmers" (Boserup, 1970:57).

Further, the European policy of recruiting men to voluntary or forced work in road building, mining, and other heavy construction was detrimental to women as well as men. The migration of husbands and sons to cities or plantations or mines increased the agricultural workload of women. Their independence was not increased. Men still retained the rights to land, to cattle, and to the sale of the cash crops that women cultivated. Women were responsible for cultivating their own land and that of their husbands without any personal benefit.

These practices continue in independent African states, like Kenya and Zambia, where Europeans control mining companies and plantations. Judith Van Allen (1974:61) reports that wages to migrant laborers are set too low to support a whole family. The husband, then, treats his wages as his alone and does not, and cannot, spend them for housing and food for his family. Where provisions are made for nearby housing of workers' families, farm plots are provided so that women produce food for the family. In both situations, then, women are primarily responsible for the feeding and housing of their families. The economic pattern is one of exploitation. Wages are kept at a minimum and women's farming subsidizes both the mining company and plantation wages. The companies, in their turn, make exorbitant profits.

> The small wages migrant laborers receive are not enough to provide for the accumulation of capital for agricultural development. The companies themselves, especially the mining companies (which account for almost half of African exports), are not integrated into local economies; the profits they make are taken out of Africa. Yet their high rates of profit would not be possible except for the unpaid labor of the wives of their African workers, who feed, clothe, and care for themselves and their children at no cost whatsoever to the companies. Far from the traditional agricultural sector being a "drag" on the modern sector, then, as it is sometimes claimed, the modern sector is dependent for its profits on the free labor done by women. (Van Allen, 1974:61)

In summary, the loss of women's rights and status can be seen as a result of agricultural land-reform policies of colonial European administrations. The Europeans were against the involvement of women in agricultural work, which they viewed as antithetical to the proper roles of men and women. This discriminatory policy continues in independent African states that are dependent on foreign aid and investment. The result is that for women in Africa, "modernization means more dependency" (Van Allen, 1974:60).

Living Under Apartheid

The word *apartheid* was coined as an election promise by the powerful Nationalist party in 1948 and literally means "separatehood." It is a segregationist policy designed to restrict and enforce strictly the control by the state over blacks in their movement to urban areas and in their employment and residential opportunities.

Ghana's Women Maintain Their Corner on the Marketplace

BY SHELIA RULE

ACCRA, Ghana— To the market women of this tropical West African country, the sale is everything. Their eyes dart back and forth, scouring the crush of higgledy-piggledy stalls and people for someone who looks willing to spend a little cash. They compete vociferously for attention. Once they attract some interest, they persuade with gilded flattery and hard bargaining.

"Agoooo," shouts one determined market woman to several others in her path, using the often-heard cry that loosely translated means "get out of the way and let me pass." She has spotted a shopper who is gingerly maneuvering around the mud and puddles of the Makola Markets in downtown Accra. The woman coaxes the prospective customer to a stall of brightly colored fabrics.

"Nice colors for you, Madame," she coos, draping a piece of purple and blue cloth over the shopper's shoulder and then standing back, hands on hips, to admire the look. "Make yourself happy, Madame. Buy. Buy."

Despite the emergence of Western-style department stores and shopping centers in black Africa, the open-air market is still where most people do their buying and selling. In Ghana, as in some other West African countries, women have for years held a near monopoly on the wholesaling and retailing of consumer products. Many of these "market mammies" or "market mummies" are illiterate, but know the value of money, how to price and sell goods and when to take financial risks. It is not uncommon for them to keep track of their products without record books. Some have become wealthy, after starting off as teenagers with only a few cents as capital.

Under the military Government of Flight Lieut. Jerry J. Rawlings, some of Ghana's market women have lost their businesses and are now trying to start over. In 1979, after Mr. Rawlings overthrew the Government of Lieut. Gen. Frederick W. K. Akuffo, soldiers demolished stalls and goods in one of the marketplaces in this rundown capital. According to several officials, the action was taken because the market women were selling goods at prices above those set by the Government. A local publication discussing the achievements of the Rawlings Government said the women had "dictated prices without thinking of the suffering workers."

Mr. Rawlings, a former pilot in the Ghanaian Air Force, voluntarily stepped down as the nation's leader in September 1979 in favor of a civilian Government. But he overthrew the civilians in 1981, reclaiming leadership of a country whose economy had been deteriorating for several years. The new Rawlings Government barred the market women from selling certain essential commodities, including milk, sugar and textiles.

One official said that with economic improvement brought about by austerity measures, the order regarding the selling of essential items had been "relaxed— not canceled, but relaxed." Other officials said that the destruction of one of the markets in 1979 had been "misguided." According to their reasoning, the women are the mothers, wives and daughters of the workers and, in general, do not make exorbitant profits. The real enemies of the people, the officials say, are the corporations that make the products and set the initial prices. There have been other enemies lately. In the last few weeks, 11 Ghanaians have been executed after convictions for corruption or for plotting against the Government. Nine others have been sentenced to death for bank fraud.

"It stands to reason that with the economy improving, with more available to buy and sell, with factories producing more and more goods, the women's prices are bound to come down because there can be more competition," an official said. "In any case, it is impossible to keep a Ghanaian woman under one's heels for long because she is strong."

History underscores that point. The

(continued)

British found a woman, Nana Yaa Asantewa, leading the Ashanti army in the last of the Anglo-Ashanti wars in 1901. And a ruler of the people of Accra, Dede Akaibi, was assassinated in 1610 because she ruled with a rod of iron. As to why West African women are so enterprising in trade, one reason may be the ancient practice of using them to carry on trade between tribes while the men were conducting wars, Nana Asantewa and Dede Akaibi notwithstanding. Women also grew food for the family and made the clothes and were entitled to keep whatever they earned from selling any surplus at market.

Like many others, Anna Obeng began learning the trade at an early age, while still attending school.

"When I'm a young girl, I come to sell in the afternoon after school," said Miss Obeng. "Some days the market is good, good, but some days the business is small, small. It is small, small today. So you buy, please, you buy."

SOURCE. Sheila Rule. 1985. "Ghana's women maintain their corner on the marketplace." *The New York Times* (June 9). Copyright 1985 by The New York Times Company. Reprinted by permission.

Anchoring the policy was the creation of ten quasi-independent "homelands" (or *Bantustans*), based on the former tribal reserves as shown in Figure 11.1. The establishment of the "homelands" also enabled the white government to legally force blacks out of designated white areas into resettlement camps or other inferior living arrangements. Between 1960 and 1980, an estimated 1.75 million blacks were relocated in the homelands from just the "white" rural areas (Browett, 1982). The policy of the white government is to grant "independence" to these homelands and create "national states." This has occurred in the Transkei (1976), Bophuthatswana (1977), Venda (1979), and Ciskei (1981).

The homelands enable the white ruling government to use the blacks as a cheap and disenfranchised labor force. Three kinds of laborers are represented in the black population (Smith, 1982). The first and most numerous are workers who permanently and legally reside in "white" South Africa. They reside in townships attached to the "white" cities. The second are the migrant laborers who contract to work for extended periods of time in white-run businesses, factories, mines, and agricultural farms. They return to the homeland to visit their families for short spells.

The third form of migrant labor is what has been called "frontier commuters" (Smith, 1982). These are people who live with their families in the homelands and travel on a daily basis across what apartheid ideology depicts as national borders into "white" South Africa. These townships are just within the homelands in areas adjacent to the "white" urban areas. They have experienced extremely rapid growth and have taken on the character of squatter settlements. Within the township itself, there is little economic opportunity. That is only available in the "white" urban areas, and, even here, it cannot handle the burgeoning township population.

The extended family is used to produce cheap labor. The male worker on his annual return to the homeland for short spells between work contracts provides the minimum amount of family continuity that would be required for his involvement in caring of the very young and very old, the sick, and the education of the young. During the rest of the year, the wife and other members of the extended family are expected to take care of the everyday needs of family members. Apartheid uses the extended family in terms of a "social security" function (Smith, 1983). The apartheid homeland policy transforms the traditional family system from its precapitalist mode of production to a reproduction system and uses it to control a cheap African industrial labor force. In effect, the poor, rural, black homelands are subsidizing the white, urban, industrial, economically advanced areas.

The wages paid to the migrant laborers do not meet the needs for family support

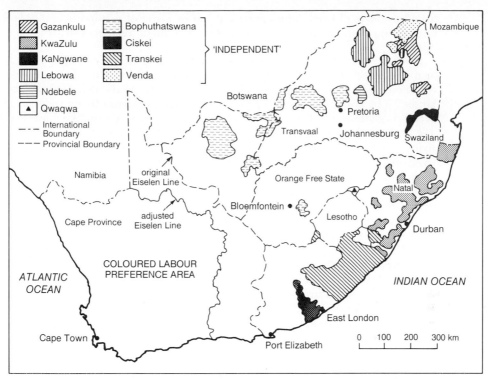

FIGURE 11.1   Homelands or *Bantustans* for the black (African) population of South Africa, and the Coloured Labor preference area of Cape Province west of the Eiselen line. The homelands are shown according to 1975 consolidation proposals.
(SOURCE: David M. Smith. 1982. "Urbanization and social change under apartheid: Some recent developments." In *Living Under Apartheid*, David M. Smith (ed.). London: George Allen & Unwin, p. 26.)

(Lemon, 1982). White municipalities and employers are saved the costs of housing, social security, food, clothing, and so forth, which the presence of families would demand. "[A] the social costs of labour—education of workers' children, social services, welfare benefits for the old, the widowed and the unemployed, housing of squatters . . . are being effectively transferred to 'independent' states" (Lemon, 1982:89). Unfortunately, however, the rural areas of these homelands have become so densely populated that there is insufficient land for the development and improvement of agriculture. The result is that "South Africa, by giving 'independence' to the peripheral areas of her space economy, is doing precisely the opposite" (Lemon, 1982:82).

Joseph Lelyveld (1986), in his Pulitzer-Prize–winning book, *Move Your Shadow: South Africa, Black and White*, observes how the legalization of apartheid laws affects the more than 800,000 black migrant workers. The law psychologically pressures black family members to succumb to a feeling of resignation that their lot in life is to be separated and fragmented. He speaks of the impact of apartheid as being measured not in dollars and cents but in "dead souls." "I could measure it only by trying to witness the system in operation, at the points where it impinges on individual lives, especially in the mazelike structure of courts and official bureaus that it has established to channel black laborers in and out of areas of economic opportunity while minimizing their chances of establishing permanent residence with their families'' (1986:82).

Black men are given jobs in white areas, including the major cities. They also work as migrant laborers in the mines or on sugar plantations, many for extended periods of time. Their wives and children, however, must live in the designated black "home-lands." The law is designed to prevent black families from living together. Housing accommodations for the black men are in single-sex, prisonlike hostels (Browett, 1982). For those increasingly smaller number of blacks who have chosen to continue living together, illegal life is very hard. One such "illegal" described by Lelyveld has lived in Cape Town for 20 years, where he, his wife, and their six children have moved from one squatter camp to another in their constant attempt to escape the authorities. They are currently sleeping in a church hall that is used as a nursery school during the day. His original home was in Transkei, a black homeland. Since then, like himself, his extended family has dispersed all over South Africa. He finds himself with no land, no extended family, and no place to go back to. He comments: "My heart is not feeling nicely. I'm the same like dead. I think of these things, the government and all, and sometimes I cry" (quoted in Lelyveld, 1986:109).

In the following passage, Lelyveld describes the situation of one man, Napthali Ngcobo, who was a uniformed watchman and handyman in the lobby of the Johannesburg building where Lelyveld had his office. He was relatively successful—well liked by blacks in the area and influential by virtue of their belief in him as a faith healer. Ngcobo's family lived in Zululand, which he was only able to visit for one month each year.

> He was earning about $235 a month, and most of it still went home: $60 to keep an eighteen-year-old-son, his hope for the future, in a boarding school; another $110 or so for his wife, who ran a household that still contained five of their eight children, plus his father, who wasn't sure of his age but recalled that he was

The day starts for the people of this shantytown outside Cape Town, South Africa, with breakfast at dawn.

supposed to be eleven in 1908. Another son had left a wife behind to come to Johannesburg, where he grilled hamburgers at a Wimpy fast-food joint in an Afrikaner neighborhood. Napthali, it seemed, had successfully fitted the disparate pieces of his life together and achieved a measure of contentment, but in his own mind, in reality, too, this had been done in spite of the system, not thanks to it. "The whites don't care at all," he said. "They are the ones who make it impossible to live with your family. Even if you have money, they won't allow it. (Lelyveld, 1986:111)

Gender Roles in Industrial Societies: The Soviet Union

It is beyond the scope of this book to document fully the entire range of social-historical changes in male – female relationships that have accompanied the advent of the Industrial Revolution over the last 200 years. But certain changes have been especially significant in how they affected gender-role relationships. The demographic revolution, the changing nature of economic life, and the changing ideology pertaining to gender-role and family relationships are important factors.

The demographic revolution includes the lengthened life span and the lowered mortality rate of mothers and infants during childbirth. Before industrialization, women were defined primarily in terms of their reproductive and maternal roles. The scientific advances in medicine that accompanied industrialization had a qualitative effect on the conceptualization of women. No longer need they be defined solely in terms of their maternal role. Their life span has increased to the extent that they no longer devote their longest phase of life to maternity. They are now free to pursue additional roles, both in the family and outside it in the economy.

Industrialization has also been a factor in changing gender roles. Children are no longer the economic necessity that they are in nonindustrial agricultural or hunting-and-gathering societies. They are an economic burden since they are unable to participate in the economic sphere until completing a long period of training. This has resulted in the loss of the importance of women's reproductive role as the entire rationale for their existence. Also, the economic value of the housewife has declined; her economic contribution no longer justifies the housewife role. Evelyne Sullerot (1971:79–80) has observed that the increased use of labor-saving and relatively expensive prepared-food items has made the housewife a consumer rather than an earner through her production in the home. The result is that for women who wish to contribute to the economic well-being of their families, it is more efficient to do so by becoming wage earners than by staying housewives.

In addition, the increased economic demand for labor in industrial societies increases the involvement of women in the economy. Women particularly have found a place in the tertiary sector (office work and service jobs) of the Western industrial economy; they hold jobs in occupations that are clearly related to traditional female gender-role activities and personality traits. Betty Yorburg (1974:68) has observed that there is an overwhelming concentration of women in canning and clothing factories, teaching, nursing, social work, and dietetics, and at occupational levels that require little or no organizational leadership or organizational characteristics. As we will see, the pattern is somewhat different in the Soviet Union and Eastern Europe.

The third element, the changing ideology pertaining to gender-roles and family relationships, intersects with the other two factors in influencing the changes in the relationship between men and women. The lessened economic importance of children as producers has fostered a shift in values regarding children. Children are socialized in a more permissive manner than when they were of high economic value. The increased life span of the husband and wife has also allowed for the development of a more romantic love ideology, the development of a companionate notion of marriage, and the seeking of erotic gratification within the marital relationship. This

Apartheid's Rules Leave a Black Family Sundered

BY SHELIA RULE

OKKERNOOTBOOM, South Africa — The letter came not long ago to this village and preparations for celebration began immediately. Sainah Zitha's husband was coming home.

Mrs. Zitha and her four children had not seen him since the four days he spent with them at Easter in Okkernootboom, in the impoverished, so-called homeland of Gazankulu.

Now they would have a month together before he took the 16-hour train ride back to Johannesburg and his job as a construction worker. It is a situation that has repeated itself for 20 years of marriage. In all those years, the family has been together a total of about 20 months.

The homecoming represents one of the peculiar rituals of many black people in a country where the laws of apartheid can transform a loving family into so many scattered pieces.

72-HOUR LIMIT

Under laws intended to control the influx of blacks into urban areas, no black can remain for more than 72 hours in a "white" city unless a stringent group of requirements are met.

Among other things, a black must have lived somewhere in the area continuously since birth, worked there continuously for at least 10 years or be the wife, unmarried daughter or son under the age of 18 of a person who meets these regulations.

Others, specifically migrant workers from the "homelands," must have special permission to be in the urban areas to work at certain jobs for specific employers. They are barred from bringing their families to live with them.

It is this last regulation that forces Mrs. Zitha's husband to live in a drab single-sex hostel hundreds of miles away from home for most of the year, as the woman goes about life's chores and waits for his infrequent return.

A MONTH'S REUNION

She speaks of how the children miss their father and how joy flowers within the household when the letters bring news of his imminent arrival. The intense happiness wilts when, all too soon, he must board the train once again for the long ride to Johannesburg and work that brings an income equivalent to about $76 a month.

But there are few other options in this patch of Gazankulu, a place of inferior soil where people can grow only enough vegetables to last five months and where half of the children die before they are 5 years old. No major industries or cities are nearby to absorb the employable adults. Those who stay face unemployment rates of as much as 90 to 100 percent, by some estimates, and so they board the trains to distant cities.

The absence of large numbers of men leaves many children with no strong male role models and families with little to guard against slow disintegration. By custom, the man of the family is the judge and jury and word of a crisis at home must be relayed by telephone, telegraph or letter. News of the death of a child, for example, may take two weeks to reach him. The family waits anxiously, hoping that the head of the household will be allowed to return for the burial. No one is to be buried without the presence of the man of the family. It is tradition.

A WAITER IN PRETORIA

"We miss him," said Mrs. Zitha, two of whose children died in infancy of what, to her, were unknown ailments. As she talked, she sat on a stoop outside the modest rectangle of hardened mud and paint that is her home. Candles were lit for her visitors, as night lowered its veil of darkness.

The Rev. Reckson Sithole, a minister who aids refugees from Mozambique living in the homeland, was at one time among the thousands who took the long journey. He was a waiter in Pretoria and would work there for two months before coming home for a weekend. He would leave Pretoria on a Thursday, arrive home Friday and head back to work on Sunday afternoon. The

(continued)

round-trip train ride cost the equivalent of $15.20. He was earning about $66 a month.

"It was a hardship on the family," Mr. Sithole said, driving through the arid countryside. "When you stay away and then come back, the children may not know who their father is. Small babies will not recognize you, which is very bad.

"Children must grow in a family life. Children who grow without parents, especially their father, are lacking something; something is missing to them. The wife, she is not to remain alone. She needs a partner who will be with her all the time. It was not allowed to take the family to Pretoria. I was staying at a hostel, which is like a hall with many beds and a shelf for our clothes. They only needed me because I was a qualified waiter for them. But I had to leave the home. There was no work around here."

The situation has changed little since Mr. Sithole made the journey. Thus, Mrs. Zitha remains behind and waits with children in this place that her mother traveled to on foot 20 years ago. Sarah Mkhonto once lived on fertile farmland about 12 miles from what is now Okkernootboom.

One day, as she tells it, white men came. She had no idea who they were, but they ordered her and the 1,000 others in her village to leave their land. Mrs. Mkhonto said the villagers moved out that same day, asking no questions because "they were white men." The villagers walked over the course of about two days to reach this barren brown spot of earth, leaving behind homes and belongings and starting over.

It is not uncommon for people such as Mrs. Mkhonto, her daughter and others in this remote area to have never heard the word "apartheid" and to look perplexed when a definition is offered. They simply live it.

SOURCE. Sheila Rule. 1985. "Apartheid's rules leave a black family sundered." *The New York Times* (Dec. 20). Copyright 1985 by The New York Times Company. Reprinted by permission.

has been concomitant with the increase in the number of years that the husband and wife can spend with each other in activities other than childbearing and child rearing.

We return to the discussion of the changing ideologies of men and women in the marital relationship in the next chapter. The discussion of the demographic revolution and its impact on parent–child relationships is a theme discussed more fully in later chapters. We examine the relationship of men and women within the economy of industrial societies. To put the examination of occupations into perspective, we review recent developments in the Soviet Union and contrast them with those in the United States, Sweden, and Israel. These industrial societies, which are based on varying ideological perspectives, have differentially involved men and women in the economy. Yet, there is similarity underlying all of them. These differences and similarities are the concern of the remaining pages of this chapter.

The socialist countries of Eastern Europe, along with the Soviet Union, have made a strong and conscientious effort to bring women into positions of equality in the economy. They have been ahead of Western industrial societies in this endeavor and thus the problems and solutions that they have experienced can provide guidelines for Western societies in their attempts to bring women into full participation in the occupational world. Two major elements, ideological and economic considerations, have been the forces behind this movement. Let us examine each in turn.

Ideology has been a prime factor influencing the relationship between the sexes in the Soviet Union. The Marxists, and particularly Friedrich Engels in his *The Origin of the Family, Private Property, and the State* (originally published in 1884), saw monogamy as a tool of economic capitalism. The division of labor between men and women in the monogamous household, according to this argument, has as its effect the subjugation of women and children to the capitalistic patriarchal system. The division of labor between the sexes is viewed as the prototype of the class struggle between the men who own the means of production and those who toil in their behalf. Engels conjectured that the socialist revolution would dissolve the monogamous family system. Women would be able to achieve equality by entering the economic system and there would be created public household services and public centers for the socialization of children.

> At all events, the position of the men thus undergoes considerable change. But that of the women, of *all* women, also undergoes important alteration. With the passage of the means of production into common property, the individual family ceases to be the economic unit of society. Private housekeeping is transformed into a social matter. (Engels, 1884/1972:83)

The Marxists believe that the housewife role is alienating. Work and social interactions outside the household are necessary to realize one's full potential. Housewives who are cut off from such outside contacts are cut off from the creative source and thus can never realize their full capabilities. Ultimately, the family and the society are the losers by this underutilization of women. This philosophy serves as the foundation for the policies of the Soviet Union after the Russian Revolution of 1917. Lenin, echoing Marx and Engels, saw the necessity of removing women from the "slavery" of the household to full participation in the socialist economy:

> You all know that even when women have full rights, they still remain downtrodden because all housework is left to them. In most cases, housework is the most unproductive, the most savage and the most arduous work a woman can do. It is exceptionally petty and does not include anything that would in any way promote the development of the woman. . . . To effect her complete emancipation and make her the equal of the man it is necessary for housework to be socialised and for women to participate in common productive labour. Then women will occupy the same position as men. (Lenin, 1919/1966:69)

Following the Russian Revolution, legislation was passed that aimed to achieve the liberation of women from the household and their equality in all spheres of life. Laws regulating family relationships and questions concerning divorce and abortion were designed to aid in this task. Marriage and divorce regulations were simplified. Abortions were legalized in 1920. The goal was to bring women into full participation in the social economy and into government. The means to accomplish this were seen in the transfer of economic and educational functions from separate households to the society as a whole. Barriers to educational institutions were removed for women. Communal household services, kitchens, dining halls, laundries, and repair shops were established. Infant-care centers, kindergartens, and educational institutions for older children were expanded.

However, economic considerations and demographic realities caused vicissitudes in Soviet family law and the implementation of many programs. Throughout Soviet history women have constituted a majority of the population. The Soviet Union had over 25 million war deaths in World War II. These were mostly men. This was in addition to the massive losses in World War I, the revolutionary civil war, the famine and epidemics of the 1920s, the industrialization drive, the forced collectivization of agriculture, and the purges of the 1930s—all brought about a most uneven sex ratio. Census reports from the 1920s, 1930s, 1940s, and 1950s show a significantly greater number of women in the population than men. The range is from 51.7 percent of the population in the first census report of 1926 to 57.4 percent more women than men in the postwar census of 1946. This latter figure represents an excess of 25 million women in a total population of 176 million (Field and Flynn, 1970:260)

It must be emphasized that, for the post–World War II population, this difference is at its highest in the marriage-age groups. The census of 1959 reflects this: although more than 90 percent of Soviet men between the ages of 30 and 69 were married, only 72 percent of the women between 35 and 39, only 62 percent of those between 40 and 44, only 54 percent of those between 45 and 50, and less than half of all women over the age of 50 were married (Field and Flynn, 1970:261). In human terms, the loneliness of Soviet women is reflected in the poem by Vladimir Semenov addressed to a Soviet girl:

> You tried to find him everywhere
> He must exist
> He is someplace.
> You asked:
> Where is he? Where?
> There was no answer.
> Your youth is gone.
> You paled and withered.
> You, whose beauty shone once,
> You do not know the verity
> That a wife to no one
> You long since are
> A widow . . .
> You do not know that he was killed
> in War
> Before you met him.
> (Semenov, 1959, cited in Field and Flynn, 1970:261)

In addition, then, to the ideological factors, the severe shortage of men in the Soviet Union necessitated women's involvement in the economy. This involvement is not as in Western societies where women constitute a reserve labor force, but rather women are integrated into and indispensable to the Soviet labor force. Although the labor shortage encouraged the employment of women, it also required an emphasis on childbearing to replace the decimated population. The stress placed on childbearing modified the application of the Marxist ideology.

In 1936, abortions were once again made illegal, except in exceptional medical circumstances. Divorces were made more difficult and costly. Unregistered marriages lost their validity and equality with registered marriages. In 1944, a decree was passed encouraging large families by establishing the honorific title, heroine mothers. These were women who had more than five children. They received special economic rewards and honors.

At the onset of these changes, child-care facilities proved inadequate. Eventually, they were expanded, particularly in industries that employed a large percentage of married mothers. Since 1953, the end of the Stalinist era, there has been a return to a more ideological implementation of the Marxist principles regarding male and female relationships. But the general pattern through Soviet history has been one of vacillation in ideological implementation, which has depended on the needs of the Soviet economy.

This discussion gives us some overview of the history of the factors that have influenced the involvement of Soviet women in the labor force. Gail Warshofsky Lapidus (1982)—who has written extensively of Soviet women—in reviewing labor statistics and current research, points out that women are heavily concentrated in certain types of economic activities and significantly underrepresented in others. In the service sector, public health, social welfare, education, and culture, women account for three-fourths or more of the labor force. Only one-fourth of the labor force is female in construction and transportation. In industry, where women represent almost half of all production personnel, they constitute over 80 percent of food and textile workers and over 90 percent of garment workers.

Mark G. Field and Karin I. Flynn (1970), in examining employment data from the Soviet census of 1959, found that women were underrepresented in occupations that entail directive, managerial, and executive functions. They also tended to be overrepresented in subordinate and minor positions, as well as in menial jobs. Citing data from almost a quarter of a century later, Lapidus (1982) finds a continuation of this pattern. She observes that, occupationally, women predominate in the lower and middle levels of white-collar employment and the paraprofessions. Virtually all nurses, technicians, librarians, typists, and stenographers are female. Yet, women are underrepresented in supervisory and managerial positions. There is also much disparity in male and female earnings, with women frequently making less money for doing the same work as men.

TABLE 11.1   Proportion of Women in High-Level Positions in Selected Fields and Institutions

Enterprise Management	*1959*	*1970*
Enterprise directors (including state farms)	12	13
Heads of shops, sections, departments, and foremen	15	15
Heads of production-technical departments, sectors, groups, offices	20	24
Scholarly Research and Teaching	*1970*	*1979*
Academician, corresponding member, professor	9.9	10.7
Senior research associate	25.1	22.5
Junior research associate and assistant	49.8	47.7
Scientific personnel	38.8	40.0
Candidate in science	27.0	28.0
Doctorate in science	13.0	14.0
Education	*1960/1961*	*1979/1980*
Directors of secondary schools	20	32
Directors of 8-year schools	23	37
Deputy directors of secondary schools	53	67
Directors of primary schools	69	80
Teachers	70	80
Medicine	*1959*	*1975*
Chief physicians	54	53
Physicians	79	74
Midwives and feldshers	84	83
Nurses and pharmacists	99	99
Communist Party	*1976*	*1981*
Politburo	0	0
Central Committee		
Full members	2.8	2.5
Candidates	4.3	6.0
Urban and district party secretaries	4 (1973)	na
Party membership	24	25
Executive Committee of a Leningrad District Soviet	*1962*	*1966*
Chairman, his deputies and secretary of executive council	24.9	24.9
Directors and deputy directors of divisions, directors of sectors	63.1	40.0
Specialists (instructors, inspectors, etc.)	87.2	92.9
Clerical personnel	100.0	100.0

SOURCE: Gail W. Lapidus. 1982. "Women, work, and family: New soviet perspectives." In Gail Warshofsky Lapidus (ed.), *Women, Work, and Family in the Soviet Union.* Armonk, NY: Sharpe, pp. xxii–xxiii. Reprinted by permission.

Explanations on why women do not fare as well in the labor force are beginning to focus on social factors and not biological constraints as the most salient factors. Soviet social scientists are recognizing the fact that differential educational opportunities and family responsibilities work against women. Lapidus observes how all these social factors create a "vicious circle" that severely retards and restricts women's economic equality and advancement:

> . . . women have lower expectations of occupational mobility than their male counterparts; they gravitate toward jobs which are most compatible with their domestic responsibilities; they have less time available for study and are not able to improve their qualifications as rapidly as men; they tend to become stuck in less rewarding and stimulating jobs with few incentives or opportunities for upward mobility; and they are viewed by enterprise managers as less promising and productive, which reduces their leverage and opportunity still further. (Lapidus, 1982:xxv)

However, if we compare the Soviet figures for professions—including engineering and medicine—with those of Western countries, one is astonished by the greater proportional participation of Soviet women. Sullerot (1971:151–157) examined data gathered in the 1960s on women's participation in the medical, legal, and engineering professions in the Soviet Union and in Western societies. The differences are overwhelming. For example, there are more women surgeons, specialists, and hospital directors in the Soviet Union than in all the Western countries put together. In the engineering profession, there are over 500,000 engineers (37 percent) in the Soviet Union compared to only 6,000 (3.7 percent) in France, the country with the next highest percentage.

Despite the great progress that women have made in the Soviet Union, there still remain problems in the achievement of complete equality. As mentioned previously, a greater proportion of women are found in subordinate positions and menial labor. They also tend to be discriminated against in jobs that demand directive, managerial, and executive skills. A survey of Soviet women by David K. Shipler (1976) reports that women do not reach the upper echelons of responsibility in occupational institutions, the professions, or in governmental politics. They are overrepresented in the lower ranks where the prestige and pay are less. To illustrate, although some 71 percent of secondary-school teachers are women, 72 percent of the principals are men. Similarly, in the medical profession, which is 70 percent composed of women, the heads of hospitals and other medical facilities are usually men; women are, at best, assistant directors. The large number of women in medicine is explained by the relatively low salaries that doctors make. Doctors earn about 100 rubles a month, and $135, which is about three-quarters of the average industrial wage.

TABLE 11.2   Percentage of Women in the Professions

	Medical Profession	*Barristers*	*Engineers*
USSR	76.0	38.0	37.0
Great Britain	25.0	4.0	0–0.06
France	22.0	19.0	3.7
West Germany	20.0	5.0	1.0
Austria	18.0	7.0	nd
Sweden	13.0	6.7	nd
Denmark	nd	10.0	nd
USA	6.0	3.0	0–0.07

Note: nd = no data.

SOURCE: Adapted from Evelyne Sullerot. 1971. *Woman, Society and Change.* New York/Toronto: McGraw-Hill (World University Library), pp. 151–152. Copyright 1971 by World University Library, McGraw-Hill Book Company. Reprinted by permission.

Shipler (1976) reports a similar pattern existing in light industry and factory work. Women are discriminated against in salary, overrepresented in the more-tedious jobs, and underrepresented in administrative posts. This is attributed to the underrepresentation of women in politics. Membership in the Communist party is mandatory for many of those who hold key positions in industry and the professions, and women make up only 24 percent of the total number of Communist party members. Here, again, men hold the important positions.

The pattern of discrimination continues in the academic world. Women comprise only 13.7 percent of the membership of the Union of Writers and in the prestigious Academy of Sciences just three of the 243 full members are women. More than two and one-half times as many men as women hold the academic degree of candidate in science, which is equivalent to something between the master's and doctorate degree in the American system. At the doctorate level (the equivalent of a "superdoctorate"), men outnumber women by six to one (Shipler, 1976:9)

Thus, although the Soviet Union has advocated a public policy designed to stimulate women's involvement in the economy, and although it has pioneered in the development of maternal and child-care services, it still does not have full equality of women in the work sphere. There are a number of reasons to explain this situation. Examination of these reasons may prove instructive to Western countries in their attempts to develop policies are procedures.

First, there is the continuation of patriarchal attitudes. Traditionally, the people of the Soviet Union share the patriarchal ideology that has characterized Western countries. Even today, despite the introduction of Marxist egalitarian principles over 60 years ago, patriarchy still flourishes. The following quotation by a woman who had made a career commanding cargo ships reflects the prevalence of sexism in the Soviet Union. She advises women not to become sea captains and endorses the regulation that closed seafaring schools to women in 1944:

> In the previous 20 years probably hundreds of girls studied to become ship commanders, but only four in the whole country made it. So is it worthwhile to continue spending money teaching girls? You cannot fight against life. To command a ship is still a man's business.
>
> Let men go to sea and women remain on shore to raise children, to occupy themselves with things traditionally feminine. (Anna I. Schchetinina cited in Shipler, 1976:9)

Despite the remarkable achievements of women in the Soviet economy, many men and women share patriarchal assumptions of women's intellectual inferiority and emotional frailty. This attitude is most representative in the women's dual role, which demands that they continue to keep a home (without expecting much help from their husbands) at the same time that they hold down a full-time job. The result is that women work longer hours than their husbands; in addition to their full-time jobs, they put in an additional five to six hours a day in household activities. Their task is complicated by the fact that there is little domestic help, there are few labor-saving devices available, and few conveniences, such as supermarkets and prepackaged food. Traditional sexist attitudes persist in the household. Soviet men view household tasks as "feminine" and refuse to do their fair share. David Shipler observes that "it is common to go into the homes of Moscow intellectuals and discover women professionals with their own careers, who participate fully in conversation and are accustomed to having their views respected. Yet it is rare to see men clearing tables, shopping for food or doing housework" (1976:9).

A second factor is the emerging patterns of marriage in the Soviet Union and the changing ideas regarding child rearing and family roles. The Soviet Union originally conceived of a minimal role for the family and placed higher stress on family members' involvements with outside institutions. This has changed in recent years to a greater emphasis on the closeness and intimacy of the family and its concern with its members' formation and emotional support (Fogarty, Rapoport, and Rapoport, 1971:85). Tied to this conceptualization is the desire for the mother to spend more time with her children, especially the very young. The implications are that the wife should restrict her commitments in outside involvements.

Also occurring is a change in the assessment of institutionalized nursery care and early childhood day care. There has been some discrediting of these institutions in terms of their potentially negative effects on children. The result is a tendency to make less use of them, and there also has been considerable popular resistance to them. The result has been a dilemma that still has not been resolved. On the one hand, there is the desire of the state that women should continue to be involved with their jobs during the early child-rearing years and, on the other hand, there is the desire of the couple for greater involvement of the wife with her children. Although some congruity of these objectives is now occurring, sentiment has swayed toward a greater emphasis on individual and personal development and on the family as a central agent to it (Fogarty et al., 1971:84–91).

A third reason for the dilemma between women's work and family roles is the failure of employment agencies to develop recruitment, training, and promotion practices adapted to the life cycle (for example, maternity) of married women. Michael T. Fogarty and his associates (1971) report that this failure is combined with the failure to develop career patterns for women that would assist them in making it to top-echelon positions.

Fogarty and his associates (1971) believe that the fourth reason in the uncertain record of women's career achievement is related to the ambiguity regarding feminine identity and its implication for working life. The traditional conceptualization of femininity is still echoed in the Soviet economy. Roles related to sex differences are still prevalent in Eastern Europe and the Soviet Union:

> . . . girls and women tend to be more conscientious and disciplined than boys and men, but less path-breaking; that girls' interests tend to run to the humanities, to "maternal" fields such as teaching or medicine and to menial work, rather than to outdoor work, technology, or mastering nature as such; that women tend to be more emotional, personal, and concerned with detail than men, and less able to deal logically and objectively with broad issues; that they tend towards ancillary rather than leadership roles; that married women tend to defer publicly to their husbands, and to be reluctant to earn more or reach higher than them; and that both women and men tend to accept that a mother, unlike a father, will treat her domestic role as primary. (Fogarty et al., 1971:95)

Extensive attempts have been made to remove these alleged and real sex differences. There have been developments in coeducational curriculums to provide girls with equal opportunities to develop technological skills and to enter into all fields of work. Further, new attitudes are emerging, encouraged by governmental programs, such as the belief that feminine roles can include both career and motherhood. The choice of career should be based on a principle of equal opportunities and the free choice of men and women. But Fogarty and his co-authors conclude that there still remains uncertainty between the old and new conceptualizations that have not been fully realized. The dilemma is to reach some accommodations in terms of the acceptance of some new criteria relating to sex differences and the achievement of the goals relating to equal opportunity.

The Impact of Soviet Women's Work on the Family

The impact of women's work on the family has become a major concern in the Soviet Union. The focus is on three broad areas: its effects on patterns of marriage and divorce, on fertility, and on the sexual division of labor (Lapidus, 1982). The widely held view that female education and employment are inversely associated with family stability is supported by statistical data. High divorce rates are associated with women who are more likely to initiate divorces. This is, in part, attributed to their greater economic independence and relative unwillingness to hold together an unsatisfactory marriage. Divorce rates vary by region, age, and ethnic make-up. The overall divorce rate is 3.5 divorces per thousand population. This figure is exceeded only by the figure for the United States. However, for the European parts of the USSR and particularly in major cities like Moscow (5.1) and Leningrad (5.6), the divorce rate is much higher.

Peter H. Juviler (1984), a leading American expert on the Soviet family, reports that experts of the family interpret the divorce rate as a sign of greater family instability that has troubling implications for the demographic situation in the Soviet Union. These experts estimate that about 15 percent fewer children will be born because of family breakup. Further, family strains may serve as a deterrent against having children. This problem is seen as being particularly acute in the Russian Soviet republic rather than in the less European Asian Soviet republics with their large Islamic population.

Gary Lee Bowen (1983), in his examination of Soviet family policy, points out that the high divorce rate for urban couples reflects the fact that these couples represent the technological and professional elite of Soviet society. They are characterized by dual-careerism, conjugal-family systems, and neolocal residence—all factors that cause high divorce rates. In comparison, rural families in the Soviet Union continue to be characterized by lower divorce rates, reflecting the continued prominence of extended-family networks and stable familial and traditional cultural values. Bowen further states that, "in some ways the marital pattern presently found in the Soviet Union reflects that which Engels envisioned: one based on true love with the capacity to be dissolved when this love ceases" (1983:309). Indeed, Lapidus (1978) cites one Soviet sociologist who interprets the rising divorce rate not in terms of marital disorganization but as a sign of strength and adaptability to new conditions.

Women's employment is also seen as affecting the family through its influence on childbearing. The urban and industrial areas where there is a declining birthrate are also the areas where there is a high level of female employment. Lapidus (1982) observes that some officials have suggested that to counter this trend there should be a reduction in female employment. "Deploring the fact that the one-child family has become the norm in the urban regions of the European USSR, a number of Soviet authors call for reducing the level of female labor force participation and even restricting abortions in order to increase birthrates to a socially optimal level" (Lapidus, 1983:xxxiv).

In addition to the full-time employment of many urban women, the trend of having small families can also be explained by the general lack of living space and the low standard of living for many families. The Soviet government is particularly concerned with the low fertility rate and the trend toward single-child families. It goes counter to the ideological belief that children of such families are likely to be indulged and fail to develop the intellectual and emotional characteristics of self-discipline, joint participation, and unselfishness that are necessary for integration into a socialist society (Bowen, 1983).

Bowen (1983), in his analysis of Soviet family policy, believes that the present strategy to provide incentives to fertile families and penalize families with three or less children will not be effective. The problem does not lie in the attitudes of parents toward children but rather in the detrimental social and economic circumstances that permeate Soviet society. He concludes that policies will continue to address themselves to the current demographic indicators that depict Soviet marriage as popular, but relatively weak, characterized by high divorce rates and low fertility, especially in urban centers. "The demographic trends of higher divorce and lower fertility will undoubtedly remain the focus of anxious discussion among Soviet officials, for they challenge the very foundation of the socialist state: namely, that female emancipation and the reform of the family proceed concomitantly, generating both marital stability and high rates of fertility" (Bowen, 1983:310).

The third way in which female employment is seen by Lapidus to impact on the family is on the sexual division of labor within the family. The consensus among Soviet authors is that working women now have greater authority within the family. A more-democratic pattern of family decision making — including a more-equal sharing of family responsibilities — is seen as another consequence of women's employment (Lapidus, 1982). Juviler supports this observation: "Women these days are making greater demands than their mothers did for equality in family burdens, decency and sobriety on the part of their husbands, and emotional supports. They have more options and make more demands than their mothers and grandmothers did" (1984:98). He also attributes this rise in family equality to the elimination of illiteracy and cultural backwardness and to the movement from village to city and the breakdown of the extended family. This movement effectively destroyed the power and social control of the villages over couples, while it also removed the nuclear family from extended-family controls.

Lapidus (1982), however, cautions us not to exaggerate this movement toward gender-role equality. She cites voluminous Soviet time-budget investigations that reveal that, while men and women devote equal time to paid employment, women are still devoting an additional 28 hours per week to housework. Men's contributions are only an additional 12 hours. As a consequence, men have 50 percent more leisure time than women. She further observes that a reduction in the time that women spend on housework is not a consequence of husband involvement but rather the result of the use of labor-saving household appliances. In short, she argues that the "double burden" still exists.

> While Soviet authors routinely decry the "double burden" which working women continue to bear and enjoin men to assume a greater share of the responsibility for domestic chores, few directly confront the fundamental sources of the problem. The household continues to be viewed as predominantly a female domain, and the family as a female responsibility. The fundamental assumption of Soviet economic and family policy — that women, and women alone, have dual roles — is a continuing barrier to fundamental improvements in women's position. (Lapidus, 1982:xxxv)

In summary, the Soviet Union has to a large extent been in the forefront of the effort to establish equality between the sexes and has made giant steps toward the accomplishment of that goal. Yet, formal and traditional barriers to women's progress still exist. However, in light of the relatively minor advances of Western countries in the quest for sexual equality of opportunity, the achievements of the Soviet Union are notable. Further, its experience provides a useful perspective from which to anticipate the development of problems and ultimate solutions of Western countries in their movement toward achieving sexual egalitarianism.

The Western Experience: Sweden

For almost half a century, Sweden had been under the influence of the Social Democratic party. In that time, Sweden has created one of the most progressive social-welfare systems in the world. Comprehensive governmental programs and services exist in the fields of health, education, and welfare. Parents receive family allowances for their children. Education is free and universal. Old-age pensions and benefits are available to all citizens, regardless of the amount of their prior contributions. Day-care facilities are numerous and are well utilized. Birth-control information, contraceptive devices, and abortions are readily available.

Sweden has made great strides in bringing about gradual equality between men and women in politics, education, employment, and the family. To accomplish this goal, the Swedes approach the problem through far-reaching policies carefully conceptualized and pragmatically implemented. To illustrate, Sweden during the depression of the 1930s had a dramatically declining birthrate. People could not afford to have children. The Swedish government realized that, if it wished the population to rise, it must implement a comprehensive and supportive social welfare program. This was essential to encourage marriage and childbearing and to protect the lives and health of both the parents and the children. The policy that was developed was multifaceted and included the following elements: "encouragement of sex education and contraception; state-financed housing; a child-allowance benefit for all families; the creation of mother-baby health clinics throughout the country; a commitment to feed every schoolchild every day; and medical services for all" (Herman, 1974:77).

Although Sweden has been notably successful in its attempt to equalize the relationship between the sexes, vestiges of traditional patriarchal ideology still are manifest. In work, women are predominantly employed as office workers and sales help. They are overrepresented in the lowest civil service grades—81 percent are women—and underrepresented—only 3 percent—in the highest-paid grades. According to the 1972 tax tables, women's income was almost half that of men's, 14,600 crowns to 28,600 crowns (Herman, 1974:78). This variation reflects women's lower job status and the proportionately greater number of women who are employed part-time. This persistence of part-time employment and lower-echelon positions for women reflects the traditional viewpoint that women's place is in the home.

The double burden of the employed wife is as prevalent in Sweden as it is in the Soviet Union and in Eastern European societies. The old idea that women have greater responsibility in the home for both domestic activities and child care still predominates. This has handicapped the drive for the advancement of women in the field of employment, in labor unions, and in political organizations.

The Swedish approach to bringing about changes in these traditional ideas has been to broaden the discussion concerning women's rights and "the problem of women" in relation to the overall problem of gender roles. In 1962, a controversial book was published that has stimulated this debate. This book, *Kvinnors Liv och Arbete* [*The Life and Work of Women* (Dahlström, 1962)], consists of a series of essays by noted Scandinavian sociologists, social psychologists, and economists who center their attention on the overall problem of gender-role discrimination in society. The book was a major breakthrough in that it placed the discussion about the "women's question" into the larger social context. One of the contributors to this book, Rita Liljestrom, summarizes by alluding to the similarity between gender-role discrimination and racial discrimination:

> If a society shows sexual discrimination in the labor force, if its decision-making bodies, councils, and parliament contain an overwhelming majority of men, if sexual discrimination is practiced in connection with household tasks, it is as unreasonable to talk about "the problem of women" as to lay the blame for racial prejudice upon the Negro. (Liljestrom, 1970:204)

The placing of the "women's problem" into the broader social issue relating to discrimination and civil rights was a significant turning point in changing traditional ideas. The widening of the debate beyond the conventional focus of discussions on the conflict between women's two roles—family and work—to encompass the two roles of men has also had an effect on men. Liljestrom (1970:200–201) notes the use of the expression "men's emancipation" means the rights of husbands and fathers to become involved in child care and domestic activities. Further, the phrase is taken to mean that options for men and women should be expanded in both economic and family institutions.

Sweden is of particular interest to us in terms of how it is seeking to handle the disadvantaged economic position of families vis-à-vis individuals or married couples who are childless. Liljestrom (1978) speaks of a "new kind of poverty" characterizing families who cannot make ends meet. Childless individuals or couples are able to maximize their spending and investing power. Through their ability to focus their economic resources, they are driving up the price of commodities, including housing, transportation, and other consumer goods. Families with full-time employed husbands and wives are finding that they cannot economically compete given the financial costs of child rearing. In turn, seeing this, younger people are making decisions either to postpone or to never have children. As a consequence of this trend, Sweden has been experiencing a declining birthrate. "The Population Commission saw as the most important cause of the declining birthrate the lower living standard of families with children *relative* to that of the childless at corresponding income levels" (Liljestrom, 1978:26).

The Swedish government was concerned that if this trend continued unchecked, it would produce more childless couples and accentuate the divergence in living styles. To combat this problem, Sweden adopted the family allowance as a "pronatalist" measure. The government pays a fixed allowance to all parents with children. It also advances payments of private child support that are due.

Sweden is also aware of the impact that these programs have on the lives of women. Taken by itself, a family allowance could easily function as a strong incentive to remain at home for the married woman. If she subsequently divorces, she may find herself ill-prepared, lacking the necessary job skills and experience to enter the job market. To combat such eventualities, Sweden has developed a parent-insurance program that allows either or both parents to take a nearly full-paid employment leave of up to nine months after the birth of a child. This system is financed through taxes and employers' contributions.

The Swedish system reflects a substantial commitment to child-care responsibility. In addition to cash allowances, the government has undertaken to provide widespread public child-care services. This is very important for women who are divorced; the burdens of child care are shared with the state. The government does not operate under the principle of equalizing the financial burden with the father. However, the state, rather than women, absorbs much of the impact of divorce.

Unfortunately, Sweden's patriarchal ideology has limited the full realization of these programs. For example, one of the central goals of the parent-insurance program was to encourage men as well as women to participate in child rearing. Yet, in 1983, nearly ten years after the introduction of this program, only 25 to 30 percent of the fathers eligible for parental leave at the time of childbirth actually utilized it. When they did it was for a relatively short period ranging from ten days to one month. Pressures from fellow male workers who did not approve, plus the workers' own mixed feelings, account for this (Trost, 1983).

Another shortcoming is that, despite the strong emphasis to provide for child-care facilities, as of 1980 only 30 percent of the children from birth to age six could be accommodated in existing centers (*Fact Sheets on Sweden*, 1982). While it is true that the existing schools are of the highest quality and stringent requirements for high-quality centers have curtailed their development, there is an urgent need for additional preschool facilities. This is particularly the case with so many young women entering the labor force.

In conclusion, what has been occurring in Sweden can be insightful for other Western industrial countries and the United States. Sweden is far ahead of the United States in achieving the ultimate goal of gender equality. Its government has been progressive and farsighted. It has supported and led meaningful programs and reforms. However, the traditional idea of masculine dominance still persists and hinders the drive for equal opportunity for men and women.

Swedish Government Panel Urges Male Child-Caring

BY LARS FOYEN

STOCKHOLM, Sweden—The Swedish male has been inspected and found wanting by a government panel that believes fathers would be happier sharing child-caring and other domestic duties equally with their working wives.

"Warm, skin-close child-caring could make men open up emotionally and give them a safety net of intimate relations as a backup in a personal crisis," says Stig Ahs, who chaired the committee.

Most Swedish men appear to be ignoring that advice, even though government policy and financial realities have pushed 83 percent of Swedish women with preschool children into the labor market. The losers, Ahs says, are the men.

"We have paid a very high price for the traditional male role, which tends to make us emotionally castrated," he said in an interview.

Suicides, alcoholism and criminality are much more common among Swedish men than women, he noted.

Newly appointed Foreign Minister Sten Andersson showed signs of being among the new Swedish males recently when he vowed he would attend only a few cocktail parties in his new job.

"I have to make dinner for my kids when my wife is working late," Andersson said.

Swedes have spent decades tinkering with the welfare state. Much of the effort in recent years has been aimed at encouraging equality between the sexes.

Sweden offers both mother and father almost a full year of parental leave at government expense, to be taken one at a time by either parent, married or unmarried.

A recent government study found, however, that 80 percent of all eligible fathers keep right on working. The remaining 20 percent, mostly well-educated men working in the public sector, take an average of only 47 days leave.

Although younger men do somewhat better, Swedish men on average spend only seven or eight hours a week on domestic duties, compared to 35 hours for women, the study says.

Sweden is also one of the few countries to have a minister of equality. The minister, Social Democrat Anita Gradin, set up Ahs' panel in 1983 to discuss men's roles and suggest changes.

The panel's recently published report, "The Male in Change," proposed ways to increase contacts with children and thus give men "a better life."

It also proposed obligatory education and discussion among conscripts and officers on male roles in the military services and in society, and the establishment of centers for men in crisis, such as those recovering from a divorce. The military is expected to respond formally to the proposal by March.

Some Swedish men have had enough of equality.

"It's men who are oppressed these days. The attacks from feminists have made them feel ashamed and uncomfortable," says Jan Gronholm, 40, a behavioral scientist and lecturer on male roles.

Gronholm contended in an interview in the Stockholm daily *Expressen* that Ahs' panel is proposing that men become clones of women.

Referring to "soft men on paternal leave," he said Swedish teenage boys were watching more violent video tapes because they were being "starved in their immediate surroundings of real men to imitate."

Two female psychologists, appearing on a much-discussed radio program, attacked the notion of parents sharing equally in infant care.

"There is a special relation, a psychological umbilical cord, between the infant and the mother," said psychologist Gunilla Guva.

Her colleague Kristina Humble added that parents who share parental leave might cause the child a "separation trauma" that would have repercussions when the child grows up.

Both psychologists said that clouded sexual role models might hamper the father's crucial task of breaking the "symbiosis" between the mother and the child at age 4 or 5.

(continued)

However, American scientist Michael Lamb, author of *The Role of the Father in Child Development,* said during a visit to Sweden that "there is so far no proof that the development of a child's sexual identity would be disturbed by shared child-caring."

"I may be an amateur," wrote Gudrun Nordgren in the Stockholm daily *Aftonbladet,* "but based on my experience as a mother and a grandmother I want to say: Don't trust the experts. Trust daddy."

Surveys show that most Swedish men and women support shared diaper-changing and cuddling. Many men at traditional male-dominated work places avoid paternal leave, however, because they think employers and colleagues would disapprove.

Swedish trade unions earlier this year complained that some companies had moved employees to less attractive jobs because they took parental leave.

To increase incentives, Ahs' panel suggested that couples who split parental leave should be reimbursed with 90 percent of their salary, not only during the first nine months but also for the remining three during which they now only get $6 a day.

Older generations of men may also get a second chance.

Noting that "middle-aged men often are more interested in their grandchildren than they were in their own children during their career-oriented years," the panel suggested government-paid "grandpaternal leave."

SOURCE. Lars Foyen. 1986. "Swedish government panel urges male child rearing." *The Philadelphia Inquirer* (Nov. 19). Reprinted by permission of the Associated Press.

The Western Experience: Israel

Our last societal illustration in this chapter is that of Israel. We focus on the kibbutz movement, which is a prime illustration of communities whose major goal is the emancipation of women and the establishment of complete equality between men and women in all aspects of life. The kibbutz is a collective agricultural settlement comprising between 100 to 2,000 inhabitants. There are some 230 kibbutzim (plural of kibbutz) in Israel, with a total population of about 100,000. This is a little less than 5 percent of Israel's population.

The kibbutz movement originated in the beginning of the twentieth century by East European Jews who settled in what was then Palestine. It represented an attempt to implement the ideologies of Zionism (the belief in a Jewish homeland), socialism, and the ideals of Tolstoy and his disciples concerning the virtues of agricultural pursuits and the belief that the greatest happiness is a return to mother earth.

There are a great number of different types of kibbutzim in Israel. Politically, they range from mild social democratic ideologies to extreme-left Marxian positions. Generalizations, therefore, must be made cautiously. Most, generally, try to maintain the belief in economic collectivism. Essentially, this principle eliminates private property and the opportunity to accumulate wealth. The common feature of these collective settlements is the shared ownership of property and the communal organization of production and consumption. Except for a few personal belongings, all property belongs to the community. All income goes into the common fund. Everything is provided by the community, based on the collective decision of the community. Through a general assembly and an extensive committee system, the members' needs are provided on an egalitarian basis.

A most striking feature of the kibbutzim is their attitudes and practices regarding the family. Kibbutz founders expounded their revolutionary and collectivist ideology toward the family. The kibbutz philosophy demanded the complete commitment and involvement of all its members (kibbutzniks). It was felt that this goal could be best accomplished if family and kinship ties were minimized. The late Israeli sociologist

A community celebration on one of the first Israeli communes, known in Hebrew as a kibbutz, in 1948.

Yonina Talmon (1965b:146) stated that the kibbutz founders saw the family as an obstruction to the desired collectivist community. Individuals' attachment to the family and their intense emotional involvement with family members were seen to infringe on the loyalties to the kibbutz. They also believed that involvement with the family members might impede the ideological and work goals of the kibbutz. Finally, it was felt that "inasmuch as they act as buffers and protect the individual from the direct impact of public opinion, they reduce the effectiveness of informal collective control over members" (Talmon, 1965b:261).

With this antifamily ideology, the kibbutz founders rejected the double standard for men and women and the traditional patriarchal structure of the Jewish family. This traditional structure required women and children to be subservient to the husband and father in the family. The division of labor was rigidly segregated in the Jewish family. Women had little involvement with external family matters in the social, cultural, religious, and economic life of the community. Women were confined primarily to the house; their activities revolved around children and domestic chores.

The kibbutz movement seeks to counter the debilitating effects of the family on women and its accompanying double standard through a series of dramatic steps designed to limit drastically the function of the family. Men and women are given jobs based on egalitarian principles. Although husbands and wives are housed in separate household units, their meals are cooked in communal kitchens and taken in the communal dining room. Clothing is purchased, washed, and ironed by assigned kibbutzniks. The community is run as a separate household. From infancy, children are raised in a separate children's house with other children of their own age group. They sleep, eat, and study in these houses. The children are allowed to visit their parents and siblings for several hours daily, but they are raised as a group by community members assigned to this task. Thus many of the tasks traditionally performed by the wife-mother are transformed in the kibbutz into occupational roles requiring trained and professional staffs.

This, then, is the philosophical basis of the kibbutz movement and the implementation of that philosophy. However, in recent years there is evidence that the collectivist system is losing ground to the reemergence of individual values and patriarchal patterns.[1] Manifestations of this change are apparent in the development of discriminatory gender differentiation patterns in the work sphere and the reestablishment of family and kinship ties. Talmon, who had done extensive studies on the kibbutz movement before her untimely death, examined (1965a) the developing division of labor between the sexes in both the internal system of the family and the external system of the occupational and leadership areas. She found that whereas the predominant egalitarian ideology is formally applauded, in reality a segregated gender division of labor exists.

In the sphere of the family, there has been a gradual increase of family functions. Parents are now taking a more-active role in raising their children. This is a partial reversal of the collective's role in the care and socialization of the children. Further, although the role differentiation between the mother and the father is not as segregated as it is in the United States, there is a trend to a division of labor between the parents. Women become more involved in taking care of the children in the home. Women also are becoming more involved in the domestic activities of the home; cleaning, washing clothes, and so on. Men, in turn, have their responsibilities geared to work outside the home—in the yard, on the farm, and in dealing with communal affairs of the kibbutz. The result is that "in the eyes of the growing child, the father emerges gradually as the representative of the kibbutz, and its values within the family, while the mother acts primarily as the representative of the family in the kibbutz" (Talmon, 1965a:147).

Gender-role differentiation is also developing in outside-work assignments and in the involvements of kibbutz committees. Men's work activities are concentrated mainly in agriculture and in the production services, transportation, equipment- and machinery-maintenance shops, and the like. Women are found in extensions of traditional women's occupations. Workers in the communal kitchens, in the clothing

---

[1] For an extensive review of contemporary patterns in the kibbutzim, albeit with a different interpretation than that given here, see Lionel Tiger and Joseph Shepher, *Women in the Kibbutz* (1975).

shops, and stores are almost exclusively women. In education, women are found teaching in the primary grades, men at the high-school level.

Talmon found a gradual trend toward growing gender-role differentiation in the participation on committees and in the overall leadership of the community. Generally, men predominate in overall leadership and in the central governing committees. The committees on which women are predominant are those involving education, health, and consumption. Thus, here too, the gender-role division of labor begins to follow traditional patriarchal male-female patterns.

Talmon attributes the growing gender-role differentiation in the kibbutz to two major reasons. First, there are the vestiges of traditional patriarchal thought that surfaced again in the kibbutzim. Second, there are the factors attributed to pregnancy and lactation. Childbearing necessitates that women become involved with activities that do not jeopardize their child-care role. Tied to pregnancy and child rearing is the overall increase in family function. The family thus regains some of its lost functions and becomes more active in internal activities. In addition, "the identification with the specifically and typically feminine role of mother undermines the masculine image of the feminine role upheld by the official ideology and weakens the resistance to sex-role differentiations" (Talmon, 1965a:151).

The role differentiation within the family gradually exerts pressure and influences the work sphere. Lines between appropriate work for men and women become more sharply delineated. The egalitarian basis for the designation of occupations becomes lost. The result is the continued acceleration of gender-role differentiation.

The implication of these findings is that the differentiation of gender roles is ultimately based on physiological factors—the reproductive function of women. The argument is that even when a social group desires to construct a community based on sexual equality, the biologic differences between the sexes have a determining role. Tiger and Shepher (1975), in a polemical study of women in the kibbutz, continue this argument by postulating that biologic reasons may ultimately be the determining causal factor in the allocation of gender-role patterns. It is our opinion that biology, although influential, is not deterministic, that is, although it would be negligent to ignore the influence of biology on human activities, we believe that the pervasive influence of the traditional patriarchal ideology combined with other social factors can best account for the reemergence of discriminatory gender-role differentiation patterns.

Further, it must be emphasized that the kibbutz movement is not an isolated social phenomenon. It occurs in a society that is predominantly a Western-oriented capitalistic system. A study by Dorit D. Padan-Eisenstark (1973) found that women have not achieved an appreciably higher degree of equality in Israeli society than their counterparts in other Western industrial societies. More specifically, the findings—based on a secondary analysis of surveys and studies conducted in Israel from 1930 through 1971—reveal that women's employment is concentrated in various service occupations. Almost three-quarters of the women held jobs in teaching and nursing occupations, clerical and service occupations, and the catering industries. Padan-Eisenstark points out that these occupations are those that have been traditionally linked to women and represent the professionalized form of the domestic household tasks. In addition, a large number of women held jobs that had flexible hours and were part-time. This allowed them to be less committed to employment and more involved with family and domestic tasks. Finally, Israeli women are underrepresented in all managerial and high-status professional occupations. Thus, the kibbutz pattern is a reflection of the larger societal pattern.

In conclusion, the kibbutzim are not isolated from the dominant Israeli society that continues to discriminate against women following patriarchal sexist guidelines. Nor are its members immune to this ideology. The kibbutz movement cannot be studied and treated as if it were a totally autonomous and independent entity.

In Wages, Sexes May Be Forever Unequal

BY PAUL LEWIS

THROUGHOUT the industrial world, women are catching up with men in education and earning power. But if some current trends continue, they may never achieve equality.

According to the Organization for Economic Cooperation and Development, women claim a much higher share of places in higher education than they did a decade ago. In the United States, Canada, Norway, Sweden and Denmark, the proportion of women at universities and other institutions of higher education is roughly in line with their proportion in the population, and in a few instances is higher. But many countries, including Japan, Luxembourg, Switzerland and Britain, are lagging in this regard.

The O.E.C.D. found that the gap between what men and women earn is narrowing but persists despite legislation in most of its 24 member nations requiring equal pay for equal work.

The findings are in two recent reports, one on education and the other on women's roles in the economy, that grew out of decade-long studies. Each country supplied its own data.

The statistics show women's earnings are closest to men's in Australia, the Scandinavian countries and the Netherlands; O.E.C.D. officials said the figures turned in by Italy and Portugal are not credible. The data from the United States, while not readily comparable to that provided by other countries, suggest that American women are singularly disadvantaged in their earnings.

The percentage of working-age men who are employed has been falling in most Western countries as a result of the prolonged decline of manufacturing. At the same time, the percentage of women in the labor force has risen. Despite women's gains in education, however, most of the new positions they fill are service jobs that require few skills and pay comparatively poorly.

Part of the explanation, according to the O.E.C.D., is that women are still underrepresented in the most prestigious schools, such as France's "grands écoles," and specialize in subjects least likely to lead to well-paid jobs. Women tend to concentrate in literature, languages, education and sociology, for example, while young men dominate science, engineering, business studies and law.

But the O.E.C.D. also found that in any given job category men are paid more than women. The report said women tended to be kept in less lucrative positions and to receive less overtime, for example.

"Serious inequalities between girls and boys and between men and women persist," the report said. "A serious gap remains between the official objectives and actual practice."

SOURCE. Paul Lewis. 1986. "In wages, sexes may be forever unequal." *The New York Times* (Dec. 21). Copyright 1986 by The New York Times Company. Reprinted by permission.

Although the kibbutz movement can be viewed as a noble experiment and although it has not achieved the long-sought goal of sexual equality, its failure in this area can be attributed to specific social factors rather than to unproved biologically determined theories of causality.

Conclusion

This chapter presents a broad range of topical areas regarding gender-role relationship patterns. We began the chapter with an examination of the arguments that seek to explain the almost universal female subordinate patterns that exist cross-culturally and historically. Two factors—one physiologically based, that is, women's reproductive role and their lesser physical strength; and the second ideologically based, that is, patriarchy—have served as the philosophical and moral justifications for discriminatory gender-role differentiation. These ideologies have held sway in Greco-Roman, Semitic, Indian, Chinese, Japanese, and Western Christian civilizations.

Next, investigation of different economic systems and the accompanying gender-role differentiation patterns was undertaken. We found that in shifting agricultural economies the prevalent pattern was egalitarian. On the other hand, in plow agricultural systems the patriarchal ideology held sway. As a result of imperialistic colonization, many shifting agricultural systems, most notably in Africa, were forcibly transformed to plow agricultural systems. In addition, the Western patriarchal ideology accompanied this transformation. The result was a decided loss of feminine status and power. Our concern was also how modernization processes have impacted on African women. We observed that often "modernization means more dependency." Our final topic in this section of the chapter was what living under apartheid in "white" South Africa means to black families. The debilitating, demoralizing, and exploitative system was analyzed.

The nature of the male–female division of labor in industrial societies was then investigated. To dramatize the continued impact of patriarchal sexist thought, we looked at societies that have adopted the goals of female liberation and of sexual equality as official policy. European Marxist countries and the Western societies of Sweden and Israel espouse the egalitarian ideology, but they have not achieved total equality. They still are plagued by vestiges of the discriminatory ideology of patriarchy. Although great strides have been taken by women in the occupational economy, they are overrepresented in service occupations and underrepresented in managerial and executive positions. Further, they are burdened by a dual role that expects that in addition to their full-time occupational involvements they must also be involved full-time with home tasks—domestic and child-care activities. Husbands and fathers, although equally involved in the occupational sphere, continue to be relatively noninvolved in the home sphere.

The examination of gender-role differentiation patterns occurring in these industrial societies provides Americans with an interesting comparative perspective. The pitfalls, problems, and experiences of these societies, more advanced than we are in sexual equality, can serve as important models in our own drive toward gender-role liberation. By profiting from the experiences of other countries, we may be able to develop alternative strategies in assuring sexual equality.

CHAPTER 12

Marital Relationships: The World of Work and the World of the Family

"Peasant Wedding Dance in the Open Air" (1624), by Pieter Breugel II.

CHAPTER OUTLINE

This chapter is a continuation of the previous one since many of the same underlying issues that were discussed there are also pertinent here. In the previous chapter, we emphasized different types of economic systems and how they are related to the male–female relationship. These underlying conditions, which have influenced the differentiation between the sexes, are notably manifest in the marital relationship. The economic-variable framework will allow further exploration and insight into the relationship between the sexes in marriage.

Our orientation in this discussion is on the activities of males and females in public and private spheres. The differentiation of these spheres of activities has been a factor dominating the expression of marital roles. They are important in determining power, privilege, respect, and deference patterns within the family. We begin our discussion by looking at this differentiation in preliterate societies, and then shift our attention to a social-historical examination of marriage in Western Europe and the United States since the Industrial Revolution.

Work and the Family in Nonindustrial Societies

William N. Stephens (1963), in his excellent cross-cultural survey of the family, examined three aspects of husband–wife roles: togetherness versus separateness, men's work versus women's work, and power and privilege. Stephens used existing ethnographic data and interviews with ethnographers on family deference customs and power relations. These data comprise the "ethnographer-interview" and total 53 cases. Stephens found that traditional barriers curtail the intimacy, sharing, and togetherness of husbands and wives. Many nonindustrial societies practiced avoidance customs in public: the ethnographers interviewed said that these societies did not allow husbands and wives to share affection in public. Only 11 societies allowed this. Further, in over half of the reported cases, husband and wife may not even touch each other in public (Stephens, 1963:275). These avoidance customs were carried over into the private sphere. In the home, traditional barriers ordained that the husband and wife sleep in separate beds, live in separate houses, own separate property, eat separately, and go separately to community gatherings.

Stephens also found that the sexes worked at separate tasks. As we have seen in previous chapters, this task differentiation was not based on biologic capabilities or limitations of the two sexes. Yet, the women's capacity for bearing and nursing children tends to influence the work allocations of men and women. Stephens uses George P. Murdock's (1937) cross-cultural survey of the division of labor by sex and his own ethnographer-interview data. He finds that men were assigned the following tasks: metalworking, stonecutting, lumbering, and killing or herding large animals. They were also given tasks that required geographic mobility: hunting, fishing, warring, and trading away from home. These tasks were allocated to men not so much because of their alleged superior physical strength or ability but because of their exemption from childbearing and child care. This was a chronic condition for women in precontraceptive eras. A wife's work was centered in the home and in nearby locations because she could tend to her babies at the same time she completed other tasks. These tasks were nearly always done by women: cooking, water carrying, and grain grinding as well as housekeeping and care of young children. Stephens also notes that in most preliterate societies women's work was not solely confined to the home; they also were involved in the subsistence work of getting, growing, and processing food. In hunting-and-gathering societies, women gather plant food while the men hunt. In agricultural societies, particularly those that practice shifting agriculture, women do a large share of the farm work.

The third aspect of husband–wife roles examined by Stephens was power and privilege. He found that power tends to be controlled by men.

> If there are social inequities between the sexes, women tend to be the "underprivileged minority group" in matters of marriage form (polygyny), sex restrictions, marital residence (moving far from home), and access to public gatherings and public office. (Stephens, 1963:305)

Stephens concludes that traditional rules having to do with power relationships tend to be made for men: deference patterns (the ritual expression of cultural expectations of an unequal power relationship) and real power (who dominates and who submits, who makes the family decisions, who commands, who obeys, and so forth, in the family) are in the majority of cases determined by men. Stephens examines some of the widespread transcultural discrimination against women. The following findings are based on his ethnographer-interview sample:

THE DOUBLE STANDARD

In a good many societies, sex restrictions are more severe for women than they are for men. For thirteen sample societies, premarital sex restrictions bear more heavily on girls than on boys. . . . For no society is it reported that premarital sex regulations are stricter for men than for women. Likewise, I know of no society in which restrictions on adultery are more severe for men than for women. On the other hand, in eight cases, husbands are free to practice adultery, but wives are supposed to remain faithful. . . . For two other cases, adultery rules seem to be stricter for wives than for husbands.

DEFERENCE

In six societies in my ethnographic notes, a wife must kneel or crouch before her husband. . . . In six societies, the woman is reported to walk behind her husband. . . . For five cases, the husband is said to get the choice food. . . . For no society in my ethnographic notes is there any mention of husband-to-wife deference customs.

POWER

In the language of politics, husbands and wives may be viewed as two separate and opposing interest groups. If a husband gains in power, his wife must lose power; if he gains in privilege, his wife loses privileges, and vice versa. Marriage—seen in these terms—is a power struggle. The husband may "win" (and become a dominating patriarch) or "lose" (and be a hen-pecked husband), or they may "tie" (and have an egalitarian marital relationship). One gets the impression that men usually have an initial advantage in this struggle. It looks as if men often make the rules to suit themselves; the deference customs, the jural rights, generally point in the direction of a power advantage for the husband. (Stephens, 1963:290, 294, 302)

Many investigators have asked why there is almost a universal classification of women to secondary status. Sherry Ortner (1974:69), an anthropologist, observes that "everywhere, in every known culture, women are considered in some degree, inferior to men.'' She provides some answers when she observes the types of criteria particular cultures use to assign women inferior roles. The first type of data are the statements of cultural ideology that explicitly devalue women, their roles, their tasks, and their products. Second, there are the symbolic devices, such as the attribution of defilement, associated with women. Last, there is the exclusion of women from participation in or contact with areas believed to be most powerful in the particular society, whether religious or secular. We concentrate our discussion on the third element in this analysis.

A recent explanation on the universality of women being allotted secondary status is offered by sociologists and anthropologists who see this stemming from the relegation of women to the domestic, private domain of the household, whereas men remain in the public sphere of activities. The greater involvement of women with childbearing and child rearing leads to a differentiation of domestic and public spheres of activity. Michelle Zimbalist Rosaldo (1974:36)—in her introductory essay to the excellent anthology of cross-cultural writings on women, *Woman, Culture, and Society*—argues that ''women's status will be lowest in those societies where there is a firm differentiation between domestic and public spheres of activity and where women are isolated from one another and placed under a single man's authority in the home.'' Rosaldo believes that the time-consuming and emotionally compelling involvement of a mother with her child is unmatched by any single involvement and commitment made by a man. The result is that men are free to form broader associations in the outside world through their involvement in work, politics, and religion. The relative absence of women from this public sphere results in their lack of authority and power. Men's involvements and activities are viewed as important, and cultural systems give authority and value to men's activities and roles. In turn, women's work, especially when it is confined to domestic roles and activities, tends to be oppressive and lacking in value and status. Women are only seen to gain power and a sense of value when they are able to transcend the domestic sphere of activities. Societies that practice sex discrimination are those in which this differentiation is

© Marj Van der Puy

An Auca Indian family at their settlement in Ecuador. The young man is making darts for use in hunting jungle animals to feed his wife and son.

TABLE 12.1   Comparative Data on the Division of Labor by Sex

	Number of Societies in Which Activity is Performed by				
	Men Always	Men Usually	Either Equally	Women Usually	Women Always
Metalworking	78	0	0	0	0
Weapon making	121	1	0	0	0
Pursuit of sea mammals	34	1	0	0	0
Hunting	166	13	0	0	0
Manufacture of musical instruments	45	2	0	0	1
Boat building	91	4	4	0	1
Mining and quarrying	35	1	1	0	1
Work in wood and bark	113	9	5	1	1
Work in stone	68	3	2	0	2
Trapping or catching of small animals	128	13	4	1	2
Work in bone, horn, and shell	67	4	3	0	3
Lumbering	104	4	3	1	6
Fishing	98	34	19	3	4
Manufacture of ceremonial objects	37	1	13	0	1
Herding	38	8	4	0	5
House building	86	32	25	3	14
Clearing of land for agriculture	73	22	17	5	13
Net making	44	6	4	2	11
Trade	51	28	20	8	7
Dairy operations	17	4	3	1	13
Manufacture of ornaments	24	3	40	6	18
Agriculture—soil preparation and planting	31	23	33	20	37
Manufacture of leather products	29	3	9	3	32
Body mutilation—for example, tattooing	16	14	44	22	20
Erection and dismantling of shelter	14	2	5	6	22
Hide preparation	31	2	4	4	49
Tending of fowls and small animals	21	4	8	1	39
Agriculture—crop tending and harvesting	10	15	35	39	44
Gathering of shellfish	9	4	8	7	25
Manufacture of nontextile fabrics	14	0	9	2	32
Fire making and tending	18	6	25	22	62
Burden bearing	12	6	33	20	57
Preparation of drinks and narcotics	20	1	13	8	57
Manufacture of thread and cordage	23	2	11	10	73
Basket making	25	3	10	6	82
Mat making	16	2	6	4	61
Weaving	19	2	2	6	67
Gathering of fruits, berries, and nuts	12	3	15	13	63
Fuel gathering	22	1	10	19	89
Pottery making	13	2	6	8	77
Preservation of meat and fish	8	2	10	14	74
Manufacture and repair of clothing	12	3	8	9	95
Gathering of herbs, roots, and seeds	8	1	11	7	74
Cooking	5	1	9	28	158
Water carrying	7	0	5	7	119
Grain grinding	2	4	5	13	114

SOURCE: Adapted from George P. Murdock, 1937. "Comparative data on the division of labor by sex," Reprinted from *Social Forces*, vol. XV, May 1937 p. 552. Copyright The University of North Carolina Press. Reprinted by permission.

most acute. Those societies in which men value and participate in domestic activities tend to be more egalitarian.

Rosaldo points out that in contemporary America—although giving perfunctory lip service to the idea of sexual equality—society, nonetheless, is organized in such a way that it heightens the dichotomy between private and public, domestic and social, female and male. Further, through the restrictions of the conjugal family, women tend to be relegated to the domestic sphere. Yet, when the society places values on men's work and women's work, the tendency is to place greater value and higher priority on the public work associated with men rather than the domestic work associated with women. This is symbolized by the phrase, "only a housewife." This dichotomization is encouraged by the admonitions placed on women to cease work and take almost exclusive care of small children and to sacrifice their career aspirations to those of their husbands. These normative strictures perpetuate the assignment of women to the domestic, private sphere, whereas men are almost exclusively involved in the higher valued and higher status activities of the public sphere.

The question then arises as to why this particular state of affairs exists and what the factors are that account for its prevalence. We believe that it would be useful to trace this development in Western civilization back to the beginning of industrialization.

The Public World of the Preindustrial Western Family

When we switch our attention to the impact of industrialization on the family, we find a heightened dichotomization between private, noneconomically productive domestic work and the public world of finance, industry, commerce, and wage-earning work. It would be instructive to contrast the preindustrial world of Western Europe at the advent of industrialization with our contemporary era.

Philippe Ariès, a French social historian, has written a seminal work on the analysis of the historical evolution of the Western family. Ariès' *Centuries of Childhood: A Social History of Family Life* (1962) traces the developments in the conceptualization of the family from the Middle Ages to the present. His data sources include paintings and diaries, the history of games and pastimes, and the development of schools and their curricula. Ariès' basic thesis is that the contemporary conceptualization of family life and the modern image of the nature of children are recent phenomena. He argues that the concept of the family did not emerge until the seventeenth century. He does not deny the existence of the family prior to that time but makes a critical distinction between the family as a *reality* and the *idea* of the family, which is sensitive to change. Ariès states that the physical existence of the family is not in question: Fathers and mothers and children exist in all societies. But the point is that the ideas entertained about family relations can be radically dissimilar over lengthy periods of time.

> . . . it would be vain to deny the existence of a family life in the Middle Ages. But the family existed in silence: it did not awaken feelings strong enough to inspire poet or artist. We must recognize the importance of this silence: not much value was placed on the family. (Ariès, 1962:364)

The low valuation placed on the family in preindustrial Europe occurred because of the individual's almost total involvement with the community. People lived in their communities; they worked, played, and prayed in them. The communities monopolized all their time and their minds. They had very little time for their families. The gathering point for the community was the "big house," which contained up to 25 people, including families, children, and servants. They fulfilled a public function by serving as places for business and sociability. Here friends, clients, and relatives met and talked. The rooms of the house were multifunctional: they were used for domestic activities as well as for professional purposes. People ate, slept, danced, worked, and received visitors in them.

> They ate in them, but not at special tables: the "dining table" did not exist, and at mealtimes people set up folding trestle-tables, covering them with a cloth. . . . It is easy to imagine the promiscuity which reigned in these rooms where nobody could be alone, which one had to cross to reach any of the communicating rooms, where several couples and several groups of boys or girls slept together (not to speak of the servants, of whom at least some must have slept beside their masters, setting up beds which were still collapsible in the room or just outside the door), in which people foregathered to have their meals, to receive their friends or clients, and sometimes to give alms to beggers. (Ariès, 1963:394–395)

The general situation was one in which most activities were public and one where people were never left alone. The density of social life made isolation virtually impossible. Families were part and parcel of the society and were intertwined with relatives, friends, clients, protégés, debtors, and so on. Ariès argues that the lack of privacy attributed to this overwhelming community sociability hindered the formation of the concept of the family. The concept of the family developed as other specialized institutions relieved the home of its multifaceted functions. The growth of the tavern, cafés, and clubs provided alternative outlets for sociability. The establishment of geographically distinct business and occupational places freed the family from its business functions. The strengthening of the family was to be seen in the increased privacy for family life and a growing intimacy among family members. Gradually, the family cut itself off from the outside world and a separate and distinct family life emerged. As we see, this isolation has had critical implications for women and children.

Edward Shorter—in a provocative book, *The Making of the Modern Family* (1975)—continues the general theme of Philippe Ariès. He sees the family tied integrally with the community. Shorter states that ordinary families in western and central Europe from 1500 to the end of the eighteenth century were "held firmly in the matrix of the larger social order" (Shorter, 1975:3). The family was secured to the community by two ties: one was the intricate web of extended kin, including uncles, aunts, and cousins; the other was to the wider community. The family had no sense of privacy or separation from the community. The marital roles were not viewed as independently important. Marriage was frequently arranged on the basis of advancing the extended family's economic interests.

Shorter's central argument is that the history of the family can be seen in the shift in the relationship between the nuclear family and the surrounding community. During the preindustrial period, the physical matrix discouraged privacy and intimacy within which the traditional family found itself. However, unlike Ariès—who presents a rather rosy, idealized depiction of preindustrial life, where all peoples of different ages, sexes, and classes intermingled in a Bruegelesque scene—Shorter stresses the negative characteristics of marital and family life. Shorter argues that family life was characterized by emotional coldness between husband and wife and an emotional isolation through a strict division of work assignments and gender roles. The emotional detachment of the marital pair and their demarcation of tasks are seen to be revealed in the following French regional proverbs:

> —"Mort de femme et view de cheval font l'homme riche." (Brittany) (Rich is the man whose wife is dead and horse alive.)
> —"Deuil de femme morte dure jusqu'a à la porte." (Gascony) (Your late wife you so deplore until you enter your front door.)
> —"L'homme a deux beaux jours sur terre: lorsqu'il prend femme et lorsqu'il l'enterre." (Anjou) (The two sweetest days of a fellow in life are the marriage and burial of his wife.)

—"Les femmes a la maison, comme les chiens, les hommes a la rue, comme les chants." (Gascony) (Women belong at home, like the dogs; men belong in the streets, like the cats.)

—"Femme fenestriere et courriere n'est en rien bonne menagere." (Gascony) (If you hang out the window or run around, you'll have the sorriest home in town.)

—"Jamais femme ni cochon ne doivent quitter las maison." (Dauphine) (Never let go out the doors either the women or the boars.) (Shorter, 1975:58, 73. Copyright © 1975 by Basic Books)

Unlike other social historians—who stress the importance of women in domestic industry in preindustrial England—Shorter sees the life of women in preindustrial continental Europe as being relatively removed from economic enterprises and confined to having children and doing household tasks. The significance of this is spelled out in the considerable inequality between working men and domestically confined women. This finding is a notable contrast to the status and treatment of working women in England.

Shorter finds women having considerable power within the household but "women's control over certain domestic spheres, which were isolated from the economy as a whole, did not free them from subordinate social rules" (Shorter, 1975:66–67). Women's roles were subservient and they were expected to be inferior. Three specifically feminine roles are delineated: passivity of women in external relations and with men in general, self-abnegation and personal sacrifice for the family, and finally "women's work was found in sex and reproduction: sleeping with husbands on demand and producing babies to the limits set by community norms" (Shorter, 1975:75).

Both Ariès and Shorter, then, observe that the preindustrial family was one which was characterized by a lack of privacy and intimacy. However, Ariès emphasizes the positive qualities of preindustrial community life, which compensated for the lack of marital "togetherness." Shorter, on the other hand, decries the lack of emotional involvement as being detrimental to the individual well-being of men and women; he does not regard community involvement positively. For our purposes, a more-rounded picture of the nature of husband-and-wife relationships can be seen when we examine the couple's lives in terms of their involvement in work and in the home and the impact of their marital relationship on the power and status of women.

In the preindustrial period, the family was the unit of production. There was relatively little role differentiation among men, women, or children working together in the home and in the fields. Life was characterized by an interweaving of the husband's and wife's involvement with domestic life and with a productive work life. Women were involved in both the care of the home and the children as well as being participants in the family's basic economic productive system. Family industry was common. The food or goods produced did not yield much more than a bare subsistence. The family was the unit of production, with its members tied together in economic partnership. With the husband working in the home as well as the wife and children, there existed an integration of the public and private spheres of activities.

Alice Clark, in 1919, wrote an important work entitled *The Working Life of Women in the Seventeenth Century*. She examined women's work in agriculture, textiles, and the woolen trade in England during this period. All these activities were performed under a system of family industry. All goods and services produced by the family were intended for either family consumption or for sale or trade. Work, then, was not distinguished between that for domestic consumption or that for sale or trade. Cotton production illustrates this. The home was set up like a miniature factory; the entire process of cotton production from raw material to finished cloth was contained within the home. Men and women worked side by side. Both were actively involved in all aspects of the work. Clark summarizes her observations on the role of women in the preindustrial economy in the following manner:

> Under modern conditions, the ordinary domestic occupations of English women consist in tending babies and young children . . . in preparing household meals, and in keeping the house clean. . . . In the seventeenth centry [the domestic role] embraced a much wider range of production; for brewing, dairy work, the care of poultry and pigs, the production of vegetables and fruit, spinning flax and wool, nursing and doctoring, all formed part of domestic industry. (Clark cited in Oakley, 1974:15)

Ann Oakley (1974), who has written a valuable work of the social history of the housewife, observes that women at the time of marriage were expected to be economically productive, whether in agriculture or in the handicraft trades. The notion of women's economic dependence was foreign to the family system. Men were not viewed as the economic supporters of women. To demonstrate, Oakley (1974:22) examined the list of the occupations of married couples taken from the Sessions Papers of the Old Bailey. These were couples who were either witnesses, prosecutors, or prisoners of the court. She found that only 1 out of 86 married women did not have an occupation of her own. The remaining 85 women's occupations ranged from plumber to poultry dealer to seller of old clothes.

Traditionally, the husband was seen as the head of the household. He presided over the division of labor in various work and domestic tasks. Michael Young and Peter Willmott (1973) argue that the doctrine of St. Paul — "Wives submit yourself unto your own husbands, as it is fit in the Lord" — was still the canon in the seventeenth century. The husband's power was tempered by the importance of the wife's economic contribution and also that of the children. Thus, although most wives were in fact beaten (some beaten severely), it was not to the husband's economic advantage to antagonize his wife too much. "Her economic value was her saving, especially if she not only worked herself but also produced for her employer other workers, so putting him in the state recognized in the words of the psalm — 'Happy is the man who hath his quiver full of children' " (Young and Willmott, 1973:67).

In summary, traditional life in preindustrial Europe can be seen as being characterized by a much greater involvement of the family with the surrounding community. The relationship between husband and wife was not as intimate or private as it is in today's contemporary industrial societies. In addition, the status and treatment of women can be seen to vary with their involvement in economically productive work. When a woman contributed, she had more power and control over her own life. When she did not, her life was that of a domestically confined slave; servile and subservient to her master — her husband.

From Public to Private: The Early Industrial Western Family

The Industrial Revolution shattered the domestic economy centered in the household. Looking at mid-eighteenth-century England, we are best able to observe its impact. England was primarily rural with men and women largely engaged in some form of domestic industry. This activity occurred within the home. In the cities, women as well as men were involved in some form of trade, frequently serving as partners in joint work activities. The agrarian revolution at the end of the eighteenth century saw the lessening of the necessity for productive work at home. Industrial development deprived them of their involvement in the older domestic industries and trades:

> If you go into a loom-shop, where there's three or four pairs of looms,
> They are all standing empty, encumbrances of the rooms;
> And if you ask the reason why, the older mother will tell you plain
> My daughters have forsaken them, and gone to weave by steam. (J. Harland,
> *Ballads and Songs of Lancashire,* 1865. Cited in Thompson, 1963:308)

Family members were absorbed into the new economy as wage earners. This led to the differentiation between work and the home. E.P. Thompson, the English historian, in his *The Making of the English Working Class* (1963) comprehensively examines the changes occurring in people's ways of life between 1780 and 1832. In the following passage, he contrasts the differences between two economies:

> Women became more dependent upon the employer or the labour market, and they looked back to a "golden" period in which home earnings from spinning, poultry and the like could be gained around their own door. In good times the domestic economy supported a way of life centred upon the home, in which inner whims and compulsions were more obvious than external discipline. Each stage in industrial differentiation and specialisation struck also at the family economy, disturbing customary relations between man and wife, parents and children, and differentiating more sharply between "work" and "life." It was to be a full hundred years before this differentiation was to bring returns, in the form of labour-saving devices, back into the working woman's home. Meanwhile, the family was roughly torn apart each morning by the factory bell. (Thompson, 1963:416)

During this period, the family lost its productive function to industry. Work was now separated from the family. The differentiation of the family from the economy necessitated by the new industrial economy was accompanied by the differentiation of roles within the family. For men, it meant involvement in the outside world and in the expanding occupational marketplace; for women, it increasingly meant confinement within the home. "The woman became the nonemployed, economically dependent housewife, and the man became the sole wage or salary earner, supporting by his labour his wife—the housewife—and her children" (Oakley, 1974:34).

At the outset, women gained by the transference of economic production from the home to the workplace. It was instrumental in improving domestic conditions. The grime, filth, and industrial wastages associated with industrial production were now being removed from the home. Ivy Pinchbeck (1930), another English historian, observed that with the home no longer a workshop, women for the first time in the history of the industrial age were now able to turn their attention to homemaking and the care of children.

Shorter (1975) also is impressed by the positive consequences of industrialization. Shorter believes that the family underwent some major changes with the advent of market capitalism. By market capitalism, Shorter is referring to the development of the modern marketplace economy with the linking of local markets with regional and national ones. The effect was that local tradesmen, artisans, craftsmen, and small shop owners developed a less parochial orientation. For the family, this translates into a more-cosmopolitan attitude with a lessening of importance given to local lineage concerns. Further, market capitalism contributed to the growth of the philosophy of individualism and freedom. The wish to be free emerges in gender-role relationships as romantic love and conjugal marriage.

Shorter is concerned with the changes in the relations between husbands and wives and parents and children since 1750. He believes that there was a great onrush of emotions and sentiment in family life and he examines changes in three areas: courtship, the mother–child relationship, and the relationship of the family with the community.

In courtship, he notes the emergence of sentiments of affection and friendship and the romantic love ideology. The result was that marriage became more and more a matter of free choice rather than an arranged concern determined by the parents on the basis of economic and social considerations.

The second area, mother–child relationships, is depicted as of secondary importance to the needs of domestic work and activities in the traditional preindustrial era. Shorter presents a shocking picture of mothers' neglect and disinterest in their children. The result is an all too frequent occurrence of unattended children burning to death or being eaten by the pigs or succumbing to the indifference of wet nurses. The absence of bereavement at the death of the infant or child supports Shorter's belief that mother–child relationships were unimportant. Although his description of events is parallel, in some respects, to Ariès' social history of childhood, it is embroidered with horrific analysis and commentary.

Shorter downplays the importance of economic factors. He de-emphasizes both the fact that "ordinary" families were living under bare subsistence conditions as well as the lack of medical sophistication needed to combat the epidemic diseases rampant throughout Europe. Instead, he stresses the prevalence of an ideology of maternal neglect and indifference.

> The high rate of infant loss is not a sufficient explanation for the traditional lack of maternal love *because precisely this lack of care was responsible for the high mortality.* . . . It came about as a result of circumstances over which the parents had considerable influence: infant diet, age at weaning, cleanliness of bed linen, and the general hygienic circumstances that surrounded the child—to say nothing of less tangible factors in mothering, such as picking up the infant, talking and singing to it, giving it the feeling of being loved in a secure little universe. . . . The point is that these mothers did not *care,* and that is why their children vanished in the ghastly slaughter of the innocents that was traditional child-rearing. (Shorter, 1975:203, 204)

Shorter believes that attitudes toward children began to change in the nineteenth century. New sentiments of affection and love emerged and neglect and indifference became less common. The result was an increase in the growth of maternal care, defined in terms of maternal breast-feeding and the development of a more loving attitude toward children by their mothers.

The relationship of the family to the community is seen to have undergone dramatic changes with these shifting sentiments. The family became more of an emotional unit rather than a mainly productive and reproductive one. The affectional and caring sentiments tied the husband–wife relationship tighter. It began to replace lineage, property, and economic considerations as the foundation of the marriage. Simultaneously, there was a lessening of the couple's involvement with the community. Peer-group pressures lessened and with it the ending of community controls on the young couple. The emphasis was on a value system that exalted personal happiness and self-development as opposed to a value system that emphasized generational allegiances and responsibility to the community.

These new sentiments manifested themselves in the rise of the companionate family and domesticity. The companionate family is one in which the husband and wife become friends rather than superordinate and subordinate, and equally share tasks and affection. Domesticity, which Shorter (1975:227) defines as "the family's awareness of itself as a precious emotional unit that must be protected with privacy and isolation from outside intrusion," is a central feature of the companionate family. Domesticity serves to sever the involvement of the family from the surrounding community. Thus, two processes are at work: the first is the couple's almost complete withdrawal from the community; the second is the corresponding strength of the ties of the couple with each other and with their children and close relatives.

Shorter has been criticized on both methodological and theoretical grounds. Reviewers, notably Richard T. Vann (1976), have criticized the inadequacies and inconsistencies of Shorter's analysis of admittedly impressionistic data culled from contemporary accounts by physicians, priests, local magistrates, and family members. For our purposes the criticisms of Shorter on theoretical grounds (Gordon, 1977; Plumb, 1975; Vann, 1976) are more relevant. These critics question the theoretical conclusion on the relationship among sentiment, the family, and industrialization. A basic viewpoint is that Shorter overemphasizes the importance of the "sentimental revolution." He tends to overlook the enormous impact the loss of women's economic involvement and their confinement to the home have for their power and status. Let us look at another perspective on the relationship between early industrialization and the family. This orientation differs from Shorter's in two ways. It stresses the negative consequences of both the Industrial Revolution and the Victorian patriarchal ideology, which sought to fight the evils of industrial labor practices with a highly protective philosophy that secluded and confined women and children to the household.

We have discussed the fact that the family ceased to be a productive unit in society. The world of work was separated from the family household, and there was an increased differentiation of roles between husband and wife. These changes had dramatic effects on the family. The separation of workplace and home meant that husbands and wives were also physically separated during working hours, which were quite long. Husbands' work became isolated from family contact. The wife no longer knew what the husband was doing or how much he was earning. The lack of occupational visibility also meant that children could not be socialized into their father's profession by their father. People no longer worked as a family; now men were employed as individuals for a wage. If the wages were good the husband could support his family; unfortunately, too often, they were low and inadequate to provide for the family.

Young and Willmott (1973) observe that this new economic system had disastrous consequences for the family. They cite nineteenth-century sources in England to argue their case. They note that the husband as the prime breadwinner controlled the economic resources of the family. All too frequently this was much to the family's detriment. There was an extraordinarily high consumption rate of spending on such items as betting, tobacco, and liquor. The quantity and quality of food purchased for the home was also disproportionately distributed, the husband getting the most and the choicest. Physical abuse of the wife and children, which was held in check by their economic contribution in the preindustrial family-oriented economy, now occurred with greater frequency and duration. The husband's actions become more understandable if one takes into consideration the relatively low wages that these men were paid. Employees were not paid according to the number of dependents that they had. The inadequate income of these men combined with the low status and power of women and children led to the last two being a convenient scapegoat for the former.

The subjugation and subordination of women during the nineteenth century were a central concern of the great English humanists of the Victorian era: Henry Mayhew, John Stuart Mill, and Friedrich Engels. Mayhew, in his investigations of the poor in London, reported on the great prevalence of wife beatings in his classic work, *London Labour and the London Poor:*

> They can understand that it is the duty of the woman to contribute to the happiness of the man, but cannot feel that there is a reciprocal duty from the man to the woman. The wife is considered as an inexpensive servant and the disobedience of a wish is punished with blows. She must work early and late, and to the husband must be given the proceeds of her labour. Often when the man is in one of his drunken fits — which sometimes last two or three days continuously — she must by her sole exertion find food for herself and him too. To live in peace with him there must be no murmuring, no tiring under work, no fancied cause for jealousy — for if there be, she is either beaten into submission or cast adrift to begin life again — as another's leavings. (Mayhew cited in Young and Willmott, 1973:76)

John Stuart Mill (1869/1966), in his essay "The Subjection of Women," attacks the condition of legal bondage and debilitating education, and the oppressive ethic of "wifely subjection." Mill views the home as the center of a system of domestic slavery, the wife a bondservant within marriage. He observes that under Victorian law women have less rights than slaves. Women and children are owned absolutely by the husband-father. Unlike slaves, who were sometimes spared coercion into sexual intimacy, wives could not be entitled to any household items and, if the husband so desired, could be compelled by the courts to return to him. There was little legal opportunity for women's freedom through divorce. Mill also observed the prevalence of physical brutality in marriage, it being the logical conclusion of women's subjection.

> And how many thousands are there among the lowest classes in every country, who without being in a legal sense malefactors in every other respect, because in every other quarter their aggressions meet with resistance, indulge the utmost habitual excesses of bodily violence toward the unhappy wife, who alone, at least of grown persons, can neither repel nor escape from their brutality; and toward whom the excess of dependence inspires their mean and savage natures, not with generous forbearance and a point of honor to behave well to one whose lot in life is trusted entirely to their kindness, but on the contrary with a notion that the law has delivered her to them as their thing, to be used at their pleasure, and that they are not expected to practice the consideration towards her which is required from them towards everybody else. (Mill, 1966:467–468)

Mill advocated legal change—suffrage and a just property law—to alleviate the debilitating conditions of women. He also saw the need for women to enter the labor market and the professions and urged the right of women to work.

Friedrich Engels, as you recall, took a more-radical approach. He argued that the monogamous family system was created by the industrial capitalist economy to enslave women and use them as a cheap source of domestic labor. He felt that the attainment of legal equality for women was not enough unless it was also accompanied with total social and economic equality. Further, it was necessary to broaden the opportunities of women to assure personal fulfillment in productive work. The dependent status of women was seen as antithetical to equality. And equality can only be assured with the end of masculine dominance over economic production and the entrance of women into the economic world on a parallel level.

Contributing to the lowly position of women during the Victorian industrial period was the development of an ideology whose explicit goal was to assure the safety and well-being of women but that implicitly added to her political and social demise—the ideology of domestic confinement. A central tenet of this philosophy was the belief in women's natural domesticity. This belief prevented and restricted the employment of women outside the home. It advocated the economic dependence of married women on their husbands and their sole involvement with household tasks and child care. This ideology was in direct contrast to the practices of the preindustrial era when women were a part of domestic industry. It can be seen as the Victorian answer to the harshness and severity of early industrial labor practices.

Numerous laws were passed that restricted or prevented female and child labor in mining, factories, and the textile industries. This protective legislation led to the creation of the modern housewife role that has become the prime source of feminine subservience. It is ironic that this legislation passed by "chivalrous" Victorian gentlemen to alter the brutality of industrial work had as its ultimate effect the substitution of a different form of subjugation.

Ann Oakley (1974) investigated contemporary Victorian documents to find the rationale for the confinement of women to the household and their restriction or prevention from seeking outside employment. Four main reasons are delineated: "female employment was condemned on moral grounds, on grounds of damage to physical health, on grounds of neglect of home and family, and lastly, simply on the grounds that it contravened the 'natural' division of labour between the sexes" (Oakley, 1974:45).

Oakley reports that from 1841 to 1914, housewifery increasingly became the sole occupation of women. She cites figures from England to show that 1 of 4 married women were working in 1851, compared to only 1 in 10 by 1911. The ideology of women's confinement to the home originated in the middle and upper classes. A woman's idleness was seen as a mark of prosperity. The leisured lady at home was the ideal. The development and elaboration of society and rules of etiquette became the epitome of the later Victorian era. For the working classes, the doctrine of female domesticity began to crystallize in the last quarter of the nineteenth century. It ran counter to the economic needs of the family, yet became prevalent. For the working classes, too, "the idea that work outside the home for married women was a 'misfortune and a disgrace' became acceptable" (Oakley, 1974:50). A closer look at Victorian society and its accompanying etiquette rules can be enlightening, for it was these rules established by the emerging bourgeois upper class that proved to be influential in affecting gender-role relationships not only for that class but also for the entire society.

Sexual Politics in Victorian Etiquette[1]

In an insightful monograph, Leonore Davidoff (1975) examined the significance of manuals of etiquette within the larger context of Victorian England "society." Davidoff observed that during the nineteenth century, England saw a radical transformation of its ruling classes. As newly rich families began to gain eminence, these families—through individual achievement in industry and commerce—were supplanting the traditional rich whose positions were based on heredity and family connections. To govern the social mobility of these new personnel, an elaborate formalized society developed. The rules of etiquette set down in housekeeping books, etiquette manuals, and advice columns in magazines were most relevant for highly structured social gatherings. Presentations at court, country and city house parties, and the round of afternoon calls regulated the behavior of all participants.

The rules of "society" were created to control entrance and involvement within social classes. This was viewed as necessary since Victorian "society" was undergoing unprecedented social change; rigid rules of social acceptance provided a haven of stability. The elaborate code of etiquette created barriers to social entry. Ceremonial behavior can be seen as rites of passage, especially during certain important events as births, marriages, and deaths. The introduction of new individuals and families into group membership and activities was also a sensitive area and it, too, was marked by etiquette rules. Introductions, visits, and dining patterns became formalized and vastly elaborate.

The home became increasingly an important area for social gatherings. It served to control and regulate the contacts that the "ins" wished to have with their equals and the new people seeking entrance into their group. The private clubs served a similar function. The "society" can be seen as controlling access to and involvement with those of the upper classes. For the newcomer it necessitated the abandonment of old allegiances, family and nonfamily, for this new prestigious social group (Davidoff, 1975:27).

The role of women was paradoxical. Influenced by the male-dominant patriarchal

---

[1] The following discussion is based on Pearl W. Bartelt and Mark Hutter, "Symbolic interaction perspective on the sexual politics of etiquette books." Paper presented at the meeting of the American Sociological Association, Chicago, September 1977.

Historical Pictures Service, Chicago

Strict Victorian rules of etiquette in England controlled interaction between the sexes in public places.

ideology, Victorian "society" was elaborated by its women. Women were exhorted to act as guardians of the home; men were exhorted to leave the home for the struggles of the business world, the army, the church, or politics. Women's duties were to regulate and control social gatherings and thus keep order in the ever-changing social scene. However, their sequestration in the home, and the confinement of their activities to domestic and "society" matters, occurred at the same time that men were expanding their influence and involvement in the new industrial world. This, ultimately, proved disastrous for women's independence and autonomy.

Socialization practices reinforced this dichotomy. Men were being socialized to operate in the ever-changing and complex world of industry, finance, and commerce. Women were socialized into the complexities of etiquette and the running of the home with its hierarchy of servants. Dress was a sign of social position and achievement. It serves as a good illustration of the extent to which etiquette rules were elaborated:

> Every cap, bow, streamer, ruffle, fringe, bustle, glove and other elaboration symbolised some status category for the female wearer; mourning dress being the quintessence of this demarcation. A footman, with long experience in upper-class households, said "jewelry was a badge that women wore like a sergeant major's stripes or field-marshall's baton; it showed achievement, rank, position." It is not

surprising, then, that girls and women of all classes were preoccupied with dress. (Davidoff, 1975:95)

The rules governing sexual behavior for women were also paradoxical. The emphasis was on respectability through control of sexual behavior and desire. Victorian women gained status by denying their own sexuality and treating the Victorian masculine sex drive as sinful. Purity beliefs and the elaborate etiquette norms—which stressed modesty, prudishness, and cleanliness—as well as the rules governing demeanor and appearance served to provide a sense of order, stability, and status in the everyday world. However, they also served to be psychologically stultifying. Further, the placing of women on a virginal pedestal, limiting their involvement to the home, and excluding them from the economic sphere served to reinforce the patriarchal ideology. Through idolatry, subservience emerged.

Gender Roles in the Industrial Western Family

Industrialization and a patriarchal ideology led to the development of a conjugal-family system with a clear delineation of roles between husband and wife. The breakdown of larger community involvements was supposed to be compensated for by an increased intimacy and emotionality between family members. Unfortunately, many husbands, burdened by inadequate wages to support their families and finding themselves isolated from domestic everyday activities, did not provide the necessary emotional as well as economic supports for their wives and children. An all-too-frequent occurrence was family neglect and physical abuse. Thus, the breakdown of community involvement with the family and the disintegration of the traditional extended family, which characterized preindustrial rural life and domestic industry, led to an intolerable situation for women and children. They were dependent both economically and emotionally on the whims of detached, autocratic, and often despotic husbands.

Young and Willmott (1973), in their astute history of the family in England, developed the thesis that women—after acclimating themselves to industrial-based city life—eventually developed a family organization based on mother–daughter maternal bonds. They did this to protect themselves and their children from the unreliability and indifference of their husbands. With the husband absent from the household and working elsewhere, daughters developed strong ties with their mothers. They lived near them and mothers served as an oasis of security for both married daughters and grandchildren. In addition, mothers could provide day-care services if their daughters got jobs, and they were also able to pass on gifts and money during periods of need.

We have discussed this family system earlier in our analysis of working-class communities and families in England and the United States. Young and Willmott base their thesis on the working-class community of Bethnel Green in London.[2] As you may recall, these communities were labeled closed communities by John Mogey (1964) and urban villages by Herbert Gans (1962a). These communities were depicted as ones in which intense interfamilial cooperation exists. They also are cohesive and homogeneous in cultural values, and are closed to nonmembers. In our discussion of working-class family life in Bethnel Green, we saw that husbands and wives performed a separate set of household tasks. In times of emergency, aid for

---

[2] In addition to Young and Willmott's *Family and Kinship in East London* (1957), the following monographs are pertinent: Willmott and Young's *Family and Class in a London Suburb* (1960), Peter Townsend's *The Family Life of Old People* (1957), and Peter Marris' *Widows and Their Families* (1958).

either the husband or wife is provided by other husbands and wives in the area. Frequently, these are same-sex relatives. Under these conditions, a strict role segregation of tasks is maintained. Leisure-time activities are similarly segregated. Within segregated role-pattern families, mother–daughter relations tend to be stronger than father–son relations. This is particularly the case when the married couple takes up residence in close proximity to the wife's mother. Intimate, emotional, and isolated conjugal families did not live in these communities.

When we examine these internal family structures in more detail, we find the opposite of the conjugal-family form. Elizabeth Bott (1957), in an interesting typology, focuses on the husbands' and wives' involvement with social networks comprised of kin, friends, and neighbors in the community as well as their relationship and involvement with each other. Bott found that if neither family members maintained ties with a network of friends, neighbors, and relatives who knew one another and interacted, husband–wife ties would be minimal. Husbands and wives who are members of such close-knit networks when they marry and continue to maintain such relationships during their marriage have a marital-role organization based on a clear differentiation of tasks with few shared interests or activities. If either needs assistance, whether economic or emotional, he or she does not ask the spouse but rather seeks help from network members. The result is that the husband–wife relationship is not close. The couple live in relatively separate worlds with different involvements and activities.

The picture presented is quite different from that drawn by Edward Shorter (1975) of families emotionally and intimately involved with each other. It is a family that has weak marital ties and strong lineage ties. It is an industrial-age version of the community dominating the family pattern, which was characteristic of preindustrial society. This developed out of the felt need of economically and emotionally dependent women and their children to assure some stability and continuity in their lives. Young and Willmott (1973) observe that this family system becomes self-perpetuating. Once the female-centered system developed, it served to exclude men from the intimacies of domestic family life and force them to seek other ways to satisfy their needs:

> This sort of structure—weak on the family of marriage, strong on the family of origin—tended to perpetuate itself. Husbands were often squeezed out of the warmth of the female circle, and took to the pub as their defence against the defence. They had to put up with mothers-in-law who were constantly interfering, as the man might see it, with the arrangements in his own home. His wife could seem more her daughter than his wife, and both of them belonged to a group which did not award men a high place in its order of values. He could find himself undermined, in a hundred ways, subtle and unsubtle. He could be pushed into becoming an absentee father, so bringing on the insecurity which the extended family in this form was established to counter. (Young and Willmott, 1973:92)

In this section, we have seen that the Industrial Revolution had important and long-lasting effects on the family. It meant the separation of men and women into two isolated worlds—the world of work and the world of the household. This had the effect of setting apart the life of the husbands from the intimacies of everyday domestic activities and estranging them from their wives and children. Women found themselves outside of the work force and involved solely in housework and child care. Economic factors coincided with a misguided Victorian patriarchialism that saw economic employment as a threat to womanly virtue and bad for her from both a physical and emotional standpoint. Not, incidentally, that a woman working for wages was seen as an indication of her husband's failure to earn sufficiently to support her and the family. The increased sentiments, emotions, and intimacies of the newly emerged conjugal family did not compensate for women's economic dependence on their husbands and their resultant decline in social status. Particularly, this became a problem as it occurred at the same time that the ties with extended kin and with the surrounding community diminished. Thus the emotional supports of these "outsiders" collapsed, and the increased emotional dependency of the marital couple on each other — heretofore called on far too infrequently — occurred. To help compensate for their loss, working-class women in England developed an alternative family system that emphasized mother–daughter ties and de-emphasized the ties between husband and wife.

However, the predominant ideology was focusing more and more on the belief in the primacy of the conjugal family with its accent on intimacy and emotionalism between husband and wife. At the same time, an integral aspect of the ideology of the conjugal family, female domesticity, worked against it. Thus the conjugal family system found itself in a dilemma. Its advocacy of differentiated spheres of activity — masculine public life and feminine private life — was antithetical to the very intimacy it sought; that is, female dependency ran counter to conjugal intimacy. It is now time to examine the contemporary conjugal-family system and see how it attempts to resolve this issue.

From Private Family to Symmetrical Family

The theme running through this chapter is the distinction between public and private spheres of activity and their respective implications for male and female marital relationships. The trend has been gradual, from a more-public family system with high community involvement to a more-private closed family system. The public family was one in which there was little distinction made between work and the home

A dual-income couple "sharing" breakfast before work.

and where community played a major role in shaping and determining family relationships. Community control and scrutiny was primarily responsible for the limitations on family intimacy and privacy. Women in the preindustrial period were actively involved in work. In fact, the distinction between work and domesticity hardly existed. The ideology of the private family emerged during the Industrial Revolution. Work was separated from the household and there was a greater differentiation and specialization of the roles of husband and wife. Coinciding with industrialization was the development of an ideology that stressed the importance of sentiments regarding emotionality, intimacy, and privacy among conjugal family members. However, through much of the history of industrialization, the reality of the private family was relatively uncommon since it was restricted to the more affluent middle classes of the society. The upper classes, desiring to maintain and control their family wealth and power, continued to maintain a family system that placed great importance on extended kinship lines. For the working classes, especially in the city, maternal-centered, three-generational family systems developed to compensate for the husband's emotional distance and the too-frequent economic unfeasibility of the conjugal-family form.

Certain conditions have become prevalent in contemporary industrial society that have had great significance for family relations. Demographic changes, the lengthened life span, the decline in infant and child mortality rates, the decline in maternal deaths in childbirth, lower birthrates, the dissociation of reproductive from sexual activities, and the decline in the period of life devoted to maternity in relation to the total life expectancy have contributed to attitudinal and behavioral changes in the family. For example, the typical couple now spend a great number of years together outside of parental concerns. This has helped foster the emergence of the conjugal role ideology. The emphasis on love, emotional support, friendship and companionship, and erotic and sexual gratification can transform the marital relationship into the ideal conjugal family.

Feminism has also been influential in the reshaping of the family. Through the twentieth century, women have been gaining in legal equality. Areas of legal change include the women's suffrage rights, rights of separation and divorce, and rights of equal employment and opportunity. Although equality has not been fully realized, as the struggle over the Equal Rights Amendment (ERA) can testify, there has been marked improvement in the power and status of women compared to life in the nineteenth century. The result has been a growth of female independence.

The higher standard of living for ordinary families and the migration of families from rural to urban and from urban to suburban residences has contributed to these changes. As we saw in our earlier discussion on suburban families, the emphasis became more and more focused on conjugal family ties at the expense of the extended family. The acquisition of better homes has made the household a more attractive place in which to spend time and on which to spend money. Husbands are devoting more time to their families, and there is a diminishing of the segregation of marital couples that characterized working-class couples of the earlier industrial period.

Observing these changes in England, Young and Willmott (1973) have postulated the emergence of a new family form that epitomizes the ideals of the conjugal family but with some notable differences. This is the symmetrical family. The *symmetrical family* is seen as one in which there is recognition for the continued differences in the work opportunities and ways of life of husbands and wives but in which there is marked egalitarianism between the sexes. Young and Willmott note a similarity between this family form and the family of domestic industry. Both families emphasize the relationships among husband, wife, and children. However, unlike the domestic industrial family, which functioned as a productive entity, the symmetrical family functions as a unit of consumption:

> When husband, wife, and children worked together on a farm or in handicrafts the family was *the* productive unit even if it did not yield much more than a bare subsistence to its members. When individual wage-employment became almost universal (except for housewives) the family had to give way to a wider division of labor. But in the course of time the family has re-established a new kind of primacy, not as the unit of production so much as the unit of consumption. (Young and Willmott, 1973:xxi)

Couples, particularly husbands, see themselves as no longer having to devote as much time to earning a living and providing for a family. They are now able to spend more time with their families in leisure and home-centered activities. The new egalitarianism is realized in the assumption of joint responsibility in the planning of children and the increased tendency for greater husband involvement in the rearing of the children. Feminism is evinced in the symmetrical family as the belief that there should be no monopolies for either husband or wife in any sphere of activity. Women, then, are entitled to the same rights as men to become involved in work outside the home as well as in it. The result has been a movement of women back to the labor force, the usual pattern being the wife staying at home during the early years of child-rearing, then taking first a part-time job, and later a full-time job as the children grow older.

Young and Willmott (1973) believe that the traditional pattern of the husband being the primary wage earner will continue.

> The devotion of a husband to a career, if it goes with scant sympathy for a partner who does not have one, may drive his wife to espouse the same values as himself and follow him out. But that is exceptional. (Young and Willmott, 1973:276)

These authors observe a similar phenomenon to the one that we discussed in our analysis of the Soviet Union, where the wife has become responsible both for her outside work and for all domestic tasks. This dual role or double burden for women is practiced among the London families interviewed by Young and Willmott.

Notably, Young and Willmott see positive gains in the strength of the feminist movement. They believe that just as the worlds of work and leisure are merging, so too will the worlds of men and women merge. The result will be an eventual sharing of the tasks by men and women in both domestic and outside work. They recognize the strains that will have to be overcome: the caring of children as well as arrangement of work and leisure schedules so that the family can spend time together. Generally, they are optimistic for the future: technology and family wants can both be fulfilled.

This hopeful and sanguine portrait of family life is not shared by many contemporary sociologists. They see the various social movements that have become manifest in recent years—the youth counterculture; the women's liberation movement; the rise in experimental forms of family life, particularly swinging, communal marriage, and so on—as reflections of the dissatisfactions with the dichotomization of public and private worlds and the growing privatization of the family. Barbara Laslett (1973), in an intriguing article, observes that the private family—manifested to an advanced degree in the United States—is a central feature of contemporary life. Its development is a consequence of the separation of work and family activities. The privatization of the family results in less community and social control over how family members behave toward each other as well as providing less social support for family members. Barbara Laslett speculates that the experimentation with alternative family styles, such as communal living, group marriages, and single-parent families, has been one adaptation to the strains of nuclear family living. This view sees the final development of the intimate private conjugal family as not achieving the long-sought needs of individualism and equalitarianism. Instead, the private conjugal family is seen as mired with problems. Let us look at this position in some detail.

The above arguments by the critics of the conjugal family bear a striking similarity to those of Peter L. Berger and his associates in *The Homeless Mind: Modernization and Consciousness* (1974). By integrating Berger's analysis with those of the scholars we discussed, we may be better able to grasp the dynamics of contemporary marital dynamics.

In Chapter 3, we saw that *The Homeless Mind* is concerned with the consequences of modernization and the privatization of the family. The authors argue that modernization was supposed to free the individual but has, instead, increased feelings of helplessness, frustration, and alienation and has beset individuals with threats of meaninglessness. Berger and his associates develop the argument that technology's primary consequence has resulted in the separation of work from private life. Further, work is characterized by anonymous and impersonal relations; individuals interact with each other in terms of the functions they perform in their jobs. There is no need to be aware of each other's uniqueness as individuals. To combat this situation, private institutions like the family are developed. In them, individuals can express their subjective identities and the individualism that is denied them in the work situation.

Berger and his associates argue that the reality of the world is sustained through interaction with significant others and an individual who is deprived of relationships with significant others will feel a sense of anomie and alienation. This is the case of the individual at work. However, the marriage relationship is designed to provide a nomos versus an anomic situation. Here intimacy can occur and a meaningful world can be constructed. Marriage is viewed as a "dramatic" act in which the two participants come together and redefine themselves through the unfolding of the marital relationship and the involvement they have with others.

The contemporary character of middle-class marriage, then, has its origins in the development of a private sphere of existence that is separated and segregated from the controls of such public institutions as politics and economics. It is designed to be a haven of security and order. It is a world in which the husband and wife can create their own social reality and social order. This is seen to be of crucial importance to wage earners—it provides them with an environment in which they can gain a sense of control in contrast to their jobs, which are often viewed in terms of powerlessness and unfulfillment, or to politics, which is viewed cynically.

It is important to note that in an earlier work Peter L. Berger, in collaboration with Hansfred Kellner (1964), saw marriage as accomplishing these outlined objectives. In that work, "Marriage and the Construction of Reality," the marital relationship is viewed as a nomos institution that helps establish a meaningful reality sustained through the interaction of the marriage partners. However, Berger and Kellner's view of the positive nature of marriage is seen from the man's perspective. They virtually ignore women in their analysis. Although noting how the family may serve as a refuge for men from the debilitating reality of the workplace, they do not address themselves to the problems of domestically confined housewives who have no refuge from their mundane and repetitive household chores or from the unceasing demands of their children. Further, they overlook the greater demand placed on women to satisfy the demands and morale of their husbands than the reverse.

In *The Homeless Mind,* Berger and his associates come to the realization that marriage is insufficient to satisfy the demands of all family members, including the husband. In this book, they also come to the implicit recognition that the *ideology* of marriage as a nomos institution is one thing and that *reality* is another; that is, marriage, which was seen as providing a meaningful world for the participants, is in fact unable to overcome the modern condition of "homelessness," which results from the separation of work and the family. This "pluralization of life-worlds," which is distinguished by the dichotomy of private and public spheres of activities, fosters both a world of work that is insufficient to give people a feeling of worth and a world of marriage that is unable to provide ample satisfactions in people's private lives.

Two Views of Marriage Explored: His and Hers

BY DANIEL GOLEMAN

Every marriage, researchers are discovering, is actually two marriages: his and hers. The differences suffuse even the happiest of relationships between husbands and wives.

Some of the new research suggests that, paradoxically, the differences need not be divisive, but can be sources of marital growth.

Psychologists say that couples who openly acknowledge these differences improve their chances of avoiding strife. And those who seek to free their marriages of such male–female differences are better able to do so if they are aware of how powerful, though largely hidden, the differences are.

One of the great gaps between husbands and wives is in their notions of emotional intimacy and how important they feel it is in a marriage. For many men, simply doing such things as working in the garden or going to a movie with their wives gives them a feeling of closeness. But for their wives that is not enough, according to Ted Huston, a psychologist at the University of Texas at Austin who has studied 130 couples intensively.

"For the wives, intimacy means talking things over, especially talking about the relationship itself," Dr. Huston said. "The men, by and large, don't understand what the wives want from them. They say, 'I want to do things with her, and all she wants to do is talk.' "

While women expect more emotional intimacy than their husbands do, "many men seem to feel they've fulfilled their obligation to the relationship if they just do their chores," said Robert Sternberg, a psychologist at Yale University who has studied couples. "They say, 'I took out the garbage; now leave me alone.' "

In courtship, Dr. Huston has found, men are much more willing to spend time talking to women in ways that build a woman's sense of intimacy. But after marriage, and as time goes on, the men tend to spend less and less time talking with their wives in these ways, and more time devoted to their work or with buddies. The trend is strongest in marriages that follow

---

MARRIAGE: DIFFERENT PERCEPTIONS

What's the main attraction?
Men: Her looks.
Women: His earning potential.

What counts in a marriage?
Men: Her ability to make love; shared interests.
Women: How well he handles her parents; how well each gets along with the other's friends; marital fidelity.

How well is the couple doing?
Men: Well, in communication, finances, relationship with parents, listening to each other, tolerating each other's flaws, romance.
Women: Not so well, in all of the above.

These descriptions of how men and women tend to view marriage differently are drawn from recent studies at Yale, the University of Illinois and the University of Michigan.

---

traditional patterns, and most of the current research suggests the traditional patterns are still prevalent despite two decades in which these conventional attitudes and mores have been assailed for the stereotypes they breed.

"Men put on a big show of interest when they are courting," Dr. Huston said. "But after the marriage their actual level of interest in the partner often does not seem as great as you would think, judging from the courtship. The intimacy of courtship is instrumental for the men, a way to capture the woman's interest. But that sort of intimacy is not natural for many men."

As with all such differences, there is a lesson to be learned. The starkness of the husband's apparent change in behavior after marriage can lead to disappointment, demands and acrimony—in short, a relationship in trouble. Dr. Huston suggests that in more successful marriages there is a middle ground in which the couple share experiences that naturally lead to more intimate conversation.

"You can't force intimacy," Dr. Huston said. "It has to arise spontaneously from shared activities."

(continued)

Husbands' and wives' differing stances toward intimacy signify deeper disparities between the sexes, in the view of Carol Gilligan, a psychologist at Harvard University. Dr. Gilligan says young boys take pride in independence and are threatened by anything that might compromise their autonomy, while young girls tend to experience themselves as part of a network of relationships and are threatened by anything that might rupture these connections.

"Boys, as they mature, must learn to connect, girls to separate," said Kathleen White, a psychologist at Boston University, who, with her colleagues, is the author of an article on intimacy in marriage in the current issue of *The Journal of Personality and Social Psychology.*

In adulthood this means women tend to be uncomfortable with separateness, while men are wary of intimacy. Some psychologists have proposed that one lesson teen-age boys learn from their girlfriends is how to be emotionally intimate, a lesson that can extend into marriage, particularly for those who never really master it.

The more comfortable a husband is with intimacy, Dr. White's research shows, the more satisfied with the marriage is the wife likely to be.

CHANGING VIEW TOWARD PARENTS

Another telling finding is that marriage typically makes a woman draw closer to her parents, while a man often becomes more distant from his. For a woman, closeness to her parents ranks among her most important expectations, the new research shows, while husbands tend to rank a warm association with either set of parents comparatively low.

For the men, the marriage evidently supplants earlier closeness to parents. What the men often seem to be saying, according to Dr. White, is "I don't need my parents anymore; I have my wife."

But for women, Dr. White has found, the marriage seems to offer a crucial footing from which they can set aside earlier rebelliousness and make peace with their parents, particularly their mothers, and develop a new warmth.

Other factors may be at work, too.

"Because many husbands focus their lives outside the marriage, on their work or their friends, many wives have a sense of being abandoned," Dr. Huston said. "They turn to their mothers for an intimate involvement they do not get from their husbands."

Other research has found that wives place more emphasis than their husbands do on preserving ties with both sets of parents, not just their own. Some experts say a couple that blends the stances of the wife and the husband toward their parents can find a healthy balance in which independence and family ties coexist.

The disparities between husband and wife in such areas as intimacy and family ties are part of a wide range of differences that men and women bring to marriage, according to many experts.

DIFFERING SETS OF VALUES

Some of the starkest evidence of these differences has come from a study by Dr. Sternberg of people 17 to 69 years old, some of whom have been married for as long as 36 years. The men in the study rated as most important in their marriage their wives' ability to make love and the couple's shared interests. But the wives listed marital fidelity and ties to family and friends as most important. The wives were particularly concerned with how well the husband handled both sets of parents, especially hers, and also how well the couple got along with each other's friends.

Dr. Sternberg's study found evidence that the double standard still holds for many couples. Wives said fidelity was very important for both spouses; husbands said it was more important for wives than for husbands.

Perhaps the most dramatic difference is in evaluating the relationship. "The men rate almost everything as better than do the wives," Dr. Sternberg said. Men have a rosier view of lovemaking, finances, ties with parents, listening to each other, tolerance of flaws and romance.

"The only thing the women rate better than the men is the couple's degree of fidelity," Dr. Sternberg said.

Wives generally complain more about the state of their marriage than husbands do.

(continued)

Jesse Bernard, a sociologist, has proposed in *The Future of Marriage* (Yale University Press) that this is because marriage is harder on women than on men. Dr. Bernard, citing a wide range of studies, says the "psychological costs of marriage seem to be considerably greater for wives than for husbands."

Other marital experts, though, say wives appear to suffer more than husbands because women are more willing than men to admit their problems. Men often feel it is "unmanly" to admit depression or anxiety.

According to John Gottman, a psychologist at the University of Illinois who has studied happy and unhappy couples, wives are more willing to complain about problems in marriage than men are, and this is particularly so among unhappy couples. Men generally try to avoid conflicts in marriage, he has found, while women are more willing to confront them.

"Men and women have different goals when they disagree," Dr. Gottman said. "The wife wants to resolve the disagreement so that she feels closer to her husband and respected by him. The husband, though, just wants to avoid a blowup. The husband doesn't see the disagreement as an opportunity for closeness, but for trouble." Dr. Gottman believes this is because men are more vulnerable than women to physical stress from emotional confrontations, at least as he reads the research evidence.

The preferences that draw couples together also show a major, and perhaps unsurprising, difference between the sexes: women, by and large, place great importance on a man's earning potential, while men place great stress on a woman's attractiveness, according to Dr. White's study in *The Journal of Personality and Social Psychology*.

Some psychologists say that one lesson to be learned from the differences is that each partner in the psychological alliance that is marriage can be enriched by learning from the other. In this view, marriage offers a unique opportunity for psychological growth. "Men and women," said Dr. White, "need to take on each other's strengths."

The differences also point to what people mean when they say that it takes work to make a marriage work. Those who are complacent about the differences between spouses, who see no need to accommodate the partner's perspectives, may be putting the marriage at risk, the experts say.

"It's too easy to portray the expressive wife as good and the stoic husband as horrible; in fact, they are just different," said Carol Tavris, a social psychologist whose book *The Longest War* (Harcourt, Brace Jovanovich) reviews sex differences.

"While you want to understand the differences, it is probably futile to try to change your partner to be just like your best friend," Dr. Tavris said. "It's better for husbands and wives to develop a sense of humor and tolerance, and to accept their mates as they are."

SOURCE. Daniel Goleman. 1986. "Two views of marriage explored: His and hers." *The New York Times* (Apr. 1). Copyright © 1986 by The New York Times Company. Reprinted by permission.

Berger and his associates conclude that the modern private family is in trouble. Evidence of this is the development of processes of demodernization that manifest themselves in various forms of rebellious movements, such as the youth counterculture and the women's liberation movement. Further evidence is apparent in the dramatic rise in the divorce rate, which reflects the desire of individuals to seek more satisfactory private meanings and relationships than those that exist within the marriage.

Problems of the Dual-Career Family

In an insightful article, Hunt and Hunt (1982) observe that an examination of the contemporary dual-career family provides important insights on social-change processes and their impact on the family. They, like Berger and his associates, are not as sanguine about the future of what Young and Willmott have labeled the symmetrical family. They challenge the view that dual-career families—in which both husbands and wives have significant and fulfilling occupational careers as well as meaningful, intimate, and involved family roles—represent the wave of the future. Instead, they theorize that *both* men and women will have to make decisions regarding their commitments *either* to occupational careers or to the family. The result will be a polarization of the worlds of career and family, and institutional separation of the world of work and the world of the family will be even more complete. "[T]he movement of women into careers and of men into family involvement will break down the integration of these spheres and promote the evolution of more distinct lifestyles organized around either careers or families" (1982:508).

The dual-career family of the 1960s and 1970s was characterized by the unequal distribution of self-commitments to careers (work involvements that are continuous, developmental, demand a high level of commitment, and have intrinsic value and reward) and families by men and women. Essentially, while both men and women worked, men gave differential commitment and involvement to their careers, while women toned down their career aspirations and gave differential commitment to their familial roles. Women, especially highly educated women, pursued a "career of limited ambition" (White, 1979). This family form did not challenge the male role and departed little from the conventional domestic division of labor among dual-career couples. The career wife performed dual roles or the "double burden" through skillful allocation of her time and resources.

Profamily coercion by employers further reinforced this pattern. Women often found themselves in dead-end careers with restricted employment, fewer professional opportunities, and lower salary scales. Implicitly, this was legitimated by beliefs that wives' careers were secondary, with their primary identification being the family, and that their wages were supplemental family income. The consequence of this pattern was a dual-career family form that "permitted the lives of dual-career men to be similar to those of other career men, while the lives of dual-career women were

Michael Weisbrot/Stock, Boston

A young businesswoman nurses her infant while she takes a phone call.

carefully balanced to provide a measure of career involvement as long as the family was not inconvenienced" (Hunt and Hunt, 1982:501).

However, changing attitudes since the mid-1970s have questioned this family form and alternative patterns are emerging. Many women are entering the labor force and are making greater commitment to their occupational careers. This factor, combined with the occasional enforcement of antidiscrimination laws, has pressured and forced employers to move away slowly from discriminatory gender employment practices. At the same time, many women are also choosing to avoid the stresses of dual commitments by postponing or permanently deciding against marriage and parenthood. Concomitantly, men observing the continued erosion of the acceptance of women's double burden may themselves be reluctant to assume greater commitment to familial and domestic roles and may make similar decisions regarding marriage and parenthood. Hunt and Hunt observe that in fact the incidence of the two-person career family has decreased in the 1980s. They believe that growing employment for women may actually cause a decline in the formation of the family.

While these trends continue for a significant segment of the population, many other people continue to marry and have children. However, Hunt and Hunt speculate that for the men and women who are family-oriented, they will tone down their career aspirations. This will occur as a realization that they cannot effectively compete occupationally with their counterparts who have made decisions to be solely committed to their careers. The consequent result will be two dominant lifestyles. Men and women who pursue careers will begin to resemble each other and the world of work will become more gender-neutral. For those who marry and become family-oriented, there will also be a blurring of the lines of gender-role differentiation.

> We are suggesting, then, that U.S. society is evolving toward a social order which is less overtly sexist yet which extends the legacy of patriarchy. What has been polarized by sex roles will remain polarized: public power versus family involvement. In the past this meant that men were assigned work roles that resulted in truncated family lives, while women were assigned family roles that often precluded satisfying work lives. Now women can become "sociological men" — persons who emphasize their public lives and enjoy the resulting power and independence — and men can become "sociological women" — persons who invest themselves primarily in their families and forfeit power and control of their personal destinies. (Hunt and Hunt, 1982:503)

Most important, however, the polarization of career and family has wide-ranging family policy implications. Polarization will result in a widened gap between parents and nonparents. Those without children will monopolize the highest-paying jobs. Without worrying about the costs of raising children, singles or "child-free" couples will be able to afford the bounties of an affluent consumer society. The "Yuppiefication" of many cities points to the growing disparity in resources between these professionals and their family-oriented, less economically successful counterparts. Family-oriented couples may find themselves priced out of the market for the more-attractive rewards, housing, automobiles, and consumer goods available to the wealthy. It will become apparent to families that they cannot compete effectively in a consumer market stimulated by the spending and investing power of child-free adults. As a consequence, more and more people may reach the decision that parenthood is too costly an option that prevents them from pursuing other attractive lifestyles.

A significant decline in a nation's birthrate has the potential to become a serious social problem. "The birth of fewer children and/or their failure to develop into healthy and productive adults would be economically depressing and would increase the ratio of non-employed to the population of employed adults" (Hunt and Hunt, 1982:508). This could ultimately undermine the viability of benefit systems such as social security. It is for that reason that Hunt and Hunt argue for social policies that would support family life. They call for policies that would subsidize family incomes to reduce the disparity in living standards between families and nonfamilies. These policies provide for greater sharing of the costs of children through such programs and policies as publicly funded child care and health care, family allowances (payments per child), housing allowances, and paid maternal (or paternal) leave to care for infants and sick children. Such tax-financed services and income-transfer policies are in effect in European societies like Sweden, which has a large proportion of the female population in the work force. Unfortunately, the policy of the U.S. government has been less enlightened. The consequences will be the further dichotomization or polarization of the worlds of work and the family, with particularly negative consequences for the American family.

> Families will survive, but not thrive. They will be idealized like motherhood and ignored like mothers. They will be forced to trade efficacy for security. Under these conditions, people will be free to choose families, but those who do so will continue to suffer the age-old effects of being women in a man's world. (Hunt and Hunt, 1982:510)

Conclusion

This chapter concludes our five-chapter analysis of the effects of patriarchy on male–female premarital and marital relationships. It is a continuation of the previous analysis that emphasized the interrelationship of patriarchy and economic systems and how they influence the division of labor of husbands and wives.

We demonstrated how the differentiation of activities of males and females in public and private spheres has been a dominating factor in establishing marital roles and responsibilities. The differential involvement of men and women in the worlds of work and in the household is important in determining the power, privilege, respect, and deference patterns within the family. Comparatively, we examined cross-cultural and Western historical evidence to develop our thesis. We concurred with the views of a significant number of social scientists that the greater and more exclusive the involvement of women is in the domestic sphere, devoting their time to household tasks and child-rearing, then the less freedom, authority, and power women have in relation to men. Concomitantly, the more exclusive the involvement of men in the outside world of work, politics, and religion, the greater is their authority and power over women.

A large segment of this chapter was devoted to an historical analysis of the effects of the Western Industrial Revolution on male–female relationships. We discussed the relationship of modernization processes to the privatization of the family (referring back to our opening chapters) and saw striking parallels in the conclusions reached by social scientists coming from different subdisciplines. The common thrust of our presentation was on the negative consequences of the dichotomization of private and public spheres of activities and the privatization of the family. We argued that such developments as the women's movement, the youth counterculture movements, and the new family form (perhaps idealized) of the symmetrical family represented reactions against the privatized family. We concluded with a discussion of dual-career families. The optimism that initially greeted this family form has been tempered by the realization that family members may withhold some of their commitments to careers because of familial obligations. The implications of this potential problem in terms of economic and career competition with single individuals or couples without children was noted.

In Part IV, we examine the family in terms of generational relationships. These represent a different expression of patriarchal ideology, authority, and power differentiation.

PART IV

Generational Relationships

CHAPTER 13

Fertility Patterns and Parenthood

A pregnant woman and her husband participating in a childbirth class at a hospital.

Paul Fortin/Stock, Boston

CHAPTER OUTLINE

An inescapable fact of contemporary life is the overwhelming increase of the world's population. Today's population is increasing at a rate faster than ever before in history. It is taking less and less time for the world's population to double. During the Stone Age, when man was hunting and foraging for subsistence, the total world population is estimated to have been about 10 million. By the beginning of the Christian era, the world population was about 250 million people. If it took about 35,000 years for the first one-quarter billion people to appear, it took only about 1,650 years for the population to double to one-half billion. But, in a mere 200 years (A.D. 1850), it doubled again. Then, in a time span of only 80 years—from 1850 to 1930—the population increased to 2 billion. By 1975, 45 years later, the population again doubled to approximately 4 billion people. Demographers predict that by the end of this century the human population will have again doubled to 8 billion people. This change is depicted graphically in Figure 13.1.

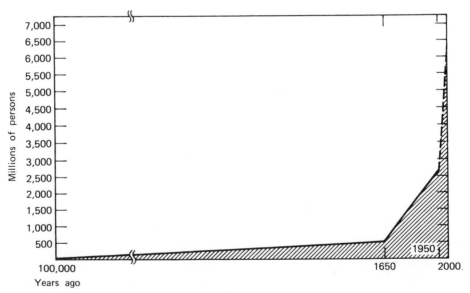

FIGURE 13.1   A schematic representation of the increase in the human species. (Adapted from William Petersen, 1975. *Population*, 3d ed. New York: Macmillan. Copyright © by William Petersen, reprinted with permission.)

Rapid population growth and the size of the contemporary world population are among the most urgent concerns of the twentieth century. The consequences for the quality of life and for the future are subject to extensive analyses, discussions, and speculations. Population-control programs have been implemented throughout the world. Within the contexts of modernization and the family, our analysis will examine some of the elements that account for this phenomenon. In addition to examining the broad demographic trends, we discuss changing attitudes and values regarding parental roles and the transition to the parenthood period of Americans. We conclude the chapter by studying the impact of abortion on the family.

Fertility Patterns in Preindustrial Family Life

Earlier, we noted a distinction between mating and marriage. Mating refers to a biologic phenomenon, whereas marriage, as a sociologic concept, refers to a social institution. Marriage controls sexual activity and reproduction. Throughout the world, we find copulation and reproduction reinforced by cultural norms. William Petersen, the noted demographer, has observed that "a society's demographic and cultural persistence depends on the fact that the physical care, socialization, and social placement of its young are not left to the sometimes haphazard dictates of sexuality alone" (Petersen, 1975:202). Reproduction, which is vital to a society's continuation, is always controlled by cultural norms about family size and such related matters as marriage, frequency of intercourse, and abortion. It is never a matter left up to the individual couple alone.

There are notable differences in fertility rates for underdeveloped preindustrial societies and more developed industrial societies. Demographers (Freedman, 1963:68; Davis, 1955) have observed that, generally, underdeveloped societies have higher fertility levels. These fertility levels are related to various factors found in these societies. Ronald Freedman (1963/68) presents two very general explanations. High fertility can be seen as an adjustment to high mortality and to the centrality of kinship and family structures to community life. Let us examine each factor in more detail.

High infant and child mortality along with a relatively short and precarious life expectancy require a high fertility rate to assure a society's perpetuation. Calvin Goldscheider (1971) observes that many families have "extra" children as a hedge against infant and child death and the probable early death of one of the parents. He cautions against making an unwarranted assumption that high birthrates are necessarily associated with large family-size norms. The high birthrates he observed occurred in conjunction with the high mortality of infants and children. Thus, families may have had a large number of children so that some of them would survive.

In support of this notion, Freedman (1963/68) finds that a number of studies in contemporary underdeveloped areas reveal a discrepancy between the number of children desired, usually three or four, and the actual number of children that a couple has, frequently six or more. Freedman interprets this finding as a result of the decline in infant and child mortality rates. It is not seen as reflecting a new attitudinal preference for a small family size. It reflects previous historical circumstances when, owing to high mortality, six or more children were required if three or four children were to survive. Freedman reports on data from India where social scientists are surprised that surveyed families express a desire for three or four children yet practice little or no birth control.

> However, wanting three or four living children in a high-mortality country is quite consistent with the much higher average number of births. Even if mortality is declining, the peasant who has learned from his culture to depend on his children

for labor on the farm, for old-age security, and for other essentials cannot be expected to extrapolate declining mortality with the demographer and to calculate a long-range need for fewer children. (Freedman, 1963/1968:164)

Significantly, however, families that have three or four surviving children are more inclined to have favorable attitudes toward family-planning information and supplies. This is consistent with their belief that birth control practices are irrelevant until the essential minimum number of children exist (Freedman, 1963/68).

The second element that accounts for the high fertility rate in preindustrial countries is the dominance of kinship and family groupings. Prior to modernization, a wide range of activities involved interdependence with kinfolk, especially children. Economic production and consumption along with leisure activities and assistance to the elderly and the infirm occurred largely within family and kinship structures. Freedman (1963/68) states that large numbers of children are desired when the society is based on and its values are achieved through kinship and family ties rather than through other social institutions. Under high-mortality conditions, high birthrates become desirous to assure the survival of the kinship groupings.

Goldscheider (1971), in a comprehensive review of the demographic literature, reaches a similar conclusion. He finds that in kinship-dominated societies pronatalist sentiments are prevalent. Children are a source of protection and prestige. The social strength of a given kinship unit is dependent on its size. Tied to this attitude is the domination of the kinship group over the individual. Kinship ascription provides an occupation for a man and his placement in the society is determined by the family or kin group to which he belongs. Children enable families and the kin group to achieve socially desired goals.

In such instances, high value is placed on large families. Further, the viability of extended-kinship involvements diminishes the personal responsibilities of the couple in the care and maintenance of their children. The burdens of a large family, economic and social costs, and social and personal care are shared and controlled by the larger kinship-family structure: "Parents not only had personal rewards for having large families but they could escape from direct responsibilities of their many children" (Goldscheider, 1971:142).

The gender-role segregation that predominates in these kinship-based societies is another important facet in encouraging a large family. The role and status of women is clearly linked with their childbearing function. Prestige and other social and economic rewards and benefits can only be obtained through motherhood. The production and survival of healthy offspring for the continuation of kinship lines provide the chief source for rationalizing a woman's existence.

The familial-based economic system found children to be important productive assets. Children were an integral part of the labor force. Thus the more offspring, the more workers within the family. Further, the larger the number of offspring, the greater the chances of their providing for their parents when they got old. Children, then, represented one type of old-age insurance (Goldscheider, 1971:153). The lack of geographic and social mobility combined with the lack of personal aspirations also increased the desire for large families.

Taken altogether, the kinship-based society was dependent on high fertility for the perpetuation of its social system. Demographic, social, familial, and economic conditions resulted in the institutionalization of high fertility. The entire society—its values and goals as well as the various aspects of its cultural and religious life—were organized around high-fertility values and behavior.

Turning our attention to the industrialized nations of the world, we find that the rate of population growth has decreased after an earlier rapid increase. Demographers have referred to this phenomenon as the demographic transition. Simply put, the demographic transition refers to the movement from high-fertility and high-mortality rates to low-fertility and low-mortality rates. Demographers have traced the historical sequence of population growth in the Western world over the last 200 years. They observed three broad stages of population dynamics.

During the preindustrial period, birth and death rates were high, variations occurring during periods of famine and epidemics. Population size was relatively stable. Industrialization ushered in the second stage. It was accompanied by improvements in sanitation and sewage systems, better transportation systems for shipping foods, and more-productive family techniques. Improvements in these conditions led to a reduction in the death rate. Although the death rate was reduced, there was no commensurate reduction in the birthrate. This resulted in a period of rapid population growth. By the end of the nineteenth century, through the twentieth century, and continuing until today, the high birthrate has been reduced. The disparity that existed between birthrates and death rates, which was characteristic of the second stage, is reduced in this, the third stage. Today, the industrialized nations of the world have a low, steady death rate and a low, but somewhat fluctuating birthrate.

How can we explain this dramatic decline in the rate of population growth in contemporary industrial societies? Goldscheider (1971) has developed an argument that is similar to that articulated by William J. Goode (1963) in his *World Revolution and Family Patterns*. Goldscheider (1971:148–151) believes there are three key social processes that can account for the transition from high to low fertility and family size. First, there is the shift from kinship dominance to the conjugal-family unit. He sees the breakdown of the dominance and centrality of the kinship-based consanguineal family as one of the significant features of modernization. The extended-family system can no longer dictate the number of children that a given nuclear family should have. Individual couples emphasize their family of procreation rather than their family of orientation. They have their own economic and social responsibilities and the welfare of their children is primarily in their hands. The break with the extended-family system allowed for the development of new behavioral and value patterns. It coincided with the processes of migration, urbanization, and social mobility.

Second, there is a marked improvement in living standards accompanied by increased economic opportunities. These contribute to rising aspirations for social mobility. This aspiration is frequently in conflict with the desire for a large family. These social and economic changes are seen to have exerted direct pressures toward fertility control and reduction. The decline in family-based agricultural and preindustrial enterprises diminished the importance of children. Children are no longer productive assets. The decline in fertility is accentuated by the rapid urbanization that accompanied industrialization. Urban conditions contribute to the decline of the traditional classical extended-family system. It frees the conjugal family from the socioeconomic controls of the extended-family system. Further, urban lifestyles, living standards, and aspirations all run counter to the traditional values that encouraged large family size and high fertility.

The third and last factor is the development of new values and attitudes that stress individualism, secularism, and rationalism. These values all share a common belief in the desirability of limiting family size. Values in favor of smaller families are also shared by the emerging value of achievement versus ascription. Together, these three processes greatly affect the decline in fertility and family size in industrialized societies. Let us examine how these factors operate by looking at India as a case study.

India: A Case Study

India is one of the world's largest nations. It is also one of its poorest. Second only to the People's Republic of China in population size, in mid-1975 India had a population of 608.5 million (Population Reference Bureau, 1976). In a land area one-third the size of the United States, India has three times as many people. India's population represents one-eighth of the entire world's population. Demographers predict that unless the current growth rate is substantially reduced, India will have a population of well over 1 billion by the end of the twentieth century.

The Indian government has viewed its population growth as a major deterrent to economic and social development. Initially, however, Mahatma Gandhi, Jawaharlal Nehru, and other government leaders were ambivalent about the need to reduce fertility, but eventually family-planning programs became more and more important, culminating in the coercive sterilization policies of Indira Gandhi and the Congress Party during the "emergency" of 1976–1977. The general position held is that the economic development of the country is dependent on the investment of the national income. However, a rapidly increasing birthrate diverts income to food consumption, housing, education, and other social needs. A lower birthrate would allow for greater modernization, economic development, and increased total production. Population, then, is seen as being a crucial variable in the complex interrelationships of economy, social structure, and culture. In the transition to a modern industrial state, the population growth of the society must be regulated through governmentally sponsored population-planning programs. Since independence in 1948, India has been developing programs to slow its population growth. The result is that the birthrate has dropped from 42 per 1,000 in 1951–1961 to 35 per 1,000 by 1974 (Population Reference Bureau, 1976). However, the decline in the birthrate has been partially offset by lower mortality rates. Life expectancy in India has risen to about 50 years today. This reflects the great strides India has made in industry, agriculture, education, and public health. However, India's population today is increasing at a rate of 2 to 2.5 percent. At this rate of growth, *every five years* India's population will grow by an additional number that equals the combined population of East and West Germany or more than the population of Australia and New Zealand together (Petersen, 1975). At this rate, its population will double in approximately 35 years.

In 1952, India became the first country to adopt an official family-planning program. At the outset, the program was poorly funded. This reflected the ambivalence of Indian officials to reduce fertility. During the first five-year plan (1951–1956), 147 clinics were established in all of India, 126 in the cities and 21 in rural areas. During the succeeding five-year period, 1956–1961, over 4,000 clinics were established. Contraceptives were distributed at subsidized rates or were given out free. Petersen observes that by 1960, only 1.4 million families of the 75 to 80 million families in India were given family-planning advice (Petersen, 1975:652).

The slow rate of growth of the population programs reflects the initial hesitation of the central government to implement family planning. Nehru in 1956 asserted that family planning was being assisted "not in a major way but in experimentation" with emphasis on medical reasons to promote the "health and happiness" of the family (Nehru cited in Petersen, 1975:651). The program also reflected the inefficiencies and inaccessibility of the clinics to the vast majority of the Indian population.

The census of 1961 provided a major impetus for the government to develop population-control programs. The continued rapid growth of the population was seen as having detrimental economic and social consequences. The third plan, 1962–1967, saw the beginning of a heightened commitment to population-control programs. The family-planning program was decentralized with federal allocations now dispersed through state projects. The principal means of contraception advocated in the earlier plans, the rhythm method and *coitus interruptus,* were now seen as being ineffectual. Diaphragms and spermicides were also viewed as being inappropriate. An oral contraceptive, the pill, was too expensive and the general feeling was that women would forget to take it daily. In 1965, two new techniques were introduced: male sterilization (vasectomy) and the intrauterine device (IUD).

Shortly after its introduction, the IUD fell into disfavor. William Petersen (1975) summarizes a number of Indian studies that found that whereas less than 1 percent of the women who had IUDs inserted became pregnant, almost one-tenth of the users automatically expelled the devices and as many as one-third of the women had them removed. These women either experienced excessive bleeding, pain, or discomfort, or had them removed because of the fear generated by the failures of others. In all, about 800,000 IUDs were inserted during the first year (1965–1966), but only about 790,000 or (19 percent) of the target population of 6 million were reached during the following year.

Increasingly, male sterilization was gaining favor by government officials. During 1965–1966, 600,000 men had vasectomies. Through various cash-incentive payments, the number rose in the following year but started to decline toward the end of the 1960s and the early 1970s. The low vasectomy rates did not approach the governmental goals. Further, most of the men who underwent the operation had already fathered as many children as they wanted.

The failure of the vasectomy program paralleled the failure of the other population-control programs. India's programs have been continually hampered by bureaucratic inefficiency, inadequate funds, poor planning, and the monumental size of the task. Further, India has never been able to convince its people on the necessity for population limitation. As previously noted, although the birthrate has dropped somewhat since the implementation of these programs, the population is still increasing by a rate of 57,000 new births every day. In 1974, a panel of Indian social scientists predicted that by the year 2000 half the Indian population would be homeless and the country would be stripped bare of its resources for fuel and food (McKee and Robertson, 1975:45).

To combat this trend, the Indian National Congress, the ruling party of India since independence, accelerated its family-planning programs. A multitude of programs were implemented. IUDs, condoms, and other contraceptive devices were distributed free. The oral birth-control pill was available only through pilot projects and distribution had begun in rural and urban family-planning centers. The mainstay of the program was sterilization.

During the authoritarian "state of emergency" of Indira Gandhi and the Congress Party, a mass vasectomy campaign sterilized millions of Indian males. At the time the program was initiated, Karen Singh, the Health Minister, described the problem this way:

> We are facing a population explosion of crisis dimensions, which has largely diluted the fruits of the remarkable economic progress that we have made. The time factor is so pressing, and the population growth so formidable, that we have to get out of the vicious circle through a direct assault upon this problem, as a national commitment. (Karen Singh cited in Borders, 1977)

Although ostensibly a voluntary program, the government pressured, cajoled, and forced people to undergo sterilization. The national campaign set a target of 4.3 million sterilizations. Over 7.8 million sterilizations were actually performed in the "emergency" between April 1976 and January 1977. The excessiveness of the aggressive birth-control program led to a high number of forcible operations.

The sterilization issue was one of the major factors contributing to the dramatic defeat of the ruling Congress Party and of Indira Gandhi in the elections of March 1977. In the so-called vasectomy belt, the populous states of north and central India, which felt the full brunt of the aggressive family-planning campaign, the Congress Party suffered overwhelming defeat. This was particularly the case in the constituencies of Indira Gandhi and her son Sanjay. After the election, an Indian diplomat provided the following explanation for the startling and unpredictable election results:

> The emergency would never have filtered down to the villages if all that was involved was press censorship and random jailings. But when you corral people without explaining that sterilization is not castration, when you take away their capacity to produce children to care for them in their old age and when you ignore the fact that Hindu philosophy has glorified fertility for 2,000 years, you've got to lose in the end. (Jensen in *Newsweek*, 1977:42)

Soon after the election, Raj Narain, who became the Minister of Health and Family Planning, ended the government sponsorship of sterilization and the cash-incentive payments to individuals who underwent sterilization operations. He called for a considerable modification in the birth-control program and the elimination of all elements of compulsion. He said that the new program would concentrate on increasing the number of condoms and birth control pills distributed, and it would also encourage other methods of preventing conception, including self-control or abstinence. The immediate result was a dramatic curtailment in sterilization operations: "In the northern state of Haryana, where sterilization was perhaps the single most important campaign issue — and where the Congress Party lost every single seat — 20,000 operations were performed last December; the number performed in March was less than 20" (Borders, 1977).

The success or failure of population-planning programs can best be understood when examined in the contexts of people's lives. Demographic statistical patterns are, of course, meaningful, but to get a more in-depth understanding of why they occur it is necessary to look at real people and real families. A study by Mahmood Mamdani, *The Myth of Population Control: Family, Caste and Class in an Indian Village* (1972), does just that. Mamdani is concerned with why the birth control movement was such a dismal failure in a small northern Indian village, Manupur. He looks at the structure of village life, at its caste and class structure, and at its families to determine why the population-planning program was so unsuccessful.

Before we look at Mamdani's study, let us provide some additional information on the joint-family system and the village-based caste system. The joint family coupled with the village-based caste system are the main core units of traditional Hindu life. The Indian family is based on an extended- or joint-family system. The family, in turn, is centered around the village, which is and still remains the most significant geographical entity for the vast majority of the contemporary Indian population.

Irawati Karve, an Indian social scientist, provides a precise definition of the traditional joint family: "A joint family is a group of people who generally live under one roof, who eat food cooked at one hearth, who hold property in common and who participate in common family worship and are related to each other as some particular type of kindred" (Karve cited in Ross, 1961:9). The head of the joint family is the oldest male member. His family, his younger brothers, his sons and their wives and children, and his grandchildren reside in the family compound. Relationships of family members are regulated by interlocking patterns of mutual dependence and assistance in times of need, mutuality of interests, and strong primary-group controls. In general, the younger generation is controlled by the elders. Individuality is subordinated to the collective. The marital relationship has little structural importance in the Hindu joint family. Traditionally, all marriages were arranged, and this procedure is only slowly disappearing. Marriage serves as a reaffirmation of a network of caste alliances and hierarchical gradations: "For the ancient sages declare that a bride is given to the family of her husband, and not to the husband alone" (Āpastamba cited in Lannoy, 1971:102).[1]

The joint family is supported and reinforced by the caste system. The numerous castes and subcastes are arranged in a vertical hierarchical pattern. In the Indian census of 1901, the last one to tabulate the many different Indian castes, there were

---

[1] Āpastamba lived about the fourth century B.C.

2378 "main" castes (Ross, 1961). They ranged in size from those that had several million people to others that had only a few. The caste system evolved out of a desire by ruling groups to provide an effective and stable division of labor. Each caste became identified with a particular occupation. Mamdani (1972), for example, discusses such "low" castes as the *Jheevar*, who are water carriers, and the *Marasi*, who are drum beaters. Both, incidentally, have been rendered obsolete as a result of technological change; the water carriers were replaced by the water pump and the drum beaters are no longer needed as the *Gurudwaras* (Sikh houses of worship) have become equipped with loudspeakers. Each caste member is assigned a given position, and all are fully aware of their standing and those of their superiors and inferiors.

Together, the joint family and the caste system serve to promote the stability of the social order. Kingsley Davis (1951) has outlined how they have helped to retard social change and the industrialization of Indian society. The joint family coupled with the village-based caste system lowers social mobility and serves to minimize competition.

> [The family system] . . . strongly limits social mobility and social change because it binds the individual to others on the basis of birth, forces him to contribute to the support of a large group independently of their ability, introduces nepotism into both business and politics, and assures control of the younger generation by the elders. (Davis, 1951:216)

The ascription-based caste system rejects qualification by achievement and "introduces unusual rigidities into the social order" (Davis, 1951:216). The caste system "is an effective brake on geographical mobility, ready contact with strangers, and the formation of large-scale business organizations" (Davis, 1951:216).

In modern times, the joint family remains a crucial factor in influencing individuals' lives. Aileen D. Ross (1961) cites a number of studies that provide evidence of the continued viability of the joint family even when family members move to the city. The emerging pattern is for the maintenance of connections with extended kin. The village continues to be the primary source of an individual's family identity. Authority remains vested in the family patriarch who still is the arbitrator of family matters. Family members return "home" on special occasions, such as festivals and marriages. Men who go into the cities to work send money back to their families and seek to return to the village after they have made money in the city, which enables them to buy land or live more comfortably in their village. Karve reports on this pattern:

> . . . instead of founding independent families in the towns where they are employed they tend to keep their ties with the family at home. They send money to the impoverished farmers at home, send their wives home for childbirth and go themselves for an occasional holiday or in times of need. The urge to visit the family for certain festivities and at sowing and harvesting times is so great that there is seasonal migration of mill-labourers in all industry towns. Even if a man earns good wages it is difficult for him to find a bride from a decent house if he has no family with some land in some village. (Karve cited in Ross, 1961:22)

The continued viability of the joint-family system and the caste system in contemporary India have been instrumental factors in explaining the dismal failures and problems of India's population-planning programs. Mahmood Mamdani (1972) examines family, caste, and class in an Indian village in the Punjab and demonstrates their influence on a big birth-reduction campaign.

Under the sponsorship of the Indian government and the Rockefeller Foundation, the *Khanna Study* was the first major field study in birth control in India. The field study was from 1954 to 1960, and the follow-up study occurred in the summer of 1969. This birth-control program was conducted in seven villages with a total population of 8000 people at a study cost of approximately $1 million.

Mahmood Mamdani believes that the primary reason for the failure of the *Khanna Study* was its deep-rooted political conservatism and its inability to understand the realities of village life. The family-planning program implicitly was considered as a substitute for structural and institutional change. The population controllers sought to bring about population control without any fundamental changes in the underlying relationships of the villagers. He argues that to be successful population-planning programs must understand individuals within the given social structure. It is foolhardy to believe that the simple dissemination of birth control information is sufficient to change people's behavior. Such a policy completely ignores the inequalities inherent within the caste and class structure.

Mamdani convincingly demonstrates that poor families will not restrict their family size because large families are economically viable. The only hope that the poor have in raising their status and economic position is to have a large family of sons. They can either work land for their parents and so help them accumulate savings so that they can buy land or they can emigrate to the cities and send back monetary remittances. To overcome poverty, large families are needed. The land can be worked with the manpower available within the family. One farmer puts it this way: "Why pay 2500 rupees for an extra hand? Why not have a son? . . . Instead of land fragmentation more sons increase your land" (Mamdani, 1972:77).

Mamdani points out that in a society that has a low level of technology, large families have high value among agricultural laborers. Under such conditions economic competition is determined by numbers, and the more laborers you have the better off you are. For these people, family planning means voluntarily reducing the family labor source. This would mean economic suicide and would be extremely irrational behavior. For the overwhelming majority (nearly 95 percent) of the people who participate in the agricultural economy, a large family is a necessity. For the small minority, the wealthy, civil servants, teachers, and others who live under radically different material conditions the importance of children is significantly less. Attitudes and perceptions of the villagers toward birth control varied according to their relationship to the economy.

> The majority in Manupur found it difficult to believe that the *Khanna Study* had actually come to introduce contraceptive practices. Even though the *Khanna Study* was a reality obvious to all, even though the whole enterprise "must have cost an incredible amount of money," the majority of the villagers never understood why so much money and effort were being spent on family planning when "surely everybody knows that children are a necessity in life." (Mamdani, 1972:144)

The failure of the birth-control program does not stem from either the illiteracy or the ignorance of the people. Nor would the demographic education of the villagers change their behavior. It would only change when it becomes economically viable for families to restrict their numbers. And that can only occur when the caste and class system is changed and when technological development economically warrants such a move. Mamdani quotes a low-caste water carrier who, mistaking him for a *Khanna Study* worker, proudly exclaims:

> You were trying to convince me in 1960 that I shouldn't have any more sons. Now, you see, I have six sons and two daughters and I sit at home in leisure. They are grown up and they bring me money. One even works outside the village as a laborer. You told me I was a poor man and couldn't support a large family. Now, you see, because of my large family, I am a rich man. (Mamdani, 1972:109)

This examination of population dynamics in India reveals that it is interrelated with family conceptualizations and dynamics along with social, political, and economic factors. In the next section, we see how the interrelationship of these factors is manifested in Western societies, particularly in the United States. Our focus of

Eight Indian children sit on top of an exhortation to limit the size of one's family.

concern centers on the conceptualization of parenthood and its influence on marital and parental relationships.

Fertility Patterns in the West: Parenthood and Ideologies

Paradoxically, although the emerging industrial system propagated ideologies that fostered low fertility and small family size, there were opposing ideologies gaining ascendancy that advocated domesticity and motherhood; that is, doctrines placing high value on the domestic confinement of women and their exclusive involvement with housework and child rearing were being set forth at the same time forces were motivating couples to want fewer births and to restrict their family size. Thus, women's entire functions were being defined in terms of motherhood at the same time the societal demands for children were diminishing. This situation was of course inherently unstable. The women's movements, the delay in marriage and child bearing, and the increased participation of women in the labor force can all be seen as protests to the untenable position of women in industrial society. We have discussed some of these ideologies and the conditions underlying them in Chapter 12. A brief review would be beneficial to help put this discussion of fertility and parenthood in perspective.

The rise of industrialization in the mid-nineteenth century saw a vast migration of people from rural areas to the factories and bureaucracies of a modern urban society. Work became more and more removed from the family setting. Men took jobs away from the home. They became increasingly independent of the previous prevailing domestic economy. With work becoming independent of the home, so did men.

These processes had an opposite effect on women and children. They became more economically dependent on the financial contributions of husbands and fathers. Domestic constraints, household tasks, and the care of children became solely the province of women. They were prevented from participation in extrafamilial occupations. Increasingly, they became cut off from the outside world of work. The resultant picture was that women and children were now economic liabilities who were almost totally dependent on the economic viability of men. Ann Oakley (1974:59) summarizes three lasting consequences associated with industrialization: "the separation of the man from the intimate daily routines of domestic life; the economic dependence of women and children on men; the isolation of housework and child care from other work."

We have discussed the patriarchal ideology, which advocates the domestic confinement of women. Its basis was the desire of Victorian men to shield the family from the evils of industrialization and urbanization. The isolated home was to provide a safe shelter and protection for the wife and the children. In this cloistered home the mother was to shield and protect the man's children. It was each man's castle and sanctuary. The home and women took on a sacred quality; they became the repository of goodness in a world of evil. John Ruskin has made the classic statement on the nature of the domestic scene as the province of mothers in his essay "Of Queen's Gardens" first published in 1865:

> This is the true nature of home — it is the place of Peace; the shelter, not only from all injury, but from all terror, doubt, and division. In so far as it is not this, it is not home; so far as the anxieties of the outer life penetrate into it, and the inconsistently-minded, unknown, unloved, or hostile society of the outer world is allowed by either husband or wife to cross the threshold it ceases to be home; it is then only a part of the outer world which you have roofed over and lighted a fire in. But so far as it is a sacred place, a vestal temple, a temple of the hearth watched over by Household Gods . . . so far as it is this, and the roof and the fire are types only of a nobler shade and light, shade as of the rock in a weary land, and the light as of Pharos in the stormy sea — so far as this it vindicates the name and fulfills the praise of home. (Ruskin, 1865/n.d.: 151–152)

The Victorian model, then, depicted women as the repository of virtue. The home was seen as the sanctuary protecting women and children from the evils of the outside world. The home was the working man's castle; his refuge from "the jungle out there."

The Victorian idealization of motherhood continues to linger in contemporary society. Betty Rollin talks of " 'The Motherhood Myth' — the idea that having babies is something that all normal women instinctively want and need and will enjoy doing — they just think they do" (Rollin, 1971:346). The motherhood myth is seen to have emerged after World War II. The economic prosperity and growth of postwar America was in striking contrast to the years of want and sacrifice during the Great Depression and the uncertainties of the war years. Rollin cites Betty Frieden who, in *The Feminine Mystique,* saw the late 1940s and 1950s as a period when the production of babies became the norm and motherhood turned into a cult.

Psychoanalysis was influential in the development of the mystique surrounding parenthood. Psychoanalysis placed undue emphasis on the mother–child relationship, oversentimentalizing it. It argued that only the biologic mother was capable of providing the emotional satisfaction and stimulation necessary for the healthy development of the infant. For the individuals involved, parenthood represented a necessary step on the road to maturation and personality development. For women, parenthood was necessary for them to achieve normality and avoid neuroticism. Freudian psychology insisted that the reproductive potential, that is, childbearing, must be actualized if women were to achieve mental health. Motherhood represented the realization of women's basic psychologic and biologic needs.

Rochelle Paul Wortis (1977) critically reexamined the concept of the maternal role as expressed in psychoanalytic theory. She concluded that the evidence used in psychological studies for the importance of the mother–child relationship was based on scientifically inadequate assumptions. The overemphasis on parenthood and particularly on motherhood encouraged "the domestication and subordination of females in society" (Wortis, 1977:361).

Wortis observed that the psychologic studies centering around the mother–infant bond reflected the provincialism of Western psychology and psychiatry. She argues that they turned a cultural phenomenon into a biologic one. Wortis notes that there are diversified ways in which children around the world are raised. Our society is relatively unique in insisting that child development lies solely within the province and responsibility of the mother. Wortis augments her argument by citing from the work of Margaret Mead:

> At present, the specific biological situation of the continuing relationship of the child to its biological mother and its need for care by human beings are being hopelessly confused in the growing insistence that child and biological mother, or mother surrogate, must never be separated, that all separation, even for a few days, is inevitably damaging, and that if long enough it does irreversible damage. This . . . is a new and subtle form of antifeminism in which men . . . are tying women more tightly to their children than has been thought necessary since the invention of bottle-feeding and baby carriages. Actually, anthropological evidence gives no support at present to the value of such an accentuation of the tie between mother and child. . . . On the contrary, cross-cultural studies suggest that adjustment is most facilitated if the child is cared for by many warm friendly people. (Mead, 1954, cited in Wortis, 1977:366)

Additional cross-cultural evidence on the variability of child-rearing patterns is provided in a study of six cultures by Minturn and Lambert (1964). The researchers found that only in the New England suburb of Orchardtown were there isolated households and exclusive mother–infant child rearing. In the five more "primitive" societies, there was a greater involvement by other kin and outsiders in the raising of the child. Thus, among the Nyansongo of Kenya, the child is cared for by an older sibling when the mother is working in nearby fields. Among the Rajputs of India, a caretaker, either an older sister or a cousin, cares for the child. Old men and, eventually, other male relatives—fathers, uncles, or grandfathers—assist in the child's care. Similar shared involvements characterize the Taira in Okinawa, the Mixteans of Mexico, and the Tarong of the Philippines. It is only in our society that women solely have this task.

Judith Blake, a world-famous demographer, argues that in contemporary Western society motherhood is actualized in "coercive pronatalism" (1972). Blake believes that motherhood, rather than being a voluntary option for women, is in fact a mandatory directive. This directive assures that women will bear children. Two pronatalist coercions characterize modern American society. The first is the prescribed primacy of parenthood in the definition of gender roles. The second is the prescribed congruence of personality traits with the demands of the gender roles as defined. Adult gender roles are defined in terms of parenthood. Americans socialize girls and boys to become the proper kinds of people they say that mothers and fathers should be.

Blake believes that the emphasis on the primacy of parenthood limits the accessibility of alternative roles. This is particularly the case for women. Nonfamilial roles are seen as deviant and pathological. Challenges to the role of motherhood arouse widespread opposition since they are viewed as threats to the gender-role expectations relegating women to domesticity and parenthood. Female labor-force participation, higher education for women, and feminism are viewed negatively by society as they run counter to the desired goal of motherhood. Motherhood is seen to represent the fulfillment of a woman's destiny.

Myths about motherhood provide the supportive ideology for the above viewpoint. Motherhood is seen to provide a woman with her most rewarding status. Fatherhood demonstrates the masculinity of the man. E.E. LeMasters (1977) has outlined several folk beliefs about parenthood that have been popular in American culture. (A folk belief is one that is widely held but that is not supported by facts.) Here are some of LeMasters' examples of these beliefs:

1. Rearing children is fun.
2. Children are sweet and cute.
3. Children will turn out well if they have "good" parents.
4. Children will improve marriage.
5. Childless couples are frustrated and unhappy.
6. Parents are adults.

LeMasters believes that these myths have been disproved by scientific evidence. However, they still serve to promote parenthood. Further, they downplay the problems associated with the transition to parenthood. Indeed, the transition to parenthood is a period often marked by crisis and marital disruption. Alice S. Rossi (1968), in an enlightening article, argues that the tensions and problems accompanying parenthood can be seen as an outgrowth of the isolation of the nuclear family and the almost exclusive involvement of the mother with infant and child care. An examination of the transition to the parenthood period is revealing in that it highlights the nature of parental roles in our modern industrial society.

Father as the Good Provider

The following discussion reviews the sociological character of men's lives in American families. Invariably, in the study of the family, greater attention is paid to the female roles of wife and mother than is paid to the male roles of husband and father. Given the dichotomization of the worlds of work and the worlds of the family, with men and women having corresponding influence in each, this is not surprising. However, the women's movement of the last 25 years has resulted in a serious reconsideration of the allocation and appropriation of the given roles of *both* women and men and their relative place in the public and private spheres of work and the home.

Jessie Bernard (1981), in a wonderful and insightful article, "The Good Provider Role: Its Rise and Fall," traces the historical development and changes in male roles in the family in the United States. She observes that the Industrial Revolution and the transition from a subsistence economy to a market economy in the 1830s led to the development of a specialized male role, that of the "good provider." It remained in effect for almost 150 years. Then, in the late 1970s, forces precipitated by the women's movement brought about changes symbolized by the 1980 census. That national census no longer assumed that a male should automatically be considered to be the head of the household. Essentially, the good-provider role defined a man as one whose wife did not have to, or should not, enter the labor force. Bernard cites Webster's second edition, which defines the good provider as "one who provides, especially (colloq.) one who provides food, clothing, etc., for his family, as he is a good or an adequate provider" (cited in Bernard, 1981:2).

The good-provider role has implications for both men and women. Bernard reminds us that in the colonial period, women such as Abigail Adams, the wife of John

In Praise of Children

BY ROBERT J. SAMUELSON

Until a year ago I was one of those slobs who thought all infants ugly. But as I write, my first child, Ruth, born last January, is climbing the stairs. Is it the greatest thing ever? Hard to tell. Two weeks ago she mastered clapping. She beams at every triumph. So do I. Everything she says—for example, "ah-yee-dee-dee-dah"—makes more sense than all the people I interview. Don't get the idea that I like being a father; it's simply the best experience of my life.

The truth, though, is that I'm part of the baby bust. I didn't marry until my late 30s, and Ruth arrived when I was 39. Like others of our generation, my wife and I have yet to reproduce ourselves. Collectively, this is an ominous failure. When we retire, the relative scarcity of workers (in relation to the elderly) could cripple social security and Medicare. And an older society may also be less energetic, less imaginative and more rigid. Ben Wattenberg of the American Enterprise Institute thinks declining population could enfeeble us as a great power.

Since Ruth's arrival, the baby bust seems a perverse consequence of "progress." Ours is an age of unrivaled wealth and individual choice. But, in a society that exalts self-expression, children are often inconvenient, because they destroy the fiction that we control our lives. The temptation is to leave them to last and, by then, it's sometimes too late. The baby bust's greatest losers may be people who do not have children and later wish they had. By delaying, some couples will have fewer than they want. And demographer Arthur Campbell thinks that more than a fifth of the women born in the mid-1950s may never have a child, almost triple the childless rate of their mothers.

WOMEN'S LIB

You will hear this ascribed to a breakdown of traditional values, or rampant selfishness. But this glib explanation misses the deeper truth, which is more subtle and less personal. People haven't suddenly become more selfish. Changing economic and social realities have simply made children less economically essential and, therefore, more a matter of choice. When people urge a return to traditional values, they're talking about the impossible: reversing centuries of economic and technological change that have altered women's roles. Women's liberation is less an idea than the result of changes that, by reducing pressures for childbearing, inevitably led to more educational and job opportunities.

Consider what's happened. In 1800 the average American woman had seven children; by 1900 the number had dropped below four, and today it is 1.8. At most, modern contraception increased the decline; the basic causes lie elsewhere. On the farm children were laborers, but in the city they added to crowding. As medicine improved, families could have fewer children and more survivors. Social security relieved parents' need for children to care for them in old age. In 1900 two-thirds of those over 65 lived with relatives; today 84 percent live by themselves.

Far from destroying traditional values, these changes fulfilled them. Our idea of progress has always been that people should live their lives as they see fit—as in "life, liberty and the pursuit of happiness." But if liberation is not radical, its results are often unintended or unwanted: for example, later marriages, more divorces and more single-parent families. Women, the greatest beneficiaries of change, have also been the greatest victims. Many working mothers experience frustration on the job and guilt at home. But, either economically or psychologically, more need to work. More than half of women with children under six work, up from 39 percent in 1975.

DIM FUTURE

The difficulty in speculating about the baby bust is that we don't know whether it will continue. By one theory, it won't. Economist Richard Easterlin argues that the

(continued)

steep drop in birthrates is a peculiar creature of the baby boom. Reared in ever-rising affluence, members of the baby boom expected the same. Instead, a lackluster economy and stiff competition among themselves for jobs depressed their wages and, by Easterlin's logic, made them less willing to assume the burdens of children. More women went to work to maintain living standards. A new generation—less populous, with more sober expectations—will fare better and have more children.

Who knows? Easterlin's theory is controversial and with good reason. Our society has created so many choices that the identity crisis—which was supposed to be a passing phase of adolescence—has become a permanent condition of life. Prediction is difficult. No one knows what an ideal population would be, and, as demographers Michael Teitelbaum and Jay Winter argue in a new book (*The Fear of Population Decline*, Academic Press), past fears of population decline have often been premature. But if the birthrate doesn't increase, our population could, depending on immigration flows, drop by the middle of the next century. The median age, already up to 31 from 28 in 1970, could go to 39 by 2020.

My hope is that Easterlin proves correct, though perhaps for different reasons. Attitudes change. The pleasures and pains of children cannot be anticipated. My sensible wife tries to educate me about what's important in life. But for her, I might have waited forever. My fear of Ruth was not dirty diapers or sleepless nights but that I might not like her. What a fool. I barely imagined the immense joys, constant surprises or sheer fun. But she is humbling. When learning to crawl, she preferred the dog to Dad. And her only use for my column is to tear it up; thank goodness, George Will gets the same treatment.

No one need remind me that my views of children are wildly romantic and unrealistic. A friend writes that his eight-year-old rebels against long car trips by singing his own version of Willie Nelson's "On the Road Again." A sample: "On the road again / I'd rather have the world come to an end." Dirty diapers are nothing next to the adventures and anxieties that lie ahead. But, for now, I'm floating in ya-ya land.

Adams, managed estates and were active in business and professional pursuits. Women were expected to provide for the family along with men. They were involved in the running of stores, shops, and businesses. The domestic economy of preindustrial America saw the household as a center for the production of food, clothing, furniture, bedding, candles, and other accessories. Women's involvement in the economic well-being of the family was taken for granted.

The development of a specialized male role devoted to economic activity had as a consequence the removal of women from labor-force participation and income-producing activities. Instead of looking after themselves and their families, they had to devote their attention to obtaining a "good provider" who would "take care of" them and their children. Throughout this book, we indicate the psychological and sociological consequences of this viewpoint for women's lives. Now let us turn our attention to the consequences for men.

Men were told to concentrate on their jobs and careers; emotional expressivity was not to be their concern. The expression of emotion was to be in the women's realm. Lack of expressivity became a defining characteristic of the good-provider role. It was even reflected in the criteria for marriage. A man was defined as a good marriage prospect if it was felt that he would be a good provider, not that he would be gentle, loving, or tender. Being a good provider was the essential quality that was looked for. While being a "family man"—setting a good table, providing a decent home, paying the mortgage, feeding and clothing wife and children—was important, loving attention and emotional involvement with the family were not necessarily seen as a part of the package. As Bernard puts it: "If in addition to being a good provider, a man was kind, gentle, humorous, and not a heavy drinker or gambler, that was all frosting on the cake" (1981:3).

A consequence of the good-provider role was the development of a predominant concept of male identity in terms of work and career activities. Success was measured by an economic criterion. The worth of a man and the meaning of his life became defined by the work place and his success and failure there; they were not measured in terms of his being a caring, loving, and nurturing husband and father. The consequence was that failure to provide economically for the family resulted in negative identity feelings regardless of how successfully the man may have fulfilled the emotional and expressive needs of family members.

Also involved in attitudes regarding the good-provider role was the belief that a wife employed was evidence of the male's failure to provide. A working wife was also viewed as ultimately undermining the man's position as head of the household.

Bernard historically examines the different ways that males have confronted the good-provider role. Two categories of males—the "role rejectors" and "role overperformers"—are delineated. The role rejectors are epitomized by the fictional character Rip Van Winkle, who slept through the 20 crucial years of marriage and child rearing. The tramp, the hobo, and today's homeless men on skid row are men who dropped out of the role entirely. The social historian John Demos (1974) depicts the tramp as follows:

> Demoralized and destitute wanderers, their numbers mounting into the hundreds and thousands, tramps can be fairly characterized as men who had run away from their wives. . . . Their presence was mute testimony to the strains that tugged at the very core of American family life. . . . Many observers noted that the tramps had created a virtual society of their own . . . based on a principle of single-sex companionship. (Demos, 1974:438)

Conversely, we speak of the overperformers as "workaholics" or men so intoxicated by work that they lose sight of the ultimate goal of providing for the family with a compulsive striving for occupational and career achievement. This often results in the complete neglect of family members. They epitomize the intrinsic strain and contradiction in the good-provider role. For, by epitomizing it, they highlight the inherent limitations of defining good providing solely in economic terms. And as Bernard points out: "Their preoccupation with their work even at the expense of their families was . . . quite acceptable in our society" (1981:7).

In the 1970s, the good-provider role underwent dramatic changes. Ideological changes brought about through the women's movement questioned male family roles. Further, the simultaneous occurrence of recession and inflationary economic conditions often necessitated a two-income family to maintain the family's standard of living. Ideological factors combined with economic conditions resulted in more and more wives and mothers entering the work force. One consequence was a welcome relief for the husband-father from the economic burden of being sole provider. Attached to women's work realities was a consequent demand for two modifications in the traditional male good-provider role. Bernard identifies these as a call for more intimacy, expressivity, and nurturance on the part of males in the family and sharing of household responsibility and child care. To some extent, changes are occurring, albeit painfully for some. Bernard closes by raising a number of questions regarding the impact of the large influx of women into the work force, the large number of men who will increase their participation in the family and the household, and the subsequent demise of the good-provider role:

> Will men find the apron shameful? What if we were to ask fathers to alternate with mothers in being in the home when youngsters come home from school? Would fighting adolescent drug abuse be more successful if fathers and mothers were

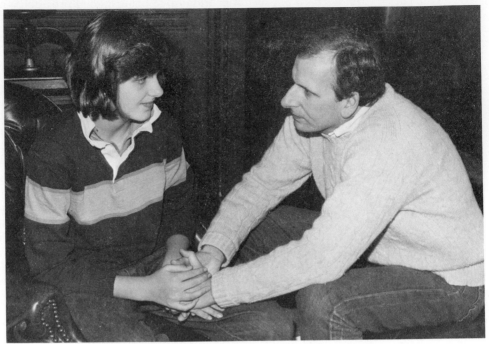

Miro Vintoniv/Stock, Boston

Father and teenage daughter having a heart-to-heart conversation.

equally engaged in it? If the school could confer with fathers as often as with mothers? If the father accompanied children when they went shopping for clothes? If fathers spent as much time with children as do mothers?

What does the demotion of the good provider to the status of the senior provider or even mere co-provider do to him? To marriage? To gender identity? What does expanding the role of housewife to that of junior provider or even co-provider do to her? To marriage? To gender identity? (Bernard, 1981:11)

The Transition to Parenthood

Only in recent years have sociologists recognized that parenthood, rather than marriage, may be the crucial role transition for men and women. Parenthood necessitates the reorganization of economic patterns of earning and spending the family income. It demands the reallocation of space, time, and attention. It necessitates the reorganization of marital decision making and the reorganization of occupation-role commitments, particularly for the wife. It calls for the reworking of relationships with extended family, friends, and neighbors. Finally, it demands the reestablishment of marital adjustment and intimacy, which have been disrupted by the period of transition to parenthood.

Despite the importance of this transition, little research effort has been directed to this concern. The behavioral sciences have almost exclusively confined their attention to the child when studying the husband–wife–child relationships. Thus, a vast body of data has been accumulated in the field of child development. There is a great deal of literature concerned with the effect parents have on their children. The corresponding issue—the effects children have on their parents—has received relatively little attention. This reflects the parenthood myth that having children is an enriching and maturing experience. The myth says parenthood enhances personality growth, solidifies the marriage, and indicates the achievement of adult status and community stability. With such positive attributes, the impact of parenthood on the parents was not seen as problematic and was, therefore, not defined as a subject worth studying. The handful of existing studies, although exploratory and having methodological weaknesses, nonetheless reveal that parenthood is not always positive.

In a widely cited article, "Parenthood as Crisis," E.E. LeMasters (1957) found that 83 percent of the 46 couples interviewed experienced extensive or severe crisis in adjusting to the birth of their first child. Some of the problems of adjustment most frequently mentioned by mothers were chronic tiredness, extensive confinement to the home with resulting curtailment of social contacts, and the relinquishing of satisfactions associated with outside employment. Women felt guilty about not being better mothers. Fathers mentioned decline in sexual response of the wife, economic pressures resulting from the wife's retirement, additional expenditures necessary for the child, and a general disenchantment with the parental role.

The amount of crisis experienced by these couples was found to be unrelated to the planning of children, to prior marital adjustment, or to the personality adjustment of the couples. Couples seemed to experience crisis even when they actively wanted the child and had a good marriage. The only variable that LeMasters found to distinguish crisis from noncrisis reactions was professional employment of the mother. All eight mothers with extensive professional work experience suffered severe crises. LeMasters concludes that parenthood is the real "romantic complex" in our culture and that this romanticizing of parenthood and the attendant lack of training for the role are crucial determinants of problems.

Everett D. Dyer (1963) studied 32 middle-class couples who had their first child within the 2 years before the study. Among these couples, 53 percent experienced extensive or severe crisis, 38 percent experienced moderate crisis, and the remaining 9 percent reported slight adjustment problems. These crises often lasted for several months and involved the reorganization of preexisting role relationships. Difficulties reported by these new mothers were similar to those reported by LeMasters: tiredness, feelings of uncertainty, and curtailment of outside activities and interests. New fathers reported the same problems as their wives and added those of adjusting to one income and getting used to new demands and routines. Overall, the findings from Dyer's study tend to support the contention that the arrival of the first child constitutes a crisis event for middle-class couples and those who undergo the severest crises have the most difficulty recovering.

Some studies, however, have found that beginning parenthood should be seen as a transitional period rather than a crisis one. Notably, the studies by Daniel F. Hobbs (1965, 1968) and that of Hobbs and Sue Peck Cole (1976) found only slight amounts of difficulty among parents adjusting to the first child. However, they did find that mothers reported significantly greater amounts of difficulty than did fathers. The Hobbs and Cole study differed from Hobbs' two earlier studies in that his samples were not limited to middle-class couples and the couples were contacted much sooner after the birth of their child. Hobbs speculates that the low proportion of couples experiencing crisis at this early period may be due to a "baby honeymoon." This is a period of early elation over parenthood but, after four to six weeks, crisis occurs. Another factor, that the samples contained lower-class couples, may indicate variations among the classes in their reaction to parenthood. Let us look at class variations in more detail.

Arthur P. Jacoby (1969), in a reassessment of the transition to parenthood literature, developed hypotheses to explain why his findings and those of LeMasters and Dyer found greater role transition problems for their middle-class samples than for Hobbs' working-class samples. The following key elements were suggested to explain the higher middle-class parenthood-crisis rate:

1. Middle-class standards may be higher. (Middle-class families are seen to have greater expectations in terms of childbearing practices and personal advancement.)
2. The working-class woman places a greater intrinsic value on having children.
3. The principal sources of gratification for the working-class woman are located within the family rather than outside it.
4. Parenthood is far more likely to interfere with career aspirations for middle-class mothers.
5. Middle-class mothers are less experienced in the care of children.
6. The middle-class husband-and-wife relationship is more strongly established as affectively positive at the time of birth of a child. (Research on lower-class marriages indicates a weaker and less affectionate conjugal tie than in the middle class. The arrival of a child represents less of a threat to the marital relationship because there is less to threaten.)

Let us build on Jacoby's speculations by analyzing the transition to parenthood within different class groups, focusing on the effect of the transition period on three major areas: (1) the marital relationship; (2) the satisfactions of the husband and wife with their marital roles and their lives; and (3) social and career aspirations, interests, and activities of the husband and wife. By comparing husbands and wives of different social classes in these three areas, we will be able to pinpoint their attitudinal and behavioral differences regarding parenthood.

Marital Interaction

Several studies (Blood and Wolfe, 1960; Campbell, 1970; Renne, 1970; Reiss, 1971) report that after childbirth, marital communication is disrupted and marital satisfaction drops for middle-class couples. Harold Feldman (1974) found that in companionate marital relationships the level of marital satisfaction decreased when a couple had a child. It was more apt to increase in differentiated marital relationships. Here, the previously nonexistent closeness between the parents was changed by the new, shared interest in the infant. This may support Jacoby's (1969) proposition that the birth of a child can easily disrupt emotional and affectional middle-class family ties.

Wives involved in household and family responsibilities may resent their husbands' nonfamilial involvements. Reuben Hill and Joan Aldous (1968) believe that this resentment may become manifest in their resistance to husbands' demands for intimacies. Peter Pineo (1961) presents evidence indicating that parenthood may have a disproportionately negative effect on women. Women's disenchantment with marriage is seen to result from parenthood, whereas occupational commitments are seen to be the major factor accounting for male disenchantment.

Working-class couples have been characterized by weak and less affectionate ties and thus a child may not represent a threat to the marital relationship. Mirra Komarovsky (1964) and Lee Rainwater (1965) found that there is a segregated pattern of decision making and task division with working-class couples as well as less expectation that husbands and wives will be companions. This is felt to aid them and better prepare them to interact as father and mother than as conjugal partners. It would seem that a key variable underlying the differences between the classes is the different types of marital relationships that existed before parenthood. Middle-class companionate relationships characterized by joint decision making and task differentiation tend to become more disrupted at parenthood than working-class noncompanionate relationships.

However, Hannah Gavron (1966) reports that for some middle-class couples with an egalitarian relationship there is a tendency for parents to establish some barriers between themselves and their children. But, during the period immediately following the birth of the child, there still is some degree of temporary segregation of spousal responsibilities. Rossi (1968) suggests that, with the strengthening of the egalitarian relationship, there may develop a greater recognition of the wife's need for autonomy and the husband's role in the routines of home and child rearing. In fact, Rossi sees such a movement becoming institutionalized through natural childbirth and prenatal courses for the husband. These developments are seen as a consequence of greater egalitarianism between husband and wife, especially when both work and jointly maintain the household before the birth of the child. If this is a coming trend, then the disruption of marital communication and marital satisfaction for middle-class parents should diminish.

A very interesting approach in the investigation of marital interactions after the birth of a child argues that the study of the allocation, utilization, and commitment of time can be useful in the analysis of the transition-to-parenthood period. Ralph LaRossa and Maureen LaRossa (1981) have made the argument that researchers have been so involved in the measurement of the attitudes that people have toward the transition to parenthood that they have neglected to study the actual behavior that occurs during this transition period. They described the experiences of 20 white upper-middle-class couples, half of whom had just had their first child and half of whom had other children in addition to their newborn one. The key variable in explaining the character of the transition into parenthood was how the couples allocated time. In answer to questions on how their lives had changed since their babies were born, the constant theme echoed by these parents was the loss of time for such everyday activities as sleep, communication, sex, and even using the bathroom. Paradoxically, they also reported that they were more likely to be bored; weight gain and television soap-opera addiction were unwanted consequences.

LaRossa and LaRossa attribute the simultaneous feeling of time being both scarce and abundant to the nature of infant care and its related activities. New infants require constant supervision and care and the parents have to be constantly available. "It is this basic pattern — child dependency resulting in continuous coverage, which means a scarcity of free time, which leads to conflicts of interest and often conflict behavior — that cuts across the experiences of all the couples in our sample" (LaRossa and LaRossa, 1981:46–47).

Among these affluent couples the distribution of time allocation for the infant is different for the mother and father. They make a distinction between playing with the infant and caring for the infant. Men are much more likely to play with their babies, while mothers are more likely to bathe, feed, dress, and change them. The spending of time at play is seen to require less attention on the part of the father than care on the part of the mother. Of course, there is also a qualitative difference in the nature of the interaction between parent and infant than between adults. Infants are unrelenting in their demand for the satisfaction of their needs, whether it be the changing of a diaper or being fed. Infants also demand that parents be present during their waking hours. This again severely restricts the activities of the parent.

In addition to the parental division of labor in infant care, LaRossa and LaRossa found that mothers are primarily responsible for their infants. When fathers assume the caring role, it is invariably defined as "helping" their wives. They found that "*every* couple would, at least once in their interviews, refer to the husband as 'helping' the wife with the baby, whereas not a single couple defined the wife's parental responsibilities in these terms. Clearly from the start, the mother is the one who is 'in charge' of the baby" (1981:57).

In a later article, Ralph LaRossa (1983) makes the theoretical distinction between "physical" time and "social" time as an explanatory variable in understanding the transition to parenthood. Physical time is astronomical time; it is quantitative, continuous, homogeneous, and objective. The examples provided include the speed of light and the rate of decay of the body. Social time, on the other hand, is qualitative, discontinuous, heterogeneous, and subjective. Here, the examples include courtship, small talk, and the sequences and durations of friendship. LaRossa builds on William J. Goode's (1960) sociological approach to time put forth in his theory of role strain. Goode conceptualizes time as being a relatively scarce resource. People face a problem in trying to meet their total role obligations given their overall activities and given the finite nature of time. LaRossa focuses on one of the 20 couples that he (along with Maureen LaRossa) studied earlier to demonstrate the utility of this distinction between physical time and social time.

LaRossa shows how both the mother and father find difficulty in fulfilling their total role obligations as a consequence of the birth of their third child. The wife-mother has to balance caring for the two other children, her career, housework, and marriage with the demands of infant care. The husband-father, who travels a lot, must make every second count when he returns home and spends time with his family. The demands of the infant, who will not socially accommodate to the temporal rules of the parents' schedule, complicates matters. LaRossa states, "Thus, the transition to parenthood makes a family more aware of their schedule—formerly a taken-for-granted system (who questions the validity of not getting up at 4:00 A.M.?) —which in turn makes them more aware of the clock, which then makes them feel that they are constantly running out of time" (1983:585–586).

Further, when, as in the case of this case-study family, the couple have an overcommitment to their work and their home, additional problems may be felt. LaRossa believes that this couple may be a prime candidate for what he calls "marital burnout," a belief that they do not have enough time to make love or have a meaningful conversation. Their overcommitment to other activities leaves them less time than they wish for their commitment to each other. They are then forced to justify their undercommitment to their relationship in terms of these other involvements. "[T]hey find themselves excusing and justifying their misconduct (i.e., their conduct that is at odds with their shared belief that they are still in love) by citing their lack of time" (LaRossa, 1983:587).

In summary, we concur with LaRossa's opinion that the future investigation of the transition to parenthood would be aided by examining it within the context of the social reality of time. By so doing, we would be able to find out how time is allocated and its trajectory and effect on the transition-to-parenthood period. Social-time analysis would also be a significant conceptual tool in understanding differential commitments, role allocations, and the definition of infant care as a scheduled event. Variations in societal norms and subcultural families' commitments to the social construction of the transition to parenthood should also be studied. Finally, the study of the resolution of apparent contradictions between articulated commitments and actual behavior of new mothers and fathers would aid in the analysis of the transition to parenthood.

Marital Roles and Life Satisfactions

The sexual relationship is disrupted and frequently discontinued during the 8 weeks prior to birth and up to 2 months after birth. This allows the woman's tissues to heal. Further, the involvement of the woman with the infant or frequent disruptions by its cries often lead to a disinterest toward sex. The fear of immediate pregnancy after the birth of a child can also be a factor. Studies of working-class families by Rainwater (1960) and Komarovsky (1962) discuss the wife's dilemma: her self-interest in avoiding another pregnancy versus her desire for sexual pleasure to gratify herself and her husband. This is of crucial importance to women who have recently given birth and who do not communicate with their husbands on sexual matters. These studies and many others report that the lack of communication in this area is more characteristic of the working class than the middle class. If this is the case, then we would suspect that middle-class couples may find postpartum sexual adjustments easier than blue-collar couples. However, the revolution in the general technology of contraception, especially the birth-control pill, has the potential to alter this factor dramatically. Unfortunately, there is virtually no systematic investigation on the extent that this occurs.

A second factor that affects sexual and marital satisfactions and adjustments after childbirth is the degree of segregation of marital-role tasks. Earlier, we reported on Hill and Aldous' (1968) contention that wives who are tied down by domestic household and child-care duties resent their husbands' external involvements. This resentment becomes evident in their resistance to their husbands' demands for conjugal intimacies. Based on this finding, we may conclude that segregated-task allocations, especially in terms of the wife's involvement with domestic and child-care tasks, will be positively related to poor sexual adjustment and potentially poor marital adjustment. Since role segregation is more prevalent in the working class, we would expect the working class to have the greater frequency of poorly adjusted marital and sexual relationships. However, confounding this expectation is one important fact: the nonfamilial career and social interests, involvements, and aspirations of the wife. This factor, discussed in the next section, is inversely related to class; that is, middle-class wives have greater conflicts with work and family roles than working-class wives. Thus, they may resent their relatively total involvement with domestic and child-care duties to a greater extent than their working-class counterparts.

Nonfamilial Career and Social Interests, Involvements, and Aspirations

Bernard Farber (1964) defines the family as a set of mutually contingent careers. Farber's approach sensitizes us to the multiple roles of men and women other than husband and wife. Other roles, such as father and mother, and occupational and career roles for men and women occur over time and make the attainment of marital satisfaction somewhat problematic. Further, Farber's orientation emphasizes that marital satisfaction and family satisfaction are not the same. Men and women place differential importance on marital and parental roles as well as on occupational and career roles. Farber has suggested that we classify families as child centered versus parent centered to highlight this variation.

Herbert Gans (1962a) has made a similar observation in his masterful work on Italian-American residents of an urban village in Boston, Massachusetts. He sees more than one set of definitions concerning the behavioral expectations of the parental role. He makes the distinction between adult-centered, child-centered, and adult-directed families and proposes that each type of family is prevalent in different class levels. In each family type, the role of the parents and the children are manifested differently.

The working-class family is characterized as adult centered. Here, the husband and wife live gender-segregated roles. They have separate family roles and engage in little of the companionship typically found in the middle class. The husband is predominantly the wage earner and the enforcer of child discipline. The wife's activities are confined to household tasks and child rearing. Children are expected to follow adult rules and are required to act "grown up." They are disciplined when they act as children. Family life is centered around the desires and interests of the adults and does not cater to the demands of the children. Husbands and wives are frequently involved with extended kin and with neighbors and friends, albeit different ones for each.

Husbands and wives of the lower-middle class have a more-companionate relationship. Their roles are less sexually segregated than those of the working class. The home and the family are the common interest points. The family is child centered, with the home being run both for adults and children. The children are allowed to be themselves and to act as children. The lower-middle-class family is a conjugal one consisting of only parents and children. The couple tends to share activities, and their social life tends to be informal and primarily involves friends and neighbors.

The upper-middle-class family is depicted by Gans as being adult directed. Predominantly college educated, this family type is interested in and participates in the activities of the larger world. Unlike the preceding two types, it does not confine its activities to the local community. Family and the home are less important to this class than to the other classes. Frequently, the wife pursues a career prior to having children and is either working or has aspirations to work as the children are growing. Domestic activities are alleviated to some extent through the employment of service help or the sharing of activities by the husband. Children serve as a common focal point of interest and concern. The upper-middle-class couples are concerned with the intellectual and social development of their children. They are highly motivated to provide direction for the lives of their children, so that family life is child centered as well as adult directed.

These variations in social-class family types have differential effects on the importance of parenthood for males and females. Thus, although males in our society derive their primary status and identification from their occupational role and women gain theirs from their familial roles, there are significant degrees of variation between the working class and the more upper-middle class. This is particularly the case for upper-middle-class women. For them, there has been a notable movement to get away from the ascribed roles of wife and mother and to incorporate additional or alternative roles in the occupational sphere. As of now, this movement has had its primary influence on the educated and affluent women of the upper-middle classes. By and large, working-class women still perceive their primary role in terms of marriage and motherhood.

Studies of working-class families have concluded that the parental role maintains a dominant position in a woman's life (Gans, 1962a; Komarovsky, 1962; Rainwater, 1965). Robert Bell (1964, 1965, 1971), in studies of married lower-income black women in Philadelphia, found that motherhood was more highly valued than wifehood. Similarly, Rainwater (1960)—in a study of sex, contraception, and family planning in a white working-class population—found that motherhood gives a woman her major rationale for existence. He reports that the experience of pregnancy and childbirth aids working-class women in establishing self-validity. It has higher significance for working-class women than for middle-class women, who may place higher value on outside interests. He also found, as did J. Mayone Stycos (1955), that impregnating a woman is a sign of masculine potency and is highly valued by working-class husbands. However, children, outside of being the proof of masculinity, have little significance for the husband in his everyday world. For the wife, on the other hand, the child provides the chief source for her psychic gratification and she defines herself mainly in her motherhood role. Rainwater (1965) makes the following observation:

> To the working-class mother caring for children represents the central activity of her life. She defines herself mainly as a mother and seeks to find gratification in life principally through this function. The children are considered mainly her property and responsibility and it is through them that she expects to fulfill herself and her potentialities. . . . (Rainwater, 1965:86)

The extent to which the ideologies of egalitarianism and individualism have infiltrated the working class remains open for investigation. Yet, although somewhat stereotypical, the above quotation draws attention to the emphasis placed on segregated role relationships of husbands and wives and the wives' main involvement defined in terms of the home and children.

In contrast, the upper-middle-class woman is caught in a dilemma. On the one hand, she has achieved a relatively high degree of educational attainment and frequently is involved in an occupation that she values and to which she has made a considerable commitment. Yet, she is faced with cultural pressures to assume the maternal role. For many, the pressure is so great that they have children in the absence of any genuine desire for them or the ability to care for them.

Alice S. Rossi (1968) points out that parental roles differ dramatically from marriage and work. With the widespread availability of effective contraceptives, parenthood can be postponed indefinitely. Before the technological advancement in contraceptive devices, pregnancy was likely to follow shortly after marriage. Then marriage was the major transition in a woman's life. Couples can now postpone having children until they are ready to have them. Today, many couples have children after they have had the opportunity to establish a workable marital relationship and have acquired sufficient capital and household furnishings to support a child financially. Occupational roles are also something that is learned over a period of time. The attainment of both roles, occupational and marital, can be seen as gradual transitional processes. However, parenthood is an immediate occurrence. All too frequently there is an almost complete absence of training for the role. Most women facing the birth of their first child have had little preparation for the maternal role other than some sporadic babysitting, or occasionally taking care of younger siblings. Suddenly, the inexperienced woman is confronted with the reality of a 24-hour job of infant care. Further, in contrast with other role commitments, parenthood is irrevocable. Rossi notes that we can have ex-spouses and ex-jobs but not ex-children.

The point may be raised that if women insist on maintaining their occupational role in addition to their maternal role the family may become more egalitarian with the husband assuming more of the responsibility for child care. This would alleviate some of the burden of the parental role incurred by a woman's double-role involvements. Earlier, we suggested that there seems to be a growing trend, especially among middle-class couples, for greater egalitarianism. Rossi states that an egalitarian base to the marital relationship may result in a tendency for parents to establish some barriers between themselves and their children. If this occurs, it may be a positive factor mitigating against the development of the crisis of parenthood for middle-class couples, especially for women. Jacoby (1969) concluded that middle-class women place a lower evaluation on having children than working-class women and that parenthood is far more likely to interfere with their career aspirations. Thus, if a coalition of support occurs between husband and wife the crisis may not occur.

Undoubtedly, many couples develop patterns to offset the debilitating aspects of parenthood, yet for most couples, particularly wives, parenthood can be a crisis period. All too frequently, the wife is faced with what we have described as the double burden. The woman is expected to hold down her occupational position and at the same time continue to be primarily involved in domestic tasks, including child rearing. This, of course, is an untenable position.

In summary, we believe that the dissatisfactions and problems associated with parenthood, particularly for the middle class, ultimately stem from the very nature of the conjugal-family system. In middle-class American society, the family is relatively isolated from the supports of extended kin and the surrounding community. They are not available to assist in the care of infants and young children. This is quite different from conditions in our historical past or in other societies.

Historically, the family was a part of the community. Philippe Ariès (1962) has observed that the contemporary family has withdrawn into the home. It has become a private place of residence for family members. The former extended-family group, who lived in common residence, is gone. The family is segregated from the rest of the world, and the home is isolated from external involvements. This has had profound effects on the wife-mother who has been relegated to domestic tasks and child-bearing. She has the major responsibility for the well-being of the child. Fathers are not required to be involved in child care. The community provides minimal institutional supports and assistance. The result has been the increased dissatisfaction with parenthood and particularly motherhood.

This has been the traditional pattern. But, as we have noted, there are movements of change. Increasingly, husbands are becoming involved in domestic activities, including relationships with their children. Another is the increased demands for child-care facilities outside the home. This would allow both the husband and the wife to pursue outside family careers. As of this writing, child-care facilities are still woefully inadequate. Finally, and most dramatically, there is the development of ideological arguments for increased options for women. The motherhood myth is less acceptable to many. This should result in a more-satisfying and more-productive parenthood and childhood. Our thoughts echo those of Betty Rollin:

> When motherhood is no longer culturally compulsory, there will, certainly, be less of it. Women are now beginning to think and do more about development of self, of their individual resources. Far from being selfish, such development is probably our only hope. That means more alternatives for women. And more alternatives mean more selective, better, happier motherhood—and childhood and husbandhood (or manhood) and peoplehood. It is not a question of whether or not children are sweet and marvelous to have and rear; the question is, even if that's so, whether or not one wants to pay the price for it. It doesn't make any sense any more to pretend that women need babies, when what they really need is themselves. If God were still speaking to us in a voice we could hear, even He would probably say, "Be fruitful. Don't multiply." (Rollin, 1970:17)

Abortion and the Family

There are a seemingly endless variety of laws, restrictions, customs, and traditions that affect the practice of abortion around the world. Christopher Tietze (1981), a preeminent expert on international abortion, wrote a report for the Population Council in New York City called *Induced Abortion: A World Review, 1981.* Tietz found that 9 percent of the world's population of 4.4 billion people live in countries that totally forbid abortion, while 38 percent live in nations that allow abortion on request at least during the first trimester of pregnancy. Since 1965, 17 countries (including Canada, India, Norway, and Great Britain) have liberalized their abortion laws. During that same period, seven nations (Bulgaria, Czechoslavakia, Hungary, Rumania, Iran, Israel, and New Zealand) have adopted tougher legislation.

Abortion is now the most common surgical procedure not only in the United States but also in the world. Some countries—such as Cuba, Rumania, and the Soviet Union—have abortion rates that are much higher than our own. Other countries—such as England, Canada, and West Germany—have much lower rates. Countries that have comparable rates to the United States include Japan and Sweden (Tietze, 1981).

Time (1981)—in an article titled "Private Lives, Public Policies"—reports on some cross-cultural variations in abortion practices. Cuba is the only Latin-American country that has legalized abortion. However, practice does not necessarily follow the law. In Brazil, the government has begun implementation of a national family-planning program while at the same time a lucrative—albeit illegal—abortion business thrives. Uruguay has readily available illegal abortion clinics that have a large Argentine clientele.

In Belgium, abortion is allowed only to save the lives of mothers. Belgians who desire abortion travel north to the Netherlands, where 75 percent of the legalized abortions are performed on foreigners. The Dutch themselves have the lowest abortion rate of any West European nation. Similarly, the countries of New Zealand and Australia have different policies regarding abortion. In 1977, New Zealand's anti-abortion activists succeeded in passing legislation that required cumbersome review procedures by medical and psychiatric consultants to determine the extent of physical or mental damage to the mother. Three thousand New Zealand women traveled to Australia to have legal abortions and thus skirt the New Zealand bureaucracy. As New Zealand women became more sophisticated in presenting the appropriate psychiatric symptoms, the abortion rate has returned to about 4,000 a year.

Feminists have viewed the patriarchal control of women's bodies as one of the prime issues facing the contemporary women's movement. They observe that the definition and control of women's reproductive freedom have always been the provence of men. Patriarchal religion as manifest in Islamic fundamentalism, traditionalist Hindu practice, orthodox Judaism, and Roman Catholicism has been an important historical contributory factor for this and continues to be an important presence in contemporary societies. In recent times, governments, usually controlled by men, have "given" women the right to contraceptive use and abortion access when their countries were perceived to have an overpopulation problem. When these countries are perceived to be underpopulated, that right has been absent. Robin Morgan — a leading advocate of worldwide women's rights — states, "The point, of course, is that this is *the right of an individual woman* herself, *not a gift to be bestowed or taken back* (1984:6).

Morgan goes on to observe that the many social agencies of the United Nations have observed the absence of contraceptive information and devices and the suppression of women's knowledge of them. As a consequence, women have often suffered by being forced to bear unwanted children, being kept from having wanted children, and having to bear children in inappropriate and often desperate circumstances. Among the cited evidence, she includes the following:

- Thirty to 50 percent of all "maternal" deaths in Latin America are due to improperly performed illegal abortions or to complications following abortion attempts.
- Fifty percent of all women in India gain no weight during the third trimester of pregnancy, owing to malnourishment.
- Every ten minutes in 1980, an Indian woman died of a septic abortion.
- More than half of all live births in Venezuela are out of wedlock. Illegal abortion is the leading cause of female deaths in Caracas.
- The average Soviet woman has between twelve and fourteen abortions during her lifetime, because contraceptives, although legal, are extremely difficult to obtain.
- In Peru, 10 to 15 percent of all women in prison were convicted for having had illegal abortions, 60 percent of the women in one Lima prison were there for having had or performed illegal abortions.
- Eighty percent of pregnant and nursing rural women in Java have anemia. (Morgan, 1984:7)

The Abortion Controversy in the United States

The United States has witnessed a revolution in the abortion situation for the last 15 years or so. In the late 1960s and early 1970s, 17 states liberalized their abortion laws. Then in January 1973, the Supreme Court issued landmark rulings that virtually wiped out both the old laws and most of the more-liberal new ones. In *Roe vs.*

Wade and *Doe vs. Bolton,* the court held that any woman anywhere in the United States can legally receive an abortion if she wants.

Since these decisions, the annual number of abortions performed in the United States has risen from 744,600 in 1973 to 1.5 million by 1980 (*Time,* "The Battle over Abortion," April 6, 1981). Abortions in 1980 terminated one-third of all pregnancies in the nation. More than a million teenagers became pregnant, and 38 percent had abortions. Almost 320,000 married women had abortions in 1980. The court's decision and the rise in the abortion rate that followed it has provoked a crusade of unrelenting commitment. This "right to life" movement has become perhaps the most powerful single-issue force in American politics.

On one side of the controversy are those who call themselves "pro-life." They view the fetus as a human life rather than as an unformed complex of cells; therefore, they hold to the belief that abortion is essentially murder of an unborn child. These groups cite both legal and religious reasons for their opposition to abortion. Pro-lifers point to the rise in legalized abortion figures and see this as morally intolerable. On the other side of the issue are those who call themselves "pro-choice." They believe that women, not legislators or judges, should have the right to decide whether and under what circumstances they will bear children. Pro-choicers are of the opinion that laws will not prevent women from having abortions and cite the horror stories of the past when many women died at the hands of "backroom" abortionists and in desperate attempts to self-abort. They also observe that legalized abortion is especially important for the 17 percent of rape victims and 25 percent of incest victims who become pregnant (Pasnau, 1972). They stress physical and mental health reasons why women should not have unwanted children.

To get a better understanding of the current abortion controversy, let us examine a very important work by Kristin Luker (1984), *Abortion and the Politics of Motherhood.* Luker argues that female pro-choice and pro-life activists hold different world views regarding gender, sex, and the meaning of parenthood. Moral positions on abortion are seen to be tied intimately to views on sexual behavior, the care of children, family life, technology, and the importance of the individual. Luker identifies "pro-choice" women as educated, affluent, and liberal. Their contrasting counterparts, "pro-life" women, support traditional concepts of women as wives and mothers. It would be instructive to sketch out the differences in the world views of these two sets of women. Luker examines California, with its liberalized abortion law, as a case history. Public documents and newspaper accounts over a 20-year period were analyzed and over 200 interviews were held with both pro-life and pro-choice activists.

Luker found that pro-life and pro-choice activists have intrinsically different views with respect to gender. Pro-life women have a notion of public and private life. The proper place for men is in the public sphere of work; for women, it is the private sphere of the home. Men benefit through the nurturance of women; women benefit through the protection of men. Children are seen to be the ultimate beneficiaries of this arrangement by having the mother as a full-time loving parent and by having clear role models. Pro-choice advocates reject the view of separate spheres. They object to the notion of the home being the "women's sphere." Women's reproductive and family roles are seen as potential barriers to full equality. Motherhood is seen as a voluntary, not a mandatory or "natural," role.

Views on sex and sexuality also differ between the two groups of activists. Pro-life people are more likely to view the proper role of sex in terms of procreational love, not amative (recreational or pleasurable) love. "Sex as fun" is an ideology not shared by pro-life activists; rather, the emphasis is on the sacred and the transcendent—to bring into existence another human life. They tend to oppose most forms of contraception. Natural family planning or periodic abstinence is the preferred form of fertility control. According to the pro-lifers, highly effective contraception would subvert the reproductive functions of marriage, and would subordinate the role and value of children.

In regard to sexuality, differing attitudes toward premarital sex, particularly among teenagers, highlight the differences between the two groups. For the pro-lifers, those who feel that sex should be procreative, premarital sexuality is very disturbing. Teenage sexuality is seen as both morally and socially wrong, as it is not directed in terms of having children. But to provide sex education, contraception, and abortion services for teenagers goes against everything in which pro-life advocates believe. It is a clear threat to their belief systems on the procreative function of sex.

Pro-choice advocates take diametrically opposite positions to these views regarding sex and sexuality. The central concern of sex should be on intimacy. Contraception enhances intimacy by allowing people the freedom to focus on the emotional aspects of sex without worrying about the procreational aspects. A belief in the procreational supremacy of sex is seen to lead to an oppressive degree of regulation of sexual behavior, particularly the behavior of women. Luker states that "In the pro-choice value system, both the double standard and "purdah"—the custom of veiling women and keeping them entirely out of the public eye, lest they be too sexually arousing to men—are logical outcomes of a preoccupation with protecting and controlling women's reproductive capacities" (1984:177).

In regard to teenage sexuality, pro-choicers have no basic objection to sexual activity provided that the people involved are "responsible." Their main concern is about teenaged parenthood. Like the pro-lifers, they take the position that teenagers are not prepared to become good parents. But given their view that sex helps create intimacy, caring, and trust, premarital sex (whether with different people or with the one person with whom they intend to make a long-term commitment) is desirable. Sex education and the availability of contraception and abortion services are deemed as proper and important for teenagers.

Luker believes that the essence of the abortion debate and the reason that it is so passionate and hard-fought is "because it is a referendum on the place and meaning of motherhood" (1984:193).

> Motherhood is at issue because two opposing visions of motherhood are at war. Championed by "feminists" and "housewives," these two different views of motherhood represent in turn two very different kinds of social worlds. The abortion debate has become a debate among women, women with different values in the social world, different experiences with it, and different resources with which to cope with it. How the issue is framed, how people think about it, and, most importantly, where the passions come from are all related to the fact that the battle lines are increasingly drawn (and defended) by women. While on the surface it is the embryo's fate that seems to be at stake, the abortion debate is actually about the meanings of *women's* lives. (Luker, 1984:193–194).

Luker found significant social-background differences between the pro-choice and pro-life women whom she examined. Pro-life women had less income than pro-choice women; 44 percent of them had incomes of less than $20,000 a year. In comparison, one-third of the pro-choice women reported incomes in the upper end of the scale, $50,000 a year. Tied to income levels are a number of interconnecting factors. Pro-choice women tend to work in the paid-labor market; earn good salaries; and, if married, have husbands with good incomes. Pro-life women were less likely to be employed; when they were, they made less money for less-skilled work or part-time or less-structured activities like selling cosmetics to friends. The education levels of these two groups also significantly differed. The pro-choice group had attained higher levels of education that often translated into employment in the major professions, as administrators, owners of small businesses, or executives in large businesses. Pro-life women were likely to be housewives, and the few who worked did so in the traditional jobs of teaching, social work, and nursing.

Women in the two groups also made different choices regarding marriage and the family. A greater percentage of the pro-choicers were not married, and for those who were married, they had fewer children than their pro-life counterparts. Religious affiliation and involvement were significantly different as well. The majority (63 percent) of the pro-choicers who were active in the movement reported that they observed no religion; the majority (80 percent) of the pro-life women were Catholic; the minorities of both groups contain Protestants and Jews. However, the major difference in regard to religion is the active involvement of the pro-lifers with their respective religions both in terms of church attendance and in terms of how religious doctrines govern their attitudes and behavior.

In summarizing her findings, Luker (1984) believes that women become activists in either of the two movements as the end result of lives that center around different conceptualizations of motherhood. Their beliefs and values are rooted to the concrete circumstances of their lives—their educations, incomes, occupations, and the different marital and family choices that they have made. They represent two different world views of women's roles in contemporary society and as such the abortion issue represents the battleground for the justification of their respective views.

> Pro-choice and pro-life activists live in different worlds, and the scope of their lives, as both adults and children, fortifies them in their belief that their own views on abortion are the more correct, more moral, and more reasonable. When added to this is the fact that should "the other side" win, one group of women will see the very real devaluation of their lives and life resources, it is not surprising that the abortion debate has generated so much heat and so little light. (Luker, 1984:214)

Peter L. Berger and Brigitte Berger (1983), in their book *The War Over the Family,* also observe the importance of the abortion issue in coalescing differing opinions on the meaning of children, marriage, and the family. They see abortion as a strategically important moral issue that raises fundamental questions of human and civil rights and not just as a topic of family policy. They see the two antagonistic and opposing groups being at loggerheads with little shared ground and with little likelihood that a consensus can easily be reached. They refer to the two warring camps as "pro-abortion" (pro-choice) and "anti-abortion" (pro-life).

They call to task the pro-abortionists who fail to see the "awe" of human reproduction in terms of the fundamental metaphysical questions of birth and death. Similarly, they are critical of the anti-abortionists who fail to recognize our ignorance about the very foundations of human life—what human nature is and when it begins. That is: When does the fetus become human? Berger and Berger observe that pro-abortionists often try to avoid the reality that the fetus has the potential to become human. They illustrate this by noting that pro-abortion advocates become infuriated when anti-abortionists parade color photographs of fetuses or (as has happened at least once) dump aborted fetuses literally in their laps. On the other hand, anti-abortionists' certainty—by virtue of divine revelation or traditional religious authority—that human nature begins at the moment of conception does not recognize our ignorance on this matter.

To arrive at a consensus on the abortion question, Berger and Berger (1983) suggest a general policy direction. This would recognize the awe of conception by setting a fairly narrow time frame (not beyond the first trimester) as the period when the abortion would be permitted. The law would lean to the side of conservatism when the fetus is to be regarded as a person. The decision on whether to abort or not must be left to the pregnant woman, in consultation with whomever *she* chooses. They reason that if the fetus is presumed to be a person, no one—neither the mother nor any other individual—has the right to kill that person. But if the fetus is not presumed to be a person, it must be presumed to be considered as part of the pregnant woman's body. This being the case, no one other than the woman has the right to make decisions regarding it.

One Issue That Seems To Defy a Yes or No

BY ADAM CLYMER

The political fight over abortion, which once provoked hopes and fears of a constitutional amendment and a Government more concerned with and involved in the morality of its citizens, has settled into trench warfare. The troops still assemble regularly. Last month, 36,000 foes of abortion marched on the Supreme Court to protest the anniversary of its decision in *Roe v. Wade* and next month, the decision's supporters hope to gather as many or more of their partisans at the Lincoln Memorial.

But neither side hopes for recent triumphs and a recent *New York Times* poll suggests that a key reason for the shift in atmosphere is that Americans do not see abortion in anything like the clear, black-and-white terms discerned by activists on the issue.

In Washington, there is no longer an imminent prospect of a constitutional amendment forbidding or limiting abortions—a fact that represents a strategic success for the groups that call themselves pro-choice. President Reagan regularly renews his calls for an amendment, but it has become clear that he will not spend serious political capital on the fight.

Instead, for organizations such as Planned Parenthood or institutions such as the District of Columbia government, which advise or pay for abortions using funds from other sources, the battle is over Federal money for abortions themselves. And there the recent record is one of tactical victories for the groups that oppose abortion, and call themselves pro-life.

Peter Gemma, head of the National Pro-Life Political Action Committee, agrees that in the last few years "there have been no dramatic gains" for his side. But he contends that more judges who oppose abortion are being appointed and that his allies have realistic hopes of "cutting off Federal appropriations for anyone who does consultation on abortions." On the other side, Ann F. Lewis, executive director of Americans for Democratic Action, is optimistic because she sees politicians competing for younger voters and concluding that a rigid anti-abortion stance is a sure way to discourage them.

ROOT CONFLICTS

But the *Times* poll indicates two deeply felt conflicts in the public that make unlikely solid support for sweeping changes in either direction. First, 56 percent of the public said they did not approve of the present legal situation, with 40 percent saying they wanted abortion legal "only in such cases as saving the life of the mother, rape or incest," and 16 percent saying it should not be permitted at all. But only three-fourths of them, or 41 percent of the population, said they wanted the Constitution amended to make their belief the law of the land.

Other important conflicts showed up. Fifty-five percent of the public said they believed that "abortion is the same thing as murdering a child," but 66 percent said they agreed with the statement that "abortion is sometimes the best thing in a bad situation." Twenty-seven percent of the public—23 percent of the men and 31 percent of the women—believed both of those statements. The margin of sampling error in the survey was plus or minus three percentage points.

On both sets of questions, it was clear that people with higher incomes and more education were least hostile to abortion. For example, 50 percent of those with family incomes of less than $12,500 but only 27 percent of those with incomes of $50,000 or more wanted an amendment to change the law. Similarly, 64 percent of those who did not have a high school education but just 36 percent of those with college or advanced degrees believed that abortion was the same thing as murder.

Age mattered more on the issue of the legality of abortion than on questions about what the procedure means morally. Forty-five percent of those 44 or younger said the practice should be legal, as it is now; only 25 percent of those 65 or older agreed. Southerners and Midwesterners were

(continued)

especially hostile to abortion; people from the Northeast were least antagonistic.

The history of polling on abortion has consistently shown that the wording of a question had a tremendous impact on the responses. To public opinion specialists, that is a clear indication of uncertainty and conflict.

To an angry Connie Marshner, head of the National Pro-Family Coalition, the recent *New York Times* poll's findings that abortion is seen as both murder and the best thing in a bad situation were "incredible." She said: "Those people who agree with both statements haven't got a leg to stand on when it comes to criticizing

Hitler. They are saying murder is all right."

But to Carol Gilligan, associate professor at the Harvard Graduate School of Education and the author of *In a Different Voice*, the figures reflected a pragmatic approach to a "very complicated moral argument" comparable to one that upholds killing in wartime. "People can imagine themselves in situations like that," she said, "and can't be quite sure what they would do, and so don't want to impose their views on others."

SOURCE. Adam Clymer, 1986. "One issue that seems to defy a yes or no." *The New York Times* (Feb. 23). Copyright © 1986 by The New Times Company. Reprinted by permission.

Given the extreme moral and metaphysical positions taken by the opposing groups, whether such a consensus can become operative remains in question. Further, given the extreme contrasting social positions regarding gender roles, sex and sexuality, and the nature of parenthood, the abortion debate promises to continue as a major political issue for years ahead.

Sex Choice: Amniocentesis and Abortion

Another issue regarding abortion that should become more prominent in future years is the social ramifications of biological technology to predict the sex of the fetus. Such techniques could allow the choice of the sex of a baby; one technique would require amniocentesis and abortion.

Amniocentesis is a biological technique that takes a sample of the amniotic fluid surrounding the fetus. A needle is inserted through the pregnant woman's abdomen into the amniotic sac. A small amount of the fluid surrounding the fetus is withdrawn. The amniotic fluid contains cells sloughed off from the fetus. These cells can be examined to detect some 70 genetic disorders such as sickle-cell anemia, Tay-Sachs disease, cystic fibrosis, hemophilia, and trisomy-21 or Down's syndrome or mongolism. Amniocentesis is usually performed at 14 to 16 weeks of pregnancy, and is often used with women over age 30 or 35 because of the increased risk of trisomy-21. It is also indicated if the couple already have a child with a genetic affliction, or if either parent is a carrier of a genetic disorder. If the woman so desires, an abortion would be performed.

The technique can also determine if the cells have XX chromosomes (girl) or XY chromosomes (boy). Some women have had the procedure done in order to discover the sex of the fetus and then choose abortion if the fetus is not the desired gender (Franke, 1982). There has been much speculation on the consequences of such sex control if it were to become prevalent (Campbell, 1976). For example, the demographer Charles Westoff suggests that sex control could lead to smaller families, defuse the population bomb, and lower the incidence of sex-linked hereditary diseases.

Proponents of sex control foresee a growing satisfaction with the composition of the family. Parents would no longer have two or three children of the same sex if they no longer wished to have them. They could choose their family composition—a boy or girl, two boys, two girls, and so forth. The late anthropologist Margaret Mead believed that such technology would finally mean that female children would at last be wanted, since they will have been chosen.

Paul DeMaria, N.Y. Daily News

Robin Morris holds a petrie dish like the one used to fertilize her eggs with her husband's sperm. Once germinated, the eggs were implanted in her womb, and nine months later New York State's first "test tube" quadruplets were born (August, 1987). Her husband, Daniel Morris, said the children will someday be told how their life began. "We'll show them the dish. It's a high-tech birth," he said proudly. (They are pictured with their doctor, Zen Rosenwaks [rear]).

Less optimistic is the sociologist Amitai Etzioni, who paints a scenerio of a world populated with boys, or a society locked into a pattern of first-born boys and second-born girls. Westoff counters by suggesting that an increase in males will eventually lead to a baby boom in girls and ultimately a balance in the sex ratio. Westoff believes that in American and European countries, the preference for boys is relatively mild and therefore the shortage of one sex will increase its value; for example, a shortage of girls would lead to a rising demand for them and presumably an increase in production. But we would argue that there may be serious problems in patriarchal societies where there is a strong preference for boys and where people would have the ability to control the sex of their population.

More specifically, many patriarchal societies place much greater emphasis on the birth of a son than on the birth of a daughter. This preference is explained by the fact that, in patriarchal societies in which descent is reckoned through the male line and where patrilocal residence is practiced, males play a more-prominent and more-continuous role in the consanguineal-family structure. A female severs her involvement with her natal family (family of orientation) after marriage and, in effect, becomes part of her spouse's family system. As a consequence, the birth of a male often brings joy while the birth of a daughter is accompanied by feelings of sorrow. We have noted earlier that in some cases female infanticide has been practiced.

This family-planning decision has become a major problem in some patriarchal

Choosing the Baby's Sex in Advance
New technique of sex selection outwits the stork

BY RICHARD D. LYONS

After the birth of their daughter three years ago, Charles and Marilyn Cox of Mason, Mich., agreed that they wanted one more child and that it was to be a boy.

In Concord, the David and Joy Delapines had arrived at the same conclusion. They also wanted a boy.

Susan Fredricks and her husband in Philadelphia decided on a girl because they already had two boys.

"Besides, I'm from a family that had four girls and I really felt that my own family would be incomplete without one," Susan Fredricks said.

In all three cases, the couples were rewarded with a child of the gender they desired through the use of a technique that aids sex determination.

The technique is not foolproof, and some specialists have expressed skepticism about claims for its success rate. But a study of about 250 births that involved the procedure shows that it appears to raise the chances of having a child of the desired sex from the 50-50 ratio that might be expected by chance—which actually is 106 males to 100 females—to more than 75 percent in cases in which a boy is desired. A slightly different technique is used to increase the chances of having a girl, and the success rate is reported to be about the same.

"I've received some complaints from feminists, and a few people have accused my husband and me of playing God, but I've recommended the method to friends," Joy Delapine said. "And if we ever change our minds and want a third child, I would use the method because I'm convinced it produces healthier babies, regardless of their sex."

The procedure used by these couples was pioneered by Dr. Ronald J. Ericsson of Sausalito, Marin Co., a specialist in reproductive physiology who grew up on a ranch in Wyoming. Ericsson, who claims to be little more than an "educated cowboy,"

holds patents for his technique and heads the company that licenses its use, Gametrics Limited.

In a laboratory, the husband's semen first is washed in a tissue medium and the sample then is run through first one and then a second glass column containing increasingly more viscous layers of human serum albumen.

Sperm containing the Y chromosome, which contains the genes for masculinity, are heavier, stronger and swim faster than sperm containing the X, the female chromosome. The female egg contains only the X chromosome, but the sperm contain both X and Y. Since a Y chromosome is necessary for the conception of a male, such chances are enhanced by an artificial concentration of Y chromosomes.

"It's like running the New York marathon," Ericsson said. "The larger and more powerful entrants are usually the faster. But as in real life, in which some women run faster than some men, some X sperm arrive at the bottom of the second column ahead of the Y's."

After the sperm have descended to the bottom of the second glass column, they are withdrawn, separated from the liquids that surround them, concentrated and injected directly into the woman's cervix shortly after ovulation. The procedure costs from $225 to $300.

Sex selection for females is somewhat more complicated, involving not only the sifting out of X chromosomes but also the use of a drug, clomiphene citrate, that both induces ovulation and, for some unknown reason, skews the sex ratio toward females.

Ericsson said sperm that are either immature or abnormal in some other way are almost completely screened out through the use of this procedure, thus reducing the eventual risks of spontaneous abortion as well as the birth of babies that are either physically deformed or mentally retarded.

(continued)

In addition, the technique also may be used to increase the sperm concentration for men afflicted with oligospermia, or low sperm count.

As sex selection comes into wider use, questions about the medical, social and religious implications stemming from the practice are becoming more widely asked.

Because parents requesting the technique have shown an overwhelming preference for male babies, would that skew the national sex ratio if the technique went into widespread use?

If the technique were more widespread, would the birth of more boys and the open acknowledgment of the preference of most couples for boys tend to undermine women's esteem of gender? If put in general use, would the practice lead to a population of younger sisters that in turn might institutionalize second-class status for women?

Moreover, because the technique involves artificial insemination, would it come into conflict with the religious beliefs of Roman Catholics and orthodox Jews?

If the method would, at least in theory, reduce the birth of unwanted second, third and fourth daughters in some families, would it not be a worthwhile family planning strategy for overpopulated countries?

And if, as its advocates believe, the method results in babies who have greater chances of being free of sex-linked genetic defects, would the general population eventually benefit by reducing the number of people suffering from such diseases as hemophilia and some forms of muscular dystrophy and mental retardation?

Mild scepticism about the value of sex determination techniques was expressed by Dr. Maurice J. Mahoney, a professor of genetics at the Yale Medical School, who said proof is lacking that the manipulation of sperm is completely safe. Also, he said, claims that the practice produces healthier babies cannot be substantiated on the basis of only 250 births.

Dr. Barton Gledhill, a biomedical researcher studying sex determination who is on the staff of the Lawrence Livermore National Laboratory, said:

"This field has a history of having more charlatans and hocus-pocus than any other that I can imagine. Aristotle advised Greeks desiring sons to have intercourse in the north wind, and since then, scores of alchemists and liniment salesmen claimed the ability to predetermine the sex of children.

"The idea really had gotten a terribly bad reputation, at least until a decade ago when serious researchers began looking into it," he added.

Ericsson, who recently visited China at the invitation of government officials directing birth-control efforts there, acknowledged that the field of sex selection is "a real mine field, but an idea that has suddenly gotten respect."

But he candidly acknowledged that the desire for genetically fit babies often was less important to parents than sex preference, especially among Asian parents, he said. He said the governments of Taiwan and South Korea have agreed in principle that the technique would be beneficial for population control, while clinics have opened in those two countries as well as Singapore, Malasia and Egypt.

One study by the Population Reference Bureau concluded that in Korea "daughters are scarcely considered part of the family," while "some Taiwanese consider daughters to be expensive luxuries."

One of the few studies of Americans who said they want to use the technique concluded that nearly all of the couples who expressed an opinion already had an average of 2.3 children and wished to limit the size of their family by having just one more child of a specific sex.

The study was conducted by Nan Chico, a sociologist at California State University, Hayward, and was based on the attitudes of 2,000 couples who had written either to Gametrics or to specific clinics requesting information about sex determination.

"The preponderant attitude was to bring childbearing to an end with the addition of only one more child of a desired sex, and just about everybody wanted the opposite of what they already had," Chico said. "I found this surprising because most sociologists had predicted that if such a technique were developed it would be used

(continued)

to select the sex of the firstborn, which certainly has not proved to be the case."

Yet Chico's conclusion runs counter to a study conducted by Dr. Roberta Steinbacher, a social psychologist at Cleveland State University in Ohio, who looked into the ethical problems that the technique might pose.

"I asked people if they would use the method if it were available and about one quarter said they would," Steinbacher said. "I then asked the members of this second group which sex they would prefer and 91 percent of the women and 94 percent of the men said they would prefer their firstborn to be a boy.

"I think this overwhelming preference for firstborn males would, if widely carried out, institutionalize a second-class status for women because of their ranking in the birth order," Steinbacher said. Firstborns traditionally have been considered to be aggressive achievers who tend to be more successful educationally and economically than siblings born later.

Social implications aside, physicians such as Dr. Robert H. Glass of the University of California Medical School in San Francisco, who is an associate of Ericsson, said the reduction of children having birth defects might be the most promising future use of the method.

At least 200 sex-linked genetic diseases have been identified, and in the United States alone these are estimated to be responsible for several thousand neonatal deaths a year, he said.

As an example of how the technique might be valuable in such cases, Glass said, a couple in which one spouse had a family history of hemophilia might opt to have only female children since women, while they may be carriers of the gene, are not usually afflicted. Males are far more likely to be afflicted with sex-linked genetic diseases than females.

SOURCE. Richard D. Lyons. 1984. "Choosing the baby's sex in advance." *The New York Times* (May 29). Copyright © 1984 by The New York Times Company. Reprinted by permission.

societies, such as India. Since amniocentesis has become readily available, there have been a number of reports from India that it has been used to detect and abort unwanted girl children. The All India Institute of Medical Sciences found that in 1974–1975, the test had been used in this manner extensively. Since then a forum of women's organizations have called for a ban on the tests and disciplinary action against doctors who perform it (Morgan, 1984). In the summer of 1986, United States news services reported that there still was a high incidence of amniocentesis being used to abort female fetuses.

Conclusion

This chapter sought to integrate demographic analysis into our sociological perspective on social change and the family. We opened with a discussion of fertility and family size, comparing extended-family systems, which emphasize kinship ties, with conjugal-family systems, which emphasize the marital and parental relationships. We observed that kinship-dominated societies were dependent on high fertility and large family size for the perpetuation of their social system. In contrast, in industrial societies where conjugal-family units prevail, there is an appreciable lower fertility rate and family size.

We then applied our sociologic perspective to understand population dynamics in India. The high birthrate was seen to be detrimental to Indian modernization, economic development, and increased total industrial, commercial, and agricultural production. The failure of family-planning programs reflects governmental policies that run counter to the economic viability of large family size for the joint-family system and the village-based caste system. It was emphasized that demographic changes could only occur when the class and caste systems are changed and when technological development makes it economically feasible for these families to limit their family size. This examination of population dynamics revealed that it was interrelated with family conceptualizations and dynamics along with social, political, and economic factors.

We then turned our attention to an examination of fertility patterns in the West. Ideologies relating to parenthood and particularly motherhood concerned us. We pointed out that contradictory demands were placed on women. On the one hand, doctrines placed high value on their confinement to the home and their exclusive involvement in household tasks and child rearing; on the other hand, doctrines were being propounded that encouraged families to restrict their family size.

Coercive pronatalism, a term coined by the demographer Judith Blake, was introduced to point out how social institutions forced women to assume exclusively the everyday parental role. Discriminatory practices in education and in work, reinforced by the myth of motherhood, relegated women to the wife and mother roles. We pointed out how supportive parental ideologies contributed to the obscuring of the possibility that the transition to parenthood can be problematic.

Our next topic was the transition to parenthood. This transition necessitates the rearrangement and reorganization of marital roles; relationships with kin, friends, and neighbors; economic patterns; and the reallocation of space, time, and attention. The implications of this transition for families received comparably little attention from sociologists until recent years. We reviewed this literature and compared the research findings on working-class and middle-class families. We indicated some of the problematic areas of concern and pointed out that changes are beginning to take place in the nature of motherhood and fatherhood and in society's responsibilities.

The concluding discussion dealt with the social issues of abortion. We presented a cross-cultural overview and indicated that abortion policies often reflect patriarchal ideologies; that is, in societies where patriarchy still predominates, antiabortion policies are adhered to. Where patriarchal interests are losing strength, more-liberal policies regarding abortion exist. Religious, economic, and political factors also play a role in legal attitudes toward abortion. In the analysis of abortion in the United States, the contrasting and conflicting views of "pro-life" advocates versus "pro-choice" advocates were delineated. A related theme regarding abortion was its utilization of amniocentesis to abort unwanted fetuses who were of the "wrong" sex. As of yet, this has not been a major concern in the United States. However, amniocentesis and abortion may seriously impact male–female sex ratios in other societies where strong preferences are made.

In the next two chapters, we continue our investigation of generational relationships. Chapter 14 concerns childhood and adolescence; Chapter 15 focuses on the role of the aged in the family.

The Family and Childhood and Adolescence

Child labor in India, against a backdrop of modern Bombay. A modern housing complex is being built alongside the makeshift shacks of refugees and poverty-stricken families.

CHAPTER OUTLINE

All human societies are differentiated on the basis of age and sex. Throughout history, the social roles of men and women have differed, as have the roles of children, adults, and the aged. Always, these differences have been linked to status differences in power, privilege, and prestige. In the previous chapters, we examined sex differentiation. A power dimension was seen to be inherent in the differentiation between the sexes. Generations are part of the permanent nature of social existence. And, likewise, conflict between generations has been a perennial force in the history of humanity.

In our earlier discussions, the family was viewed as the primary form of social organization that stratified people according to sex. It can also be seen as the basic form of social organization that stratifies people according to age. Basically, families are hierarchical social structures in which older generations or older siblings hold positions of power, authority, and prestige over their younger counterparts. There are different degrees of stratification by age. But the universal tendency is for the elders to exercise control over younger family members.

The degree of generational control also varies by the tempo of social change in given societies. Generally, in societies that are relatively stable, patterns of generation control become traditionalized. In societies undergoing patterns of rapid social change, the normal relationship between generations is disrupted and can be destroyed.

In this and the next chapter, we examine different forms of family systems and the relationships between family members of different ages. We are particularly interested in the manifestation of the power dimension that underlies the age hierarchy. We look at children, adolescents, and the aged within different forms of family life. Of noted concern is the role of social change on age differentiation within the family and its influence on generational controls.

Social Change and Generational Control

Ann Foner (1978) discusses what she has labeled an age-stratification perspective and applies it to an historical examination of nineteenth- and twentieth-century American families. This approach emphasizes that age must be conceived as a social process as well as a biologic one. Age is seen as a key component in social structure and social change. This age-stratification perspective incorporates both structural and dynamic elements that have implications at both the individual and societal levels for the analysis of the family.

Structurally, age-stratification affects how people of different ages relate to each other and influences the individual's attitudes and behavior. People of different age groupings are stratified into different role complexes with differential rewards, duties, and obligations. Dynamically, individuals pass through the different age strata as they move through the life cycle. The transition through stages in the life cycle and the transitions of a particular age cohort are historically unique. Thus, the age-stratification structure of the population is constantly subject to change.

The family is composed of members of different ages who are differentially related. The dominant perspective in sociology, structural functionalism, has stressed that the age differentiation of family members enhances the solidarity of its members. The interdependence of family members fosters emotional attachments, structural solidarity, and family cohesion. However, as Foner points out, family conflict is also a basic component of family life. Inherent in the differential age structure of family members is the potential for conflict and tension:

> For the family is itself stratified—not merely differentiated—by age. Not only do family members of different ages have diverse functions, but they also receive unequal rewards. . . . There are age differences in power, privilege, and prestige in the family. And these inequalities can generate age-related dissension—for example, resentment about the exercise of power or the way family resources are distributed—in the family unit. (Foner, 1978:S347)

The nature and rate of social change has been associated with the nature and type of generational control parents have over their children. Robert Redfield (1947), in his classic work "The Folk Society," contrasts the slow changing of rural folk society with the dynamic tempo of urban industrial societies. The tempo of change is associated with the attitudes and behavior patterns between the generations. It has also been observed that the authority and power of parents is correlated with the societal pattern that emphasizes the maintenance of tradition. S.N. Eisenstadt (1971) points out that societies that emphasize traditional practices are characterized by strong intergenerational bonds. These societies are also characterized by a strong central authority.

These tradition-oriented societies have been characterized by the rule of the old. The nineteenth-century and early twentieth-century British anthropologist Sir James George Frazer called these societies "gerontocracies." Using the Australian aborigines as the case in point, Frazer described the authority structure of that culture as

> an oligarchy of old and influential men, who meet in council and decide on all measures of importance, to the practical exclusion of the younger men. Their deliberate assembly answers to the senate of later times: if we had to coin a word for such a government of elders we might call it a "gerontocracy." (Frazer, 1922/1960:96)

In contrast, in societies that are undergoing rapid social change, generational continuity is de-emphasized. Concomitantly, the older generation has less control over the younger one. Indeed, some social observers argue that the pattern in contemporary Western society is characterized by such an appreciable loss of parental control that the family has become largely irrelevant in influencing the behavior and attitudes of children and adolescents. At the same time, and somewhat paradoxically, the argument is also being made that the family is a detrimental force that acts to frustrate and deny the fulfillment of the needs of the younger generation. Margaret Mead's *Culture and Commitment: A Study of the Generation Gap* (1970b) reflects the former position. After we examine this work, we look at the latter position, which derives from the contemporary conceptualization of the family, childhood, and adolescence.

Margaret Mead in her essay monograph (1970b) comparatively examines the generation gap in contemporary societies. She presents an historical explanation on

Portrait of a contemporary Shavante youth, Mato Grosso, Brazil. (Compare with the photograph of a Shavante initiation ceremony in Chapter 15.)

why the elders of preliterate societies exert such powers. She calls these societies postfigurative. In postfigurative cultures, children are socialized by their forebears. The children are raised so that the lives of the parents and grandparents postfigure the course of their own.

Postfigurative societies are small religious and ideological enclaves. They derive their authority from the past. Their cultures are conservative and resist change. There is a sense of timelessness and all-prevailing custom. Continuity with the past is a basic premise underlying the social order. The sacredness of custom and the lack of a written history makes the elders the repositories of societal wisdom and knowledge. The elders have high status because they know best the traditions of the past. Generational turmoil is rare. Adolescent and youth rebellion is almost entirely absent.

In postfigurative cultures, the emphasis is on generational continuity. The experiences of the young repeat the experiences of the old. Events that have occurred and that question the traditional order are redefined and reinterpreted to deny changes. To preserve the sense of continuity and identification with the past occurrences that have caused change are culturally blurred and innovations are assimilated into the traditional past. Mead provides some illustrations of elders who edit the version of the culture that is passed to the young. They mythologize or deny change:

> A people who have lived for only three or four generations in tepees on the great American plains, who have borrowed the tepee style from other tribes, may tell how their ancestors learned to make a tepee by imitating the shape of a curled leaf. In Samoa the elders listened politely to a description of the long voyages of Polynesian ancestors by Te Rangi Hiroa, a Polynesian visitor from New Zealand, whose people had preserved a sacrosanct list of the early voyages which was memorized by each generation. His hosts then replied firmly, "Very interesting, but the *Samoans* originated here in Fitiuta." The visitor, himself half-Polynesian and half-European, and a highly educated man, finally took refuge, in great irritation, in asking them whether or not they were now Christians and believed in the Garden of Eden. (Mead, 1970b:18)

The postfigurative society socializes the young so that they behave in accordance with the mores and values of the older generation. They do not question the way things are or the way things were. Indeed, they have a lack of consciousness of alternative ways of life. This sociocultural quality explains the great stability of postfigurative society. It also accounts for the minimal internal change from one generation to the next.

Mead emphasizes the importance of three-generational households in the socialization of children. In such households, parents raise their children under the eyes of their parents. This arrangement emphasizes cultural continuity and strengthens the power of the older generation. Robert O. Blood, Jr. (1972), has observed that the power of the aged was institutionalized in the extended-family system. The high priority and status of the aged gave rise to the extended-family system and was, in turn, supported by this form of family structure.

In societies undergoing social change, there is a break in generational continuity. The experiences of the younger generation are significantly different from those of their parents and grandparents. Mead characterizes these cultures as cofigurative. The recent past of American society is a prime illustration. Cofigurative cultures can be brought about by rapid technological development; migration to a new country and separation from the elders; military conquest and the subsequent forced acculturation of the captured society to the language and ways of the conquerer; religious conversion, where the younger generation is socialized into a new religious world view; and planned revolutionary changes in the lifestyles of the young. The consequent differential experiences of the younger generation necessitate the development of different attitudes and behavior. The elder generation cannot provide the necessary emulating models and the younger generation must find these models among their generational peers.

One illustration that Mead provides on how these changes have affected family relationships is of particular interest to us. In an earlier discussion in this book, we examined the Western urban family and suggested that the diminished importance of extended kinship of city families may have resulted from the differential socialization processes experienced by different-generation family members. Those who were raised in rural areas of European societies and who migrated to the United States will have had a quite different upbringing than their urban Americanized children and grandchildren.

Mead points out that the immigration situation is typified by the concentration on the nuclear family, with grandparents either absent or having very little influence. Grandparents are no longer the models for their grandchildren; parents have little control over grown children's marriages or careers. Characteristic of cofigurative American culture is the relinquishing of responsibility for the elderly. This is associated with the breakdown of sanctions exercised by the elderly over the second and third generations.

In its simplest form, Mead sees cofigurative culture as one in which grandparents are absent. The result is the loss of the individual's links with the past. The future is not anticipated through the traditional past but by the contemporary present. The result is that parents and grandparents no longer serve as dominating socialization agents. Formalized educational institutions take over this task. Concomitantly, the elders are no longer authority figures or models for youths' future behavioral and attitudinal patterns.

However, Mead emphasizes that in cofigurative cultures the break is never complete. Elders still have influence to the extent that they set the style and set the limits within which cofiguration is expressed in the behavior of the young. Thus, to a certain extent, the elders along with youths' generational peers develop a new style that will serve as the model for others of their generation.

Writing at the height of the social unrest of the late 1960s and being particularly influenced by the extensiveness of youth counterculture movements, Mead saw an emerging pattern that made both the postfigurative and cofigurative cultural models inadequate. In this newly emerging era of extreme rapid rates of change, Mead saw the development of a prefigurative culture. In prefigurative society, the future is so unknown that change within an elder-controlled and parent-modeled cofigurative culture, which also includes postfigurative elements, is inadequate.

> I call this new style *prefigurative,* because in this new culture it will be the child— and not the parent and grandparent—that represents what is to come. Instead of the erect, white-haired elder who, in postfigurative cultures, stood for the past and the future in all their grandeur and continuity, the unborn child, already conceived but still in the womb, must become the symbol of what life will be like. (Mead, 1970b:68)

Mead's analysis of permanence and social change demonstrates how it affects different cultures and their respective generational dynamics. The conceptualizations that exist to define the nature of particular age groups also play a significant role in the manifestations of generational attitudes and behavior. A careful examination of the different conceptualizations of young people and the family will now prove instructive.

Childhood and Adolescence Conceptualizations: Comparative Perspectives

As we observed here, societies define sets of people according to age. These age categories influence people's relations to one another. Expectations differ on what involvements, activities, and accomplishments are expected for each age grouping. Societies differ in the age distinctions they make. For example, among the Kikuyu of Kenya, age distinctions are prominently defined and explicit, and elaborate rites of passage mark the transition periods that carry the individual from one age category to the next. Age differentiation also has consequent implications for the conceptualization of persons placed in particular age groupings. Further, we must realize that the conceptualizations of childhood and adolescence are reflections of the conceptualization of the family, and together they must be seen in a cross-cultural and in a social-historical context.

Cross-Cultural Views of Childhood and Adolescence

Anthropologists have long observed the cultural relativity of age roles. They have noted that the conceptualization of childhood and adolescence varies cross-culturally. Probably the most famous research study in this area was done by Margaret Mead in her *Coming of Age in Samoa* (1928). Mead was concerned with the relationships between adolescents and culture. She contrasted the development of girls in the United States with patterns in Samoa. She was particularly concerned with whether the psychological disturbances and the emotional crises characteristic of Western adolescents were due to the nature of adolescence itself or to the culture. She wanted to ascertain if these disturbances were due to physiological changes occurring at puberty or were largely brought about by social and cultural conditions.

To test the universality of developmental psychologic stages of childhood and adolescence, Mead went to the South Pacific and lived for 9 months in Samoa, where she studied 50 adolescent girls. Among the adolescents of Samoa, she found no period comparable to the storm and stress that characterize their American counterparts. Samoan adolescence was not characterized by tension, emotional conflict, or rebellion. Indeed, Samoan culture did not even recognize the developmental stage of adolescence: It had no concept of adolescence. Mead concluded that the source of such characteristics in American youth stemmed from the social institutions and traditions found in the United States.

Anthropologists have also compared societies in regard to the conceptualization of childhood. Mead (1949), herself, examined societies that viewed the child as a small adult, with responsibilities similar to those of an adult, versus societies like the United States, where the child is thought to be qualitatively different. Ruth Benedict (1938/ 1973), in her classic study "Continuities and Discontinuities in Cultural Conditioning," has argued that there is less continuity in treatment and development from childhood and adolescence to adulthood in societies such as the United States than there is in those societies that employ the little-adult conceptualization.

Benedict sees as a distinctive feature of American culture the dichotomization of value patterns between those applicable to the child and those applicable to the adult. "The child is sexless, the adult estimates his virility by his sexual activities; the child must be protected from the ugly facts of life, the adult must meet them without psychic catastrophe; the child must obey, the adult must command this obedience" (Benedict, 1938/1973:100). Benedict points out that the more discrete and isolated the status of the child is from the status of the adult, the more difficult and ambiguous is the transition from one age group to the other. Further, this dichotomous pattern intensifies the status discontinuity experienced by the adolescent.

She argues that children are segregated from the adult world. This is especially the case for work and sex. The children's world is organized around play; little attention is given to the adult world of work. Similarly, strong taboos exist regarding sexual repression and children are required to be submissive to adult authority. As adults, they are expected to work, to be sexually mature, and to be assertive and autonomous. This disjunction between the role of the child and the one he or she is expected to perform as an adult makes the transition painful, awkward, and traumatic.

In contrast, Benedict reports that in nonliterate societies, the cultural discontinuities that characterize American society do not exist. For example, in contrasting cultural variations regarding responsibility and nonresponsibility, she finds that nonliterate societies encourage children to engage in adult activities and responsibilities as soon as possible. Among the Ojibwa Indians of Canada, boys accompany fathers on hunting trips and girls share the responsibility of preparing the meat and skins of animals trapped by their brothers and fathers in much the same manner as their mothers. Ojibwan children are consistently taught to rely on themselves and to see the world of the adult as not much different from the world of the young.

Similarly, among the Papago of Arizona, children are trained from infancy and are continuously conditioned to responsible social participation while, at the same time, the tasks that are expected of them are adapted to their capabilities. To illustrate, Benedict cites an observer who tells of sitting with a group of Papago elders when the man of the house turned to his little three-year-old granddaughter and asked her to close the door.

> The door was heavy and hard to shut. The child tried, but it did not move. Several times the grandfather repeated, "Yes, close the door." No one jumped to the child's assistance. No one took the responsibility away from her. On the other hand there was no impatience, for after all the child was small. They sat gravely waiting till the child succeeded and her grandfather gravely thanked her. It was assumed that the task would not be asked of her unless she could perform it and having been asked the responsibility was hers alone just as if she were a grown woman. (Benedict, 1938/1973:102)

Benedict sees American culture as viewing the adult–child or, specifically, the parent–child relationship in terms of a dominance–submission arrangement. In contrast, many American Indian tribes explicitly reject the ideal of a child's submissive or obedient behavior. To illustrate, Benedict reports on the child-training practices among the Mohave Indians that are strikingly nonauthoritarian:

> The child's mother was white and protested to its father (a Mohave Indian) that he must take action when the child disobeyed and struck him. "But why?" the father said, "he is little. He cannot possibly injure me." He did not know of any dichotomy according to which an adult expects obedience and a child must accord it. If his child had been docile he would simply have judged that it would become a docile adult—an eventuality of which he would not have approved. (Benedict, 1938/1973:104)

Benedict then contrasts how children are socialized into sexual awareness in different societies. She notes that in virtually all societies the norms concerning sexual conduct are not identical for children and adults. This is explained by the relatively late onset of puberty and physiologic maturation in human beings. Benedict defines continuity in sexual expression as meaning that the child is taught nothing it must unlearn later. Societies can, therefore, be classified in terms of whether they facilitate continuity or impose discontinuity regarding sexual matters. Adults among the Dakota Indians, for example, observe great privacy in sexual acts and in no way stimulate or encourage children's sexual activities. Yet there is no discontinuity since the child is not indoctrinated in ways it has to unlearn later. The Zuni in New Mexico regard premature sexual experimentation by children as being wicked. The sexual activity of adults is associated solely with reproduction. Our society, in contrast, associates the wickedness of a child's sexual experimentation with *sex itself* rather than as wickedness because it is sex at a child's age. The result is that adults in our culture must unlearn the belief taught them as children that sex is wicked or dangerous.

In concluding her analysis, Benedict examines age-grade societies that, as we pointed out, demand different behavior of the individual at different times during the life cycle. Persons of the same age grade are grouped into a society whose activities are oriented toward the appropriate behavior desired at that age. Although there is discontinuous conditioning, Benedict believes that cultural institutions provide sufficient supports to persons as they progress through the age-grade life stages. In striking contrast, Benedict argues that Anglo-American culture contains discontinuous cultural institutions and dogmas that exert considerable strain on both the interpersonal processes and the personality systems of young individuals.

It is clear that if we were to look at our social arrangements as an outsider, we should infer directly from our family institutions and habits of child training that many individuals would not "put off childish things"; we should have to say that our adult activity demands traits that are interdicted in children, and that far from redoubling efforts to help children bridge this gap, adults in our culture put all the blame on the child when he fails to manifest spontaneously the new behavior or, overstepping the mark, manifests it with untoward belligerence. (1938/1973:108)

The result is that American adolescents face serious problems during this transition period; problems of readjustment and ambiguity are experienced in activities, responsibilities, and the allocation of power: "The adolescent period of *Sturm und Drang* with which we are so familiar becomes intelligible in terms of our discontinuous cultural institutions and dogmas rather than in terms of physiological necessity" (1938/1973:108)

Historical Views of Childhood and Adolescence

Ruth Benedict's thesis anticipated the arguments advanced by the social historian Philippe Ariès in *Centuries of Childhood: A Social History of Family Life* (1962). In this classic study, Ariès applied a similar kind of analysis to medieval European society and its evolution to the present. He sought to document how in medieval life the child was integrated into the community and how it was not until the development of bourgeois society that the segregation of children occurred. Implicit within his discussion is a condemnation of the consequences of this segregation.

The theme of *Centuries of Childhood* is how the Western ideas about childhood and family life have changed and developed from the Middle Ages to modern times. Ariès examines the paintings and diaries of four centuries; documents the history and evolution of children's dress, games, and pastimes; and analyzes the development of schools and their curricula. This leads him to conclude that the concept of childhood as a distinct stage in the life cycle is a rather recent development, as is the conceptualization of the private family.

He argues that in the Middle Ages, children were treated as small adults. As soon as they were capable of being without their mothers, children interacted in the adult world. They shared the same world of work and play. By the age of 7 or 8, they were treated as if they had the same mental capacities for understanding and feeling as their adult counterparts and peers. In a particularly notable use of historical resources, Ariès points out that medieval painters portrayed children as "miniaturized" adults. Children were depicted in adult clothes and looked like adults, but on a reduced scale. The failure of the artists to draw children as we know them was not due to their incompetence or lack of artistic skill but rather to the lack of a conceptualization of the notion of childhood:

> In medieval society the idea of childhood did not exist; this is not to suggest that children were neglected, forsaken or despised. The idea of childhood is not to be confused with affection for children; it corresponds to an awareness of the particular nature of childhood, that particular nature which distinguishes the child from the adult, even the young adult. In medieval society this awareness was lacking. That is why, as soon as the child could live without the constant solicitude of his mother, his nanny or his cradle-rocker, he belonged to adult society. (Ariès, 1962:128)

The lack of awareness of the particular nature of childhood and the full participation of children in adult life is associated with the nature of the family and the community. Ariès pictures medieval community life as intense; no one was left alone. The high density of social life made isolation virtually impossible. Life was lived in public. The "sociability" of medieval life was lived on the public streets. The private home was virtually nonexistent. The street was the setting of work and social relations. This sociability hindered the formation of the concept of the private family. The medieval family was embedded in a web of relatives, friends, workmates, and neighbors all living in close proximity and in public. The distinct sense of privacy so characteristic of modern-day families was absent. In the following passage, Ariès dramatically provides an illustration of this point:

> The traditional ceremonies which accompanied marriage and which were regarded as more important than the religious ceremonies (which for a long time were entirely lacking in solemnity)—the blessing of the marriage bed; the visit paid by the guests to the newly married pair when they were already in bed; the rowdyism during the wedding night, and so on—afford further proof of society's rights over the privacy of the couple. What objection could there be when in fact privacy scarcely ever existed, when people lived on top of one another, masters and servants, children and adults, in houses open at all hours to the indiscretions of callers? The density of society left no room for the family. Not that the family did not exist as a reality: it would be paradoxical to deny that it did. But it did not exist as a concept. (1962:405–406)

The transition to the modern conceptualization of the child began to emerge during the seventeenth century. There was a revival of interest in education. This, in turn, introduced the idea that a period of special preparation was necessary before individuals could assume their place as adults. Childhood became defined as a period in which to train children. Children began to be treated differently, they were expected to behave differently, and their nature was viewed as being different. Children were now coddled, and a greater interest and concern for their moral welfare and development became common.

Although Ariès recognizes that this change reflects declines in mortality rates and the growing division of labor in the society, he believes that this concept of childhood developed and was given expression in the emergence of the bourgeois family. He argues that from a relatively insignificant institution during the Middle Ages, there developed a growing belief in the virtue of the intimate and private nuclear family. The rise of the private family and the growth of the sentimental bonds among its members came about at the expense of the public community.

> The more man lived in the street or in communities dedicated to work, pleasure or prayer, the more these communities monopolized not only his time but his mind. If, on the other hand, his relations with fellow workers, neighbors and relatives did not weigh so heavily on him, then the concept of family feeling took the place of the other concepts of loyalty and service and became predominant or even exclusive. The progress of the concept of the family followed the progress of private life, of domesticity. (Ariès, 1962:375)

The continued inward development of the family and its creation of a private sphere of life removed from the outside world was intertwined with the increased importance given to children. The outside community came to be viewed with suspicion and indifference. Proceeding into the industrial era, the family began to withdraw its nonproductive members, women and children, from involvement with the surrounding community. The increased division of labor of family members and the consequent isolation of women and children within the home was the result.

Ariès ends on a pessimistic note. He is highly critical of the contemporary private family. He believes that it has stifled children's autonomy and independence. He views medieval childhood as a period of free expression and spontaneity. The separation of the child from the larger community leads to the development of youths who are deprived of much experience in the outside world. They are increasingly dependent on their parents. The result is the ultimate loss of their individuality.

> The evolution of the last few centuries has often been presented as the triumph of individualism over social constraints, with the family counted among the latter. But where is the individualism in these modern lives, in which all the energy of the couple is directed to serving the interests of a deliberately restricted posterity? Was there not greater individualism in the gay indifference of the prolific fathers of the ancient regime? . . . It is not individualism which has triumphed, but the family. (Ariès, 1962:406)

Similar historical analyses on the changing conceptualization of adolescence have been made by F. Musgrove (1964) and Joseph Kett (1977). Musgrove traces the historical changes in the status of adolescents from the mid-seventeenth century, when adolescence was "invented," to the present. England provides his case in point. Kett examines how youths have viewed themselves and how these views have coincided or clashed with adult expectations in America from 1790 to the present.

Musgrove believes that youths are increasingly segregated from the adult world. This has diminished rather than enhanced their social status. He develops an argument that is similar to the one developed by Ruth Benedict. Musgrove sees the inconsistency and discontinuity of training youths for adulthood by excluding them from the world of adult concerns, and of training youths for the exercise of responsibility by the denial of responsibility. The result is the development of compliant, accommodating, and conservative security-conscious adults. He attributes this changing status to economic developments and demographic changes, and to psychological theories on the nature of adolescence that have helped to justify it.

Musgrove attributes the idea of adolescence—a special stage of development that intervenes between childhood and adulthood—to the eighteenth-century French philosopher Jean-Jacques Rousseau. Adolescence began to be seen as a period during which the individual's movement toward adult maturity should be retarded. The belief developed that the rights, obligations, and responsibilities of adulthood should be delayed by an intervening period of schooling, albeit for the more affluent and privileged segments of the society. Young people were deemed unfit to undertake serious concerns relating to work and politics. A protracted period of preparation for adulthood was deemed necessary. Further, this preparation was to be undertaken in segregated and congregate institutions of formal training that were set apart from the adult world.

Musgrove believes that the changing composition of the population has also helped bring about these changes. He emphasizes the demographic fact that more adolescents have been able to survive childhood and that more people are reaching adulthood and old age. The result is that positions of responsibility and leadership are more likely to be occupied by the older segments of the population and thus youths have reduced opportunities to assume such positions. This demographic fact is readily apparent in the economic sphere. Here, those already in the labor force have a vested interest in maintaining their economic viability as long as possible. The result is the belief that the young should be kept out of the labor force as long as possible.

The demands of a technologically complex and sophisticated society require skills. The relatively untrained labor skills of the young are not needed. Further, with the increased "professionalization" of occupations, there is an increased demand for the attainment of educational qualifications in terms of specialized courses and degrees before admittance is granted. Finally, labor unions, in their desire to maintain the security and well-being of their senior members, have successfully kept young recruits from gaining unrestricted access to skilled and semiskilled positions. They have effectively controlled the flow of the young into the labor force.

Together, all these factors are seen to hold back youth. Together, demographic circumstances, economic conditions, educational strategy and provision, and the institutionalized power of adults make it unlikely that any dramatic changes will occur in the treatment of youth in Western societies. One tangential observation may be of interest here. Musgrove wrote his book in 1964, before the development of the counterculture movements of the late 1960s. From the perspective of the late 1980s, the note of despair that echoes throughout Musgrove's book still seems to be an accurate appraisal of contemporary conditions.

Kett (1977), in his historical study of adolescence in America, observes that the economic and social relationships between youth and adolescents have significantly changed since 1790. Today's youths are characterized as being consumers rather than producers. They have been largely removed from the work force, spend most of their time in school, and tend to be segregated from adult society. The causes of these changes are traced to urbanization, industrialization, demographic changes, and child-rearing practices. It is his concern with the moral values associated with child-rearing practices that attracts his and our attention.

Kett places particular attention to the period between 1890 and 1920, when the society came to classify the time between 14 and 18 years as a distinct period of youth and labeled it adolescence. Kett seeks to demonstrate that the moral values associated with this conceptualization were subsumed under supposedly universal psychological laws and determined by a biologic process of maturation. These laws provided the basis for the subsequent development of a number of adolescent "helpers," such as educators, youth workers, parent counselors, and scout leaders. Through their efforts, they gave shape to the contemporary concept of adolescence, which necessitated the massive reclassification of young people as adolescents: "During these critical decades young people, particularly teenage boys, ceased to be viewed as troublesome, rash, and heedless, the qualities traditionally associated with youth; instead they increasingly were viewed as vulnerable, passive, and awkward, qualities that previously had been associated with girls" (Kett, 1977:6).

Kett observes that the most influential study on the nature of adolescence written during this period was by G. Stanley Hall (1904). Hall was profoundly influenced by the theories of Sigmund Freud and sought to link Freud's theory with that of Darwinian evolutionary theory. Hall developed a psychological theory of adolescence that emphasized the significance of hereditary determinants of personality. His theory of the socialization of adolescents was based on the principles of recapitulation theory, which held that every individual repeated the history of the species in his or her own development; that is, Hall took the viewpoint that children passed through the various stages of development from savagery to civilization that had already been traced by the race.

Hall postulated a "storm and stress" *(Strum und Drang)* interpretation of adolescence. Although anthropological studies, like Margaret Mead's *Coming of Age in Samoa* (1928), strongly suggested that adolescence need not be a period of turmoil and psychological disruption, Hall's viewpoint—combined with changes in industrialization, urbanization, and the developed intimacy and privatization of the nuclear family—led to the basic forms of today's concept of adolescence and to the treatment of adolescents in society.

Kett examines three dominating moral values that have continued to be influential in society's response to youth. The first is the belief that youths should be segregated according to their own age, both in school and in work. No longer were mixed-age groups of younger and older children to be allowed in the same classroom. Similarly, children were segregated out of the labor force. Increasingly, their work was restricted to part-time or summer employment. The second belief was the characterization of youth by passivity. The view was that adolescents should be easily moldable by grownups into the grownup's definition of adulthood. A third belief was the necessity for adult-directed activities for adolescents. Kett cites August de B. Hollingshead in his landmark sociologic study of adolescence, *Elmtown's Youth: The Impact of Social Class on Adolescents* (1949), on why the discontinuity in the socialization of youth can be so devastating.

By segregating people into special institutions, such as the school and Sunday school, and later into youth organizations such as Boy Scouts and Girl Scouts for a few hours each week, adults apparently hope that the adolescent will be spared the shock of learning the contradictions in the culture. At the same time, they believe that these institutions are building a mysterious something variously called "citizenship," "leadership," or "character," which will keep the boy or girl from being "tempted" by the "pleasures" of life. Thus the youth-training institutions provided by the culture are essentially negative in their objectives, for they segregate adolescents from the real world that adults know and function in. By trying to keep the maturing child ignorant of this world of conflict and contradictions, adults think they are keeping him "pure." (Hollingshead, 1949:149)

We are struck by the parallel conclusions and opinions reached by such anthropologists as Margaret Mead and Ruth Benedict and by a sociologist such as August Hollingshead—also shared by the social historian, Joseph Kett—on the negative consequences of this conceptualization of adolescence. It remains for us now to delineate fully how these conclusions and opinions on the contemporary definition and treatment of adolescents fit into our conceptual orientation on the nature of social change and the family.

Contemporary Implications of the Western Conceptualization of Childhood and Adolescence

To assess properly the contemporary condition of childhood and adolescence in the family and the society, it is necessary to re-present a brief historical sketch on the changes that have occurred. Preindustrial societies were characterized by a minimal differentiation of age groupings. Childhood and adolescence were not separated as separate and distinct chronological stages; rather, children were conceptualized as miniature adults. As they proceeded through childhood, they increasingly took on more and more adult responsibilities. There was no psychological conceptualization that prescribed an extended moratorium period when adolescents would be segregated and not be allowed to take on responsibilities. Life from childhood through adulthood to old age proceeded in a continuous process without cultural and institutionalized disruptions. The "adult" roles of parenthood and work participation were a culminating occurrence that flowed out of this nondifferentiated conceptualization of childhood and adolescence.

Demographic changes, industrialization, urbanization, and the changing conceptualizations of the family and of childhood and adolescence combined to produce the differentiation into the stages of life that characterizes today's population. Let us now be more explicit in our delineation of the contemporary condition of young people. We also observe how social scientists, coming out of different ideological persuasions, develop different assessments on what effect these changes have had. By necessity, we refer to previous arguments on the nature of the marital relationship in this discussion. By so doing, we hope to present a more-developed analysis.

Industrialization meant the loss of economic participation by young people in the labor force. Having once assumed economically viable positions in the family, they now became economic dependents. In the eighteenth and nineteenth centuries, the American family acted as a self-sufficient economic unit. Boys and girls were involved in work activities on the farm and in the home. They participated in the growing and harvesting of crops, the storing and cooking of foods, the caring of domestic animals, and the making of clothes. In short, the children were an economic asset contributing to the economic well-being of the family. By the end of the nineteenth century, the family economy was disappearing, giving way to a cash industrial economy. Kenneth

For Donahue, Sex Talk Falls Flat in Moscow

BY STEVE GOLDSTEIN

MOSCOW — For the first time in living memory, Phil Donahue could not get his audience talking about sex.

One young man said he lost his virginity at 14, which led to some conversation about contraception that, well, went nowhere. Then the majority, moral or not, asserted itself.

"Let's change the subject," someone said. Worse yet, the audience applauded.

Never had Donahue felt so homesick.

Let's face it. Back in the U.S.S.R., Phil, they don't much like to talk about these things. At least not publicly. At least not to a strange man in jeans and boat shoes and a mop of silver hair who is jumping around with a microphone and telling them that they will soon be seen on television in the United States. And telling them that everybody in America talks about sex.

"Maybe it's a big problem in your country," said one Russian teenager. "It's not such a big one here."

Wait until David Letterman hears about this.

Say one thing about his choice for the first foreign-based series of programs in the 20-year history of the show: Phil Donahue did not play it safe.

After the success of two "telebridge" shows in 1986, with Donahue and a U.S. audience talking to a Soviet host and an audience in the U.S.S.R., America's favorite *agent provocateur* decided to try to do *Donahue* in Moscow for a week. The results of the first-ever American talk show here, taped between Jan. 25 and 31, are scheduled to be shown in the United States next week — Feb. 9 to 13.

On a degree-of-difficulty scale of 1 to 5, this was about a 6½. Soviet television has yet to adopt American-style talk shows, and the Donahue method of diving into an audience to get responses is as foreign to Soviet citizens as Joan Rivers, and just as disconcerting.

Donahue is famous for wanting his topics "hot," and because Soviet television imposed no restrictions on subject matter during negotiations last fall, he went for some biggies. Chernobyl, for one, and the plight of Soviet Jews.

The former came off well, according to Donahue, as he was allowed as close to the reactor site as any newsman has been. He conducted interviews with Robert Gale, the American bone-cancer specialist, and with some resettled residents of the area.

But refuseniks proved hotter than radioactivity. When Donahue's executive producer, Pat McMillen, came to Moscow in October to negotiate with Gosteleradio (Soviet television), she won an agreement that 100 Jews who had been refused permission to emigrate would appear with 100 Soviet Jews who were happy to be here — "contentniks."

Later, the numbers were halved. When the Donahue crew arrived in Moscow, Gosteleradio officials appeared uncomfortable with the agreement, and things began to fall apart. The refuseniks wanted parity with the contentniks. Gosteleradio complained that there were more happy Jews than unhappy ones in the Soviet Union, and to grant parity was a distortion of Soviet society.

On the day of the taping, negotiations continued until it was obvious that the original plan was dead, and so was a face-to-face confrontation.

"I worked out an agreement with Gosteleradio wherein 50 refuseniks were to be permitted to enter this building [the Gosteleradio studios] for the purpose of sharing their agony with an American TV audience," Donahue said. "That agreement exploded."

Instead, Donahue went to an apartment near Moscow State University and taped an interview with some refuseniks, who had refused to debate at Gosteleradio so long as they were not accorded equal representation. Then he went back to the studio, where 25 members of a Soviet anti-Zionist group offered their views on the state of Soviet Jewry.

A few days later, in an article generally favorable to the Donahue show, the official news agency Tass reported the reaction by

(continued)

Soviet TV officials to charges by the refuseniks.

"The refuseniks simply lacked the arguments that they could use at the meeting with Soviet citizens of Jewish nationality," said Vladimir Popov, Gosteleradio's deputy chairman. "I do not rule out that they did not want to cross this threshold of Soviet television and thereby acknowledge the strengthening of the principles of openness that is now taking place in the U.S.S.R.

"But this episode did not affect our joint work with Phil Donahue," Popov said. "We both are of the opinion that it has good prospects."

Gosteleradio has agreed to show these programs on Soviet television at some later, unspecified date, according to Penny Rotheiser, Donahue's press representative. Soviet and American viewers alike will no doubt be fascinated by a woman in the studio audience during the show on Soviet lifestyle, who candidly discussed the dissolution of her marriage.

"With moisture in her eyes," Donahue said, "this woman told about a husband who was unfaithful and how she was picking her life up after this agony. It was very moving."

It was also encouraging to Donahue that his show on Soviet teenagers might really take off. On one of the previous telebridges, a teenager had said that he hadn't been taught anything about sex or birth control.

"From that, I assumed that if we gathered almost 400 people of the same age in the same room, you'll get a good deal of honest testimony," Donahue said after the teenage show had been taped. "But it didn't happen."

Sex might have been on their minds, but the teenagers didn't say so. One young woman said they were interested in communicating directly with their American counterparts.

"I think we should talk about sex when they see us and we see them," she said.

Donahue led them to sexuality through some innocent chat about dating, which came after unsuccessful attempts at getting some lively commentary about music and school. When the kids offered that their tastes in music weren't restricted, and that

they had nothing to complain about in their schooling, Donahue's smile turned from impish to ironic.

"You mean just everything is great here in the Soviet Union?" he said. "Americans aren't going to believe you."

His remarks, translated into the earpieces worn by all the participants, brought uneasy silence.

Donahue fared far better with two other topics: military service and religion. Some of the teenagers expressed anxiety about doing an army stint, for fear of dying in Afghanistan.

"I'm ready to die for my homeland, but not for someone else's," said one young man.

More typical were comments that entering the army was one's "internationalist duty," and that whether or not they liked it, they would serve. "A Soviet soldier expresses his dissatisfaction by wiggling his big toe," said one, quoting an old expression.

The audience actually got passionate during the discussion about religion—all but five said they were nonbelievers—and Donahue was in his element, bounding from one side of the room to another, picking up any notes of disagreement. "Church exists for people of weak character," said one. Another teenager accused his peers of hypocrisy. "How many of you were baptized?" he asked them, and a sizable number raised their hands.

Finally, it seemed *Donahue* had bridged the language and cultural barrier, and the emotion carried into the last topic of the show, Soviet-American relations.

One teenager suggested they close the show by singing, "We Shall Overcome," and a guitar miraculously appeared in the audience. It made one wonder just how spontaneous the suggestion was and, in fact, how average was this teenage Soviet audience.

Many of the kids spoke English. Assistant producer Marilyn O'Reilly said she came to Moscow a week early and picked teenagers at random from schools, a disco, a movie theater and a park. The only requirement was that they be between 16 and 19 years old and have seen one of the telebridges.

Random, yes. Average, no. The bulk of the audience came from two special schools

(continued)

in Moscow, one specializing in sports and the other in English. "We thought you had to speak English," said one teenager after the taping.

"Someone said they looked rather upper-middle class," Donahue said later. "I wouldn't know. It's my first visit here. We really did make an honest effort to get a cross-section of Soviet teenagers."

Donahue said it was "not his job" to be disappointed at the outcome of the show, but admitted that he was surprised that the teenagers weren't more willing to talk about sex and problems at school.

"I don't think they were holding back," he said. "I think that they are normal young people, just like you'd find in the United States. The Soviet culture is not as promoting of public debate, especially of a personal nature, as we are in the West."

Had he ever done a more difficult series of shows?

"Probably not," he said. "But that has to do more with translations and technology. In spite of this enormously complicated business of communicating with 300 citizens who speak a different language, I think these programs have been very, very lively."

SOURCE. Steve Goldstein. 1987. "For Donahue, sex talk falls flat in Moscow." *The Philadelphia Enquirer* (Feb. 3). Reprinted by permission of *The Philadelphia Inquirer* Feb. 3, 1986.

Keniston and The Carnegie Council on Children (1977) report that today children are an economic liability, with a cost of about $35,000 required to support them from birth just through high school, whereas in the preindustrial period children not only were able to pay their own way by working but also were expected to be the chief source of their parents' support when they got older. There was no government old-age assistance such as social security. Today, children can no longer be counted on to provide such an economic resource.

As we observed in Chapter 3, structural functionalists — in their analysis of these historical trends — developed the conceptualization of structural differentiation to explain the process in which the family has lost a number of functions to outside agencies. These agencies included the schools, the industrial sector, the political parties, and the judicial courts. The structural functionalists have long argued that the increased privatism of the contemporary family has led it to retain and even expand on two functions. These are the maintenance and stabilization of adult personalities and the socialization of children.

In that earlier discussion, we observed that contemporary critics of structural functionalism questioned whether the privatization of the family, female domesticity, and the isolation of children within the household were beneficial to family members and particularly to women and children. A common theme running through the criticism of the conjugal family revolved around the belief that its privatization and isolation have prevented it from achieving for its members the very intimacy and psychological gratification that it was designed to foster.

The structural functionalists, notably Talcott Parsons, viewed this development in a most positive light. This is a different interpretation than that developed by conservative analysts, such as Philippe Ariès. Richard Sennett (1974) contrasts the theoretical position of Parsons with that of Ariès on how "private and intense" family life relates to the socialization of children and their preparation for adulthood that we find quite useful. Ariès is seen as deploring the division of labor within the family since it isolates the family from the larger society. The result is the children's loss of needed experience with the outside world. This leads to subsequent difficulties in functioning in that world and in becoming adults.

In contrast, according to Sennett, the specialization of the family as seen by Parsons is a necessary consequence of the increased specialization of the entire society. Parsons favors the division of labor and role fragmentation within the family as preparing children for the division and fragmentation that they will experience in their adult activities. Sennett reports that Parsons views the socialization of children as requiring a long period of learning about themselves as fragmented beings. This belief develops out of Parsons's integration of the psychoanalytic description of child development and the structural analysis of society. Together these perspectives, as integrated by Parsons, argue that it is the "essence of ego formation to learn the proper limits and spheres of action" (Sennett, 1974:67). Sennett compares Ariès and Parsons in the following statement:

> The vices of the modern nuclear family for Ariès are, to a great extent, its virtues for Parsons. Where Ariès sees the specialization of the family as a limitation on human capacities to grow, Parsons sees this specialization as both a necessary conse-quence of the increased specialization of the whole society and a means of leading the child step by step into a position where he could act alone as an adult in a complex industrial world. For Parsons, the fact that the child in an isolated nuclear family would have "farther to go," as he puts it, in becoming an adult than children in another historical era is not an indictment of the family form, but an indicator of the increased complexity of the industrial society, in which the family plays a specialized role. (Sennett, 1974:66)

In recent years, the analysis centering around the implications of the privatized family for children has taken a new turn. There is a growing realization that the private family is not as free and autonomous as has been believed. Arguments have been raised that to study the family without taking into consideration the influence of the larger society leads to serious limitations in properly assessing the impact of the family on children. In particular, critics—such as Christopher Lasch (1977a)— argue that not only are the educational, political, and economic functions of the family now performed by the state and supporting institutions, but so also are the medical, social, and psychological functions increasingly performed by the helping professions. Lasch believes that there has been a progressive reduction in family functions to the extent that there is a growing intervention into the private life of the family. The services provided by the state and professionals are most graphically seen in compulsory education, but increasingly occur in the functions of medical practi-tioners, social workers, psychiatrists, child-rearing experts, and juvenile courts. The increased dependence of the family on these "experts" has ultimately led to the loss of its autonomy.

Christopher Lasch, in his stimulating book *Haven in a Heartless World* (1977a), is highly critical of structural functionalism *and* of what he labels "revisionist" and "radical" sociology. He asserts that critics of structural functionalism, which include Arlene S. and Jerome H. Skolnick, Kenneth Keniston in *The Uncommitted* (1965), Philip Slater, and R.D. Laing, "conjure up a fantastic picture of the isolated nuclear family as a miniature despotism in which parents enjoy nearly absolute power" (Lasch, 1977a:147). Lasch accuses them of over-romanticizing an alternative family model that echoes the medieval village and the extended-family system described by Philippe Ariès. And, most important, Lasch says, they fail to see how the private family system itself has been usurped by government social policies and social agen-cies. He asserts that the ideological shortcomings of structural functionalist sociology are

> because it took for granted the separation of private life and work, leisure and labor; assumed the alienation of labor as an inevitable by-product of material progress; gave scholarly support to the delusion that private life offers the only relief from deprivations suffered at work; and ignored the invasion of private life itself by the forces of organized domination. Revisionist sociology takes all this for granted too, and is equally oblivious to the erosion of the private realm. (Lasch, 1977a:149)

In the next section, we examine this argument by focusing on the development of the child-welfare movement. By so doing, we draw attention to the dilemma faced by children: the desire for the development of personal freedom and autonomy in the face of dependency situations, both in the home and in social institutions.

The Family and Child-Welfare Institutions

In previous discussions, we showed that there has been a systematic movement among the bourgeois middle class, begun several hundred years ago, to segregate and remove children from adult life. It was based on a belief that children and adolescents did not have the psychological capacities, intellectual abilities, and the requisite maturity to participate on an equal footing in adult affairs. Coinciding with this conceptualization was the development of the notion of the private family system.

This conceptualization was fostered by the emergence of the new industrialized urban society, which was viewed as threatening and unpredictable by the emerging middle class. For them, the same ideological currents that sought to protect women—by removing them from active participation in the outside world and sequestering them within the home—was carried over to the younger generation. Ostensibly, the desire was to protect both women and children from abhorrent labor conditions and their abuse by industry. In effect, however, this resulted in the subordination and dependence of both women and children. Before we examine its effect on the middle class, we can best understand how it came about by examining the child-welfare movement, which developed out of concern for the conditions of poor children of the nineteenth century. It was then that social policies regarding children developed and were carried over the contemporary era.

"Breaker" boys in a Pennsylvania mining town, 1911. These boys picked the slate and other impurities from the coal as it passed through the chutes and screens. They began at an early age and reached adulthood with little schooling, if any.

New York Public Library, Local History Division

Child labor and the abuse of children in industry were comon occurrences in the burgeoning factories of the late eighteenth and early nineteenth centuries of England. The prospering middle classes, aghast at the treatment of women and children in these factories, removed their own families from these harsh and brutal work conditions. Unfortunately, the children of the poor, the destitute, and the abandoned were not as fortunate. Economic and political realities resulted in their being victims of social injustice and forced employment in work situations that were inhumane and barbarous.

> With the coming of the machine age . . . mere babies were subjected to terrible inhumanity by the factory systems. . . . Children from five years of age upward were worked sixteen hours at a time, sometimes with irons riveted around their ankles to keep them from running away. They were starved, beaten, and in many other ways maltreated. Many succumbed to occupational diseases, and some committed suicide; few survived for any length of time. (Helfer and Kempe, 1968:11)

To illustrate, poor city children in England who were employed as chimney sweeps worked day and night. Death from cancer of the scrotum was frequent and pulmonary consumption was so common that it became known as the chimney sweep's disease.

The children who worked under these oppressive conditions were from the poorer classes. They were the young paupers from the workhouse, children without parents to protect them, many as young as 4 or 5 years of age. They also included the children of poor families who could not support them and reluctantly allowed their children to work in the mills and factories. Piven and Cloward (1971), writing on the societal functions of public welfare, note that pauper children relegated to parish poorhouses became an ideal labor source for the English textile industry. Parishes and orphanages supplied children to factories as cheap labor. They were motivated by both greed and the self-serving moral belief that idle children would grow up to be shiftless, idle adults. The manufacturers negotiated with them for lots of 50 or more children at a time. These children provided a very stable labor force because they were obligated to work until they fulfilled the terms of their indentures. For many, the terms of their indentures did not expire until the age of 21 and many children did not survive until that age.

In the beginning of the nineteenth century, the child-labor reform movement started in England with the passage of the First Factory Act in 1802. The act broke up the factory pauper-apprentice system, but it did not interfere with traditional parental rights over children. It did not apply to children whose parents were living and who allowed them or sent them involuntarily to work. Throughout the nineteenth century, the laws that were passed to curb the abuses of child labor in industry did not infringe on the Victorian premise that the family was a private and sacred institution into which outsiders had little right to intrude. It was not until the end of that century and the beginning of the twentieth that social-reform legislation was passed to protect children of the poor who did not pass the moralistic muster of middle-class reformers. An examination of events in the United States during this period will prove instructive.

In the last quarter of the nineteenth century, increased attention was given to the ways in which children were being abused. The first American legal action for child abuse was not brought about until 1874. In fact, laws to protect animals were enacted before laws to protect children. Indeed, the first child-abuse case was actually handled by the New York Society for the Prevention of Cruelty to Animals. In this first case, the child was treated under the rubric (legal rule) concerning a small animal.

By the turn of the century, a basic philosophy was developed on how best to handle abused and neglected children. These tenets have affected the way we look at abuse and neglect today and so deserve our attention. Muckraking journalists and social reformers argued that these children could best be "rehabilitated" by placing them under the jurisdiction of state industrial schools, reform schools, and the juvenile court system. Through their influence, such special judicial and correctional institutions were created for the labeling, processing, and managing of "troublesome and destitute" youth. An interesting twist is observed in this philosophy. The victimized child has in effect become the victimizer who must be incarcerated and rehabilitated. It is a nineteenth- and early twentieth-century version of "blaming the victim."

Anthony Platt (1969) has written a fascinating account of the child-welfare movement and the development of the conceptualization of abused children as delinquents. The social reformers — or, as he calls them, the child savers — believed that children who were brought up improperly by negligent parents were bound for lives of crime unless taken out of the parents' hands at a very early age. The child savers succeeded in the creation of rehabilitation institutions that were designed to prevent the development of criminal and deviant tendencies.

These reformers were influenced by the prevailing antiurban bias prevalent during that period and by their own middle-class Protestant morality. They reacted against the perceived "social disorganization" of the city. The city became the symbol of all the evils of modern industrial life. It was depicted as the main breeding ground of criminals. The children of the European peasant immigrants were seen as the victims of cultural conflict and technological revolution.

The social reformers extolled the virtues of the rural community and placed high value on religion, home, work, and the family. Parental discipline and women's domesticity were advocated to control children. The hope for children living in the city slums, who were described as "intellectual dwarfs" and "physical and moral wrecks," was to remove them from these debilitating surroundings (Platt, 1969). Platt cites a nineteenth-century reformer who reported to the National Prison Association in 1898 that philanthropic organizations all over the country were

> making efforts to get the children out of the slums, even if only once a week, into the radiance of better lives. Seeing the beauties of a better existence, these children may be led to choose the good rather than the evil. Good has been done by taking these children into places where they see ladies well dressed, and with their hands and faces clean, and it is only by leading the child out of sin and debauchery, in which it has lived, into a circle of life that is a repudiation of things that it sees in its daily life, that it can be influenced. (Platt, 1969:40–41)

The child savers were middle-class moralists who emphasized the values of home and family as the basic institutions of American society. They defined the problems of neglect as attributable to faulty hygiene and lax morality. They minimized or ignored the economic and political-power realities of the urban poor. By extolling such values, they fostered the movement of children out of the homes of the poorer classes that did not meet their standards. Middle-class families, of course, were by and large not affected by their zeal.

Unfortunately, the rehabilitation institutions did not function in the manner intended. They were overcrowded punitive institutions that physically punished boys and girls and that often had them working in industries contracted by their custodians. Platt describes the "educational" program of the Illinois State Reform School, which consisted of boys laboring 7 hours a day for a shoe firm, a brush manufacturer, and a cane-chair manufacturer. He argues that what were purported to be benevolent institutions for the intervention and prevention of crime became themselves abusive, punitive, and authoritarian, breeding their own abusive patterns. He summarizes his view by making four points (1969:176):

1. The reforms of the child-saving movement did not usher in a new system of justice, but rather they reaffirmed and expedited traditional policies.

2. A "natural" dependence of adolescence was promulgated. The creation of a juvenile court imposed sanctions on "premature" indulgence and behavior "unbecoming" a youth.
3. Paternalistic and romantic attitudes were developed but were anchored by authoritarian force. No conflicts of interest were perceived between the vested interests of agencies of social control and those of "delinquents."
4. Correctional programs were implemented that required long terms of forced imprisonment, involuntary labor, and militaristic discipline. Middle-class values and lower-class skills were inculcated.

The child-saving movement resulted in the forced incarceration of many urban poor children. Platt points out that the programs, which were rhetorically concerned with protecting children from the physical and moral changes of increasingly industrialized urban society, diminished the children's freedom and independence. Rather than provide remedies, they aggravated the problem. Platt makes an interesting observation on the relationship of this reform movement and Philippe Ariès' analysis of European historical family life that is worth repeating. It nicely summarizes a major point of this discussion—that ideological and moral biases often have a detrimental effect on the people they are designed to benefit.

> The child-saving movement had its most direct consequences on the children of the urban poor. The fact that "troublesome" adolescents were depicted as "sick" or "pathological," were imprisoned "for their own good," and were addressed in a paternalistic vocabulary and exempted from criminal law processes did not alter the subjective experience of control, restraint, and punishment. As Philippe Ariès observed in his historical study of European family life, it is ironic that the obsessive solicitude of family, church, moralists, and administrators for child welfare served to deprive children of the freedoms that they had previously shared with adults and to deny their capacity for initiative, responsibility, and autonomy. The "invention" of delinquency consolidated the inferior social status and dependency of lower-class youth. (Platt, 1969:177)

The child-saving movement, in summary, was based on the assumption that physical abuse and neglect were associated almost exclusively with poverty, slums, industrial exploitation, and the cultural deprivation of the poor and immigrant populations. As the physical conditions associated with abuse and neglect began to improve by the second decade of the twentieth century, the attention began to shift to concerns of the emotional neglect and abuse of children.

The 1920s and 1930s were a period in which the child-welfare movement increasingly turned its attention to the implementation of the new ideas of Freudian psychoanalysis and psychiatry. The emphasis shifted to the advocacy of the utilization of various forms of social services, either voluntary or by judicial intervention, in the hope of assuring the emotional well-being of children. This increasingly led to difficulties as the acceptable legal definition of emotional neglect and abuse was and is more difficult to define or prove than is its physical counterpart. The result was the development of an antagonism between affected families and social institutions that continues today. An examination of the works of Kenneth Keniston, Christopher Lasch, and Mary Jo Bane centers on this problem.

Parental Autonomy Versus Children's Rights

In *All Our Children: The American Family Under Pressure* (1977), the Carnegie Council on Children, headed by Kenneth Keniston, the psychologist known for his study of youth in the 1960s, reports on a 5-year examination on the way children grow up in America. The Council debunks the myth that the family is self-sufficient and self-sustaining as well as the widely held belief that parents alone are responsible for what becomes of their children.

The researchers believe that this myth developed in the nineteenth century out of the economic doctrine of laissez-faire capitalism and was built on images of the independent farmer and entrepreneur. The authors pick up a theme, which we have reported in this book, on how the family defined itself as a refuge that guarded women and children from the incursions of an increasingly alien and hostile urban environment. In the preceding preindustrial era of the seventeenth and eighteenth centuries, the family was defined by the Puritan conceptualization of the "little commonwealth." The family was viewed as essentially similar to the surrounding community and governed by the same standards of piety and respect. With the emergence of an industrialized and urbanized society in the nineteenth century, the belief developed among the affluent and privileged classes that the home must serve as a refuge protecting its frailer members, women and children, from the temptations and moral corruptions of a threatening outside world. "No longer simply a micro-cosm of the rest of society, the ideal family became a womb-like 'inside' to be defended against a corrupting 'outside.'" (Keniston and The Carnegie Council on Children, 1977:11).

The Council points out that, in reality, this family system was an ideal one that was perhaps realized by only a small segment of the upper-middle-class segment of the population. Poor families, immigrants, slaves, Indians, and growing numbers of factory workers rarely achieved this ideal of self-sufficiency and independence. Today, it is even less real for all segments of the population. Yet, the myth still persists. It fails to see that the family has been deeply influenced by broad social and economic forces over which it has little control. The Council argues that the family's authority and influence are constantly eroding and dwindling as that of outside institutions increase. Economic and social pressures of parents' jobs, the cost of raising children, the increased involvement of institutionalized health-care services and schools, and the entire social ecology—from television programming to the packaging of foods—define and limit parents' autonomy and independence.

> Today's parents have little authority over those others with whom they share the task of raising their children. On the contrary, most parents deal with those others from a position of inferiority or helplessness. Teachers, doctors, social workers, or television producers possess more status than most parents. Armed with special credentials and a jargon most parents cannot understand, the experts are usually entrenched in their professions and have far more power in their institutions than do the parents who are their clients. To be sure, professionals would often *like* to treat each child in accordance with his or her unique needs, and professional codes of conduct urge that they do so, but professionals who really listen to parents or who are really able to model their behavior in response to what parents tell them are still few and far between. (Keniston and The Carnegie Council on Children, 1977:18).

The Council concludes that the family is changing, but it is not collapsing: 98 percent of American children still live with one or both of their parents. They believe that "families—and the circumstances of their lives—will remain the most crucial factors in determining children's fate" (Keniston and The Carnegie Council on Children, 1977:xiv). But to do this, there is a need to remedy the greatest enemy of the family—poverty. The researchers find that one child out of four has the deck stacked against it by economic conditions. They cite a 1974 study that found that 33 percent of children born into the top-tenth income level would stay there, whereas only 0.4 percent of those born into the bottom-tenth income level would ever rise to the top.

To remedy this poverty, the Council recommends a major overhauling of Amer-ica's economic structure and sweeping reforms in social policies, work practices, laws, and services. Their proposals are designed to return to parents the authority they should have to raise their children, with the ability to do so under better circumstances than now exist. Among their specific recommendations are a guaranteed family income that is no lower than one-half the national median, full employment, income supplements for the working poor, and a national health-insurance plan.

Christopher Lasch (1977a, 1977b, 1979) is also concerned about the usurpation of family authority by professional social agencies. Lasch, an historian at the University of Rochester, believes that a work such as The Carnegie Institute's *All Our Children* reflects the growing disillusionment with the public institutions and welfare agencies that have taken over the functions of the family — the school, the hospital, the mental hospital, the juvenile courts, and the rehabilitation institutes. But, he argues, Keniston and his colleagues do not go far enough in their criticism of professionalism. He sees a contradiction in Keniston's advocating governmental expansion of services to the family, which includes a federal guarantee of full employment, improved protection of legal rights of children, and a vastly expanded program of health care, while also proposing to strengthen the family by its participation in these programs. He argues that the helping professions have systematically appropriated parental authority by demeaning the capabilities of parents, by arguing that only they have the scientific expertise to know what is best for the child, and by their piecemeal allowance of parents' decisions that only serve to perpetuate feelings of inadequacy and dependence:

> . . . the "helping professions," by persuading the family to rely on scientific technology and the advice of scientifically trained experts, undermined the family's capacity to provide for itself and thereby justified the continuing expansion of health, education, and welfare services. Having monopolized or claimed to monopolize most of the knowledge necessary to bring up children, the agencies of socialized reproduction handed it back in the form of "parent education," "consumer education," and other devices intended to enable the citizen to shop more efficiently among proliferating professional services. . . . Having first declared parents incompetent to raise their offspring without professional assistance, social pathologists "gave back" the knowledge they had appropriated — gave it back in a mystifying fashion that rendered parents more helpless than ever, more abject in their dependence on expert opinion. (Lasch, 1977b)

Lasch develops his argument through a social-historical analysis of the family and helping agencies. He asserts that the privatization of the family in the nineteenth century was short-lived. The bourgeois family did try to establish itself as a refuge, a private retreat, where it could become the center of a new form of emotional intensity between parents and children. Following the lines of previous historians, Lasch sees the nineteenth-century middle-class family developing a cult of the home, where the woman cared for her husband and sheltered her children from the perceived corrupting influences of the outside world. But, and this is the crux of his argument, at the same time that the glorification of private life and the family was occurring, a realization was developing that the family was inadequate to provide for its own needs without expert intervention. This led to the development of the helping professions.

Lasch states that the helping professions of the nineteenth and early twentieth centuries played on bourgeois fears by inventing and defining social needs only they could satisfy. He is particularly concerned with demonstrating how these professional social agencies condemned and appropriated parental authority and competence.

> . . . public policy, sometimes conceived quite deliberately not as a defense of the family at all but as an invasion of it, contributed to the deterioration of domestic life. The family did not simply evolve in response to social and economic influences; it was deliberately transformed by the intervention of planners and policymakers.

Educators and social reformers saw that the family, especially the immigrant family, stood as an obstacle to what they conceived as social progress—in other words, to homogenization and "Americanization." The family preserved separatist religious traditions, alien languages and dialects, local lore, and other traditions that retarded the growth of the political community and the national state. Accordingly, reformers sought to remove children from the influence of their families, which they also blamed for exploiting child labor, and to place the young under the benign influence of state and school. (Lasch, 1977a:13)

He discusses how the schools and social-welfare services expanded under the justification that the family could no longer provide for the needs of its children. Likewise, children's aid societies, juvenile courts, and visits to families by social workers became commonplace as the result of this belief that the family was not prepared to take care of the physical, mental, and social training of the child. Lasch believes that the result of these forces has been the usurpation of the family by outside professionals, doctors, social workers, the helping professions, and the schools.

Lasch is particularly critical of contemporary social scientists—sociologists, anthropologists, neo-Freudian psychoanalysts, and most of all Talcott Parsons and his school of functionalism. He believes their theoretical framework is responsible for the decline of the family. This occurred through their advocacy of "the family's indispensability while at the same time providing a rationale for the continued invasion of the family by experts in the art of social and psychic healing" (Lasch, 1977a:115–116). He maintains that Parsonian theory, although arguing the sociologic justification of the family's importance because of the intensification of the emotional climate of the family, nevertheless undercuts this importance with another line of argument that sees the family creating strains that only the helping professions' experts know how to handle.

Lasch sees this development as undermining the family with severe repercussions for its children. He reasons that, with the rise of the helping professions, parents become reluctant to exercise authority or to assume responsibility for their children's development. This, in turn, results in the weakening of the child's ability to develop an autonomous personality and prevents the development of moral values. In another work, *The Culture of Narcissism* (1979), he asserts that these developments have undermined American values and that the young are being socialized into a fake world of easygoing, low-keyed encounters. This culture of narcissism represents the decadence of American individualism and the end of the Protestant virtues of hard work, thrift, and capital accumulation. Today, the concern is with personal survival and hedonism.

In summary, both The Carnegie Council on Children report and Christopher Lasch's analysis provide a welcome shift away from the emphasis of debates on the family's psychological structure to the impact of society on the family and children. The policies advocated by the Council are designed to develop comprehensive and universally accessible public services to support and strengthen, but not to replace, families in the rearing of their children. However, to accomplish this, a fine balance must be achieved between the family's desire for autonomy and privacy and the public policies that seek to help and protect the child. Far too frequently, as Lasch emphasizes, the government acts not as a helping agency but as an opponent that seeks to legislate the family out of existence and to undermine its independence and autonomy. This tension also dominates the analysis of the family and social policy of Mary Jo Bane.

In her study *Here to Stay: American Families in the Twentieth Century* (1976), Mary Jo Bane, after careful statistical analysis, concluded that the contemporary American family is still quite viable and persists in its commitment to its children. She takes issue with the widely held notion that the American family of the past was an extended one. She supports the conclusions we reported, namely, that the nuclear family has been the predominant family form.

She opposes the belief that the declining birthrate reflects disintegration within the family. Rather, she observes that it indicates decreasing size of individual families and not the collective decision of the population to stop having children. As for divorce, she views it as a safety valve for families; it assures that only those who desire to stay together do so. Ultimately, it improves the quality of American marriages. Further, although the divorce rate has risen dramatically, most people remarry. Those that do not, tend to keep their children with them. Compared to a century ago, the loss of a parent is less disruptive to the family today.

The major thrust of Bane's study centers around the tension between public social policies designed for the protection of individuals, including children, and the desire for family privacy. She presents a detailed examination of such issues as mandatory day care for all, the Equal Rights Amendment, and Aid to Families with Dependent Children. She is particularly concerned that the rights of minors be protected from abusive and negligent adults and that the rights of children to economic sufficiency not impinge on and destroy the family's right to privacy and its viability. The argument is made that the tensions between family privacy and values pronounced in social policies can be resolved by a public stance that emphasizes the rights of individuals and assures the working out of family roles within the privacy of the family.

In conclusion, Bane argues for the view that Americans persist in their deep commitment to the family. Family ties continue to remain as persistent manifestations of human needs for stability, continuity, and nonconditional affection. Paradoxically, the greatest danger to the American family may lie in social policies that reflect the erroneous belief that the American family is dying. Consequently, those who hold that belief may advocate programs that, rather than attempting to supply helpful choices, may actually contribute to the family's decline and demise.

> Family ties and family feelings are integral to the lives of most Americans. The ethic that governs relationships between people who love and care for each other inevitably intrudes into public life, coloring people's perceptions of what they and others ought to do. Policies that ignore this ethic—that imply that public facilities can replace parental care or that the public welfare system is responsible for supporting children—will almost surely be either widely resented or essentially disregarded. Even when family service programs respond to real needs, they are often perceived as undermining the fabric of society. Until such programs are designed to incorporate the very real and very strong values that underlie family life in America, and until they are perceived as doing so, they are doomed to failure. (Bane, 1976:142–143)

From Economic Asset, to Priceless Treasure, to Responsible Family Member

We conclude this chapter by addressing ourselves to what sociologists see as the potential beginning of a trend toward the reconceptualization of childhood and adolescence. This changing viewpoint is seen to have been ushered in by such recent family changes as the outside work of both husbands and wives and the continued rise in divorce rates. The argument follows that these changes have necessitated that children and adolescents assume more-responsible family roles. These include household activities and involvements and, when necessary, outside employment. The reconceptualization is reflected in this section's title.

As we saw, between the 1870s and the 1930s there was a profound change in the

© Ulrike Welsch

A teenage boy works at home by doing the dishes.

attitudes toward children. Viviana Zelizer (1985) has traced the emergence of the modern child by documenting a shift in the value of children during this period from economically useful assets to economically "useless" but emotionally "priceless" love objects. To illustrate her thesis, Zelizer contrasts two legal cases:

> In 1896, the parents of a two-year-old child sued the Southern Railroad Company of Georgia for the wrongful death of their son. Despite claims that the boy performed valuable services for his parents of $2 worth per month, "going upon errands to neighbors . . . watching and amusing . . . younger child," no recovery was allowed, except for minimum burial expenses. The court concluded that the child was "of such tender years as to be unable to have any earning capacity, and hence the defendant could not be held liable in damages." In striking contrast, in January 1979, when three-year-old William Kennerly died from a lethal dose of fluoride at a city dental clinic, the New York State Supreme Court jury awarded $750,000 to the boy's parents. (Zelizer, 1985:138–139)

In the 1896 case, both the parents and the court argued solely on the basis of the child's economic worth. However, with the passing years, traditional forms of child's "work" were reconceived as illegitimate child "labor" and became a moral issue. Child-labor laws and compulsory schooling further reduced the economic contribution of children. Zelizer argues that by the 1920s, the strict economic approach to children's worth and judging the value of children by their potential earning power came to be seen as degrading, even immoral.

Children were redefined as precious, priceless objects of love and affection. Children's insurance became big business. It came to be viewed as protecting parents against the incalculable loss of a child by death or accident. This was an idea that would have been unimaginable half a century before. By the same token, in the 1870s there was no economic market for unwanted children. Baby farms, generally homes for illegitimate children, were paid fees to take in these unwanted children. By the 1930s, a market was created for babies that was based on their emotional worth. Adoption agencies for healthy white babies commanded fees of as much as $10,000 in the 1950s and even more today. Zelizer observes: "This startling appreciation in babies' monetary worth was intimately tied to the profound cultural transformation in children's economic and sentimental value in the twentieth century" (1985:170). And the change in the conceptualization of children is intimately tied to the historical change in the relationships of husbands and wives to a more-expressive and more-affectional pattern.

Recently, there have been a number of social commentators on the family who state that the conceptualization of children is once again undergoing transformation. Marie Winn (1983), in her book *Children Without Childhood,* and Neil Postman (1982), in his book *The Disappearance of Childhood,* advance the position that children are not allowed to be children. Instead, they believe that adults are rushing children into adultlike concerns. Winn attributes this to the disintegration of family life due in part to divorce and to the return of women to the work force. Further, the emphasis on sex on television, in the movies, and in other forms of the media, adult clothing designed for children, and the proliferation of drugs lead Winn to ponder, "What has happened to childhood innocence?" Similarly, Postman decries the "disappearance of childhood." Both advocate the restoration of a "real" childlike childhood.

Other social scientists have long advocated that letting children assume responsible roles has positive consequences for children. Zelizer picks up on a theme that we discussed earlier in this chapter on the necessity for giving children real responsibility and productivity in their lives. Citing anthropological evidence (Whiting and Whiting, 1975) that examined child-rearing practices cross-culturally, she finds that children who are taught responsibility develop a sense of worth and involvement in the needs of others. Glen Elder (1974), in his study of Great Depression children, found that children working to help fulfill some of the economic needs of their poor families developed independence, dependability, and maturity in money management.

Today, two views of childhood are being disputed that literally reverse the reform and traditional positions of the early twentieth century. "Once again, as at the turn of the century, two views of childhood are being disputed; but this time, the reform group proposes to selectively increase children's useful adultlike participation in productive activities, while traditionalists cling to the progressive ideal of a separate domestic domain for children" (Zelizer, 1985:221). The major factor that has precipitated this development has been the rapid increase in mothers entering the occupational work force.

Zelizer takes the position that as more and more women enter the work force and devote less time to domestic activities, and as more and more husbands become involved in household tasks, so too will children become more involved with, and responsible for, the maintenance of the household. "The demise of the full-time housewife may create a part-time 'househusband' and 'housechild'" (Zelizer, 1985:223). Indeed, she notes that a manual [Eleanor Berman (1977), *The Cooperating Family*] has already appeared that provides guidelines for how to get children to become actively involved in assuming household responsibilities including shopping, cleaning, and cooking. Popular magazines such as *Working Mother* and *Seventeen* have published advisory materials on how to define, negotiate, and establish rules for children's work. These articles are targeted for working mothers, divorced parents, and children on the necessity and means of establishing a new working relationship among family members. Zelizer quotes from a *Seventeen* article—"Do Your Parents Ask Too Much of You?" written by Sally Helgesen—which offers the following advice:

Try to look at things from your parents' point of view. If you don't do certain chores, who should do them? Do your parents, with all their responsibilities, really have time? . . . Examine the situation . . . to see what really is fair, and try to think of your family in terms of a unit with everyone having . . . something to contribute. (Helgesen, 1982:176–177)

With children assuming new household responsibilities, the question arises of just compensation for their labor. Many families do not consider household chores as deserving of monetary rewards; others pay their children in the form of allowances. However, we know very little on the nature and extent of children's domestic work. Further, more research is needed on the lives of children living under poverty. Estimates indicate that at least 300,000 migrant children work in the United States. In total, more than 11 million children live in poverty and many of them live in female-headed families (Zelizer, 1985). The meaning of work and money to these children, as well as their meaning to more-affluent children, is vital. Ethnic and racial variations and boy–girl variations and the age that work begins need to be investigated. Zelizer concludes on a hopeful note that the new family system that includes working parents and responsible children may well result in children becoming invaluable participants in a cooperative family unit. The result will also be a new integration of sentimental attitudes with a new appreciation of children's instrumental value.

The world of children is changing and their household responsibilities may be redefined by changing family structures and new egalitarian ideologies. The notion, inherited from the early part of the century, that there is a necessary negative correlation between the emotional and utilitarian value of children is being revised. The sentimental value of children may now include a new appreciation of their instrumental worth. (Zelizer, 1985:227)

Conclusion

The relationship between family members of different ages captured our attention in this chapter, as it will in the following one. Here, we saw how a power dimension was seen to be inherent in the differential relationships among family members of different ages. Children and adolescents were examined within an age-stratification perspective.

We showed that the nature and rate of social change have been associated with the nature and type of generational control parents have over their children. Margaret Mead's *Culture and Commitment* (1970b) was analyzed for its cross-cultural contribution to the understanding of what has been popularly labeled as the generation gap. Mead's work led us to examine how conceptualizations of childhood and adolescence are an important factor in the way generational attitudes and behavior become manifest.

Our comparative analysis drew on research in anthropology (Margaret Mead and Ruth Benedict) and social history (Philippe Ariès, Frank Musgrove, and Joseph F. Kett). It stressed the common elements in these research studies and this led to the conclusion that the contemporary Western conceptualization of childhood and adolescence emphasizes the removal of the younger family member from the outside world into the private family.

A brief digression followed to re-present the theoretical perspective of structural functionalism. This time, we focused on functionalism's microlevel analysis of children's roles in the family. We sought to demonstrate how structural functionalist conceptualizations reflected and reinforced the prevailing Western viewpoint of

Teenagers Are Passing Up High School Life for Jobs

BY SARA SOLOVITCH

Dominic Fesi used to play football for Wissahickon High School, but that was when he was a freshman, before he had a job that demanded 40 hours a week.

Now a senior, Fesi does his homework during work breaks at Donuts Galore in the Montgomery Mall. And he rarely has the time to attend a school game.

"Manage it? I really don't manage it, I just do it," said Fesi, quickly adding that "I wouldn't do it if I didn't get paid well for it. I get paid very well. I have a credit card, and at least once a month I can go to Bamberger's and throw my card down."

The majority of high school students in this affluent Montgomery County school district work after school—not because they have to work but because they want to work, according to administrators and teachers. They work to buy cars, tape decks, stereos and clothes. In many cases, they have chosen to work rather than participate in school sports and activities.

"The kids don't have time to be students," said Henry F. Van De Water, principal of Wissahickon High School. "They're too busy working in the malls."

It is a phenomenon that is being reported by nearly every suburban high school principal in the Philadelphia area, a trend made possible by a burgeoning of jobs in the malls and fast-food outlets of the suburbs. And it is a reflection of what is happening in schools across the country.

In 1980, 63 percent of the nation's high school seniors reported that they worked during the school year, according to a national survey by the Center for Education Statistics, a division of the U.S. Department of Education.

In 1982 that figure climbed to 70 percent—plus an additional 13 percent reporting themselves as unemployed, meaning that they were seriously interested in working but had been unable to find employment.

Although teenagers have always worked, this generation's industry has sparked something of a controversy. Principals complain that student employment has eaten away at school spirit; teachers say they are hard-pressed to reach students who appear apathetic but are actually overtired; bandleaders complain that some of their best players quit as soon as they turn 16 and become eligible for working papers.

"As boredom increases in a classroom I feel compelled to make myself more energetic," said Randy Quinby, a social studies teacher at Wissahickon. "A good teacher will automatically blame himself. But after a time you reach the point of diminishing returns. The kids are just tired. It has nothing to do with the electricity of your presentation."

Student employment was critically examined in a recent syndicated column by Richard Reeves, an author and columnist who spent three days at Great Valley Senior High School in Malvern only to stumble upon "a McDonald's generation of driven little materialists imitating the adult drudgery" of their parents.

Based on an annual survey of high school seniors, Jerald G. Bachman, a social psychologist at the University of Michigan, has coined the term "premature affluence" for the working teenager's acquired spending power:

"*Affluence* because $200 or more per month represents a lot of 'spending money' for a high school student," writes Bachman, "and *premature* because many of these individuals will not be able to sustain that level of discretionary spending once they have to take on the burdens of paying for their own necessities."

The notion of premature affluence is familiar stuff to the teachers at Great Valley High School in Chester County, where the student parking lot puts the faculty parking lot to shame, so goes the standing joke.

It also rings familiar at Springfield Senior High School in Delaware County, where administrators believe that at least 73 percent of the students work.

"Very few students are working to help their families," said Janet Way, chairwoman of that school's guidance department. "The majority of them are working to pay for their cars, their stereos, TVs and tape decks. All these things in their lives, that's

(continued)

what they value. So there's a lot of willingness to work for things."

Kelli Duffy's parents urged her to get a job last year because they thought it would help instill a sense of responsibility in the Springfield High student. In June, she found a job as a cashier in a department store where she now works three or four nights a week.

"I don't like working, but I like having a lot of money," said Duffy, who spends almost all her earnings on clothes.

Shelli DiRocco, a Springfield 10th grader, started working this year to finance her annual vacations to Florida.

"My mom said if I wanted to keep doing it, I'd have to start paying my own way," she explained. Her grades have "kind of gone down" since she began spending weekends at a telephone marketing research agency, and she has put little aside for her trips south.

"Every time I get my paycheck, it seems like the money disappears," she lamented.

A newly published book, *When Teenagers Work: The Psychological and Social Costs of Adolescent Employment,* draws conclusions that run counter to widely held beliefs about the positive value of work for teenagers.

"There is no evidence that holding a job in high school makes you any more employable," said Laurence Steinberg, a professor of child and family studies at the University of Wisconsin at Madison and co-author of the book. "What people need today to be successful in the work force is a good education, not experience in a fast-food setting."

The value of work has long been extolled by parents and educators as a way to teach teenagers the practical lessons of punctuality, responsibility, getting along with people, and the meaning of a dollar.

"Jobs with reasonable hours that don't interfere with school provide students with a whole set of positive opportunities," said Anthony Cost, principal of Cherry Hill High School East in New Jersey. "For a student, learning how to be responsible and independent, working with other people — these are valuable first-hand experiences that you can't get out of a textbook."

None of the recent studies argues wholly against teenage employment. But they almost all recommend that limitations should be set. Academics, teachers and principals generally agree that the negative effects of work outweigh the positive when students work more than 10 to 15 hours a week.

In its 1982 national survey of high school seniors, the Center for Education Statistics found that the typical employed student worked 18.2 hours a week — slightly less than the 20.7 hours a week reported in 1980.

When a faculty task force began looking into the causes behind falling grades at William Penn High School in New Castle, Del., last year, one of its findings was that work had become the focus of many students' lives.

"They work more hours than they really should, so they are not alert during the daytime," Principal Kenneth Wood said. "They have lost some of their ties with school because they are unable to attend any functions outside of normal classroom time."

"Six to 10 hours of work may provide enough structure that students may organize their time better," said James A. Kase 3d, principal of Great Valley High School. "Beyond 6 to 10 hours, there's no time to organize.

"We see the effects very clearly in poor grades, but also in a lack of participation in student activities."

Last year, while trying to do everything — maintain a B-plus average at Springfield High, play on the school's hockey and lacrosse teams and work 30 hours a week — Sue Byrne came down with mononucleosis.

"My boss has become a lot more lenient," said Byrne, a senior who works at a sporting-goods store. She has since cut back her hours at the store to three school nights plus Saturdays.

Several years ago, administrators at Springfield Senior High School set up a morning detention from 7 A.M. to 7:45 A.M. because so many of the students were unable to stay after school. Today, Principal Earl R. Knorr says that students' jobs have taken a heavy toll on school spirit.

"We have very poor attendance at our football games," Knorr said, "and the people who come to the games are mostly adults. That's also true of field hockey,

(continued)

soccer, you name it. It's not a function of a poor attitude on the part of the kids, it's a function of the fact that so many of them work."

But while Knorr, Kase and other principals deplore the rising tide of student employment, job boards are placed prominently in their schools' hallways. Their offices distribute applications for working papers, and most schools have designated one guidance counselor to act as a liaison between students and employers.

"Principals are leaned on by many employers in a community," said Steinberg of the University of Wisconsin. "They're leaned on in subtle ways, by employers who call to ask if a student can be released early from school in order to get to work on time. And it's good public relations, it reflects well on a school if the principal can point to the kids and say, 'Our kids are good kids, they're out there working.'"

SOURCE. Sara Solovitch. 1986. "Teenagers are passing up high school for jobs." *The Philadelphia Inquirer* (Nov. 9). Reprinted by permission of *The Philadelphia Inquirer* Nov. 9, 1986.

---

childhood and adolescence. The implications of these conceptualizations for children and adolescents were discussed in the section on child-welfare institutions. The idea of juvenile delinquency developed by child-saving professionals was analyzed. This was part of our larger discussion on the tension that exists between the sometimes conflicting concerns for preserving family autonomy while protecting children.

The chapter continued with a discussion of the ideas of Kenneth Keniston and The Carnegie Council on Children, Christopher Lasch, and Mary Jo Bane. These researchers asserted that the belief that the family is self-sufficient and self-sustaining is a myth. Public institutions and welfare agencies have had a strong impact on family autonomy and its authority over family members. Christopher Lasch, the most vocal opponent of the helping professions, is highly critical of structural functionalism and neo-Freudianism as forces that are undermining the family. Mary Jo Bane concluded this analysis by emphasizing the tensions that exist between public social policies designed for the protection of individuals, including children, and the desire for family privacy.

The concluding section reflected the growing recognition among social scientists that dual-income families and high divorce rates may foster a change once again in the way we conceptualize childhood and adolescence. More specifically, there are demands now being placed on younger family members to take on responsible positions in the family. One factor for this change is the belief that by assuming responsible roles the child and/or adolescent will be able to become a more-responsible and ultimately a more-successful adult. Another significant factor is structural change in the American family. Children and adolescents are becoming involved in the everyday activities of the household including shopping, cleaning, and cooking. With both parents working, many families need such help. Likewise, the single-parent family resulting from divorce often means that children and adolescents must take a more-responsible family role, including entering the job market while still attending school. The implications of these changes for the future are just beginning to be thought through.

The ways society conceptualizes childhood and adolescence are also factors in the phenomenon that we call child abuse, which becomes one of our concerns in the chapter on family violence. In the following chapter, we continue our analysis of generational relationships in the family by examining the relationships among older family members, their adult children, and their grandchildren. The four-generation family is also discussed and analyzed.

CHAPTER 15

The Family and the Elderly

A grandfather interacts with his grandson.

CHAPTER OUTLINE

In the previous chapter, we examined relationships within the family, with particular focus on the relationship between children, adolescents, and their parents. In this chapter, we extend the analysis of age differentiation and age stratification by looking at the relationship between elders and their married children. Here again, our concern lies with the structure of family status and authority patterns within the context of social change.

We focus our investigation by examining age differentiation in preliterate societies and contrasting it with the contemporary Western pattern. To highlight the differences in the conceptualization of age, we begin with an analysis of those preliterate societies that use age groupings rather than kinship as a basis for organizing social relationships. We then seek to demonstrate how age conceptualizations influence generational involvements in preliterate societies that do not employ age-set groupings. An in-depth examination of contemporary Western European and American societies follows. We show how these conceptualizations have implications not only for family relationships but also for government-based social policies that affect these relationships. We conclude by examining contemporary grandparenthood and the rise of the four-generation family.

Age Differentiation and Age-Set Societies

Age differences are biologically based. They are universally recognized. Age categories help shape people's relations to one another. Expectations vary, depending on the age of the person in question. Yet the categorizations of childhood, adolescence, youth, adulthood, and old age are social categories. They are not a mere product of biology. The social roles of child, adult, and the aged, for example, have varied from society to society and within given societies historically.

Yet one consistent pattern exists throughout the world. In all family systems, the superiority of parents to children is striking. Authority is vested in the parents, and children legitimate that authority. Thus, although parents treat their children "'like children,' . . . children treat their parents with respect" (Blood, 1972:457).

Robert O. Blood, Jr. (1972), lists three general reasons for the superiority of parents. First is the biological dependence of infants on their parents. This subsequently is transformed into social dependence, which continues indefinitely. Next, parents have had more experience and, concomitantly, they are wiser than their children by virtue of having lived longer. This especially holds true in nonliterate societies that depend on memory for the transmission of cultural knowledge about the proper ways of doing things. The third reason is that age gives parents a head start in achieving positions of power in the outside world. This, in turn, increases the resources that they can bring to the family. Together, these factors strengthen the power that parents have over their children.

There is a great deal of variability on the relative importance of age in a given society and on the degree to which age forms the basis of a separated social group. The importance of age as the determining factor in social relations varies with the total degree of differentiation in a given society. The extent of age differentiation varies by societal complexity and amount of industrialization. Generally, the more complexly differentiated societies, especially industrial societies, place less emphasis on age. Differences in work, socioeconomic status, ethnicity, religion, and the like are the more important determinants of group membership. In contrast, simpler societies with nontechnologically based economies tend to place primary emphasis on kinship, sex, and age. Kinship, sex, and age serve as the social-organizational basis of the society and provide the societal framework for the differentiation of relationships.

Age Sets in Preliterate Societies

Usually, age groupings are structurally and functionally subordinated to kinship as a basis for organizing people's relationships in groups. Age groupings are most frequently found as supports for kinship structures. They serve as a basis for the extension of kinship ties; rarely do they substitute for them. However, in some societies, age does form the basis of corporate social groupings in which the major criterion of membership is chronological age. These societies have formed age sets. *Age sets* are "social groups based on the principle of recruitment of persons of the same age, without regard to their kinship relations" (Williams, 1972:179). Age sets should not be confused with the mere categorizing of people who are recognized by a culture to be at the same stage of the life cycle (children, adolescents, old men). This is termed age grade. *Age grades* are comprised of collectivities of people who have no real social identity or corporate functions.

George Murdock (1957), in his world ethnographic sample of 547 cultures, found that less than 5 percent of the cultures (23) formed corporate, nonkin, exclusive social groups based solely on age. Approximately three-quarters of these cultures are located in Africa. It should be emphasized that the age-set system, which serves as a primary base of society-wide integration, is found in only 15 percent of all African cultures. Such age-set systems are most common among East African cultures, such as the Nandi, Kipsigi, Masai, Kamba, Kikuyu, and Meru. In these cultures associations based on age are central to the organization of community life and to the structure and function of the political system. A brief digression to examine one of these cultures will prove instructive.

Jomo Kenyatta (1938), in his classic account of his Gikuyu tribe (his preferred spelling of Kikuyu) *Facing Mt. Kenya*, discusses the importance of age groupings. On undergoing an initiation or circumcision ceremony, individuals automatically become members of one age set, irrespective of their family or kinship group or the geographic district to which they belong. This rite of passage marks the commencement of participation in various governing groups in the Gikuyu tribal administration. The tribal organization is stabilized by the activities of the various age groups. Together the different age groups provide the organizational basis for the political, social, religious, and economic life of the Gikuyu.

Kenyatta observes that Gikuyu society is graded by age and the differential prestige that accompanies a status is age grouped. Social obligations are arranged and differentiated according to this system of age groupings. Within age groups, men have equal standing. Among the age groups, they are differentiated into social grades of junior and senior, inferior and superior.

> When an uncircumcised youth is travelling in the same company as a circumcised youth, he may not drink water until his superior has drunk, nor bathe in the river above the spot where the latter is bathing. So in the distribution of food the order of precedence is observed. What is true of uncircumcised and circumcised is true as between the various circumcised groups. The older group takes precedence over the younger and has rights to service and courtesy which the younger must acknowledge. (Kenyatta, 1938:112)

Kenyatta points out the extent of the importance of the system of age groupings by emphasizing how it affects lesser as well as more important matters. "It determines the different salutations used, the different tasks in homestead or garden; it rules habits of dress or demeanor in the community; and it explains the rights of different people in judging cases, in exercising authority in the clan or family, in ceremonial or religious proceedings" (Kenyatta, 1938:103).

The relationship between males and females is also affected by the age groupings. Gikuyu society allows for polygynous marriage. Women are assigned to domestic roles. In the family, especially when there is more than one wife, the mother is the immediate head of her family set. The family set is made up of her children, her own hut, her personal ornaments and household utensils. She also cultivates her own fields and has her own granary for her crops. In turn, each wife shares in taking care of the common husband: cleaning his hut, supplying him with firewood, water, food, and so on. Each wife is materially independent of each other. The head wife has no superior authority over the rest but is shown deference and respect by virtue of her age and seniority.

Wives are expected to give special attention and treatment to members of their husband's age group. Kenyatta discusses what transpires when a visitor who has come from far away desires to spend the night in the homestead. Accommodations are made according to the rules and customs governing the social affairs of the given age group. A form of polyandry comes into play. This ultimately is seen to help reinforce the solidarity among the members of the age group.

> On these occasions the wives exercise their freedom, which amounts to something like polyandry. Each wife is free to choose anyone among the age-group and give him accommodation for the night. This is looked upon as purely social intercourse, and no feeling of jealousy or evil is attached to it on the part of the husband or wife. And, having all been brought up and educated in the idea of sharing, especially at the time when they indulged in "ngweko" (lovemaking), their hearts are saturated with ideas of collective enjoyment, without which there could not be strong unity among the members of the age group. (Kenyatta, 1938:174–175)

The age group composed of the elders has the greatest authority. The elders are treated with respect by virtue of their wisdom. They control economic affairs and political affairs for a period of 20 to 30 years; they then abdicate their power to the next generation. During this period, the men take on leadership roles and responsibilities. Even after they relinquish their power, they are treated with respect and deference. Simone de Beauvoir, in her massive work on the old, summarizes the attitudes of the Gikuyu toward their elders:

> The elders are looked upon as pious beings, holy men, serene and detached from the world. Their influence depends upon their abilities and upon their wealth. Generally speaking, they are regarded as being wise. The Kikuyu have a saying, "An old goat does not spit without a reason," and again, "Old people do not tell lies." The old women are much respected when they have no teeth left; they are

thought to be "filled with intelligence," and their bodies are buried with great ceremony instead of being left to the hyenas. (de Beauvoir, 1973:107)

What places age-set societies like the Gikuyu apart is the paramount importance of age in defining and regulating social integration, ritual activities, government, and military organization. The age-grade system is integrated with the kinship system, but it cuts across lineage membership. It serves as the major integration mechanism for the society. Although most of the world's societies are not organized solely around age sets, age does play an important role in determining societal interactional patterns. Let us now look at this in greater detail.

The Aged in Preliterate Societies

The general explanation given by social scientists for age grading follows on the nature of what Robert Redfield (1947) has termed folk societies. *Folk societies* are slow-changing, and emphasize tradition and cermonialism. They tend to be conservative and resist change. Continuity with the past is a basic premise underlying the social order. There is a sense of timelessness and all-prevailing custom. The sacredness of custom and the lack of a written history makes the elders the repositories of societal wisdom and knowledge. The elders have high status because they know best the traditions of the past.

In folk societies, the population clusters in small homogeneous communities. The community structure is fairly explicit, and it is anchored by stable values that are sacred rather than secular. The relationships among different age groups tend to be governed by explicitly delineated roles. These relationships are face to face and personal. Relationships among group members are multifaceted; they interact in different contexts, including work, home, and religious settings.

However, Leo W. Simmons (1945), who was one of the first anthropologists to attempt a large-scale cross-cultural study of aging, cautions us to be aware of the wide range of differences in attitudes toward and adaptations made to the problems and opportunities of aging. In a later article, Simmons (1960) observes that there is great diversity in cultural norms in terms of neglect and abandonment of old people on the one hand, and for their succor, support, and even glorification in death on the other. He finds that the influence and security of the elderly varies with the stability of the given society. Generally, the establishment of permanent residence, the achievement of a stable food supply, the rise of herding, the cultivation of the soil, and the increase of closely knit family relationships are all positively associated with the status and treatment of the old.

The status of the old tends to be inversely related to their numbers in the population. Simmons (1960:67–68) states that it is rare to find more than 3 percent of a primitive people 65 years of age and over. He also observes that in more primitive and rudimentary forms of human association there are fewer old people. Further, old age is attributed to these peoples at an earlier chronological date than in modern industrial societies. To illustrate, he cites a 1905 monograph on the Bontoc Igorot in the Philippines:

> A woman reached "her prime" at 23, at 30 she was "getting old," before 45 she was "old," and by 50 if she was so fortunate to live that long, she had become a "mass of wrinkles from foot to forehead. . . . Probably not more than one or two in a hundred lived to be 70. (Simmons, 1960:67)

Further, even though the number of those who did attain old age in some societies was small, the aging years came to be regarded as the best part of life. In fact, some preliterate peoples try to appear and wish to be regarded as older than they are. The anthropologist Leslie Milne[1] reports that the Palaung in North Burman is one such society where privilege and honor is given to the old:

> The older a person becomes, the greater is the respect that is paid her. The young women are expected to do a great deal of hard work along with the girls, such as bringing wood and water to the village before any festival; so married women are a little inclined to make out that they are older than they really are, in order that they may evade the extra work. (Leslie Milne cited in Simmons, 1960:68)[1]

Simmons hypothesizes that when the old can participate and fulfill themselves in the society, they tend to be treated with respect and deference. He examines their roles in the economic system, in government, and in the family to test his belief. He finds that when the aged have accumulated experience and familiarity with special skills, they retain directive roles in labor. For example, in the arts and crafts of basketry, pottery, house building, boat construction, and the manufacture of cloth, tools, weapons, and other implements, the old take on leadership roles based on their expertise. They are also highly valued for their roles of magician, healer, shaman, and priest. Midwifery is a prime illustration of a speciality associated with older women.

When they do not take on leadership roles, they can still find positions of usefulness. These usually involve engaging in secondary economic activities in field, camp, shop, and household. The underlying philosophy is the belief that all members of the society should participate in the society as long as they are physically and mentally able. By such activities, no matter how menial, the aged retain a sense of place and purpose in the society. The Hopi, a herding and farming people in northeastern Arizona, illustrate this principle:

> Old men tend their flocks until feeble and nearly blind. When they can no longer follow the herd, they work on in their fields and orchards, frequently lying down on the ground to rest. They also make shorter and shorter trips to gather herbs, roots, and fuel. When unable to go to the fields any longer, they sit in the house or kiva where they card and spin, knit, weave blankets, carve wood, or make sandals. Some continue to spin when they are blind or unable to walk, and it is a common saying that "an old man can spin to the end of his life." Cornshelling is woman's work, but men will do it, especially in their dotage. Old women will cultivate their garden patches until very feeble and "carry wood and water as long as they are able to move their legs." They prepare milling stones, weave baskets and plaques out of rabbit weed, make pots and bowls from clay, grind corn, darn old clothes, care for children, and guard the house; and, when there is nothing else to do, they will sit out in the sun and watch the dying fruit. The old frequently express the desire to "keep on working" until they die. (Simmons, 1960:73)

Property rights is an important area for prolonged and effective participation. The ownership or control of property on which younger people are dependent helps maintain the independence of the aged. Property rights also permit the aged to govern the opportunities of the young. Simmons, then, sees property rights as providing benefits to the old when they become sedentary and are not involved in direct economic production.

The high prestige and high status of the aged are supported by the extended-family system. The extended family is the basic social group providing economic security for the aged. It is central to the social structure. The obligations to the aged are institutionalized as formal rights; they are not simply generous benefactions of the young. In patriarchal societies, the eldest male possessed rank and authority. He had

---

[1] Leslie Milne. 1924. *The Home of an Eastern Clan.* Oxford: Clarendon Press.

David Maybury-Lewis/Antro-Photo File

Chief Abowa prepares a Shavante boy for initiation into manhood, Mato Grosso, Brazil, 1958.

absolute authority over his wife (wives) and children. He determined what they should do and whom they should marry. Disobedience meant disinheritance or even death.

The role and treatment of elderly women could be diametrically opposite that for elderly men. Simmons (1960) provides a vivid illustration of this in his discussion of the Ainu of Japan. The Ainu were a technologically primitive society before they were influenced by Japanese civilization. They lived in a very cold coastal area where they subsisted largely on raw fish. Fathers possessed great authority. They could divorce their wives or disinherit their children. The elder fathers received filial reverence and obedience to their dying days. Women throughout their lives were treated as outcasts and their fate grew harsher with advancing age. A.H.S. Landor[2] relates his visit to a hut in 1893 in which he found a feeble old woman crouched in a dark corner:

> As I got closer, I discovered a mass of white hair and two claws, almost like thin human feet with long hooked nails. A few fish bones were scattered on the ground and a lot of filth was massed together in that corner. . . . I could hear someone breathing under that mass of white hair, but I could not make out the shape of a human body. I touched the hair, I pulled it, and with a groan, two thin bony arms suddenly stretched out and clasped my hand. . . . Her limbs were merely skin and bones, and her long hair and long nails gave her a ghastly appearance. . . . Nature could not have afflicted more evils on that wretched creature. She was nearly blind, deaf, dumb; she was apparently suffering from rheumatism, which had doubled up her body and stiffened her bony arms and legs; and moreover, she showed many symptoms of leprosy. . . . She was neither ill-treated, nor taken care of by the village or by her son, who lived in the same hut; but she was regarded as a worthless object and treated accordingly. A fish was occasionally flung to her. (Landor cited in Simmons, 1960:81–82)

Simmons (1960) states that one tactic used by the old men to maintain their advantages in the family was to marry younger women. By so doing, they assured the continuation of their power. The following passage written by the anthropologist W.C. Holden[3] in 1871 describes the position of an aged Xosa or Kafir in Africa:

> The man is then supported in Kafir pomp and plenty; he can eat, drink and be merry, bask in the sun, sing, and dance at pleasure, spear bucks, plot mischief, or make bargains for his daughters; to care and toil he can say farewell, and go on to the end of life. As age advances he takes another young wife, or concubine, and then another, to keep up eternal youth, for he is never supposed to grow old as long as he can obtain a youthful bride; she by proxy imparts her freshness to his withered frame and throws her bloom over his withered brow. (Holden cited in Simmons, 1960:80)

The fate of the aged in preliterate societies was ultimately determined by the balance between their contribution to the society and their dependence on it. As long as the productivity of the old exceeded their consumption, they found places for themselves. However, for those who were regarded as a living liability—the over-aged; those at the useless stage; those in sleeping period, the age-grade of the dying; and the already dead—actual neglect or even abandonment was rather common. In Simmons' (1945) cross-cultural investigation of 39 tribes in which definite information was available, neglect and abandonment were customary in 18 tribes. He reports that among the Omaha, a nomadic North American Indian tribe, the very feeble were customarily left at a campsite provided with shelter, food, and a fire. Similar practices occurred among the Hopi, the Creek, the Crow, and the Bushmen of South Africa (de Beauvoir, 1973). The Eskimo persuaded the old to lie in the snow and wait for death or put them on an ice flow and abandoned them when the tribe was out fishing or shut them up in an igloo to die of the cold.

Yet, the abandonment, exposure, or killing of the aged was not necessarily disrespectful. It occurred out of dire necessity rather than from personal whims. It came from the hardness of preliterate life, not the hardness of the preliterate heart. Environmental necessity forced the rather drastic deaths of the few helplessly aged persons (Simmons, 1960). Simone de Beauvoir, in her comprehensive study *The*

[2] A.H.S. Landor. 1893. *Alone With the Hairy Ainu.* London: J. Murray.
[3] W.C. Holden. 1871. *The Past and Future of the Kaffir Races.* London: the author.

Coming of Age, cites anthropologist Paul-Emile Victor's dramatic example of a sick Amassalik Eskimo man in Greenland who was unable to get into his kayak. The man asked to be thrown into the sea, since drowning was the quickest way to the other world. His children did as he asked. But, buoyed up by his clothing, the man floated over the freezing water. A beloved daughter called out to him tenderly, "Father, push your head under. The road will be shorter" (cited in de Beauvoir, 1973:77–78).

Our final illustration from Simmons serves to conclude this discussion. Simmons indicates that the abandonment of the sick and very old was a reciprocal process with the "victim" actively participating in the process without harboring feelings of ill will toward the young. He quotes from J.A. Friis' 1888 monograph[4] on the Lapps of Finland:

> To carry the sick and disabled persons such a long journey is impossible, and so there is no choice but that he or she, whoever it may be, perhaps one's own father or mother, must be left behind, provided with food, in some miserable hut on the mountain, with the alternative of following later or else of dying entirely alone. . . . But a father or mother does not think this being left alone on the mountain a sign of cruelty or ingratitude on the part of their children. It is a sad necessity and a fate that perhaps had befallen their parents before them. (Friis cited in Simmons, 1960:85–86)

Simmons (1960:88) concludes by outlining five universal interests of aging people:

1. To live as long as possible.
2. To hoard waning energies.
3. To keep on sharing in the affairs of life.
4. To safeguard any seniority rights.
5. To have an easy and honorable release from life, if possible.

These five wishes are seen to be shared by people living in the most primitive societies and the most complex. Simmons believes, however, that the ability to obtain these wishes becomes more problematic with social change. He argues that in stable preliterate societies a pattern of participation becomes relatively fixed for the aged. A structured framework for participation is developed in which statuses and roles are defined, sex-typed, aptitude-rated, and age-graded. With permanence, the pattern solidifies and the aged are able to entrench themselves. However, all becomes upset with social change:

> In the long and steady strides of the social order, the aging get themselves fixed and favored in positions, power, and performance. They have what we call seniority rights. But, when social conditions become unstable and the rate of change reaches a galloping pace, the aged are riding for an early fall, and the more youthful associates take their seats in the saddles. Change is the crux of the problem of aging as well as its challenge. (Simmons, 1960:88)

We now investigate the impact of social change on the aged by looking at a type of society that differs radically from the so-called primitive societies—Western industrial societies.

---

[4] J.A. Friis. 1888. *Jajla: A Tale of Finmark.* London: G.P. Putnam's Sons.

The Aged in the West

Irving Rosow, a contemporary American social scientist, has written persuasively and elegantly on the status of the old in the industrial United States. In a thoughtful article, Rosow (1973) contrasted the role of the aged in preindustrial societies with their role in America. He wished to explain the societal variations in the welfare of the aged. He outlined seven contributing factors: property ownership, strategic knowledge, religious links, kinship and extended family, community life, productivity, and mutual dependence. All seven involve the resources that old people command, the functions they perform, and the state of social organization. We use them as the organizational framework for our discussion. In the following pages we point out how social changes relating to these factors have affected the role of the elderly in Western industrial societies.

Property Rights

Preindustrial agrarian Western societies were characterized by the elders' ownership, control, and direct operation of the principal form of productive property—the farm. In such circumstances, the aged maintained their independence at the same time that their offspring were dependent on them.

Conrad M. Arensberg's *The Irish Countryman* (1937/1959) and his *Family and Community in Ireland* written with Solon T. Kimball (1959) are classic works on the family in a farming economy. They are concerned with rural Irish communities of the 1930s, consisting of families with small farms. The family's total existence is centered around the possession and maintenance of the family farm. "Keeping the name on the land" is the central value that governs the family. The Irish farm is too small for feasible economic subdivision. Family continuity demands that the farm pass to the next generation intact. Economic necessity means that the inheritance of the farm can only be passed to one child, usually one of the elder sons. All the other sons "must travel" and seek their fortunes elsewhere. Likewise, daughters who are not provided with dowries must leave the farm.

Until the time when the father dies or retires and gives one of his sons the family farm, he controls the life of his children. Even though his sons do the major work on the farm, he mandates the direction of farm work and the distribution of the farm's income. The farm bears his name in the community and his sons are spoken of as his "boys." The subordinating of sons can continue even to the ages of 45 and 50. As long as the father has not given up the farm, the sons remain "boys" both in farm work and in the rural vocabulary:

> In 1933, a deputy to the Dail raised considerable laughter in the sophisticated Dublin papers when he inadvertently used the country idiom in expressing country realities. He pleaded for special treatment in land division for "boys of forty-five and older"—boys who have nothing in prospect but to wait for their father's farm. For "boyhood" in this instance is a social status rather than a physiological state. A countryman complained to me in words which tell the whole story. "You can be a boy forever," he said, "as long as the old fellow is alive." (Arensberg, 1937/1959:39)

The change in the "boy's" status occurs when he marries and inherits the farm. Country marriages are made through "matchmaking" and involve parental negotiations and a dowry. Marriage symbolizes the transfer of economic control and the attainment of adult status. The marriage and the transfer of land to the son accomplishes a drastic transformation in the relationships of household members. The sons and daughters must be provided for elsewhere. They feel themselves entitled to some form of inheritance, either in the form of dowries to marry into another farm or of some other form of aid to help establish themselves. Typically, they must leave the farm.

The "old people" must abandon their power and move into a new status of old age. They relinquish the farm and their economic direction of the family properly passes to the young people. For the father, it means the abandonment of the farm ownership; for the mother, it means that she is no longer woman of the house.

Marriage is a central focus of rural life. It represents a universal turning point in individual histories. Marriage coincides with the transfer of economic control and land ownership. It means the reformation of family ties, advance in family and community status, and entrance into adult procreative sex life (Arensberg and Kimball, 1968). For this reason, we can understand why Ireland had the highest rate of late marriage of all record-keeping societies in the 1930s. When Arensberg first reported on his research in 1937, 62 percent of all men between the ages of 30 to 35 were still unmarried, as were 42 percent of the women in this same age group. Late marriage can be associated with the reluctance of the old couple to renounce their leadership.

In many instances, a smooth transition occurs and father and son continue to work together. This happens when the son shows deference and respect to the accumulated knowledge of the parent. One such family is described by a neighbor who observed the old man working by the side of his son, "Look at the Careys; old Johnny gives his boy a hand in everything. You wouldn't know which one has the land" (Arensberg, 1937/1959:86). The old woman can also be of help in assisting the son's wife with domestic chores and the raising of the children.

In cases where there are disagreements between the old couple and the new farm-couple owners, it is the old people who must leave. It is only in this way that the family continuity, the giving their "name to the land," can be continued. "For the pattern of family and land must continue in the persons of the new man and woman and their children" (Arensberg, 1937/1959:88). In summary, rural Irish family life maximizes the importance and the power of the aged. The Irish rural community can be viewed as a virtual gerontocracy.

Gordon F. Streib (1973) reported on Ireland since Arensberg and Kimball's famous work of the 1930s. Streib found that for many parts of rural Ireland, the old patterns of prestige, recognition, respect, and power conferred on the old farmers still held. The elder males relinquish authority very reluctantly. They retain firm control over their sons until a late age. The sons commonly delay their marriages until they have gained control of their inheritance; they consequently marry late. When the transfer of power and ownership of the land does occur, it is done formally and legally with the older man retaining only specified limited rights and prerogatives.

However, change is occurring and is attributable to both indigenous and alien influences. More specifically, the back and forth emigration of Irish emigrants and British tourists, and the media's penetration into the rural Irish hinterland, have altered traditional patterns. Further, there is a rise in influence of young farmer organizations and rural community groups that promises to continue the change in traditional thinking. Streib believes that the result of these changes may be a "shift of Irish culture from one that was more traditional and oriented to slow changes to one which stresses youth orientation, more rapid changes, and technological development" (1973:181). The result may be that "the veneration of the old may be one of the casualties of 'progress'" (1971:181).

In recent years, the rural Irish practice of older males holding property not only to ensure their own security but also to hold adult sons in a subordinate role has been changing. In parts of western Ireland, where the land has become very unproductive and a high proportion of the farmers have no visible heirs, this system has broken down. Scheper-Hughes (1983) found that these old men are portrayed as unenvied scarecrows watching over wasted, worthless land. She refers to these people as "deposed kings."

In comparison to the control of property by the elders in an agrarian society, property ownership by the elderly is not typically found in industrial American society. Irving Rosow (1973) argues that property ownership has spread broadly through the American population. Further, capital ownership and management is not centered in the hands of elderly people. The expanded industrial economy has created new jobs occupied by younger people. Higher education also provides further opportunities for the young.

Together, these developments have increased the opportunities for the young and reduced the young's dependence on the old. Rosow concludes: "While an old property owner may be financially independent, he no longer has significant control over the life chances of the young; and they have less need to defer to him" (1973:230).

Strategic Knowledge and Religious Links

In our examination of the role of the elderly in traditional societies, we saw that the elderly are viewed as the repositories of societal wisdom and knowledge. They have full understanding and knowledge of occupational skills and techniques, as well as a virtual monopoly of strategic knowledge regarding healing, religion, warfare, cultural lore, and the arts.

Now things are vastly different. The proliferation of new occupations and newer knowledge diminishes and minimizes the elders' control of strategic knowledge. Different universes of discourse are created between the generations. This, in turn, lessens the communication between the generations. For who among the young wants to hear from the old and their "old-fashioned" and "out-of-date" ideas and opinions?

Formal education has taken on the job of teaching the young occupational and other skills. The popular media teach the new attitudes and values of the society. The peer group, not the elderly, socializes the young. The result is that the elderly are no longer considered "strategic agents of instruction nor founts of wisdom" (Rosow, 1973:230).

In the past, the aged were seen as the links to the past and were venerated. In tradition-oriented societies, classical China being the prime example, old age was honorific and the aged were religiously revered. Ancestor worship of the dead parents was the norm.

The movement from the sacred order of the traditional society to the secular one of contemporary industrial society sees no corresponding role for the elderly. In practice, the old are venerated neither by religious tradition nor as links to ancestors, gods, or the hallowed past.

Kinship and the Extended Family

As we noted, in the past, the extended family was a more highly integrated economic unit. The aged parents were at its head. The obligations of the young to the old were institutionalized as formal rights, not simply generous benefactions. In recent years, social historians have been reaching the conclusion that, in the last 200 years, the extended family in Western industrial society was not as predominant as social scientists had earlier assumed. However, Tamara Hareven (1976), a prominent social historian of the family, believes that this does not alter the nature of the elders' involvements in the family. Even when the elderly lived apart from their adult children, they maintained active family roles. Reciprocal support relationships and the exchange of services characterized integenerational relationships. These ties were reinforced by a societal value and normative system that governed children's obligations. These reciprocal relationships allowed the elderly to maintain their autonomy in a period when programs of social security and other forms of public old-age assistance were relatively nonexistent.

The reader may note a similarity between Hareven's description of the nineteenth-century family and Eugene Litwak's conceptualization of the modified extended family of the mid-twentieth century. As you recall from our earlier discussion on families in the city, Litwak was one of a number of social scientists in the post–World War II period to criticize theoretically and to test empirically the prevalent notion of what Talcott Parsons labeled the "isolated" nuclear family. These writers held that it was an oversimplification to believe that the American family was organized on a conjugal basis with no involvement with extended kin. In their collective research, they found ample evidence for the existence of linkages of conjugal families joined together on an egalitarian basis for mutual aid. Further, residential propinquity, occupational solidarity, and authoritarian control by the family did not characterize their family life.

On the surface, it would seem that the "modification" of the extended-family system is not a recent phenomenon but a process that has been occurring for a rather long time. We are acutely aware that the lot of today's elderly is not as satisfactory in most aspects of their lives as it was in the nineteenth and early twentieth centuries. The reason lies not so much in changes in family structure or residential arrangements but in ideological changes that have transformed and redefined family functions. Tamara Hareven (1976) believes that the erosion of instrumental values and the ascendancy of intimacy and sentimentality as the foundation of the family has led to the weakening of the role and function of extended family members. This change has been particularly felt by older couples.

She develops her thesis by noting that the emphasis in the twentieth century has been on domesticity and child rearing as the sole role expectation for women. This, combined with the insulation of the conjugal family and its removal and detachment from aging parents and other relatives, results in the loss of power and influence by the old people in the family.

Hareven then uses a recurring theme in family sociology—the development of the ideology of family privacy. Family privacy results in the separation of the family from the community. It also leads to the lessening of social supports to friends, neighbors, and kin. The household becomes a self-contained unit. The family develops a self-initiated isolation. This development particularly affects older parents who are no longer needed for the handling of everyday family concerns, nor is their advice solicited. For example, child-rearing "bibles" like Dr. Spock's are preferred to the guidance and advice of the grandparents. The accumulated result is the increased segregation of different age groups in the society and the elimination of older people from viable family roles.

The distinct conjugal family has shifted its responsibilities to its own members' well-being—that of the father, mother, and children. Although token attention is given to aged parents, the major responsibilities for old people has shifted to governmental programs, like social security and social welfare. Hareven points out that unfortunately the welfare system is grossly inadequate. The result is that the elderly have been caught in the middle with neither families nor the government providing the necessary resources to assure a financially secure life for the elderly. We continue discussion of this aspect later in this chapter.

Community Rights

Irving Rosow (1973) makes the following general observations. He notes that in traditional societies, the population clustered in relatively small stable communities. The community structure clearly delineated formal age gradings and definite roles, linking different ages. The interaction of community members was multifaceted; they came together in all spheres of life—home, work, and the church. In contrast, the urbanized society has less community stability. Changing neighborhoods, residential mobility, and urban impersonality are all seen to undermine the stable community. The result is that the urban community has been unable to accommodate older people.

Rosow's analysis echoes our viewpoint on the changing nature of communities and family relations. We have noted that the preindustrial family was intertwined in community life. Philippe Ariès (1962) found that in preindustrial France, the lives of the people were totally absorbed in community functions. The family played a secondary role. The family itself was caught in a web of interconnection to the small community. The public nature of the family predominated. The marital couple was prevented from living a life of intimacy and separateness. The intensity of the collective life prevented this occurrence. Community pressures and involvements assured the openness of the nuclear family. Integenerational households, with the older generation controlling individual family members, also assured this outcome. From the arrangement of marriages to the control of property, the elders held sway over the individual and prevented the development of autonomous family units.

The development of the ideologies of individualism and nuclear-family privatism and domesticity intersected with the rise of the new industrial order and contributed to the breakdown of community control and the power and control of the older generation. Gerrit A. Kooy, a Dutch sociologist, has done a number of empirical studies of family life in the Netherlands. In one of his studies, Kooy (1963) examines the rural agrarian population of Achterhoek, one of the sandy districts of eastern Holland. His description of traditional Achterhoek is very similar to Arensberg's description of the rural Irish countryside. Similar to the situation in Ireland, the large majority of farms in Achterhoek are small. The labor is provided entirely by the farmer and his immediate family.

Before 1875, Achterhoek was a relatively isolated regional community. Loyalty and identification were restricted to neighborhoods located within the district. The community was homogeneous with intensive social controls. The population was stable. Individuals were born there, were raised there, were married there, and worked on the land there until their death. The church, the neighborhood, and the family influenced every aspect of an individual's life.

The church was influential in religious concerns. In addition, it played an important role in the social life of the community. It kept the population informed on who was selling livestock. Before and after services, it gave the people an opportunity to meet and exchange bits of news and gossip. For the young, it gave them a chance to see each other, a rare occurrence in a life geared to isolated farm work. The moral standards of the people were not solely determined by the church. Rather, morality was defined within the broader rubric of proper social behavior that was set by the community's normative structure.

The extended family had a great deal of power over individuals. This included such issues as deciding on whether a child should marry and whom. Marriage was defined primarily in economic terms with young couples remaining subordinate to the parental generation even after marriage. "In this type of communal situation, each marriage has a tremendous influence on every member of both families of an engaged couple, causing significant changes in the personal relations of many relatives who customarily cooperate economically and socially" (Kooy, 1963:47–48). Grandchildren, too, were strongly influenced by their grandparents. In sum, the extended family with its generations and relatives, not the parent–child unit, controlled the education and dominated the behavior of the family members.

The family system was interlocked with the neighborhood. Neighborliness was not social in nature nor was it based solely on friendship. Common law mandated mutual duties among neighbors. These duties included "assisting at births, weddings, or funerals in a neighbor's household; helping in difficult situations; or visiting and receiving neighbors in winter. If the need arose, neighbors would not hesitate to discipline the child of someone else within the group" (Kooy, 1963:48).

The traditional neighborhood in Achterhoek began to change around 1876. Improvements in transportation and communication systems opened the district to outside influence. New farming methods and the development of educational facilities fostered the district's integration into the larger Dutch society. The result was the gradual loss of control by the neighborhood. Neighborhood stability was undermined. Today, although the tradition of the neighborhood still persists, its group loyalty is weakening. Younger members of the community view "neighborliness" as a communal burden rather than as a duty. "Personal interest and the development of professional services are replacing community cooperation in a wide range of activities including the arranging of weddings to the plowing of fields" (Kooy, 1963:48–50).

Kooy then examines how these changes have affected the position of the aged and the nuclear family. As mentioned, in the traditional neighborhood, the elders held influential positions relating to all aspects of life. The elders were the embodiment of customs and traditions. Economically, they controlled the extended family system. Socially, they held sway not only over their own children but over their grandchildren as well. They were integrally connected to all facets of communal life.

Today, although still influential, their previous all-encompassing power and high status is eroding. Kooy sees the rise of the power of the individualized nuclear family as a major contributing factor to the decline of the importance of the aged. Traditionally, the nuclear family was incorporated into the all-embracing extended family, which, in turn, was closely integrated with the neighborhood and church. A new ideology has now arisen that emphasizes the independence of the nuclear family and the opposition to the extended family role. This sentiment is expressed in the following statements of farmers and countrywomen between the ages of 25 and 45:

> Father does not trust anything beyond his hands, and the other generation never gets a chance. Such a life does not have any advantage.

> Marriage can be fully enjoyed only when husband and wife are together.

> Living with relatives is entirely wrong because a young women feels like a maidservant. Previously she accepted this, but the younger generation does not.

> In the households I know the atmosphere shows that these people should not live together. The person who has married into this extended family suffers the most. The older people do not give up their authority. The younger ones are (treated) no better than servants.

> A woman taken into an extended family loses her personality. Very often she cannot lead her own life because of the domination of her in-laws, especially her mother-in-law. The loss of personality is common.

> In my opinion only a mother and father should have authority over their children. (Kooy, 1963:52–53)

The breakdown of the local community and the increased importance of the nuclear family has resulted in the loss of status and the decline in institutional-role participation by the elderly. Instead of old age meaning higher rank in the community, it now signifies the loss of rank. Further, older persons are becoming defined as outsiders in community affairs. The loss of traditional supports has affected the elderly's need of self-maintenance and self-development. Kooy concludes that as modern ideas continue to become predominant, older people's feelings of frustration and uncertainty will increase.

Productivity

In preindustrial societies, especially those at a bare subsistence level, the elderly play a significant role in economic productivity. In such societies—which have a minimal division of labor and low technological development—each individual, regardless of age, can be of value as long as he or she is able to contribute to the small gross product. Every little bit helps. This fact explains Rosow's somewhat paradoxical finding that, "the greater the poverty and the struggle to survive, the *relatively* better off old people are by the standards of their group" (Rosow, 1973:229–230).

When we turn our attention to highly developed and technologically advanced societies, we find a minimally productive role for the elderly. The increased emphasis in these societies is to retire people who are defined as having little value in the labor market. An examination of the historical development of the conceptualization and implementation of retirement highlights the relationship of old people to productivity.

Industrial development in the West has seen a transformation in the age makeup of the work population. During the eighteenth and nineteenth centuries in America, individuals worked throughout their lives. Work involvement only ceased with illness or death. With increased specialization, the demand heightened for productive efficiency. The emerging belief in the late nineteenth century was that old people were not as productive as the young. This was in fact the case for many physically demanding jobs. In these cases, the growing practice was to shift older workers into less demanding and less productive work. The automotive industry with its notorious assembly line was a prime illustration. Its workers were relegated to nonproductive positions as soon as they were thought to be unable to keep up with the pace of the assembly line. Ely Chinoy, in his study of automobile workers, quotes a worker who complained bitterly of this practice:

Elderly people in a protest demonstration for jobs, Oakland, California.

> You see the fellows who have been there for years who are now sweeping. That's why most of the fellows want to get out. Like you take Jim, he's been there for thirty years and now he's sweeping. When you aren't any good any more, they discard you like an old glove." (Chinoy, 1955:84)

Soon, however, even this practice gave way to the retirement of the older worker, bowing to the demands of industrial efficiency.

The swift growth in technological knowledge also contributed to the dislodgment of old people's involvement in the economy. The emergence of many new specialized occupations with new knowledge requirements proved disadvantageous to the old. The young benefited with educational improvements; the elderly fell behind. The exposure of the younger generation to new educational, technological, and industrial ideas heightened the inequality between the generations. New jobs and new occupations had higher status than the old ones. The younger generation filled them. As people got older, they became more and more confined to the older, less prestigious, and, sometimes, obsolete occupations.

Accompanying the notion of elderly nonproductivity was the emerging belief in the cult of youth. No longer were older people venerated and exalted. The growing disparity between generations in occupational skills helped account for this change. So did the loss of the strategic knowledge of the elders. Stemming from the Protestant work ethic — with its emphasis on efficiency, productivity, and progress — the society increasingly placed emphasis on the virtues of modern youth as opposed to the old-fashioned ways of the elderly. The result was disparagement of the elderly. Increasingly, the older individual was being defined as useless and a drain on the social and economic well-being of the society.

The cumulative result was that by the end of the nineteenth-century age-related standards of usefulness and productivity began to be implemented. And, by the beginning of the twentieth century, retirement at a specific age became commonplace. Thus, paradoxically, although men found themselves living longer than ever before, they also found themselves being forcibly retired to a stigmatized status at an earlier age than ever before.

Older women were not directly affected by the growth of the retirement movement since relatively few women were actively involved in the work force. Yet, they, too, were affected by the demographic social and economic changes of the nineteenth century. This resulted in what best can be described as maternal retirement (Fischer, 1977:146). The great demographic changes in fertility and mortality rates of the nineteenth century had a profound effect on women's lives. More and more women began to survive childbirth and the child-bearing years. Earlier, women had had a life expectancy of about 45 years. Their life span coincided with the period when they were raising their children. As the life span of women increased, a proportionately greater number of years were spent outside the maternal period. For example, a woman today with a life expectancy of approximately 75 years can look forward to a period of about 25 years after her youngest child leaves home.

Women whose lives had been defined almost exclusively by their maternal role were now faced with a stage in the life cycle where no explicit norms or rules existed to govern their behavior and to provide meaningful direction for their lives. The postparental period, coinciding with the physiological changes of menopause, proved to be a period characterized by depression and alienation. Trained solely for domestic activities and child-rearing roles, women suddenly found themselves "retired" at a much earlier age than their spouses. Thus, although men were being retired in their late 50s and 60s, women were confronted with the fact that their last child left home before they were 50.

For many older Americans, mandatory retirement is a blessing in disguise. It frees them from boring and tedious jobs. It provides them with the opportunity to pursue leisure activities, travel, and hobbies that they could not pursue when they were employed. But, too many old people find themselves more victims than beneficiaries of mandatory retirement. A recent committee report of the American Medical Association states that the mental and physical health of many people is seriously hurt by the loss of status, lack of meaningful activity, fear of becoming dependent, and the isolation that may accompany involuntary retirement. And, it noted that suicides reached a peak in upper age brackets, 70 years and over, after retirement normally occurs (Flaste 1979:62).

In recent years, to combat the debilitating effect of compulsory retirement, the aged in America have begun to organize into pressure groups, such as the Gray Panthers, the National Council on the Aging, the National Association of Retired Federal Employees, and the National Council of Senior Citizens. They have sought the passage of social legislation to either extend or bar mandatory retirement ages. Congressman Claude Pepper, who was born in 1901, is a leading proponent of this type of legislation to halt discrimination by age. He argues:

> Ageism is as odious as racism and sexism. Mandatory retirement arbitrarily severs productive persons from their livelihood, squanders their talent, scars their health, strains an already overburdened Social Security system and drives many elderly persons into poverty and despair. (*Time,* August 8, 1977:67)

However, modifications and even the banning of compulsory retirement may have profound implications for the society. Many businesses are alarmed at the prospect of changes in compulsory retirement practices. They are concerned that promotion opportunities for hired younger workers will be severely limited—the longer older people hold their jobs, the slower the job advancement for younger people. They also believe that, despite a few exceptions, a significant number of older workers may just be deadwood. These proposed changes would hinder the productivity and progress of their businesses.

In education, for example, the extension of the mandatory retirement age coupled with the tenure system will result in schools and colleges being increasingly staffed by older faculties. Younger generations of scholars will be frozen out of academic positions. It will also hamper efforts of universities and colleges to comply with affirmative action programs for hiring women and minorities. The result will be a continued and increased predominance of older white men on the nation's academic faculties.

To counter this argument, critics of involuntary retirement argue as follows: everyone should be judged on ability and no one should be refused work because of an arbitrary age limit. Such an age barrier is discriminatory and should be rejected, just as it is for sex and race. Old people need work, too, just like everybody else.

Ironically, change in the mandatory retirement age is gaining some support from younger people. They are concerned with the rise in the elderly population in America as a result of demographic changes and its impact on the Social Security system. Younger workers, whose taxes support those who are retired under Social Security, have seen a constant rise in the money needed to provide benefits. A raising of the retirement age at which people can claim benefits will serve to cut down on the monthly deductions of younger workers. This economic fact may persuade many that it is costing too much to discriminate against older workers.

The extensive debate on the issue of mandatory retirement in the United States is also beginning to occur in Western Europe with some interesting variations (Kandell, 1977). Although the United States is moving to extend the retirement age beyond age 65, in Western Europe there is a movement to lower it. In West Germany, the Netherlands, Spain, and most of Scandinavia, retirement takes place at the age of 65 or earlier, and plans are underway in all these countries to lower it even further. France has recently passed legislation to permit employees to retire at age 60. Italy, which already has reduced the retirement age to 60, is witnessing its labor unions striving to lower the age to 55.

Although aged workers are in favor of lowering the age, provided that their retirement income remains adequate, the main thrust behind this movement occurs because of the plight of a high percentage of unemployed young people. This problem has taken on political overtones. Ruling governments, opposition parties, and labor unions, bowing to the political pressure from the young, are all trying to outdo each other to gain their political support. The early retirement programs being instituted in Belgium, for example, require employers to replace those who are being retired with unemployed workers under the age of 30; they are prohibited from hiring pensioners.

Economists are wary of the long-term effects of these policies. They point out that the increase in the inactive retired is outpacing the growth of the labor force. This will ultimately put an expensive burden on most European economies. A recent study by the Organization for Economic Cooperation and Development, which consists of the Western developed countries and Japan, argued this point:

> There may be a slowing down in the trend toward lowering retirement age over the next few years because of unfavorable demographic conditions. . . . If the fertility rate continues to drop as it has done over the last 10 years, the financial burden for pensions will be spread over a smaller number of working people and it will become more and more difficult to increase the number of those drawing pensions by systematically lowering the pensionable age. (Kandell, 1977)

The economic and social problems of the aged are also a concern of some social scientists. The aged in Europe are still counting on their families to support them during the retirement years. But, as in the United States, owing to the greater mobility of the population, the long-held values that emphasize obligatory involvement with the old by the community and the family are gradually disappearing. A spokesperson of the Institute for an Active Retirement in France, one of the largest nonprofit organizations for retired people, addresses himself to this point:

> People still have an idyllic image that they can retire to their birthplace in the countryside and find friends and family members. But they often find that friends and family are no longer there. The wife may not know how to drive. The closest pharmacy may be a mile away. And the children do not visit often enough. (Seguin cited in Kandell, 1977)

Eventually, then, the same demographic, social, and economic factors that are operating in the United States will be occurring in Western Europe. Indeed, they may have already started. Although there is still no active militancy among retired and elderly people in Western Europe, aging Europeans are beginning to press their economic demands through unions and white-collar employees' associations. These people have also voiced their dissatisfaction with their social conditions. They believe that they have been discarded by society. And, outside of their involvement with their immediate family, they are upset with their forced lack of participation in the community. Ultimately, the battle between the older generations and the young will be accelerated in Europe and in the United States over these issues.

Mutual Dependency

The development of retirement as a new stage of the life cycle has necessitated a major readjustment for men and women in our society. Unlike other transitional periods that occur throughout the life cycle, the retirement stage is one that lacks a clearly defined social position in the structure of society. In a society that places its strongest emphasis on the necessity of work for the establishment of a man's sense of identity, retirement is almost antithetical. For a woman, the maternal role has served as a primary source of self-conceptualization. As she gets older, this role is no longer viable.

In addition to these social concerns, retirement is problematic because of financial uncertainties and increasing health concerns. In earlier times, children were obligated to care for their aging parents. Since the new ideology of nuclear family privatization and independence emerged in the nineteenth century, this obligation has receded in importance. The result has been that the government is becoming more and more involved in providing financial aid and health-care facilities for the elderly. Unfortunately, governmental programs have been woefully insufficient in providing adequate help to these people. Further, the welfare programs developed by the government have not proved to be viable alternatives to the involvements, obligations, and satisfactions that were inherent in the kinship ties that the elderly had with their children and other relatives in the preindustrial period.

Irving Rosow (1973) has pointed out that in preindustrial societies there was a high mutual dependence between age groups. This great interdependence promoted the mutual aid and reciprocity between the generations. In contemporary industrial society, the relative economic affluence of the population and the rise in living standards have undermined this mutual dependence. The result has been a growth in individuality and independence at the expense of solidarity and reciprocity.

Tamara K. Hareven (1976) takes a somewhat different approach to explain the decline of mutual dependency. She believes that the transformation and redefinition of family functions have been instrumental in the growing isolation of older people in our society. The privatization of the middle-class family with its emphasis on internal sentimentality and intimacy precludes the involvement of extended kin, including aged parents. The modern family has also withdrawn from community involvements. The result has been an intensification of the segregation of different age groups within the family and the community, and the elimination of older people from viable family roles.

Suburbanization has also contributed to the geographic segregation of older people. As you recall from our discussion of families in the city, after World War II there was a marked increase in the number of conjugal families that migrated into new suburban communities. These middle-class families emphasized privatism and independence from both community and extended-kinship involvements. John Mogey's (1964) distinction between closed communities and open communities provides us with a framework to discuss these variations and the relationships that exist between the generations. A closed community is characterized as one where scenes of intense interfamilial cooperation exist. The involved relationships between mother and married daughter in the English working-class community of Bethnel Green is a prime example. Open communities are those where families have selective attachments to a variety of associations or secondary groups. These families interact with individuals and extended kin in other areas as well as in their own area. Yet, these relationships do not share the same degree of intimacy or involvement as that characterized by the families of the closed community.

Open communities and conjugal family privatism have resulted in the increased geographic segregation of old people. Two groups of old people will be discussed to demonstrate the impact of the loss of mutual dependency. The first group are old people whom Herbert Gans (1962b) referred to as the trapped. These are less affluent old people who have been forced to remain in former homogeneous working-class communities that have become dilapidated and into which poorer families of different ethnic or racial backgrounds have moved. The second group of old people are the more-affluent elderly who reside in age-segregated retirement communities.

The plight of the first group was dramatically conveyed in a series of criminal incidents that occurred in the Bronx, New York City, in 1976 (Klemesrud, 1976).

Criminals, many as young as 12 and 13, terrorized old people. Unable to defend themselves and afraid to go to court because they feared retaliation, the old fell unwitting prey to a vicious cycle of mugging, beating, rape, and murder. At the time that the newspaper article was written, 20 old people had been reported murdered in the Bronx. (The Manhattan and Brooklyn figures were 34 and 25 murders, respectively.) The headlines tell the story best: "Youth Held in Murder of Bronx Man Locked in Closet Three Days," "Grandmother Is Raped and Robbed by a Burglar in Her Bronx Home," "Elderly Bronx Couple, Recently Robbed, Take Their Own Lives, Citing Fear," "Two More of the Aged Killed in the Bronx," and "Many Elderly in the Bronx Spend Their Lives in Terror of Crime."

The sections of the Bronx that were the scenes of these horrible occurrences were once almost exclusively white. Today, their population is about 80 percent black and Hispanic and 20 percent white. The blacks and Hispanics tend to be a mixture of working-class people and welfare families with few elderly members. The whites tend to be elderly Jews living on Social Security payments. They have remained in the area because they cannot afford to move or for sentimental reasons. The racial pattern of crime against old people varies through the city, depending on the makeup of the neighborhood. Elderly blacks and Hispanics have also been victimized. It is apparent that these elderly people portray the worst consequences befalling the elderly as the result of community and familial abandonment.

The rapid rise in the number of retirement communities in the last several decades reflects the situation of elderly people in our society. As early as 1942, Talcott Parsons reflected on the circumstances that brought this phenomenon about:

> In view of the very great significance of occupational status and its psychological correlates, retirement leaves the older man in a peculiarly functionless situation, cut off from participation in the most important interests and activities of the society. . . . Not only status in the community but actual place of residence is to a very high degree a function of the specific job held. Retirement not only cuts the ties to the job but also greatly loosens those to the community of residence. Perhaps in no other society is there observable a phenomenon corresponding to the accumulation of retired elderly people in such areas as Florida and Southern California in the winter. It may be surmised that this structural isolation from kinship, occupational, and community ties is the fundamental basis of the recent political agitation for help to the old. It is suggested that it is far less the financial hardship of the position of elderly people than their social isolation which makes old age a problem. (Parsons, 1942:616)

Retirement communities were developed out of a felt need by the aged for more satisfactory community involvement. They also sought to provide residents with meaningful interpersonal relationships, which the aged were not experiencing with their former nonelderly neighbors and extended kin. The most prominently visible retirement communities are located in warmer regions of the country and have such names as "Leisure Village" and "Retirement World." These communities restrict residency to those in their retirement years, about 55 or older. In the more-affluent communities, residents tend to be white, middle- to upper-class persons with professional backgrounds. The goal of these communities is to provide their members with sufficient opportunities to become participants with "people like themselves" in a number of leisure and social activities.

In addition to the more-affluent communities, residential housing projects and urban apartments have been set up to provide a supportive social environment for older people. In a number of studies on age-segregated residential communities of all types (see the readings in Part V of Kart and Manard, 1976), researchers have found high morale and social involvement of residents. Critics, however, view them as too homogeneous and confining. They feel that life in a retirement environment is artificial, boring, and that residents have few meaningful involvements and activities.

One such critic is Jerry Jacobs. Jacobs (1976) studied a planned retirement community of approximately 6,000 affluent residents over the age of 50. This community, "Fun City," is located 90 miles from a large metropolitan area on the west coast. The sterility of everyday life is revealed in the following interview that Jacobs had with one of the residents:

MR. N. Well, for me a typical day is—I get up at 6:00 a.m. in the morning, generally, get the newspaper. I look at the financial statement and see what my stocks have done. I generally fix my own breakfast because my wife has, can eat different than I do. So I have my own breakfast—maybe some cornflakes with soy milk in it—milk made out of soybeans that they sell in the health food store. And uh, then at 8:00 a.m. my wife gets up. The dog sleeps with her all night. And uh, she feeds the dog. Then the dog wants me to go out and sit on the patio—get the sun and watch the birds and stuff in our backyard and have quite a few rabbits back in there. And I finish my paper there. And then she sits and she looks at me. She'll bark a little bit. And uh, then she'll go to my wife, stand by my wife and bark at her. She wants me to go back to bed. So I have to go back to bed with her. So about 8:30 I go back to bed again with my dog for about an hour. And then I get up and I read.

And then I walk up around here and I go over to oh, the supermarket and sit there and talk to people. We go over to the bank. They have a stockroom over there, for people that own stock. We discuss stocks and events of the day. And then I come home and maybe have lunch if I want to or not—it doesn't make any difference. *In fact, down here it doesn't make any difference when you eat or when you sleep because you're not going any place. You're not doing anything. And uh, if I'm up all night reading and sleep all day, what's the difference.* [Emphasis added.] But then, I'll sit around and read and maybe a neighbor will come over or I'll go over to a neighbor's and sit down and talk about something. And then, lots of times, we go over to a neighbor's and play cards 'til about 5:00 p.m. and then we come home and have our dinner. And the evening is . . . we are generally glued to the television until bedtime comes. And that's our day.

DR. JACOBS. Is that more or less what your friends and neighbors do?

MR. N. Some of them do. Some of them don't do that much. (Jacobs, 1976:389–390)

Jacobs argues that retirement communities can be false paradises. His example, "Fun City," had few employment opportunities and few gainfully employed persons. It was geographically isolated with no intercity or intracity public transportation and no police department. Inpatient and outpatient health-care facilities were inadequate. The failure lies ultimately in the residential community's denial of the individuality of the residents and the lack of meaningful activities and events.

On a more-optimistic note, Arlie Russell Hochschild (1973) reported on an old-age community in a small apartment building that had a viable communal life. There were active involvements among the residents. Friendships and neighboring and social-sibling bonds were prevalent. There was little feeling of alienation or isolation. Hochschild believes that the community life found here counters societal disaffiliation. It fosters a "we" feeling among the residents and an emerging old-age consciousness. Generalizing from this community, Hochschild summarizes the major virtues of retirement communities:

> Communal solidarity can renew the social contact the old have with life. For old roles that are gone, new ones are available. If the world watches them less for being old, they watch one another more. Lacking responsibilities to the young, the old take on responsibilities to one another. Moreover, in a society that raises an eyebrow at those who do not "act their age," the subculture encourages the old to dance, to

sing, to flirt, and to joke. They talk frankly about death in a way less common between the old and young. They show one another how to be, and trade solutions to problems they have not faced before. (Hochschild, 1976:383–384)

Grandparenthood in Contemporary America

There has been a significant decline in the mortality rate in the last 85 years. Since the turn of the century, we have seen a decrease in infant mortality from about 140 infants out of every 1,000 dying in their first year of life to only about 14 out of 1,000 today. At the same time, the average life span has increased from less than 50 years to 73 years. In an insightful article, the demographer Peter Uhlenberg (1980) observes: "Many of the most significant changes in the American family—the changing status of children, the increasing independence of the nuclear family, the virtual disappearance of orphanages and foundling homes, the rise in societal support of the elderly, the decline in fertility, the rise in divorce—cannot be adequately understood without a clear recognition of the profound changes that have occurred in death rates" (1980:313). This mortality rate change has had a major impact on family structure. We have addressed ourselves to many of the significant changes in the American family attributable in part by Uhlenberg to this mortality decline. In this section, we investigate the changes in grandparenthood and the four-generation family as a consequence of these demographic changes.

The decline in mortality rate has caused a profound change in the relationship between grandparents and grandchildren. Mortality rate change has greatly increased the potential for family interaction across more than two generations. There was only a one in four chance that a child at birth in 1900 would have all four grandparents alive; by 1976, almost two-thirds of all children at birth had all four grandparents still alive. By the time that that 1900-born child was 15, there was only a 15 percent probability that three or more grandparents would still be alive; in 1976, that probability increased to more than half, 55 percent. Uhlenberg (1980) points out that the demographic data cannot determine the actual role of grandparents in the lives of children. But they do indicate the increased possibility of the presence of grandparents in their grandchildren's lives.

To begin our analysis of grandparents and the relationship with their grandchildren, we must take into account the age of people when they first become grandparents. In our society, the modal age of becoming a grandparent is around 49–51 years for women and 51–53 years for men (Troll, 1983). The onset of grandparenthood can be much earlier in the case of teenage pregnancies. This often produces grandparents in their 30s. Given the increased life span, many people can now experience not only grandparenthood but great-grandparenthood as well. By the same token, many young people can have grandparents well into their adult years.

The ages of grandparents cover much of the human life span—from the early 30s to the 100s. Obviously, there will be a great variation in the relationship of grandparents with their grandchildren, depending on their respective ages. Much of the research on grandparenthood covers the period of people from 50 to 70 years of age and the birth to teenage years of grandchildren. It is in this period that most people are most comfortable about being grandparents. People much younger and much older with grandchildren are not as satisfied with that role (Troll, 1983).

Recently, Andrew J. Cherlin and Frank F. Furstenberg (1986) investigated the role of the "new American grandparent" and the subtitle of their book indicates some of their findings—"A Place in the Family, A Life Apart." Their study is based on a representative nationwide study of American grandparents. They note that improvement of the quality of life of many older people has brought about changes in the grandparent–grandchild relationship. Better health and the generally improved standard of living that older adults enjoy because of such things as Social Security combined with technological improvements in transportation (for example, automobiles and airplanes) and communication (for example, the telephone) have fostered the reshaping of the grandparental "career." They further observe that class is relatively unimportant in grandparenthood.

Another factor that has had a positive impact of the grandparental role is that due to the lower fertility rate many people have completed raising all their children by the time they become grandparents. There is less likely to be role conflict among grandparents, their children, and their grandchildren. Also contributing to changes in the grandparental role is the relaxing of the formal roles among the generations. Reflecting the societal trend toward informality and personal gratification, the grandparent–grandchild relationship can be characterized more by affection than by obligation.

There is a difference in the nature of the involvement of grandparents and grandchildren, ranging from intense involvement to remoteness. In their classic article, Neugarten and Weinstein (1964) categorize five styles of grandparenthood. They include grandparents who are formal, fun-seekers, surrogate parents, reservoirs of family wisdom, and distant figures. Variations in styles of grandparenting differed by age categories. Younger grandparents ranged from fun-seekers to distant figures with a significant number of them in the fun-seeker category. Older grandparents were more consistent in their style of behavior. They were almost always formal and distant. Cherlin and Furstenberg (1986), based on their own findings, believe that the variations in grandparental involvements are more than simply a reflection of the age of the grandparents. The age of the grandchildren is a prominent factor as well. "The fun-seeking pattern failed to emerge in our data not because our grandparents did not like fun but rather because it was not an appropriate style with older grandchildren: no matter how deep and warm the relationship remains over time, a grandmother does not bounce a teenager on her knee" (Cherlin and Furstenberg, 1986:85).

Variations in grandfather and grandmother roles seem to follow traditional patterns of male–female family roles (Troll, 1982). Gunhilde O. Hagestad (1981) has found that grandmothers seem to be more nurturant and are more likely to have warm relationships with their grandchildren. Grandfathers tend to take on the role of the "reservoir of family wisdom." Further, grandfathers usually give more attention to grandsons than to granddaughters. Grandmothers make less gender distinction in their involvements with their grandchildren. Conversational topics among grandmothers and grandchildren center on interpersonal and intrapersonal topics such as dating, family, and friendship concerns; grandfathers' conversations are more focused on wider social issues and external family concerns regarding work, education, and time management. Similar findings lead Cherlin and Furstenberg to reflect that "These gender differences can be summed up in one principle: grandfathers are to grandmothers as fathers are to mothers or, indeed, as men are to women in our society" (1986:127).

Cherlin and Furstenberg (1986) observe that the revolution in the health conditions of the elderly, combined with their economic independence, enable them to pursue independent lives and live apart from the family. Indeed, this is the tension and central concern of many grandparents. They see a conflict between their desires to remain self-reliant while at the same time to establish and maintain affectionate ties with their descendants.

Cherlin and Furstenberg (1986) believe that divorce has the potential to restructure the relationships among grandparents, their children, and their grandchildren, and ultimately to alter the structure of American kinship. A special concern of grandparents, affecting their desire to be a part of the family while living a life apart,

Grandparents: Exploding the Myths of the Past

BY FAWN VRAZO

A group of about 20 grandparents sat in a circle at the Southwest Seniors' Hospitality Center, sharing their views on being a grandparent in America today. Yes, they agreed, things were different in their own grandparents' days. Grandmothers and grandfathers seemed stricter then, and grandchildren paid them a great deal of obedience and respect.

But this did not mean the modern grandparents necessarily wanted to trade places with grandparents of the past.

For one thing, they said, their lives are easier. None of them are depending on their grown children for support, and many are having a wonderful time enjoying their independence.

The most striking moment of the group interview, the one that perhaps said the most about the grandparent of the '80s, came when the grandmothers and grandfathers were asked to imagine a hypothetical situation: How would they like it learning that all of their grandchildren were going to live with them full time?

The basement meeting room of the center was suddenly filled with shouts and moans.

"Nooooo! Nooooo!," the grandparents said in a loud chorus. "No way!"

"I love my grandchildren," said Lucy Salvatore. "But I'm happy and having a good time."

"I can keep them two weeks, and that's enough for me," said Gertrude Washington. "Then send them back. . . ."

There's a popular belief today that grandparents have somehow gotten lost.

In earlier times, the notion goes, they were the ever-present backbone of the American family, guiding their grown children and young grandchildren with the wisdom of generations past.

Now most of them don't live in their grandchildren's homes; many don't even live close by.

"Where have all the grandparents gone?" asked Arthur Kornhaber and Kenneth

Woodward in *Grandparents, Grandchildren: The Vital Connection.*

"What is missing in this brave new world of consenting adults," they complained in their 1981 book, "is any sense of prior emotional attachment to or responsibility for the young."

As widely held as this Lost Grandparent idea may be, it faces a serious new challenge by a book from two well-known American sociologists who have studied the grandparent of today. Written by Andrew Cherlin of Johns Hopkins University and Frank Furstenberg of the University of Pennsylvania and scheduled for release next Sunday, Grandparents' Day, *The New American Grandparent: A Place in the Family, a Life Apart* makes some provocative statements about modern grandparents and their predecessors.

Essentially, it says, the idea that grandparents were once highly influential family members who stuck close by their kin is mostly myth. And although modern grandparents are more independent, it maintains, their emotional ties to their grandchildren are still quite strong.

Cherlin and Furstenberg suggest that there may actually be more love between grandparents and grandchildren today than there was in the past. Once the weighty ties of economic and psychological dependence between the generations are cut, they say, pure love and sentiment are often what remain.

"I've always been skeptical of the ideal that says that families were sort of central support units and that grandparents took a very active role in at least advising and perhaps even supervising their grandchildren," Furstenberg said recently during an interview in his office on the Penn campus.

Grandparents, he said, often did not exist at all. Because of shorter life expectancy, "the chances of a child of 10 or 12 having a grandparent living close by were just much lower." Sometimes, children never knew their grandparents because they had

(continued)

stayed behind in the Old Country when families immigrated to America.

Because families were larger, grandparents who lived close by were often still busy rearing children at home even after their older children had left to form families of their own.

"The specialization of grandparenthood," Furstenberg said, "is really something that's very new. Grandparents 50 or 100 years ago were still being parents."

Furstenberg and Cherlin used several methods in their study of modern grandparents, first interviewing dozens of them at senior-citizen centers. Again and again, they were struck by the strength of the emotional ties of the seniors with their grandchildren.

"We knew we had touched upon a role that elicited deep and powerful feelings," the sociologists wrote, and "that whatever else might be said about being an older parent or a grandparent, it was a very meaningful part of these people's lives."

Later, with assistance from the Institute for Survey Research at Temple University, the researchers oversaw the 1983 interviews of 510 grandparents whose names had been gathered during an earlier study of American children. The grandparents were mostly female but included many economic and racial groups. There were many characteristics that most seemed to share. For instance:

- The modern grandparents said they went out of their way not to intervene in the lives of their grown children or grandchildren. Many felt it was the worst sin a grandparent could commit — so much so that they found themselves "biting their tongues" when they wanted to point out something that they felt was wrong. The exception was black grandparents, who, more than whites, disciplined their grandchildren and gave them advice.
- Grandparents often reported that their relationships with grandchildren were informal and affectionate. Those who saw their grandchildren fairly frequently (the largest group) said they enjoyed leisure activities together, such as joking and playing or watching television. Only a few said they did more serious things, such as

going to church or synagogue together or teaching their grandchildren games or skills.

- Most grandparents gave their grandchildren money or gifts, but "the contact is different today," Furstenberg said. "They don't do it with the notion that they are going to have any say" in the family's affairs.
- There was just one major factor that determined if the grandparents saw their children a little or a lot — and that was simply location. If they lived close to their grandchildren, they saw them more; if they lived far away, they saw them less. Although the children of divorced parents were more likely to depend on grandparents for support, factors such as race, education and income had almost no role in determining how often grandparents and grandchildren saw each other.
- Maternal grandparents saw their grandchildren as often as paternal grandparents. But if the grandchildren's parents divorced, it was usually the maternal grandparents who became more important in the grandchildren's lives; paternal grandparents, unless they had a good relationship with their estranged daughters-in-law, faced being cut off.

Furstenberg and Cherlin found that grandparents were not necessarily unhappy with their lessened role in their grandchildren's lives, though there were certainly some who wished they saw their grandchildren more.

"I think we're arguing that most grandparents want what they have," Furstenberg said. "In part, I think it's a little more complicated than that, because some are settling for what they can get and being content with it. Others probably are genuinely happy. They feel as though they've given as parents, and they want to be involved as grandparents but in a more ancillary role in the family. They don't want to be parents again.

"It's a lot like what goes on with parents today. There is competition for time, and scarce resources," he said. There are fewer full-time mothers today, he said, and fewer grandmothers "who are full-time, too."

"You can either call it a growing

(continued)

individualism," he said, "and even the new narcissism. Or you can say it's kind of a longstanding value in American society that says that autonomy and a sense of leading one's own life and pursuing one's own interests are very much a part of America."

The future of grandparenthood, Furstenberg and Cherlin predicted, will be linked to the future of the American family in general. If divorce rates remain high, for instance, grandparents may become much more instrumental in their grandchildren's lives. Ironically, the sociologists said, bad times are good for families in the sense that they increase kin dependence; in good times, family connections fall apart.

Low birth rates could have an impact on grandparents, too, they said. In the past, grandparents had far more grandchildren and less to give them. In the future they will probably have few grandchildren but greater resources to share.

At the Southwest Seniors' Hospitality Center, 63d Street and Grays Avenue, where older Philadelphians throw themselves into a heavy social schedule, including casino trips and choral-singing engagements, the grandparents talked at length and lovingly about their many grandchildren. Many pulled pictures from their wallets. One showed a favored grandson in a military uniform, another the newborn baby of a daughter-in-law who had become pregnant after trying for 10 years.

There were some sad stories: grandparents who didn't see their grandchildren enough, grandmothers who felt their grandchildren approached them only when they wanted money.

For the most part, though, the grandparents said they were happy with their lives. They valued their independence, and yet somehow they were able to enjoy their grandchildren no less for this. "I felt I got more pleasure out of them when they were smaller than I did out of my own young children because I was working odd hours, and I couldn't be with them all the time—they'd be in bed," one grandfather, William Moyer, said. "And then I had more time with the grandchildren, which I enjoy."

As a grandfather, was he different from his own grandfather?

"Well, I gave them a lot more loving," he said. "I gave them a lot of that."

SOURCE. Fawn Vrazo. 1986. "Grandparents: Exploding the myths of past." *The Philadelphia Inquirer* (Aug. 31). Reprinted by permission of *The Philadelphia Inquirer* Aug. 31, 1986.

is the impact of divorce of a child, particularly a daughter, on their lives. This event often has an impact on the grandparents and they must make a decision to sacrifice some of their independence to aid their child and grandchildren. Usually, the young woman wins custody of the children and often has a hard time coping with her situation. Emotional and economic readjustments often accompany divorce. The grandparents serve as a form of insurance providing economic support and playing a larger role in the rearing and disciplining of grandchildren.

Maternal grandparents may, as a consequence of divorce, have stronger ties to some of their grandchildren than grandparents whose daughters remain married. Concomitantly, divorce can have different effects on paternal grandparents when given current patterns of child custody, the grandchildren remain in the custody of their mother, the daughter-in-law. The authors believe that if these current patterns continue, divorce may result in a "matrilineal tilt" in intergenerational continuity (Cherlin and Furstenberg, 1986:164). However, should joint custody become more common in the future, this tilt would be minimal and paternal and maternal intergenerational ties would become more equal.

The longevity of old people, their independence, and their ability to provide support in times of crisis are all seen to contribute to the emergence of a new American kinship system that often encompasses four generations. This is a development to which we now turn our attention.

Four-Generation Families

Ours is an aging society. Demographic trends reveal that there will be a sharp rise in the elderly population in the foreseeable future. In a 1981 report, the Census Bureau found that there were 25.5 million people over 65 years old. This was a 28 percent increase since 1970. The median age, the age at which half the population is younger and half is older, rose in the decade that ended in 1980 from 28 years to 30 years. The factors accounting for this rise were that the number of elderly people increased and the number of children under 15 dropped to 51 million from 58 million ten years before (Herbers, 1985:1). These statistics indicate a sharply rising median age over the next three decades and have major implications for the elderly, for families, and for society.

Ethel Shanas (1980), in a groundbreaking lead article in the *Journal of Marriage and the Family,* centers her attention on the "new pioneers" among the elderly and their families. These are the members of four-generation families. Half of all persons over 65 in the United States with living children are members of such families. The prevalence of four-generation families is a new phenomenon; earlier in this century, such families were rare.

The relationship among members of these different generations can be quite problematic. Some of the difficulty stems from the fact that the great-grandparent generation is composed of old people whom the society views as residuals and somewhat useless. Irving Rosow (1976) has astutely observed that our society has deprived old people both of responsibility and of function. By so doing, it has provided the basis for the roleless position of the elderly. In Rosow's terms, the lives of the elderly are "socially unstructured" (1976:466); that is, these people in their 70s, 80s, and 90s have no role models that they can use to fashion their own present-day roles.

Shanas observes that the one place that the old people can find refuge and can have a role is within the family. Yet that role is not clearly defined and often the great-

Margaret Grant surrounded by two granddaughters and a great-granddaughter.

Randy Matusow/Archive

grandparent generation is found to strain the emotional as well as the economic resources of the younger generations in the family. Particularly caught in the middle is the grandparent generation. These people are experiencing their own stresses associated with their own stage in the family life cycle. Many are contemplating their own aging, facing retirement, and perhaps their own financial and health problems. This generation has the brunt of generational responsibility thrust on it. They often are asked to assist their own children as they enter early adulthood and married and family life, while at the same time they are expected to care for their aged parents. Shanas speaks for this generation: "I've raised my family. I want to spend time with my husband or my wife. I want to enjoy my grandchildren. I never expected that when I was a grandparent, I'd have to look after my parents" (1980:14).

Gelman and his associates (1985), in a feature study in *Newsweek* citing studies of family functioning and stress among elders and their caretakers, found high psychological stress among the caretakers. This took the form of depression and anger as they coped with their parents. One respondent, a member of the American Association of Retired Persons, sums up these feelings this way: "There is a constant feeling of depression in the inability to bring happiness to the older person whose friends are gone, whose body is worn down and who knows he is disrupting his child's life" (Gelman et al., 1985:64).

Women within that grandparent generation are the ones who often take on a disproportionate share of the time and emotional involvement with their elderly parents. These women are often working mothers and caretakers. They provide both for their parents and for their children while often holding down a full-time job. Elaine Brody of the Philadelphia Geriatric Center has found that among her clientele, working wives are taking on the same responsibilities as nonemployed women. "They don't give up caring for their parent. They don't slack off on responsibility to their jobs or their husbands. They take it out of their own hides" (Brody quoted in Gelman et al., 1985:68). In this book, we talked about the "double burden" or "dual roles" of women. For these women, we see a "triple burden." And yet, as Brody laments, there is little attention paid to the problems of these women by the government, industry, and the women's movement.

Many elders are managing their own lives. Those that are more affluent live in retirement communities and senior-citizen homes. Others live in their own homes. An estimated 75 percent of the old remain in independent living situations. Eighteen percent live with an adult child. A relatively small number live in isolation. About 80 percent of older people see a close relative every week, according to Dr. Franklin Williams, director of the National Institute on Aging (Gelman et al., 1985).

Shanas (1980), however, cautions that we still know relatively little about the quality of the living arrangements of the elderly. "In much the same way, we do not know whether the visits between older parents and their children and relatives are brief or lengthy, friendly and warm, or acrimonious and hostile" (Shanas, 1980:13). We know that they do occur and that there is social exchange, but "[t]he nature of such an exchange may just be, as people say, 'a visit,' or it may involve actual help and services between the generations" (1980:13).

In a later review of the literature on adult children with aging parents, Victor G. Cicirelli (1983) found that among the approximately 80 percent of all elderly people that have living children, 78 to 90 percent of them see their children once a week or more often. They also are in frequent contact with them via the telephone. Most adult children feel very close to their older parents and the feeling is shared. Yet, Cicirelli observes, while the relationships are seen as gratifying and compatible, there is rarely much sharing of intimate details of life or consultation over important decisions. He conjectures that this may be accounted for by the fact that interpersonal conflict between adult children and their parents is reported by only a very small percentage of them. "It may be that most parents and adult children are able to

Denmark Seeks a Better Life for Its Elderly

BY JOSEPH LELYVELD

Even in winter, when the birches have been stripped of their leaves and icy winds beat back all but the most fanatical joggers from the beach, the Strandlund complex in the affluent suburb of Gentofte here has the look of a resort or condominium community for the idle rich. With the first buds of spring, the impression is reinforced.

It is, in fact, a housing project for the elderly built with public funds, the top of the line in a welfare state that promises free health services and institutional care to the aged.

Basic choices in social planning and the use of public money for the care of the aged are in the hands of local councils in Denmark, most of which have less to spend than Gentofte. Therefore Strandlund is not typical in either design or setting: 210 units in two-story brick structures that are snug and secure in winter, light and leafy in summer, with windows facing what was once a rich shipowner's estate on the strait separating Denmark's western extremity from Sweden's southern tip.

But the idea behind Strandlund has become the centerpiece of advanced Danish thinking on the care of the aged. And that idea—summed up in the term "self determination"—is the antithesis of the nursing home (it is, in fact, illegal to operate nursing homes for profit in Denmark). The aim is to enable old people to remain in their own homes and eventually to die in them, unless advanced senility makes it impossible.

Each apartment is connected by a signal system to a nurses' station that is staffed around the clock. Unless a resident asks to be omitted, each apartment gets a call each morning to make sure all is well. For those who cannot get to the nearby supermarket, there are helpers to do the shopping, and the complex includes a small store.

Services can be stepped up according to a resident's needs. If necessary, the helpers can cook hot meals and do the laundry, and nurses can stop by every two to three hours. "We haven't rejected anyone for being physically disabled," said Maria

Ropke, the administrator, who oversees 40 full-time and 75 part-time workers.

The other side of the story is equally important. When help is not needed, it is not pushed. "We try to inspire our nurses to say, 'Hands off, it's not our responsibility,'" Mrs. Ropke said, "They're trained in hospitals, where they take over everything. Here we have to learn how to let go."

The Strandlund apartments for the elderly are known as sheltered flats. These started coming into vogue about eight years ago as an alternative to nursing home care. More recently the trend has been to put such serviced apartments in ordinary housing complexes, rather than to concentrate them.

Strandlund has no waiting list, but only because the turnover has been so slow that list-keeping is impractical. When one of the 144 subsidized rental units becomes available, it is assigned by the local authorities on the basis of need. The 66 remaining units, which are owned privately, sell to elderly people of means when they become available, for as much as $175,000.

In Denmark, welfare state commitments, fiscal prudence and the belief in promoting self-reliance in the elderly combine to produce an even more straightforward solution to the problem of keeping old people in their own homes: it is cheaper, the authorities have found, to renovate a home at state expense to make it suitable for its elderly resident than to move the resident to another home; and it is much cheaper than to institutionalize him or her in a nursing home.

Municipalities stand ready to widen doorways and remove doorsills at public expense to enable elderly residents to move about their homes in wheelchairs. They will redo bathrooms as well, to install safety devices. The apartment can be linked to a nursing station and morning telephone calls can be arranged, making it possible for the elderly to remain in their accustomed surroundings.

The thrust of public policy is to avoid

(continued)

treating old age as a disease. But as the proportion of the elderly rises, the ambitions of the welfare state collide with its available means. This is conspicuously true within Copenhagen, where the elderly account for 22 percent of the population, compared with 14.5 percent in the nation as a whole.

Strandlund and the Old People's Town in Copenhagen — the largest old-age home in Scandinavia, with 1,123 inhabitants — are separated by only a 20-minute cab ride. But a gulf exists between the prospects of the elderly in the well-off suburb and those in the city. Administrators of the Old People's Town, which is run by the municipality, would like to build sheltered flats, but they have a waiting list for single rooms. Residents who have to share rooms with two or three others may wait as long as 18 months for rooms of their own.

The old buildings are pleasantly painted, and the care seems humane. But the poignancy of three octogenarian widows sharing one room while waiting for individual rooms to become free through the death of a resident is a reminder that even the most enlightened social planning cannot smooth out the suffering of lonely old age. One of the three, a frail white-haired woman on her first day in an institution she would probably never leave, sat with her blue eyes welling with tears next to a vase of purple tulips sent to her by the administration to make her feel welcome.

Strandlund houses a small social center where residents meet to play cards or pursue crafts projects; a swimming pool with physical therapists, and a small restaurant, where hot meals are served at midday. The staff has been seeking ways to open up these facilities to old people in the wider community of Gentofte but has met with resistance from Strandlund residents.

In the tidy apartment of Greta and Otto Kalmeyer, who have lived in the complex for seven years and who welcomed visitors late on a recent morning, pale sunlight streamed through a skylight on furnishings they had brought from their previous home. Mrs. Kalmeyer, who cannot walk unassisted, was still able to manage in the kitchen. Although husband and wife are both frail, they do without the morning call from the nurses' station because they have each other.

The Danish Government is under no illusion that it will be able to phase out nursing homes, but it is so convinced that self-determination and self-reliance for the elderly are practical goals that it has ruled that no new nursing homes can be built after Jan. 1, 1987.

SOURCE. Joseph Lelyveld. 1986. "Denmark seeks a better life for its elderly." *The New York Times* (May 1). Copyright © 1986 by The New York Times Company. Reprinted by permission.

avoid conflict by limiting the scope of the relationship to less intimate and important areas of their personal lives. At the same time, they manage to enjoy certain satisfying aspects of the relationship, such as the sense of shared warmth and affectional closeness" (Cicirelli, 1983:35).

Cicirelli also found much evidence that a mutual helping relationship continues throughout life. The exchange of aid is both instrumental (for example, transportation, housekeeping) or affective (for example, companionship, sympathy). Early in life, parents are primarily donors of both types of aid and continue to help and provide for their children through early adulthood. As they get elderly and experience disability, illness, or economic stress, the balance of help shifts from parents to their adult children. The exchange of help between parents and adult children shifts through the life cycle depending on who needs help and who is able to offer help.

The support and helping patterns between adult children and aged parents are most likely to occur when the elder generation is still relatively healthy and economically independent. Unfortunately, it is in circumstances when the elders become dependent (whether because of illness or financial matters) that adult children will develop negative feelings toward them. This would especially be the case when there is a potential for conflict between adult children's commitments to their children or their own lives and their aged parents.

Of crucial concern in the years ahead is the increasing number of people over the age of 65 and the increased number who will live beyond 85. By the year 2040, the Census Bureau predicts that the over-85 group will have grown from the present 2.2 million to nearly 13 million. During this same period, the number over 65 will grow from the current 26 million to 66.6 million (Gelman et al., 1985). The prospects, then, are of an aging population taking care of a very old population, with all the consequent emotional and financial strains. Given these demographic trends, the problems of the elderly and the four-generation family will multiply in ways that we really are only first beginning to comprehend. There is an obligation for cooperation between the government and the family to care for our old. Nursing care and nursing homes will become even more significant in the future as more elderly people find that they do not or cannot live with their families. The cost for such care, as well as the increased share of the national budget needed to be devoted to health care for the old, must be confronted now. And yet, we find little systematic governmental attention to this future problem.

Shanas is optimistic that the four-generation family and the emerging kinship ties will continue to demonstrate the amazing resiliency that they have through the centuries. "They may be different for old people in the future from what they are now, but they will continue to provide safe harbor for their members however long they may live" (Shanas, 1980:14). The *Newsweek* article concludes:

> If a society can be judged by the way it treats its elderly, then we are not without honor—so far. But as we all grow older, that honor will demand an ever higher price. (Gelman et al., 1985:68)

Conclusion

Our analysis of age stratification focused on the role of elders in the family. We opened with an examination of age set, a system of age groupings in which paramount importance is given to age in defining and regulating social, political, economic, and family and kinship relationships.

The main emphasis of the chapter was to compare the statuses and roles of elders in preliterate societies with their Western industrial society counterparts. Following the approach of Irving Rosow, we identified seven contributing factors that influence the position of older people in given societies. These factors are property ownership, strategic knowledge, religious links, kinship and extended family, community life, productivity, and mutual dependence.

The effects of family privatization once again proved to be a key factor in the generational relationships of the elderly with other family members. The elderly have little importance in an industrial society that emphasizes individual welfare, social and economic progress and change, and that is opposed to the ideology of family continuity and tradition. The elders of an industrial society—in contrast to elders of a nonindustrial society, which views its elders as the embodiment of the societal customs and traditions—are too often treated as unwanted and unknowledgable representatives of a bygone era who have little function in contemporary society. The de-emphasis of the role of the elderly, both in the family and in the society, has led to the general erosion of normative patterns of conduct and behavior between generations. The result has been the creation of a sense of futility and uselessness by the elderly and is typified by the development of institutions catering to the elderly. These range from old-age homes with minimal social and medical facilities for the poor to the segregated "leisure towns" for the elderly rich to lead atemporal and often purposeless lives.

Recent research has demonstrated that the significant decline in the mortality rate in the last 85 years has changed the character of contemporary grandparenthood and accounts for the rise of the four-generation family. This demographic change has greatly increased the potential for family interaction across more than two generations. For those who are grandparents, this time in their life cycle represents a period when there is a desire to maintain autonomy while at the same time participate in the family life of their children and grandchildren. The increase in longevity has resulted in the emergence of a four-generation-family system whose implications are not fully appreciated. Opportunities exist for the development of innovative and satisfying kinship ties across the generations, but the disruptive potential of the great-grandparent generation straining the emotional and economic resources of the younger generations in the family is quite real. Given these demographic trends, the study of gerontology within the context of the sociology of the family should prove to be a most important area of research and investigation in the years ahead.

PART V

Families in Crisis and Change

CHAPTER 16

Family Violence

A staff member of a battered women's shelter consulting with a resident.

CHAPTER OUTLINE

A major aim of this book is to demonstrate that the concepts of power and stratification are crucial in explaining familial relationships. In our discussion of marital gender roles and generational differentiation patterns, we sought to demonstrate that those who had higher status, power, and authority often used these to dominate and control relationships. Thus, in regard to gender-role relationships, a patriarchal ideology supported by economic, social, political, and religious institutions enables men to have the upper hand in most aspects of the marital relationship. This is particularly manifested in their control of the public world of work, politics, and religion. Women are relegated to the less powerful and less prestigious private world of the household and of child-rearing. Similarly, the domination of the older can be seen in age-stratification patterns in political, economic, and religious organizations.

In this chapter and the next, we examine two topics that focus on some of the negative consequences of family life. The first deals with the ultimate abuse of stratification and power differentials—family violence. Our analysis of family violence includes two predominant patterns, wife battering and child abuse. In recent years, sociologists and the lay public alike have become increasingly aware of the frequency of family violence. We study why it has so recently been discovered when all apparent evidence indicates that it has prevailed for centuries. We also examine the factors that account for its prevalence.

The second topic of concern is divorce. Divorce is a major form of marital dissolution. It represents an ultimate manifestation of marital and familial instability. Divorce has been viewed by some as an indicator of the breakdown of the American family and as a reflection of societal decline. Conversely, others see it as the outcome of a positive individual act, ultimately beneficial to all family members and as such, therefore, a sign of societal strength. A comparative analysis of divorce is undertaken. We look at divorce patterns and processes in the United States and in Islamic Egypt. Moslem divorce patterns and processes were selected as the comparative illustration because they are a prime example of a Western stereotype—the patriarchal wish fulfillment for simplicity in divorce (Rosen, 1973). By debunking this stereotype, we hope to gain a better understanding of this phenomenon.

Violence in the Family: Comparative and Theoretical Perspectives

Throughout this book, we examined different theoretical orientations that have been applied to the study of the family in change. We noted how certain perspectives, such as structural functionalism, have tended to view family conflict and disruptions as somewhat deviant phenomena. Other perspectives, notably conflict theory, have seen such disturbances as natural outgrowths of family dynamics. Until recently, conceptualizations that viewed family consensus and cooperation as the "natural" state predominated in sociology. In a ground-breaking article published in 1971 in the most prestigious sociological journal devoted solely to the study of the family, *Journal of Marriage and the Family*, John F. O'Brien pointed out that from its inception in 1939 through 1969, not a single title in this journal contained the term violence (O'Brien, 1971). He argued that this absence may reflect a desire by sociologists to avoid an issue that may be too touchy or may be thought of as too idiosyncratic a feature of "normal" families.

The entire issue of the *Journal of Marriage and the Family* containing O'Brien's article was organized around the common theme of "Violence and the Family." It was an outgrowth of the 1970 meeting of the National Council on Family Relations, which was also oriented around this theme. In the years since that conference, social scientists have become increasingly involved in the study of the phenomenon of family violence. It is part of the more-general realization that those orientations that view family disorganization as peculiar, abnormal, or as a strange deviation are limited. Instead, violence appears to be an expectable event and process and, therefore, has some legitimacy for study. The popular media also has turned its attention to this concern with particular emphasis on the most dramatic forms of family disorganization: violence between husbands and wives and between parents and children. In this section, these concerns will also be ours.

Prior to the 1970s, the social sciences had given relatively little attention to the extent that violence occurs within the family. Suzanne K. Steinmetz and Murray A. Straus (1974) surveyed the literature on violence and the family. They compiled a bibliography of over 400 sources and found little material on everyday domestic violence between husbands and wives, which includes fights, slaps, or the throwing of things. The most extensive and accurate data available was on more-extreme forms of violence—murder and child abuse.

The avoidance of this topic is shared by anthropology. The prominent anthropologist Paul Bohannan suggested two possible reasons for this neglect: Middle-class anthropologists share the middle-class horror of violence, and—possibly more significant—people in cultures under colonial situations did not conduct their family quarrels in the anthropologist's presence; nor did they discuss the violent episodes that might characterize their private lives for fear of governmental-agency intervention (cited in Steinmetz and Straus, 1974:v).

Although relatively little data had accumulated on the prevalence and extent of intrafamily violence, within the last 18 years there has been a notable increase in the scholarly attention given to this concern. One of the most active pioneer scholars on family violence, Murray A. Straus, has reviewed most of this literature and has presented certain tentative formulations to account for its cross-cultural prevalence. Straus (1977) believes that aggression and violence of all types are so widespread that they can almost be labeled as a cross-cultural universal.

Straus examined the cross-cultural evidence on the most dramatic form of conjugal violence—murder. He found that for many societies, a high proportion of homicides occur within the family. Further, other less drastic forms of aggression are quite common. Straus conjectures that high rates of conjugal violence occur in urban-industrial, agrarian, and nonliterate societies, but the highest rates of conjugal violence occur in societies that have high violence rates in other institutional spheres. He develops this supposition by examining six factors that provide some explanations for the ubiquity of intrafamily violence.

The first three factors regarding family violence are the extent of time involvements of family members with each other, the number of overlapping activities and interests that the members share, and the intensity of their involvement and attachment. The development of the private conjugal family, particularly in Western industrial societies, can thus be seen as latently contributing to the increased occurrence of intrafamily violence. Because the traditional nuclear family is more involved in community and consanguineal extended family activities, aggressive incidents can less frequently be attributed to these factors.

The fourth factor is sexual inequality. Straus observes the linkage between male dominance and wife beating. He attributes this to the high conflict potential built into a system that ascribes a superior position to the husband, and the likely possibility that not all husbands may be able to achieve leadership roles or have wives who will be submissive and subordinate. Segregation by gender contributes to this problem by further aggravating and heightening the antagonism between the sexes. Straus presents the argument, which we have discussed elsewhere, regarding the detrimental effects of such segregation, showing how it leads to the inability of women to escape from a violent husband, particularly in Euroamerican societies:

> Such societies throw the full burden of childrearing on women, deny them equal job opportunities even when they can make alternative child-care arrangements, inculcate a negative self image in roles other than those of wife and mother, and reinforce the dependency of women on their husbands by emphasizing the idea that divorce is bad for children. Finally, in most societies, there is a male-oriented legal and judicial system, which makes it extremely difficult for women to secure legal protection from assault by their husbands except under the most extreme circumstances. (Straus, 1977:723)

Straus (1977) illustrates this point by describing a pattern of male behavior labeled as protest masculinity, which has been examined in the machismo pattern of Latin-American males. Joseph P. Fitzpatrick (1971) states that *machismo*, literally maleness, refers to a combination of qualities associated with masculinity. It professes a style of personal bravado by which one faces challenges, danger, and threat with calmness. Through machismo, the individual seeks to develop a personal magnetism that attracts and influences others. It is associated with sexual prowess and power over women. This, in turn, is reflected in vigorous romanticism and jealousy of lover or wife, and it fosters premarital and extramarital sexual relationships.

Machismo fathers may have little importance or saliency in mother–child households or when the father may be physically present but not psychologically relevant. This often occurs in the extreme gender-role differentiation of the urban lower class. It is a pattern that is often associated with frequent wife beating and the glorification of physical aggression (Straus, 1977).

The privacy of the family is listed as the fifth factor to help account for family violence. The private family insulates the family members from the social control of neighbors and the extended family. Here again, the conjugal family found in Western industrial societies would be the family type most affected by this factor. The strength of the communal norm regarding the sanctity of family privacy is such that even when neighbors overhear family arguments and see the physical results of family aggression they try to ignore such evidence. More than likely they will neither contact appropriate public agencies nor make personal inquiries of the abused family member on the circumstances of the injury. Nor will they offer assistance.

The sanctity of family privacy is an important variable in Murray A. Straus' analysis of family life. He argues that cultural norms often legitimize the use of violence between family members, even if such aggression is illegal or a serious breach of normative proscriptions in nonfamilial circumstances. "In Euroamerican societies, to this day, there is a strong, though largely unverbalized, norm that makes the marriage license also a hitting license" (Straus, 1977:720).

Straus then builds on the relationship between family violence and aggression and various societal patterns. Citing cross-cultural research, Straus argues that the more pervasive the existence of societal violence, the higher is the level of family violence.

More than this, Straus postulates the existence of a reciprocal relationship between the aggression and violence in the society and the level of violence within the family: "As societal violence increases, there is a tendency for intrafamily violence to increase; and as intrafamily violence increases, there is a tendency for societal violence to increase" (Straus, 1977:725).

One final point that we wish to emphasize in this summary of Straus' article is his assertion that there is a strong link between violence in one family role with violence in other family roles. Thus, in families where violence between husband and wife is prevalent, there is more likely to be violence by parents toward their children. Further, battered or abused children often become parents who batter and abuse their children.

Murray Straus (1983), who has become a leading figure in the cross-cultural investigation of family violence, raises the question of whether or not physical aggression between family members is frequent enough to be considered a "near universal." That is: Does intrafamily violence occur with such frequency in all societies that it must be related to the most fundamental aspects of human association? Such speculation essentially places the causes of family violence outside the individual and demands that the understanding and assessing of violence and abuse is best found by studying a given society's structure and its operations. Straus (1983) himself believes that the level of interfamily violence is related in part to the ecological conditions in which a society is operating and the society's technical and economic adaptation to these environmental realities. It is also influenced by societal changes in the subsistence basis of the society.

A classic anthropological example of this point of view is Colin Turnbull's (1972) study of the Ik, a small group of nomadic hunters in the mountains separating Uganda, the Sudan, and Kenya. The Ik were driven from their natural hunting grounds, where they were a group of prosperous and daring hunters, into a barren mountainous waste where they were forbidden to hunt the animals that once were their food. The National Game Reserve sought to change them into farmers in a land without rain, without providing them with the technology and the social organization that would make farming possible.

As hunters and foragers, the Ik were nonaggressive and practiced food-sharing reciprocity. In less than three generations, they became a scattered band of hostile people whose social bonds disintegrated, and the only goal was individual survival. To survive, they learned that the price to pay was to give up compassion, love, affection, kindness, and concern—even for their own children. They lived in fear of their neighbors and were indifferent to anything but their own individual welfare. Turnbull depicts a society that has evolved whose ethics and beliefs derived from their ecological predicament. He chronicles episodes of almost unspeakable cruelty and callousness. Ik children steal food from the mouths of their aging parents; throw children as young as 3 years out to fend for themselves; and abandon the old, the sick, and the crippled. Turnbull accounts in one unforgetable passage how, for amusement, children and young men pushed and threw to the ground old men, and shrieked with laughter as the old men struggled to stand up.

However, Straus does not go so far as Turnbull, who in effect argued that the destruction of the Ik economy and the resulting cruelty and inhumanity reveal the basic features of human nature. Straus argues that Ik aggressiveness in the face of economic hardship is just one component of human nature as was their peacefulness and cooperative sharing when the ecological structure was more bountiful and when food was plentiful. Straus summarizes his position this way: "Rather, what the Ik tell us is that the level of aggression within families is governed by the complex interrelation of the constraints and resources of the particular ecological niche occupied by a society, the social organization of that society that evolved in relations to their particular ecological niche, the position of the family in that social organization, and the behavioral and personality characteristics that are congruent with these life circumstances" (1983:36).

Richard Gelles (1983), in a review of studies of wife abuse in East and Central Africa and in Scotland, sees some underlying shared patterns that provide insights into cultural patterns and wife batterings. Marriage customs often support the male point of view and wife abuse is highly correlated with domination, control, and chastisement of women due to the inferior position of wives. There is also a relationship between cultural legitimacy and extent of spousal violence. Where abuse is not positively sanctioned, the rates of wife victimization tend to be lower than in societies where violence against wives is positively sanctioned.

We conclude this discussion of intrafamily violence by examining one extreme manifestation of violence that occurred both within the family and outside it. We are referring to the destruction, in the later Middle Ages, of a large part of the female population because they were labeled witches. Misogyny, the hatred of women is one outcome, albeit extreme, of the sexist patriarchal view that asserts the superiority of men over women in all spheres of life. We have seen how this ideology was evidenced in marital-role relationships and the sexual division of labor, both in the home and in the workplace. Before we begin our discussion of the persecution of witches, a most dramatic form of patriarchy that is associated with familial and nonfamilial violence, we would like to inform the reader of the origin of the commonly used term "rule of thumb." It derives from Blackstone's codification of English common law in 1768 that legally sanctioned the practice of disciplining one's wife with a switch or rod — provided it was no wider than the husband's thumb. However, as we now discuss, more-severe beatings and discipline were common in the Middle Ages.

Violence Toward Women: The Case of Witches

Probably the most extreme example of the violence toward women was the persecution of women during the later Middle Ages for allegedly being witches. In our earlier discussion of courtly love during the medieval period, we considered the dichotomy that existed in the conceptualization of women. On the one hand, they were seen as the embodiment of the virtues of goodness reflected by the Virgin Mary; on the other, they were seen as evil incarnate, the temptress Eve, who formed pacts with the devil, Satan. At the same time the ideology of courtly love was developing, there was a counter movement based on the inherent evilness of women that grew from the eleventh to the fourteenth centuries and reached its violent peak in the Renaissance belief in witchcraft.

To counter the threat of "evil" women, the church sanctioned the absolute subjection of women to their husbands. The supremacy of the husband was espoused and the physical punishment of nonobedient and nonsubmissive wives was condoned. A wife's loyalty to her husband was likened to the fidelity of dog to master; all the husband's orders — whether just or unjust, important or trivial, reasonable or unreasonable — had to be obeyed (Powers, 1975:16). Implicit obedience was part of the ideal of marriage. Disobedient wives could be brought to compliance by force. Canon law specifically allowed wife beating. Divorce was impossible; even obtaining a separation from a brutal and violent husband was extremely difficult. Elizabeth Gould Davis (1971), in her book *The First Sex*, asserts that noblemen and squires beat their wives with such regularity that a fifteenth-century priest, Bernard of Siena, took pity on the lot of wives and urged his men parishoners to exercise a little restraint and treat them with as much mercy as they would their hens and pigs. However, to

Wife Beating Veiled in a Cloak of Silence

BY IRMA HERRERA

Those secrets most deeply hidden within the family — such tragic matters as incest, child abuse and wife beating — have become acceptable topics for public discussion, even the subject of major magazine cover stories.

But for many in minority groups, admitting the existence of these problems is not so simple. They fear such revelations will reinforce stereotypes that already allow others to cast them out. So it is that a cloak of silence surrounds the issue of wife beating in the Latino community.

Wife beating is not restricted to any one culture or social class. Lenore E. Walker, a pioneer researcher on this subject, found battered women in all age groups, races, ethnic and religious groups, educational levels and socio-economic groups.

In spite of such findings, the myth still persists that "hot-blooded Latins" are the chief offenders. Lupe Arellano, co-founder of a battered women's shelter in Gilroy, Santa Clara Co., often has encountered this, even among people working in the field. A colleague once suggested she tell them about wife beating since Latins have been putting up with it from "machos" all these years.

White society's idea of "machismo" has been particularly destructive, Arellano says. Blaming media portrayals, she explains that in the Latino community machismo comes from a tradition where men protect and provide for their families in ways that bring honor and pride to the family members.

This stereotype also affects others who deal directly with wife abuse. Sophia Esparza, director of the Chicana Service Action Center in Los Angeles, has learned that some local officers are reluctant to answer domestic violence calls in the Chicano community because they assume wife beating is part of macho culture.

In the end, such thinking also feeds the community's own reluctance to acknowledge the problem, since a group that is misunderstood naturally becomes self-protective.

Actual figures on spousal abuse among Latinos are available. Groups such as

Esparza's have seen complaints multiply, but this may reflect the fact that people with problems are reluctant to talk with someone from a different background, and, until recently, few community agencies had Latino staffs.

Then, too, there is a real increase in family violence in all segments of society. Dr. Guillermo Bernal, a psychiatrist at San Francisco General Hospital, notes this happens in all technological societies as the traditional functions of the family erode.

For Latino families, trying to enter the mainstream and survive despite higher unemployment, less education and language barriers, the stresses are even greater, he says. And this is the type of pressure that results in increased family violence.

This is compounded by changes within the family. Latino children often act as brokers, assisting their elders in dealings with the larger society. Parents feel threatened and confused, Bernal adds, and a common way to establish power within a family is through physical force.

Recent arrivals have special problems. Concha Saucedo, director of Instituto Familiar de la Raza, a health-care agency, sees many Central American refugees seeking assistance. They often are overwhelmed by their changed circumstances.

"Many have left their extended families behind, and they know they will never see them again," she explains. "They feel lost in the United States. The women may find work more easily than the men, which greatly affects men's perceptions of themselves as *hombres resonsables,* men who should provide for their families."

The resulting frustration can lead to violence. Refugees often report that battering began only after they arrived here.

Cultural values, especially the pressure to keep a family together, also can work to hide problems of abuse.

"There is tremendous shame (in the Latino community) whenever our families fall apart," says Mesha Irizarry, a former

(continued)

battered woman now with Woman, Inc., which helps battered women.

She also points to the role of the Catholic Church.

"In many instances, if assistance is sought anywhere outside the family, it is with the priest," she says. "Often the priests have advised women of the need to sacrifice for the family and to stay with their husbands."

Such advice can be harmful, Irizarry says, as research and experience show that it is important to separate abusive men from their families for at least a short time.

While legal intervention can reduce family violence, many Latinos avoid this, partly because of a strong tradition of resolving problems within the family. They also believe courts and police will not treat them fairly.

"There is great reservation about turning a family member, someone they love, into a system which they feel has already victimized them," says Irizarry.

For undocumented women, there is the added fear of immigration authorities. Many have lived here illegally for years but have children who are U.S. citizens, Esparza points out. They believe that if police or service providers learn of their immigration status, their children will be taken from them or they will be deported and never see their children again.

Women activists have fought long and hard to make the legal system, which long ignored or even allowed wife beating, more responsive to the needs of women who experience violence at home.

Today, new legislation, changed police practices and the existence of shelters and other supportive services all work together to tell women, "No one has the right to beat you up, not even your husband or boyfriend."

The message has reached some, but stereotypes and well-grounded fears in the Latino community suggest the problem there will remain hidden for some time to come.

SOURCE. Irma Herrera. 1984. "Wife beating veiled in a cloak of silence." *Sunday Woman, The Sacramento Bee* (July 1). Reprinted by permission of The Pacific News Service.

An illustration from a sixteenth-century German pamphlet entitled *Malleus Maleficarum* ("The Witches' Hammer").

encourage women to win their husband's good will, the church urged that they be submissive, devoted, and obedient.

By the later Middle Ages and the Renaissance, the violent treatment of women reached its most extreme form in the belief in witchcraft and the resultant persecution and execution of witches. A manual of witchcraft written near the close of the fifteenth century at the request of the reigning Pope reached the following conclusions:

> A woman is beautiful to look upon, contaminating to the touch, and deadly to keep . . . a foe to friendships . . . a necessary evil, a natural temptation . . . a domestic danger . . . a evil of nature, painted with fair colors . . . a liar by nature . . . [She] seethes with anger and impatience in her whole soul. . . . There is no wrath above the wrath of a woman. . . . Since [women] are feebler both in mind and body, it is not surprising that they should come under the spell of witchcraft [more than men]. . . . A woman is more carnal than a man. . . . All witchcraft comes from carnal lust, which is in women insatiable. (*Malleus Maleficarum* cited in Hunt, 1959:177)

The cited document, *Malleus Maleficarum* (The Witches' Hammer) [that is, a hammer with which to strike witches], was very influential for the next two centuries. It professed to document actual testimony of witnesses and confessed witches on the evil doings of women, ranging from summoning plagues of locusts to causing sexual problems (including infertility, impotence, frigidity, painful coitus, nymphomania, and satyriasis), to drying up a mother's milk. Witches allegedly were able to fly at night, could turn themselves into beasts of burden, and would kidnap, roast, and eat children (Hunt, 1959:195).

The belief in witchcraft was the culmination of the ideology of the evilness of women. Witchcraft was seen as a women's crime, and the ratio of women to men executed has been variously estimated at 20 to 1 and 100 to 1 (Dworkin, 1974:130). In her discussion of witchcraft, Andrea Dworkin (1974) estimates that the number of executions that may have occurred during this period may easily have reached as high as 1 million. E. William Monter (1977) sets the figure at a much lower number, 100,000. In any case, although the exact number of victims of the witchcraft mania is unknown, judicial records for particular towns and areas provide some statistical indicators of its prevalence:

> In almost every province of Germany the persecution raged with increasing intensity. Six hundred were said to have been burned by a single bishop in Bamberg, where the special witch jail was kept fully packed. Nine hundred were destroyed in a single year in the bishopric of Wurzberg, and in Nuremberg and other great cities there were one or two hundred burnings a year, as there were also in France and in Switzerland. A thousand people were put to death in one year in the district of Como. Remigus, one of the Inquisitors, who was author of *Daemonolativa*, and a judge at Nancy boasted of having personally caused the burning of nine hundred persons in the course of fifteen years. Delrio says that five hundred were executed in Geneva in three terrified months in 1515. The Inquisition at Toulouse destroyed four hundred persons in a single execution, and there were fifty at Douai in a single year. In Paris, executions were continuous. In the Pyrenees, a wolf region, the popular form was that of the loup-garou [werewolf], and De L'Ancre at Labout burned two hundred. (Hughes, 1971:63)

Women were declared witches and burned at the stake for many reasons. Davis recounts the many pretexts: "for threatening their husbands, for talking back to or refusing a priest, for stealing, for prostitution, for adultery, for bearing a child out of wedlock, for permitting sodomy, even though the priest or husband who committed it was forgiven, for masturbating, for Lesbianism, for child neglect, for scolding and nagging, and even for *miscarrying,* even though the miscarriage was caused by a kick or a blow from the husband" (1971:252).

The significance of witchcraft for the history of women lies in the fact that it is attributable to the long history of misogyny in European religion and law. Misogyny, the hatred of women, has taken many historical forms. Although the witchcraft mania was unique in providing a legal method for killing thousands of women, it was one culmination, albeit extreme, of this misogynistic heritage.

It is ironic that the medieval period, which saw the development of the ideology of romantic love, also witnessed the most terrible persecution of women. Yet, this has been women's fate in Western culture. The medieval historian, E. William Monter, makes the final summary observation:

> Although both courtly love and witchcraft were created by medieval European patriarchy, their historical consequences were grotesquely different. The sad truth is that, in women's "real" social history, the pedestal is almost impossible to find, but the stake is everywhere. (1977:135)

Conjugal Violence

Steinmetz and Straus (1974) attribute the avoidance of examination of intrafamily violence to an idealized concept of the family: by definition, the family is nonviolent and a center of love and gentleness. Conflict and violence are perceived as abnormalities that only occur in abnormal families, that is, among "sick" people. Steinmetz (1977) later points out that this belief leads families to fail to acknowledge family conflict or to exhibit what Richard Sennett has labeled the guilt-over-conflict syndrome:

> To most people it appears that good families, upright families, ought to be happy, and it also appears that happy families ought to be tranquil, internally in harmony. . . . For many people, the emergence of conflict in their family lives seems to indicate some kind of moral failure; the family, and by reflection the individual, must be tarnished and no good. (Sennett, 1973:86)

Richard Gelles (1972), in his study of violence in the home, suggests that the societally shared definition of the family as nonviolent and the belief that violence within the home is pathological leads family members to reconstruct and redefine instances in which physical force is employed into something other than "violence." This prevailing viewpoint is shared by the theoretical orientation that has dominated American sociology, structural functionalism. Structural functionalism is a consensus and integration perspective that labels violence, abrupt change, and tension as deviant or abnormal. It advocates the avoidance of conflict and tension because they are seen as detrimental to group cohesiveness. This is especially the case for groups, such as the family, where great importance is attached to its maintenance and continuation. Steinmetz and Straus (1974) rightly point out that frequently the conflict and tension are not eliminated but are merely covered up, glossed over, or ignored until they reach uncontrollable proportions.

Steinmetz and Straus, as well as an increasing number of family sociologists, find a conflict-theory perspective on the family more useful in understanding family structure and dynamics. The conflict-theory perspective challenges structural functionalism by viewing such struggles as natural occurrences between subordinate and superordinate individuals. This is not to say that the conflict perspective approves of family violence, but rather that it sees the potential for family violence is as fundamental as the potential for affection and love. This view stresses that family violence does occur and is a regular part of family life. As such, it needs to be studied. Unfortunately, the idealized portrayal of family life that dominates structural functionalism blinds the investigator to family violence.

A question remains regarding the prevalence of force and violence in the family. Steinmetz and Straus insist that it is a fundamental feature of family life:

> It would be hard to find a group or institution in American society in which violence is more of an everyday occurrence than it is within the family. . . . Underneath the surface is a vast amount of conflict and violence—including bitter feelings, anger, hatred, much physical punishment of children, pokes and slaps of husbands and wives, and not altogether rare pitched battles between family members. (1974:3, 6)

They also report that a survey of the National Commission on the Causes and Prevention of Crime and Violence estimated that between one-fourth and one-fifth of all adult Americans believe that it is acceptable for spouses to hit one another under certain circumstances. In the survey's large representative sample, it was found that about one-third of the population had been spanked frequently (and almost all at least once) as children. Further, one-fifth of the husbands felt that it was acceptable to slap a wife's face.

In a survey of 385 college students, Murray A. Straus (1974) found 16 percent reported that their parents used physical force to resolve marital conflicts during a recent 1-year period. These were couples who had been married for many years and who would, the respondents claimed, if at all possible, keep their domestic struggles from their children. Richard J. Gelles (1972), after interviewing 80 families, reported that 55 percent of them had had at least one incident of physical violence. John E. O'Brien (1971), in his study of divorce applicants, noted that more than one-third of the wives complained of the use of physical force by their husbands and almost one-fourth also complained of verbal abuse.

Suzanne K. Steinmetz (1972), in an exploratory study of 78 students at a large urban university, found that about 30 percent of their families had marital conflicts and that, in about 70 percent of cases of parent–child and sibling conflicts, physical aggression was used to resolve intrafamily conflicts. She classified four types of problem solvers. Screaming sluggers, the first type, were characterized as couples who both physically and verbally abused each other. Silent attackers, the second type, sought to avoid quarreling, but, when it became unmanageable, released their frustration through physical assaults. The third type, threateners, were verbally abusive and although they threatened physical violence, did not resort to it. Finally, some families were able to resolve their problems without resorting to either physical violence or verbal abuse. They were labeled pacifists.

The accumulated research reported by Steinmetz and Straus (1974) in their anthology reveals that violence in the family is indeed widespread. Actually, this research may have only uncovered the tip of the iceberg of family violence. Gelles (1972), in his study of physical aggression between husbands and wives, also emphasizes that violence may be more widespread and severe than previously thought:

> Taking into account the figures on the extent of conjugal violence . . . we estimate that violence is indeed common in American families. Furthermore, these incidents of violence are not isolated attacks nor are they just pushes and shoves. In many families, violence is patterned and regular and often results in broken bones and sutured cuts. (Gelles, 1972:192)

He argues that the extent of conjugal violence and its intensity indicate that violence between family members is a social problem of major proportions. Further, he points out that marital violence, even if frequent and severe, may not lead to divorce or separation. The reasons why marriages continue are complex. Steinmetz (1977) observes that the physically violent are also more likely to be highly demonstrative in affection, engaging in a great deal of kissing, hugging, and embracing.

Del Martin (1976) suggests that fear may account for battered wives staying married. The predominant reason may be fear. Fear may immobilize them and rule their actions, their decisions, and their very lives. Martin illustrates with this dramatic account:

> When he hit me, of course I was afraid. Anybody would be if somebody larger than you decided to take out their anger on you. I really couldn't do anything about it. I felt as if I was completely helpless. (Martin, 1976:76)

The fear of reprisal also prevents the abused wife from seeking help. She may be afraid of endangering her children or any neighbors that may become involved. She sees only one alternative — sacrificing herself.

Martin (1976) also sees the contemporary definition of the woman's role in our society as being highly influential in the decision to stay married. A woman assumes that she is accountable for the failure of the marriage, even if she is the one being beaten. The failure of the marriage represents her failure as a woman. Probably even more important than the loss of a woman's self-respect is the fact that more often than not, she is economically dependent on her husband. Even in those circumstances where the wife is working, she frequently is forced to surrender her paycheck to her husband. Martin argues that although women's roles are changing and women are increasingly establishing new values for living on their own, the changes are not occurring fast enough for many women who have long ago given up hope: "Only by bringing the buried problems of wife-beating and financial exploitation into the open can we begin to inspire the imaginations of those women who silently wait out their time as scapegoats in violent marriages" (Martin, 1976:86).

The prevalence and severity of family violence is particularly acute in our society because of the ideology that stresses the privacy of the family. Throughout this book, we have observed that the rise of the private family is one of the major characteristics of contemporary times. Increasingly, the family has withdrawn from community and extended kinship involvements. Granted that this withdrawal is not absolute and that viable relationships do exist for most families with relatives, friends, and neighbors, nonetheless, the privacy and sanctity of the household is normative and usually nonviolated. The result is that violent outbursts usually occur in private and outside witnesses are rare. Del Martin (1976) refers to the book *Scream Quietly or the Neighbors Will Hear,* written by Erin Pizzey (1974), to illustrate this point:

> People try to ignore violence inside the home and within the family. Many abused wives who came to Chiswick Center told Pizzey that their neighbors know very well what was going on but went to great lengths to pretend ignorance. They would cross the street to avoid witnessing an incident of domestic violence. Some would even turn up the television to block out the shouts, screams, and sobs coming from next door. (Martin, 1976:16–17)

Richard J. Gelles (1973) observes that the sociologist Erving Goffman's concept of "backstage" is quite relevant in understanding domestic violence. It is in the home, away from the prying eyes of the community, that violent family members find a place where they can fight in private: "Protected by the privacy of one's own walls there is no need to maintain this presentation of family life as harmonious, loving, and conflict-free" (Gelles, 1973:96). Gelles finds three rooms in the house as centers of family violence: the kitchen, the living room, and the bedroom. The first two rooms are focal points of family activity and as such are scenes of much nonlethal violence. It is in the bedroom where most homicides occur and where much nonlethal violence also is prevalent: conflicts regarding sex and intimacy are frequent; it is a room, used at night, from which many undressed victims find it difficult to leave. For where are they to go? The bathroom, the most private room for family members, sees relatively few violent episodes.

Family violence also occurs during particular periods of time of the day and the week. Gelles (1972) found that aggression usually occurs in the evening or late evening during the weekend. He accounts for this by observing that it is at these times that the family is usually alone and when the abused family member feels that there is no one to turn to. It is an inconvenient time to disturb neighbors, friends, or relatives with domestic quarrels. All too frequently, the only alternative is the police, and most are reluctant to take this step.

The pattern that emerges is that violence is often associated with the presence or absence of other people. The more alone the couple, the more likely violence will occur. The violent family member is often reluctant to abuse his spouse in the presence of others. Further, neighbors not wanting to intrude or become involved in domestic arguments actively seek noninvolvement in what we define as the private affairs of others.

Gelles (1972) also found that the isolation of the family from the community is a contributory factor in family violence. He contrasts his respondents who had viable neighborhood ties with those who had few friends in the community and rarely visited with neighbors or friends. He found that violent families tended to be those isolated from their neighbors; nonviolent families had viable neighborhood ties and had many friends in the neighborhood. The result was that the victims of a violent family member had minimal social supports and resources in the community to which they could turn for help when they encountered family problems. To highlight the effect of neighborhood involvements on family violence, Gelles compares two neighbors — Mrs. (44) and Mrs. (45). Mrs. (44) owns her own home and has never hit nor been hit by her husband. Mrs. (45) lives across the street and has been involved in some serious knockdown, drag-out physical brawls with her husband. Mrs. (44) discusses her neighbors:

MRS. (44): I like the neighborhood quite well, surprisingly well for just having moved here two years ago. They have been quite friendly and hospitable. The woman next door is my close friend. She is quite a bit older and has children who are married and are my age. But she has been a very good friend. It's a friendly neighborhood.

In contrast, Mrs. (45) knows few neighbors, has few friends, and does not socialize much with her neighbors:

MRS. (45): I don't bother with them and they don't bother with me. I don't mean it that way . . . we say hello or they might wave. I'm not the type that goes from one house to the next. I'm not that type of social gatherer anyway. We help them, they help us, things that are needed. They are good neighbors.

Mrs. (45) thinks that they are good neighbors, but does not know the first thing about them. Mrs. (44), however, was able to inventory the family problems in many of her neighbors' families (Gelles, 1972:133–134).

One final series of factors associated with family violence stems from sexist patriarchal ideology. A number of investigators — Goode (1971), O'Brien (1971), and Gelles (1972) — report that the role people play outside the family is important in understanding family violence. Husbands who have not achieved the societal definition of success in their occupational roles frequently take out their frustration on their wives. The investigators' explanation for this occurrence is that although patriarchy asserts that husbands should have a superior position in the household, that position must be legitimated by the husbands' achievements in the outside world of work. In situations where the husband has failed to achieve the necessary societal criteria of success, this can precipitate a conflict situation within the home.

Goode (1971) theorized that family violence is likely to occur in situations where the husband fails to possess the achieved statuses, skills, and material objectives necessary to support his ascribed superior status within the household. John E. O'Brien's (1971) research investigation supported this hypothesis. Likewise, Gelles (1972) found in his study of physical aggression between husbands and wives that it is most likely to occur when husbands have lower educational and occupational statuses than their wives. Gelles believes that in such circumstances the husband's inability to measure up to his and his wife's expectations are compounded by the husband's frustration over his inability to provide adequately for his family, and thus leads to outbreaks of aggressive behavior.

In summary, we investigated some of the dominating factors that are associated with conjugal violence. It is beyond the scope of our discussion to include such additional elements as socialization processes, psychological factors, and societal stress factors, which include unemployment and financial and health problems. We emphasized those factors that have governed our attention throughout this book. They include gender-role relationships influenced by patriarchal ideology and the family's relationships and involvement in the community. Continuing with this same orientation we turn our attention to child abuse.

Child Abuse in Cross-Cultural Perspective

The abuse of children denotes a situation ranging from the deprivation of food, clothing, shelter, and love to incidences of physical wounding and torture, to selling and abandonment, to outright murder. Although it has received an unusual amount of attention in recent years, violence toward children is as old as humankind. Historically, parents have had the prerogative to wield absolute power over their children's life and death.

Violence against children is not a recent phenomenon; it is the term, abuse, that is relatively new. Abortion, abandonment, and infanticide—the willful killing of children, usually infants—have been practiced in varying degrees throughout history and in most of the world's societies. One scholar argues that infanticide "has been responsible for more child deaths than any other single cause in history other than possibly the bubonic plague" (Solomon, 1973).

The most extreme form of child violence, infanticide, was usually related to beliefs concerning religion and superstition. But throughout human history, a more-prevalent reason for infanticide has been population control or maintenance of a physically healthy population. William Graham Sumner, in his classic work *Folkways*, describes the common solution to overpopulation.

> It is certain that at a very early time in the history of human society the burden of bearing and rearing children, and the evils of overpopulation, were perceived as facts, and policies were instinctively adopted to protect the adults. The facts caused pain, and the acts resolved upon avoiding it were very summary, and were adopted with very little reasoning. Abortion and infanticide protected the society, unless its situation with respect to neighbors was such that war and pestilence kept down the numbers and made children valuable for war. (Sumner, 1906:308)

Sumner also observes the differential treatment given to boys or girls, depending on their importance for the family. Where girls were valuable and could bring a bride-price to the father, they were treated well. In circumstances where they were economic burdens, they might be put to death. Another common practice was to kill newborn babies with congenital weaknesses and deformities. Sumner reasons that this occurred "in obedience to a great tribal interest to have able-bodied men, and to spend no strength or capital in rearing others" (1906:313).

Class variations also played a determining role in infanticide decisions. David Bakan (1971) in his *Slaughter of the Innocents,* discusses the ubiquity of infanticide and abortion. He cites the observations of Reverend J.M. Orsmond who visited Tahiti in the late 1820s. Orsmond noted the relationship between infanticide and social class. The members of the higher social class were not obligated to kill their children, whereas the lower caste were obligated to kill their babies after the first or second. Failure to do so brought shame and disgrace: "More than two-thirds of the children were destroyed 'generally before seeing the light of day. Sometimes in drawing their first breath they were throttled to death, being called tamari'i hia (children throttled)'" (Bakan, 1971:31).

A common reason for infanticide was to avoid shame and ostracism of unmarried mothers. Up to the dawn of the industrial era about 200 years ago, the killing of illegitimate children was extremely common in Europe. The unmarried woman was confronted with two negative options. If her maternity was discovered, she was excommunicated and lived as a social outcast. Nathaniel Hawthorne, in his American classic *The Scarlet Letter*, novelizes this situation in his account of Hester Prynne in colonial Salem, Massachusetts.

Bakan reports that in eighteenth-century Germany, the most common punishment for infanticide was sacking. The mother was put in a sack and thrown into a river accompanied by a live animal or two to make the death more painful. Frederick the Great, the King of Prussia in 1740, felt that this practice was too inhumane and substituted decapitation as a more acceptable alternative.

Women who committed infanticide were tried and prosecuted as witches. In the seventeenth century, Benjamin Carpoz was credited with the execution of over 20,000 women for witchcraft, a large number having committed infanticide. The manner of execution ranged from sacking to burning, to burying alive, to impalement (Bakan, 1971). Bakan cites a very popular English ballad, "The Cruel Mother," which appeared in B.H. Bronson's (1959)[1] definitive work on child ballads, that illustrates the relationship between illegitimacy and infanticide:

1. There was a lady came from York
   All alone, alone and aloney
   She fell in love with her father's clerk
   Down by the greenwood siding.
2. When nine months was gone and past
   Then she had two pretty babes born.
3. She leaned herself against a thorn
   There she had two pretty babes born.
4. Then she cut her topknot from her head
   and tied those babies' hands and legs.
5. She took her penknife keen and sharp
   and pierced those babies' tender hearts.
6. She buried them under a marble stone
   And then she said she would go home.
7. As she was (going through) (a-going in) her father's hall
   She spied those babes a-playing at a ball.
8. "Oh babes, oh babes if (you were) (thou wast) mine
   I would dress you up in silks so fine."

[1] B.H. Bronson. 1959. *The Traditional Tunes of the Child Ballads,* vol. 1 Princeton, N.J.: Princeton University Press.

 9. "Oh mother dear when we were thine
    You did not dress us up in silks so fine,
10. "You took your topknot from your head
    And tied us babies' hands and legs.
11. "Then you took your penknife (long) (keen) and sharp
    And pierced us babies' tender hearts.
12. "It's seven years to roll a stone
    And seven years to toll a bell.
13. "It's mother dear oh we can't tell
    Whether your portion is heaven or hell. (Bronson cited in Bakan 1971:39)

Phyllis Palgi (1973), in her report of a case of infanticide in contemporary Yemen, demonstrates the continued prevalence of this theme in patriarchal societies. In Islamic Yemen, premarital pregnancy is viewed as a horrible, shameful tragedy that disgraces the entire family. A young woman who was able to hide her pregnancy up to the birth of the baby killed the just-born infant at the prodding of her mother. The baby was then wrapped in a bundle and was given to the young woman's brother and uncle, who were not told the contents of the package. They were told to bury the bundle. They did not carry out their task, and the next day the infant's body was discovered and the mother was arrested:

> The [young woman's] father first threatened to kill himself and his daughter, and then he fell ill. Later he said he could not understand what had happened: perhaps something supernatural caused the pregnancy. If not, it was rape by design—this other family, the family of the baby's father, wished to have revenge upon him. Furthermore, he stated categorically that a child produced from rape is *dirt,* a sinful object, and must be destroyed. In Yemen the authorities would have no problem in understanding this, he claimed. The mother remained bitter and angry, although she agreed that it would have been impossible for her daughter to tell what happened that night. She felt cheated that she had always managed her family, and life in general, so successfully and new events had been stronger than she. It appears as if the family held council and it was decided that the mother would change her evidence. It was not her idea to kill the baby, she now maintained; the daughter was solely responsible. The daughter apparently obligingly changed her evidence accordingly. The rationale was simple: the mother was needed at home to look after her husband and small children. And in any case it was only Sara who really felt guilty. She told how she had sat opposite the baby, not seeing it until it sneezed. Suddenly she was confronted with the concrete evidence of her sin which she had denied for nine months and so blindly plunged with knife to destroy it and, perhaps, all her bad thoughts as well. (Palgi, 1973)

The child was killed to avoid a family scandal. In this patriarchal society, the killing of the child was a less-onerous task than to bear the child and suffer the shame and ostracism that would inevitably occur not only to the unmarried woman but also to her entire family.

Infanticide continues to prevail in contemporary industrial societies, such as Japan, despite the prevalence and acceptability of abortion. It can be seen as one consequence of modernization and the breakdown of the traditional extended family system. Naomi Feigelson Chase (1975) reports that the Japanese have practiced infanticide for over 1000 years. During the feudal era, the seventeenth through the nineteenth centuries, infanticide served as a means of population control. The scarcity of resources and the economic burden of a large number of children caused farmers to kill their second and third sons at birth. Many females were spared because they could be sold into prostitution, servitude, or—for the more fortunate—they could become geishas. This practice, *Mabiki,* an agricultural term that means thinning out, accounted for the death of 60,000 to 70,000 infants each year for a period of over 250 years (from about 1600 to 1850s) in northern Japan alone. The practice was prohibited with the onset of industrialization. The national policy encouraged population growth for industry and the army.

After World War II, infanticide reappeared briefly, reaching a peak of 399 cases in 1948, but it then dropped for the next 10 years. In 1958, the incidence of infanticide began to rise. By 1973, more than 100 deaths were reported and an additional 110 children were found abandoned in Tokyo alone. Chase believes that the rise of infanticide and abandonment, despite the existence of a liberal abortion law and the widespread availability of contraceptives, is attributable to rapid urbanization and the shift from the traditional extended family to the more segmentalized nuclear family. Most cases of infanticide occur in nuclear families. A second factor is the belief that the young mother lacks the confidence to raise her children without the supports of the extended family. Infanticide in Japan is not due to promiscuity (illegitimacy) or cruel stepmothers. Chase observes that it is likely in families where the mother spends a lot of time alone with the baby. Chase cites another study that suggests that infanticide or abandonment may be one way of coping with unwanted children by unprepared Japanese mothers. In comparison, their American counterparts are more prone to child abuse.

In summary, infanticide may be seen as an extreme reaction to the stress of having children. It has been a basic practice for the handling of overpopulation. Sumner provides an apt concluding remark on the inherent conflicting relationship between parents and children:

> Children add to the weight of the struggle for existence of their parents. The relations of parent to child is one of sacrifice. The interests of children and parents are antagonistic. The fact that there are, or may be, compensations does not affect the primary relation between the two. It may well be believed that, if procreation had not been put under the dominion of a great passion, it would have been caused to cease by the burdens it entails. Abortion and infanticide are especially interesting because they show how early in the history of civilization the burden of children became so heavy that parents began to shirk it. (1906:309–310)

The considerable attention spent on examining infanticide should not perplex the reader. For infanticide is logically related to child abuse. As David Bakan (1971) observed, there is a similar underlying motivation for both. The largest category of abused children is the very young. Abused children also suffer from systematic neglect. The result is that, over time, the injurious treatment of the child has a cumulative effect with a high proportion of abused children dying as a result of their injuries:

> Thus, the most parsimonious explanation of child abuse is that the parents are trying to kill the child. However, in our culture murder of children is a serious criminal offense. The method of cumulative trauma allows infanticide to take place with relative immunity from detection, prosecution, and conviction. (Bakan, 1971:56)

Gelles and Cornell (1983), reviewing the cross-cultural literature on violence and abuse toward children, observe that there are variations in cultural meanings and norms concerning children and family life. Further, there are social-structure variations and family-structure variations. Variations also pertain to the definitions of violence and abuse. Given this caveat, they report that the accumulated evidence from both empirical studies and position papers is that child abuse is probably most common in Western, industrialized, developed nations. China and the Scandinavian countries are notable in that they are characterized by very little child abuse. Violence and child abuse are relatively rare in developing countries. However, the problems that do exist in the Third World are seen to stem from social disorganization caused by modernization and the resulting changes in family, clan, tribal, and social situations.

In their review of the factors that account for the low rate of child abuse and violence in Scandinavia, Gelles and Cornell (1983) point to some key factors that also account for positive parent–child relationships. They report that social conditions are relatively good; poor economic circumstances has been associated with child abuse and violence. There is widespread use of contraceptives and free abortions are readily available, thus reducing the number of unwanted babies. Premature infants are kept in neonatal wards until they achieve sufficient weight and strength. Parents are taught how to handle the newborn, alleviating some of the tensions that often accompany the transition to parenthood. Finally, many mothers work, and day-care institutions are provided. This also lessens some of the difficulties experienced by working couples who require day-care facilities for their young children.

Researchers who study abuse in developing nations place considerable emphasis on social change, social disorganization, and cultural attitudes toward children in generating explanations regarding child abuse (see Gelles and Cornell, 1983). These researchers voice concern that urbanization and industrialization are breaking down traditional values and family structures, leading to increases in abuse and neglect. Studies in Nigeria, Zululand, and Kenya have focused on the hypothetical increase in child-abuse problems as a consequence of the disruption of traditional clan life. Research in Africa also examines the impact of poverty and malnutrition on the impaired development and even the death of children. For example, "nutritionally battered" children is a term referred to by A.K. Bhattacharyya (1983) for a form of abuse stemming from severe protein-energy malnutrition in India and other Third World countries. Indeed, any adverse environmental factors that could have been prevented by way of scientific knowledge or adequate health services often fall under the definition of abuse.

We close this section by observing that there are other forms of child abuse that need to be given increased attention. Taylor and Newberger (1983) have observed that in many countries children are used as soldiers and are victims of wars they do not choose to fight. Recent news reports have documented that children, some only 7 and 8 years old, serve in the militia in Uganda and teenagers fight in the Iran–Iraq war. The horrors of warfare are commonplace in the everyday life of many children in Ireland, Lebanon, Cambodia, and South Africa. Children, close to 52 million under the age of 15, are in the international labor force. Forty-two million of them work without pay.

Finally, corporal punishment still remains a time-honored and sanctioned form of discipline in most countries, although it is increasingly undergoing scrutiny given current concerns (Taylor and Newberger, 1983). The United Kingdom and other members of the Commonwealth that include Australia, Barbados, Canada, New Zealand, South Africa, Swaziland, Trinidad, and Tobago, as well as 46 states in America still permit corporal punishment in the schools. The practice is illegal in most Western and East European countries. Japan, China, and the Soviet Union view corporal punishment as an unsatisfactory form of discipline. Attempts to extend the ban to the home often meets with resentment. For example, even an enlightened country like Sweden has aroused controversy among its citizens when it made corporal punishment at the hands of the parents illegal.

In concluding their analysis of child abuse conducted in 1979 — the "International Year of the Child — Taylor and Newberger (1983) call for worldwide action that will help to prevent child abuse. This would include international exchanges of information to generate better understanding of child rearing throughout the world. This would help in the understanding of how people could make life better for all children. They plea for a sustained and increased effort to further the rights of children in the years to come. "At a time when enough weaponry exists to destroy the population of the world, we have everything to gain by rearing the next generation in peace (Taylor and Newberger, 1983:56).

Child Abuse in America

The ideology that argues for the sanctity and privacy of the family household not only hides the extent of domestic violence between spouses but also prevents the full examination of the prevalence of child abuse. In 1972, only 60,000 child-abuse incidents were brought to the attention of governmental agencies. Five years later, the number passed the 500,000 figure. In 1977, the National Center on Child Abuse and Neglect projected that between 100,000 and 200,000 children are regularly abused and assaulted by their parents. Compounding the problem of the reporting of incidents of child abuse is the fact that agents of social institutions—physicians, nurses, social workers, teachers, police, and judges—tend to report actual cases differentially. Particular statistics from given agencies and institutions may be typical only for them or for their geographic locality and may not be an accurate representation of the national rate.

Richard J. Gelles, in a recent study of child abuse, estimates that almost 4 percent of children under the age of 17 are subjected to abuse (Schumacher, 1978). This

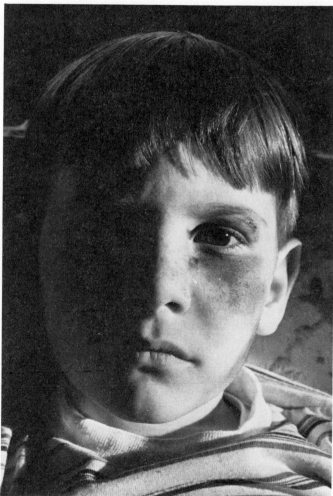

Frank Siteman/EKM–Nepenthe

A child suffering from the disciplinary beating of a troubled parent.

extrapolates to nearly 2 million children who are stabbed, kicked, bitten, punched, shot, or sexually molested by their own parents. This figure is double that estimated earlier by the Federal Center on Child Abuse and Neglect. The growing awareness of child abuse and the resultant publicity has undoubtedly encouraged people to report incidents more frequently. The earlier figures compared to the later ones probably reflect our ignorance about the frequency of occurrence rather than indicating a startling new rise in the rate of child violence.

Studies of abused children and their parents find it difficult to identify conclusively the traits of the abusive parent. Such parents come from the complete range of socioeconomic classes. Many potential child abusers are "normal" parents who over-react to the normal frustrations of being a parent:

> Is there any mother or father who has not been "provoked" almost to the breaking point by the crying, wheedling, whining child? How many parents have not had moments of concern and self-recrimination about having, in anger, hit their own child much harder than they had expected they would? How many such incidents make a "child abuser" out of a normal parent? (Zalba, 1974:412–413)

Steele and Pollack (1968), in one of the early studies of what they termed the battered-child syndrome, found no particular psychopathological or abnormal character types among the parents. What differentiated the abusive parent was an exaggeration of the contemporary pattern of child rearing:

> There seems to be an unbroken spectrum of parental action towards children ranging from the breaking of bones and the fracturing of skulls through severe bruising, through severe spanking and on to mild "reminder" pats on the bottom. To be aware of this, one has only to look at the families of one's friends and neighbors, to look and listen to the parent-child interactions at the playground and the supermarket, or even to recall how one raised one's own children or how one was raised oneself. The amount of yelling, scolding, slapping, punching, hitting, and yanking acted out by parents on very small children is almost shocking. Hence we have felt that in dealing with the abused child we are not observing an isolated, unique phenomenon, but only the extreme form of what we would call a pattern or style of childrearing quite prevalent in our culture. (Steele and Pollack, 1968:104)

The realization of the extent of this social problem reflects our increased awareness that the contemporary private conjugal American family is not as conflict-free as previously idealized. Thus, although the privatization of the nuclear family has maximized emotional intensity, it has also made it problematic and difficult.

As we discussed earlier, the battered-child syndrome is not a new problem; it existed historically and it exists cross-culturally. What is new is the attempt to control child abuse legally. And, as we described previously in our analysis of the child-welfare movement, it has its drawbacks and deficiencies. An examination of the law regarding child abuse also reveals similar problems.

In the nineteenth century, the law supported the premise that the family is a private and sacred institution into which outsiders have little right to intrude. As mentioned in Chapter 14, the first American legal action for child abuse was not brought about until 1874. Laws, in fact, were enacted to protect animals before there were laws to protect children. Indeed, the first child-abuse case was actually handled by the Society for the Prevention of Cruelty to Animals. In this first case, the child was treated under the rubric (legal rule) concerning a small animal. At about this time, problems of child abuse were handled loosely by various voluntary agencies. When court action was deemed necessary, the child was treated as a "neglected" or "dependent" child under the juvenile court laws.

Despite the recent enactment of laws to protect the legal rights of children, the child-abuse statutes do not protect children adequately. There is great reluctance on the part of governmental agencies to prosecute parents or to remove the child from the home. Further, there is a natural queasiness by social agencies and by doctors and medical institutions to report cases: It is exceedingly difficult to accuse a parent who brings in a child for treatment. This is especially the case in incidents of child abuse among the middle class, where the parents may have the legal access to contest the issue.

Most of the reported cases are from hospital admissions. Generally, these are clinic cases, where the parent or foster parent (of the poorer class) rushes a badly injured child to a hospital. Pediatricians in private practice are reluctant to report child-abuse cases. For example, in 1976 in Westchester County, New York (an affluent suburb of New York City), private physicians reported only 6 of the 891 cases of child abuse investigated by the local child-protective-services agency (Feron, 1977). David C. Honigs, the director of the county's Child Protective Services Program, questions whether private doctors even ask questions about how the child's injury occurred. One possible motive is the physician's desire to avoid the possibility of spending time in testifying in family courts. Further, they share the prevalent viewpoint of family court judges that public placement for the child may be far worse than returning the abused children to their parents.

Aggravating the problem is the lack of a unifying policy. This reflects the prevalent belief that deemphasizing the extent of child abuse and the reluctance to handle this problem. Social-welfare people argue for joint planning and cooperative arrangements between government and private sectors, between agencies and voluntary groups. There is also a need on both the administrative and case level for parent training and self-help for abusing parents.

But, we are reluctant to invade the privacy and sanctity of the home. If and when we do, we have become increasingly aware that the prosecution of negligent and abusive parents does not solve the problem of the victimized children or their parents. Programs designed to treat these parents to maintain the structural integrity of the family are woefully inadequate. In addition, the removal of children from their homes and placement in foster homes or other placement facilities may have negative consequences.

Related to the issue of parental versus social control is the extent to which our society is willing to make investments in broad-based social services that are supportive of the family structure and protective of children. Unfortunately, caught in the dilemma of values supporting parental privacy, control, autonomy, and desire to avoid overzealous intervention by social agencies, the child is all too frequently victimized.

Although it is beyond the scope of this discussion to present comprehensive solutions to the problem of child abuse, the following passage written by Serapio R. Zalba provide some initial guidelines:

> What, then, is to be done about child abuse? We cannot wait for all men and women to become angels to their children. One sensible, concrete prosposal has been made to offer preventive mental and social hygiene services at the most obvious points of stress in the family. One such point is reached when a child is born and introduced into the family. This may be especially true for the first child, when husband and wife must now take on the additional roles of father and mother. Assistance for men and women who seem under unusual strain because of this role might lead to fewer incidents of child abuse. More effective remedial efforts will await our willingness to spend greater sums of money on community-based health and welfare services. Protective services are under-staffed for the number of cases requiring their help and surveillance. And, the additional child care resources — whether they are institutions or paid individual or group foster homes — require additional sources if they are to be adequate either in terms of the number of children they can handle or in the quality of personnel. (Zalba, 1974:408)

Child Abuse: Some Answers

BY HAPPY FERNANDEZ

Why are parents, political leaders and others so shocked at recent reports of child abuse in day-care centers? Why do we have to be stunned by the death of a child or outraged by the sexual abuse of 3- and 4-year olds before we demand action to protect children?

The facts on the urgent need for responsible child care have been presented many times before. But only now, after a series of jolting incidents across the nation, are we paying attention to them.

At least three of the root causes of sexual, physical and emotional abuse of youngsters have obvious solutions.

One cause is the glaring lack of legal protection. At the present time, we have stricter laws for the registration and inspection of automobiles than we do for the day care of boys and girls.

A remedy for this situation is tough, clear laws to protect children, and careful monitoring of the implementation of those laws. The measures taken in the last decade to reduce child abuse in families points the way to what is needed to safeguard children in day-care centers, schools and other institutions.

Fifteen years ago, child abuse was occurring daily in rich, poor and middle-income households in every part of the United States. Very few people thought much of it because there were no laws saying it was wrong and no system to report suspected child abuse. But new laws were passed in 1975 that have revolutionized the way child abuse is reported, investigated, treated and monitored.

The legal protection of children in day-care centers is less effective. Centers are licensed by the state, but monitoring is minimal and underfunded. Day care provided in homes, commonly referred to as "family day care" rather than center day care, is not licensed.

Family day-care providers need only be registered with the state. Estimates are that only half of the people taking children into their homes for pay are registered.

Pennsylvania has not gone as far as Iowa, which requires that anyone being paid to care for more than two children in a home must register.

There is little, if any, monitoring of the registered family care homes. In the other, nonregistered homes, any type of sexual, physical, or emotional abuse could take place, and no one is responsible to monitor or remedy it. State elected officials have not yet focused attention on these procedures nor developed ways to protect children in family day-care homes.

Day care is also a very low priority for federal officials, who are merely reflecting the values of voters. No federal legislation provides for comprehensive quality day-care services. Congress passed the Comprehensive Family Services Act in 1974, but it was vetoed by President Nixon.

To strengthen the legal protections for children, we need state legislation requiring registration and inspection of all home-based and center day care, and federal legislation similar to the Comprehensive Family Services Act to provide a system of community-based child-care services.

A second cause of the problem is the lack of carefully trained staff in day-care centers and family care homes. Many children are being cared for by people who have no training or certification. Again, we require registered and certified electricians, accountants, nurses and teachers, but do not yet require training and certification of people who are influencing young children up to 10 hours a day.

Meanwhile, the demand for child care is growing. Each weekday morning the parents of seven million preschoolers go off to work. More than 50 percent of the mothers of pre-school and school-age children are employed outside the home. Forty-five percent of women with children under one year of age are now in the labor force—a 30 percent jump in just five years. As many as 17 percent of children under the age of 13, including many pre-schoolers, are left to care for themselves.

To ensure professional care for children, we must have carefully trained people who

(continued)

are paid a decent wage for their services. We must set basic standards and be willing to pay adequate salaries to attract and keep the brightest and the best caregivers to be substitute parents for our next generation.

A third cause of abuse of young children in day-care centers is lack of well-informed, vigilant parents. When selecting a day-care center, how many parents have thought to ask if parental visits are welcomed at any time?

One parent was wise enough to ask that question of a pre-school in California. She did not place her son there when she was told parents could not pick up children early or visit the center without an appointment. That center is now under investigation for systematic sexual abuse of dozens of young children.

A friend recently called a public agency requesting information she could use to select a day-care center. The parent was sent a thick package of regulations. What is needed is an easy-to-read guide or check list of parents so they can ask the right questions as they "shop" for the best care. City and state governments should make it their business to distribute the check list or guide.

In some cities, including Philadelphia, a Child Care Hotline is now available. Parents in the Philadelphia area can call the CHOICE Child Care Hotline for information and assistance. Many parents are desperate for care and do not know where to find the best child care.

We must do more than express horror and outrage at the reports of abuse and damage to our next generation. We must engage in constructive actions to improve the present quality and availability of day-care services.

(Happy Fernandez is chairperson and associate professor in the Child Care Department, School of Social Administration, Temple University.)

SOURCE. Happy Fernandez. 1984. "Child abuse: Some answers." *The Philadelphia Inquirer* (Aug. 23). Reprinted by permission of Happy Fernandez.

In summary, what complicates the treatment of child abuse is the prevailing tension between the rights of parents and the intervention of social agencies. Since the privatization of the family, parental rights regarding the rearing of children have been of paramount importance. However, as we have been indicating, there has been a gradual encroachment of helping agencies, which provide "expert" advice and which ultimately subvert the autonomy of the family. In cases of child abuse, society finds itself in a dilemma. It is reluctant to interfere with parental prerogatives and often leaves the child in the family and subject to further neglect and abuse. Taking the child from the home, on the other hand, often means subjecting the child to inadequate foster-care programs and institutional facilities.

Other Forms of Family Violence

Violence Against the Aged

"Granny-bashing" is the starkly graphic phrase coined in England to refer to the abuse of elderly parents by their grown children. In an English study, Freeman (1979) found a cycle of violence in operation. Family members who were exposed to a high degree of physical punishment as children were more likely to resort to family violence as adults. Children who were reared in an environment of everyday violence later tended to batter their children and spouses and in turn found themselves exposed to violence later in life from their own children — who, in effect, had been brought up by violent parents. Suzanne K. Steinmetz in her study of battered parents remarked: "It may well be that the 1980's will herald the 'public' awareness of the battered aged—elderly parents who reside with, are dependent on, and battered by their adult, caretaking children (1978:54–55).

Richard Gelles (1983) estimates that about 2.5 million parents are abused by their children in America. Of this number, about 1 million are seriously injured. Steinmetz (1981) estimates that 10 percent of the aged are at risk of abuse, which takes many forms that include verbal harassment, physical assault, withholding food, theft, threats, and neglect. It is present at all socioeconomic levels.

Researchers (Giordano and Giordano, 1984; Pedrick-Cornell and Gelles, 1982; Rathbone-McCuan, 1980; and Steinmetz, 1981) point to a number of unique characteristics of this form of abuse. Many of the caregivers are women who, as the ones primarily responsible for aged parents, are also the ones most likely to abuse them. One explanation is that the caretaker, overburdened with other family responsibilities coupled with the additional stress of an aged parent, resorts to violence as an emotional outlet. The scenario is that of a 60-year-old daughter taking care of an 85-year-old parent while trying to help her children and grandchildren at the same time. Another unique characteristic is that the victim may at an earlier time have been the abuser; that is, the aged parent may have abused the child at earlier stages in the family life cycle and may now be reaping the sad consequences of that earlier abuse—chickens coming home to roost. While there is some research evidence of this and given the cyclical nature of violence, Gelles and Pedrick-Cornell (1983) caution that more knowledge must be gained before firm conclusions can be drawn.

Lau and Kosberg (1979), in a retrospective study of 39 cases of elder abuse (30 of whom were women), suggest three possible reasons for abuse. The first is that the abuser was himself or herself harmed. A second reason for physical and emotional abuse lies in the possibility of financial gain. The third reason is laid to the societal placement of little value on the aged that is reflected in a misconstrued belief that this condones abuse.

Rape

Rape is the ultimate form of male sexual coercion. It is an act of pure violence. It can happen to any woman. In many societies, including our own, rape in marriage was not a crime, nor was it generally disapproved (Dubois and Gordon, 1984). In this section, we discuss rape with particular focus on rape in marriage.

In a review of some of the ethnographic studies on rape, Scully and Marolla (1985) conclude that culture is a factor in rape. They note that cross-cultural data from pre-industrial societies on variations in rape are somewhat suspect, given the fact that in traditional ethnography researchers rarely systematically collected data on sexual attitudes and behavior. When they did, the information was often sketchy and vague. Ethnographic evidence does show the existence of rape-free cultures (Broude and Green, 1976; Sanday, 1979). Where rape and other forms of sexual violence do occur, Sanday attributes it to cultural values that manifest contempt for female qualities. She suggests that rape is part of a culture of violence and an expression of male dominance. Blumberg (1979) takes a similar view believing that the physical and political oppression of women in pre-industrial societies is more likely to occur when women lack important life options and economic power relative to men; that is, women win some immunity from men's use of force against them only when they have relative economic power.

In a later cross-cultural study of 156 tribal societies, Sanday (1981) found strong support for an association between the level of nonsexual violence in the society (for example, whether warfare is frequent or endemic) and rape. Sanday argues that "where interpersonal violence is a way of life, violence frequently achieves sexual expression" (1981:18). There is cross-cultural evidence on the relationship of cultural support for violence and physical punishment in child rearing (Lambert, Triandis, and Wolfe, 1959), higher murder rates (Archer and Gartner, 1984) and higher rates of child abuse (Shwed and Straus, 1979). Based on this evidence, Larry Baron and Murray A. Straus (1985) articulated a ''cultural spillover'' theory to explain the relationship of cultural support for rape with cultural elements that indirectly legitimate sexual violence.

They observe that, in addition to beliefs and values that directly refer to rape, there are aspects of culture that indirectly serve to increase the probability of rape. The central proposition of their theory is that ''the more a society tends to endorse the use of physical force to attain socially approved ends (such as order in the schools, crime control, and international dominance), the greater the likelihood that this legitimation of force will be generalized to other spheres of life where force is less socially approved, such as the family and relations between the sexes'' (Baron and Straus, 1985:3).

Baron and Straus wished to test their theory by examining variations in the rape rate of all the American states and the rate of ''legitimate violence'' (for example, the cultural approval of violence) for each of those states. To do this, they utilized the 1980 rape rate as recorded in the annual FBI *Uniform Crime Reports.* They then developed an instrument to measure ''legitimate force.'' The ''Index of Legitimate Force'' combined 12 indicators of noncriminal violence that fall into three broad groups. These are (1) mass-media preferences of television programs and magazines with a high violence content; (2) governmental use of violence, such as state legislation permitting corporal punishment in the schools, prisoners sentenced to death per 100,000 population, and executions per 100 homicide arrests; and (3) participation in legal or socially approved violent activities that include such indicators as hunting licenses per 100,000 population, National Guard expenditures per capita, and lynchings per million population during the period 1882–1927.

They found a positive association of states that ranked high on the Index of Legitimate Violence and the rape rate. (The five highest ranked states were the District of Columbia, Nevada, Alabama, California, and Florida. The five states that had the lowest rates were Wisconsin, Iowa, Maine, South Dakota, and North Dakota with the lowest ranking.) Other factors that also contributed to the rape rate were the degrees of social disorganization, urbanization, economic equality, and percentage of single males. They concluded that their findings support structural theories explaining the origins of violent cultural or orientations and for a ''cultural spillover'' theory of rape.

Given this cross-cultural and societal overview, what about the individual rapist and the victim? What are they like? And under what circumstances does rape occur? Contrary to popular belief, most women are raped by people they know, not by strangers. These include coworkers, neighbors, dates, friends, and family members. Let us look at two groups of people who are often not associated with rape—dates and husbands.

Physical (including sexual) abuse can take place in dating relationships, especially committed relationships before marriage (Cate, 1982; Makepeace, 1981; Roscoe and Benaske, 1985). ''Date rape'' accounts for about 60 percent of all reported rapes, but the actual percentage is probably much higher (Seligmann, 1984). Barrett (1982) observes that it is one of the least reported and potentially one of the most emotionally damaging forms of sexual assault. As Ellen Doherty, coordinator of a Rape Intervention Program at a New York City hospital, observes that women find rape under these circumstances very hard to talk about, even with close friends, because ''Not only has her body been violated, but her trust in another human being has been betrayed, and her faith in her own judgment has been shaken'' (quoted in Barrett, 1982). Amy Levine, the director of the Rape Prevention Program at the University of California at San Francisco, observes that ''It's hard to make women understand that if they get raped while they're in college, it's more likely to be on a date than in a dark alley" (quoted in Barrett, 1982:48).

Studies have reported that at least one-third of battered women have also been sexually abused by their partners (Finkelhor and Yllo, 1985; O'Reilly, 1983). Although at least 17 states now have laws permitting the prosecution of husbands for raping their wives, a number of states expressly prohibit women from charging their husbands in these cases. When California adopted a marital rape law, Senator Bob Wilson protested, "If you can't rape your wife, who can you rape?" (O'Reilly, 1983). Marital rape has been a particularly difficult violent situation to legislate against because sexual intercourse is considered a right of marriage. The states that have passed laws recognize that forced intercourse by a husband as being no different than forced sexual acts by someone else.

Richard Gelles (1979) calls attention to two violence situations where wives are particularly at risk — marital rape and beatings during pregnancy. He views married men who rape their wives as lacking resources, including economic resources, that could act positively in the power balance in marriage. They use marital rape as a way to exercise nonlegitimate power. Gelles believes that these men see this act as a way to coerce or humiliate or dominate their wives. These men react violently to the possibility that they may be forced to relinquish the power and privilege inherent in the traditional male role. Wife battering during pregnancy is associated particularly with tensions brought about by anticipated economic and social stresses as a consequence of the birth of a child. Another explanation offered is that it may result from sexual frustrations by the uninformed belief that abstinence is required during pregnancy. Also, husbands may batter their wives because the prospective child is unwanted.

Gelles points out that research indicates the lowest rates of marital violence are found in those families where decision making is shared by husbands and wives. He argues for a reconsideration of marital roles in terms of interest or ability rather than the assignment of tasks and responsibilities on the basis of sex and age as a way of reducing family violence. "An elimination of the concept of 'women's work,' elimination of the taken for granted view that the husband is and must be the head of the family, and an elimination of sex-typed family roles are all prerequisites to the reduction of family violence" (Gelles, 1979:19).

Rape traditionally was blamed on the victim, reflecting the sexist biases of many societies. If a man committed rape, it was somehow the woman's fault for provoking him. This belief was reinforced by a parallel belief that women expected or enjoyed being forced into sexual relations. This unfortunate view contributed to the massive underreporting of rape; victims feared disapproval from family and friends. In recent years, however, the feminist movement has vigorously challenged this false assumption. Through the operation of antirape groups, attempts have been made to re-educate people and to counsel rape victims and persons close to them. Groups such as these have fought the mistreatment of rape victims by the police, the courts, hospital personnel, the media, and the society as a whole. Still, despite changing attitudes and public policies many women believe that it is best not to report rape. In a *Good Housekeeping* (1982) article on rape, the Federal Bureau of Investigation estimates that in 1980 there were 165,000 to 700,000 unreported cases of rape compared to the reported 82,000 cases.

The traditional view of the rapist has also been under challenge. In two papers reporting on their research with convicted rapists, Scully and Marolla (1984, 1985) provide evidence that seriously questions the belief that rape is committed by a relatively few "sick" men who have idiosyncratic mental disease and uncontrollable sexual urges. Rather, they found evidence that rapists viewed and understood their behavior from a popular cultural perspective that condones or underemphasizes rape as violent abuse against women. They are led to the conclusion that explanations of this form of sexual violence must include culture and social structure as predisposing factors. From this perspective, rape is seen as the endpoint in a continuum of sexually aggressive behaviors that reward men and victimize women. Through an analysis of interview data of 114 convicted incarcerated rapists, Scully and Marolla report that "[E]vidence indicates that rape is not a behavior confined to a few 'sick' men but many men have the attitudes and beliefs necessary to commit a sexually agressive act" (1985:251).

Through an analysis of interview data of 114 incarcerated rapists, Scully and Marolla found that rape was frequently a means of revenge and punishment. Victims were often substitutes for the woman they wanted to avenge or women whom the offenders perceived as collectively responsible and liable for their problems. In other cases, rape was used as a means of gaining access to unwilling or unavailable women. It often occurred during a robbery or burglary and was seen as an added bonus. Finally, rape represented a recreational activity and excitement. "Gang" rape is an example of rape being viewed as a recreational activity. Impersonal sexual violence was exciting as it gave the offenders a sense of power and control over their victims. It also gave some a feeling of elation and even elevated their self-image. For these men, women are objectified. They are seen and treated as sexual commodities, not as human beings with rights and feelings. One rapist who murdered his victim because she would not "give in" expressed this contemptuous view of women this way:

> Rape is a man's rape. If a women doesn't want to give in, the man should take it. Women have no right to say no. Women are made to have sex. It's all they are good for. Some women would rather take a beating but they always give in; it's what they are for. (Quoted in Scully and Marolla, 1985:261)

Scully and Marolla see as very significant the rapists' belief that they would never go to prison for their actions. Many did not fear imprisonment because they redefined their behavior as not being rape or a sexually violent act. They knew that many women would not report it, and if they did, the likelihood of their being convicted was very low. These offenders perceived rape as a low-risk act that was rewarding. Scully and Marolla conclude that these men have "learned that in this culture sexual violence is rewarding" (1985:262). They end by raising the question that given the apparent rewards and cultural supports for rape, why is it that all men do *not* rape or sexually assault women. "Instead of asking men who rape 'Why?', perhaps we should be asking men who don't 'Why not?'" (Scully and Marolla, 1985:251).

Update on Intrafamily Violence

In a recent study, Straus and Gelles (1985), two of the leading researchers and scholars in the area of family violence, compared statistics in the areas of child abuse and conjugal violence. The two studies, one conducted in 1975 and the other conducted in 1985, used nationally representative samples containing 2,143 families and 3,520 families, respectively. The researchers found extremely high incidences of severe physical violence against children and a high incidence of violence against spouses in both samples.

An encouraging note, however, was that there were substantially lower rates (47 percent) of child abuse in the more-recent study. There was a similar decline (27 percent) in the wife-abuse rate. Straus and Gelles note that some of the differences may be accounted for by different methodology of the studies and an increased reluctance to report incidences of abuse. But they are encouraged that some of the reduction in intrafamily violence is due to the effectiveness of the 10 years of effort of prevention and treatment. They are also of the opinion that changes in American society and family patterns may have contributed to the reduction of intrafamily violence even without the help of ameliorative programs. These changes include a more-favorable economic outlook, a more-negative assessment of family violence, increased marital and familial alternatives for women, better social processes, and greater availability of treatment and prevention services.

While pleased that the national effort to do something about intrafamily violence is showing results, they caution against too much optimism. They observe their findings indicate that an intensified effort is still needed. For, even with the reduction in rates of child abuse and wife beating, there still leaves a minimum estimate of over a million abused children aged 3 through 17 in two-parent households and a million and a half beaten wives each year in the United States.

Conclusion

This chapter was concerned with different manifestations of family violence. Predominant attention was given to wife battering and child abuse. Both were depicted as irrational outgrowths of the excesses of patriarchal authority. In the first case, wife battering, we sought to demonstrate that the legitimation of male prerogatives, privilege, authority, and power can be abused, and too often it is. This results in the severe mistreatment of women. Both cross-cultural and historical evidence was cited. However, our predominant concern was to study contemporary American society and its recent "discovery" of the prevalence of the marital abuse. We indicated that structural conditions inherent in the private conjugal family plays a contributory role. Further, the belief that "normal" conjugal marriages are happy and well adjusted and that violence is an aberration has led to the underestimation of such abuse and to the treatment of it erroneously as a psychologically determined pathology and not as a social phenomenon.

In many ways, our discussion of child abuse can be seen as a continuation of our previous analysis of childhood and adolescence. We stressed that the conceptualization of children and adolescents as essentially inferior and subordinate human beings makes them particularly vulnerable to child abuse. Structural characteristics of the conjugal family play important contributory roles. Governmental policies and the underlying assumptions of the helping professions too often work against the best interests of children.

The chapter's concluding section included discussions of violence against the aged, rape, and an update on intrafamily violence. The growing concern of abuse of elderly parents by their grown children can be explained by a number of salient factors. Here again, we saw that inadequacies of the conjugal family in their treatment and regard for the elderly is a significant contributory explaination of this abhorent phenomenon. Likewise, in our discussion of rape we stressed how it is a manifestation of an ultimate form of male sexual coercion. What may have surprised the reader is that rape in dating and marriage is not uncommon. Finally, our update pointed out the devastating impact that intrafamily violence has on the character of the contemporary American family.

CHAPTER 17

Divorce, Single Parenthood, and Remarriage

A young mother rides the bus holding her newborn infant.

Stephen Shames/VISIONS

485

CHAPTER OUTLINE

There are many internal and external situations, events, and activities that require major readjustments on the part of the family. These include death, physical disabilities, and illnesses; social and psychological maladjustments, such as mental illness, alcoholism, and drug abuse; marital infidelity, separations, desertions, and divorce; and family violence. External factors that also play a role in family instability include war, unemployment, poverty, and such catastrophes as floods and earthquakes. All of these require changing conceptualizations by family members of their marital and family-role definitions. For example, the women's movement has necessitated the rethinking of family roles for all members of the family as has new-role conceptualizations regarding the aged, children, and youth. In this section, we focus on divorce and see how divorce processes and outcomes are responded to by different family systems.

Greater attention is given to divorce than other forms of marital dissolution because it often represents the culmination of other types of family disruption. In this, we follow the example of William J. Goode (1976)—one of the few structural functionalists who has given extensive attention to family disorganization—who reasons that differential consideration should be given to the study of divorce "because so many other types of family disorganization are likely to end in divorce sooner or later, because it is the focus of so much moral and personal concern, and because changes in the divorce rate are usually an index of changes in other elements in the family patterns of any society" (Goode, 1976:517).

The United States has the highest divorce rate among industrialized societies. The noted demographer Paul C. Glick (1975) reports that other societies with high divorce rates include the Soviet Union, Hungary, and Cuba. Other societies that have had high divorce rates in the recent past include Japan (1887–1919) and Egypt (1935–1954). In Table 17.1 comparative divorce rates are presented to illustrate some of these trends. In this discussion, we first examine divorce in the United States and why it has risen in the twentieth century. Then we look at the situation in Japan, Egypt, and Iran and try to explain why the divorce rate has declined in these societies.

Our attention is drawn to the common opinion that the high frequency of divorce is associated with the decline of marriage and threatens the very existence of the family. Tied to this belief is the feeling that contemporary marriages are less harmonious and gratifying than "traditional" marriages. Further, the argument follows

TABLE 17.1 Divorces per 1,000 Marriages in Selected Countries, 1890–1974

Country	1890	1900	1910	1920	1930	1940	1950	1971–1974
United States	55.6	75.3	87.4	133.3	173.9	165.3	231.7	424.0[c]
Germany[a]		17.6	29.9	40.7	72.4	125.7	145.8	186.0[d]
England and Wales				8.0	11.1	16.5	86.1	279.0[e]
France	24.3	26.1	46.3	49.4	68.6	80.4	106.9	117.0[f]
Sweden		12.9	18.4	30.5	50.6	65.1	147.7	380.0[g]
Egypt					269.0[b]	273.0	273.0	204.0[h]
Japan	335.0	184.0	131.0	100.0	98.0	76.0	100.0	98.0[i]

SOURCES: Adapted from William J. Goode, 1976. "Family Disorganization." In Robert K. Merton and Robert Nisbet (eds.), *Contemporary Social Problems,* 4th ed. New York: Harcourt Brace Jovanovich, p. 526. Reprinted by permission of the publisher. All figures calculated from governmental sources and from United Nations. 1974. *Demographic Yearbook.* New York: United Nations.

NOTE: A better measure of divorce frequency is the number of divorces per 1,000 existing marriages, but the latter figure is not often available. The above rate compares marriages in a given year, with divorces occurring to marriages from *previous* years. However, changes from one year to another or differences among countries may be seen just as clearly by this procedure.

[a] 1950–1971, West Germany. [d] 1971. [g] 1972.
[b] 1935. [e] 1972. [h] 1971.
[c] 1974. [f] 1971. [i] 1972.

that a lowering of the divorce rate would enhance the stability of the family. We examine the assumptions underlying these beliefs and test their validity by looking at the implications of divorce for the individual, the family, and the society.

We conclude by analyzing changes in divorce laws that reflect changes in traditional concepts of marriage and the family. Coming under scrutiny are the consequences of divorce for the resultant single-parent family. Our analysis ends with a discussion of family structures and the dynamics of remarriage.

Divorce in Non-Western Societies

We begin our analysis by looking at divorce in preliterate societies. George Murdock (1950) has compiled systematic cross-cultural descriptive data on divorce in 40 small and preliterate societies in Asia, Africa, Oceania, and North and South America. In all but one society (the Incas), institutionalized provisions existed for dissolving marriages; in three-fourths of these societies both sexes had equal rights to initiate divorce. Murdock estimates that divorce rates in about 60 percent of all preliterate societies are higher than in the United States. On the basis of these findings, he concluded that: "Despite the widespread alarm about increasing 'family disorganization' in our society, the comparative evidence makes it clear that we shall remain within the limits which human experience has shown that societies can tolerate with safety" (Murdock, 1950:197).

The higher divorce rates in preliterate societies does not mean that divorce is associated with social disorganization. The society reintegrates the divorced person into the family and that person is not stigmatized and can remarry. Further, a variety of devices are employed to preserve the stability of marital relationships. These include prohibitions against incest, dowries and bride prices, and parental influence and supports. A most important stabilizing practice is the custom of vesting parents with the right to arrange the marriage for their sons and daughters. In societies where marriages are arranged, marriage is usually not defined by characteristics associated with Western romantic love. These marriages do not exhibit the same

Shao Bano, an Islamic woman who successfully sued
her former husband of forty-three years for support
payments. Soon thereafter, however, she dropped her claim,
bowing to the clamor of Muslim demonstrators who argued
that the court decision was an unwarranted intrusion into
their religious affairs.

degree of intimacy and emotionality as their Western counterpart for they are not based on the personal attraction between the persons getting married. Their solidarity derives from the obligations, duties, and rights of members of consanguineally related extended families.

High divorce rates can be, and often are, associated with stable extended-family systems. When divorce does occur, there are clear norms that specify what will happen to family members after the separation. Many societies have provisions for the reintegration of the divorced husband and divorced wife back into their respective kinship group. The children usually remain within the prevailing unilineage's locality. Further, high divorce rates do not necessarily mean that the family system is being undermined nor is it necessarily associated with societal disorganization. High divorce rates may not reflect family breakdown; in fact, they may reflect culturally prescribed ways of eliminating disruptive influences.

Family sociologists have found it useful to distinguish between the instability of the family unit and the instability of the family system in a given society. William J. Goode (1966) points out that both types of instability must be distinguished from social change and family disorganization. He observes that high divorce rates have been common in many Arab Islamic societies for centuries, and they did not reflect, until recently — when the divorce rate declined — changes in the family system. The high divorce rate remained unchanged for many generations and the essential structure of the Arab family created it and has coped with it.

Goode further observes that the direction of change in the divorce rate of a given family system depends on the characteristics of the system prior to the onset of change. For example, the divorce rate in Arabic Islam and in Japan were decreasing rather than increasing when the reverse pattern was occurring in the West. Thus, he reaches the somewhat paradoxical conclusion that social change, rather than bringing about disorganization, may actually reduce the rates of occurrence of such disorganizational phenomena as divorce.

> With respect to change, it is evident that if the rates of occurrence of major family happenings, such as the percentage eventually marrying, percentage married at certain ages, divorce rates, fertility, patterns and so on, are changing, then it may be that the family system is also changing and that at least some parts of it are dissolving or undergoing disorganization. On the other hand, some of these changes may actually reduce the rates of occurrence of such phenomena classically called "disorganization," such as divorce, separation, illegitimacy or desertion. Thus, for example, the rate of desertion has been dropping in the United States. In Latin American countries in the process of industrialization, with all its predictable *anomie,* the rate of illegitimacy has been dropping. Japan's family system has been undergoing great changes over the past generation and thus by definition certain parts of it must have been "dissolving," but the divorce rate has steadily dropped. Finally, even though the old family patterns may be dissolving, they may be replaced by new ones which control as determinately as the old. (Goode, 1962/1966:388)

These conclusions bring us to our next concern: Why are divorce rates changing in contemporary societies? Goode (1963), in his influential *World Revolution and Family Patterns,* attributes the relatively high divorce rates in the West to the emergence of the conjugal-family system and the decline of the consanguineal extended-family system. The large kin groups associated with unilineage systems in non-Western societies subordinate their younger members and arrange their marriages. Love as a basis for marriage is discouraged as the affectional ties between the couple may undermine their loyalty to the extended family. Nothing is permitted to conflict with the obligations and loyalties one has to the larger kin group. The development of the conjugal family leads to the assumption that greater emotional ties between husband and wife will be present. The diminished importance of the larger family group removes the alternative source for emotional sustenance and gratification. The conjugal relationship now becomes all important. The consequent mutual dependence of spouses on one another for support combined with the comparative isolation of the conjugal unit from kin fosters a relatively more unstable relationship with a concomitant rise in the divorce rate.

> Thus the emotions within this unit are likely to be intense, and the relationship between husband and wife may well be intrinsically unstable, depending as it does on affection. Consequently, the divorce rate is likely to be high. (Goode, 1963:9)

Goode cites the experiences of Japanese and Arabic Islamics to provide the illustrative cases of cultures whose high divorce rates have declined in the twentieth century. He attributes this decline to the development of the independent conjugal family. A brief examination of Japan and a somewhat more-detailed look at Islamic Egypt demonstrates some of the dynamics operating in the lowering of the divorce rate. We conclude this section by examining the impact of the Islamic revolution in Iran on divorce rates.

Divorce in Japan

Goode (1963) reports that in the early Meiji period of the late 1860s and 1870s, as well as for many prior generations, Japan had a high divorce rate in a very stable society. Marital instability did not affect the stability of the family system nor did it undermine Japanese social structure.

The Japanese conception of marriage and divorce differed from that of the West. They were neither sacramental affairs nor a concern of the state. Marriage was arranged by extended families through go-betweens. The typical pattern after marriage was for the wife to move into her husband's family's household. This was especially true for the wealthier families. But, regardless of wealth, the wife was expected to accommodate herself to her in-laws. This included showing deference, respect, and obeying them by performing all the assigned tasks. Failure to comply or meet the approval of in-laws would result in the termination and repudiation of the marriage. This was done without regard to the relationship between the woman and her spouse.

This system permitted rather free divorce and the divorce rate was higher in the lower social strata than in the upper strata. Goode attributes this to a system that allowed noblemen to obtain concubines if marital problems existed. If a wife got along with her in-laws and if she bore sons, the marriage continued. The purpose of marriage was not for the emotional gratification of the couple, but rather for the development of the extended family alliances. Divorce could be too disruptive and could cause unnecessary conflict between the two families.

In a later work, Goode (1976) presents statistical data (see Table 17.1) that reveals that the Japanese divorce rate has declined since 1890. He sees this decline as related to the increased proportion of marriages that are based on personal choice or preference and only then approved by the respective parents. The result is that the relationship between spouses has increased in importance as the influence of the extended family has declined in importance.

In the traditional Japanese family, members of the family included only those who actually lived and worked together. Children were viewed as the property of the father, and he almost always retained custody of the children after separation and divorce. He was the one who initiated divorce, and after divorce the mother left, severing all ties with her husband, his family, and her children. The children would be raised by the women in the patrilineal family. Thus, from the man's perspective, divorce had little impact on his everyday life. He could divorce without much regard to its future consequences for himself or his children.

Divorce was an option that could be exercised by men alone. There were seven reasons that a man could provide for easily divorcing his wife. They included her inability to bear children, her immorality, being argumentative with her in-laws, too talkative, dishonest, jealous, or diseased (Condon, 1985). A letter such as the following, sent to the proper authorities, would accomplish divorce: "You are incompatible with the customs in my family. So you are no longer needed and are free to seek happiness elsewhere" (quoted in Condon, 1985:45). A divorced woman was returned to her family.

Women's divorce options were limited to running to a Buddhist temple or nunnery where, if she was admitted, she could stay for a 2-year period and then would be declared officially divorced. It was not until the Meiji Civil Code of 1898 that women were given the right to divorce. But even with that legal option, a divorced woman had few economic opportunities for self-support.

After World War II, when most women's rights were gained, there was an appreciable change in the initiation of divorce proceedings. Today, 74 percent of all family court petitions for divorce are initiated by women (Condon, 1985). Similarly, there has been a change in which parent gets custodial rights. In 1950, 49 percent of the fathers got custody compared to 40 percent for the mother. However, by 1981, mothers received custody in 69 percent of the cases and the father in only 24 percent (O'Kelly and Carney, 1986).

In the last 15 years, the Japanese Health and Welfare Ministry statistics show that the divorce rate has doubled (Condon, 1985). In comparison to the United States (1.5 per 1,000 population compared to 5.3 per 1,000), the divorce rate is still low. In comparison to a world scale, Japan's divorce rate is still one of the lowest. This low rate is attributed to the fact that divorce is still disapproved of and stigmatizes the family name.

Recent surveys that have found that more than 70 percent of men and women are in disagreement with the view that people should feel free to divorce (cited in O'Kelly and Carney, 1986). Divorce creates scandals. Children of divorce find that their marriage prospects are diminished. The dominant belief is that divorce is bad for children and that couples with children should not divorce. However, since 1963, the divorce rate has risen especially among older couples, reflecting the fact that couples have delayed divorce until after their children have married. Often it is women who initiate these divorces. "Husbands are said sometimes to be taken by surprise when an otherwise dutiful wife declares that she wants a divorce now that they are older and their parental responsibilities have been completed. Husbands who saw nothing wrong in their marriages can be faced with wives who suddenly tell them they have loathed them for years" (O'Kelly and Carney, 1986:210–211).

A major factor accounting for the low divorce rate is the fact there is no provision for alimony in Japanese law. A divorce agreement usually includes only one lump-sum settlement payment that is relatively small. The reason for this stems from the traditional practice of a divorced woman returning to her family. Indeed, as Condon (1985) points out, the Japanese word for "divorcee" *(demodori)* means someone who *de* (goes out) and *modori* (comes back). This is particularly hard on the divorced woman who is often faced with economic difficulties. Japanese social services and public assistance provide minimum assistance.

Another factor that minimizes the divorce rate is that child support is often minimal or nonexistent. Condon cites figures that indicate that more than 75 percent of divorced men do not keep up the payments. Social services and public-assistance programs provide some help, but often are inadequate. The result is that divorced mothers often find that they cannot make ends meet. Her average annual income is less than half the national average for heads of households (Condon, 1985). The lack of social supports, combined with the lack of family supports, often makes divorce a

Women's Views on Divorce Are Changing in Japan

BY TERRY TRUCCO

TOKYO, June 10 — Last fall, Mieko Enomoto became the most talked-about divorced woman in Japan.

In the long-running trial of former Prime Minister Kakuei Tanaka, accused of receiving bribes from the Lockheed Corporation, Mrs. Enomoto disclosed that her former husband, Toshio Enomoto, admitted that he had accepted $1.8 million on the Prime Minister's behalf.

Mrs. Enomoto's testimony became the talk of Japan, and opinion was sharply divided. Many men were critical of what they called "treachery," but a number of women cheered. They viewed Mrs. Enomoto's testimony as a form of revenge in this male-dominated country where divorce settlements are low and divorced women are often treated as outcasts.

CONSTITUTIONAL GUARANTEE

The Constitution of 1946 guarantees equality of the sexes, but in practice, the Japanese have seldom acted as equals. Elderly women still walk a few paces behind their husbands, and women's salaries generally are half of those of men, according to figures for 1979 from the Ministry of Labor.

"In the prewar period, the adulteress was dead to society, but the divorced woman was considered even worse," says Fumiko Kanazumi, a lawyer who has handled divorce cases for nearly a decade. "She had failed as a wife, the one role a Japanese woman is expected to fulfill," Mrs. Kanazumi said. "Even today, Japanese girls are still educated to believe that marriage is the main goal in life."

Japan boasts one of the world's lowest divorce rates. According to United Nations figures, there were 1.22 divorces per 1,000 Japanese in 1980. In contrast, there were 5.19 divorces per 1,000 Americans that year.

While it can hardly be termed epidemic, Japan's divorce rate has risen steadily since 1965, and in the last decade the divorce rate has doubled. Last year, 154,000 couples decided to end their marriages, 12,000 more than in 1980. In 1981,

780,000 couples were married, 5,000 more than in 1980.

Some social observers see the rising divorce rate as evidence of a breakdown in the structure of the postwar Japanese family. Others contend that it shows a healthy improvement in the status of Japan's women. "Women are beginning to realize they don't have to continue in miserable marriages," said Yoriko Madoka, a Tokyo marriage counselor and author of four books on divorce.

Women now file for 55 percent of the divorces, men initiate 35 percent, and parents, usually the wife's, instigate the remainder, according to 1978 figures, the most recent available from the Health and Welfare Ministry.

In part, these numbers reflect notable changes in women's attitudes toward marriage. Schooled for centuries in the Confucian principles of endurance and compliance, women were once expected to obey their fathers in childhood, their husbands in marriage and their children in old age. "Japanese girls would laugh at you if you suggested anything like that today," says Mrs. Madoka, who is divorced.

An increase in so-called "love marriages," as opposed to the traditional "o-miai," or arranged unions, has also swelled the divorce rate, some believe. They argue that couples who have married for love, not convenience, enter a marriage with higher expectations and may well divorce when they find those expectations shattered. On the other hand, they theorize that couples involved in arranged marriages hold more traditional views and find it difficult to end an "o-miai" relationship without embarrassment. But the Rev. Yukio Saito, who operates a telephone counseling service here, says that an arranged marriage may also be easier to break these days "because the couple can say to their parents, 'You made me do this. I didn't want this marriage.'"

The most persuasive reason for the rise in divorce, however, is economic. "Women now make up more than one-third of the

(continued)

labor force," said Mrs. Kanazumi. "They no longer have to depend on their husbands for their only support."

Working mothers are viewed more favorably in the larger cities, although they are still scorned in the provinces, said Teiko Seki, a freelance translator in Tokyo who was divorced almost two years ago. She now uses her maiden name. "I had worked before my marriage, and I knew it wouldn't be easy to support myself and my son," said Miss Seki, "but I never doubted I would get a job."

Women contemplating divorce expect to work, since financial settlements in Japan are notably low. Japan's largest divorce settlement was recorded in 1980, when a court ordered a Yokohama businessman to pay his estranged wife $740,000. But the average divorce settlement—usually involving cash, not property—is for less than $4,350, and such settlements are most often made in one or two chunks, much like severance pay. Only 10 percent of the payments exceed $25,000, and just 2.7 percent of all women who divorce receive alimony. The figures, for 1978, were compiled by the Health and Welfare Ministry.

Like so much else here, tradition is largely the reason for the small settlements. A divorced woman was usually sent back to her family, which was expected to support her. Now fewer divorced women return home and instead support themselves and their children, if any.

NOT MUCH FOR CHILD CARE

Child-care payments aren't much better than the settlements. In 1978, more than half of Japan's divorced women provided all living expenses for their children, the Health and Welfare Ministry has reported.

"There's no precedent for higher settlements between divorcing couples, so the amount will probably continue to be small," said Mrs. Kanazumi.

Many divorced women say they sense job discrimination. Yukiko Hashimoto, a 29-year-old assistant secretary who was divorced two years ago and now uses her maiden name, recalled that she was interviewed by a number of companies after her divorce. "But they seemed disinterested in me as soon as I told them I was divorced," she said. Fluent in English, she eventually found a job with an American company in Tokyo.

Yet some employers prefer to hire divorced women. Kiyoshi Yazawa, editor of Cosmo '82, a Japanese science magazine, said she believes divorced women work harder. "Women just out of the university expect to get married in a couple years and are not serious about their careers," she said, "but a job means a lot to a divorced woman."

Many blame the Government for the social stigma still surrounding divorce. Though a mutual-consent divorce is quick, easy and inexpensive, the Government has actively discouraged divorce. Since 1949, Japan's Family Court has provided state-sponsored marriage counseling. But couples are never interviewed together, divorce is seldom offered as a solution, and the most frequent advice, usually for wives, is "gam batte"—"hang in there."

Japan's divorce rate is expected to continue to rise. Japanese women today have fewer children and are well educated. "Living just for your children is no longer enough," said Mrs. Madoka. "Women want companionship from their husbands, not just financial stability. Many Japanese men don't realize this."

Indeed, a second marriage is not a goal for many of Japan's divorced women. While a newspaper survey here found that many divorced men would like to remarry, a little more than half of the women interviewed were interested. Miss Hashimoto, for example, said that while she enjoys dating, she finds that most men want to remarry because they need help with the house and children. "They want servants and slaves; it's very difficult to find a man who isn't looking for a wife," she said.

difficult and discouraging option for unhappy wives. The result is that they often stay married. One Japanese lawyer sums up the situation for these women: "More than 50 percent of married women are unhappy, but they tell themselves 'Be patient. Be patient'" (quoted in Condon, 1985:59).

Divorce in Egypt

Table 17.1 also documents that the divorce rate has declined in Egypt, an Arab Islamic society. Goode attributes this lowering of the divorce rate to the loss of the absolute right of a man to repudiate and divorce his wife. "Where the union under the earlier system was fragile because of the elders, as in Japan, or dependent on the whim of the man, as in Arab countries, the new system, with its greater independence of the young couple, more-intense emotional ties of husband and wife with one another, and the increased bargaining power of the woman may mean a somewhat greater stability of the family unit" (Goode, 1976:528).

Islam derived its origins in seventh-century Arabia. It reflected a combination of the seminomadic tribal and the feudal conditions present at that time. Prior to the rise of Islam, women had no rights and were viewed as qualitatively different and inferior to men. With Islam, the position of women greatly improved. Women were freed from the domination of the male. This social revolution included the right to education, the right to buy and sell property, and the right to hold a job and go into a business. Islam gave women legal rights and protections that were incorporated into the Koran as a series of permissions and prohibitions that have continued to be influential to this day. Islam, then, as an integral religion formulated a total pattern of living rather than focusing primarily on theology.

From the perspective of pre-Islamic Arab society, Islam appeared to be a great social revolution in the history of women's rights. Unfortunately, as the centuries proceeded, the advances of Islam stagnated and reversed. Influenced by pre-Islamic culture, a strong tradition developed that led to the total exclusion of Arab women from the world of public affairs. We observed how the veil and the gradual exclusion of women from the public world has lowered the general status of women, has reduced their awareness of the subjugation of their rights, and has robbed them of the opportunity to exercise those rights. Eventually, men gained dominance over women. This dominance included not only power over women's involvement in public matters, including business, wealth, and education, but also in private matters regarding marriage, the family, and in personal decisions regarding their own destiny. Islam has come to emphasize patriarchal authority of the husband-father along with the corresponding subservience of women and children. The marriage bond is subsumed under patriarchal authority and polygyny and easy divorces are permitted.

The situation has begun to change with the liberating and social revolutionary movements of recent times. In the Arab countries today, there is a recognition that to develop and achieve national identities and goals, the equality of women must be achieved. The more-Westernized segment of the Arab population has been in the forefront of the movement to achieve and regain women's rights. But this view is held by only a small, rather limited group. Even in those Arab countries that have sought to re-establish women's legal rights there is a large segment of the population that has been fighting a successful battle to deny these rights. The situation in Egypt is a good case in point. Although a new constitution has been written that is very strong in securing equality for women in public matters, it is weak in terms of achieving equality in personal matters within the family structure. Aminah al-Sa'id, a leading Egyptian feminist, voices the following opinion.

> If we look at the new Egyptian constitution which in my opinion is one of the leading documents in terms of women's emancipation, we find it rich in laws designed to assure equality between men and women *except* in matters relating to personal status. These laws (the *Shari'ah*, or canon, laws governing the family, divorce, inheritance, marriage) were established in the time of ignorance and are based on faulty interpretations which are no longer suitable for the needs and the spirit of our institution within the nation, that is, the family. The fact that they are still in operation leads to the biggest contradictions to be found in our new life. It is hard for the mind to connect these two situations: the home and family situation, in which the Arab woman's position is very weak, and the public and social situation, in which she has achieved so many victories—victories which have placed her in importance cabinet posts, in positions as deputy ministers in the government, as judges in the courts, and as representatives in important economic and political conferences. (al-Sa'id, 1977:385)

An examination of Egyptian marriage and family conditions today provides the necessary evidence to support her sentiments.

The pre-Islamic inhabitants of the Arabian peninsula had no limitations on the number of wives a man was allowed. The Koran, although permitting a man to have as many as four wives, signifies a rise in the status of women. Further, it restricts the men to provide equal treatment, both sexually and in the matter of support. Indeed, it was this Koranic provision that justified the legal prohibition against polygyny in 1955 in Tunisia. The view taken was that it was an obvious impossibility for wives to be treated equally, and thus polygyny was specifically disapproved; few Islamic men ever managed to obtain more than one wife at a time (Goode, 1963). Informal forces against polygyny are strong and its economic advantages are minimal.

Divorce has been the alternative method for having more than one wife during the course of one's life. Divorce in Islam is the unlimited right of the man, provided he follows the proscribed forms. Women do not have the same rights of divorce as men. According to Islamic law, a husband is allowed to divorce his wife by simply saying, "I divorce thee," three times before two witnesses. The husband need have no ground for divorce. However, it is rarely used. The more-typical pattern is for a final and terminal divorce to go through three stages. During the first two stages a man may remarry the same woman. But should he divorce her a third time, he is forbidden to remarry her unless in the meantime she has been married and divorced by another man. Forbidding remarriage to a thrice-divorced couple follows the logic that they have not and probably will not be able to get along in the future. The pronouncement "I divorce thee," three times on the same occasion counts as a triple divorce and remarriage must follow this same rule. Therefore, it is rarely used.

Goode (1963) asserts that this procedure disproves the popularly supposed belief held by non-Moslems that the male perogative of divorce is unqualified under Islam: "The Koranic tradition did not evaluate divorce very highly: 'Of all that he has permitted, God detests nothing more than divorce'" (Goode, 1963:155). Koranic tradition assumed that a man would not express the formula, "I divorce thee," three times at a single conflict. Rather, ethical injunctions held that only after three successive trials would a man finally and irrevocably divorce a woman. The usual pattern was that, after the first conflict, a husband could reverse the divorce process merely by living together with her again within a 3-month period, the *'iddah:*

> The *'iddah* is a period during which the woman cannot marry another man. Its main purpose is to make sure that, if the woman is carrying a child fathered by the husband, there will be no conflict regarding paternity. If the husband does not take back his wife during the *'iddah* period, he cannot thereafter do so without a new contract. The divorce in the latter case is called *ba'in*, or absolute, in contrast to the *rag'i*, or temporary divorce during the *'iddah* period. If the husband exercises his right of absolute divorce three times, he cannot remarry his wife unless the latter is

married first to another man, or *muhallal,* and then divorced by him. (Mohsen, 1974:41)

The emphasis in Koranic tradition, therefore, is placed not on the simplicity of the verbal formula, but on the necessity of the three stages before the dissolution is completed. However, although Islamic strictures regard divorce seriously, the extraordinarily high rate of divorce leads us to conclude that the religious tradition is not strictly followed. One explanation is that divorce is not viewed with the same stigma and negative consequences for women as it is in most Western Christian societies. Goode (1963) observes that, under the Arab institutional structure, the wife's family does not pressure an unhappy wife to remain in an unsatisfactory marriage. If her divorce is irrevocable, when she returns to her family they can obtain another bride-price for her.

Smock and Youssef (1977), in their study of women's roles and statuses in Egyptian society, found that the proportion of adult women reported in a census count as "currently divorced" was only 2 percent in 1960 and 1.7 percent in 1966. They attribute this low figure to the fact that most divorced women are young and remarry quickly. Further, the woman's extended family has moral and financial obligations to provide her status placement and economic support. Children, if any, are not a problem because the legal code and religious family statutes assign guardianship of young children to either the maternal or paternal grandparents. The slight social stigma attached to divorce allows the divorced woman to be placed back on the marriage market and to compete with single girls: "All these factors produce a situation in which the divorced woman is thought of as an 'expectant wife' and as such is often subjected to the same family restrictions and controls imposed on the single girls so as to secure a remarriage that will reflect favorably on her own standing and that of her family" (Smock and Youssef, 1977:46).

Of particular interest to us is the effect of modernization processes on the traditional Islamic way of life. Egypt, which has been in the forefront of social change, makes an interesting case study of how Westernization has affected Islamic divorce practices. Mohsen (1974) observes that there have been legal changes that aim at achieving the equality of women. However, "despite the appearance of modernity, the attitude toward the role of women in public life—as well as in private—still remains a fairly conservative one" (Mohsen, 1974:38). Mohsen's analysis concentrates on practices and attitudes relative to the role of those women who have been most immediately affected by Western ideas—urban middle-class and upper-middle-class women.

The divorce laws in Egypt has been changed to make it easier for a woman to obtain a divorce. Yet, economic factors are an important deterrent, preventing unhappily married women from resorting to divorce. This is especially true for women who have no independent financial resources and who must rely on their parents. If children are involved, even more pressure is placed on the woman to remain with her husband. Her family does not wish to assume the responsibility of child support. Unlike the traditional situation, where little significant social stigma is attached to divorce, these "modern" women, even if they have independent sources of income, experience enough social stigma that they think twice before divorcing their husbands. Mohsen cites an article written by Aminah al-Sa'id (1977) on the plight of these women; in this article, al-Sa'id reports that letters received from divorced women describe how friends avoid them and that men colleagues in their places of work view them as easy sexual prey and make sexual advances. These women discuss their loneliness and the difficulty of finding suitable second husbands. Available men turn out to be much older than they are and the men are socially and economically less desirable than their first husbands.

Mohsen (1974) argues that the desire for a new conception of the role of women based on equal participation and rewards can only come about through changing the conservative cultural practices and attitudes of men and women. It is not enough simply to change the laws of personal status and family relations:

> Men's conservatism stems from the need to maintain the status quo, which is to their advantage. Women's conservative attitude stems partly from the fear of having to compete in areas for which they have not been culturally trained. The home for the woman is the domain of her authority and the source of her security. Some women view equality (especially if it entails cooperation between husband and wife in domestic activities) as a sacrifice of the woman's only stronghold. It will take more than legislation to change some of these attitudes. It might take a few generations for women to achieve the self-confidence needed to compete in the man's world. But until this happens, any attempt to change the role of women by mere legislation is bound to effect minimal results. (Mohsen, 1974:58)

In 1979, a new law was passed that essentially maintained the existing statutes with some minor, insignificant changes (El Saadawi, 1984). Husbands still have an absolute right to divorce; women have no such right. The wife's right to divorce is limited to cases in which the husband fails to support his wife financially, suffers from an incurable disease or disability, physically maltreats or damages the wife, and if he is absent more than 5 years.

The divorce rate remains very low compared to Western rates. In Cairo and Alexandria, a 1980 study showed that divorce rates were 2.9 percent of the married population that year (Morgan, 1984). In outlying provinces, the rates fall below 2 percent. The divorce rate was highest among women in the labor force. The traditional practice of men being allowed easy divorce remains, as well as his ability to force his wife to return if she has left him, or has been conditionally divorced. Alimony payment is often not made and there is little recourse for enforcement.

Child maintenance is the father's responsibility (tutelage), despite the fact that children are allowed to remain with the divorced mother until the age of 9 for boys and 11 for girls. Dependent children are defined as either male minors and unmarried, widowed, or divorced daughters. The power of the father under the tutelage practice is illustrated in the following personal account by Nawal El Saadawi, an Egyptian feminist:

> In 1976, my daughter, then nineteen years old, was invited to Algeria to participate in a tennis tournament. I had divorced her father a few months after she was born, and by mutual agreement he allowed her to live with me. Throughout the years I remained solely responsible for her livelihood and for everything concerning her. Nevertheless, the passport autorities refused to allow her to travel without her father's permission. Since he was working in Saudi Arabia as a medical doctor I was unable to obtain an official document from him in time for her departure, and so she missed the opportunity to visit Algeria and participate in the tournament. (1984:206)

In summary, what we discover is that in the traditional Islamic family there are structured safeguards for women in the form of extended kinship institutions. The relative ease with which a man can gain a divorce is compensated for by various forms of social and familial supports for both women and children. Obviously, the Islamic sanctioning of polygyny, the unilateral power of the husband in divorce, and other religious-legal sanctions and prohibitions against women mitigate against their achieving equality. Yet, modernization in the form of legal reforms in Egypt has not led to the achievement of an equitable position for married and divorced Egyptian Islamic women. This can only be achieved when the cultural attitudes and practices of Egyptian society are changed to accommodate the egalitarian elements of Islam with those of modernization.

Court Ruling on Wives Divides Egypt

BY JUDITH MILLER

CAIRO, June 9—The abolition of a women's rights law last month by Egypt's Supreme Court has touched off a furious debate here and put the Government of President Hosni Mubarak in a politically awkward position.

On May 6 the court struck down on procedural grounds the "personal status" amendments of 1979. While Egyptian law never banned polygamy, the amendments required a man to notify his wife officially if he took a second wife. If she objected, she could divorce him within a year, receive alimony promptly and retain custody of young children in their apartment, or in another that the husband was required to provide.

Feminists and liberals have protested the court's ruling that struck down these provisions. Although she rarely criticizes Egypt publicly, Jihan Sadat, wife of the late President Anwar el-Sadat, said in an interview here that she was "shocked and deeply dismayed" by the abolition of the law, which she had championed and her husband had issued by decree. "Egyptian women must fight this," said Mrs. Sadat, who taught classes this spring at American University in Washington and the University of South Carolina. She recently returned to Cairo.

FUNDAMENTALISTS LIKE DECISION

Islamic fundamentalists and other conservatives have disagreed with Mrs. Sadat and have applauded the court's decision. Though the country's Islamic religious establishment supported the 1979 law, fundamentalists argued that it was inconsistent with Sharia, the 1,300-year-old Moslem code. The Constitution says Sharia is the "principle source" of Egyptian law.

The court action has forced President Mubarak to choose between competing demands of liberals that the law be reintroduced in the Parliament and of the Islamic fundamentalists, who oppose a new statute.

President Mubarak has tried to steer a middle course. He says he will reintroduce a bill that is consistent with Sharia, or at least with Egypt's interpretation of it.

But some Egyptians warn that he may wind up pleasing neither camp. "The effort to codify Sharia as it applies to sensitive issues of sex, marriage and divorce risks is opening the Government to charges of heresy by those who disagree with the Government's interpretation of religious law," warned Said el-Ashmawi, a judge, a Moslem and an opponent of Egyptian fundamentalism.

The complex and highly sensitive debate over the law highlights ways in which Egypt's pressing economic problems have affected interpersonal relationships.

"This has been portrayed as a struggle over women's rights and over whether or not Egypt will adhere to the principles of Islamic law," said Ahmed Baha el-Din, an influential Egyptian writer and a supporter of the 1979 law. "But what is really at issue is who gets the apartment after a divorce."

The housing shortage in Egypt is acute, particularly in Cairo. Marriages are often delayed, some up to 10 years, because a couple cannot find an apartment it can afford.

As a result, many men in this highly traditional, male-dominated society fiercely resented the requirement that, in the event of a divorce, a man either find his first wife and young children a new flat or move out of his own.

Many intellectuals, especially leftists, have also been slow to criticize the court's ruling because they favor elimination of laws they say President Sadat promulgated illegally.

"The court's action has pitted our feminism against our desire to see all these laws obliterated," conceded Nawal Saadawi, a writer and leader of the campaign to restore the amendment.

The repeal of the law has shocked liberals, who take pride in Egypt's historical role as a pioneer of the women's rights movement in the Arab world.

Even today, said Aisha Rateb, Egypt's first and only female ambassador, who now teaches law at Cairo University, Egyptian

(continued)

women enjoy rights denied women in much of the developing world and in the Persian Gulf. They work in all sectors and are guaranteed equal pay by law. They vote and have been allocated at least 30 seats in the People's Assembly. Women make up 45 percent of university students and 25 percent of university staff, Mrs. Rateb says.

CONFLICT WITH KORAN IS DENIED

Defenders of the 1979 law dispute the fundamentalist contention that it conflicted with Sharia and the Koran, the holy book of Islam.

Some defenders of the law acknowledge privately, but almost never publicly, that the Koran is, as Mr. Baha el-Din put it, "a man's document." In some respects, they concede, the Koran discriminates against women. Men can have up to four wives simultaneously, for example, while women can have only one husband. Female children are entitled to one-half what is due a male heir.

Some Egyptians, fearful of being labeled anti-Islamic, argue that the Koran affords women even greater rights than many Western women enjoy. Under Sharia, women keep their father's names in marriage and their own property.

They say the Koran, as interpreted in Egyptian law, places so many conditions on polygamy—such as requiring a man to treat all his wives equally—that multiple marriages are virtually impossible.

But Egypt's fundamentalists reject the more liberal interpretations of Sharia upon which Egyptian law has traditionally been based.

Zenab el-Ghazali, an influential member of the Moslem Brotherhood, maintains that the 1979 statute was anti-Islamic because it effectively penalized men for multiple marriages by allowing the courts to intervene and limit his right to take a second wife or divorce his first.

"Only Sharia is acceptable to Moslem women," said Mrs. Ghazali, whose late husband was simultaneously married to two other women.

Mrs. Ghazali, whose party is part of a coalition that constitutes the only opposition group in Parliament, vowed to oppose Government efforts to pass a substitute law.

Under the 1920 and 1929 personal status laws now in effect, with the repeal of the 1979 act, a woman no longer need be officially notified if her husband divorces or takes a second wife. No longer is a second marriage automatically grounds for divorce; a woman must once again prove in court that the second marriage has harmed her.

ALIMONY NOT AUTOMATIC

She is no longer entitled to immediate alimony. She no longer automatically wins custody of daughters over the age of 7 and sons over 9. She no longer has the right to remain in her apartment until the father gains custody.

Women are already being affected by the court action, as the case of Zakia Ahmed shows. Last March, before the amendments were struck down, Mrs. Ahmed, a mother of four who is about 45 years old, returned to her apartment in Shubra, a poor section, and found her husband "betraying" her, as it is said in Arabic, with this secretary, whom he later married. When Mrs. Ahmed refused to leave their home, he attacked her with a knife, inflicting injuries that required hospitalization. She eventually returned home, the only place she had to go, but found her husband's second wife well ensconced there.

"She was sleeping in my bed, wearing my clothes," Mrs. Ahmed told a women's meeting two weeks ago, her fury and anguish undiminished.

Given the abolition of the 1979 law, if Mrs. Ahmed wishes to take legal action now, she will have to prove injury in a protracted court proceeding that will be difficult for her to afford.

Aziza Hussein, a family planning expert, argued that even when the 1979 law was in force, Egypt's conservative traditions and practices discouraged women like Mrs. Ahmed from insisting on their rights. But without the law, women face additional psychological hardships, she said.

"Polygamy is not widespread in Egypt, only about 3 to 4 percent," Mrs. Hussein said. "But most women, especially the lower classes, live in terror that their husbands will take second wives and that they will lose their homes."

This, in turn, has prompted them to have

(continued)

more children, in order to bolster their
standing within the family and to make it
more difficult for a husband to support
more than one wife.

"Population is Egypt's number one
problem," said Mrs. Hussein. "This is more

than a woman's issue. Our national
interests are at stake."

SOURCE. Judith Miller. 1985. "Court ruling on wives
divides Egypt." *The New York Times* (June 10).
Copyright ©1985 by The New York Times
Company. Reprinted by permission.

Divorce in Iran

Iran, like Egypt, is an Islamic country. However, it is not an Arab country. Unlike
Egypt and other Arab countries that practice Sunni Islam, Iran is a Shi'ite Islamic
country whose people practice a more-fundamentalist form of Islam. The story of
Iran in the last 25 years is the story of the trials and tribulations of modernization
processes and its impact on family dynamics. Mohammed Reza Shah Pahlavi was the
reigning monarch from 1941 until he was ousted by the Islamic revolutionary forces
of the Ayatollah Ruhollah Khomeini in February 1979.

Under the shah, the attempt was to build a country that would approximate
European standards and would be one of the advanced nations of the world. Economically supported by its rich oil fields, modernization processes were instituted to
accomplish this goal. Urbanization and industrialization occurred, with Teheran
becoming the symbol of the new Iran. Under pressure from the United States to
liberalize his regime, a series of laws designed for social and land reform were passed
during the 1960s and 1970s. However, this program of land reform, parliamentary
elections, and improvements in education and social services—grandiloquently
dubbed the "White Revolution"—proved to be very inadequate and did not end the
underlying social inequality, injustices, and lack of civil rights prevailing in the
country. Military expenditures continued to climb, political freedom actually lessened, and land reform did little good.

In the late 1970s, there was a coalescing of forces against the shah; his policies were
seen to have resulted in foreign social and cultural domination. There was bitterness
over political repression and the wasting of the financial gains from oil sales (Apple,
1979). Popular sentiment called for the shah's overthrow. The Shi'ite faith and its
leaders, the ayatollahs (holy men) and mullahs (priests), was seen as the embodiment
of Iranian nationalism, integrity, and selflessness that would replace the corruption
and hedonism of the shah's regime. The revolution occurred in late 1978 and early
1979 and, after a quick succession of caretaker governments, they were finally
replaced by a government controlled by the Shi'ite leaders who installed a Shi'ite
Islam state based on fundamentalist Islamic jurisprudence.

The impact of Shi'ism on women's rights and divorce in Iran captures our attention here. Under the shah, women gained the right to vote in 1963. The land-reform
policies that were implemented during the 1960s had little effect on women since
they were prohibited from getting land grants. The Family Protection Law was
passed in 1967 and amended in 1975. Before the law, in the 1960s, Iran had one of
the highest divorce rates, compared to other countries (Aghajanian, 1986). The
reason for this is that the common practice allowed husbands to divorce their wives
with relative ease and whenever they decided to do so. The only requirement was the
presence of two male witnesses to hear the husband say *talagh* (I divorce you).

The 1967 law allowed divorce only through legal procedures. It called for disputes
between married persons to be filed in court, and recognized divorce by mutual
consent and divorce by judicial decree through annulment or dissolution. It gave
women the right to divorce under special circumstances. The impact of the new law

was a depressive effect on the rate of divorce that was nearly halved from 1.0 per thousand population in 1965 to 0.6 in both 1970 and 1975. Aghajanian (1986) attributes this decline in part to the slowness of the judicial process and the requirement that Iranian husbands had to produce evidence to justify a divorce. The law was repealed by the revolutionary government in 1979.

The new law replaced the Family Protection Court with a Special Civil Court based on Islamic laws. This law is anchored by the Islamic belief that to protect a family from instability and divorce an Islamic judge first tries to reconcile the divorcing couple. Mutual consenting couples who seek divorce can obtain it by simply registering their divorce before two witnesses at a notary-public office. Aghajanian (1986) observes that the ease of divorce under this new law can be abused in the case of "mutually consenting" couples. The Iranian family is patriarchal, and women may be forced to consent and all sorts of pressures may be used. Coercion may also be used to affect the wife's "consent" to forfeit her property (dowry). "This practice has such a long tradition in the Iranian society that there is a saying that a man may persist in annoying his wife so that she says: 'Get my *Mahr* [dowry] and free my life'" (Aghajanian, 1986:751).

The rate of divorce has been rising in Iran since 1981. Aghajanian (1986) attributes this rise to a number of factors that include the legal and social changes introduced in Iran since the revolution, increasing unemployment and unfavorable economic conditions, and the ongoing war with Iraq. Among the legal changes was the minimum age for females has been reduced from 18 to 13 (18 for males). In accordance with Shi'ite ideology, there was strong encouragement for early marriage and having children. The number of marriages increased from 184,000 in 1979 to 280,000 only one year later (Aghajanian, 1986). Aghajanian believes that the lack of preparation for family responsibilities of many of these young couples accounts for the rise in divorce. In addition, the increasing number of remarriages of war widows, some into polygynous marriages, may also account for this rise in divorce.

Family instability and resultant divorce is seen by Aghajanian (1986) particularly to affect urban middle-class families. These people have had to make major readjustments to the Islamic value system. Educated women have had to accommodate themselves to the new values and lifestyles of fundamentalist Islam. This is seen as a major source of conflict in urban middle class families and has contributed to marital tension and divorce. In general, Aghajanian (1986) sees a deterioration in the psychological and economic conditions of divorced women in Iran. Indeed, the history of the Iranian revolution has had serious negative consequences for women and their civil rights.

The aftermath of the Iranian revolution has seen a continuous policy in which women's rights won under the shah's monarchy have been abolished by the Shi'ite government. From the inception of the Khomeini government, an antifeminist campaign was conducted. In media campaigns just before and after the revolution, attacks were made on women who were active in the overthrow of the shah but who were against Shi'ite fundamentalism. They were accused of immorality, of weakening family ties, and of sexual misconduct. Pictures of women in bathing suits were used to support charges of prostitution against women working in the government bureaucracy. The goal was to belittle and discredit women leaders (Afkami, 1984).

In March 1979, more than 8,000 women marched in protest — under the slogan "In the dawn of freedom, there is no freedom" — of the Khomeini's fundamentalist policies (Morgan, 1984). Similar demonstrations occurred in other major Iranian cities. However, Shi'ite activists countered by attacking and stoning these marchers. More-repressive practices quickly followed. In 1981, women were banned from most sports events. In April 1983, veiling was made compulsory for women. In June 1981, 50 schoolgirls were shot and thousands were arrested for their "counterrevolutionary" or "anti-Islamic" activity. Morgan cites reports that by 1983 more than 20,000 women have been executed, including pregnant and elderly women, and young girls.

In December 1984, John Kifner (1984) the chief of the *New York Times* bureau in in Beirut, Lebanon, visited Iran. He gives us a rare glimpse of life under the Khomeini government. The following passage is indicative of some of these changes in everyday life:

> Islamic virtue reigns in every aspect of public life. Alcohol is strictly forbidden, of course, and every woman on the street wears either the traditional black chador, a cloth wrapping that must be grasped with hands and teeth to keep it in place, or the more practical hijab, a dark scarf pulled over the forehead, a baggy, dark smock and loose trousers. Indeed, the Government seems obsessed by sex. *Time, Newsweek* and other Western publications are regularly available, but a Government functionary goes through them first, carefully inking over with felt pen all but the face in any woman's picture, particularly in the cases of the starlets in the newsmaker sections. An Islamic skiing garment has been designed, at some cost in wind resistance, for women who want to try the snow at the ski resorts in the Elburz mountains—separate slopes, of course—and a solid fence is being constructed down the middle of the beach along the Caspian Sea for segregated bathing . . .
>
> . . . there are patrols of Islamic enforcers in white Nissan jeeps who can grab a woman off the streets if they do not like her garb—perhaps her scarf is set too far back, showing a fringe of hair—and carry her off to Evin prison, where she is treated as a prostitute.
>
> Of the untidy alliance that opposed the Shah—Westernized intellectuals, leftist students educated abroad, disaffected government officials and technocrats, traditionalist merchants of the powerful bazaar, slum dwellers of south Teheran and the militant fundamentalist mullahs—it is the clergy who have survived and triumphed. (Kifner, 1984:47, 48, 52)

Divorce in the United States

Paul H. Jacobsen (1959), in his much-cited work on American divorce patterns from 1860 to 1956, reports that at about the time of the Civil War (1860–1864), the divorce rate per 1,000 of existing marriages was 1.2. By the turn of the century (1900–1904), the rate had risen to 4.2, and 25 years later (1925–1929), the rate climbed to 7.6. Through the Depression years of the 1930s, the rate stayed relatively stable; but, near the end of World War II and the postwar 1940s, the rate hit a high of 13.7, which was not reached again until the 1970s. The high rates reached during the 1940s can be seen as an aftermath of a stressful period when many marriages deteriorated. The divorce rate declined steadily through the 1950s until the end of that decade, at which time the rate (9.4) reached approximately the same level as that for 1940. However, since the beginning of the 1960s, the divorce rate has dramatically risen (Carter and Glick, 1976). It more than doubled between 1960 and the mid-1970s. Carter and Glick (1976) predict that at least one-third of the first marriages of couples about 30 years of age would eventually end in divorce.

The annual divorce rate published by the National Center of Health Statistics (NCHS) indicates that the divorce rate has leveled off after showing a steep rise between 1966 and 1976 (Saluter, 1983). Paul C. Glick and Sung-Ling Lin (1986) corroborate this finding in their own anlaysis of vital statistics by NCHS, the Census Bureau's data and Current Population Surveys. Their study, in fact, indicates that the level during the early 1980s were slightly below the peaks reached in 1979 and 1981. Glick and Lin share the belief of Theodore Kemper (1983) that the leveling, and possible slight decline in the number, of divorces may reflect the trend toward lower remarriage rates, which would lower the pool of eligibles for redivorce. Also, the rising age at marriage and the presumed maturity of young adults in their choice of marriage partners and a growing concern or fear with the consequences of divorce are all seen as possible indicators for the stability of divorce rates, albeit high rates, for the immediate future. The following discussion examines why the divorce rate is so much higher today than it was in the past.

The rise in the divorce rate in the United States can best be seen by relating it to other family and social changes. Probably the most important change is the relation of the family to the economic process. In earlier times, the family had greater economic self-sufficiency. Both men and women were involved in the economic process. Men worked in an agricultural and hunting setting to produce food, clothing materials, and other economic necessities. Women's work was interdependent with that of the men. In addition to domestic household and child-rearing activities, women processed the food, made the clothing, and assisted the men whenever needed. In situations where domestic industry prevailed, the home served as a production unit, with all family members involved in labor participation. The result was an economic interdependence that often translated into an emotional interdependence as well.

With technological development, all this has changed. Domestic activities, once exclusively the province of women, were taken over by outside institutions. The manufacturing of clothing and many aspects of food processing and production moved outside the home to commercial establishments. The husband became a wage earner, and work became separated from domestic activities. The family became more a center of consumption than of production.

A second major change that has affected marital relationships has been the urbanization and increased geographical mobility of the American population. This has effectively diminished the controls and sanctions of the community and religious institutions over family members and their treatment of each other. As we observed, the family was once integrally tied to the community. The community exerted pressure and control over family members. The family's openness to community scrutiny assured the conformity of the family to community standards. Community influence was enhanced by religious institutions that, through church religious and secular activities for all members of the family, tied the family even more tightly to the community. The church served as a reinforcer of the parental-authority structure and imposed prescribed attitude and role patterns to govern the relationship between husband and wife and between parents and children. Collective religious ritual and family religious and secular devotions and rituals reinforced the ideology on the sanctity of marriage and the abhorrence of divorce. In essence, then, there may be some truth to the adage that "the family that prays together, stays together."

These changes interacted with the changes occurring in family ideology—that is, the new emphasis on the independence and the privatization of the nuclear family. New marital orientations and expectations developed that sought maximum and almost exclusive personal and emotional involvements within the nuclear family. The husband and the wife became dependent on each other for their emotional gratification and allowed few external sources of additional support—unlike the earlier period when marital solidarity and interdependence were tied to an interdependent familial economy. However, the new economic system does not foster such interdependence. The development of specialized services in an industrialized economy permits one to purchase many domestic goods and services, such as clothing, laundry services, prepared foods, and housing. The wife finds increased opportunities to enter the labor force and thus has obtained self-supporting economic options.

The increasing economic independence of women allows them greater opportunity to dissolve unsatisfactory marriages. Ross and Sawhill (1975) observed that as the wife's earnings increased, so did the likelihood that her marriage would end in divorce. One may interpret this finding to mean that occupational involvement takes too much time away from a woman's domestic and marital life or that the woman sought employment in preparation for divorce. A more likely and plausible explanation, however, is that financial security gives her the options to pursue more satisfactory possibilities than remaining in an unhappy marriage. We would argue, then, that part of the explanation for the lower divorce rates of several decades ago was that the great majority of women were financially dependent on their husbands and thus did not have the financial independence to leave them. Their increased involvement in the labor force has led to the removal of this economic barrier to divorce.

Taken together, all the above-mentioned factors lead to a highly unstable situation. Unrealistic or hard-to-satisfy expectations are placed on the marital relationship. Marriage is expected to lead to the exclusive attainment and fulfillment of an individual's affectional, personal, and communal needs. When it proves incapable of meeting those needs, marital unhappiness and often divorce occur. The increased independence of men and women combined with the lessened stigma attached to divorce and the possibilities of remarriage help account for the rise in the divorce rate. In sum, the rising divorce rate is an indication that, for an increasing number of people, divorce with all its future unknown uncertainties is a preferable option to continuing in a marriage relationship that has proved debilitating and unsatisfactory.

We now make a more-detailed examination of the implications of marital, family, and social changes on American divorce and remarriage structures and processes. We begin by looking at how these changes are reflected in American divorce laws. Our attention centers on an analysis of no-fault divorce laws and the adjudication of child custody. An examination of the single-parent household and the effects of divorce on children follows. We conclude with a discussion of remarriage.

Legal Aspects of American Divorce: No-Fault

Weitzman and Dixon (1980), in an excellent analysis of the implications of no-fault divorce, emphasize that the laws governing divorce reflect the society's definition of marriage, provide the parameters for appropriate marriage behavior, and point out the reciprocal rights and obligations of marriage partners. Further, divorce laws are also seen to define the continued obligations that the formally married couple have to each other after divorce: "One can generally examine the way a society defines marriage by examining its provisions for divorce, for it is at the point of divorce that a society has the opportunity to reward the marital behavior it approves of, and to punish spouses who have violated its norms" (Weitzman and Dixon, 1980:355). Given this viewpoint, the authors assert that a study of changing divorce laws will reflect social changes in family patterns. For this reason, they chose to examine no-fault divorce laws to demonstrate how "this new legislation seeks to alter the definition of marriage, the relationship between husbands and wives, and the economic and social obligations of former spouses to each other and to their children after divorce" (1980:354).

Prior to no-fault divorce in America, divorce laws followed Anglo-American legal tradition. Divorce was cast in the traditional common-law model of an adversary procedure. The plaintiff's success depended on proving defendant's fault. Both parties were assumed to be antagonists and were expected to be at odds and were expected to bring forth all the relevant facts to be assessed by the judge in reaching his or her verdict. No-fault divorce laws are based on a new concept of marital dissolution. The first such law in the United States, the Family Law Act, was passed in 1970 by the California legislature. The suggested procedure begins with a neutral petition—"In re the marriage of John and Jane Doe" rather than "Doe vs. Doe"— requesting the family court to inquire into the continuance of the marriage.

The California law abolished completely any requirement of fault as the basis to dissolve the marriage. One spouse is not required to bring charges against the other nor is evidence needed of misconduct. Under traditional divorce laws, the division of property and the allocation of alimony payments are determined under the concept of fault. Property and support are given to the judged "innocent party" as a reward extracted from the "guilty party" as punishment. The no-fault law gives legal recognition to "marital breakdown" as a sufficient justification for divorce. Indeed, the Californian legislation eliminated the term *divorce* replacing it with the phrase, "dissolution of marriage." The dissolution is granted on the basis of "irreconcilable differences" that have caused the irremediable breakdown of the marriage. Under the no-fault law, property is substantially divided equally, and alimony is based on the duration of the marriage, the needs of each party, and their respective earning ability.

By 1977 provisions for no-fault divorce existed in all but three states. Its popularity reflects the increased recognition that the cause for the marital dissolution is usually a result of a number of factors and is shared by both partners. Carter and Glick (1976) point out the positive aspects of no-fault divorce laws:

> No-fault divorce procedures avoid exploring and assessing blame and concentrate on dissolving the marriage and tidying up the inevitable problems—responsibility for the care of the children (there still are children involved in the majority of divorce cases despite the decline in the birth rate), financial support of children, division of jointly owned property, and spousal support (alimony) if this seems indicated. The moment it is established that the question of blame is irrelevant to settlement of the case, some of the bitterness (but by no means all of it) goes out of the divorce proceedings. (Carter and Glick, 1976:458)

Weitzman and Dixon argue that no-fault divorce reflects changes in the traditional view of legal marriage. By eliminating the fault-based grounds for divorce and the adversary process, the new law recognizes the more contemporary view that frequently both parties are responsible for the breakdown of the marriage. Further, the law recognizes that the divorce procedure often aggravated the situation by forcing the potentially amicable individuals to become antagonists.

No-fault divorce laws advocate that the financial aspects of marital dissolution are to be based on equity, equality, and economic need rather than on fault- or gender-based role assignments. Alimony is also to be based on the respective spouses economic circumstances and on the principle of social equality, not on the basis of guilt or innocence. No longer can alimony be awarded to the "injured party," regardless of that person's financial needs. The new law seeks to reflect the changing circumstances of women and their increased participation in the labor force. By so doing, it encourages women to become self-supporting and removes the expectation that husbands have to continue support of wives throughout their lives. Although it considers custodial care for children, the thrust of the law is on financial criteria. California judges are directed to consider the following in setting alimony: "the circumstances of the respective parties, including the duration of the marriage, and the ability of the supported spouse to engage in gainful employment without interfering with the interests of the children of the parties in the custody of each spouse" (California Civil Code 4801, cited in Weitzman and Dixon, 1980:363).

Weitzman and Dixon (1980) see the overall impact of no-fault legislation as its redefinition of the traditional marital responsibilities of men and women by instituting a new norm of equality between the sexes. No longer are husbands to be designated as the head of the household and solely responsible for support, nor are wives alone obligated to domestic household activities and child-rearing. Gender-neutral obligations, which fall equally on husband and wife, are institutionalized. These changes are reflected in the new considerations for alimony allocation. In addition, the division of property is to be done on an equal basis. Finally, child-support expectations and the standards for child custody reflect the new equality criteria of no-fault divorce legislation. Both father and mother are equally responsible for financial support of their children after divorce. Mothers are no longer automatically given custody of the child; rather, a sex-neutral standard instructs judges to award custody in the "best interests of the child."

In conclusion, Weitzman and Dixon (1980), while praising the changes in divorce legislation, raise one importance caveat. They see the law as reflecting idealized gains for women in social, occupation, and economic areas, gains toward equality that may, in fact, not reflect women's actual conditions and circumstances. This can have extremely detrimental effects on women's ability for self-sufficiency after divorce:

> Thus, while the aims of the no-fault laws, i.e., equality and sex-neutrality are laudable, the laws may be instituting equality in a society in which women are not fully prepared (and/or permitted) to assume equal responsibility for their own and their children's support after divorce. Public policy then becomes a choice between temporary protection and safeguards for the transitional woman (and for the older housewife in the traditional generation) to minimize the hardships incurred by the new expectations, versus current enforcement of the new equality, with the hope of speeding the transition, despite the hardships this may cause for current divorces. (Weitzman and Dixon, 1980:365)

No-Fault Divorce: Unexpected Consequences

By 1985, the new no-fault divorce laws had been adopted in some form by every state except Illinois and South Dakota. The new laws were designed to reduce accusation, acrimony, and manufactured marital misconduct as the necessary grounds for divorce. They sought to base monetary awards on need and ability to pay rather than treating them as rewards on punishments for alleged sins. They were intended to correct an outmoded legal code that was seen as degrading and humiliating to all parties involved in the divorce process and often unfair in the outcome. However, an unintended consequence is that they may help undermine the very conceptualization of marriage, and husbands' and wives' roles in marriage. This is the provocative view Lenore J. Weitzman (1985), one of this country's leading divorce researchers, has reached in her provocative book, *The Divorce Revolution*.

Weitzman (1985)—after studying the results of these laws and focusing her attention mostly on California, which initiated the first no-fault, no-consent statute 15 years earlier—finds "unexpected," "unfortunate," and "unintended" social and economic consequences for women and children in America. Her research is based largely on an analysis of 2,500 California court cases, supplemented by interviews of hundreds of recently divorced men and women as well as lawyers and judges in Los Angeles and San Francisco.

Weitzman's major finding is that, under no-fault divorce, divorced women and their children are becoming a new underclass, suffering an average decline of 73 percent in their standard of living in the year after the divorce. Men, on the other hand, experience an average increase of 42 percent in the same period. According to Weitzman, if a man makes $1,000 a month, a judge will usually award him $700 and give $300 to the ex-wife and two children. She found that older women, women with young children, and former wives of middle-class professionals experienced the most deprivation.

Divorced women are often impoverished by no-fault because courts, in dividing property, interpret "equality" at divorce by disregarding the economic inequalities created during marriage. Further, the equal division of property often forces women to sell their homes to divide what usually constitutes the couple's only real property. Less tangible, and often more valuable, the husband's property and assets such as education, professional licenses, career advancements, pensions, and health insurances are often not taken into account in court decisions. As a consequence, rather than alleviating the injustice, no-fault exacerbates it.

Divorce settlements also assume self-sufficiency for both husband and wife as soon as possible (usually in about 2 years). While this is a laudable goal, Weitzman points out that as our society is currently structured, it is naive, to say the least, that women who may have been out of work for many years devoting full attention to child rearing can become self-sufficient that quickly. The problem is compounded by a child-support system that is often inadequate, unpaid, and uncollectable. Weitzman reports that 60 to 80 percent of all fathers, regardless of social class, do not comply with court orders. Adding to the problems is that no-fault divorce continues to follow the old-law divorce patterns with 90 percent of custodial parents being women. But some gender-neutral provisions now force women to fight for what used to be their custodial right. The result of these provisions is that to win custodial rights, women often are forced to bargain away support.

Weitzman argues that no-fault divorce laws reflect the larger cultural themes of individualism, personal fulfillment, and self-sufficiency. These new norms imply that neither spouse should invest too much in marriage or place marriage above self-interest. She alludes to Lawrence Stone's term *affective individualism,* which historically gave rise to the emotional closeness between nuclear-family members as well as to a greater appreciation for the individuality of each member. At the same time, this norm helped develop and strengthen the husband–wife bond at the expense of extended-kinship contacts and involvements. Now, the strength of the husband–wife unit, the conjugal family, is declining as values of "pure" individualism are emerging. The rise in divorce rates and the new no-fault divorce laws reflect this evolution of individualism and the importance of personal primacy.

This contemporary version of individualistic norms implies a new view of marriage that sees marriage as a means of serving individual needs. It replaces the traditional dictum that individuals should submerge their personal desires whenever they conflict with the "good of the family." Norms of reciprocity and mutual dependency are challenged: "If men are no longer solely responsible for support, and if women are no longer responsible for homemaking and child care, then neither sex can count as much on the other for support or services" (Weitzman, 1985:375). The implications of Weitzman's important study are clear. For women who wish to devote themselves to home-making and child rearing, they may be pursuing a perilous and foolhardy course. They may find themselves impoverished and abandoned by a society that no longer shares their priorities or values their skills. Indeed, this is the implication of the new divorce laws.

> The new divorce laws alter the traditional legal view of marriage as a partnership by rewarding individual achievement rather than investment in the family partnership. Instead of the traditional vision of a common financial future within marriage, the no-fault and no-consent standards for divorce, and the new rules for alimony, property, custody, and child support, all convey a new vision of independence for husbands and wives in marriage. In addition, the new laws confer economic advantage on spouses who invest in themselves at the expense of the marital partnership. (Weitzman, 1985:374)

The far-reaching consequence of the new divorce laws is that marriage is likely to become increasingly less central to the lives of individual men and women. Weitzman believes that traditional family law gave privileged status to marriage. It placed protections and restrictions on its inception and dissolution. These laws reinforced the importance of marriage, and encouraged husbands and wives to invest in and to make marriage the center of their lives. In contrast, the new laws are based on belief in absolute individualism and reflect the values of the "Me Decade." They discourage the conceptualization of marriage as a shared partnership investment and encourage both husbands and wives to pursue individual self-fulfillment. The result, in Weitzman's view is that "[a]s more men and women follow the apparent mandate of the new laws, it seems reasonable to predict that marriage itself will lose further ground" (1985:376).

Legal Aspects of American Divorce: Child Custody

Another legal change regarding divorce involves decisions of which parent should be given custody of children. Robert S. Weiss (1979b) reports that mothers are currently awarded legal custody of children in about 90 percent of American divorce cases. However, in recent years there has been an increased recognition of fathers' rights regarding custody. It reflects a recognition of the changing role of American fathers. This change has been popularized in the 1980 Oscar-winning motion picture, *Kramer vs. Kramer*. In addition, courts are now beginning to view joint custody as another legal option. To understand the basis for custody adjudication decisions, a brief review of the historical changes in parental roles and their relationship to the judicial principle of "best interest" is necessary.

Weiss points out that courts have historically been governed by the "best interests" principle in awarding custody of children. Judges are supposed to treat as irrelevant the issue of which parent was at "fault" in the divorce; rather, their sole concern is to ascertain which parent would best serve to maximize the children's future well-being and welfare. Prior to the mid-nineteenth century, fathers were judged as the parent who could best take care of and educate the child. Women were thought to be too dependent on men, whether it was their fathers, husbands, or related kin. Since they too needed the protection of men, the courts judged them as not being the parent best able to provide for the children.

Beginning in the mid-nineteenth century, there was a change in judicial decisions in custody awards, which became almost standard by the end of the century. Mothers came to be seen as better able to serve the child's "best interests." This change reflected the changing popular belief about the aims of the family and the raising of children. With increased industrialization, fathers withdrew from taking an active role in domestic matters, including child care, and they devoted more of their attention to earning a living outside the home. This movement away from domestic-oriented economic involvements to commerce and factories also affected children. They were gradually removed from the work force and were no longer economic assets. The family household began to be viewed in Christopher Lasch's eloquence as a "haven in a heartless world" (1977a). The home was designed to protect the child from the incursions of a changing and threatening outside world. The family was viewed as a place where children should be nurtured and protected, and, increasingly, it was the mother who was considered the preferred parent to do this.

In the twentieth century, this pattern continued. It reached its culmination in the post–World War II period of the 1950s and 1960s. The affluence and materialism of this era, embodied in the development of middle-class suburbia, heightened the division between husband-father and wife-mother. The feminine mystique and the motherhood myth dominated—only the mother was deemed as the appropriate parent and was thus given almost complete responsibility for child rearing. The total responsibility for child care carries over to divorce. The legal assumption regarding the mother's natural superiority in parenting is reflected in custodial dispositions. As mentioned earlier, women are awarded custody in over 90 percent of divorce cases.

Leonore Weitzman (1977) has made some interesting observations on the implications of courts' automatically granting custody to the mother. Although it is true that most divorcing women want custody of their children, this practice also tends to reinforce the women's social role as housewife and mother. It also frequently reinforces women's dependency on their husbands for support. Further, this judicial preference may coerce women to accept custody even if they do not wish to do so. They may bow to social pressures and be subject to feelings of deviance and guilt.

Fathers are also subjected to discrimination by this practice. They are often legally advised of the futility of contesting custody, particularly in the case of young children. The burden of proof is on them, either to document the unfitness of the mother or to show that they could do a qualitatively better job of parenting. In those cases where the father could be the better parent, both his interests and the "best interests" of the child are denied.

In recent years, the increased recognition of the changing role of father has begun to influence the judicial decision-making process of custodial award. In addition, inherent contradictions in the principle of "best interests" has also led to a reevaluation of the practice of automatically giving mothers custody of the children. Let us look at each of these changes in turn.

With the end of the period of prosperity of the 1950s and 1960s, there was a growing disenchantment with family-role segregation, which extended from the end of the 1960s on through the 1970s. The feminist movement began to articulate fully women's dissatisfaction with their confinement to the home and exclusive parenthood. In addition, fathers were re-evaluating their role involvements. An increasing number of them began to express doubts about lives characterized by an almost total involvement in occupational careers and almost complete withdrawal from family matters, including the raising of children. Kelin E. Gersick (1979) expresses these changes this way:

> In recent years . . . the role of the American father has been enjoying a resurgence. Several factors may be involved: a decrease in the average man's working hours and resulting increase in leisure time; the woman's dissatisfaction with her role limitations and movement toward greater economic and social flexibility; and the spreading disenchantment with material acquisition as the exclusive measure of the good life, along with the espousal of close relationships as a principal measure of happiness. Whatever the reasons, there appears to be a recent upswing in father's involvement in their families. (Gersick, 1979:307)

Additional factors particularly apparent as we entered the 1980s included the change in the economic fortunes of Americans inflation and recession became a way of life. This has increased the economic necessity for women to work. The transition of women into the labor force has been made smoother as a result of the women's movement, which has persuaded most men and women of the legitimacy of women's work. This has led to the growth of dual-income families with more and more households composed of working parents who are also sharing domestic involvements and child care. These changes have played a contributory role in the re-assessment by judicial court systems on the adjudication of custody of children when parents separate.

Robert S. Weiss (1979a) observes that criticism of the legal presumption in favor of the mother began to appear in the 1960s and by the early 1970s some state statutes that had required mothers be preferred had been repealed. In 1973 the bellwether state of California, repealed such a statute and replaced it with the "best interests" principle. The growing sensitivity to sexual discrimination has also played a contributing role in these changes. One way that this has been shown is in the increased debunking of the belief in the natural superiority of women in parenting. It is now argued in several states that a presumption in favor of the mother constitutes unfair discrimination owing to sex and deprives the father of his right to equal protection by the law (Weiss, 1979a:327). Weiss mentions a second element contributing to this change, which ties in with the arguments against job discrimination because of gender. He says that "defenders of fathers rights pointed out that if men are to have no advantage over women in the competition for jobs, and if most single mothers can be expected to work, then women should not be seen as having more right to the children: 'A man can hire a babysitter as well as a woman'" (Weiss, 1979a:327).

An additional issue, which we wish to draw to the reader's attention, is the way the idea of children's rights is tied to the "best interests" principle. Weiss observes that many key states have adopted the custody statute proposed by the American Bar Association that "direct[s] judges to consider the wishes of the child's parents and of the child, the relationship of the child and the parents, the child's adjustment to home, school, and community, and the mental and physical health of all involved" (1979b:330). Further, in some states judges are required to take into consideration the economic potential of each parent, their cultural background, and a catchall other-relevant-factors clause. Increasingly, judges have turned to investigations by members of the helping professions, including social workers, probation officers, and psychiatrists, to help them in their decision-making on which parent is to be awarded custody so that the best interests of the child can be maximized.

With this concern over children's rights, the courts are focusing attention on the pros and cons of whether children should be consulted during the judicial process. Weiss states that although there are obvious reasons why the child should be consulted, there are also pitfalls including the child's immaturity. Weiss questions whether some children might make decisions on the basis of one parent's leniency regarding homework, chores, and discipline. Further, after divorce, the parent not chosen may become spiteful and voice resentment, which could endanger his or her future relationship with the child.

One final issue concerns Weiss: the inherent contradiction of awarding custody to one parent and allowing visitation rights to the other. The problem is to what extent does the visitation parent have custody rights when the child is in that parent's care. Two solutions have been offered. One would place visitation rights solely at the option of the custodial parent. By so doing, it would increase that parent's authority and would strengthen his or her dealing with the other parent, who may be viewed as a disruptive or dangerous influence on the child. Weiss uses recent research to demonstrate that children desire free access to the noncustodial parent and rarely is it disruptive to their development.

The second solution, more to Weiss's liking, requires joint custody with both parents having custodial rights and responsibilities. Children would be under the custodial care of the parent with whom they were living at a given time. Weiss indicates that preliminary studies, which are somewhat impressionistic, indicate that such a solution may work. However, he cautions that this favorable outcome may be restricted to situations where both parents are in agreement and when the parting was amicable. More evidence is required before an adequate assessment can be made.

In summary, as Weiss (1979b) points out, the full implications for children and their parents of these different procedures and approaches are still not known. The courts, in their deliberations on custody and visitation, are well advised to keep abreast of the empirical evidence, which seeks to determine the consequences of various arrangements after parents separate and divorce.

The Effects of Divorce on Children

"'What will happen to me if anything goes wrong, if Mommy dies or Daddy dies, if Daddy leaves Mommy or Mommy leaves Daddy?'" (Mead, 1970a:113). This question has particular meaning to American children since our society stresses the impor-

Deborah Kahn/Stock, Boston

A single father reading a newspaper with his daughter and son in his daughter's bedroom.

tance of parents in raising children. Father's kin or mother's kin, including the respective grandparents, have no legal responsibility for children as long as the parents are alive. Further, cultural norms emphasize parental independence and freedom from extended-family involvements in child rearing. In contrast, the larger extended family, or clan, which still exists in many societies, has formally defined rights, duties, and obligations over each member of the family grouping, including children. For such children, the question of death, divorce, or separation of their own parents is less problematic than in the American situation. Extensive kinship ties provide sufficient sources of intergenerational involvement so that marital disruption or dissolution has relatively minimal impact on children's psychological well-being. In the contemporary United States, these wider kinship networks are lacking at a time when many families are dissolving because of divorce. This fact is complicated by the lack of sufficient preparation or the development of alternatives for the child's psychological dependence on his or her parents. Margaret Mead addresses herself to this anomaly:

> We have constructed a family system which depends upon fidelity, lifelong monog-
> amy, and the survival of both parents. But we have never made adequate social
> provision for the security and identity of the children if that marriage is broken, as it
> so often was in the past by death or desertion, and as it so often is in the present by
> death or divorce. We have . . . saddled ourselves with a system that won't work.
> (Mead, 1970a:115)

Mary Jo Bane (1979) observes that since 1900, the proportion of children affected
by marital disruption has been between 25 and 30 percent of the total population of
children under the age of 18. There has been a change, however, in the dominant
cause of the disruption. At the turn of the century, the ratio of disruption by death
was much higher than disruption by divorce and long-term separation. By 1980, the
ratio was reversed; divorce is now affecting more children, particularly at an earlier
age, than is the death of a parent. The number of children involved in divorces has
risen sharply since the 1950s. In 1955, 348,000 children under 18 years of age were
involved in divorce cases (National Center for Health Statistics, 1977, 1978). The
figure almost doubled by 1965 to 630,000. In 1972, for the first time, more than 1
million children were annually affected by divorce. This figure has remained relatively stable through the 1970s. Bane (1979) estimates that about 30 percent of the
current generation of children will witness the breakup of their parents' marriage.
There are currently 12 million children under the age of 18 whose parents are
divorced.

Bane goes on to discuss the economic effects of marital disruption. She projects
that two-fifths of children born in the 1980s are likely to experience parental divorce.
These children will be living in a single-parent household for an average of 5 years.
During these years, financial resources will be limited. This results from the following
causes: the greater prevalence of divorce among low-income families; irregular and
low levels of alimony, child support, and public assistance; fewer adult wage earners
in the family; fewer opportunities for females heading the household to find employment; and the lower wages paid women as compared to men (Bane, 1979:283).

Bane is concerned with the effect of family poverty on the physical well-being of
the children of divorced parents. She also believes that economic deprivation could
result in psychological stress, tension, and frustration. She calls for the development
of governmental programs, such as a guaranteed maintenance allowance, to improve
the situation for separated, divorced, and widowed mothers who share the brunt of
the responsibility in raising children. Bane observes that in many European countries
programs exist to meet the needs of single-parent families. Sweden is the cited
example. It provides all families with children with housing and child allowances.
Widows receive pensions. Divorced and separated women receive a major part of
their income in the form of guaranteed maintenance allowance regardless of the
husband's ability or willingness to pay for support or alimony. It is the government's
responsibility to recover the allowance from the husband. Bane provides the following statement on why such an allowance policy is needed in the United States:

> A guaranteed maintenance allowance, or something like it, could dramatically
> improve the situation of single-parent families in the United States. It would take
> from women the burden of collecting alimony and child support and ensure that
> payments were steady and adequate. It would take most single-parent families off
> welfare, and if designed correctly would provide strong incentive to work. (Bane,
> 1977:285)

The recitation of statistics and the delineation of the economic difficulties accompanying divorce cannot reveal the potentially negative effects on children's psychological well-being. For the parents involved, divorce often produces anger and a sense
of failure. For children it raises issues of conflicting loyalties and it necessitates their

readjustment from a two-parent family to a single-parent household. The popular impression is that divorce contributes to the development of children's psychological disorganization and has other ill effects. Recent evidence, however, indicates that this view is an oversimplification of what actually occurs. It is worth examining some of the research on this issue.

Early research by the criminologists Sheldon and Eleanor Glueck (1951) and others seems to support the belief that children from broken homes are more likely than others to be psychologically disturbed, low achievers, and delinquents. However, critical analyses of these studies by Lawrence Rosen (1970) and Karen Wilkinson (1974) disprove these conclusions. Separately, these reviewers argue that the earlier studies lacked adequate controls and asked wrong and biased questions. Rosen's analysis of 11 of these studies demonstrates that there is no significant relationship between broken homes and juvenile delinquency. Wilkinson reaches a similar conclusion: ideological biases distort this relationship.

Studies by Lee G. Burchinal (1964) and Judson T. Landis (1962) provide evidence that unhappy, unbroken homes may have more detrimental effects on children than do broken homes. Burchinal's findings reveal either few differences or that the children from broken homes have better personality development and demonstrate less stress and deviancy than children living with parents.

His findings are based on a comparison of seventh and eighth graders in Cedar Rapids, Iowa, who were grouped into five categories: unbroken families, those living only with their mothers, and those from three types of reconstituted families — mothers and stepfathers, both parents remarried, fathers and stepmothers. Burchinal concludes that his findings "require the revision of widely held beliefs about the detrimental effects of divorce upon children" (1964:50).

In an earlier study, Landis (1960) studied 295 university students whose parents divorced when they were children. He concludes that divorce of parents affects children in various ways, depending on such factors as the age of the children at the time of divorce and the children's evaluations of their parents' marriage and their own feelings of security. Those who viewed their homes as happy prior to the divorce experienced more trauma than those who perceived the home as being unhappy and characterized by parental conflict. This latter group often felt relief that their parents' troubled relationship ended.

In a systematic review of the literature, Cynthia Longfellow (1979) concluded that the emotional impact of divorce on children relates to the family relationship, the single mother's mental state, and the child's own viewpoint. In support of Landis's and Burchinal's studies, Longfellow reports that a body of research finds that a child who experiences parents' marital discord is likely to face great psychiatric risk. The child's stress may, in fact, be reduced if the parents separate or divorce. However, if the conflict persists after the marriage is dissolved, through each parent demanding exclusive loyalty from the child or by conflict over other issues, the child may experience adjustment problems.

Longfellow also examined the extensive research that has been accumulating on the effect of divorce on different age categories of children. She reports that young children are more adversely affected and experience greater stress than older children. Preschoolers are found to be cognitively less able to cope with divorce. This inability is also associated with the fact that single-parent mothers with young children are the most vulnerable to economic instability and are among the most highly stressed group of women:

> Age, then, appears to be an important mediator of the effects of divorce on children. In two contexts, it is the younger child who is more adversely affected: preschoolers create a greater psychological strain on their divorced parents and at the same time seem cognitively less able to cope with the divorce. . . . A family with

young children is also often at the point in its life cycle when job and financial pressures are the greatest. Therefore, we might expect that a divorce at this time simply overtaxes the family, placing both mothers and children at greater psychiatric risk. (Longfellow, 1979:305)

Longfellow ends her review by briefly mentioning some of the factors that may help mitigate the impact of divorce on children. These include the beneficial effects of a good parent–child relationship, a supportive network of friends and relatives, and an ex-husband who continues to be supportive toward his family. Her concluding remarks lead us to our next area of examination, the single-parent household.

Single Parenthood

Single parenthood is becoming more common in our society. Paul C. Glick and Arthur J. Norton (1979), in their review of governmental statistics, report that the proportion of children living with one parent has more than doubled from 1960 to 1978. By 1978, a little more than 5.5 million American families with children were headed by a single adult. This represents 19 percent of the 30 million families with children in the United States. Five years later, in 1983, there were almost 6 million children living with divorced parents in single-parent households. Most of these children lived with divorced mothers (U.S. Bureau of the Census, 1984a: Table D).

The total number of children living with one parent (as a result of death, divorce, separation, or parent never marrying) has increased sharply during the last 15 years. In 1970, 7.4 million children under the age of 18 lived with a single parent. This was 11 percent of all children in that age group. By 1983, the number had risen to 13.7 million, an 85 percent increase. This comprises 22 percent of the population of children (Glick, 1984b). Paul C. Glick (1984a) predicts that 59 percent of all children born in the early 1980s will spend at least one year of their childhood in a single-parent household.

Alvin L. Schorr and Phyllis Moen (1980), citing early 1970s statistics, observe that the popular image of the conventional family — husband, wife, and children — is, in fact, a minority family form in the United States. Single parenthood, couples without children, and reconstituted families (remarrieds with and without children) represent 55 percent of American families; the conventional form accounts for only 45 percent of American families.

Mary Jo Bane (1979) estimates that nearly 30 percent of the children born around 1970 will experience parental divorce by the time they are 18. An additional 15 to 20 percent may live in a one-parent household because of death, long-term separation, or birth to an unmarried mother. Together, then, 45 to 50 percent of the children born around 1970 will live for a period of time with a single parent. Further, as Robert S. Weiss notes, "among all children who now live with either their mothers or their fathers alone, 93 percent live with their mothers" (1979a). As pointed out earlier, mothers currently become the custodians of children in over 90 percent of all American divorces.

Variations in the single-parent experience depend on the circumstances that resulted in the single parent raising children alone. Payton (1982), citing governmental statistics, states that 71 percent of single-parent households are created by separation (27 percent) and divorce (44 percent). The remaining 29 percent result from death (13 percent) and unwed parents (16 percent). Between 1960 and 1983, the number of children living with a separated parent increased by 30 percent, those living with a divorced parent tripled, and the number living with a parent who never married increased by more than five times (Glick, 1984b). Collectively, these demographic realities dictate that the main part of our discussion focus on legally separated and divorced mothers. First, however, we examine variations in the single-parent circumstance. Also, we examine teenage mothers and conclude with an analysis of the growing phenomena of single-parent households headed by fathers.

Single-parent families are more likely to be found among the lower-income, lower-education, and lower-occupational-status population. One-half of all children in single-parent families have a parent with less than a high-school education, compared to only one-fourth of those in two-parent households. Furthermore, there were three times the proportion of black children living with a single parent in 1981 than there were white children; 46 percent of all black children were in single-parent situations, compared with only 15 percent of the white children (Glick, 1984a).

One common characteristic shared by all female-headed single-parent families is poverty. The mother, in the vast majority of cases, must provide for the child's care as well as be the principal, and—in the case of no employable older children—the only, wage earner in the family. Often this proves an impossible task, with an appreciable number of such families falling into poverty. Single-parent families have lower average income than do two-parent families. In 1983, the median income of woman-headed households ($11,790) was only 43 percent of the median income of two-parent households ($27,290) (U.S. Bureau of the Census, 1984b). The differential is even greater when both wife and husband work in two-parent households. Aggravating the situation, female-headed households with no husband present have 29 percent more children under the age of 18 years than do married-couple families (U.S. Bureau of the Census, 1984a). Ross and Sawhill, in their study of the problems of female-headed households, provide the following explanation of the situation:

> The inadequate incomes of most female-headed families stem from the loss of a male earner, the mother's continuing responsibility for the care of young children, and the inability of most women to earn enough to support a family. However, the loss of a male earner within the household need not mean the loss of all of the father's income. Alimony and child-support payments as well as more informal gifts of money and other items help to maintain women and children living on their own. But indications are that the flow of those private transfers is somewhat smaller than is commonly believed. They are certainly inadequate to the task of keeping many women and children out of poverty. (Ross and Sawhill, 1975:175)

Variations in the Single-Parent Experience: A Brief Sketch

Separated or divorced single parents, the widow or widower now raising children alone, and the unwed mother or father will have different attitudes and experiences toward single parenthood. Weiss (1979a) finds many divorced and separated parents have feelings of wariness and self-doubt. Another result of an unhappy marriage is that the divorced often have disparaging, critical, and untrustworthy images of each other. In contrast, single parenthood brought about by death often results in an idealization of the marital relationship and reinterprets it, emphasizing only the happier moments. The widow or widower also dispays greater commitment to the former marriage; he or she begins to date later and does not contemplate new attachments as early as divorced parents.

Weiss contrasts divorced parents, widows, and widowers in terms of their involvement with their children and the larger community. Widows or widowers often turn to their children for solace and comfort. The divorced parent finds it difficult to talk about his or her marriage with the children; their marital difficulties are seen as a private matter. The larger community is more sympathetic to widows and widowers; the divorced are often stigmatized. Weiss also makes the following distinction between the separated and divorced from widows and widowers in regard to the role of the other parent in their lives:

There are many ways in which a separated parent's relationship with the other parent may develop, yet almost always that relationship has aspects of discomfort. The other parent almost always continues to have rights and responsibilities to the children that the separated parent must acknowledge. The other parent can be regularly intrusive, telephoning or appearing at unexpected times. Furthermore, the children of separated and divorced parents are likely to be loyal to both their antagonistic parents and to search for some method by which they can preserve their identifications with both parents despite the parents' criticisms of each other. Insofar as the children attempt to defend their relationships with the absent parent, they may enter into conflict with the parent with whom they live. (Weiss, 1979a:9)

The role of kin and the financial situation can also vary between these two groups. For the widow and widower as well as the separated or divorced, kinship bonds can be of immeasurable importance. A supportive atmosphere is almost automatic for the widows and widowers. However, it can be somewhat problematic with the divorced. This depends on the circumstances surrounding the marital breakdown. Parents and other relatives of the single parent as well as the deceased spouse's family may and often do provide various forms of aid. With the separated and divorced, the spouse's family may not be as willing to help, particularly when they feel that their son or daughter was not at fault. Further, continuation of aid may be longer for the living spouse, in that family members may feel greater obligations.

Unwed single parents' circumstances differ from the others. Although it is beyond the scope of this discussion to deal with this matter in great detail, a few points will be mentioned. Weiss (1979a) observes that for the majority, although the pregnancy is often unwanted, the child is wanted. Weiss distinguishes between the younger and older unwed mother. Older women tend to be more realistic and more self-reliant than younger women. The younger mother's adjustment is often associated with her parents' willingness to have the child raised in their home, their assistance in child care, and their financial help.

The children of never-married mothers are particularly vulnerable to abuse and neglect. In contrast to the widowed mother—who can blame fate, medicine, or God for her circumstances—and to the separated or divorced—who can blame their failings on their spouse—the unwed mother can only blame herself or her child (Weiss, 1979a). Based on data gathered from a national sample conducted by Nicholas Zill, Weiss (1979a) states that 30 percent of never-married mothers say that, if they had to do it again, they would not have children. This compares to the 20 percent of separated mothers, 15 percent of divorced mothers, and 10 percent of widowed mothers. More disturbingly, the never-married group are more likely to abuse their children physically. The study found that 27 percent of never-married mothers are most likely to admit that at some point in their relationship with their children they lost control and may have hurt them. The figure for the separated or divorced is 15 percent and for widowed mothers it is 5 percent.

Female-Headed Single-Parent Families

The female-headed single-parent family can be studied best within the larger context of the "proper" roles of the husband-father and wife-mother and the importance of the intact, or unbroken, family. Social scientists (see Brandwein, Brown, and Fox, 1974, and Schorr and Moen, 1980) have pointed out that our society is dominated by the assumption that families headed by a single parent, particularly when that parent is a woman, are deviant and pathological. Such families are characterized as broken, disorganized, or disintegrated, rather than being recognized as a viable alternative family form. Rather than being seen as a solution to circumstances and examined in terms of their strengths, they are viewed negatively with emphasis on their alleged weaknesses and problems.

Similar to the simplifications and distortions of poverty-level families taken by culture-of-poverty advocates, depicting the single-parent family in these terms denies the realities of this family form and misrepresents it. This has led to biased governmental, employment, and social policies that have proved detrimental to single-parent families. Further, many separated and divorced women reacting to their stigmatized status have often incorporated the negative images into their own self-images. This can prove particularly disabling in their attempts to readjust their lives after separation and divorce. Thus taken together, a self-fulfilling prophecy can come into effect and thus limit the capabilities of the single-parent family. Let us see how this operates in more detail.

Our society has believed that men should be primarily involved in outside-the-home matters. Through such activities they dominate the economic resources of the family and are legitimated as the head and brains of the family. This situation forces women to be dependent on husbands, particularly when they are parents and society dictates that their appropriate roles are housewives and mothers. This dependency situation becomes even more problematic and acute if a woman is granted custody of the children after divorce. Far too often she does not have access to resources comparable to her husband's. Janet A. Kohen, Carol A. Brown, and Roslyn Feldberg (1979) make the following observations on this situation:

> If a couple divorces, the woman loses most of her right to the man's resources, but she also loses her personal dependence and obligations of service. She now stands in direct relationship to society as the head of her family. But male-dominated society neither recognizes a divorced woman's right to head a family nor makes available to her, as a woman, the necessary resources. The divorced mother has exchanged direct dependence on one man for general dependence on a male-dominated society. Employers, welfare officials, lawyers, judges, politicians, school authorities, doctors, even male relatives and neighbors, set the parameters of her ability to take on successfully the role of family head. (1979:229)

Economic discrimination particularly affects divorced mothers. The traditional view that the proper role for women is housework and child care has fostered the opinion that women are marginal workers and should be given only marginal jobs, which pay less, have less status, and are less secure than those given to men. The result is that women, regardless of marital status, do not earn the same salaries as men in comparable jobs. They also are found in more dead-end jobs that have little or no possibilities for promotion. The jobs are more likely to be nonmanagerial and nonadministrative. These biases and discrimination make it extremely difficult for women raising their children alone to support a family.

Inadequate, unreliable, and, when available, expensive child-care facilities complicate the divorced mother's situation. The scarcity of child-care facilities reflects society's values—that the only acceptable setting for the care of children is in the home and by the mother. Child-care facilities are viewed negatively; they can only hinder the psychological development of the child and thus they are deemed undesirable and unnecessary. Unfortunately, for single parents the absence of alternative child care prevents their full involvement in the labor force and limits them to marginal, part-time, or seasonal jobs. Such women often suffer severe economic hardships because far too frequently their insufficient earnings are not offset by other forms of child support. The child-support payments from the ex-husband are often inadequate, irregular, or nonexistent, as is welfare and assistance from governmental programs and social agencies. Ironically, then, the parent least able to support the family is often left with the major economic responsibility. The effects of this downward income mobility can be severe.

> Lowered income means not only a drop in consumption within the home, but often a change in housing to poorer accommodations in a poorer neighborhood. . . .

> Moving is itself a stress . . . in this case often compounded by problems of reduced personal safety, higher delinquency rates, and poorer schools. A rapid change in socioeconomic status is associated with anomie . . . adding to the problems of emotional support. . . . Some of the correlation between multi-problem families and divorced parents has been explained in terms of lowered SES and poorer housing. (Brandwein, Brown, and Fox, 1974)

In our society, men are commonly depicted as the household member with the power and authority to command respect within the family, and as the one who can act on behalf of the family in dealings with outside social agencies and institutions. The divorced mother may legally be the head of the family, but her family group is considered deviant because she and not a man heads it. Kohen, Brown, and Feldberg, in their study of 30 mothers who were divorced or separated from 1 to 5 years, report that intrusions that did not occur when these mothers were married, occurred in their new status. These intrusions included "schools and hospitals ignoring their requests for their children, men attempting to break into the house, landlords refusing to rent to them, [and] their own parents interfering in their lives" (Kohen, Brown, and Feldberg, 1979:236). These researchers believe that such incidents provide indications of the lack of social legitimacy to females heading families. Additional evidence is the disproportionate number of divorced mothers who are confronted with discrimination by businesses, credit-granting institutions, and mortgage banks who, in effect, deny these women their head-of-household status.

The divorced mother's authority within the home can also be undermined by these patriarchal ideas. This is a difficult task because of the lack of external social institutions to provide such services. We have already described this factor in our discussion of child-care facilities. The same holds true for other institutions, such as schools and businesses, that, in their independent demands on single-parent mother, often require her to be in two places at the same time. In addition, the cultural denial of the legitimacy of the female-headed family can affect both the women herself and her children. She is now required to assume both the mother and father roles within the family. Neither she nor her children may be ready to accept this amalgamation. However, research reported by Brandwein, Brown, and Fox (1974) show that women's ability to overcome this difficulty should not be underestimated. Likewise, Kohen, Brown, and Feldberg (1979) point out that their sample of divorced and separated mothers report that they developed increased feelings of mastery over their relationships with their children. They were also able to take on new responsibilities and perform unfamiliar tasks around the household and outside it — tasks that were exclusively in the province of the husband-father before the separation or divorce. Finally, they developed more positive self-images and stronger self-concepts.

The future for female-headed single-parent families can improve if and when governmental and social policies provide adequate financial supports — either directly or by enforcing spouses' child-support agreements — as well as such services as child care and crisis intervention when needed. Finally, societal attitudes toward women must change to allow them to gain employment opportunities that would provide them with the financial security to take care of themselves and their families.

Teenage Mothers

Much media attention has been given to the rise in teenage pregnancy and parenthood. In a 1985 cover story, "Children Having Children," *Time* reports that four out of five of the more than one million American teenage girls who will become pregnant in the next year will be unmarried. Of this number, 30,000 are under the age of 15. Further, the estimate is that fully 40 percent of today's teenage girls will be pregnant at least once before the age of 20.

These teen mothers are many times as likely as other women with young children to live below the poverty level. Claudia Wallis (1985), the *Time* writer, cites a study that only one-half of those who give birth before age 18 complete high school (as compared with 96 percent who don't become pregnant). They will earn, on the average, half as much money than their non–child-bearing counterparts and are far more likely to be dependent on welfare. Seventy-one percent of females under the age of 30 who receive Aid to Families with Dependent Children had their first child as a teenager. In effect, teen pregnancy imposes hardships on at least two generations: parents and children. Lucille Dismukes, of the Council on Maternal and Infant Care in Atlanta, a state advisory group, observes: "A lot of the so-called feminization of poverty starts off with teenagers' having babies. So many can't rise above it to go back to school or get job skills" (quoted in Wallis, 1985:79).

Blacks living in urban ghettos are particularly affected by teenage pregnancies. Nearly half of all black females in the United States are pregnant by age 20. The pregnancy rate among those between the ages of 15 and 19 is almost twice as high as it is among whites. Ninety percent of the babies born to blacks in this age group are born out of wedlock and most are raised in fatherless homes.

The incidence of white teenage pregnancy is also very high. The Alan Guttmacher Institute (a nonprofit research center in New York City), based on a 37-country study, concludes that the United States leads nearly all other developing nations in its incidence of pregnancy among girls ages 15 through 19. Their researchers compared in detail five Western countries—Sweden, Holland, France, Canada, and Great Britain—with the United States. They found that, while American adolescents were not more sexually active than their European counterparts, they were more likely to become pregnant. Further, even omitting black teenagers in the United States, who have a higher pregnancy rate than whites, whites alone had nearly double the rate of British and French teenagers and six times the rate of the Dutch. These figures leads Jeannie Rosoff, the president of the Alan Guttmacher Institute, to conclude that "It's not a black problem. It's not an East Coast problem. It's a problem for all of us" (quoted in Wallis, 1986:80).

The Guttmacher researchers believe that the lack of openness in American society about birth control constitutes a striking difference between American teenagers and their European peers. The policy in Sweden, to cite another country's handling of this problem, is to educate children from the age of 7 on reproductive biology. By the time Swedish children are 10 or 12, they are knowledgeable about the various types of contraceptives. The goal, as one Swedish educator states, is "The idea is to dedramatize and demystify sex so that familiarity will make the child less likely to fall prey to unwanted pregnancy and venereal disease" (Annika Strandell quoted in Wallis, 1985:82).

Holland has a similar sex-education program that seeks to demystify sex. Contraceptive counseling is available at government-sponsored clinics for a minimal fee. Media attention is also given to the sex education. The result is that birth control is commonly used by Dutch teenagers. In contrast, in the United States, public opinion prevails that minimizes public sex education. Faye Wattleton, president of the Planned Parenthood Federation, believes that our puritanical heritage accounts for this orientation. She states: "While European societies have chosen to recognize sexual development as a normal part of human development, we have chosen to repress it. At the same time, we behave as if we're not repressing it" (quoted in Wallis, 1985:82). The birth-control result is a double standard that allows teenagers to have sex as a result of a spontaneous passion. But to plan for sex by taking the pill or using a diaphragm is viewed as something wrong.

The Guttmacher researchers in their cross-cultural data analysis conclude that the result of this practice is that societies that have the least open attitudes toward sex are the ones that have the highest teenage pregnancy rates. They are also the societies with the highest teenage abortion rates. They also report that countries like Holland, Sweden, and France—while providing far more generously for indigent young

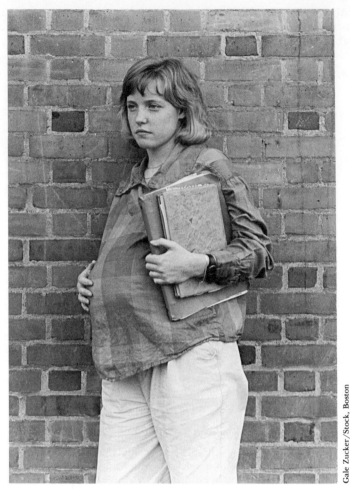

A pregnant teenager.

mothers—still have low pregnancy rates. Research by Frank Furstenberg (Vrazo, 1986) further refutes the notion that teenagers who become pregnant are simply looking for a welfare handout. Furstenberg and his research team from the University of Pennsylvania interviewed in 1967 a group of about 300 Baltimore black teenager mothers, then re-interviewed them 5 years later in 1972 and again in 1984. He found that during this 17-year period, only one-quarter of them were receiving welfare assistance. Most of them finished high school, got jobs, and improved their circumstances.

Male-Headed Single-Parent Families

It is an unusual development for a father to assume custody of his children after divorce. As discussed previously, in over 90 percent of the cases women are granted custody. Kelin E. Gersick (1979) points out that this results not solely because of court-mandated decisions but also because a very high percentage of divorcing couples have reached pre-court agreement that the wife will have custody. This agreement primarily reflects the role allocation of the couple during their marriage and their anticipation of the postdivorce roles as well as their assumption that the court will award custody to the mother if the custodial issue is contested. Gersick explains:

> Men have been more likely to be employed full time, to be making the larger income, to have higher status jobs, and to be in a career progression. Following the divorce, it has usually been easier for the father to continue his occupation than for a non-working mother to leave the home and start a new career. Regardless of the man's emotional attachment to his children, the couple's pre-divorce division of labor was most likely to have assigned the primary childcare role to the mother. This not only increased her childcare skills and the dependence of the children on her, but also established patterns of many years' standing which would take great effort to reverse, and at best would require a major adjustment for all the family members. In addition, the social pressure on mothers to take custody has been overwhelming. (Gersick, 1979:308).

The beginnings of the breakdown in parental roles and postdivorce parental roles has begun to affect custodial outcomes of divorce. Concomitantly, a small but growing number of fathers are now taking custody of their children. Gersick (1979) reports on his exploratory study of 20 single-parent fathers awarded custody of their children and a comparable group of noncustodial fathers. He observes that four complex variables appear to play the determining factor of whether the father would consider gaining custody. The first variable is that the custodial fathers reacted against their own families' relationships with them when they were children. In particular, they wished to overcome in their own relationship with their children the emotional detachment they had experienced with their own fathers. This was not an important consideration for the noncustodial fathers.

The second factor was the feelings concerning the departing wife. Most of the men who sought custody believed that their wives betrayed them and their children through their involvements with another man. Their concern for the future well-being of the children was combined with a desire to punish their wives. A third and possibly the determining factor related to fathers getting custody of the children was that, in 18 of the 20 cases, the wives gave pre-trial consent. The last factor was their respective attitudes toward their attorneys. In the control group of fathers who did not receive custody, a dominant belief was that their attorney's reluctance to contest the issue played a decisive role in their decision to agree on giving custody to the wife. The fact that so many of the custodial fathers had their wives give pre-trial consent made this a nonfactor for them.

In summary, the issue of a father's custody is tied explicitly to the underlying premises of the proper roles of fathers and mothers after divorce and on the "best interest" principle concerning children. These premises are reflected in the court's orientation. Gersick's description of the 20 father-headed single-parent families can serve as a fitting summing up of this little-researched phenomenon:

> In addition to *caring* deeply about their children, the fathers in the custody sample also felt that *raising* them was important enough to be worth sacrifices in other areas; in some instances, particularly regarding their careers, sacrifices did have to be made. It is interesting to note that many of the difficulties the men faced as a result of taking custody were exactly the same as those widely experienced by single-parent mothers. Money was tight. Childcare became a problem, which made work more difficult. Visits by the mother were often anticipated with wariness and anxiety. In addition, for some of the men the strain of the divorce, combined with the emotional demands of parenthood, made the development of a new life very

difficult. Yet none of these fathers said he regretted his decision to take custody. (Gersick, 1979:322–323)

Remarriage After Divorce

Even with today's liberalizing attitudes toward divorce, individuals report varying degrees of loneliness, confusion, and depression after divorce (see Goode, 1956b; Bohannan, 1971; and S. Gordon, 1976). Many find that they are not able to confide in their friends and relatives. The failure of the society to provide clear-cut normative standards to guide the divorced individual aggravates the situation. Further, the social ideologies that stress individualism and separation from extended kinship structures often prevent divorced persons from seeking aid or involvements with their families. The individual's ties and interpersonal relationships with married friends are also often shattered by divorce. The somewhat stigmatized identity combined with the necessity to change old relationships often prove difficult to resolve.

Combined, all these factors often result in the desire of the divorced person to remarry. Indeed, a society that provides few alternate emotional resources outside of marriage limits the institutionalized options of the divorced person. The ideology that stresses the marital relationship as the most beneficial institution for the realization of individual emotional gratification and happiness almost mandates that the individual seek a new marital partner. The result is that remarriage is increasingly becoming more predominant. Almost one out of five currently married people were married previously; one out of four marriages is a remarriage for one of the spouses. Furthermore, the divorced are remarrying sooner after their divorce.

William J. Goode (1956) in his seminal study *After Divorce*, argues that high divorce rates do not imply social disorganization. The high remarriage rate provides corroborating evidence. It leads us to reconsider divorce as a temporary state rather than a permanent one for many people committed to marriage:

> Indeed, the divorce system then becomes in effect part of the courtship and marriage system: that is, it is part of the "sifting out" process, analogous to the adolescent dating pattern. Individuals marry, but there is a free market both in getting a first spouse, and in getting a second spouse should the individual not be able to create a harmonious life with the first one. Indeed, to the extent that marriage becomes a personal bond between husband and wife, and they marry after they are formed psychologically, there would seem to be at least some ideological arguments for their being free to shift about in order to find someone who fits better (Goode, 1962/1966:387).

The American Experience

Remarriages have always been common in the United States. During the colonial period and through the nineteenth century, the death of a spouse was almost always followed quickly by remarriage. The harshness of life demanded that a single parent obtain a spouse to help care and provide for children. Although remarriage after the death of a spouse has been an accepted institution, our society rejected the remarriage of divorced individuals. Duberman (1977) states that the American clergy were disinclined to remarry divorced individuals. State laws also existed to discourage this practice.

However, after World War I, the divorce rate in the United States began to rise. This gradually affected the attitudes and rates of remarriage of divorced people. Jacobson (1959) estimates that into the 1920s there were still more remarriages after the death of a spouse than after divorce. But, beginning in the 1930s, this pattern changed. Arthur J. Norton and Paul C. Glick (1976), reporting on remarriage patterns, have observed that at the present time the overwhelming majority of remarriages occur as a result of the divorce or one or both of the new partners.

The proportion of remarriage to all marriages occurring is steadily increasing. At the turn of the century, about nine-tenths of all marriages were first marriages; most of the remaining one-tenth involved widows or widowers. Jacobson (1959) calculates that only about 3 percent of all brides were previously married in 1900. The figure increases three-fold to 9 percent by 1930. The current estimate is that about one-fourth (25 percent) of all brides are previously divorced (Carter and Glick, 1976).

Concurrent with the rise of divorced persons who remarry is the increasing presence of children found in these remarriages. Andrew Cherlin (1980), citing U.S. Bureau of the Census figures, reports that nearly 9 million children lived in two-parent families where one or both parents had been previously divorced. He conjectures that a significant number of the children were from previous marriages.

In an analysis of long-term trends in remarriage focusing on changes in recent years, Glick and Lin (1986) report that remarriage rates went up during the 1960s, but then started a steep decline that continued until the late 1970s, after which the decline moderated. Among the significant findings was that remarriage rates are higher for men (84 percent) than for women (77 percent). One finding that is highlighted is the fact that young divorced women with children were becoming more likely than their childless counterparts to remarry and to do so quickly.

The childless divorced women stayed divorced longer than the divorced mothers. The reluctance of young, childless, divorced women to remarry was seen as reflecting an alternative lifestyle. They included cohabitation outside marriage, the experience of costs and benefits of living alone, and an option to deliberate in seeking an acceptable unmarried man to marry. On the other hand, the ability of young divorced mothers to remarry soon after divorce is perceived by Glick and Lin to reflect the increased acceptability of divorce. Early remarriage for divorced mothers reflects a desire to increase the divorcee's financial security. Typically, remarriage means adding not only an additional income but additional support in the running of the household.

Given the acceleration of remarriage figures, we would estimate that an even larger number of children are involved in these families of remarried divorced people today. The existence of such large numbers of remarried families necessitates an in-depth examination of the adjustments that these family members have to make after remarriage occurs.

Adjustment of Members of Remarried Families

There is a myth surrounding remarriage that says that the second marriage is more successful than the first. In popular parlance, "love is better the second time around." The explanations given include the belief that remarried individuals are now older, wiser, and more mature. Also, it is assumed that divorced persons who remarry will work harder to assure a more successful second marriage. Yet, the divorce rate for persons who remarry after divorce is higher than for persons who marry for the first time (Cherlin, 1980). Paul C. Glick, the senior demographer of the Bureau of the Census, estimated that in 1975 about 36 percent of all first marriages may end in divorce, whereas about 40 percent of remarriages after divorce may also dissolve (cited in Westoff, 1977).

An apparent contradiction is noted by William J. Goode who cautions against viewing the divorced remarrieds as divorce-prone. Instead of comparing divorce rates, he suggests that one should ask all those who have remarried to compare their second marriages with their first. He reasons:

> Granted that the divorced who remarry are somewhat more prone to divorce than those who marry for the first time; nevertheless, the only comparison that makes sense to those divorced people is between their second marriage and *their own first marriage*. Our divorcees are not, after all, asserting that their second marriages are better than marriages of *others* who are first married. They are only claiming that their second marriages are "happier" than their *own first* marriages. (Goode, 1956:334–335)

Andrew Cherlin (1980), however, argues that the divorce rate *is* the best indication of the differences in the unity between families of remarriages after divorce that include children from previous marriages and those of first-marriage families. Cherlin contends that there are insufficient institutional supports and guidelines to assure optimal success of these remarriages. He observes that family members of such remarriages face unique problems that do not exist in first-marriage families. He believes that the origins of these problems lie in the complex structure of remarried families and the normative inadequacies to define these familial roles and relationships:

> These families are expanded in the number of social roles and relationships they possess and also are expanded in space over more than one household. The additional social roles included stepparents, stepchildren, stepsiblings, and the new spouses of noncustodial parents, among others. And the links between the household are the children of previous marriages. These children are commonly in the custody of one parent — usually the mother — but they normally visit the noncustodial parent regularly. Thus they promote communication among the divorced parents, the new stepparent, and the noncustodial parent's new spouse. (Cherlin, 1980:375)

Cherlin is of the opinion that our society's overemphasis on first marriages provides little guidance for the handling of the potential problems of remarriages stemming from these complexities. To support this contention, he refers to the study by Paul Bohannan (1971) that calls attention to the inadequacies of our kinship terminology. Bohannan states that the term *stepparent* originally meant the individual whom the surviving parent married to replace a parent who had died. A stepparent after divorce is an additional parent, not a replacement. Our society has not developed norms on how to handle this situation. We do not have norms to govern our behavior and expectation, nor do we have norms to show the differences between parent and stepparent. The difficulties in what we call these stepparents highlights this problem. If a noncustodial biological parent is still alive and maintains contact with his or her child, does the child also call the stepparent "Mom" or "Dad"? Cherlin points out that the lack of appropriate terms also exists for the new complex of extended relationships, including uncles, aunts, and grandparents. The significance of these absent terms is stated by Cherlin:

> Where no adequate terms exist for an important social role, the institutional support for this role is deficient, and general acceptance of the role as a legitimate pattern of activity is questionable. . . . These linguistic inadequacies correspond to the absence of widely accepted definitions of the form of many of the roles and relationships in families of remarriage. The absence of proper terms is both a symptom and a cause of some of the problems of remarried life. (Cherlin, 1980:376, 377)

Legal and social difficulties also confront the families of the persons who remarry after divorce. The social and financial obligations of former spouses who have also remarried as well as the obligation incurred as the result of subsequent divorces and remarriages further complicate matters. Bohannan (1971) indicates that there is a whole series of social groups that emerge with remarriage. He refers to them as quasi-kinship groups as a result of the chain of relationships that are formed among spouses and their ex-spouses. These "divorce chains also result from complications which exist within the household which contains stepparents, stepsiblings, and half-siblings and by the ways that these household members behave in relation to ex-spouses and *their* families" (Bohannan, 1971:128–129).

Margaret Mead (1971) has identified the legal regulations regarding incest and consanguineal marriages that become problematic for remarried family members. She argues that incest taboos allow children to develop affection for and identification with other family members without risk of sexual exploitation. But incest prohibitions are drawn to blood or genetic relationships rather than to domestic relationships among household members. This failure in incest taboos can lead to inadequate security and protection of children. In more dramatic situations, it can lead to the sexual abuse and exploitation of individuals by their stepparents or stepsiblings. In ordinary circumstances, it can lead to psychological confusion and inability to develop adult relationships.

> As the number of divorces increases, there are more and more households in which minor children live with stepparents and stepsiblings, but where the inevitable domestic familiarity and intimacy are not counterbalanced by protective, deeply felt taboos. At the very least, this situation produces confusion in the minds of growing children; the stepfather, who is seen daily but is not a taboo object, is contrasted with the biological father, who is seen occasionally and so is endowed with a deeper aura of romance. The multiplication of such situations may be expected to magnify the difficulties young people experience in forming permanent-mating relationships, as well as in forming viable relationships with older people. (Mead, 1971:120)

Indeed, most customs and conventions of family life are not applicable to remarried families after divorce. These include such everyday activities as discipline of children (how much authority should stepparents have) the relationships of individuals with their spouse's ex-spouse, and the relationship among siblings and stepsiblings resulting from the various combinations that could come about when individuals remarry, divorce, and remarry. In all, the everyday nature of family life can be seen as problematic to these remarried family members.

Another concern is the impact of remarriage on grandparents, both natural and stepgrandparents. In a study of remarried couples living in central Pennsylvania, Spanier and Furstenberg (1982) observe that children in these families have at least one extra pair of grandparents. While children get a new set of grandparents, these new grandparents' roles are not clearly delineated. However, the researchers found that grandparents were usually quick to accept their "instant" grandchildren. Most of the remarried persons studied reported that the process of introducing their children to their new partner's families was comfortable and pleasant. Similar findings were found by Cherlin and Furstenberg (1986) who report that only 9 percent of the stepgrandparents agreed with the statement, "'You've had problems accepting your stepgrandchildren as grandchildren'" (1986:160). In addition, in both studies, the contact with stepgrandparents did not diminish the children's involvements with their biological grandparents. Further divorces and remarriages would result in more than three sets of grandparents. Cherlin and Furstenberg (1986), in their examination of this potential situation, feel that the nature of these new, post-divorce relationships, is still unknown.

The necessity for a critical examination of remarriage after divorce, especially when children are involved, is vitally apparent. Such empirical research and analysis not only will increase our understanding of these family structures and processes, but can also be of immeasurable aid in understanding the nature of the institutional relationship between the family and society in the transmission of social norms

Stepfamily Is an Overlooked, Growing Problem for Society

BY BETTY CUNIBERTI

WASHINGTON—By 1985, 40 percent of all children in the United States will have seen their parents divorce and remarry. Put another way, in a few years almost half the nation's children will be stepchildren.

Despite the mushrooming phenomenon of stepfamilies in America, little research has been done on the art of treating their special, social-psychological problems.

The literature that most commonly comes to mind is "Cinderella." And everyone knows what that did for the image of stepmothers.

At the conference of the National Association of Social Workers here recently, Thomas A. Hlenski—a psychiatric social worker and a stepfather—gave a presentation on the subject to a group of colleagues who not only filled every available chair but also sat on the floor, stood in the back of the room and spilled out into the hallway.

Hlenski, from Huntington, N.Y., encouraged his co-workers to insist that their clients explore the complex web of old and new relationships present in the stepfamily, even if the clients balk at opening old wounds or think their new living arrangement has nothing to do with whatever problem they came to talk about.

Mostly, the approach to dealing with stepfamilies has been no approach at all. If a member or members of a stepfamily seek a social worker's help, the fact that the family involved is a *stepfamily* often is not dealt with.

Partly because of the negative social stigma attached to stepfamilies and the guilt involved in breaking up a family and creating a new one, therapists and stepfamily members alike often ignore the fact the people involved are part of a stepfamily. It is more comfortable to view the new family and its problems as being just like a natural, biological family.

But it isn't.

"Stepfathers, stepmothers and stepchildren have become, as it were, ecological refugees in an environment that tends to ignore their special culture and fosters instead a negative or indifferent view," said Hlenski. "Legal, school, medical and other impacting systems remain archaic in their delivery of service to the stepfamily population."

"Myths and negative societal stereotypes continue to flourish, unchecked by the real facts. In the immediate environment of the stepfamily, members of extended families, grandparents, relatives and friends remain unclear as to how to interpret the stepfamily situation. Members of stepfamilies remain confused as to their respective roles, and often feel the strain of being viewed as second-class citizens."

What role to play is often the central issue.

"How much to be a parent?" said Hlenski. "How much to love? How much to hold back?"

Children are confused, too. Many appoint themselves as mediators to try to get their biological parents back together.

"They always have a flicker of that fantasy," said Hlenski.

So when the biological parent remarries, there can be trouble right from the start.

"The marital couple is celebrating their union, and the children are facing an end to any fantasy of parental reunion," said Hlenski.

Once the remarriage has occurred, both the stepparent and the absent biological parent must struggle to decide how much parenting to do. Often, they struggle with each other, overtly or covertly. But more often, said Hlenski, "the biological parent is getting lost."

"The problem that hasn't been addressed is the relationship between the stepfather and the biological father. Often there's no relationship of directness, but [only] strong undercurrents. They can easily become competitors. This may account for why a lot of natural fathers don't visit much. There's a high suicide risk among fathers who don't remarry or visit their children. It's important that the formerly married couple work closely together in raising the children."

But this, Hlenski warns, can cause strains

(continued)

for the stepparent, who feels threatened by the continued relationship of his spouse with the ex-spouse.

One of Hlenski's clients came to see him because of anger and depression.

Hlenski discovered, through questioning, that the client was a stepfather, "and his anger and depression were very much related to his struggle with his wife and stepson over who is in charge of the house."

This problem of the "parental child" was given particular attention.

The parental child most often assumes the role of the absent father during separation. He literally takes charge, often to the relief of the mother. One of Hlenski's clients, an 11-year-old parental-child boy, "went after his father to duke it out because of what he had done to the mother. Think of the Oedipal stuff," said Hlenski.

"It did come down to the father spanking the kid, treating him like a kid."

Recognizing a parental child and taking firm action to return him to child status is one of the key challenges for social workers, Hlenski said.

Many problems in stepfamilies occur because issues from the earlier marriage were left unresolved. Hlenski woud like to see social workers be firm in their insistence to go back and take care of these matters, even though the clients may resist.

"The worker needs to carefully balance the family's need to move on and their need to go back into the past," he said. "He must serve as a bridge for the family in order to undo the problems created by unclear messages from the past."

But Hlenski does not by any means believe that the stepfamily situation is hopeless. A little patience, insight, honest discussion and tolerance can go a long way for these increasingly prevalent American families.

SOURCE. Betty Cuniberti. 1982. "Stepfamily is an overlooked, growing problem for society." *The Philadelphia Inquirer* (Dec. 1). Copyright 1982 Los Angeles Times. Reprinted by permission.

governing individuals. This point is the central concern of Andrew Cherlin and captures our attention:

> We need to know what the institutional links are between family and society which transmit social norms about everyday behavior. That is, we need to know exactly how patterns of family behavior come to be accepted and how proper solutions for family problems come to be taken for granted. And the recent rise in the number of remarriages after divorce may provide us with a natural laboratory for observing this process of institutionalization. As remarriage after divorce becomes more common, remarried parents and their children probably will generate standards of conduct in conjunction with the larger society. By observing these developments, we can improve our understanding of the sources of unity in married—and remarried —life. (Cherlin, 1980:380–381)

Conclusion

All societies permit divorce or the dissolution of marriage. In our cross-cultural examination of divorce, we saw that there is no necessary association between divorce rates and societal breakdown or disorganization. Indeed, for many preliterate societies high divorce rates often serve to stabilize extended family systems. In our study of divorce in Japan and Egypt we observed that their respective rates of divorce have declined in the twentieth century, whereas the rates in the United States have risen. Yet, as William J. Goode (1963) has observed, these changes in the divorce rates, although going in opposite directions, reflect a similar pattern—a growing tendency for both women and men to have equal rights of divorce. The impact of the Islamic revolution on Iran and women's rights and divorce was then examined.

Our attention then turned to an in-depth examination of divorce in the United

States. The steady climb in the American divorce rate was shown to be related to social and familial changes closely associated with the family's relationship to economic processes. Changes in family ideology reflecting an emphasis on the independence and the privatization of the nuclear family have also played an important role in changes in the divorce rate. Of particular interest is the relationship of working wives and their increased economic independence, and the possibility that their marriages may end in divorce.

Changes in law regarding divorce and child custody were shown not only to reflect changes in familial roles, but also to serve as an impetus for bringing about changes in the definition of marriage and the responsibilities of husbands and wives with each other and with their children. Further, divorce laws and custody decisions also define the continued obligations that the formerly married couple have to each other and to their children after divorce.

What happens to the wives, husbands, and children following a divorce and how familial roles change with the dissolution of the marriage was the next topic of concern. The effects of divorce on children were seen to be associated with the child's conceptualization of the parents' marriage. They were also associated with the child's age. We emphasized the need for more systematic research in this area and cautioned against imputing solely negative consequences of divorce on children. The readjustments, problems, and solutions of single parents' raising children alone was then investigated. In the case of female-headed single-parent households, we saw the interrelated effects of government and social policies regarding financial support— either directly or by enforcing spouse's child-support agreements—social services— such as child care and crisis intervention—and social attitudes toward divorced women, especially in terms of employment opportunities and their ability to cope with circumstances.

Our final discussion was on remarriage. Remarriage rates, divorce rates of remarrieds, and the problems confronted by reconstituted families were analyzed. Here again, we saw the necessity for more systematic investigation of remarriage.

Epilogue: The Family in China

A Manchu family in Wang Yeh Fu, Mongolia, ca. 1924.

CHAPTER OUTLINE

This concluding chapter differs from summaries generally found in other texts. We apply the themes discussed in previous chapters to an analysis of a family system that we have only briefly discussed previously—the Chinese family.[1] Thus, the utility of the conceptual frameworks introduced earlier in this book can be tested by looking at changes in the Chinese family system. Our analysis uses modernization processes, the family's relationship with the wider kinship networks and surrounding communities, premarital and marital relationships, and age-and-gender differentiation and stratification patterns. In the following pages, we trace the changes that the traditional Chinese family system has undergone in the twentieth century.

China is a vast country with almost 1 billion people. Its urban population, 200 million, is probably the largest urban population in the world. Yet, almost 80 percent of the population lives in the rural countryside. In the twentieth century, many changes have occurred. It has moved from a semifeudal country to a world force. It has undergone major political and social revolutions that have shaken the world. It has fundamentally transformed traditional agricultural and industrial ownership, production, and distribution. Its traditional family system, with its emphasis on the needs of the collective rather than the individual, has been influential in the development of a modern family form that differs fundamentally from the Western private conjugal family.

An understanding of these changes and the underlying issues involved is of immeasurable value, not only in the understanding of the Chinese experience, but also in understanding much of the sweeping social, political, and economic changes occurring in the contemporary world. Such an understanding serves to illuminate much of our concern with the nature of social change and the family.

---

[1] A brief footnote on the English spelling of Chinese names and places used in Chapter 18 may be appropriate. The reproduction of Chinese sounds in written English is, at best, an approximation. The Chinese spellings in this chapter are drawn from the Wade-Giles system named for two nineteenth-century British linguists. This is the familiar system for Chinese personal and place names that has long been in use. But in 1979, China officially adopted another system, known as Pinyon (phonetic spelling). In the same year, the United States government began to use Pinyon exclusively for Chinese names and places. While some of the printed media have also adopted the new system, others have not. This has complicated the translation period from Wade-Giles to Pinyon. With Pinyon, "Mao Tse-tung" is transformed into "Mao Zedong," "Hua Kuo-feng" becomes "Hua Guofeng," and "Teng Hsiao-ping" turns into "Deng Xiaoping." The spelling of China's capital changes from "Peking" to "Beijing." "Hong Kong" becomes "Xianggong." Indeed, if there wasn't a concession by the Chinese government "China," itself, would become known as "Zhonggo." To minimize confusion and given the historical emphasis of this chapter the author has decided to utilize the more familiar Wade-Giles system that already is well known to readers.

Modernization Processes and the Chinese Experience: The Setting

In Chapter 3, we discussed some of the implications of modernization processes on the individual, the family, and the society. The themes developed by Szymon Chodak (1973) and Peter L. Berger, Brigette Berger, and Hansfried Kellner (1973) helped us to examine modernization processes in Third World societies. Chodak referred to two types of modernization—accultural and induced. Both types were characterized by the absence of industrialization and were aimed at creating favorable conditions for future industrialization.

Accultural modernization, which was typical of the African colonial systems, emerged from direct confrontation and the superimposition of European colonial culture on the traditional culture. This frequently led to a phenomenon called detribalization. Detribalization is a process in which there was substitution of traditional positions and roles by a new system of positions and roles based on the Western model. Chodak sees the acculturative process as leading to alienation: the individual becomes marginal to both his traditional and modern worlds.

Berger and his associates (1973) voice similar conclusions. They observe that detribalization is a process of radical social reclassification. Not only is the world redefined, but the social relationships are also reclassified and the individual's sense of identity is undermined: "At this point, all of reality becomes uncertain and threatened with meaninglessness—precisely the condition that sociologists commonly call anomie" (Berger, Berger, and Kellner, 1973:153). This is a condition that they say leads to the development of the "homeless mind."

In contrast, induced modernization, as described by Chodak, is a process of nation-building and the generation of national identities. Its primary purpose is to transform the society into a new, national entity by integrating significant parts of the traditional culture into the new social order.

Berger's group examines modernization processes and its effect on traditional ways of life, kinship patterns, and "social constructions of reality." Although these authors do not explicitly make the distinction between acculturated and induced modernization, they reach a conclusion similar to Chodak's in his discussion of induced modernization. They view this phenomenon as representing a later stage of the modernization process occurring in the Third World. With political independence and with the installation of revolutionary socialist governments, the state itself becomes the agent of development. The basic goal is to relate the ideologies of nationalism to socialism and to combine the benefits of modernity with the traditional tribal community that offers the individual meaning and solidarity. The aim is to prevent the alienating, fragmenting, and disintegrating processes related to the destruction of tribal and communal solidarity.

This task is extremely difficult because modernization brings with it reclassification of social relationships based on economic status, occupation, and national relationships rather than having social relationships based on tribal and kinship criteria. Berger, Berger, and Kellner see modernization as both liberating and oppressing. Modernization liberates individuals from colonization and from the controls of family, clan, and tribe. It oppresses individuals in the quest for the development of technological and bureaucratic institutions. The tensions of the processes at work in induced modernization are dramatically presented in China after the revolution of 1949.

William Hinton (1966) titles his vivid account of revolutionary change in a rural Chinese village, *Fanshen*— is a Chinese word meaning a complete turnabout in the nature of the social world:

Every revolution creates new words. The Chinese Revolution created a whole new vocabulary. A most important word in this vocabulary was *fanshen*. It means "to turn the body," or "to turn over." To China's hundreds of millions of landless and land-poor peasants it meant to stand up, to throw off the landlord yoke, to gain land, stock, implements, and houses. But it meant much more than this. It meant to throw off superstition and study science, to abolish "word blindness" and learn to read, to cease considering women as chattels and establish equality between the sexes, to do away with appointed village magistrates and replace them with elected councils. It meant to enter a new world. (Hinton, 1966:vii. Copyright © 1966 by William Hinton. Reprinted by permission of Monthly Review Foundation.)

The Communist revolution was a total revolution. Not only was there a change of the political and economic system but also of the social system. The fundamental social relationships among individual, family, and community were dramatically transformed. This chapter is devoted to an examination of that transformation.

The Traditional Chinese Family

The traditional extended Chinese family persisted without substantial structural change for almost 2000 years. There had been a general pattern of continuity and gradual assimilation of some changes into basic Chinese society. This long period without major social changes is partially accounted for by a deeply rooted tradition of paternalistic authority and control. Michael Gasster (1972) points out that the relationships between leaders and followers is central to all societies, but in China these relationships, especially the questions concerning duties, social obligations, and conflicting loyalties, were a primary concern of China's philosophers and statesmen throughout its history.

To ensure stability, an elaborate code developed that was anchored on fundamental family relationships. A rigid structural hierarchy became dominant and dictated proper attitudes and behaviors among people of different social statuses. The hierarchy of submission and dominance, which so characterized the family, was reflected in the larger semifeudal economic system. By the nineteenth century, China was divided into two groups: a very small, privileged group, the gentry; and the vast majority group, the peasantry. The gentry claimed the position akin to the father's position in the family. Their claim was based on tradition and built on the foundation of family life. To understand fully the traditional family system, it is vitally necessary to see how it operated in this larger context. China's struggle to achieve modernization can best be studied by focusing on this relationship.

Marion J. Levy, Jr. (1949), characterizes the gentry as having the following characteristics:

1. Their primary source of income was from land, which they did not cultivate themselves, as well as income from government offices.
2. They held most, if not all, of the intellectual and academic positions.
3. They controlled the administrative, judicial, and legislative systems of the state.
4. They controlled the economy by absentee land tenure. As China moved into the twentieth century, the gentry also became involved in industry and commerce— as owners and managers—and in banking. The gentry constituted less than one-fifth of the population.

China was basically agricultural, and the peasantry, which accounted for more than 80 percent of the population, was predominant. The peasantry cultivated the land of the gentry. The peasantry did contain members who cultivated their own land, but, generally, they were tenants or hired non–land-owning agricultural laborers. Those groups that fall outside the status dichotomy are the handicraftsmen, the merchants, the servants, the soldiers, the domestic industry workers, the factory workers, and a miscellaneous group containing priests and entertainers. These latter groups, according to Levy, were relatively unimportant in the social structure and generally followed the social patterns of the peasantry.

Levy claims that the picture of the gentry has been taken as representative of the entire population. He points out that the confusion is due to the fact that gentry family patterns were considered ideal patterns by almost the entire society. Western observers, therefore, have had great difficulty separating the ideal from the empirically valid descriptions of Chinese society. But, given this caveat, one should realize that the influence of the gentry cannot be overemphasized. Their ways were the ideal patterns and served as the standards for the entire country.

The Chinese peasantry was faced with a dual system of oppression based on a hierarchy of domination and subservience that was enforced with brutality and violence. Oppression came from a semifeudal economic system and from the traditional family. Traditional family and village life was characterized by omnipresent exploitation. William Hinton describes it in his study of Long Bow, a rural village, during the transition period to Communist rule in the mid-1940s:

> Violence was chronic at all levels of human relationship, husbands beat their wives, mothers-in-law beat their daughters-in-law, peasants beat their children, landlords beat their tenants, and the Peace Preservation Corps beat anyone who got in their way. The only living creatures that could hope to avoid beatings, it seemed, were adult male gentry and draft animals—the donkeys, mules, horses, oxen, and cows that were the basis of Long Bow's agriculture. (Hinton, 1966:51)

In his graphic presentation of prerevolutionary family and village life, Hinton sees the entire system as being characterized by barbarity, terror, and cruelty. The system originated in the division of the society into the two classes of gentry and peasantry and extended this ideology to age and gender relationships. Two of the tales told to Hinton provide some indication of the pervasiveness of this everyday torment:

> There were three famine years in a row. The whole family went out to beg things to eat. In Chinchang City conditions were very bad. Many mothers threw newborn children into the river. Many children wandered about on the streets and couldn't find their parents. We had to sell our eldest daughter. She was then already 14. Better to move than to die, we thought. We sold what few things we had. We took our patched quilt on a carrying pole and set out for Changchin with the little boy in the basket on the other end. He cried all the way from hunger. We rested before a gate. Because the boy wept so bitterly a woman came out. We stayed there for three days. On the fourth morning the woman said she wanted to buy the boy. We put him on the *K'ang*. He fell asleep. In the next room we were paid five silver dollars. Then they drove us out. They were afraid when the boy woke up he would cry for his mother. My heart was so bitter. To sell one's own child was such a painful thing. We wept all day on the road. (Hinton, 1966:42–43)

The family life of both peasants and gentry was dominated by a rigid authoritarian hierarchy based on age and sex. The family strongly influenced every aspect of an individual's life. Three interlocking factors—generation, age, and proximity of kin—resulted in the placement of each person into a fixed kinship group that determined one's ascribed status and determined one's obligations, rights, and privileges. These factors, particularly age hierarchy, laid the foundation for the hierarchy of status and authority of the family organization and the clan.

The oldest man had the highest status and unquestioned control of all important family decision-making. Women's status was lower than that of all men, but increased with age and with the birth of male offspring. A great emphasis was placed on respect for age differences. Just as the wishes of the woman were subjugated to those of the man, the wishes of the young were subjugated to those of the old. There was dominance by parents, and stratification of status and distribution of functions by sex and age. C.K. Yang observes that the Confucian canon of the kinship relation of Mencius (372–289 B.C.)[2] was followed: "Between father and son there should be solidarity and affection; . . . between husband and wife, attention to their separate functions; between old and young, a proper order" (Yang, 1959:6–7). The relationship between father and son was held to be of primary importance.

The familial hierarchy of status and authority was anchored on the dual principles of filial piety and veneration of age. C.K. Yang[3] states that "filial piety demanded absolute obedience and complete devotion to the parents, thus establishing the generational subordination of the children" (Yang, 1959:89). Ideally, filial piety benefited both parents and children. Filial piety did not operate solely through coercion; it also included an emphasis on mutual interdependence, parental affection, and the child's moral obligation to repay parental care and affection. This is reflected in the Chinese proverb that says, "Men rear sons to provide for old age; they plant trees for shade" (Chao, 1977:123). Thus, Paul Chao observes that filial piety can be related to group insurance.

Filial piety, the devotion of sons to their parents, was considered to be a vital necessity for family stability and order. It served as a major force of formal and informal social control. It was extended and institutionalized in the tradition of ancestor worship (the worship of dead male ancestors from the patrilineal group).

The veneration of age was the second pillar of social control. The elderly, the closest living contacts with ancestors, received deference, respect, and obedience. They were depicted as the repositories of wisdom. They held important positions both in the family and the community. They were considered the models of skill and knowledge in all areas, ranging from handicrafts to farming. Yang provides the following personal experience to emphasize the position of importance and prestige the elderly held in traditional China:

> In 1949 the writer tried to introduce into a village an improved weeder which worked much more effectively than hand weeding or hoeing. The younger peasants tried it and liked it very much, but a few days later nobody wanted to use the new instrument because "the old people concluded that it will hurt the root system of the plant." The writer challenged the younger peasants to experiment with the instrument by offering to pay for any damage resulting from it, but to no avail. Confucius' advice of learning to farm from an "old farmer" still stood firm. (Yang, 1959:92)

Yang attributes the long stability of the traditional family institution to the strength of filial piety and the veneration of age. However, he is quick to point out that this great stability was achieved at the price of strenuous repression of the young and their almost complete lack of equality and freedom. Parents had absolute authority over their children including the right to put them to death:

> The proverb "The son must die if so demanded by the father" was a means of compelling obedience from the young in traditional China, especially in rural communities, although the carrying out of the threat was extremely rare. A childhood that passed without frequent physical punishment was an exception rather than the rule. When a child reached his mid-teens, his increased physical strength and his

[2] Mencius, born a century after Confucius' death, is generally regarded as one of the great developers of Confucian thought.

[3] C.K. Yang. 1959. *Chinese Communist Society: The Family and the Village.* Reprinted by permission of The MIT Press, Cambridge, Mass. © 1959 by the Massachusetts Institute of Technology.

ability to run away bolstered his security, but the requirement of filial piety kept a tight rein on him. The necessity of observing this moral code was not merely impressed upon him in the operation of the family institution and group pressure of the community; it was also enforced by formal law. In the Ch'ing period sons were flogged or banished by the court merely on the charge of disobedience brought by the father. (Yang, 1959:93)

Together, filial piety and the veneration of age assured the preservation of a status system dominated by a hierarchy of age for the operation of family authority and control. In effect it was a system designed for the perpetuation of the traditional family institution and the rule of the old over the young.

Mate Selection

The domination of the elders over the young can be readily illustrated through an examination of mate-selection processes. Marriages were arranged by the families and were considered to be too important to be left to the whims and desires of the young. Since marriage served to draw two families together, it took precedence over the fact that it also brought together two individuals. In this and in other situations, the needs of the family took precedence over the needs of the individual. Of utmost importance was the desire to arrange a marriage that would produce a male offspring and thus assure continued ancestor worship.

Traditionally, there was little emotional involvement between the selected prospective marriage partners. Further, such involvement among eligible marriage partners was frowned on and was seen as a potential threat to the extended family. When emotional involvement was perceived by the elders, another suitable marriage was arranged. The disruption of such relationships provided a popular theme in Chinese literature. But, it should be emphasized, rarely did children disobey the wishes of their parents.

Arranged marriages were particularly difficult for the women. With marriage, the bride moved into her husband's family residence. Marriage often meant a complete uprooting of the wife from her family, friends, and community. Katie Curtin (1975) cites a study of a Chinese village in the 1920s that found that although almost 97 percent of the farm operators were born in the village and 94 percent of their fathers, only 6.6 percent of their wives had been.

The husband's parents sought a prospective bride who would be submissive to her new relatives, particularly her mother-in-law. The relationship between a new bride and her mother-in-law was frequently quite antagonistic. The daughter-in-law had to be resocialized and integrated into her new household and coercion was the popular mode to accomplish this.

Burgess and Locke (1945)—in their now classic textbook, *The Family from Institution to Companionship*—provide us with a document secured in 1932 from a Chinese student in Burgess's class at the University of Chicago. It records an interview with an aged woman in Chicago's Chinatown. Burgess and Locke point out that this document is of particular interest in that it depicts the traditional conception of the roles of mother-in-law and daughter-in-law in the context of the changing conceptualization of these roles. This is revealed by the younger woman's inner rebellion against the traditional power and authority of the older woman:

> Mother-in-law was deeply religious, a faithful follower of Buddhism. My husband and I were Christians. Before I was married friends frankly warned me that it is impossible for a Christian to marry into a pagan family without domestic troubles. Some told me that mother-in-law was cruel. Accordingly, the double image of the tender Buddha and devilish mother-in-law constantly appeared in my mind. But I had to sacrifice my own happiness for the sake of my beloved husband.

A part of the marriage ceremony involves the giving of presents between the mother-in-law and daughter-in-law. Mother-in-law gave me a gold bracelet and I gave her the customary present of a skirt made by my mother. This signified the resignation of family duties by the mother-in-law. According to the old idea a full-dress was inconvenient for work; and hence the removal of a skirt signified taking on the duties of work. I thought this signified that the wife was to be the successor of the mother-in-law in carrying on family duties. My mother-in-law, however, interpreted it in a very restricted sense. Family duties to her were but the hard labor and the rest of the duties she kept for herself. Family policies were devised and executed by her, as a queen sitting on the throne of her kingdom.

Every morning, while the sun was still lying behind the morning dews, I went quickly to prepare morning tea for mother-in-law. Afterward I came back to my room to comb my hair, and then, I put on my formal dress. The skirt was indispensable for a full dress.

Going to her bedroom, I found that she was still asleep. I stood beside her bed for an hour waiting to attend her. At last she awoke. I bowed to her humbly; then I gave her my arm in support until she reached her armchair. I went to the kitchen and took a basin of hot water to her bedroom and helped her wash her face. Then I presented her a cup of hot and fragrant tea with all the eastern virtue and politeness I could command.

It was nine now; I had to prepare breakfast. We had servants, but did they help me do anything at all? No. My own status was lower than any of them. I had no experience in cooking. The criticisms of my cooking were hardly bearable. Such criticism as "It is too salty." "It is tasteless," etc. prevented me from being calm; my tears flowed like an inexhaustable fountain. I came back to my private room, crying and crying.

At night I had to take care of her bed. I had to hang down her mosquito net in order to keep mosquitoes out. Besides, I had to say good night while leaving.

I disliked two things particularly. The prohibition against having a private talk with my husband destroyed the best part of my marriage life. Occasionally we talked in our private room. As soon as she discovered it she would call me out with a scornful voice. In her own philosophy private talks were undesirable at home since everything in the home was opened to every individual. There was no privacy at all.

Second, I was not permitted to visit my mother's home often. I was permitted to go to her home once a year, though she was living near by. Once when I went to my mother's home for five days, I suddenly found out that a carriage was waiting outside for my return. Mother-in-law tried to cut me off from both my husband and my mother. (Burgess and Locke, 1945:46–47).

(From *The Family: From Institution to Companionship* by Ernest W. Burgess and Harvey J. Locke. Copyright 1945 by American Book Company. Fourth Edition by Ernest W. Burgess, Harvey J. Locke, and Mary M. Thomes. © 1971 by Little Educational Publishing, Inc. Reprinted by permission of D. Van Nostrand Company.)

Marriages generally occurred when girls were between the ages of 15 and 17 and boys were between the ages of 16 and 18. Child marriages were frequent occurrences for girls. The young bride became the property of her husband's family and was discouraged from having any contact with her own family. Symbolizing her new life was a new name, which reflected her position in her new household. Her wishes and desires were subordinated to those of her new family. Thus, she had no alternative means of financial support. She was in effect in bondage to her husband and his family. And, since she was separated from her own kin, she had no external kin supports.

Divorce

Divorce occurred infrequently in the traditional family system of China. It was discouraged and uncommon, although the husband had the right to divorce his wife on several grounds; these included disobeying the husband's parents, failing to have children, acquiring a loathsome disease, committing adultery, displaying jealousy, being overly talkative, or stealing (Leslie, 1979:119). But husbands rarely resorted to this measure. The poor could not afford it; the wealthy found it stigmatizing. Further, the structural reality of the extended family mitigated against it.

Husbands also had alternatives to divorce that were quite acceptable. They could find relief from an unhappy marriage through prostitutes or by obtaining a concubine. Concubines, although not legally wed, could become members of the man's household. For women, however, there was no emotional or sexual institutionalized outlet outside of marriage. Marion J. Levy, Jr. (1949), in his discussion of divorce, observes that a distraught daughter-in-law had only two options, either to run away or to commit suicide. Divorce was not a viable alternative. Its occurrence was viewed as a tragedy for a woman. Her repudiation by her mother-in-law or by her husband necessitated that she return to her own family in shame. She was no longer deemed suitable for marriage. She had minimal rights within her parents' household, and she was denied the opportunity of becoming wife, mother, and mother-in-law—her only source of status, prestige, and power.

In extremely unbearable situations, unhappy wives saw suicide as the only way out from the rigidities of the marital bond. William J. Goode (1963), in his examination of suicide statistics in China during the pre-Communist twentieth century, argues that the prevalence of suicide may have been exaggerated by romantic legend. He further states that the young bride, realizing that suicide was her only alternative, reduced her motivation to struggle against her mother-in-law. He also declares that, "Conversely, since suicide was a great disgrace for the family that caused it, it is likely that most families *reduced* their pressures on the daughter-in-law when she showed any such intention" (Goode, 1963:312).

C.K. Yang (1959), on the other hand, provides us with some evidence—vivid testimony of the difficulties and "solutions" encountered by wives in domestic situations that proved to be irresolvable—that may be indicative of a prevailing pattern:

> In sixteen counties in southern Shansi, from July to September of 1949, there were twenty-five women who died of inhuman treatment by their husbands or their fathers- or mothers-in-law. In Hotsin and Wanchuan counties of the same province, in the second half of 1949, twenty-nine women committed or attempted suicide by hanging themselves or jumping into the well for the same reason. In the months of July to September in Wenshui county and in November in Taiku county there were twenty-four legal cases involving the loss of human lives; among these fourteen were women who met death for the same reason. In Pingyao county the wife of Chao Ping-sheng demanded a divorce and Chao killed her. In Lingchuen county, Li Shao-hai, a young married woman, commited suicide on account of maltreatment by her husband and mother-in-law. (Communist report cited in Yang, 1959:66)

Women's Status

Women were considered inferior in traditional China, although their status increased with age, the bearing of male heirs, and ascending to the head of the domestic household in older age. In the prerevolutionary years female babies were considered an economic liability and throughout their lives females were downtrodden and suffered.

> How sad it is to be a woman!
> Nothing on earth is held so cheap.
> Boys stand leaning at the door.
> Like Gods fallen out of heaven.
> Their hearts brave the Four Oceans,
> The wind and dust of a thousand miles.
> No one is glad when a girl is born;
> By her the family sets no store.
> (Fu Hsuan cited in Curtin, 1975:13)

The practice of female infanticide was common, particularly in time of famine, drought, high taxes, and other economic catastrophes (Levy, 1949:99). Although the actual killing of a female child at birth may not have occurred with great frequency, the child frequently suffered neglect with a resultant higher death rate among female children than among their male counterparts. The selling of female children into slavery occurred frequently among the peasantry. The neglect and maltreatment of female children was tied to the oppressive feudal economic system. William Hinton (1966), in his analysis of rural village life, presents the following case study on the integral relationship of child neglect and economic conditions:

> In Chingtsun one old woman said, "I sold four daughters because I had to pay back a landlord debt. I wept the whole night, and the tears burned my eyes. Now I am blind. Poverty forced me to sell my own daughters. Every mother loves her child." Others said, "In the old society no one loved a daughter because you brought them up and they left the house. Many parents drowned their little daughters. In the old society feet were bound with cloth. Small feet were thought to be one of the best qualities of women. But to bind a woman's feet is to tie her body and soul. Small feet are a symbol of the old society." (Hinton, 1966:397–398)

A heartrending illustration of the abuse of females was the prevalent practice of foot binding. Young girls between the ages of 5 and 7 had their feet bound. This practice, which was introduced into China in the tenth century, continued well into the 1940s, although it was officially banned in 1911. Ostensibly, the bound foot was romanticized as a mark of femininity and beauty; in actuality it became a symbol of the subordinate role of women in China. An old Chinese proverb states its essential purpose: "Feet are bound, not to make them beautiful as a curved bow, but to restrain women when they go out of doors" (Curtin, 1975:10). The binding process, which was excruciatingly painful, required the flexing and pressing of four toes over the sole of the foot. The feet were then bound in bandages, and the girl was forced to walk in shoes that became progressively smaller until, after a two- or three-year period, the feet were reduced to three or four inches in length from heel to toe.

The inferior position of women was actualized within the marriage structure and in their seclusion and lack of education. C.K. Yang (1959) observes that the seclusion of women was not only to prevent them from contact with men outside the family, thus forestalling romantic love as a basis of marriage, but also to prevent them access to opportunities for independence in political, economic, and social activities. The following passage illustrates how the traditional ways still survived in the early years of Communist rule:

> Restricting and interfering with women's participation in social activities is a form of mistreatment. After the victory of the Chinese people's revolution, due to the growth of political awakening, the broad masses of women have begun to participate in social activities, but they face a great deal of resistance. Some women who participated in the women's association, in literacy classes, or in newspaper-reading groups, have come home to confront the long faces of a husband and mother-in-law. Some women have returned from a meeting and the family would not give them food to eat, and some have even been locked out of the house. Some husbands and mothers-in-law summarily forbid women from participating in any social activity. Still other women are beaten up or even tortured to death by their husbands and mothers-in-law because of participation in social activities. Such conditions occur not only among peasants and workers, but also among urban bourgeoisie, and even among the intelligentsia. (Yang, 1959:112)

In summary, the rigidity of the class lines that separated the gentry from the peasantry provided for the strength and stability of the traditional family system. But such stability was achieved at the price of immeasurable repression and suffering.

Within the rigidity of the family hierarchy, women and the young were subjected to harassment and punishment by men and the old. The subjugation of individual rights as well as the rights of women and the young were traditionally justified as practices that preserved and strengthened the family. Ultimately, the traditional age and gender hierarchy and the system of family status and authority facilitated its very downfall. To document the changes in the family, we now turn to an examination of the historical processes and forces both before and after the Communist revolution.

The Communist Revolution and the Family

Prior to the founding of the People's Republic of China in 1949, the traditional social order was already undergoing changes. Beginning in the mid-nineteenth century, the eastern seaboard and inland river ports were industrializing and open to Western trade. Improved means of transportation and the development of new economic opportunities brought many peasants and intellectuals into the emerging cities. Western ideas, norms, and material goods introduced through religious missions, trade, education, and political intervention led to the rapid disintegration of the traditional family among the intellectuals. They demanded a less-authoritarian family structure, equality of women, free choice in marriage selection, greater freedom for the young, and the end of footbinding, concubinage, and female slavery.

The traditional family system, with its rigid hierarchy and institutionalized subjugation of women, the young, and the individual, was challenged by the intellectuals and by the oppressed age and gender groups. In 1911, with the overthrow of the Ch'ing Dynasty and the rise to power of Sun Yat-sen, these groups demanded a new family system. Despite the intensive and extensive resistance of traditionalists, modern changes were gradually legitimated through a series of legal statutes that stressed equality of the sexes and individual rights over those of the kinship group. Through the 1910s, 1920s and 1930s, a series of civil codes were formulated that sought to change the family system into a more egalitarian one. However, the movement had its greatest impact on the already liberalized higher status intellectual groups located in the urban centers. It had relatively little impact on the vast agricultural region that contained more than three-quarters of the population. Further, there is very little evidence that the Nationalist government enforced any of these codes, and it is relatively certain that there was minimal change when the Communists gained political control of the country in 1949.

The Chinese Communist Party (CCP), from its inception in the early 1920s, realized that the traditional family system was dependent on the traditional ideological, political, and class systems as well as the semifeudalistic agricultural economy. Its persistence through 2,000 years without major substantive changes was attributed to the fact that it was thoroughly integrated with the traditional system and, indeed, served as the center of all social activities. From its beginning the CCP desired to replace the Confucian-based virtues and ethics of the family with a new family system based on Marxist ideology. The family was conceived of as the institution basic to providing the necessary link to the building of the new socialist individual and the socialist society. Reflecting the views of Marx, Engels, and Lenin, the CCP attacked the old family system for its maltreatment and oppression of women. Mao Tse-tung's report to the Executive Committee published at the Second National Congress of Representatives of the Soviets held in March 1934 demonstrated the Communist emphasis on the liberation of women from the tyranny of the family:

> This democratic marriage system destroys the feudal shackles which have fettered humanity and in particular the women and it establishes new norms in accordance

with human nature. It is one of the greatest victories in human history, however this victory depends on the victory of democratic dictatorship. Only when, after the overthrow of the dictatorship of the landlords and capitalists, the toiling masses of men and women — in particular women — have acquired political freedom in the first place, and economic freedom in the second, can freedom of marriage obtain its final guarantee. (Mao Tse-tung cited in Chao, 1977:126–127)

This historical concern of the CCP formed the basis of the Marriage Law of 1950. It was the first civil code announced by the CCP after the establishment of the People's Republic of China. According to Teng Ying-chao, vice-president of the All-China Democratic Women's Federation and the wife of Chou En-lai, the purpose of the law was "to ensure to people the full freedom of marriage, and to deal a death blow to the old marriage system" (cited in Curtin, 1975:35).

The Marriage Law of 1950 is based on the equality of the sexes. It excludes the influence of extended family members in the selection of marital partners and abolishes arranged marriages. It outlaws polygamy, concubinage, child marriage, and the practice of paying a price in money or gifts for a wife. The new law, which actually is a moral code for the regulation of many aspects of family life, also prescribes new methods of contracting marriages, defines the rights and duties of the husband and wife, redefines the relations of parents and children, and protects the rights of children. The articles on divorce allow for divorce by mutual consent or on the insistence of either spouse. It describes the obligations of divorced parents to their children and defines the division of property after divorce.

To destroy the authority base of the traditional family system, a multifaceted attack was launched in the form of land reform, economic innovation, class struggle, class consciousness, and thought reform. It was deemed necessary to destroy the authority structure of the gentry, which was based on land ownership and the power of the *tsu* (clan.)

The CCP viewed the traditional family, the clan organization, and the landlord system as interlocking agents of the old feudal system and, therefore, as obstacles that must be removed for the society to modernize. The *tsu*, in particular, came under attack. The *tsu*, which was the largest corporate kin group, included all persons with a common ancestor. The *tsu* could be composed of thousands of people and could include both gentry and peasantry. It varied in importance from one section of the country to another, but it could often include all the inhabitants of a village. In such cases, it served as the judicial and enforcement authority, and it acted as a governmental agency in the collection of taxes. The educational system was controlled by the *tsu*. It ultimately had control over individual families and served as the final mediator in their disputes. It maintained ancestral graves and the extensive *tsu* property.

The interrelationships among families of the same *tsu*, who often have the same surname, are depicted in the following document written in the pre-Communist era:

Every family in X village where I live bears the surname "Chu." These families are all descended from Ting Ling Chu who moved from a village twenty miles away to X about three hundred years ago. The X village is one of six villages which make up the Chang River clan of Chus with fifteen villages. Our family has intimate relations with the group of Chu families in the village. The village has an ancestral hall which is the center of social and religious life of the Chu families in X. When some extraordinary thing happens to some one family, other families are willing to help. Therefore, there is no need of any philanthropic institution. When a person of the village dies a tablet made of wood bearing his or her title and name is put in the shrine of the ancestral hall and the ceremony of ancestor worship is conducted there.

The families of the village are well organized. A board of elders consisting of the oldest member of each family is in charge of the village affairs. At regular meetings the birth of every male child and every marriage are recorded. The board of elders also has judicial power. When there is a dispute between two families, they refer the matter to the board for decision. The board of elders then calls a meeting in which not only the elders of the board but all influential members of the village are present. The two parties present their claims and arguments and after discussion, persuasion, and compromise, a certain agreement is brought about.

The Chu county clan has no definite organization. All Chu families of the same county have good will toward each other and under some extraordinary circumstances they may combine. About fifty years ago a member of a family in a Chu village was mistreated by the magistrate of a neighboring county. He presented his case to the members of the Chang River Chu and they decided to take revenge. Chus from two districts of the county joined the crusade. About a thousand people marched to the neighboring county and caught the magistrate. They brought him to the office of the perfect and demanded that he be dismissed from office. The prefect consented. This incident reflects how members are protected by family organizations in China. (Burgess and Locke, 1945:39–40)

Land-reform practices sought to attack the *tsu* at its base. Traditionally, the family farm was viewed as a family enterprise, as were other kinship-based industries. Even the farming equipment was the joint property of the extended family. All deeds and contracts were signed in the family name. The CCP acted through an atomizing land reform. They proceeded to redistribute land regardless of the two bastions of traditionalism, age and gender. It was presumed that, by undermining the traditional economic base, the traditional social structure would also be undermined. Confiscation of land and subsequent redistribution to the peasantry was to create a new social base, tear down the class structure, and, in turn, help reorder the state.

Social classes were reclassified. Village social life was no longer centered on the *tsu*. Only approved social meetings took place under party scrutiny. All informational sources were placed under party control. The educational system underwent drastic revisions. The CCP recognized the importance of education and sought to implement a new system that would nullify and destroy the old ways. Education became available to all, especially women, who had been systematically excluded under the traditional system.

In *China Shakes the World,* Jack Belden gives a vivid illustration of the major changes that took place in the lives of peasant women as Mao's Eight Route Army was liberating areas of the country from Japanese control during the years 1938 to 1945. The CCP was committed to the equality of women. When they gained control of large areas, they initiated land reform and won the support of the peasants. They found that women were important allies. The CCP adopted a radical social program to mobilize the population in the continued fight against the Japanese and the Chinese Nationalists.

In the women of China the Communists possessed, almost ready made, one of the greatest masses of disinherited human beings the world has ever seen. And because they found the key to the heart of these women, they also found one of the keys to victory over Chiang Kai-shek. (Belden, 1970:275)

One of the first acts was to organize a women's association. A cadre (political group) would get some women together and would encourage them to talk about their lives. The cadre would tell them that they no longer were in bondage to men, that they had the right to equality, the right to eat well, and should not be beaten by their husbands or in-laws. At first, the women were reluctant to speak of their bitterness and misery. But slowly, they began to speak up. And so was born the Speak Bitterness sessions.

The Speak Bitterness sessions can be compared to the consciousness-raising groups of contemporary American women. In these meetings groups of women would gather in the village and publicly recount the brutality of the old system. Women soon realized that their personal torments were not unique but rather reflected social conditions under which they had all been living. Their individual concerns were transformed into a collective force against the oppressive system. It led to their unification.

Belden dramatically describes this process in "Gold Flower's Story" (Belden, 1970:275–307). Gold Flower gave her account of her problems and received the encouragement of other women to change her unhappy situation. She returned to her in-laws' home and attempted to force them and her husband to alter their brutal treatment of her and consider her as an equal. When her wife-beating husband did not comply, the women's association took collective action and vented their fury and anger.

> The crowd fell on him, howling, knocked him to the ground, then jumped on him with their feet. . . . Those in the rear leaped in, tore at his clothing, then seized his bare flesh in their hands and began twisting and squeezing till his blood flowed from many scratches. . . . Chang let out an anguished howl. "Don't hurt me anymore." Under the blows of the women, his cries were soon stilled. The women backed off. Gold Flower peered down at her husband. He lay there motionless on the ground, like a dead dog, his mouth full of mud, his clothes in tatters and blood coming in a slow trickle from his nose. "That's how it was with me in the past," Gold Flower thought. Unable to restrain a feeling of happiness, she turned to the other women. "Many thanks, comrade sisters, for your kindness. If it had not been for you, I would not have been able to get my revenge." (Belden, 1970:302)

The tensions and conflicts were not simply between the wife and husband. There was also an inherent problem between woman of different generations that surfaced. Mothers-in-law saw the drive for female equality as a real threat to their status and interest, with a resultant loss in their economic and social security in old age. Equality, they perceived, would mean that they no longer would be able to control their sons' wives and force them to assume their workload. William Hinton (1966) illustrates this conflict in his account of a man who was criticized for favoring his wife over his mother and thus was not fulfilling his filial piety.

In the decades since the revolution of 1949, China has experienced four major campaigns all directed in part to assure the emancipation of women and the destruction of the traditional patriarchal family system. The first thrust was the passage of the Marriage Law of 1950, which sought to free the individual from the old traditional feudal system. The second, the Great Leap Forward of 1958, was intended to achieve greater productivity in agriculture and independence in industrial development. Through the establishment of communes, it sought to achieve women's equality by circumventing traditional male prerogatives in the family and household. The third campaign was the Great Proletarian Cultural Revolution, which began in 1965. With the death of Mao Tse-tung in 1976 and the ascendancy to power of Teng Tsaio-ping, China can be seen to have entered into the present phase of social and family change. Our account will continue by examining events after the passage of the Marriage Law of 1950, which culminated in the Great Leap Forward campaign of 1958.

Although the Marriage Law of 1950 made important inroads toward the achievement of women's equality and the destruction of the patriarchal family, significant problems were encountered. National priorities after land reform focused on increasing production, nationalization, and the collectivization of agriculture. Lower priorities were given to the struggle against the traditional family institution. These economic and political factors resulted in the downplaying of women's rights and increased emphasis was placed on mobilizing women while admonishing them to perform traditional family duties as well.

This, in turn, led to a revival of traditional family practices in rural areas. Aline K. Wong (1974) examined Chinese documents that revealed that the practice of early marriage, arranged marriage, and the payment of exorbitant bride prices still prevailed well into the second half of the 1950s. For example, Inger Hellstrom (1963) reports that, in 1953 in two rural counties, 90 percent of all marriages were arranged. He also cites a study undertaken in 1953 to investigate enforcement of the Marriage Law of 1950, which concludes the following:

> The law was only partially effective in the Central-South and East China, and hardly at all observed in Northwest and Southern China, where parents still arranged marriages, reared daughters-in-law for their sons, and married off their children too young; even female slavery and concubinage were still practiced. (Hellstrom, 1963:272)

The Great Leap Forward and the Cultural Revolution

The period 1953 through 1958 was designated as the "transition to socialism" period and was governed by policies of the first Five Year Plan. This period was marked by unbalanced production: industry experienced enormous growth, but agriculture proceeded at a much slower pace, barely keeping up with the increase in production. The dissatisfaction with the unbalanced production and countrywide economic problems led the CCP to adopt a new policy, the Great Leap Forward, which stressed more balanced economic growth in agriculture as well as in heavy and light industry. This plan also desired to achieve a more-efficient balance between centralized planning and local initiative. The result was the development of the commune system in rural and urban areas. This was essentially a major reworking of provincial political boundaries and a new administrative system. The primary thrust was to encourage communes in the countryside to combine all functions, from industry and agriculture to education and self-policing. The second Five Year Plan began in 1958 and was to initiate "the construction of socialism." An allied objective of the Great Leap Forward was to bring women into full economic partnership with men.

The Chinese Communists, following in the intellectual position of Marx, Engels, and Lenin, believed that women could not achieve a full position of equality in the society if they were confined to household tasks. Tied to this belief was the allied idea that as long as production centered on the family unit, women would be restricted to the home. If the family continued as the unit or production, women would be solely involved in the care of the children and of housework. The solution to this problem was seen in the collectivization of the land and with everyone, women and men alike, working it:

> In the old society, women were generally regarded as men's dependents, no matter how hard they worked at home. The profession of housewife did not pay. Apart from political and social discrimination against women, the economic dependence of women was the source of men's superiority complex and their undisputed authority as head of the family. Under such circumstances, notwithstanding all talk to the contrary, inequality between men and women existed in fact so long as women had to depend on men for their support. . . .
>
> Liberation brought political and social discrimination against women to an end [*sic*]. But the problem of economic dependence of women took a long time to solve, with the result that women were usually at a disadvantage in public life. This unfortunate state of affairs changes rapidly when women stand on their own feet economically and become equal partners with men in supporting the family. In this

Women and children working in a people's commune near Peking (Beijing).

> way the status of women is raised. . . . Thus women acquire an increasing sense of
> their economic independence and the old practice of the male head of the family
> bossing around the home is on the way out. (Cited in Johnson, 1976:300)[4]

The CCP's introduction of the system of the commune in 1958 was claimed to
represent a stage in the development of the ultimate communist form of common
ownership and equal distribution according to need. A major objective of the communes was to facilitate the destruction of the clan and its replacement by the commune itself. It sought to replace the pre-existing pattern of familism with communal-
ism. It developed out of the traditional family values that stressed the extended
family over the individual. Individualism continued to be submerged within the
newly emergent unit—the commune.

Ancestral graves were converted into farmlands, and economic life fell under the
domination of the commune, not the clan. The political control exercised by the clan
was surrendered. Rural populations were resettled—to break up the local village
ties, which often were under the domination of the *tsu*. The *tsu* was attacked as the
embodiment of the old feudal system, which served to perpetuate the corrupt Nationalist government. It was also seen as the basis for the dominance of both the older
generation and males. In general, the aim was to replace the *tsu* with the commune
and its own network of authority and loyalty.

By the end of 1958 the government had taken ownership of almost all heavy
industry. It established some 26,000 rural communes, each averaging 5,000 households and about 2,400 acres of land. The commune became the administrative

---

[4] The quotation is from Yang Kan Ling. (1950.) "Family Life—The New Way." *Peking Review.*
(Nov. 18): 9–10.

standard of rural community organization. It sought to be self-sufficient by manufacturing its own tools, fertilizers, and clothing, as well as its food.

To get women into the labor force, many household tasks were collectivized. As part of the program, the rural communes set up communal dining rooms, kitchens, nurseries, and child-care centers, and kindergartens and schools. Additional services, developed to reduce further the need for individual women's work within the family, included laundries, weaving and sewing cooperatives, barber shops, and shoe-making and repair shops.

William J. Goode (1963) astutely points out that the establishment of the communal system and its accompanying collective domestic services can be seen as one way of radically revamping gender-role relationships without insisting that men get involved in traditionally female-defined tasks. Further, this collectivization had as its primary aim not so much the destruction of gender-based division of labor, but rather the socialization of women's work so that they could enter the labor force and get out of the home.

> In certain respects, the development of communal dining halls, nurseries and kindergartens, laundry services, and so on may be more acceptable to the Chinese male than would be any serious attempt to force him to conform to egalitarian values that would direct him to share the household tasks equally or to give up the services which were traditionally his male right. Under the communal system, he may still obtain these services, even though they are not so individualized as they would be in his own household; at least he does not have to take part in such "women's activities," himself. . . . after many generations of ideological debate in the West, men have not yet conceded egalitarianism in the home or in the economic life. How much less, then, would Chinese men have accepted such a move. To this degree, then, the communal solution bypasses the still strong insistence on male prerogatives among Chinese men. (Goode, 1963:302)

The communes brought about a massive introduction of women into the labor force. In 1959, 90 percent of the total female labor force worked in the rural communes. Johnson (1976) cites figures that report that men worked an average of 249 days in rural areas before the Great Leap Forward; in 1959, their workload had increased to 300 days. For women, the figures almost double: 166 days in the precommune year and 250 days at the height of the commune movement. Most of the jobs women obtained were not in heavy industry — these still remained male-defined occupations — but were in such new industries as water conservancy, afforestation, construction projects, as well as in increased sideline jobs in fisheries and animal husbandry. Several hundred million women were employed in these newly created labor markets. Thus, in these occupational areas as well as in the collectivization of such domestic services as food preparation and child care, the CCP was careful to avoid generating hostility among men: "The Great Leap policies, it seems, did not attack norms that operated against women's participation in certain types of work so much as it created new jobs in areas that women could enter more easily" (Johnson, 1976:301).

However, soon after the implementation of the policies of the Great Leap Forward, China experienced great economic difficulties. In 1959 almost half of the cultivated land was affected by heavy floods or serious drought. The following year more drought, typhoons, floods, and insect pests seriously affected almost three-quarters of the cultivated land. Soon after the creation of the communes, a rift developed between the Soviet Union and China, which led to the withdrawal of Soviet economic aid in 1960. This caused critical problems in heavy industry and was a severe setback to China's industrial progress.

In addition to these difficulties, organizational problems in the communes compelled a slowdown in the rate of economic growth and expansion. This centered around the anger of the peasants toward communal administrative policies. Katie

Curtin (1975) points out that the reasons for the failure of the Great Leap Forward were not directly related to its reforms of family life. Rather, the difficulties stemmed in part from the attempt to radically reorganize traditional villages under a central commune administration. This centralism changed the work pattern by drastically lengthening the workday and by transferring a large part of the harvest out of the hands of the peasants for distribution to the cities and for industrial uses.

William Gasster describes the failures of the Great Leap Forward in the following summarization of the analysis by Ta-Chung Liu:

> The Great Leap Forward was based on a sound diagnosis of the basic weakness of the mainland economy but a serious misconception of the proper way to deal with it. The poorly conceived treatment included excessive regimentation in rural life, impossibly long working hours, removal of incentives (such as family plots), unworkable farming and water control techniques, excessive pressure on industrial enterprises to expand production, and total miscalculation of technical possibilities in introducing the backyard furnaces. . . . The whole economy suffered a serious leap backward from 1958 to 1961. (Gasster, 1972:122)

During the 1960s, almost immediately after the implementation of the Great Leap Forward in 1958, the massive economic difficulties experienced in China led to a reversal in the policy concerning the mobilization of women into the labor force. In 1959 and 1960 the Great Leap Forward began to be abandoned. The communes were radically altered. Gasster (1972) reports that the 26,000 large communes were divided into about 74,000 smaller ones—a three-fold increase. This approximated the number of townships that existed before 1958. The organizational structure of a given commune was also reduced in size. Families were given small private plots. Land that they farmed collectively with other families coincided with the land that they had always farmed. The communes still controlled a variety of functions, including birth, death, and marriage registry, regulation of civic disputes, and management of schools and hospitals. They were still viable administrative entities.

For women, the collapse of the Great Leap Forward meant a retrenchment in their drive for equality. Nurseries, dining halls, and other collective domestic services were scaled down or abolished. The many special industrial and agricultural projects that had been newly created and that employed a high percentage of women were consolidated or shut down. The result was that a large number of women who had just entered the labor force found themselves laid off or unemployed. The CCP, although recognizing that this retarded the achievement of women's equality and prevented the redressing of serious inequities, felt that first priority was overcoming the economic reversals.

> Concerning the status of women, marital status and family relationships, survivals of old ideas and viewpoints still remain.
> On top of this, the extent of women's participation in social labor, viewed either from the number of persons employed or from the role they have played, still suffers a certain limitation although it is the correct proportion in relation to the present stage of development of our national economy. As a result of this limitation, there is still a difference in fact though not in law for women in the enjoyment of equal rights with men both in society and in the home. This difference will gradually disappear following the further development of production. That is to say, to do away completely with the old survivals in marriage and family relationships, it is necessary to create the more mature socio-economic and ideological conditions this requires. (cited in Johnson, 1976:301–302)[5]

---

[5] The quotation is from Yang Liu. (1964.) "Reform of Marriage and Family Systems in China. *Peking Review,* (March 18):19.

China underwent political and economic turmoil throughout the 1960s. In the years from 1961 through 1966, China experienced a retrenchment in many of the radical political, economic, and social policies advocated by Mao Tse-tung. During this period Mao was replaced as head of state by Liu Shao-ch'i. Liu's primary concern was to proceed with economic development and he saw no need to insist on the rigorous following of Maoist policies. Western models or those of the Soviet Union could be adopted if they would increase industrial and technological developments.

Liu emphasized material incentives, private plots were encouraged, and free markets flourished. His policies relaxed Mao's demand for political indoctrination and party discipline. Liu also wished to strengthen the family to help establish higher production outputs. The result of these policies was an increase in the standard of living and a relaxation of the military-style aspects of everyday life, but it also led to the increased power of the family.

Liu's policies meant a return of women to domestic life and a reaffirmation of traditional family roles, albeit with a Communist twist. Ai-li S. Chin (1969), in a content analysis of Chinese fiction from 1962 to 1966, reports that it stressed the solidarity of the nuclear family, the renewal of wider kinship ties, and a respect for elders in general and the father in particular. Chin observes that the stories that emphasize family unity have as a common theme the partial return to the old pattern of paternal authority and filial piety. They emphasize the solidarity of the father – son tie and the reassertion of younger generation subordination. Father relationships with daughters include strictness with an element of affection, a pattern that repeats the traditional practice of fathers disciplining their daughters less severely than their sons. Interestingly, Chin finds ambivalence in the stories dealing with the proper roles of women. Two rival ideologies are present: the first emphasizes the authority of elders; the second concerns the basic doctrine of individual responsibilities. Further, the stories reflect a dilemma on the correct position for liberated women: Should she be independent or demure? Should her place be with her family and the household or as a full participant in the labor force in the building of the socialist state?

In 1966, Mao wrestled political control away from Liu and his supporters through his brilliant use of the Red Guard and the subsequent launching of the Great Proletarian Cultural Revolution. The objective was to wipe out the "four olds" — old ideas, old culture, old customs, old habits. According to a Maoist document of the period, the aim was to "use the new ideas, culture, customs and habits of the proletariat to change the mental outlook of the whole of society" and to "touch people to their very souls" (cited in Gasster, 1972:130). Integral to this view was Mao's desire to prevent the development of a Soviet-style bureaucratic ruling class.

Handwritten posters were pasted on walls, posts, and kiosks throughout the country. The Red Guards, consisting primarily of the young, attacked the Liu-led leadership and their followers as well as the intellectuals and the bureaucrats, who in their view, had lost sight of the needs of the masses and who no longer followed the objectives of the revolution. There was a wholesale purge of party members at all levels. Liu Shao-ch'i was disgraced and purged from the party.

The years 1966 through 1969 were marked by turbulence. The remnants of traditional society were violently attacked and suppressed. Traditional artifacts, such as old art objects, were smashed and old books were burned. It was as if all visual evidence of the past had to be destroyed.

The Red Guard entered people's homes and shattered family altars that denoted allegiances to the Confucian reverence for ancestors. Churches, mosques, and temples still serving religious functions were closed and put to secular use. These included the great Buddhist, Lama, and Taoist temples of Peking, which had been allowed to remain open partially because of tourists. All religious statues, altars, and other artifacts were removed.

Tillman Durdin (1971), writing for the *New York Times,* vividly described the effects of these policies based on his observations of a three-week visit to the vast coastline of China. He reported that not a single home that he visited had any family altar; nor were there tablets to ancestors or any representation of the old gods worshipped by the Chinese masses — which would still be found in family homes in Hong Kong. Women no longer wore the traditional sheath dresses, nor did they use cosmetics. They wore the same garments as men: frumpy blue or gray trousers and jackets. The traditional large Chinese family was not visible. Indeed, housing could only accommodate a husband, wife, and one to three children. He observed the absence of traditional art, music, and literature, which had been replaced by Maoist equivalents. He concludes the following:

> In the Chinese People's Republic there is no "mysterious East" any more, just workaday people following workaday routines that seem essentially familiar and ordinary to the Westerner, even though they operate within a Marxist totalitarian framework. . . . A new generation has appeared and though much of the old China is too indelible to erase as yet, a new China with ways quite different from the old is in existence. (Durdin, 1971:125–126)

It can be seen that the ultimate aim of the Cultural Revolution was to revive and expand many of the goals of the Great Leap Forward. Mao hoped that this would enable China to overcome the "Three Great Differences — the differences (or contradictions) between town and country, industry and agriculture, and mental and manual labor" (Gasster, 1972:130). Mao believed that to build a proletarian society it was necessary to have a viable commune system:

> In Mao's view, the ultimate solution to problems of political unity, social change, and economic development continues to be the commune system, in which a relatively high degree of administrative decentralization encourages the people's sense of participation, releases their energies and productive capacities, and avoids excessive bureaucratization; and ideological solidarity, which means common allegiance to Mao's thoughts, provides national unity. Indeed, it sometimes seems that ideological solidarity, which means common allegiance to Mao's thoughts, provides national unity. Indeed, it sometimes seems that ideological unity is intended as a substitute for political and economic centralization. If so, Mao's China bears a certain resemblance to traditional China. But Mao believes that only the commune system can permanently eliminate the Three Great Differences. (Gasster, 1972:134)

The implementation of the policies of the Cultural Revolution had a significant impact on the family and on women's roles. Once again, emphasis was placed on the need for women to engage in the collective economy to achieve full equality. Women, including working women and housewives, were politically mobilized. They were encouraged to criticize and question the power structure, whether it was in the home, at work, or in the community. The authoritarian structure of the family came under attack.

> Over thousands of years our family relations have been that son obeys what his father says and wife obeys what her husband says. Now we must rebel against this idea. . . . We should make a complete change in this. . . . It should no longer be a matter of who is supposed to speak and who is supposed to obey in a family but a matter of whose words are in line with Mao Tse-tung's thought. (Johnson, 1976:310)

However, despite some additional gains, the pendulum once again swung toward conservative norms and values. By 1972, the revolutionary zeal subsided and the concern for women's political mobilization, equal education, and full involvement in the collective economy once again died down. Kay Ann Johnson (1976) makes the following points in her concluding remarks on the women of China, which presents, in succinct form, an overall assessment of the Cultural Revolution.

> However, the Cultural Revolution may have accelerated the creation of a new generation of young women leaders. These women, without personal knowledge of the wretched female oppression of the past, may be more conscious of the persistence of serious discrimination of the present. Like the Red Guards who, taking their elders' socialist ideal seriously, became critically aware of the elitist nature of established institutions before their elders in authority, young educated women may be more likely to take the propagated ideals of sex equality to demand more complete equality in politics, family life, and work. What is certain is that the struggle to make families, jobs, and opportunities equal has only begun. Liberation will be won only through protracted struggles—struggles that persistently raise issues of sex inequality to the level of political saliency and that overcome the ever present tendency to shelve these issues and mask continued inegalitarian practices and values. (Johnson, 1976:315–316)

China After Mao

New policies for social change were revised dramatically in China during the 1970s. The Cultural Revolution of 1966–1972 weakened the economy. In addition, the excesses of revolutionary zeal among radical Maoists curtailed the development of education, science, and technological knowledge. In 1971, the U.S. Secretary of State, Henry Kissinger, and, in 1972, President Richard M. Nixon visited China. In addition to the broader perspective of global politics, the process of diplomatic normalization can be seen as a desire by the Chinese to obtain scientific and technological know-how.

In 1974, two years before their deaths, Chairman Mao and Premier Chou put forward the Four Modernizations Program. It was not until after their deaths and the ascendancy to power of Teng Hsaio-p'ing that the ambitious plan calling for the complete modernization of China by the year 2000 began to be implemented. This plan calls for four modernizations—in farming, industry, science and technology, and defense. Its primary aim is to accelerate scientific, technological, and industrial development to increase economic growth.

The Four Modernizations Program has three phases. The first, covering the years 1978–1980, is aimed at the nationwide mechanization of agriculture and the consolidation and restructuring of existing industry. Phase two covers the next 5 years, 1980–1985. It calls for major developments in factory production. The final stage, 1985 to the year 2000, seeks further expansion of production by including more sophisticated consumer goods and such advanced technological items as electronics and computers. All indications of military modernization are given lower priority in the creation of a technological and industrial base (*Newsweek*, 1979).

To improve planning, make administration more efficient, and raise productivity, greater stress is being put on material incentives, adopting relatively elitist policies to foster the development of needed talent, and using market forces to spur competition and foster development. Teng Hsaio-p'ing has reversed Mao's view of human nature. Mao argued that individuals are motivated to work their hardest for the common good, whereas Teng takes the view that individuals are primarily motivated by material encouragements. The range of material incentives introduced by Teng include bonuses for productive factory workers, bigger incomes, larger private plots, and the lowering of the costs for agricultural equipment for hard-working agricultural workers. Students with the highest grades are given preferential treatment in entering colleges and studying abroad.

In January 1979, in an attempt to take advantage of the unused talents of the prerevolutionary capitalists, landowners, and other members of the gentry still residing in China (whose power and influence were stripped during the Cultural Revolution), China restored their citizens' rights. In announcing these policy changes, the CCP began a blistering attack leveled against those who were instrumental in the programs, implementations, and practices of the Cultural Revolution. Coming under attack was Lin Piao, the former defense minister, and Mao's leftist associates, known as the Gang of Four. By October 1979, Mao himself was criticized, and the Cultural Revolution was described as appalling and leading to catastrophe.

The implications of these changes for the Chinese family are beginning to be felt. An integral aspect of the Four Modernizations Program is the desire for stability and unity. This means a reinforcement of family values over individual concerns. It has led to a hardening of attitudes regarding divorce. Divorce is now viewed as "going against the feeling for social harmony and economic efficiency" (Butterfield, 1979). The reading on a divorce trial illustrates this change.

The Four Modernizations campaign has led to a change in Chinese population policies. The CCP believes that a high growth rate could wipe out most of the anticipated development gains. "The rapid growth of the population has brought a lot of difficulties to the national economy, the people's livelihood and employment, creating a roadblock for socialist construction. Fast population growth has hampered the four modernizations and the raising of the people's living standards" (Chinese official cited in Sterba, 1979). This is a radical change from the earlier philosophy that population growth was beneficial to the national interest.

China has launched an extensive birth-control educational campaign, using radio, television, newspapers, commune reading rooms, and exhortative songs at concerts to spread the new policy about population size. Birth-control devices are readily available and are distributed without cost. Sterilization operations for both men and women are encouraged. Abortions are largely free and given on request. Abortion does not carry the same emotional overtones that it does in the United States, and it never has been a political issue. The operations last about an hour and are either acupuncture abortions or Western-style procedures. Unless there are complications, women are expected to return to work the next day. In addition to birth control and abortions, the Chinese are encouraging later marriages, usually not before 28 for men and 25 for women. Legally, women cannot register for marriage until age 23. The minimum marriage age for men is 26 in urban areas and 25 in rural areas. This modifies the Marriage Law of 1950 which prescribed the minimum marriage age of men at 20 years and women at 18 years of age.

Economic incentives are used to curb population. Economic rewards are given to families who have the required number of children (one or two), and those families who exceed that number (three or more) are punished economically. In Sichuan province — with 90 million people, it is more populous than all but seven countries in the entire world — cash subsidies and other incentives are provided to families who have only one child, and 10 percent bonus in monthly income is offered. Such families are also eligible for the same type of housing as larger families. Their child would also receive preferential treatment in admission to schools and in job assignments. In other provinces, salaries of those who have a third child are reduced 10 percent until that child reaches the age of 14. The child will also be denied free education and medical care.

China's approach to population control includes using group pressures. Factory managers and commune leaders maintain records on the number of children each woman has borne as well as the type of contraceptive she uses. Women's groups reach communal decisions on which family will be allowed to have a baby. Decisions are

In Cheng-chou, a rural area of China, a loudspeaker truck decorated with slogans emphasizes the importance of the policy of one child per family.

reached by checking with the provincial family planning committee of the factory or agricultural production team's birth quota. In addition, women's groups monitor the menstrual cycles of the female employees to check compliance. In this way, they hope that the unit's productivity will not be adversely affected by having too many women out on maternity leave (Butterfield, 1979).

Men are not exempt from social pressures. Publicly kept birth-control charts report on the techniques used by men to control their family size, and the charts are open to scrutiny by all members of the production unit. Butterfield (1979) reports that on one wall of the clinic of a production brigade there is a listing of the 29 officials and how they are complying with the birth-control campaign. Of the 27 men named (2 are women), the chart shows the 10 who have had vasectomies and the 14 whose wives are using the pill or the interuterine loop. Of the remaining 5, 2 of the men are married but are not practicing family planning and 3 others are too young to marry under China's strict policy of delaying wedlock until the prescribed age.

Recent newspaper dispatches have reported changes in Chinese attitudes toward heterosexual relationships. Under headlines with such titles as "Love Blooms Again,"[5] "Chinese Discover Love and other Feelings,"[6] and "First Cautious Steps: Dancing in a Changing China,"[7] these news stories report a loosening up of the strict moral codes covering relationships between men and women. Noticeable increases in the number of young men sporting mustaches and longer hair are being seen on Peking's streets. The young are increasingly shedding their Mao tunics and are wearing such fashions as tweed coats and leather jackets. These changes indicate that there is less pressure for social conformity. Finally, romance itself is making a come-

[5] *Newsweek,* February 5, 1979, pp. 51, 53.
[6] *Philadelphia Inquirer,* March 12, 1978.
[7] Fox Butterfield in *The New York Times,* December 31, 1978.

back, or at least a Western version of romance. Western observers report that there are now young persons holding hands or sitting on public benches and gazing into neach other's eyes. We must caution the reader to be wary of misreading these events as evidence that certain Chinese customs are emerging as Oriental versions of Western courtship, marriage, and family patterns and values. That is far from the case.

Westerners in their assessments of Chinese culture frequently fail to acknowledge one of the most significant differences in their culture and that of the Chinese: the differential value placed on individual rights versus group values. Westerners place primary emphasis on individual rights, whereas the Chinese favor the role of the individual in the group. Ross Terrill (1979), one of the most astute Western authorities on China, observes that all rights and duties flow from "self fulfillment of the person" and "shared values among the people." Occidentals favor the former, Chinese the latter. The group emphasis stems from the Confucian tradition and the Communist ideology. The contemporary social structure of Chinese society is based on the need for self-sacrifice in the building of an advanced industrialized nation. The imposition of Western values has led Americans, in particular, to misjudge and misunderstand developments in Chinese policy regarding modernization and the family.

Since the Communist revolution, China has been influenced by two goals that sometimes coincide, sometimes conflict with each other. One is the desire to create antiauthoritarian social relationships within a collectivist social organization. The other is to develop heavy industry and reach economic and development parity with the Soviet Union and the United States. After the 1949 revolution, China embarked on a policy that stressed heavy technological development and rural modernization. The development of an elitist class of managerial experts and the potential for the creation of a managerial and bureaucratic new class led to the Great Leap Forward and the establishment of the communes in 1958. Emphasis was placed on more-egalitarian social relationships and on women's equality and involvement in the labor force. The failure to develop medium and light industry in the rural countryside led to a retrenchment in the drive for egalitarian social relationships.

From 1962 to 1966, China was governed by the conservative policies of Liu Shao-ch'i. The emphasis was on the development of heavy industry and a hierarchical division of labor; greater stress was placed on material incentives and market-capitalism considerations. The issue of women's liberation and the development of a more-egalitarian family system was ignored. The Cultural Revolution of 1966 through 1972 was a return to a concern for the development of labor-intensive industry and more-egalitarian social relationships. Technologically intensive heavy industry and its inherent hierarchical division of labor fell into disfavor.

The post-Mao period, under the leadership of Teng Hsaio-p'ing, once again called for technological and heavy industrial development. That is the essence of the Four Modernizations program. In the past, similar programs have meant the re-emergence of autocratic social relationships, including the domination of the individual by the family system. It remains to be seen what the future holds for the individual and the family in China.

China in the 1980s

In examining changes in the Chinese family structure in the 1980s, we are struck by the development of two emerging forms. These forms are a consequence of the differential experiences of people living in rural and urban areas. As a consequence of these differential experiences, rural people's identities and particularly women's identities continue to be rooted in family relations. However, in the cities, governmental agencies and work units have taken over many of the family's functions and

For "Older Boys and Girls" of China, Matchmaking

BY EDWARD A. GARGAN

SHANGHAI—Chen Gaixin is a fussy romantic.

Her future husband, she insists, must be an intellectual, work for a research institute or the city government, have a house and be around 45 years old. He also should be "frank, good-mannered and thoughtful."

"Oh yes," she adds, he must be taller than 1.70 meters—a hair under 5 feet 7 inches.

At 36, Miss Chen is one of a growing number of middle-aged singles. Once past 30, people like Miss Chen usually live with their parents and find that potential spouses are to find.

"There are a lot of 'older boys and girls,'" said Jiang Yuedi, a merry woman in her 50's who has devoted several years to matching lonely hearts. "It is difficult for them to find someone. So we decided to set up this introduction room. This is a new thing and a good thing for society."

A CENTURIES-OLD PRACTICE

In Shanghai, introduction rooms like Mrs. Jiang's are cropping up all over town. In many cases, retired workers like Mrs. Jiang have taken over the role of matchmaker, once performed by friends or relatives in a practice that is centuries old in China.

A "love corner," as it was known, used to flourish in People's Park here. "Older boys and girls" would gather by the hundreds, size one another up and, in many cases, drift off hand in hand. Over this past summer, the number of people who descended on People's Park seeking partners mushroomed and, according to the local press, hawkers began roosting on benches shouting such things as "one, aged 34, is looking for a 28-year-old."

The press denounced this activity as auctioneering, and the "love corner" was banned.

"It is a real problem," said a young woman, whose shyness about giving her name was leavened by her willingness to try her English. "There are not many situations where boys can meet girls. There is not much privacy. Many people wait too long. They want someone with a house or with a good job. By the time they don't find someone, they are already old."

The woman said her brother's plant, a glass factory with a predominantly male work force, sponsored monthly dances with a nearby textile factory that employs women. A few late-night coffee shops have sprung up downtown, where, the woman said, "boyfriends bring girlfriends for privacy."

"But it is hard to meet new people there," she added.

Distressed over these difficulties, Mrs. Jiang and a handful of her friends persuaded their neighborhood street committee to allocate them a room in an apartment building.

"When we first started, people did not want to come because it meant they were unable to find someone on their own," said Kang Maoying, a neighborhood official who works with Mrs. Jiang.

The women printed forms asking love-seekers a battery of personal questions —none too personal—about jobs, salaries, education, their housing situation, habits and hobbies, their needs, and, of course, their height. Space is provided for a photograph. The women collect a fee of about 40 cents.

'PROBABLY LIE ABOUT HEIGHT'

"When they fill in the form, they probably lie about their height," Qu Jieda, one of the matchmakers, said. "Of course, when people see each other, they realize this."

Height, it appears, is the most crucial consideration in a spouse, and Mrs. Jiang puts it at the top of her list of why young women cannot find spouses.

"The young men are not tall enough," Mrs. Jiang. "The girls want men taller than they are. Of course, another problem is housing. If the boy does not have his own place, the girl does not want him as a husband. For some girls, the requirements are so high, they wait and wait and get past 30."

One of the applicants, Qu Leimeng,

(continued)

noted on his form that he was born in 1958, "the Year of the Dog," and was a college graduate and technician. His salary, he said, was the equivalent of $34.50 a month, but he had no apartment of his own. He lived with his parents. Mr. Qu professed to a height of 5 feet 7 inches and wanted a woman who was "a little cute to do housework and be tender."

COLLEGE EDUCATION A FACTOR

Mrs. Qu leafed through a stack of applications.

"Men who are tall and good-looking will probably have no problem," she said. "Those a little bit ugly or not too tall may have to wait a while. Girls all hope the boys will be taller than they are. You are allowed only one child, so if the husband is tall, the child will be tall. It is kind of a tradition for women to have tall men."

"Of course," she said, "men who are not very tall but are college graduates will have no problem. But if a boy is not tall and, on top of that, is not a college graduate, well, it probably will be difficult."

Mrs. Jiang said applicants could pore through application forms and select someone from a photograph.

"Then we send out a letter setting up an appointment," she said.

Discretion requires that the letter go out in a plain envelope without a return address, Mrs. Jiang said. "Some people don't want others to know that they use our services," she added.

The initial meeting occurs in the introduction room at the end of a six-foot table on two folding chairs.

"Sometimes they come and, after a moment, they say they will go out and talk elsewhere," Mrs. Jiang said.

"If it does not work, we start over," she said. "We try to be more careful next time. There was one girl, 36, who saw 10 people and at last succeeded this year. She wanted an articulate, open, faithful person who would not try and dominate her. She got someone who works in a milk research institute."

SOURCE. Edward A. Gargan. 1987. "For 'older boys and girls' of China, matchmaking." *The New York Times* (Nov. 4). Copyright © 1987 by The New York Times Company. Reprinted by permission.

---

have diminished family authority. This section examines these changes. We conclude by looking at the future implications of China's population increase in terms of the family and Chinese society.

The Four Modernizations program called for the balanced growth and modernization of four sectors—agriculture, industry, science and technology, and defense. The sector that has taken the brunt of the responsibility for growth has been agriculture. The goal has been to achieve a favorable balance between agricultural development and population growth. To achieve higher agricultural productivity, the government is actively encouraging family farming under the loose supervision of communes. A governmental directive was implemented in 1981 that recommended the nationwide reorganization of the communes, with the family as the basic unit of production. The family signs a contract with the village commune that fixes output quotas by household and assigns work tasks to each. Surpluses are controlled by the family and can be sold to enhance family income. Incentives are given to peasant families to cultivate waste land, plant trees, step up output of handicrafts, breed fish, and collect herbal medicines. In essence, the family has been given an increasingly positive role in the economic sphere. It has become the main contracting work-group under the family responsibility system.

While this policy has reaped economic benefits by expanding the scope of the peasant-family economy, the domain of local male kinship-based solidarity groups has also been strengthened. The economic success of this policy has resulted in the increased power and control of the patriarchal family over rural women. Judith Stacey (1985) observes that, as a result, the government has been reticient in curbing patriarchal authority and undertaking anti-patriarchal campaigns that would facilitate greater equality and participation by women in the agricultural labor force.

Margery Wolf (1985b), a leading authority on women in China, observed how this program, variously called the family responsibility system or the household production system, operated in a rural section of China, which she visited in 1981. The large production teams of 20 to 40 households that collectively held land, draft animals, and tools, and shared the profits were replaced by individual families who bid to work particular plots of lands. Wolf states that under the (replaced) communal system, women were protected from the autocratic elder males in their household by the collective's social pressure and state regulations. However, under the new household responsibility system the limited independence of rural women will be lost. For under the new program, the head of the production unit is now also the head of the household. As a consequence, women, being either young or old, will find themselves subservient to the economic decisions of males. And, as long as the family is economically productive, the niceties of governmental regulations will be overlooked. Wolf believes that, "In effect, the state has handed back to men as individuals their full patriarchal authority over women in what amounts to a decollectivization of Chinese agriculture" (1985b:43).

The massive social transformation of the Chinese countryside that has occurred since the revolution has wrought many changes. However, while the landlord gentry system that existed in prerevolutionary China and the organized lineage systems have been destroyed, the bonds of kinship remain a significant force that the government has used to fit their economic, political, and social purposes. Similarly, the underlying philosophy of using the family to fit the needs of the state has resulted in different outcomes regarding the family and kinship structures in cities.

Wolf (1985a) observes that in the cities, the state has done everything possible to destroy the bonds, moral debt, and filial duty to patrilineal kin. The goal of Communist ideology was not to destroy the family as a domestic unit, but rather to break up and destroy the old family system and its underlying patriarchal authority. She analyzes the impact of the state on the family through an examination of marriage. Her findings are based on 300 interviews of women in two cities and four rural communes conducted in 1980–1981.

Urban marriages are still controlled, but the control has shifted from the family and the lineage to the collective. In the cities, a marriage-registration system was developed that in effect enables the party to control who gets married, when, and to whom. Couples who marry must obtain permission from the party secretary of their work unit. On the other hand, in rural areas, couples seeking to marry may simply register within their brigade office. The age at marriage also varies between urban and rural areas. Urban women marry at a later age than rural women. This reflects the relative power of the family and the party. In the rural areas, power is held by the family. The goal is to get children married so that they can have children and consequentially continue the extended kinship structure. In the cities, the power of the party is supreme. The party's preference is that people marry later and have fewer children. Their policy is to control population growth.

The desired orientation of the newly married couple should not be themselves, or to their lineage, but to the collective. Arranged marriages by kin are no longer sanctioned and the ideal is for young people to marry whom they want and not be subjugated to the extended family. Obligations to the society are to replace kinship obligations. Wolf found that, in rural areas, the family still remains very strong in controlling marriage and three-quarters of her rural respondents were strongly influenced by their families as to whom they married. In the cities, parents served in an advisory capacity and extended kin—uncles, grandfathers, and cousins—were largely irrelevant in marriage decisions. Many people met at work or at school. Wolf reports that her urban informants were developing changing attitudes regarding

Jean-Pierre Laffont/Sygma

A contemporary Chinese family in Shanghai. Mrs. Lee, 30, is a bookkeeper and her husband, 33, is a computer engineer. Wu, their baby, is 9 months old.

arranged marriages. Of the 41 women she interviewed, a little more than one-half (23) felt that women should find their own mates, and the remaining 18 thought that they should have parental help or at least parental approval.

China's urban marriages are seen by Wolf to bear a superficial resemblance to the Western conjugal form. Based on her urban interviews and the reading of numerous marital guidebooks, Wolf finds the development of a "companionate marriage without the romance" (1985a:229). Interviewed women reflected the official version of the purposes of marriage: "a good marriage was one in which both parties were willing to work for the good of the country, studied hard to increase their knowledge so that they could contribute to their work units, and were not afraid of hard work" (Wolf, 1985a:229–230). Housing shortages and work-place involvements further influence and prevent the formation of the private culture intrinsic to conjugal marriage. Wolf reports that home is "less a love-nest than a staging ground for separate lives centered on their workplace" and the result is "to transfer the center of a person's life from her home to the unit where she works" (Wolf, 1985a:231).

Wolf concludes by noting that the traditional Chinese rural family is still highly viable but that is no longer the case in urban areas. "In a sense, in the countryside, the family has won; in the cities, in contrast, the state has won because it has taken on so many of the functions of the family" (1985b:48).

The Marriage Law of 1980 and Population Policy

In 1980, a new marriage law was passed that has had important implications for family reform and for population policy. The new law is particularly focused on family planning. China has a population of approximately 1 billion people. That is about 22 percent of the total world population. China has only 7 percent of the

Some Stirrings on the Mainland
Sex Rears Its Head in China, but Ever So Cautiously

BY JOHN LEE

After a night of frenzied dancing, Zhen Zhen came to grief when her boyfriend entered the room while she was taking a bath. Yen Li, who yearned to be an actress, lost her virtue when a wily actor insidiously told her that Ingrid Bergman and Sophia Loren devoted their lives—and their bodies—to art. The pivotal event of Li Na's life occurred when her date tricked her into watching a porn movie. "She was shocked by the movements on the screen, and she felt warm and suffocated. As she was about to unbutton her collar to breathe a little, a hand grasped her."

These cautionary tales confront wide-eyed readers of the new book *Girls, Be Vigilant!*, an official publication of the Chinese government. The usually puritanical press is blossoming with articles on sex, one sign that traditional policies of sexual repression are undergoing attack. The sex-crime rate has soared, particularly cases of rape, which is sometimes defined to include simple seduction. Divorce is also up, and the New China News Agency reports that "disharmonious sexual life arising from a lack of sexual knowledge" is now placing great strain on many families.

Opinion polls conducted by various journals show that attitudes are rapidly changing. As recently as 1982, 80% of those surveyed in one study said premarital sex was immoral. In late 1985 polls put the figure between 60% and 65%. To no one's surprise, sexual repression is less popular among the young than the old. In a fall 1985 survey of married people in the Peking area, only half of the under-30s, in contrast to three-quarters of the over-50s, said they opposed sex before marriage.

To some extent the findings of the polls are a by-product of the government's decision to bring sex out of the closet by allowing new sex manuals and setting up courses on sex and marriage. In September, Shanghai opened its first School for Newlyweds, offering two-week instruction on sexual life, hygiene and contraception.

Couples who had been married several years, still feeling ignorant in the field, signed up for refresher courses. Forty of the city's more than 400 secondary schools are experimenting with sex-ed courses for 12- and 13-year-olds. These courses concentrate on physiology and hygiene and a few "moral concepts of sex." The emphasis on physiology is hardly standard. Chinese society has been so reticent and the Communist regime so straitlaced that sexual anatomy was usually omitted from physiology courses. Many newly married couples take to the bridal bed with only a foggy notion of what they are supposed to do.

The government plays on the wide-spread ignorance of sex by issuing dark warnings about many sexual practices. A 1984 government book for newlyweds on health says that promiscuity brings brief pleasure but also a loss of will, a generally low character and possibly neurasthenia. Even the wedding night has its perils. The book warns that husbands who do not know the location of the female genitals can cause severe damage. "Though such cases are rare," the book says, "they are worth noting."

While China's leaders do not believe that masturbation results in hairy palms and blindness, the book states that the practice can lead to "dizziness, insomnia, too much dreaming, exhaustion, aching in the back and waist, worsening of the memory, absentmindedness, lack of appetite, palpitation, shortness of breath, headache, dimmed vision, mental decline." *Girls, Be Vigilant!* helpfully lists some of the traditional remedies for illicitly roaming hands, including the cultivation of a "rhythmically arranged life" and good habits such as avoiding tight clothes and not sleeping on your stomach.

In the cities, China's high-ranking officials have access to prostitutes, porn films and a varied sex life. But most of the population finds itself hemmed in sexually.

(continued)

Nearly every relationship is monitored by neighbors and subject to fevered interpretation. Getting away from prying eyes is so difficult that at nightfall parks fill up with courting pairs, and adventurous lovers couple on the ground.

Outside the cities, sex involves greater risk. In some rural areas, if a single man walks a single woman to her door, the stroll is equivalent to a declaration of marriage. The misreading of a relationship by neighbors or an accusation can bring social ruin. As in most other countries, the woman bears the brunt of the blame for sexual misconduct, though that may slowly be changing. One weekly managed to be both antisex and antisexist when it wrote that "virginity education should be carried out with females and males at the same time. A girl and a boy who have illegal sex should both face social accusation." Such accusation may have drastic implications; China's legal system lumps almost all sex crimes under the category of rape, which carries severe penalties; including long imprisonment or death in cases of serious injury or homicide. The possibility of a rape charge can haunt almost any male in China.

Many of the rapes recounted in *Girls Be Vigilant!* and in the daily press are either seductions or panicky charges leveled by young girls. Normally, consensual-sex "rape" results in prison terms of three to five years.

Despite the chilling effect of law and custom, liberal ideas and practices surface and are customarily blamed on the West. To many Chinese, Westerners seem enslaved by their animal instincts and unconcerned about family unity. Still, more open attitudes seem to continue. The usually stern Shanghai *Liberation Daily* raised eyebrows last summer with an evenhanded treatment of the loss of virginity, calling it "not a good thing, but it is not necessarily an irredeemably bad thing." And like other countries, China is learning that courses and books aimed at keeping the lid on sexual activity help feed it. Young women are now reading *Girls, Be Vigilant!* for tips on the erotic life.

SOURCE. John Lee. 1986. "Some stirrings on the mainland." *Time* (Feb. 10). Copyright 1986 Time Inc. All rights reserved. Reprinted by permission. from TIME.

world's arable land (Redmond, 1986). Her land mass, however, is only slightly larger than that of the United States. Further, only a small portion of the land is suitable for growing crops, while there is plentiful agricultural land in the United States. In essence, China has half the usable farmland that America has and five times as many people.

China's huge population and continued growth of that population has aroused much concern. It is for that reason that a "one couple, one child" policy has been implemented. This policy has prevented an estimated 100 million births since 1980 (Redmond, 1986). The goal is to hold the population down to 1.2 billion by the year 2000. If the policy fails, and family size stays at just over two children, it will have a population of 1.4 billion. In effect it would add twice the population of the United States in just 15 years.

The new marriage law raised the minimum age for marriage by two years to 22 for men and to 20 for women, and made family planning mandatory. It made family planning the duty of both husband and wife and articulated a new statement of obligation among family members (Stacey, 1985; Wolf, 1985a). The principle of equal status of men and women was re-affirmed and neither spouse was allowed to restrict or interfere with the other's production, work, study, or social activities. The norm of extended-family relations was shifted from a patrilineal form to a bilineal direction. Family members now have obligations to both maternal and paternal relatives extended over three generations; that is, grandchildren, parents, and grand-parents have reciprocal obligations to support and assist each other. The motive for this change was to diminish and undermine the social and economic logic of son preference and thus alleviate the potential problem of the birth of a daughter in the new birth limitation program of one child.

China's Only Child

BY EDWARD GOLDWYN

NARRATOR

In Mrs. Wu's neighborhood there are some 200 women whose contraceptive is an intra-uterine device.

She sees that they are all checked regularly every four months. The check is said to be necessary to see the I.U.D. is in the right place. But the check also shows if there's an accidental pregnancy underway — or if the I.U.D. has been removed, which would be illegal and very serious.

Mrs. Wu always goes along, both to be friendly and to see that there's no deception, that a woman is not hiding a pregnancy by sending a neighbor along as a stand-in.

Hospital Worker: A coil check? This way.

Mrs. Wu: I'll tell you a joke to show why I love birth control work.

NARRATOR

Early one morning Mrs. Wu was in the street. She saw Mr. and Mrs. Li on their way to work. She overheard Mrs. Li say, "We've just had our wage increase. Why don't we have another baby."

That was at seven o'clock.

MRS. WU

After I overheard that I rushed to her factory. I was there at nine o'clock. I looked for the party secretary, that's Party Secretary Wang. At 12 o'clock he went to find her and have a talk. He asked her very seriously, "Is it true you want another child?" She said, "I'm not going to, I use contraception all the time." He asked again. That made her cross and she said, "No! Of course I'm not going to!" "But this morning you said you would, that you could afford it now." She said, "I was only making a joke." Afterwards she found me. She apologized and said it was a joke. Then she asked me: "Why did you take it seriously?" But I must, the minute you let go, someone's tummy starts to get fatter.

MR. MING

We of Zuang Tang brigade have done well in family planning and been rewarded. But we must be modest and work even harder next year.

NARRATOR

Mr. Ming is the leader of a brigade of 500 families in a commune in the country close to Changzhou. His 100 percent record is being threatened by a couple who has fought very hard to have a second child.

Jinghu — and his wife ManXue have just given in after weeks of "persuasion." ManXue is six months pregnant, but she has agreed to have an abortion tomorrow.

The person who had to make ManXue agree is Mrs. Feng — the brigade's family planning official.

Mrs. Feng's duties are to control the quota and to see no one breaks the rules.

She's just decided which women can have a child. So she moves their names from "being on pills" to "waiting to be pregnant."

They are the last two women to get places in this year's quota of 32 babies.

Who gets them is worked out from a simple formula that gives priority to couples who are older and who have been married longest.

MRS. FENG

You've been allocated a birth permission card. Here it is. I hope you have an intelligent healthy child. Here's your book.

NARRATOR

The book is called "How to Have Healthy Child," and it's given to couples when they get their permission so they can get off to a good start.

Mrs. Feng has to tell six couples they must wait.

In this household the young couple live with the husband's parents.

When Mrs. Feng came to tell them the new wife was out.

The woman is his mother.

Mrs. Feng: You are one of the youngest couples.

(continued)

I'm asking if you can wait? What do you have to say?

Husband: I have nothing to say. The important thing is the country's call. We have to give emphasis to work and study. Don't you agree, mother?

Mother: Yes.

NARRATOR

Most people accept the new rules. The defiance that their neighbor, ManXue has been showing is very unusual.

The story of how Mrs. Feng made ManXue agree to an abortion shows how the persuasion is done.

ManXue and Jinghu work their fields under the new "responsibility system." That means they hand over to the commune a fixed amount of the vegetables as payment for using the field. They sell in the market any extra they grow.

They have made a great deal of money this year—from the work they've put into the crops—from the chickens ManXue keeps and because Jinghu not only has a factory job as a carpenter, but makes furniture in the evening.

They have become quite wealthy, and have made for themselves about three times an average salary. They already have a son aged one-and-a-half but they felt they could afford a second child. They had not taken out a one-child certificate.

JINGHU

Go to mummy. Dad is going to work.

NARRATOR

Six months ago Jinghu and ManXue stopped using birth control. The thick winter clothing made it easy to hide her swelling figure.

ManXue is an outspoken woman. Just a month ago she went to Mrs. Feng and said, "I'm pregnant, and I'm having this baby."

Next day Mrs. Feng came by and said, "I have to tell you why you musn't have this child."

ManXue said, "Fine, come back and tell me after the baby is born."

Mrs. Feng brought along the leaders of the brigade who spent several evenings telling her, "One child is good for the country. It's also good for you. Why won't

you agree to an abortion? If you're worried about your health, we'll guarantee you get the best doctors. Why won't you agree!"

ManXue said, "No."

The next night more senior officers of the commune came to the house. They went through it all again and again very slowly. The next night an even more senior official came and he said the same things.

So it went on night after night. Repeatedly she was asked, "Why *won't* you agree?"

In the end ManXue got worn down. She said, "After a while I knew they would just keep on and on and on."

None of her friends stood up for her—they kept silent.

She offered a deal to Mrs. Feng. "I'll have the abortion if you get me a job in the commune shoe factory."

Mrs. Feng tried to arrange that. She came back to report, "They'll agree provided you agree to be sterilized too."

ManXue said, "No—I don't want that."

But finally she agreed to have the abortion in her sixth month of pregnancy.

Hospital Worker: So she wants an abortion but not to be sterilized?

Mrs. Feng: That's right.

Hospital Worker: Bring her at eight o'clock tomorrow.

Mrs. Feng: ManXue, are you in?

Jinghu: Should we bring a quilt?

Mrs. Feng: Just a change of clothes. Let me carry it.

NARRATOR

ManXue will be given an injection into her womb that will kill the fetus and cause its premature delivery within 24 hours.

MRS. FENG

Personally I feel sympathy for couples wanting a second child. It's reasonable to want two. But in the interest of the country, we can't let them have it. If one couple is allowed, too many others will want a second. That would make our work impossible. So we must do our job well. Don't let second children be born. But personally, I sympathize.

NARRATOR

Why do the rebels in the end give in?

(continued)

Why is it that these women don't get support from friends and neighbors?

Why do the people of this town accept these intrusions?

And why are the persuaders so proud of their work?

Madame Chen says it's because of the huge effort she has made with public education and propaganda.

The thing she proudly shows her visitors is the first ever neon sign in Changzhou. It says, "Please practice contraception carefully."

Over the last three years she has filled Changzhou with slogans for the one-child policy. "Fewer people but higher quality." "Birth control is every citizen's responsibility." "One child allows us to modernize."

It says on this boat: "Take pride in your single child." And "Have fewer children but raise the quality."

"A single child is cause to be proud."

NEIGHBORHOOD WORKERS (SINGING)

Neighborhood workers are in high spirits. We grasp the work of birth control. We work together with one aim. We shall never waver.

CHILDREN (SINGING)

Ee - yo - ei - hai - ei - hai - yo. Mummy only had me. We don't want brothers or sisters. Everyone is happy. The whole house rejoices, laa . . . , la, la.

NARRATOR

Each brigade is told monthly one couple — one child, and why.

MR. MING

If the one-child policy is followed to the year 2000, it guarantees that food and industrial production will first double and then redouble.

NARRATOR

Afterwards they break into their production teams to say what they think, and to discuss local problems.

This meeting of Mrs. Feng's group was attended by ManXue and her neighbors. They all knew of her fight.

Mrs. Feng: Now we've heard Comrade Ming's speech, are there any questions? Anything to discuss?

Brigade Member: The whole country and the party should concentrate on family planning work. The members of our team must answer the government's call. I respond to the government's call strongly, I want only one child.

Young Brigade Member: We young people have strength. Now the government asks us to marry late and use birth control. This is good for young people.

NARRATOR

Nobody mentioned ManXue's recent ordeal. What they felt, they hid. ManXue said, "The hardest part of the last weeks has been that no one stood up for me — or said anything."

ManXue agreed to take out the one-child certificate, but she has remained adamant that she won't be sterilized.

So Mr. Ming's brigade has met all of this year's targets — and he'll receive another certificate at the Changzhou award ceremony for birth control.

On the platform sit the mayor and the other important bureaucrats who will present the awards.

The audience are all delegates from units which have met their targets — it's an honor to be invited.

The applause and awards conclude a year of difficult — often painful — work and persuasion.

These efforts have made China the only developing nation in the world today to significantly slow its population growth. And with one-fourth of the people on earth, China's success is crucial to controlling world population.

Changzhou is the Chinese dream.

It's had a huge investment of government money to develop its factories.

Most of the old people here have pensions. They don't need sons to support them.

Elsewhere that's not so.

Eighty percent of the Chinese live in the countryside. They are peasants who must have a son. The officials there understand — and turn a blind eye when a couple has two children. In the countryside, results fall short of 100 percent.

But in Changzhou people can actually see the wealth the publicity promises.

Changzhou is not a typical city, it's the

(continued)

ideal. It's to show the Chinese people what the sacrifice is for—the wealth there could be for all in two generations.

If they don't control the population, the future will be catastrophic.

It's very rare to see a government trying to deal with problems 30 years ahead. The Chinese are saying this: if the population were reduced to 700 million, they would have twice today's living standards.

If it steadies at one billion, they can continue to keep people fed and housed. At one-and-a-half billion they see a descent to poverty. Above that, severe hardship. Above two billion, it's a fight for food.

This will be their future at three children per family. This for 2.3 children per family. Two children each. One and a half children each.

One child.

If we were faced with this future, how would we try to deal with it?

First, we would educate and convince everyone there is a problem. Then limit births. And finally ensure the rules are applied equally to all.

That's what the Chinese are doing. It is harsh. But is there an alternative?

MADAME CHEN

To be honest, my own opinion is if couples had two children, it would be quite all right. Two children is very desirable and people would easily accept it. Our work would be easier if we could allow two children. But we think of our country's future. We have to keep our population under 1.2 billion in the year 2000.

SOURCE. *Nova.* 1984. "China's only child." Edward Goldwyn and Terry Kay Rockefeller BBC/WGBH.

Restrictive measures and incentives are combined to augment the new population policy. In urban areas, workers must meet the new age requirements and have their factories' permission to get married. They must have received instruction in family planning, and passed a written test. Once married, they have to get the permission of the family-planning officer when they can try to have children. A bureau chief at the factories in the city of Changzhou expresses the goals of the factory in fulfilling the policy this way:

> Recently we have met all our targets 100 percent. Couples using birth control is 100 percent. One-child families is 100 percent. Late marriage is 100 percent. We have attained the so-called "three withouts." "Without" permission, no one is pregnant. We are "without" any second child. We are "without" early births. We have no under age mothers. ("China's Only Child," *Nova*, February 14, 1984)

Married couples who obtain a "one-child certificate," which pledges their intention not to exceed the norm, are rewarded in terms of wage increases, preferential housing assignments, and special considerations for their child in terms of free education and priority for a university place and priority for a job. Unauthorized pregnant women who are carrying either their first or their second child are pressured to have abortions. Those that have a second child lose these rewards and various sanctions are applied including the loss of wages, promotions deferred, maternity leaves denied, loss of preferential housing and educational supports for their children, and reductions in their food allotments.

The "one couple, one child" law is not as stringently enforced in rural areas; bowing to the importance of the family, a two-child norm is the goal. Similar collective pressure tactics are used to reach this goal. For those who voluntarily restrict their family size to one child, they become eligible for preferential treatment regarding work, grain rations, and private land plots. There are inducements for women who agree to be sterilized after the birth of one child that include sewing machines, additional food allocations, and money. Couples who do not enter such agreements experience social and economic pressures and are required to refrain for at least five years the having of a second child. Forced sterilization after the birth of a second child or becoming contractually obligated to abort unauthorized pregnancies has been practiced in a number of different regions (Stacey, 1985). The dynamics of these policies was illustrated in one segment of the *Nova* television program, "China's Only Child," which was originally broadcast on PBS on February 14, 1984.

Stacey (1985) believes that one of the consequences of the "one couple, one child" policy may be a dramatic shift in family structure and gender relationships. "A one-child family system could level a serious challenge to patrilineality by making parents as dependent upon their daughters as their sons. . . . This could significantly raise the family status of daughters and dissolve the patrilocal marriage system" (Stacey, 1985:279). However, such an outcome is not seen as likely to materialize. A two-child norm is seen to be feasible, and this would tend to weaken, but not to destroy, the patrilineal base of rural family structure. However, the overall consequences of this new marriage law and population policies should in the long run diminish the power of patriarchal interests.

Conclusion

Winston Churchill once described the Soviet Union as "a riddle wrapped in a mystery inside an enigma." For many, this description is even more fitting in describing China. We chose to study the Chinese family extensively in the concluding chapter of this book for a number of reasons. In its own right, the permanence and change of the Chinese family are unique. In the twentieth century, there has occurred an accelerated development of the Chinese family system that, although strongly influenced by Western technology and ideologies, remains fundamentally Chinese. We pointed out how the traditional family system with its emphasis on the needs of the collective—family, clan, village, and China—rather than the individual continues to be reflected in the development of a modern family form that differs fundamentally from the Western private conjugal family.

However, the themes throughout this book—modernization and social change, consanguineal and conjugal family forms, the family's relationship to the community and the society, premarital and marital relationships, parent–child relationships, and age- and gender-differentiation and stratification patterns—can be better understood through an examination of the modern Chinese family system, which is in change. We examined these topics historically through an analysis of the convoluted changes of the Chinese revolutions of the twentieth century. The tensions existing between different ideological positions—first between the Nationalists and the imperial Manchu dynasty, next between the Communists and the Nationalists, and finally between the radical Maoist wing of the Communist party and the more pragmatic wing, represented today by Teng Hsaio-p'ing (Deng Xiaoping)—was investigated. This investigation was not directed at world political implications but rather at the implications for the Chinese people and their family system.

In conclusion, we reminded the reader that the revolution in twentieth-century China was a total revolution. The political, economic, social, and family revolution that occurred in China during this period was unique in its totality and its fundamental effects on the individual. The social relationships between the individual, the family, and the community are being transformed radically. Yet, it is this acceleration of change that has made the study of the Chinese family so fascinating and useful. It highlights, in a most dramatic fashion, the themes relating to social change and the family. In sum, we trust that our examination of the Chinese family experience will increase the reader's knowledge and understanding not only of China, but also of much of the sweeping social, political, and economic changes occurring in today's world and how they affect families and their members.

References

Abu-Lughod, Janet L. 1961. "Migration adjustments to city life: The Egyptian case." *American Journal of Sociology* 67:22–32.

Adams, Bert N. 1975. *The Family: A Sociological Interpretation.* 2d ed. Chicago: Rand McNally.

Adler, Jerry, with Nikki Finke Greenberg, Mary Hager, Peter McKillop, and Tessa Namuth. 1985. "The AIDS conflict: Ignorance and uncertainty fuel an epidemic of fear that could be almost as destructive as the disease itself." *Newsweek* (Sept. 23):18–24.

Afkhami, Mahnaz. 1984. "Iran: A future in the past—The 'prerevolutionary' women's movement." Pp. 333–341 in Robin Morgan (ed.), *Sisterhood is Global: The International Women's Movement Anthology.* Garden City, N.Y.: Anchor Press/Doubleday.

Aghajanian, Akbar. 1986. "Some notes on divorce in Iran." *Journal of Marriage and the Family* 48 (Nov.):749–755.

Aldous, Joan. 1968. "Urbanization, the extended family, and kinship ties in West Africa." Pp. 297–305 in Sylvia Fleis Fava (ed.), *Urbanism in World Perspective: A Reader.* New York: Thomas Y. Crowell.

Allon, Natalie, and Diane Fishel. 1981. "Singles bars as examples of urban courting patterns." Pp. 115–121 in Peter J. Stein (ed.), *Single Life: Unmarried Adults in Social Context.* New York: St. Martin's Press.

al-Sa'id, Aminah. 1977. "The Arab woman and the challenge of society." Pp. 373–390 in Elizabeth Warnock Fernea and Basina Qatan Bizirgan (eds.), *Middle Eastern Women Speak.* Austin: University of Texas Press.

Anderson, Michael. 1971. *Family Structure in Nineteenth-Century Lancashire.* Cambridge, England: Cambridge University Press.

———. 1980. *Approaches to the History of the Western Family 1500–1914.* London and Basingstoke: The Macmillan Press Ltd.

Anderson, Nels. 1923. *The Hobo.* Chicago: University of Chicago Press.

Apple, R. W., Jr. 1979. "Iran: Heart of the matter." *The New York Times Magazine* (Mar. 11):19, 101–102, 104–106.

Applebaum, Richard P. 1970. *Theories of Social Change.* Chicago: Markham.

Archdeacon, Thomas J. 1983. Becoming American: An Ethnic History. New York: Free Press.

Archer, Dane, and Rosemarie Gartner. 1984. *Violence and Crisis in Cross-National Perspective.* New Haven, Conn.: Yale University Press.

Arensberg, Conrad M. 1937. *The Irish Countryman.* Gloucester, Mass.: Peter Smith. (Reprinted 1959.)

————, and Solon T. Kimball. 1968. *Family and Community in Ireland,* 2d ed. Cambridge: Harvard University Press.

Ariès, Philippe. 1962. *Centuries of Childhood: A Social History of Family Life.* Robert Baldick (trans.). New York: Knopf.

Arungu-Olende, Rose Adhiambo. 1984. "Not just literacy, but wisdom." Pp. 394–398 in Robin Morgan (ed.), *Sisterhood is Global: The International Women's Movement Anthology.* Garden City, N.Y.: Anchor Press/Doubleday.

Axelred, Morris. 1956. "Urban structure and social participation." *American Sociological Review* 21:13–18.

Aziz-Ahmed, Shereen. 1967. "Pakistan." Pp. 42–58 in Raphael Patai (ed.), *Women in the Modern World.* New York: The Free Press.

Bachofen, J.J. 1948. *Das Mutterecht.* Basel: Beno Schwabe. (Originally published, 1861.)

Bakan, David. 1971. *Slaughter of the Innocents.* Boston: Beacon Press.

Bane, Mary Jo. 1976. *Here to Stay: American Families in the Twentieth Century.* New York: Basic Books.

————. 1979. "Marital disruption and the lives of children." Pp. 276–286 in George Levinger and Oliver C. Moles (eds.), *Divorce and Separation: Context, Causes, and Consequences.* New York: Basic Books.

Bardos, Panos D. 1964. "Family forms and variations historically considered," Pp. 403–461 in Harold T. Christensen (ed.), *Handbook of Marriage and the Family.* Chicago: Rand McNally.

Baron, Larry, and Murray A. Straus. 1985. "Legitimate violence and rape: A test of the cultural spillover theory." Mimeograph of paper presented at the 1985 meeting of the Eastern Sociological Society.

Barrett, K. 1982. "Date rape: A campus epidemic." *Ms.* (Sept.):48–51, 130.

Bartelt, Pearl W., and Mark Hutter. 1977. "Symbolic interaction perspective on the sexual politics of etiquette books." Paper presented at the meeting of the American Sociological Association, Chicago, Ill. (Sept.)

Bascom, William. 1968. "The urban African and his world." Pp. 81–93 in Sylvia Fleis Fava (ed.), *Urbanism in World Perspective: A Reader.* New York: Thomas Y. Crowell.

Belden, Jack. 1970. *China Shakes the World.* New York: Monthly Review Press.

Bell, Robert R. 1964. "The lower-class Negro mother and her children." *Integrated Education* (Dec.):23–27.

————. 1965. "Lower-class negro mothers' aspirations for their children." *Social Forces* 44:483–500.

————. 1971. "The related importance of mother-wife roles among lower class black women." Pp. 248–254 in Robert Staples (ed.), *The Black Family.* New York: Wadsworth.

Bell, Wendell. 1958. "Social choice, life styles and suburban residence." Pp. 225–247 in William Dobriner (ed.), *The Suburban Community.* New York: G.P. Putnam's Sons.

Bell, Wendell, and Marion D. Boat. 1957. "Urban neighborhood and informal social behavior." *American Journal of Sociology* 62:391–398.

Bellah, Robert N. 1957. *Tokugawa Religion: The Values of Preindustrial Japan.* New York: Macmillan.

Bendix, Reinhard. 1967. "Tradition and modernity reconsidered." *Comparative Studies in Society and History* 9:292–346.

Benedict, Ruth. 1973. "Continuities and discontinuities in cultural conditioning." Pp. 100–108 in Harry Silverstein (ed.), *The Sociology of Youth: Evolution of Revolution.* New York: Macmillan. (Originally published in *Psychiatry* 1:161–167, 1938.)

Berger, Brigitte. 1971. *Societies in Change.* New York: Basic Books.

————, and Berger, Peter L. 1983. *The War Over the Family: Capturing the Middle Ground.* Garden City, N.Y.: Anchor Press/Doubleday.

Berger, Miriam E. 1971. "Trial marriage: Harnessing the trend constructively." *The Family Coordinator* 20:38–43.

Berger, Peter L., 1963. *Invitation to Sociology: A Humanistic Perspective.* Garden City, N.Y.: Doubleday (Anchor Books).

Berger, Peter L., Brigitte Berger, and Hansfried Kellner. 1973. *The Homeless Mind: Modernization and Consciousness.* New York: Random House.

Berger, Peter L., and Hansfried Kellner. 1964. "Marriage and the construction of reality." *Diogenes* 46:1–25.

Berger, Peter L., and Thomas Luckmann. 1966. *The Social Construction of Reality.* Garden City, N.Y.: Doubleday.

Berkner, Lutz K. 1975. "The use and misuse of census data for the historical analysis of family structure." *Journal of Interdisciplinary History* 4:721–738.

Berman, Eleanor. 1977. *The Cooperating Family.* Englewood Cliffs, N.J.: Prentice-Hall.

Bernard, Jesse. 1981. "The good provider role: Its rise and fall." *American Psychologist* vol. 36, no. 1 (Jan.):1–12.

———. 1975. *The Future of Motherhood.* New York: Penguin Books.

Berrol, Selma. 1976. "Turning little aliens into little citizens: Italians and Jews in New York City public schools, 1900–14." Pp. 32–41 in Jean Scarpaci (ed.), *The Interaction of Italians and Jews in America.* Staten Island, N.Y.: The American Italian Historical Association.

Berry, Brian J.L. 1973. *The Human Consequences of Urbanization: Divergent Paths in the Urban Experience of the Twentieth Century.* New York: St. Martin's Press.

Berube, Allan. 1981. "Marching to a different drummer." *Advocate* (Oct. 15).

Billingsley, Andrew. 1969. *Black Families in White America.* Englewood Cliffs, N.J.: Prentice-Hall.

———. 1969. "Family functioning in the low income black community." *Social Casework* 50:563–572.

Blake, Judith. 1972. *Coercive Pronatalism and American Population Policy.* (Preliminary paper no. 2 on results of current research in demography). Pp. 17–22 in *International Population and Urban Research.* Berkeley: International Population and Urban Research, University of California.

Blood, Robert O., Jr. 1967. *Love Match and Arranged Marriage: A Tokyo–Detroit Comparison.* New York: The Free Press.

———. 1972. *The Family.* New York: The Free Press.

Blood, Robert O., Jr., and Donald M. Wolfe. 1960. *Husbands and Wives.* New York: The Free Press.

Blumberg, Leonard, and Robert R. Bell. 1959. "Urban migration and kinship ties." *Social Problems* 6:328–333.

Blumberg, Rae Lesser. 1979. "A paradigm for predicting the position of women: Policy implications and problems." Pp. 113–142 in Jean Lipman-Blumen and Jessie Bernard (eds.), *Sex Roles and Social Policy.* London: Sage Studies in International Sociology.

Bohannan, Paul. 1971. "The six stations of divorce." Pp. 33–62 in Paul Bohannan (ed.), *Divorce and After.* Garden City, N.Y.: Doubleday Anchor.

Bolig, R, P. Stein, and P. McKenry. 1984. "The self-advertisement approach to dating: Male-female differences." *Family Relations* 33:587–592.

Borders, William. 1977. "India will moderate birth-curb program." *The New York Times,* (Apr. 3).

Boserup, Ester. 1970. *Women's Role in Economic Development.* London: Allen & Unwin.

Bott, Elizabeth. 1957. *Family and Social Network.* London: Tavistock Publications.

Bowen, Gary Lee. 1983. "The evolution of Soviet family policy: Female liberation versus social cohesion." *Journal of Comparative Family Studies* 14 (Autumn):299–313.

Brandwein, Ruth A., Carol A. Brown, and Elizabeth Maury Fox. 1974. "Women and children last: The social situation of divorced mothers and their families." *Journal of Marriage and the Family* 36:498–514.

Briggs, Kenneth A. 1981. "Reform Jews to seek conversion of non-Jews." *The New York Times* (Dec. 9).

Broude, Gwen, and Sarah Greene. 1976. "Cross-cultural codes on twenty sexual attitudes and practices." *Ethnology* 15:409–428.

Browett, John. 1982. "The evolution of unequal development within South Africa: An overview." Pp. 10–23 in David M. Smith (ed.), *Living Under Apartheid*. London: Allen & Unwin.

Brozan, Nadine. 1983. "Family issues of Jewish couples." *The New York Times* (Nov. 3).

Bruner, Edward M. 1963. "Medan: The role of kinship in an Indonesian city." Pp. 1–12 in Alexander Spoehr (ed.), *Pacific Port Towns and Cities*. Honolulu: Bishop Mussua Press. (Reprinted pp. 122–134 in William Mangin (ed.), 1970, *Peasants in Cities: Readings in the Anthropology of Urbanization*. Boston: Houghton-Mifflin.)

Burchinal, Lee G. 1964. "Characteristics of adolescents from unbroken, broken, and reconstituted families." *Journal of Marriage and the Family* 26:44–51.

Burgess, Ernest W., and Harvey J. Locke. 1945. *The Family from Institution to Companionship*. New York: American Book.

Butterfield, Fox. 1979. "As population nears a billion, China stresses curbs." *The New York Times* (Apr. 24).

Campbell, Colin. 1976. "What happens when we get the manchild pill." *Psychology Today* 10 (3) (Aug.):86–91.

Campbell, F.L. 1970. "Family growth and variation in family role structure." *Journal of Marriage and the Family* 32:45–53.

Carter, Hugh, and Paul C. Glick. 1976. *Marriage and Divorce: A Social and Economic Study*, rev. ed. Cambridge: Harvard University Press.

Cate, Rodney. 1982. "Premarital abuse: A social psychological perspective." *Journal of Family Issues* 3 (1) (Mar.):79–90.

Chao, Paul. 1977. *Women Under Communism*. Bayside, N.Y.: General Hall.

Chase, Naomi Feigelson. 1975. *A Child Is Being Beaten*. New York: McGraw-Hill.

Cherlin, Andrew. 1980. "Remarriage as an incomplete institution." Pp. 368–382 in Arlene S. Skolnick and Jerome H. Skolnick (eds.), *Family in Transition: Rethinking Marriage, Sexuality, Child Rearing, and Family Organization*, 3d ed. Boston: Little Brown. (Reprinted from *American Journal of Sociology* 1978, 84:634–650.)

———. 1981. *Marriage, Divorce, Remarriage*. Cambridge, Mass.: Harvard University Press.

———, and Frank F. Furstenberg, Jr. 1986. *The New American Grandparent: A Place in the Family, A Life Apart*. New York: Basic Books.

Chin, Ai-li S. 1970. "Family relations in modern Chinese fiction." Pp. 87–120 in Maurice Freedman (ed.), *Family and Kinship in Chinese Society*. Stanford, Calif.: Stanford University Press.

Chinoy, Ely. 1955. *Automobile Workers and the American Dream*. Garden City, N.Y.: Doubleday.

Chodak, Szymon. 1973. *Societal Development: Five Approaches with Conclusions from Comparative Analysis*. New York: Oxford University Press.

Christensen, Harold T. (ed.). 1964. *Handbook of Marriage and the Family*. Chicago: Rand McNally.

Cicirelli, Victor G. 1983. "Adult children and their elderly parents." Pp. 31–46 in Timothy H. Brubaker (ed.), *Family Relations in Later Life*. Beverly Hills, Calif.: Sage Publications.

Clark, Alice. 1919. *The Working Life of Women in the Seventeenth Century*. London: G. Routledge & Sons. (Reissued by Frank Cass, 1968.)

Clark, Matt, with Vincent Coppola. 1985. "AIDS: A growing 'pandemic'?" *Newsweek* (Apr. 29):71.

Clark, Matt, with Mariana Gosnell, Deborah Witherspoon, Mary Hager, and Vincent Coppola. 1985. "AIDS: Once dismissed as the 'gay plague,' the disease has become the no. 1 public-health menace." *Newsweek* (Aug. 12):20–24, 26–27.

Clayton, Richard R. 1979. *The Family, Marriage, and Social Change,* 2d ed. Lexington, Mass: D.C. Heath.

Clendinen, Dudley. 1985. "Schools in New York will admit an AIDS pupil but not 3 others: 'Epidemic of fear' in U.S." *The New York Times* (Sept. 8):1, 22.

Coles, Robert. 1968. "Life in Appalachia—the case of Hugh McCaslin." *Transaction* (June):22–33.

Collins, Randall. 1971. "A conflict theory of sexual stratification." *Social Problems* 19:3–21.

Condon, Jane. 1985. *A Half Step Behind: Japanese Women of the 1980s.* New York: Dodd, Mead.

Cooper, David. 1970. *The Death of the Family.* New York: Random House (Vintage Books).

Cortes, Carlos E. 1980. "Mexicans." Pp. 697–719 in Stephen Thernstrom (ed.), *Harvard Encyclopedia of American Ethnic Groups.* Cambridge, Mass.: The Belknap Press of Harvard University Press.

Cott, Nancy. 1979. "Passionlessness: An interpretation of Victorian sexual ideology, 1790–1850." Pp. 162–181 in Nancy F. Cott and Elizabeth H. Pleck (eds.), *A Heritage of Her Own.* New York: Simon and Schuster.

Covello, Leonard. 1967. *The Social Background of the Italo-American School Child.* Leiden, the Netherlands: E.J. Brill.

Curtin, Katie. 1975. *Women in China.* New York: Pathfinder Press.

Dahlström, Edmund (ed.). 1962. *Kvinnors Liv och Arbete* (The Life and Work of Women). Stockholm: Studieförbundet Näringsliv & Samhälle.

———. 1971. *The Changing Roles of Men and Women.* Boston: Beacon Press.

D'Andrade, Roy G. 1966. "Sex differences and cultural institutions." Pp. 174–204 in E.E. Maccoby (ed.), *The Development of Sex Differences.* Stanford, Calif.: Stanford University Press.

Darwin, Charles. *Origin of Species.* New York: Random House, Modern Library. (Originally published, 1859).

Davenport, William H. 1977. "Sex in cross-cultural perspective." Pp. 115–163 in Frank A. Beach (ed.), *Human Sexuality in Four Perspectives.* Baltimore, Md.: The Johns Hopkins University Press.

Davidoff, Leonore. 1975. *The Best Circles: Women and Society in Victorian England.* Totowa, N.J.: Rowman & Littlefield.

Davis, Elizabeth Gould. 1971. *The First Sex.* New York: G.P. Putnam's Sons.

Davis, Kingsley. 1951. *The Population of India and Pakistan.* Princeton, N.J.: Princeton University Press.

———. 1955. "Institutional patterns favoring high fertility in underdeveloped areas." *Eugenics Quarterly* 2:33–39.

———. 1976. "Sexual behavior." Pp. 219–261 in Robert K. Merton and Robert Nisbet (eds.), *Contemporary Social Problems,* 4th ed. New York: Harcourt Brace Jovanovich.

de Beauvoir, Simone. 1973. *The Coming of Age.* New York: Warner Books (Warner Paperback Library).

Degler, Carl N. 1980. *At Odds: Women and the Family in America from the Revolution to the Present.* New York: Oxford University Press.

de Jesus, Carolina Maria. 1962. *Child of the Dark: The Diary of Carolina Maria de Jesus.* David St. Clair (trans.). New York: E.P. Dutton.

D'Emilio, John. 1983a. "Capitalism and gay identity." Pp. 100–113 in Ann Snitow, Christine Stansell, and Sharon Thompson (eds.), *Powers of Desire: The Politics of Sexuality.* New York: Monthly Review Press.

———. 1983b. *Sexual Politics, Sexual Communities.* Chicago: University of Chicago Press.

Demos, John. 1970. *A Little Commonwealth.* New York: Oxford University Press.

———. 1974. "The American family in past time." *American Scholar* 43:422–446.

Dinnerstein, Leonard, and David M. Reimers. 1975. *Ethnic Americans: A History of Immigration and Assimilation.* New York: Dodd, Mead.

Donzelet, Jacques. 1979. *The Policing of Families*. New York: Pantheon.

Dore, R.P. 1965. *City Life in Japan: A Study of A Tokyo Ward*. Berkeley/Los Angeles: University of California Press.

Duberman, Lucile. 1977. *Marriage and Other Alternatives*, 2d ed. New York: Praeger.

Dubois, Ellen Carol, and Linda Gordon. 1984. "Seeking ecstasy on the battlefield: Danger and pleasure in nineteenth-century feminist sexual thought." Pp. 31–49 in Carole S. Vance (ed.), *Pleasure and Danger: Exploring Female Sexuality*. Boston, Mass.: Routledge & Kegan Paul.

Durdin, Tillman. 1971. "Elimination of 'four olds' transform China." Pp. 123–126 in *The New York Times* (ed.). *Report from Red China*. New York: Avon Books.

Durkheim, Emile. 1915. *The Elementary Forms of the Religious Life*. Joseph Ward Swain (trans.). London: Allen & Unwin. (Originally published, 1912.)

———. 1933. *The Division of Labor in Society*. George Simpson (trans.). New York: Macmillan. (Originally published, 1893.)

———. 1951. *Suicide: A Study in Sociology*. John A. Spaulding and George Simpson, (trans.). New York: The Free Press of Glencoe. (Originally published, 1897.)

———. 1964. *The Division of Labor in Society*. George Simpson (trans.). New York: The Free Press. (Originally published, 1893.)

Dworkin, Andrea. 1974. *Women Hating*. New York: E.P. Dutton.

Dyer, Everett D. 1963. "Parenthood as crisis: A restudy." *Marriage and Family Living* 25:196–201.

Economic Commission for Africa. 1984. *Report of the Second African Population Conference* (Addis Ababa).

Eisenstadt, S.N. 1971. *From Generation to Generation*. New York: The Free Press.

Ekong, Sheilah Clarke. 1986. "Industrialization and kinship: A comparative study of some Nigerian ethnic groups." *Journal of Comparative Family Studies* 12 (Summer):197–206.

Elder, Glen H., Jr. 1974. *Children of the Great Depression*. Chicago: University of Chicago Press.

Engels, Friedrich. 1972. *The Origin of the Family, Private Property, and the State*. New York: Pathfinder Press. (Originally published, 1884.)

Epstein, A.L. 1969. "Urbanization and social change in Africa." Pp. 246–287 in Gerald Breese (ed.), *The City in Newly Developing Countries: Readings on Urbanism and Urbanization*. Englewood Cliffs, N.J.: Prentice-Hall.

Eshleman, J. Ross. 1978. *The Family: An Introduction*, 2d ed. Boston: Allyn & Bacon.

Fact Sheets on Sweden. 1982. "Child care programs in Sweden."

Fact Sheets on Sweden. Stockholm: The Swedish Institute (Oct.).

Fanon, Frantz. 1965. *The Wretched of the Earth* (Preface by Jean Paul Sartre). Constance Farrington (trans.). New York: Grove Press.

———. 1967. *Black Skin White Masks*. Charles Lam Markmann (trans.). New York: Grove Press.

Farber, Bernard. 1964. *Family: Organization and Interaction*. San Francisco: Chandler.

Feldman, Harold. 1974. *Development of the husband–wife relationship* (research report). Mimeographed. Ithaca, N.Y.: Cornell University.

Feron, James. 1977. "Suburban child abuse: Its subtle forms hinder identification." *The New York Times* (Apr. 11).

Feuer, Lewis S. 1969. *The Conflict of Generations: The Character and Significance of Student Movements*. New York: Basic Books.

Field, Mark G., and Karin I. Flynn. 1970. "Worker, mother housewife: Society woman today." Pp. 257–284 in Georgene H. Seward and Robert C. Williamson (eds.), *Sex Roles in Changing Society*. New York: Random House.

Finkelhor, David, and Kersti Yllo. 1985. *License to Rape: Sexual Abuse of Wives*. New York: Holt, Rinehart and Winston.

Firestone, Shulamith. 1970. *The Dialectic of Sex: The Case for Feminist Revolution*. New York: William Morrow.

Fischer, Claude S. 1982a. "The dispersion of kinship ties in modern society: Contemporary data and historical speculation." *Journal of Family History,* 7 (Winter):353–375.

———. 1982b. *To Dwell Among Friends: Personal Networks in Town and City.* Chicago: University of Chicago Press.

Fischer, David Hackett. 1977. *Growing Old in America.* New York: Oxford University Press.

Fitzpatrick, Joseph P. 1971. *Puerto Rican Americans: The Meaning of Migration to the Mainland.* Englewood Cliffs, N.J.: Prentice-Hall.

Flandrin, Jean-Louis. 1979. *Families in Former Times: Kinship, Household, and Sexuality.* Richard Southern (trans.). Cambridge, England: Cambridge University Press.

Flaste, Richard. 1979. "Research begins to focus on suicide among the aged." *The New York Times* (Jan. 2):C2.

Fogarty, Michael P., Rhona Rapoport, and Robert N. Rapoport. 1971. *Sex, Career and Family.* Beverly Hills, Calif.: Sage.

Foner, Ann. 1978. "Age stratification and the changing family." Pp. S340–S365 in John Demos and Sarane Spence Boocock (eds.), *Turning Points: Historical and Sociological Essays on the Family.* American Journal of Sociology 89(suppl).

Ford, Clellan S. 1970. "Some primitive societies." Pp. 25–43 in Georgene H. Seward and Robert C. Williamson (eds.), *Sex Roles in Changing Society.* New York: Random House.

———, and Frank A. Beach. 1951. *Patterns of Sexual Behavior.* New York: Harper & Row.

Foucalt, Michel. 1978. *The History of Sexuality. Volume 1, An Introduction.* New York: Random House.

Franke, L.B. 1982. *The Ambivalence of Abortion.* New York: Random House.

Frazer, Sir James George. 1960. *The Golden Bough: A Study in Magic and Religion.* One volume, abridged ed. New York: The Macmillan Company. (Originally published, 1922.)

Freedman, Ronald. 1963. "Norms for family size in underdeveloped areas." Proceedings of the Rural Society, B 159: 220–245. Reprinted pp. 157–180 in David M. Heer, (ed.), 1968, *Readings on Population.* Englewood Cliffs. N.J.: Prentice-Hall.

Freeman, Linton C. 1974. "Marriage without love: Mate-selection in non-Western societies." Pp. 354–366 in Robert F. Winch and Graham B. Spanier (eds.), *Selected Studies in Marriage and the Family,* 4th ed. New York: Holt, Rinehart & Winston.

Freeman, M.D. 1979. *Violence in the Home.* Westmean, England: Saxon House.

Gans, Herbert. 1962a. *The Urban Villagers: Group and Class in the Life of Italian-Americans.* New York: The Free Press.

———. 1962b. "Urbanism and suburbanism as ways of life: A reevaluation of definitions." Pp. 624–648 in Arnold Rose (ed.), *Human Behavior and Social Process.* Boston: Houghton-Mifflin.

———. 1967a. "The Negro family: Reflections on the Moynihan report." Pp. 445–457 in Lee Rainwater and William B. Yancey (eds.), *The Moynihan Report and the Politics of Controversy.* Cambridge: M.I.T. Press.

———. 1967b. "Culture and class in the study of poverty: An approach to anti-poverty research." Pp. 201–228 in Daniel P. Moynihan (ed.), *On Understanding Poverty.* New York: Basic Books.

———. 1982/1979. "Symbolic ethnicity: The future of ethnic groups and cultures in America." Pp. 495–508 in Norman R. Yetman and C. Hoy Steele (eds.), *Majority and Minority,* 3d ed. Boston: Allyn & Bacon. [First published in *Ethnic and Racial Studies* 2, 1 (Jan. 1979)]

Garvon, Hannah. 1966. *The Captive Wife.* London: Routledge & Kegan Paul.

Gasster, Michael. 1972. *China's Struggle to Modernize.* New York: Knopf.

Gee, Emma. 1978. "Japanese picture-brides." Pp. 53–60 in Marjorie P.K. Weiser (ed.), *Ethnic America. The Reference Shelf* Vol. 50, No. 2. New York: H.W. Wilson Company.

Gelles, Richard J. 1972. *The Violent Home.* Beverly Hills, Calif.: Sage.

———. 1979. *Family Violence.* Beverly Hills, Calif.: Sage.

———. 1983. "An exchange/social control theory." In David Finkelhor et al. (eds.), *The Dark Side of Families.* Beverly Hills, Calif.: Sage.

———, and Claire Pedrick Cornell (eds.). 1983. *International Perspectives on Family Violence.* Lexington, Mass.: Lexington Books/D.C. Heath.

Gelman, David, with Pamela Abramson, George Raine, Peter McAlvey, and Peter McKillop. 1985. "The social fallout from an epidemic: A 'safe sex' movement—an aura of fear." *Newsweek* (Aug. 12):28–29.

Gelman, David. et al. 1985. "Who's taking care of our parents?" *Newsweek* (May 6):61–68.

Gersick, Kelin E. 1979. "Fathers by choice: Divorced men who receive custody of their children." Pp. 307–323 in George Levinger and Oliver C. Moles (eds.), *Divorce and Separation: Context, Causes, and Consequences.* New York: Basic

Ghurayyib, Rose. 1984. "The harem widow." Pp. 419–423 in Robin Morgan (ed.), *Sisterhood is Global: The International Women's Movement Anthology.* Garden City, N.Y.: Anchor Press/Doubleday.

Gil, David G. 1971. "Violence against children." *Journal of Marriage and the Family* 33:637–648.

Giordano, N.H., and J.A. Giordano. 1984. "Elder abuse: A review of the literature." *Social Work* 29:232–236.

Gist, Noel P., and Sylvia Fleis Fava. 1974. *Urban Society,* 6th ed. New York: Thomas Y. Crowell.

Glenn, Norvell D. 1982. "Interreligious marriage in the United States: Patterns and recent trends." *Journal of Marriage and the Family* 44 (Aug.):555–566.

Glick, Paul C. 1975. "A demographer looks at American families." *Journal of Marriage and the Family* 37:15–26.

——— 1984. "Marriage, divorce and living arrangements: Prospective changes." *Journal of Family Issues* 5:7–26.

———. 1984. "American household structure in transition." *Family Planning Perspectives* 16:205–211.

———, and Arthur J. Norton. 1979. "Marrying, divorcing, and living together in the U.S. today." *Population Bulletin,* vol. 32, no. 5. Washington, D.C.: Population Reference Bureau.

Glick, Paul C., and Graham B. Spanier. 1980. "Married and unmarried cohabitation in the United States." *Journal of Marriage and the Family* 42:19–30.

Glick, Paul C., and Sung-Ling Lin. 1986. "Recent changes in divorce and remarriage." *Journal of Marriage and the Family* 48 (Nov.):737–747.

Glueck, Sheldon, and Eleanor Glueck. 1951. *Unraveling Juvenile Delinquency.* New York: The Commonwealth Fund.

Goldscheider, Calvin. 1971. *Population, Modernization and Social Structure.* Boston: Little, Brown.

Goldwyn, Edward (writer and producer). 1984. "China's Only Child." *Nova.* This program was originally broadcast on PBS on February 14, 1984.

Goliber, Thomas J. 1985. "Sub-Saharan Africa: Population Pressures on Development." *Population Bulletin* Vol. 40, No. 1 (Feb.).

Good Housekeeping. 1982. "Rape: The likeliest time, place, and victim." (July):195.

Goode, William J. 1956. *After Divorce.* Glencoe, Ill.: The Free Press.

———. 1959. "The theoretical importance of love." *American Sociological Review* 24:38–47.

———. 1960. "A theory of role strain." *American Sociological Review* 25 (Aug.):483–496.

———. 1962. "Marital satisfaction and instability: A cross-cultural analysis of divorce rates." Pp. 377–387 in Reinhard Bendix and Seymour M. Lipset (eds.), *Class, Status, and Power,* 2d ed. New York: The Free Press.

——. 1963. *World Revolution and Family Patterns.* New York: The Free Press.

——. 1964. *The Family.* Englewood Cliffs, N.J.: Prentice-Hall.

——. 1971. "Force and violence in the family." *Journal of Marriage and the Family* 33:624–636.

——. 1976. "Family disorganization." Pp. 511–554 in Robert K. Merton and Robert Nisbet (eds.), *Contemporary Social Problems,* 4th ed. New York: Harcourt Brace Jovanovich.

Goodwin, John. (ed.). 1972. *The Nuclear Family in Crisis: The Search for an Alternative.* New York: Harper & Row.

——. 1973. *The Mating Trade.* Garden City, N.Y.: Doubleday.

——. 1977. "Review of *The Making of the Modern Family,* by E. Shorter." *Contemporary Sociology,* 169–171.

——. 1978. *The American Family: Past, Present, and Future.* New York: Random House.

Gordon, Michael. 1981. "Was Waller ever right? The rating and dating complex reconsidered." *Journal of Marriage and the Family.* 43:67–76.

Gordon, Suzanne. 1976. *Lonely in America.* New York: Simon & Schuster (Touchstone Books.)

Gough, Kathleen. 1971. "The origin of the family." *Journal of Marriage and the Family* 33:760–770.

Greeley, Andrew. 1961. "American sociology and the study of ethnic immigrant groups." *The International Migration Digest* I (Fall):107–113.

Greer, Scott. 1957. "Urbanism reconsidered: A comparative study of local areas in a metropolis." *American Sociological Review* 21:19–25.

Greven, Philip J., Jr. 1970. *Four Generations: Population, Land, and Fertility in Colonial Andover, Massachusetts.* Ithaca, N.Y.: Cornell University Press.

Gusfield, Joseph R. 1967. "Tradition and modernity: Misplaced polarities in the study of social change." *American Journal of Sociology* 72:351–362.

Gutkind, Peter C. W. 1969. "African urban family life and the urban system." Pp. 215–223 in Paul Meadows and Ephraim H. Mizruchi (eds.), *Urbanism, Urbanization, and Change: Comparative Perspectives.* Reading, Mass.: Addison-Wesley.

Gwartney-Gibbs, Patricia A. 1986. "The institutionalization of premarital cohabitation: Estimates from marriage license applications, 1970 and 1980." *Journal of Marriage and the Family* 48 (May):423–434.

Hagestad, Gunhild O. 1981. "Problems and promises in the social psychology of intergenerational relations." Pp. 11–46 in Robert W. Fogel et al. (eds.), *Aging: Stability and Change in the Family.* New York: Academic Press.

Hall, G. Stanley. 1904. *Adolescence: Its Psychology and Its Relation to Physiology, Anthropology, Sociology, Sex Crime, Religion and Education.* New York: Appleton.

Hance, William A. 1970. *Population, Migration, and Urbanization in Africa.* New York: Columbia University Press.

Haraven, Tamara K. 1971. "The history of the family as an interdisciplinary field." Pp. 211–226 in Theodore K. Rabb and Robert I. Rotberg (eds.), *The Family in History: Interdisciplinary Essays.* New York: Harper (Torchbooks).

——. 1975. "Family time and industrial time: Family and work in a planned corporation town, 1900–1924." *Journal of Urban History* 1:365–389.

——. 1976. "The last stage: Historical adulthood and old age." *Daedalus* 105:13–27. (Fall issue titled, "American Civilization: New Perspectives.")

——. 1978. "The dynamics of kin in an industrial community." Pp. 151–182 in J. Demos and S.S. Boocock (eds.), *Turning Points: Historical Points: Historical and Sociological Essays on the Family.* Chicago: University of Chicago Press.

——, and John Modell. 1980. "Family patterns." Pp. 345–354 in Stephen Thernstrom (ed.), *Harvard Encyclopedia of American Ethnic Groups.* Cambridge, Mass., and London, England: The Belknap Press of Harvard University Press.

Harris, Marvin. 1968. *The Rise of Anthropological Theory: A History of Theories of Culture.* New York: Thomas Y. Crowell.

Heer, David M. 1980. "Intermarriage." Pp. 513–521 in Stephen Thernstrom (ed.), *Harvard Encyclopedia of American Ethnic Groups.* Cambridge, Mass., and London, England: The Belknap Press of Harvard University Press.

Heesterman, J. C. 1973. "India and the inner conflict of tradition." *Daedalus* 192:97–114. (Winter issue titled, "Post-Traditional Societies.")

Helfer, Ray E., and C. Henry Kempe (eds.). 1968. *The Battered Child.* Chicago: University of Chicago Press.

Helgesen, Sally. 1982. "Do your parents ask too much of you?" *Seventeen* (Apr.):176–177.

Hellstrom, Inger. 1963. "The Chinese family in the Communist Revolution: Aspects of the changes brought about by the Communist government." *Acta Sociologica* 6:256–277.

Henretta, James A. 1971. "The morphology of New England society in the colonial period." Pp. 191–210 in Theodore K. Rabb and Robert I. Rotberg (eds.), *The Family in History: Interdisciplinary Essays.* New York: Harper (Torchbooks).

Herbers, John. 1981. "Sharp rise of elderly population in 70's portends future increases." *The New York Times.* (May 24).

Herman, Sondra R. 1974. "The liberated women of Sweden." *The Center Magazine* 7:76–78.

Hill, Robert. 1972. *The Strengths of Black Families.* New York: Emerson-Hall.

Hill, Reuban, and Joan Aldous. 1969. "Socialization for marriage and parenthood." Pp. 885–950 in David A. Goslin (ed.), *Handbook of Socialization Theory and Research.* Chicago: Rand McNally.

Hinton, William. 1966. *Fanshen: A Documentary of Revolution in a Chinese Village.* New York: Random House (Vintage).

Hobbs, Daniel F. 1965. "Parenthood as crisis: A third study." *Journal of Marriage and the Family* 27:367–372.

———. 1968. "Transition to parenthood: A replication and an extension." *Journal of Marriage and the Family* 30:413–417.

Hobbs, Daniel F., Jr., and Sue Peck Cole. 1976. "Transition to parenthood: A decade replication." *Journal of Marriage and the Family* 38:723–731.

Hochschild, Arlie Russell. 1976. "Communal life systems for the old." Pp. 367–384 in Cary S. Kart and Barbara B. Manard (eds.), *Aging in America: Readings in Social Gerontology.* Port Washington, N.Y.: Alfred Publishing. (Reprinted from *Society* 10, 1973.)

Hogan, David. 1983. "Ethnicity and education." Paper presented at "Making It in America," a conference sponsored by the Balch Institute for Ethnic Studies and the American Jewish Committee, Philadelphia, Apr. 21.

Hollingshead, August de B. 1949. *Elmtown's Youth: The Impact of Social Class on Adolescents.* New York: John Wiley & Sons.

Howell, Joseph T. 1973. *Hard Living on Clay Street.* Garden City, N.Y.: Doubleday (Anchor Books).

Horowitz, Ruth. 1983. *Honor and the American Dream: Culture and Identity in a Chicano Community.* New Brunswick, N.J.: Rutgers University Press.

Hughes, Pennethorne. 1971. *Witchcraft.* Harmondsworth, England: Penguin Books.

Hunt, Janet G., and Larry L. Hunt. 1982. "The dualities of careers and families: New integrations or new polarizations?" *Social Problems* 29(June):499–510.

Hunt, Morton M. 1959. *The Natural History of Love.* New York: Knopf.

Hutter, Mark. 1970. "Transformation of identity, social mobility and kinship solidarity." *Journal of Marriage and the Family* 32:133–137.

Internal Medicine World Report 1987. "Roundup, AIDS—The Year in Review" (Nov.) 2:2–4; 34–35.

Jacobs, Jerry. 1976. "An ethnographic study of a retirement setting." Pp. 385–394 in

Cary S. Kart and Barbara B. Manard (eds.), *Aging in America: Readings in Social Gerontology.* Port Washington, N.Y.: Alfred Publishing Co. (Reprinted from *Gerontologist* 14:483–487, 1974.)

Jacobson, Paul H. 1959. *American Marriage and Divorce.* New York: Rinehart.

Jacoby, Arthur P. 1969. "Transition to parenthood: A reassessment." *Journal of Marriage and the Family* 31:720–727.

Jensen, H. 1977. "Cobblers tale." *Newsweek* 89 (Apr. 4):42.

Johnson, Colleen Leahy. 1977. "Interdependence, reciprocity and indebtedness: An analysis of Japanese American kinship relations." *Journal of Marriage and the Family* 39 (May):351–365.

Johnson, Kay Ann. 1976. "Women in China: Problems of sex inequality and socioeconomic change." Pp. 286–319 in Jean I. Roberts (ed.), *Beyond Intellectual Sexism.* New York: David McKay.

Jones, Maldwyn Allen. 1960. *American Immigration.* Chicago: The University of Chicago Press.

Juliani, Richard N. 1980. *The Social Organization of Immigration: The Italians in Philadelphia.* New York: Arno Press.

Juviler, Peter H. 1984. "The urban family and the Soviet state: Emerging contours of a demographic policy." Pp. 84–112 in Henry W. Morton and Robert C. Stuart (eds.), *The Contemporary Soviet City.* Armonk, N.Y.: M.E. Sharpe.

Kandell, Jonathan. 1977. "Retirement age falling in Europe." *The New York Times,* (Dec. 4).

Kart, Cary S., and Barbara B. Manard (eds.). 1976. *Aging in America: Readings in Social Gerontology.* Port Washington, N.Y.: Alfred Publishing Co.

Kemper, Theodore D. 1983. "Predicting the divorce rate: Down?" *Journal of Family Issues* 4:507–524.

Keniston, Kenneth. 1965. *The Uncommitted: Alienated Youth in American Society.* New York: Harcourt, Brace and World.

———. 1968. *Young Radicals: Notes on Committed Youth.* New York: Harcourt, Brace and World.

Keniston, Kenneth, and The Carnegie Council on Children. 1977. *All Our Children: The American Family Under Pressure.* New York: Harcourt Brace Jovanovich.

Kenkel, William F. 1977. *The Family in Perspective,* 4th ed. Santa Monica, Calif.: Goodyear.

Kenyatta, Jomo. 1938. *Facing Mt. Kenya.* New York: Random House (Vintage Books).

Kett, Joseph F. 1977. *Rites of Passage: Adolescence in America 1790 to the Present.* New York: Basic Books.

Key, William H. 1961. "Rural urban differences and the family." *Sociological Quarterly* 2:49–56.

Kifner, John. 1984. "Iran: Obsessed with martyrdom." *The New York Times Magazine.* (Dec. 16):36–42, 47, 52, 54, 56.

Kikumura, Akemi, and Harry H.L. Kitano. 1981. "The Japanese American family." Pp. 43–60 in Charles H. Mindel and Robert W. Habenstein (eds.), *Ethnic Families in America: Patterns and Variations.* 2d ed. New York: Elsevier.

Kinsey, Alfred C., Wardell B. Pomeroy, and Clyde E. Martin. 1948. *Sexual Behavior in the Human Male.* Philadelphia: Saunders.

Kitano, Harry H.L. 1980. "Japanese." Pp. 561–571 in Stephan Thernstrom (ed.). *Harvard Encyclopedia of American Ethnic Groups.* Cambridge, Mass. and London, England: The Belknap Press of Harvard University Press.

Kleinman, Dana. 1979. "The dating game on videotape." *The New York Times* (March).

Klemesrud, Judy. 1976. "Many elderly in the Bronx spend their lives in terror of crime." *The New York Times* (Nov. 22).

Knox, David, and Kenneth Wilson. 1981. "Dating behaviors of university students." *Family Relations* 30:225–258.

Kohen, Janet A., Carol A. Brown, and Roslyn Feldberg. 1979. "Divorced mothers:

The cost and benefits of female control." Pp. 228–245 in George Levinger and Oliver C. Moles (eds.), *Divorce and Separation: Context, Causes, and Consequences.* New York: Basic Books.

Komarovsky, Mirra. 1962. *Blue Collar Marriage.* New York: Random House.

Kooy, Gerrit A. 1963. "Social system and the problem of aging." Pp. 45–60 in Richard H. Williams, Clark Tibbits, and Wilma Donahue (eds.), *Processes of Aging: Social and Psychological Perspectives* (Vol. 2). New York: Atherton Press.

Laing, R.D. 1969. *Self and Others.* Baltimore: Penguin Books.

Lambert, William W., Leigh Minturn Triandis, and Margery Wolf. "Some correlates of beliefs in the malevolence and benevolence of supernatural beings: A cross-societal study." *Journal of Abnormal and Social Psychology* 58 (Mar.):162–169.

Landis, Judson T. 1962. "A comparison of children from divorced and nondivorced unhappy marriages." *Family Life Coordinator* 11:61–65.

———. 1960. "The trauma of children when parents divorce." *Marriage and Family Living* 22:7–13.

Lannoy, Richard. 1971. *The Speaking Tree: A Study of Indian Culture and Society.* New York: Oxford University Press.

Lapidus, Gail Warshofsky. 1978. *Women in Soviet Society.* Berkeley, Calif.: University of California Press.

———. 1982. "Introduction: Women, work, and family: New Soviet perspectives." Pp. ix–xlii in Gail Warshofsky Lapidus (ed.), *Women, Work, and Family in the Soviet Union.* Armonk, N.Y.: M.E. Sharpe.

LaRossa, Ralph. 1983. "The transition to parenthood and the social reality of time," *Journal of Marriage and the Family* 43 (Aug.):579–589.

———, and Maureen M. LaRossa. 1981. *Transition to Parenthood: How Infants Change Families.* Beverly Hills, Calif.: Sage Publications.

Lasch, Christopher. 1975a. "The emotions of family life." *New York Review of Books* (Nov. 27).

———. 1975b. "The family and history." *New York Review of Books* (Nov. 13).

———. 1975c. "What the doctor ordered." *New York Review of Books* (Dec. 11).

———. 1977a. *Haven in a Heartless World: The Family Beseiged.* New York: Basic Books.

———. 1977b. "The siege of the family." *New York Review of Books* (Nov. 24).

———. 1979. *The Culture of Narcissism.* New York: W.W. Norton.

Laslett, Barbara. 1973. "The family as a public and private institution: An historical perspective." *Journal of Marriage and the Family* 35:480–492.

Laslett, Peter. 1965. *The World We Have Lost: England Before the Industrial Revolution.* New York: Charles Scribner's Sons.

——— (ed.). 1972. *Household and Family in Past Time.* Cambridge: Cambridge University Press.

Lau, E.E. and Kosberg, J.I. 1979. "Abuse of the elderly by informal care providers." *Aging:*10–15.

Leerhsen, Charles, with Andy Murr and Deborah Witherspoon. 1985. "Epidemics: A paralyzing effect." *Newsweek* (Sept. 23):23.

Lelyveld, Joseph. 1986. *Move Your Shadow: South Africa, Black and White.* New York: Penguin Books.

LeMasters, E.E. 1957. "Parenthood as crisis." *Marriage and Family Living* 19:352–355.

———. 1977. *Parents in Modern America.* Homewood, Ill.: Dorsey.

Lemon, Anthony. 1982. "Migrant labour and frontier commuters: Reorganizing South Africa's black labour supply." Pp. 64–89 in David M. Smith (ed.), *Living Under Apartheid.* London: George Allen & Unwin.

Lenin, V.I. 1966. "The tasks of the working women's movement in the Soviet republic." (Speech delivered at the fourth Moscow City conference of nonparty working women, September 23, 1919.) Pp. 66–72 in *The Emancipation of Women: From the Writings of V.I. Lenin* (Preface by Nadezhda K. Krupskaya). New York: International Publishers.

Le Play, Frédéric. 1855. *Les Ouvriers Européens.* Paris: Imprimerie Royale.

Lerner, Daniel. 1958. *The Passing of Traditional Society: Modernizing the Middle East.* Glencoe, Ill.: The Free Press of Glencoe.

Leslie, Gerald R. 1979. *The Family in Social Context,* 4th ed. New York: Oxford University Press.

Leslie, J. A. K. 1963. *A Social Survey of Dar es Salaam.* London: Oxford University Press.

Lévi-Strauss, Claude. 1957. "The principle of reciprocity." Pp. 84–94 in Lewis A. Coser and Bernard Rosenberg (eds.), *Sociological Theory: A Book of Readings.* New York: Macmillan.

———. 1971. "The family." Pp. 333–357 in H. L. Shapiro (ed.), *Man, Culture and Society.* New York: Oxford University Press.

Levy, Marion J., Jr. 1949. *The Family Revolution in Modern China.* Cambridge: Harvard University Press.

———. 1966. *Modernization and the Structure of Societies.* Princeton, N.J.: Princeton University Press.

Lewis, Hylan. 1965. "Agenda Paper No. 5: The family: Resources for change—Planning session for the White House Conference to fulfill these rights." November 16–18, 1975. Pp. 314–343 in Lee Rainwater and William B. Yancey (eds.), *The Moynihan Report and the Politics of Controversy.* Cambridge: M.I.T. Press.

Lewis, Oscar. 1966. *La Vida: A Puerto Rican Family in the Culture of Poverty—San Juan and New York.* New York: Random House.

Libby, Roger W. 1977. "Creative singlehood as a sexual life style: Beyond marriage as a rite of passage." Roger W. Libby and Robert N. Whitehurst (eds.), *Marriage and Alternatives: Exploring Intimate Relationships.* Glenview, Ill.: Scott Foresman.

Liebow, Elliot. 1967. *Tally's Corner: A Study of Negro Street Corner Men.* Boston: Little, Brown.

Light, Richard J. 1974. "Abused and neglected children in America: A study of alternative policies." *Harvard Educational Review* 43:556–598.

Liljestrom. Rita. 1970. "The Swedish model." Pp. 200–219 in Georgene H. Seward and Robert C. Williamson (eds.), *Sex Roles in Changing Society.* New York: Random House.

———. 1978. "Sweden." Pp. 19–48 in Sheila B. Kamerman and Alfred J. Kahn (eds.), *Family Policy: Government and Families in Fourteen Countries.* New York: Columbia University Press.

Little, Kenneth. 1965. *West African Urbanization: A Study of Voluntary Associations in Social Change.* Cambridge: Cambridge University Press.

———. 1973. *African Women in Towns: An Aspect of Africa's Social Revolution.* London: Cambridge University Press.

Litwak, Eugene. 1959–1960. "The use of extended family groups in the achievement of social goals." *Social Problems* 7:177–188.

———. 1960a. "Geographical mobility and extended family cohesion." *American Sociological Review* 25:385–394.

———. 1960b. "Occupational mobility and extended family cohesion." *American Sociological Review* 25:385–394.

Lloyd, Peter Cutt. 1969. *Africa in Social Change: Changing Traditional Societies in the Modern World.* Baltimore: Penguin Books.

Longfellow, Cynthia. 1979. "Divorce in context: Its impact on children." Pp. 287–306 in George Levinger and Oliver C. Moles (eds.), *Divorce and Separation: Context, Causes, and Consequences.* New York: Basic Books.

Lowie, Robert H. 1937. *The History of Ethnological Theory.* New York: Holt, Rinehart & Winston.

Luker, Kristin. 1984. *Abortion and the Politics of Motherhood.* Berkeley, Calif.: University of California Press.

Mace, David, and Vera Mace. 1960. *Marriage: East and West.* Garden City, N.Y.: Doubleday.

Macklin, Eleanor D. 1972. "Heterosexual cohabitation among unmarried college students." *The Family Coordinator* 21:463–472.

———. 1978. "Nonmarital heterosexual cohabitation." *Marriage and Family Review* 1:1–12.

———. 1981. "Cohabitating college students." Pp. 210–220 in Peter J. Stein (ed.), *Single Life: Unmarried Adults in Social Context.* New York: St. Martin's Press.

Maine, Henry Sumner. 1960. *Ancient Law.* London: J.M. Dent & Sons. (Orginally published, 1861.)

Makepeace, James. 1981. "Courtship violence among college students." *Family Relations* 30 (1) (Jan.):97–102.

Mamdani, Mahmood. 1972. *The Myth of Population Control: Family, Caste and Class in an Indian Village.* New York: Monthly Review Press.

Mangin, William. 1960. "Mental health and migration to cities." *Annals of the New York Academy of Sciences* 84:911–917.

———. 1968. "Tales from the barriadas." *Nickle Review,* September 25–October 8, 1968. Reprinted pp. 55–61 in William Mangin (ed.), 1970, *Peasants in Cities: Readings in the Anthropology of Urbanization.* Boston: Houghton-Mifflin.

——— (ed.). 1970. *Peasants in Cities: Readings in the Anthropology of Urbanization.* Boston: Houghton-Mifflin.

Marris, Peter. 1958. *Widows and Their Families.* London: Routledge & Kegan Paul.

———. 1961. *Family and Social Change in an African City: A Study of Rehousing in Lagos.* Evanston, Ill.: Northwestern University Press.

Marsh, Robert. 1967. *Comparative Sociology.* New York: Harcourt, Brace and World.

Martin, Del. 1976. *Battered Wives.* San Francisco: Glide Publications.

Martindale, Don. 1960. *The Nature and Types of Sociological Theory.* Cambridge, Mass.: Houghton-Mifflin.

———. 1962. *Social Life and Cultural Change.* Princeton, N.J.: Van Nostrand.

Masnick, George, and Mary Jo Bane. 1980. *The Nation's Families: 1960–1990.* Boston: Auburn House.

Mbate, Robert Muema. 1969, Nairobi. "Identity." *Bursara* 2, no. 3:31–34.

McCall, Michal M. 1966. "Courtship as social exchange: Some historical comparison." Pp. 190–200 in Bernard Farber (ed.), *Kinship and Family Organization.* New York: John Wiley & Sons.

McKee, Michael, and Ian Robertson. 1975. *Social Problems.* New York: Random House.

Mead, Margaret. 1928. *Coming of Age in Samoa.* New York: William Morrow.

———. 1949. *Male and Female: A Study of the Sexes in a Changing World.* New York: William Morrow.

———. 1954. "Some theoretical considerations on the problems of mother-child separation." *American Journal of Orthopsychiatry* 24:471–483.

———. 1963. *Sex and Temperament in Three Primitive Societies.* New York: William Morrow. (Originally published, 1935; Reprinted in 1950.)

———. 1966. "Marriage in two steps." *Redbook* 127:48–149.

———. 1970a. "Anomolies in American postdivorce relationships." Pp. 107–125 in Paul Bohannan (ed.), *Divorce and After.* Garden City, N.Y.: Doubleday (Anchor Books.)

———. 1970b. *Culture and Commitment: A Study of the Generation Gap.* New York: Natural History Press/Doubleday.

———. 1975. *Blackberry Winter: My Earlier Years.* New York: Pocket Books.

Metzker, Isaac (ed.). 1971. *A Bintel Brief.* New York: Ballantine Books.

Mill, John Stuart. 1966. *On Liberty, Representative Government, The Subjection of Women. Three Essays.* London: Oxford University Press (The World Classics). (*The Subjection of Women* was originally published in 1869.)

Millett, Kate. 1970. *Sexual Politics*. Garden City, N.Y.: Doubleday.

Minturn, Leigh, and William W. Lambert. 1964. *Mothers of Six Cultures: Antecedent of Child Rearing*. New York: John Wiley & Sons.

Mogey, John. 1964. "Family and community in urban-industrial societies." Pp. 501–534 in Harold T. Christensen (ed.), *Handbook of Marriage and the Family*. Chicago: Rand McNally.

Mohsen, Safia K. 1974. "The Egyptian women: Between modernity and tradition." Pp. 37–58 in Carolyn J. Matthiasson (ed.), *Many Sisters: Women in Cross-Cultural Perspective*. New York: The Free Press.

Montague, Ashley. 1973. *Man and Aggression*, 2d ed. London: Oxford University Press.

Monter, E. William. 1977. "The pedestal and the stake: Courtly love and witchcraft." Pp. 119–136 in Renate Bridenthal and Claudia Koonz (eds.), *Becoming Visible: Women in European History*. Boston: Houghton-Mifflin.

Montero, Darrel. 1981. "The Japanese Americans: Changing patterns of assimilation over three generations." *American Sociological Review* 46 (Dec.):829–839.

Montiel, Miguel. 1970. "The social science myth of the Mexican American family." *El Grito: A Journal of Contemporary Mexican American Thought* 3 (Summer):56–63.

———. 1973. "The Chicano family: A review of research." *Social Work* 18 (March):22–31.

Moore, Wilbert E. 1964. "Social aspects of economic development." Pp. 882–911 in Robert E. L. Faris (ed.), *Handbook of Modern Sociology*. Chicago: Rand McNally.

Morgan, Lewis Henry. 1963. *Ancient Society*. Edited with an introduction and annotations by Eleanor B. Leacock. New York: World (Meridian Books). (Originally published, 1870.)

Morgan, Robin. 1984. "India" Pp. 294–305 in Robin Morgan (ed.), *Sisterhood Is Global: The International Women's Movement*. Garden City, N.Y.: Anchor Press/Doubleday.

———. 1984. "Planetary feminism: The politics of the 21st century." Pp. 1–37 in Robin Morgan (ed.), *Sisterhood Is Global: The International Women's Movement Anthology*. Garden City, N.Y.: Anchor Press/Doubleday.

——— (ed.). 1984. *Sisterhood Is Global: The International Women's Movement Anthology*. Garden City, N.Y.: Anchor Press/Doubleday.

Morris, Desmond. 1970. *The Human Zoo*. New York: McGraw-Hill.

Moynihan, Daniel Patrick. 1986. *Family and Nation: The Godkin Lectures at Harvard University*. San Diego, Ca.: Harcourt Brace Jovanovich.

Murdock, George. 1937. "Comparative data on the division of labor by sex." *Social Forces* 15:551–553.

———. 1949. *Social Structure*. New York: Macmillan.

———. 1950. "Family stability in non-European cultures." *Annals of the American Academy of Political and Social Science* 272:195–201.

———. 1957. "World ethnographic sample." *American Anthropologist* 59:664–687.

Murillo, Nathan. 1971. "The Mexican American family." Pp. 99–102 in Nathaniel N. Wagner and Marsha J. Haug (eds.), *Chicanos: Social and Psychological Perspectives*. St. Louis: Mosby.

Murray, Charles. 1984. *Losing Ground: American Social Policy 1950–1984*. New York: Basic Books.

Musgrove, Frank. 1964. *Youth and the Social Order*. Bloomington: Indiana University Press.

National Center for Health Statistics. 1977. "Marriage and divorce." *Vital Statistics of the United States 1973, Vol. III*. Washington, D.C.: U.S. Government Printing Office.

———. 1978. "Births, Marriages, Divorces and Deaths for 1977." Monthly Vital Statistics Report, vol. 26, no. 12. Washington D.C.: U.S. Government Printing Office.

Newsweek. 1979. "Special report: The new China" (Feb. 5):32–59.

Newsweek. 1986. "Special report: AIDS: Future Shock" (Nov. 24):30–47.

Neugarten, Bernice, and Karol K. Weinstein. 1964 "The changing American grandparent." *Journal of Marriage and the Family* 26 (2) (May):199–204.

Nisbet, Robert A. 1966. *The Sociological Tradition*. New York: Basic Books.

Norton, Arthur J., and Paul C. Glick. 1976. "Marital instability: Past, present, and future." *Journal of Social Issues* 32:5–20.

Novak, Michael. 1971. *The Rise of Unmeltable Ethnics*. New York: Macmillan.

———. 1977. *Further Reflections on Ethnicity*. Middletown, Pa.: Jednota Press.

O'Brien, John E. 1971. "Violence in divorce-prone families." *Journal of Marriage and the Family* 33:692–698.

O'Kelly Charlotte G., and Larry S. Carney. 1986. *Women and Men in Society: Cross-Cultural Perspectives on Gender Stratification*. 2d ed. Belmont, Calif.: Wadsworth.

O'Reilly, Jane. 1983. "Wife beating: The silent crime." *Time* (Sept. 5).

Oakley, Ann. 1974. *Woman's Work: The Housewife, Past and Present*. New York: Pantheon Books.

Ogburn, William F. 1922. *Social Change*. New York: Viking Press.

———, and Meyer F. Nimkoff. 1955. *Technology and the Changing Family*. Boston: Houghton-Mifflin.

Pace, Eric. 1975. "A changing Iran wonders whether the gain will exceed the loss." *The New York Times* (Jan 16).

Ortner, Sherry. 1974. "Is female to male as nature is to culture?" Pp. 67–87 in Michelle Zimbalist Rosaldo and Louise Lamphere (eds.), *Woman, Culture and Society*. Stanford, Calif.: Stanford University Press.

Pace, Eric. 1975. "A changing Iran wonders whether the gain will exceed the loss." *The New York Times* (Jan 16).

Packard, Vance. 1966. *The Sexual Wilderness*. New York: David McKay.

Padan-Eisenstark, Dorit D. 1973. "Are Israeli women really equal? Trends and patterns of Israeli women's labor force participation: A comparative analysis." *Journal of Marriage and the Family* 35:538–545.

Palen, John J. 1975. *The Urban World*. New York: McGraw-Hill.

Palgi, Phyllis. 1973. "Discontinuity in the female role within the traditional family in modern society: A case of infanticide." In E. James Anthony and Cyrille Koupernik (eds.), *The Child in His Family: The Impact of Disease and Death* (vol. 2). New York: John Wiley & Sons.

Parillo, Vincent N. 1985. *Strangers to These Shores: Race and Ethnic Relations in the United States*. New York: John Wiley & Sons.

Park, Robert E. 1967/1916. "The city: Suggestions for the investigation of human behavior in the urban environment." Pp. 1–46 in Robert E. Park, Ernest W. Burgess, and Roderick D. McKenzie, *The City*. Chicago: University of Chicago Press. (Originally published, 1925.)

———. 1952/1926. "The urban community as a spacial pattern and a moral order." In Everett C. Hughes et al. (eds.), *Human Communities*. Glencoe, Ill.: The Free Press. Originally published in Ernest W. Burgess (ed.). 1926. *The Urban Community*. Chicago: University of Chicago Press, pp. 3–18.

———, and Herbert A. Miller. 1925. *Old World Traits Transplanted*. Chicago: Society for Social Research, University of Chicago. Copyright 1921, New York: Harper and Bros.

———, Ernest W. Burgess, and Roderick D. McKenzie. 1925. *The City*. Chicago: University of Chicago Press.

Parsons, Talcott. 1942. "Age and sex in the social structure of the United States." *American Sociological Review* 7:604–616.

———. 1943. "The kinship system of the contemporary United States." *American Anthropologist* 45:22–38.

———. 1949. *Essays in Sociological Theory, Pure and Applied*. Glencoe, III.: The Free Press.

————. 1955. "The American family: Its relation to personality and to the social structure." Pp. 3–33 in Talcott Parsons and Robert F. Bales (eds.), *Family, Socialization and Interaction Process*. New York: The Free Press.

————, Robert F. Bales, James Olds, Morris Zelditch, Jr. and Philip E. Slater. 1955. *Family: Socialization and Interaction Process*. New York: The Free Press.

Payton, Isabelle S. 1982. "Single-parent households: An alternative approach." *Family Economics Review* (Winter):11–16.

Pedrick-Cornell, Claire, and Richard J. Gelles. 1982. "Elder abuse: The status of current knowledge." *Family Relations* 31 (July):457–465.

Peterson, William. 1975. *Population*, 3d ed. New York: Macmillan.

Pinchbeck, Ivy. 1930. *Women Workers and the Industrial Revolution 1750–1850*. London: Routledge & Kegan Paul. (Reissued by Frank Cass, 1969; reissued by Augustus M. Kelley, New York, 1971.)

Pineo, Peter. 1961. "Disenchantment in the later years of marriage." *Marriage and Family Living* 23:3–11.

Pitt-Rivers, A. Lane-Fox. 1916. *The Evolution of Culture and Other Essays*. Oxford: Oxford University Press.

Piven, Frances Fox, and Richard Cloward. 1971. *Regulating the Poor*. New York: Vintage Books.

Pizzey, Erin. 1974. *Scream Quietly or the Neighbors Will Hear*. London: IF Books.

Platt, Anthony M. 1969. *The Child Savers: The Invention of Delinquency*. Chicago: University of Chicago Press.

Population Reference Bureau. 1976. *World Population Growth and Response*. Washington, D.C.: Population Reference Bureau.

Postman, Neil. 1982. *The Disappearance of Childhood*. New York: Laurel Books.

Power, Eileen. 1975. *Medieval Women*. Cambridge: Cambridge University Press.

Queen, Stuart A., Robert W. Habenstein, and Jill S. Quadagno. 1985. *The Family in Various Cultures*, **5th ed. New York: Harper & Row.**

Rabin, A.I. 1970. "The sexes: Ideology and reality in the Israeli kibbutz." Pp. 285–307 in Georgene H. Seward and Robert C. Williamson (eds.), *Sex Roles in Changing Society*. New York: Random House.

Rainwater, Lee. 1960. *And the Poor Get Children*. Chicago: Quadrangle.

————. 1965. *Family Design*. Chicago: Aldine.

————. 1966. "Crucible of identity." *Daedalus* 95:172–216.

————, and William B. Yancey (eds.). 1967. *The Moynihan Report and the Politics of Controversy*. Cambridge: M.I.T. Press.

Rathbone-McCuan, E. 1980. "Elderly victims of family violence and neglect. *Social Casework* 61:296–304.

Redfield, Robert. 1941. *The Folk Culture of Yucatan*. Chicago: University of Chicago Press.

————. 1947. "The Folk Society." *The American Journal of Sociology* 52:293–308. Reprinted in pp. 180–205 in Richard Sennett, (ed.), 1969, *Classic Essays on the Culture of Cities*. New York: Appleton-Century-Crofts.

————. 1953. *The Primitive World and Its Transformations*. Chicago: University of Chicago Press.

————. 1955. *The Little Community*. Chicago: University of Chicago Press.

Redmond, Ron. 1986. "China to tighten its population controls." *The Philadelphia Inquirer* (July 31).

Reiss, Ira. 1960. *Premarital Sexual Standards in America*. New York: The Free Press.

————. 1971. *The Family System in America*. New York: Holt, Rinehart & Winston.

Reiss, Paul J. 1965. "The extended kinship system: Correlates of and attitudes on the frequency of interaction." *Marriage and Family Living* 24:333–339.

Reissman, Leonard. 1972. *Inequality in American Society: Social Stratification*. Glenview, Ill.: Scott, Foresman.

Renne, K. S. 1970. "Correlates of dissatisfaction in marriage." *Journal of Marriage and the Family* **32:54–68.**

Riis, Jacob A. 1957/1890. *How the Other Half Lives: Studies Among the Tenements of New York.* New York: Hill and Wang.

Rimmer, Robert H. 1966. *The Harrad Experiment.* Los Angeles: Sherbourne Press.

Ritter, Malcolm. 1985. "Fearful hospital staff gives poor care." *Courier-Post* (Sept. 15):15f.

Rodman, Hyman. 1965. "Middle-class misconceptions about lower-class families." Pp. 219–230 in Hyman Rodman (ed.), *Marriage, Family, and Society: A Reader.* New York: Random House [Originally published in Arthur B. Shostak and William Gomberg (eds.), 1974, *Blue-Collar World: Studies of the American Worker.* Englewood Cliffs, N.J.: Prentice-Hall.]

———. 1971. *Lower-Class Families: The Culture of Poverty in Negro Trinidad.* New York: Oxford University Press.

Rollin, Betty. 1970. "Motherhood: Who needs it?" *Look,* September 22, 1970, pp. 15–17. Reprinted pp. 346–356 in Arlene S. Skolnick and Jerome H. Skolnick (eds.), 1971, *Family in Transition: Rethinking Marriage, Sexuality, Child Rearing, and Family Organization.* Boston: Little, Brown.

Rosaldo, Michelle Zimbalist. 1974. "Woman, culture and society: A theoretical overview." Pp. 17–42 in Michelle Zimbalist Rosaldo and Louise Lamphere (eds.), *Woman, Culture and Society.* Stanford, Calif.: Stanford University Press.

Roscoe, Bruce, and Nancy Benaske. 1985. "Courtship violence experienced by abused wives: Similarities in patterns of abuse." *Family Relations* 34 (3) (July):419–424.

Rosen, Lawrence. 1970. "The broken home and male delinquency." Pp. 489–495 in Marvin Wolfgang, Norman Johnson, and Leonard Savits (eds.), *Sociology of Crime and Delinquency.* New York: John Wiley & Sons.

———. 1973. "I divorce thee." Pp. 39–43 in Helena Z. Lopata (ed.), *Marriages and Families.* New York: Van Nostrand.

Rosow, Irving. 1973. "And then we were old." Pp. 229–234 in Helena Z. Lopata (ed.), *Marriages and Families.* New York: Van Nostrand.

———. 1976. "Status and role change through the life span." Pp. 457–482 in R.H. Binstock and E. Shanas (eds.), *Handbook of Aging and the Social Sciences.* New York: Van Nostrand.

Ross, Aileen D. 1961. *The Hindu Family in its Urban Setting.* Toronto: University of Toronto Press.

Ross, Heather L., and Isabel V. Sawhill. 1975. *Time of Transition: The Growth of Families Headed by Women.* Washington, D.C.: The Urban Institute.

Rossi, Alice S. 1968. "Transition to parenthood." *Journal of Marriage and the Family* 30:26–39.

———. 1977. "A biosocial perspective on parenting." *Daedalus* 106:1–31.

Rothman, David J. 1971. "Documents in search of a historian: Toward a history of children and youth in America." Pp. 179–190 in Theodore K. Rabb and Robert I. Rothberg (eds.), *The Family in History: Interdisciplinary Essays.* New York: Harper (Torchbooks).

Rothman, Ellen K. 1984. *Hands and Hearts: A History of Courtship in America.* New York: Basic Books.

Rubin, Gayle. 1984. "Thinking sex: Notes for a radical theory of the politics of sexuality." Pp. 267–319 in Carole S. Vance (ed.), *Pleasure and Danger: Exploring Female Sexuality.* Boston: Routledge & Kegan Paul.

Ruskin, John. *Sesame and Lilies: Three Lectures.* New York: Chatterton-Peck Company. (Originally published, 1865.)

Ryan, William. 1971. *Blaming the Victim.* New York: Random House (Vintage Books).

El Saadawi, Nawal. 1984. "Egypt: When a woman rebels . . . " Pp. 202–209 in Robin Morgan (ed)., *Sisterhood is Global: The International Women's Movement Anthology.* Garden City, N.Y.: Anchor Press/Doubleday.

Safilios-Rothschild, Constantina. 1970. "Toward a cross-cultural conceptualization of family modernity." *Journal of Comparative Family Studies* 1:17–25.

Salholz, Eloise, et al. 1986. "Too late for Prince Charming?" *Newsweek* (June 2):54–57, 61.

Saluter, Arlene. 1983. *Current Population Reports.* Washington, D.C.: U.S. Government Printing Office, Series P-20, No. 380.

Sanday, Peggy Reeves. 1979. *The Socio-Cultural Context of Rape.* Washington, D.C.: United States Department of Commerce, National Technical Information Service.

———. 1981. "The socio-cultural context of rape: A cross-cultural study." *Journal of Social Issues* 37:5–27.

Sandler, Jack, Marilyn Myerson, and Bill N. Kinder. 1980. *Human Sexuality: Current Perspectives.* Tampa, Fla.: Mariner.

Scheper-Hughes, Nancy. 1983. "Deposed kings: The demise of the rural Irish gerontocracy." Pp. 130–46 in J. Sokolovsky (ed.) *Growing Old in Different Cultures.* Belmont, Calif.: Wadsworth.

Schorr, Alvin L., and Phyllis Moen. 1980. "The single parent and public policy." Pp. 554–566 in Arlene S. Skolnick and Jerome H. Skolnick (eds.), *Family in Transition: Rethinking Marriage, Sexuality, Child Rearing, and Family Organization.* Boston: Little, Brown.

Schumacher, Edward. 1978. "Child abuse is twice as common as estimated earlier study finds." *Philadelphia Inquirer* (Nov. 20).

Schwartz, Pepper, and Janet Lever. 1976. "Fear and loathing at a college mixer." *Urban Life* 4 (Jan.):413–430.

Scully, Diana. 1985. "'Riding the bull at Gilley's: Convicted rapists describe the rewards of rape." *Social Problems* 32 (3) (Feb.):251–263.

Scully, Diana, and Joseph Marolla. 1984. "Convicted rapists' vocabulary of motive: Excuses and justifications." *Social Problems* 31 (5) (June):530–544.

Seeley, John R., Alexander Sim, and E.W. Loosley. 1956. *Crestwood Heights: A Study of the Culture of Suburban Life.* Toronto: University of Toronto Press.

Seligmann, Jean. 1984. "The date who rapes." *Newsweek* (Apr. 9):91–92.

Seller, Maxine. 1977. *To Seek America: A History of Ethnic Life in the United States.* Englewood, N.J.: Jerome S. Ozer.

Sennett, Richard. 1973. "The brutality of modern families." Pp. 81–90 in Helena Z. Lopata (ed.), *Marriage and Families.* New York: Van Nostrand.

———. 1974. *Families Against the City: Middle Class Homes of Industrial Chicago.* New York: Random House (Vintage Books).

Shanas, Ethel. 1980. "Older people and their families: The new pioneers." *Journal of Marriage and the Family* 42 (1) (Feb.):9–15.

Sharma, Ursula. 1980. *Women, Work and Property in North-West India.* New York: Tavistock.

Shipler, David K. 1976. "Life for Soviet woman all work, little status." *The New York Times* (Aug. 9).

Shorter, Edward. 1975. *The Making of the Modern Family.* New York: Basic Books.

Shwed, John A., and Murray A. Straus. 1979. "The military environment and child abuse." Mimeographed manuscript.

Simmons, Leo W. 1945. *The Role of the Aged in Primitive Society.* New Haven: Yale University Press.

———. "The aging in preindustrial societies." Pp. 62–91 in Clark Tibbitts (ed.), *Handbook of Social Gerontology: Societal Aspects of Aging.* Chicago/London: University of Chicago Press.

Sirjamki, John. 1964. "The institutional approach." Pp. 33–50 in H.T. Christensen (ed.), *Handbook of Marriage and the Family.* Chicago: Rand McNally.

Skolnick, Arlene S. 1973. *The Intimate Environment: Exploring Marriage and the Family.* Boston: Little, Brown. (Revised, 1978.)

Skolnick, Arlene S., and Jerome H. Skolnick. 1971. *Family in Transition: Rethinking Marriage, Sexuality, Child Rearing, and Family Organization.* Boston: Little, Brown. (Revised 1977, 1980.)

Slater, Philip. 1970. *The Pursuit of Loneliness.* Boston: Beacon Press.

Smelser, Neil J. 1959. *Social Change in the Industrial Revolution.* Chicago: University of Chicago Press.

————. 1973. "Processes of social change." Pp. 709–761 in Neil J. Smelser (ed.), *Sociology: An Introduction,* 2d ed. New York: John Wiley & Sons.

Smith, David M. 1982. "Urbanization and social change under apartheid: some recent developments." Pp. 24–46 in David M. Smith (ed.), *Living Under Apartheid.* London: George Allen & Unwin.

Smith, Joel, William H. Forn, and Gregory P. Stone. 1954. "Local intimacy in a middle-sized city." *American Journal of Sociology* 60:276–283.

Smock, Audrey Chapman, and Nadia Haggag Youssef, 1977. "Egypt: From seclusion to limited participation." Pp. 33–79 in Janet Zollinger Giele and Audrey Chapman Smock (eds.), *Women: Roles and Status in Eight Countries.* New York: Wiley-Interscience.

Solomon, Theodore. 1973. "History and demography of child abuse." *Pediatrics* Part 2, 51, 4:773–776.

Southall, Aidan. 1961. "Introductory Summary." Pp. 1–66 in Aidan Southall (ed.), *Social Change in Modern Africa.* London: Oxford University Press.

Spanier, Graham B. 1983. "Married and unmarried cohabitation in the United States, 1980." *Journal of Marriage and the Family* 45 (May):277–288.

————, and Frank J. Furstenberg, Jr. 1982. "Remarriage after divorce: A longitudinal analysis of well-being." *Journal of Marriage and Family* 43 (Aug.):709–720.

Spencer, Herbert. 1897. *The Principles of Sociology* (3 vols.). New York: Appleton.

Stacey, Judith. 1983. *Patriarchy and Socialist Revolution in China.* Berkeley, Calif.: University of California Press.

Stack, Carol B. 1974. *All Our Kin.* New York: Harper & Row.

Staples, Robert. 1971. "Towards a sociology of the black family: A theoretical and methodological assessment." *Journal of Marriage and the Family* 33:119–138.

————, and Alfredo Mirandé. 1980. "Racial and cultural variations among American families: A decennial review of the literature on minority families." *Journal of Marriage and the Family* 42 (Nov.):157–173.

Starr, Joyce R., and Donald E. Carns. 1973. "Singles in the city." Pp. 154–161 in Helena Z. Lopata (ed.), *Marriages and Families.* New York: Van Nostrand.

Steele, Brandt F., and Carl B. Pollock. 1968. "A psychiatric study of parents who abuse infants and small children." Pp. 103–113 in R.E. Helfer and C. H. Kempe (eds.), *The Battered Child.* Chicago: University of Chicago Press.

Stein, Maurice. 1964. *The Eclipse of Community.* New York: Harper (Torchbooks).

Stein, Peter J. 1975. "Singlehood: An alternative to marriage." *Journal of Marriage and the Family* 24:489–503.

————. 1976. *Single.* Englewood Cliffs, N.J.: Prentice-Hall.

————. 1981a. "The never-married." Pp. 5–8 in Peter J. Stein (ed), *Single Life: Unmarried Adults in Social Context.* New York: St. Martin's Press.

————. 1981b. "Understanding single adulthood." Pp. 21–34 in Peter J. Stein (ed.), *Single Life: Unmarried Adults in Social Context.* New York: St. Martin's Press.

Steinberg, Stephen. 1981. *The Ethnic Myth.* New York: Atheneum.

Steinmetz, Suzanne K. 1977. *The Cycle of Violence: Assertive, Aggressive and Abusive Family Interaction.* New York: Praeger.

————. 1978. "Battered parents." *Society* 15 (July–August):55–56.

————. 1981. "Elder abuse." *Aging:* 6–10.

————, and Murry A. Straus (eds.). 1974. *Violence in the Family.* New York: Dodd, Mead.

Stephens, William N. 1963. *The Family in Cross-Cultural Perspective.* New York: Holt, Rinehart & Winston.

Sterba, James P. 1979. "Chinese Will Try to Halt Growth of Population by end of Century." *The New York Times* (Aug. 13).

Stone, Gregory P. 1954. "City shoppers and urban identification: Observations on the social psychology of city life." *American Journal of Sociology* 60:36–45.

Stone, Lawrence. 1977. *The Family, Sex and Marriage: In England 1500–1800*, abridged ed. New York: Harper/Colophon Books.

Stonequist, Everett V. 1937. *The Marginal Man*. New York: Scribner.

Straus, Murray A. 1974. "Leveling, civility, and violence in the family." *Journal of Marriage and the Family* 36:13–29.

———. 1977. "Societal morphogenesis and intrafamily violence in cross-cultural perspective." *Annals of the New York Academy of Sciences* 285:719–730.

———. 1983. "Societal morphogenesis and intrafamily violence in cross-cultural perspective." Pp. 27–43 in Richard J. Gelles and Claire Pedrick Cornell (eds.), *International Perspectives on Family Violence*. Lexington, Mass.: Lexington Books/D.C. Heath.

———, and Richard J. Gelles. 1985. "Societal change and change in family violence from 1975 to 1985 as revealed by two national surveys." *Journal of Marriage and the Family* 48 (3) (Aug.):465–479.

Streib, Gordon F. 1973. "Old age in Ireland: Demographic and sociological aspects." Pp. 167–181 in Donald O. Cowgill and Lowell D. Holmes (eds.), *Aging and Modernization*. New York: Appleton-Century-Crofts.

Stycos, J. Mayone. 1955. *Family and Fertility in Puerto Rico*. New York: Columbia University Press.

Sullerot, Evelyne. 1971. *Women, Society and Change*. New York: World (University Library).

Sumner, William Graham. 1906. *Folkways*. Boston: Ginn.

Sussman, Marvin B. 1953. "The help pattern in the middle class family." *American Sociological Review* 18:22–28.

———. 1959. "The isolated nuclear family 1959: Fact or fiction?" *Social Problems* 6:333–340.

———, and Lee Burchinal. 1962. "Kin family network: Unheralded structure in current conceptualizations of family functioning." *Marriage and Family Living* 24:231–240.

Tallman, Irving. 1969. "Working-class wives in suburbia: Fulfillment or crisis." *Journal of Marriage and the Family* 31:65–72.

———, and Romona Morgner. 1970. "Life style differences among urban and suburban blue collar families." *Social Forces* (March):334–348.

Talmon, Yonina. 1964. "Mate selection in collective settlement." *American Sociological Review* 29:468–508.

———. 1965a. "The family in a revolutionary movement—the case of the kibbutz in Israel." Pp. 259–286 in Meyer Nimkoff (ed.), *Comparative Family Systems*. Boston: Houghton-Mifflin.

———. 1965b. "Sex-role differentiation in an equalitarian society." Pp. 144–155 in Thomas F. Lasswell, John H. Burma, and Sidney H. Aronson (eds.), *Life in Society*. Chicago: Scott, Foresman.

Tambiah, S. J. 1973. "The persistence and transformation of tradition in Southeast Asia, with special reference to Thailand." *Daedalus* 102:55–84. (Winter issue titled, "Post-Traditional Societies.")

Taylor, Lesli, and Eli H. Newberger. 1983. "Child abuse in the international year of the child." Pp. 45–62 in Richard J. Gelles and Claire Pedrick Cornell (eds.), *International Perspectives on Family Violence*. Lexington, Mass.: Lexington Books/D.C. Heath.

Terrill, Ross. 1979. *The China Difference*. New York: Harper & Row.

Theodorson, George A. 1968. "Cross-national variations in eagerness to marry." Pp. 119–134 in H. Kent Geiger (ed.), *Comparative Perspectives in Marriage and the Family*. Boston: Little, Brown.

Thomas, William I., and Florian Znaniecki. 1918–1920. *The Polish Peasant in Europe and America,* 5 vols. Chicago: University of Chicago Press.

Thompson, E.P. 1963. *The Making of the English Working Class.* London: Gollancz.

Thrasher, Frederic M. 1927. *The Gang.* Chicago: University of Chicago Press.

Tietze, Christopher. 1981. *Induced Abortion: A World Review, 1981.* New York: Population Council of New York City.

Tiger, Lionel, and Robin Fox. 1971. *The Imperial Animal.* New York: Holt, Rinehart & Winston.

Tiger, Lionel, and Joseph Shepher. 1975. *Women in the Kibbutz.* New York: Harcourt Brace Jovanovich.

Time. 1977. "Jobs: Challenging the 65 barrier" (Aug. 8):67–68.

———. 1981. "The battle over abortion" (Apr. 6):20–28.

———. 1981. "Private lives, public places" (Apr. 6):27.

———. 1987. "Stretching their options" (Jan. 26):23.

Tischler, Henry L., Phillip Whitten, and David E.K. Hunter. 1986. *Introduction to Sociology,* 2d ed. New York: Holt, Rinehart & Winston.

Tönnies, Ferdinand. 1963. *Community and Society [Gemeinschaft und Gesellschaft].* Charles P. Loomis (trans. and ed.). New York: Harper (Torchbooks). (Originally published, 1887; original translation, 1957.)

Townsend, Peter. 1957. *The Family Life of Old People.* London: Routledge & Kegan Paul.

Troll, Lillian E. 1983. "Grandparents: The family watchdogs." Pp. 63–74 in Timothy H. Brubaker (ed.), *Family Relationships in Later Life.* Beverly Hills, Calif.: Sage.

Trost, Jan. 1975. "Married and unmarried cohabitation: A case of Sweden, with some comparisons." *Journal of Marriage and the Family* 37:677–682.

———. 1978. "A renewed social institution: Non-marital cohabitation." *Acta Sociologica* 21:303–315.

———. 1983. "Parental benefits—A study of men's behavior and views." *Current Sweden.* Stockholm: The Swedish Institute (June):1–7.

Turnbull, Colin M. 1962. *The Lonely African.* New York: Simon & Schuster.

———. 1972. *The Mountain People.* New York: Simon & Schuster.

Turner, John F.C. 1969. "Uncontrolled urban settlement: Problems and policies." Pp. 507–534 in Gerald Breese (ed.), *The City in Newly Developing Countries: Readings on Urbanism and Urbanization.* Englewood Cliffs, N.J.: Prentice-Hall.

———. 1970. "Barriers and channels for housing development in modernizing countries." Pp. 1–19 in William Mangin (ed.), *Peasants in Cities: Readings in the Anthropology of Urbanization.* Boston: Houghton-Mifflin.

Uhlenberg, Peter. 1980. "Death and the family." *Journal of Family History* 5 (Fall):313–329.

U.S. Bureau of the Census. 1983. *Statistical Abstract of the United States 1984,* 104th ed. Washington, D.C.: U.S. Bureau of the Census.

———. 1984a. *Current Population Reports.* Washington, D.C.: U.S. Government Printing Office, Series P-25, No. 949.

———. 1984b. *Current Population Reports.* Washington, D.C.: U.S. Government Printing Office, Series P-20, No. 358.

U.S. Department of Commerce, Bureau of the Census. 1981. *Marital Status and Living Arrangements: March, 1980.* Current Population Reports, Series P-20, No. 365. Washington, D.C.: U.S. Government Printing Office.

———. 1983. *Marital Status and Living Arrangements: March 1982.* Current Population Reports, Series P-20, No. 380. Washington, D.C.: U.S. Government Printing Office.

U.S. Department of Labor. 1965. *The Negro Family: The Case for National Action.* U.S. Department of Labor, Office of Policy Planning and Research. Washington, D.C.: U.S. Government Printing Office.

Valentine, Charles. 1968. *Culture and Poverty: Critique and Counter-Proposals.* Chicago: University of Chicago Press.

Van Allen, Judith. 1974. "Modernization means more dependency: Women in Africa." *The Center Magazine* 7:60–67.

Vann, Richard T. 1978. "Review of *The Making of the Modern Family*" by E. Shorter." *Journal of Family History* 3:106–117.

Vrazo, Fawn. 1986. "Study disputes stereotype of black teen mothers." *The Philadelphia Inquirer* (Mar. 13).

Vreeland. Rebecca S. 1972a. "Is it true what they say about Harvard boys." *Psychology Today* 5:65–68.

———. 1972b. "Sex at Harvard." *Sexual Behavior*: 3–10.

Walkowitz, Judith. 1980. *Prostitution and Victorian Society*. Cambridge: Cambridge University Press.

Waller, Willard. 1937. "The rating dating complex." *American Sociological Review* 2:727–734.

———. 1938. *The Family: A Dynamic Interpretation*. New York: Dryden.

Wallis, Claudia, with Melissa Ludtke. 1985. "AIDS: A spreading scourge." *Time* (Aug. 5).

Wallis, Claudia. 1985b. "Children having children: Teen pregnancies are corroding America's social fabric." *Time* (Dec. 9):78–82, 84, 87, 89–90.

Webb, Craig. 1987. "New odds: Marriage data disputed." *The Philadelphia Inquirer* (Jan. 13).

Weber, Eugen. 1976. *Peasants into Frenchmen*. Stanford: Stanford University Press.

Weber, Max. 1949. *The Methodology of the Social Sciences*. Edward H. Shils and Henry A. Finch (trans. and eds.). New York: The Free Press.

Weeks, Jeffrey. 1981. *Sex, Politics and Society: The Regulation of Sexuality Since 1800*. New York: Longman.

Weiner, Myron (ed.). 1966. *Modernization: The Dynamics of Growth*. New York: Basic Books.

Weiss, Robert S. 1979a. *Going It Alone: The Family Life and Social Situation of the Single Parent*. New York: Basic Books.

———. 1979b. "Issues in the adjudication of custody when parents separate." Pp. 324–336 in George Levinger and Oliver C. Moles (eds.), *Divorce and Separation: Context, Causes, and Consequences*. New York: Basic Books.

Weitzman, Lenore J. 1977. "To love, honor and obey." Pp. 288–313 in Arlene S. Skolnick and Jerome H. Skolnick (eds.), *Family in Transition: Rethinking Marriage, Sexuality, Child Rearing, and Family Organization*, 2d ed. Boston: Little, Brown.

Weitzman, Lenore J., and Ruth B. Dixon. 1980. "The transformation of legal marriage through no-fault divorce." Pp. 354–367 in Arlene S. Skolnick and Jerome H. Skolnick (eds.), *Family in Transition: Rethinking Marriage, Sexuality, Child Rearing, and Family Organization*, 3d ed. Boston: Little, Brown.

Westermarck, Edward A. 1905. *The History of Human Marriage*, 5th ed. (3 vols.). New York: Macmillan. (Orginally published, 1891.)

Westoff, Leslie Aldridge. 1977. *The Second Time Around: Remarriage in America*. New York: Penguin Books.

White, Morton, and Lucia White. 1962. *The Intellectual Versus the City*. Cambridge: Harvard University Press/M.I.T. Press.

Whiting, Beatrice B. and John W.M. Whiting. 1975. *Children of Six Cultures*. Cambridge, Mass.: Harvard University Press.

Wilkinson, Karen. 1974. "The broken family and juvenile delinquency: Scientific explanation of ideology?" *Social Problems* 21:726–733.

Williams, Tomas Rhys. 1972. *Introduction to Socialization: Human Culture Transmitted*. St. Louis: C. V. Mosby.

Willie, Charles V. 1979. *Caste and Class Controversy*. Bayside, N.Y.: General Hall.

———. 1981. *A New Look at Black Families*. Bayside, N.Y.: General Hall.

Willmott, Peter, and Michael Young. 1960. *Family and Class in a London Suburb*. London: Routledge & Kegan Paul.

Wilson, Edmund. 1975. *Sociobiology: The New Synthesis.* Cambridge, Mass.: Belknap and the Harvard University Press.

———. 1978. *On Human Nature.* Cambridge, Mass.: Harvard University Press.

Wilson, William J. 1978. *The Declining Significance of Race.* Chicago: University of Chicago Press.

Winn, Marie. 1983. *Children Without Childhood.* New York: Pantheon.

Wirth, Louis. 1938a. *The Ghetto.* Chicago: University of Chicago Press.

———. 1938b. "Urbanism as a way of life." *American Journal of Sociology* 44:1–24.

Wolf, Margery. 1985a. "Marriage, family, and the state in contemporary China." Pp. 223–251 in Kingsley Davis (ed.), *Contemporary Marriage.* New York: Russell Sage Foundation.

———. 1985b. "The People's Republic of China." Pp. 33–48 in Jennie Farley (ed.), *Women Workers in Fifteen Countries.* Ithaca, N.Y.: ILR Press, Cornell University Press.

Wong, Aline K. 1974. "Women in China: Past and present." Pp. 229–259 in Carolyn J. Matthiason (ed.), *Many Sisters: Women in Cross-Cultural Perspective.* New York: The Free Press.

Wortis, Rochelle Paul. 1977. "The acceptance of the concept of the moral role by behavioral scientists: Its effects on women." *The American Journal of Orthopsychiatry* 41:733–746. [Reprinted pp. 362–378 in Arlene S. Skolnick and Jerome H. Skolnick (eds.), *Family in Transition: Rethinking Marriage, Sexuality, Child Rearing, and Family Organization,* 2d ed. Boston: Little, Brown.]

Yancey, William L., Eugene P. Ericksen, and Richard N. Juliani. 1976. "Emergent ethnicity: A review and reformulation." *American Sociological Review* 41 (June):391–402.

Yang, C.K. 1959. *The Chinese Family in the Communist Revolution.* Cambridge: M.I.T. Press.

Yans-McLaughlin, Virginia. 1971. "Patterns of work and family organization." Pp. 111–126 in Theodore K. Rabb and Robert I. Rotberg (eds.), *The Family in History: Interdisciplinary Essays.* New York: Harper (Torchbooks).

Ybarra, Lea. 1982. "When wives work: The impact on the Chicano family." *Journal of Marriage and the Family* 44 (Feb.):169–178.

Yorburg, Betty. 1974. *Sexual Identity: Sex Roles and Social Change.* New York: John Wiley & Sons.

Young, Michael, and Peter Willmott. 1957. *Family and Kinship in East London.* Baltimore: Penguin Books. (Rev. ed., 1963.)

———. 1973. *The Symmetrical Family.* New York: Pantheon Books.

Zalba, Serapio R. 1974. "Battered children." Pp. 407–415 in Arlene S. Skolnick and Jerome H. Skolnick (eds.), *Intimacy, Family, and Society.* Boston: Little, Brown.

Zelditch, Morris, Jr. 1964. "Cross-cultural analysis of family structure." Pp. 462–500 in Harold T. Christensen (ed.), *Handbook of Marriage and the Family.* Chicago: Rand McNally.

Zelizer, Viviana A. 1985. *Pricing the Priceless Child.* New York: Basic Books.

———, and Merle E. Frampton. 1966. "Theories of Frederic Le Play." Pp. 14–23 in Bernard Farber (ed.), *Kinship and Family Organization.* New York: John Wiley & Sons.

Zimmerman, Carle C., and Merle E. Frampton. 1966. "Theories of Frederic Le Play." Pp. 14–23 in Bernard Farber (ed.), *Kinship and Family Organization.* New York: John Wiley & Sons.

Zorbaugh, Harvey W. 1929. *The Gold Coast and the Slum.* Chicago: University of Chicago Press.

Author Index

Subject Index

Date Due